The
Revolution in Virginia
1775–1783

by
John E. Selby

With a new foreword by Donald Higginbotham

The Colonial Williamsburg Foundation
Williamsburg, Virginia

Distributed by the University of Virginia Press
Charlottesville, Virginia

20 19 18 17 16 15 14 13 12 11 10 09 08 07   4 5 6 7 8 9 10

Printed in Canada

Paperback cover designed by Helen M. Olds

ISBN-10: 0-87935-233-7 (pbk.)
ISBN-13: 978-0-87935-233-2 (pbk.)

The original publication of *The Revolution in Virginia, 1775-1783,*
was made possible in part by a grant from the Division of Research Programs
of the National Endowment for the Humanities.

The Library of Congress has cataloged the hardcover edition as follows:
Selby, John E.
The revolution in Virginia, 1775-1783.
Bibliography: p. 409
Includes index.
1. Virginia—History—Revolution, 1775-1783.
I. Title.
E263.V8S45   1988   978.3'09755   87-29983
ISBN 0-87935-075-X

Colonial Williamsburg is a registered trade name of
The Colonial Williamsburg Foundation, a not-for-profit
educational institution.

The Colonial Williamsburg Foundation
PO Box 1776
Williamsburg, VA 23187-1776
www.colonialwilliamsburg.org

FOR MARY, HILARY, HOLLY,
JON, AND CHRIS

Maps

Western Territories, 1774–1777   37
Eastern Virginia, 1775–1776   65
View of Great Bridge, 1775   71
Commerce and Manufacturing in Virginia, 1775–1783   164
Western Territories, 1778–1783   185
Virginia and the Carolinas, 1776–1783   212
Virginia, 1781   278
Siege of Yorktown   304

Contents

Foreword		vii
Preface		xi
Prologue	The Magazine	1
Chapter 1.	"The malignancy . . . and the wickedness . . . in their plans of despotism"	7
Chapter 2.	Britain's Oldest Dominion	23
Chapter 3.	The Collapse of Royal Government	41
Chapter 4.	War	55
Chapter 5.	Independence	80
Chapter 6.	"How few . . . have ever enjoyed . . . an election of government"	100
Chapter 7.	The War Continues	124
Chapter 8.	Perfecting the Republic	138
Chapter 9.	The Economy in War	163
Chapter 10.	The War in the West	184
Chapter 11.	British Strategy Shifts Southward	204
Chapter 12.	Reform and Taxes	227
Chapter 13.	"Barely sufficient to keep us joging along"	245
Chapter 14.	Defeat	265
Chapter 15.	Victory	286
Chapter 16.	"The most painful suspense with regard to events in Europe"	310
Endnotes		325
Bibliographical Essay		409
Index		421

Foreword

W hen I look back over John Selby's multitudinous professional activities and his record of scholarly publications, I am reminded of a question the historian Carl Becker asked after enumerating a typical day in the life of Thomas Jefferson: But "when do we eat?" Besides a variety of essays, articles, and short monographs, Selby is remembered for two highly regarded books, one of which you hold in your hands. The other, on which he collaborated with Thad W. Tate, another William and Mary professor, and with Warren M. Billings, a University of New Orleans professor and William and Mary graduate, is *Colonial Virginia: A History,* one of the best, if not *the* best, volumes in KTO Press's History of the American Colonies series.

The Revolution in Virginia, 1775–1783, published in 1988 by the Colonial Williamsburg Foundation, was warmly praised by most reviewers. It has certainly stood the test of nearly two decades and deserves to be republished at this time. In fact, there is no better study of a state at war between 1775 and 1783. *The Revolution in Virginia* is characterized by judicious treatment and careful analysis, not by strikingly new interpretations. Selby's statement that, for its white population, "Virginia was more united in support of the Revolution than any other state in the rebellion" (p. xi) is correct. Even so, a few recent scholars, reflecting the influence of the new social history, would put more emphasis on those who either opposed the Revolution or wanted to shape it in a more democratic direction. They examine more closely than Selby and historians of his generation the story of African Americans, Native Americans, and sometimes disgruntled white smallholders. But, certainly Virginia's ruling elite remained in control and shaped the political and institutional changes that took place.

What then was revolutionary about the Revolution in Virginia? The creation of a written constitution with its Declaration of Rights and the eventual disestablishment of the Anglican Church, explained and justified in republican terms, stand out. If one acknowledges the contributions of the new social historians, Selby remains on sound ground in his declaration that the most significant changes "lay in the intellectual rather than the social realm" (p. 160). In the short run, at least, the author believed that most of Virginia's political institutions functioned as they had in the late colonial period. The authority of the county courts remained undiminished, and the House of Delegates acted much as the House of Burgesses had done before 1776.

The book is most persuasive in describing the state's war effort. Virginia turned back the challenge of its royal governor, Lord Dunmore, who sought to plant a permanent base on the coast for rallying the loyalists and encouraging a massive slave uprising. During the first five years of the conflict, the state made major contributions to the Continental armies and to the economic costs of the struggle. After that, as the war turned south, the Old Dominion suffered a succession of British invasions, resulting in heavy losses in men and the collapse of its economy. Even the victory at Yorktown did not erase the bitterness of countless Virginians who felt that Congress and the northern states had been slow to come to their assistance. Nationalistic sentiments gave way to a new provincialism, which, according to the author, helps to explain why Virginia became one of the most Anti-Federalist states. This well-researched, readable volume should attract a new generation of both historians and general readers.

On a more personal note, I welcome this opportunity to say something about John Selby as a person and as a scholar and teacher. A native of Massachusetts, John always retained his distinctive New England accent. He received his Ph.D. at Brown University, studying under Edmund S. Morgan, and then taught for some years at the University of Oregon prior to taking a position as assistant director of Research at the Colonial Williamsburg Foundation. In 1966, he moved down the street to the College of William and Mary's Department of History, where he held forth until his retirement in 1999. He was a visible and effective leader and administrator. After a long tour of duty as graduate dean of arts and sciences, he served two terms as chair of his department. For five years, he was William E. Pullen Professor of History. In 1989, he received the college's Thomas Jefferson Award for distinguished service. The following year, he became president of the faculty assembly.

In addition to teaching a variety of courses on colonial Virginia and early America, John directed a substantial number of doctoral dissertations as well as master's and honors theses. Somehow, he also made the time to play an active role at the Omohundro Institute of Early American History and Culture. Founded in the mid-1940s and jointly sponsored by the Colonial Williamsburg Foundation and the College of William and Mary, the Institute publishes the leading scholarly journal in colonial and Revolutionary studies: *The William and Mary Quarterly*. For over twenty-five years, John held the position of book review editor, and, for a time, he stepped in as acting editor of the journal itself.

For more than thirty years, our paths repeatedly crossed. John and I just missed an initial meeting in Williamsburg. I taught briefly at the College of William and Mary in the late 1950s, and John arrived in town shortly thereafter. During the two decades prior to his death in 2001, John and I lectured on the same day each July at the Monticello–Stratford Hall Summer Seminar for Teachers at the Lee ancestral home, Stratford Hall, in Virginia's Northern Neck. We and our wives spent the night in one of Stratford Hall's guesthouses and had dinner together. Somehow John Selby did find time to eat.

Don Higginbotham, 2007
Dowd Professor
University of North Carolina at Chapel Hill

Preface

This book is a political, administrative, and military history of Virginia during the years of the War for American Independence, 1775 to 1783. Much of the story has been told before, most often in biographical form. The brilliance of Virginia's Revolutionary generation explains why the genre is a favorite among historians of the era. After preparing portions of Chapter 3 as interpretive studies for Colonial Williamsburg and an essay on Lord Dunmore for the Virginia Bicentennial Commission, I decided to expand the research to fill the need for a general narrative of the state's role in the conflict.

Virginia was more united in support of the Revolution than any other state in the rebellion. Its leaders enjoyed virtual unanimity regarding the constitutional issues in contention with Great Britain. A long controversy over claims to the western territories notwithstanding, the Virginia leadership stood firmly behind the Continental Congress from that body's inception, first because colonial union held the only hope of bringing the mother country to terms, later because unity offered the best chance of national victory. After the last battle, attitudes in the state toward central authority altered dramatically.

While insisting on their terms, Virginia leaders clung to the possibility of remaining in the British Empire almost to the eve of the final decision for independence. Then, with separation declared, a wave of excitement over the opportunities that political self-determination afforded swept the state. Some Virginians plunged enthusiastically into redesigning their government to improve on the British system which they had so long admired; others turned with equal zest to economic endeavors that imperial monopolies and the structure of the colonial economy previously impeded. The political changes the Revolutionary generation achieved—creating a republic and disestablishing the monarchy and eventually its church—had enormous consequences for future ages. The survival of most other colonial institutions, however, suggests a relatively high degree of satisfaction, at least among the politically active classes, with the way the colony generally had been run.

At the onset of the conflict, while most of the rest of the continent concentrated on the fighting around Boston, Virginians defeated their royal governor Lord Dunmore with a minimum of outside aid in a fourteen-month campaign. Although the triumph is overshadowed by the northern battles, Continental commanders understood full well that, had the governor held on and the British significantly reinforced him, as on at least one occasion might easily have occurred, the king's forces could have split the union and most likely suppressed the rebellion. Instead, Virginians expelled the governor and freed the manpower and food stocks of the largest and most populous state in the uprising to assist in other theaters. The Chesapeake's tobacco, too, provided the only credits the Continent earned abroad.

The Revolution lasted a long while. The extent of the mobilization it required exceeded any effort Virginians had previously undertaken. In government and economic affairs they never had to do so much so expeditiously. They proved capable of periodic bursts of intense energy in defense of their land right up to the end of the struggle. After the initial years, however, the attempt to fashion a lasting economic and administrative structure collapsed completely. Four invasions in the last three years of the fighting proved more than the system could handle. Many contemporaries believed the root of the failure to be moral, and the resulting recriminations probably did as much to diminish the earlier idealism and weaken the cause as the actual suffering that successive defeats, inflation, and scarcities inflicted. Victory in the end came from a combination of French intervention and British ineptitude. The Virginians' contribution came from hanging on as long as they did until they won.

During the writing of this book I have become indebted to many individuals for their generous assistance and support. Most of all, I thank the director emeritus of research of the Colonial Williamsburg Foundation, Edward M. Riley, who many years ago introduced me to the study of Virginia history. Under his auspices the Foundation Library compiled one of the best collections in existence of printed and microform materials on eighteenth-century Virginia. Rose Belk, Dorothy Shipman, Cynthia Zignego Stiverson, and John E. Ingram gave unstintingly of their time in making the collection manageable. Margaret C. Cook similarly guided me through the manuscript holdings of the Earl Gregg Swem Library of the College of William and Mary. I thank, too, Thad W. Tate, director of the Institute of Early American History and Culture, association with whom for many years has greatly enriched my understanding of Virginia history. The Institute's monthly colloquiums frequently afforded new insights as did many conversations about history with my former colleague at the Institute, Norman S. Fiering, now director of the John Carter Brown Library, with the editor of the *William and Mary Quarterly*, Michael McGiffert, and with members of the Colonial Williamsburg Research Department, the present director and vice president, Cary Carson, Kevin P. Kelly, John M. Hemphill, Peter V. Bergstrom, and Harold B. Gill, Jr. Anne Kelly, managing editor of the *Quarterly*, taught me the essentials of the computer program for preparing the index. Emory G. Evans of the University of Maryland shared numerous discoveries as he conducted research parallel to mine. Several anonymous editorial readers have been similarly generous, as has Peter R. Henriques of George Mason University. I appreciate, too, the strong encouragement for publication from Robert C. Birney, senior vice president of the Colonial Williamsburg Foundation, and the steady hand of Joseph N. Rountree, director of publications, in guiding the project. Publication was made possible in part by a grant from the Division of Research Programs of the National Endowment for the Humanities. Richard J. Stinely contributed his artistic talent in designing the book and drafting the maps. Finally, I will be ever grateful for the eagle eyes and stylistic sense of Colonial Williamsburg's managing editor, Donna C. Sheppard, and of her assistant, Sharon Thelin, and to Donna's spouse and my colleague in the William and Mary history department, Thomas F. Sheppard, who often found himself pressed into courier service. The errors remaining are unquestionably mine and not the editors'. Finally, I owe everything to the support and patience of Mary T. Selby and our children during the long hours away from home that it takes to write a book.

PROLOGUE

The Magazine

I N the governor's "Palace," as it was known in Williamsburg, Virginia,
a group of angry men confronted the royal governor, John Murray,
fourth Earl of Dunmore. At their head stood the Speaker of the
House of Burgesses, Peyton Randolph. With him were other magistrates
including the mayor of the city, John Dixon, and the treasurer of the
colony, Robert Carter Nicholas. The men indignantly protested the removal by British soldiers of gunpowder from the public magazine early
that morning, April 21, 1775. They had just come from a heated meeting at the courthouse at which they had barely persuaded a furious citizenry to let them confront the governor instead of assaulting the Palace.
The city's independent company of volunteers waited ominously under
arms on the green a short distance away.[1]

Everyone knew that the British secretary of state for the colonies, William Legge, Earl of Dartmouth, had sent circular letters to royal governors at the beginning of the year instructing them to seize any munitions
brought into the colonies and to prevent elections for a second Continental Congress.[2] In March the Virginia Convention in Richmond had
called upon the colony to assume "a posture of Defense" and had de-
fiantly selected representatives for the next Congress in Philadelphia.[3]
The day after the Convention adjourned Dunmore published the proclamation forbidding the election. Would he try to do more to interfere?
For several days the schooner H.M.S. *Magdalen* under Lieutenant Henry

Collins had been moored at Burwell's Landing on the James River four miles from Williamsburg, and local leaders knew that Dunmore had obtained the keys to the public magazine from the keeper. To forestall what the governor seemed to be contemplating, members of the city's volunteer company had been thinking of seizing the powder themselves.[1] Then, before dawn on April 21, Collins and his men slipped into town and carried off fifteen half-barrels from the magazine. Soon drums beating the alarm brought the volunteers and most of the population to the market square.

To the governor's surprise the address of the delegation before him was milder than the uproar in town had led him to expect, although he still deemed their statement "one of the highest insults."[5] The address pointed out that the powder belonged to the colony, not the crown, and demanded its immediate return in view of recent rumors of slave unrest. Clearly the city fathers intended to go no farther than they had to. They could not ignore the incident and wanted to be certain that Dunmore had no other moves in mind. On the other hand, Randolph and most other delegates had scheduled their departure soon for Congress. At Philadelphia they would have reliable news of the imperial government's answer to the petitions for redress of grievances that Congress had sent to Britain during its first session the fall before. More important, whatever happened, the response of delegates united in Congress would have greater effect than the rioting of a mob in Williamsburg.

Dunmore, too, did not want a showdown. He had expected his display of force to overawe the few rabble-rousers whom he considered to be behind the recent dissension. The extent of public reaction took him completely by surprise. To "sooth" the delegation, the governor later wrote to the British ministry, he replied that he had only taken the powder to protect it from the slaves—there actually were rumors of a possible uprising—and promised to return it promptly if needed. Impatiently the magistrates reminded him of the temper of the mob and he made preparations to defend himself. But again to his amazement, when the delegation returned to the courthouse, they represented his response as entirely satisfactory, and the crowd dispersed.[6]

That evening another mob gathered upon the rumor that the *Magdalen*'s men were coming again. Once more the city elders quieted the crowd. The next morning, his self-assurance regained, Dunmore flew into a violent rage in a chance encounter with an alderman and in a few words painted himself as more diabolical than the most suspicious had imagined. Incensed at the insolence shown him, he threatened to raise the slaves against the colonists and, swearing "I have once fought for the Virginians, and by God I will let them see that I can fight against them," ordered the arrest of William Finnie and George Nicholas, leaders of the volunteer company, before—Dunmore said—they could cause more trouble.[7] Fearful, some prominent citizens sent their families from the city, but peace returned to Williamsburg a third time.

Five days later three horsemen, Mann Page, Jr., Lewis Willis, and Benjamin Grymes, Jr., dashed into town after a hectic twenty-four-hour ride from Fredericksburg. Word of Dunmore's action had reached there just as that town's volunteers were mustering. Hugh Mercer and other officers immediately summoned neighboring companies to rendezvous on Saturday, April 29, for a march on Williamsburg and dispatched the riders to find out if Dunmore had restored the powder. Alarmed at their quest, Speaker Randolph sent them back after only a few hours' rest with assurances that the governor's explanation entirely satisfied Williamsburg leaders and a warning that "violent measures may produce effects, which God only knows the consequence of."[8] In Randolph's view an unruly mob at Fredericksburg served Virginia no better than one at Williamsburg.

Throughout the colony reports of the magazine incident were like sparks falling on dry brush. Spontaneously county committees offered protection to Williamsburg, and volunteer companies set out on the road to the capital. Recurring news of troop movements in Great Britain over the past months caused many to fear that Dunmore's raid was a prelude to invasion. The recent orders to colonial governors to prevent the second session of Congress spread the rumor that there was a blacklist of prominent Americans to be seized for trial in England. Although there is no evidence that such a list existed, Richard Henry Lee confidently informed Landon Carter that it contained thirty-two names in all, including several from Virginia.[9]

Faced with this possibility, the Virginia delegates hesitated to leave for Philadelphia until they learned what more Dunmore would do. As chairman of the Caroline County committee, Edmund Pendleton marshaled the men of his area but held them in camp pending word from the Speaker. Farther north George Washington hastened to meet the independent companies gathering at Alexandria. Then, as information indicated that Williamsburg was calm, Washington turned aside offers of a command on the grounds that the situation did not warrant delaying his return to Congress. On his way north, Randolph joined Pendleton in another appeal to the men at Fredericksburg. Richard Henry Lee, too, added his counsel to the chorus urging patience until Congress had a chance to act.[10]

On April 29 over six hundred mounted men gathered at Fredericksburg with more at Bowling Green in Caroline County and contingents en route from as far away as Berkeley and Frederick counties. All day a representative committee of 102 officers and men debated the delegates' advice. The evening before news arrived of the battles of Lexington and Concord in Massachusetts on April 19 when the military governor, General Thomas Gage, had sent troops to seize prominent New England leaders and stockpiles of arms. The similarity seemed too close to be coincidental. Nonetheless, the committee at length agreed to disband in deference to the Speaker but pledged "at a moment's warning" to defend "this or any sister colony, from unjust and wicked invasion." The troops unanimously ratified the decision, and word went to the others at Bowling Green and elsewhere to return home.[11]

Some were not dissuaded so easily, however. In Albemarle County volunteers voted to ignore the Fredericksburg decision and, after drumming out of their ranks two who wanted to disband, marched on. Down the road, they met others from Orange County. In Hanover County, as his fellow delegates to Congress turned northward, Patrick Henry, who was already famed for his ringing oratory in defiance of the king, put off his own departure for Philadelphia to revive the march on Williamsburg.[12]

At first the Hanover County committee refused to sanction Henry's plan, but in view of the news from Massachusetts gave their consent after a day-long debate on May 2. Late that evening Henry dispatched a small force to capture the receiver general, Richard Corbin, at his home in King and Queen County to force payment for the powder from the king's revenues in his possession. The next day the remainder of the force, about 150 men, reached Doncastle's Ordinary, some fifteen miles from the capital city.[13]

Fortunately for Corbin, he was at the Governor's Palace in Williamsburg for a Council meeting to deal with the threat from Fredericksburg. Lady Dunmore and her children had already boarded H.M.S. *Fowey* off Yorktown, and an appeal for reinforcements was on its way to General Gage and Admiral Samuel Graves in Boston. Threatening again to arm the slaves and spread "Devastation wherever I can reach," Dunmore fortified the Palace, and at word of Henry's movements ordered forty marines and sailors—"boiled crabs" the *Virginia Gazette* called them—from the *Fowey*.[14] When Henry asked the York County committee to block

Dunmore's retreat, Captain George Montagu of the *Fowey* bluntly threatened to bombard Yorktown, causing some to flee and shocking many more when they realized that the British navy was ready to treat them like a foreign enemy.[15]

On the evening of May 3 Corbin's son-in-law, Carter Braxton, rode into Williamsburg with a message from Doncastle's Ordinary. Returning from Caroline County, where he had been with Pendleton, Braxton had learned of the attempt on the receiver general and hastened to propose a truce to Henry while he arranged payment for the powder. The next morning Braxton brought a bill of exchange for £330 to Henry, who rejected the offer but accepted a note signed by Thomas Nelson, Jr., a prominent merchant-planter of Yorktown, instead. Henry promised to buy more powder with the money and to account for it at the next convention. At the same time Henry wrote Robert Carter Nicholas offering to continue into Williamsburg to protect the public treasury, but the Hanover County committee reported that Nicholas frigidly replied he had "no apprehension of the necessity or propriety of the proffered service." The treasurer also declined a similar offer from the New Kent County committee.[16] Thereupon Henry harangued his troops on the need for vigilance and sent them home. He himself headed northward. When Dunmore proclaimed Henry an outlaw, county after county voted to defend him, and three volunteer companies in full dress escorted him to the Maryland border.

The magazine incident and its immediate aftermath reveal the nuances within the political opposition to Great Britain in Virginia. Once again Henry was the hero. His defiance of British authority repeatedly dramatized the sentiments of many Virginians in a moment of crisis. On the other side, his willingness to risk rebellion and war distressed many, however firmly opposed to British policy they may have been. As Edmund Pendleton summarized the situation, "The Sanguine are for rash Measures without consideration, the Flegmatic to avoid that extreme are afraid to move at all, while a third Class take the middle way and endeavor by tempering the first sort and bringing the latter into action to draw all together to a Steddy, tho' Active Point of Defense."[17] Some like Braxton and Nicholas wanted to censure Henry at the next convention, causing the orator enough concern to ask Francis Lightfoot Lee to defend him when it met since Henry expected to be still in Congress. Most Virginia leaders, once Dunmore's intentions became clear, however, preferred to drop the matter for the sake of unity. Pendleton wrote from Philadelphia that as far as the other delegates were concerned, the episode had ended. Promising protection if Dunmore foolishly tried to arrest Henry, Pendleton urged that the affair be "as little Agitated as may be, lest difference of Sentiment should be wrought into dissentions, very injurious to the common Cause."[18]

CHAPTER 1

"The malignancy . . . and the wickedness . . . in their plans of despotism"

T HE magazine episode in Virginia released passions rising to the combustion point over the preceding decade. By the Treaty of Paris that ended the French and Indian War in 1763, Great Britain had expelled France from the North American mainland and more than doubled the area of the British American empire to include Canada and all the territory east of the Mississippi River, except the city of New Orleans. Faced with the added expense of these new possessions on top of the crushing debts of the war, the British government asserted the right of Parliament to tax the American colonies to help pay for their own defense and administration. The virtually unanimous reply from America was that by ancient right colonists could be taxed only by their representatives in colonial legislatures. There followed more than ten years of abstract but acrimonious debate over the extent of Parliament's authority, debate punctuated by death and destruction of property as colonists upon occasion resisted British claims by force.

Throughout the controversy Virginians had been in the forefront of the protests. In 1765 Patrick Henry's resolutions in response to the Stamp Act, and his speech comparing King George III to Caesar and the American resisters to Caesar's assassin Brutus, were among the most forceful statements of colonial legislative autonomy at the time. Because the royal governor Francis Fauquier refused to convene the General Assembly to elect delegates, Virginia was not represented at the Stamp Act Congress in New York, but its grass roots reaction to the new stamp tax was similar to that in several other colonies. An angry crowd cornered the stamp collector, George Mercer, on the porch of a tavern in Williamsburg. Although rescued by Fauquier, Mercer saw the wisdom of resigning the next day. Virginia courts closed rather than use stamped paper, and citizens almost universally observed boycotts of British goods. Largely because of the economic impact on British merchants of such boycotts throughout the colonies, Parliament repealed the Stamp Act the next year.[1]

In 1767 Parliament tried again to raise a revenue by enacting the Townshend Duties on items imported into the colonies: paper, paint, glass, and tea. Like many other colonists, Virginians again protested, and in June 1769, when the House of Burgesses passed a resolution rejecting Parliament's claims, the new governor, Norborne Berkeley, Baron de Botetourt, dissolved the assembly. A majority of the burgesses foiled him, however, by moving down the street in Williamsburg to the Raleigh Tavern. There, in extralegal session, they voted to join other colonies in an association binding signers a second time to boycott British imports. Within a year the Townshend Duties, too, except for that on tea, were repealed.[2]

Virginians employed the same tactic in May 1774 when the next governor, Lord Dunmore, dismissed the assembly for declaring a day of fast in support of Boston after that city's famous Tea Party the previous December when a band of Bostonians disguised as Indians dumped casks of dutied tea into Boston harbor. Confronted by this deliberate act of violence against British property, Parliament responded by closing the port of Boston and severely restricting Massachusetts's government until reparations were made. Once again members of the House of Burgesses thwarted the governor by adjourning to the Raleigh Tavern, where they formed another association against British imports and called for an annual meeting of colonial delegates in a "general congress . . . to deliberate on those general measures which the united interests of America may from time to time require."[3] This resolution was one of the earliest proposals for a Continental Congress.

Dissolution of the legislature played into the hands of the resisters because it occurred before the assembly could reenact the schedule of court fees, which had expired. Richard Henry Lee and others may have been looking for an excuse to close the courts again as had been done to protest the Stamp Act, but their chance of success came only after the news of the punishment of Boston arrived. In June county courts began to cease operations on the grounds that they could not legally assess fees. Dunmore denied any responsibility and blamed the closings on the Virginians' hope of evading payment of debts to British merchants. That motivation doubtless brought resisters important support since owing the British money would hardly have been a reason not to oppose the mother country. But critics of British taxation had already found frustrating British creditors good strategy in pressuring Parliament to change its policies, and now with marvelous irony the immediate cause of the cessation could be laid at the royalists' door. Questions arose over how far to pursue the tactic because of the impact on domestic litigation. Edmund Pendleton opposed any interference at all with the courts, but the tide of opinion against the British led him to be silent and go along. The refusal of lawyers to serve in the General Court the next fall compelled the suspension of civil proceedings in that body, too, although criminal hearings continued for another year.[4]

A few days after the meeting in the Raleigh Tavern, a circular letter arrived from Boston urging a halt to exports to Great Britain as well as imports. Twenty-five burgesses still in the vicinity summoned a convention to meet in Williamsburg on August 1, 1774, to consider the proposal. The call received enthusiastic response from the rest of the colony. In towns and about two-thirds of the counties meetings of "Freeholders and other inhabitants" endorsed Boston's cause as Virginia's own and hailed, albeit with some differences in detail, the idea of restrictions on trade.[5] Some meetings voted funds and supplies for the beleaguered northern city and, when the Council persuaded Dunmore to convene a new assembly in early August, held elections for it as well. Again the governor inadvertently handed his opponents an advantage by proroguing the new session before it met. Since local meetings had generally chosen the same representatives for both the convention and the assembly—most of whom, moreover, had been members of the previous legislature—the extralegal convention gained legitimacy.

A shadow government began to form to circumvent royal authority on one issue after another until the old regime became the shadow. The assembly had established a committee to correspond with other colonies in moments of crisis, especially between sessions, but otherwise the opposition in Virginia had needed little formal organization aside from the legislature itself until the call for a ban on British trade arrived. Virginia's port towns acted first, having received the circular letter about the same day as Williamsburg. Alexandria, Dumfries, Fredericksburg, Norfolk, and Portsmouth, followed by some of the county meetings, formed committees of correspondence to communicate "their sentiments on the present . . . Alarming situation of America" and "to take such steps for . . . the establishment of the rights of the colonies, as . . . shall appear most expedient and effectual," as one committee explained.[6] By the time the convention met, at least five counties—Dunmore, Fairfax, Frederick, Norfolk, and Stafford—had also given their committees the responsibility of enforcing a boycott as sentiment for once more adopting that strategy against the British grew.[7]

The Virginia Convention convened in Williamsburg during the first week of August. The delegates selected Peyton Randolph, Richard Henry Lee, George Washington, Patrick Henry, Richard Bland, Benjamin Harrison, and Edmund Pendleton to represent them in Congress and formed an association whose members agreed to halt imports from Great Britain after November 1, 1774, and shipments to the mother country after August 10, 1775. The Convention issued instructions to the congressional delegates that were calmly reasoned but firm. Briefly recounting the issues of taxation and representation that were in dispute, the directions emphasized Virginia's willingness to endure the "great Inconvenience" of curtailing trade to obtain redress and concluded with the abrupt warning that enforcement of the decrees against Massachusetts would "justify Resistance and Reprisal."[8]

In Philadelphia that October Congress took much the same stand. Electing Peyton Randolph president, the members adopted a Continental Association patterned on Virginia's, but delayed the dates for prohibiting imports to December 1, 1774, and exports to September 10, 1775. Congress also published as its own the Suffolk County Resolves of Massachusetts, a bristling declaration which Samuel Adams introduced that the punitive acts directed against Boston ought to be resisted with violence if enforced. Acceptance of these resolves and the rejection of a conciliatory proposal from Joseph Galloway of Pennsylvania to establish a separate parliament for America constituted victories for the more militant delegates, especially those from

New England. Even so, Congress declared, its purpose in endorsing the Suffolk Resolves was to "carry such conviction to the British nation, of the unwise, unjust, and ruinous policy of the present administration, as quickly to introduce better men and wiser measures." To this end it dispatched petitions to the king and people of Great Britain.[9]

Congress did not realize how committed to a confrontation with the colonies, beginning with Massachusetts, British officialdom had become. Although clearly prepared for the possibility of violence, neither Congress nor the Virginia Convention had yet concluded that British rule per se was bad and independence the only alternative. Congress's petitions rested on the same assumption that had guided colonial leaders since the onset of the controversy, that American troubles sprang from corruption in the British government which allowed wrongheaded ministers to work their wiles upon king and Parliament, but that otherwise the British system was essentially sound. The Convention, too, had emphasized in the instruction to its delegates that Virginians had no objection to the mercantilistic regulations that gave Great Britain a monopoly of the tobacco trade. The Convention stressed, however, that it regarded the burden of the tobacco monopoly on Virginians to be the principal contribution that the colonists should be expected to make toward the expenses of the empire.[10]

The American reluctance to part from the mother country is quite understandable, for colonists had always believed that, as Englishmen, they were the freest people on earth. The renowned political philosopher Baron de Montesquieu, although a subject of a nation with which Britain had often been at war over the past half-century, had declared after studying the constitutions of the world that the British form of government guaranteed freedom best. Montesquieu pronounced the British constitution a "beautiful system" of checks and balances with multiple separations of power between monarchy, aristocracy, and democracy, between the executive, legislative, and judicial branches, and between the two houses of the legislature. Little wonder that translations of his work, *The Spirit of the Laws,* became popular in Great Britain and the colonies.[11]

History recorded the same story. Americans read how Parliament had wrested freedom from Stuart tyrants during two revolutions in the seventeenth century. Most recently, victory in the Seven Years' War over the autocratic Louis XV of France combined the joys of liberty with the glory of belonging to the mightiest empire in the world—a "second Rome" some called it—a heritage not blithely cast away.[12] Here lies the anomaly of the American Revolution. It established for the modern world the right of a people to revolt against oppression and foreign domination. Yet unlike many of the revolutions for national self-determination that followed, it began, not with seething hatred for alien rulers, but with demands that Americans be accorded all the rights of Englishmen, that they be allowed to be even more English than they were.

Just as perplexing is the attitude of colonists toward the king. Eventually they renounced George III with the bitterness of disillusioned children who believe their parent has failed them, but until several months after fighting broke out colonists repeatedly appealed to the monarch for protection against the alleged corruption of ministers and Parliament. The resisters' insistence that George could help them requires explanation since the principle of parliamentary supremacy within the government was firmly established by that time.[13] For contemporaries in Great Britain and America, however, that principle did not mean that the king should be a figurehead. Ministers still functioned primarily as the crown's servants rather than as parliamentary leaders, and most Britons and Americans expected the monarch to have a significant voice in their selection.[14]

The trouble was that ministers also had to have support in Parliament, particularly in the House of Commons, to stay in office. Since early in the 1700s they relied on the "influence of the crown," as critics termed it, to line up votes. Barring other more pressing considerations, monarchists naturally tended to let the prince have his way and habitually supported any minister he appointed. In addition, the crown had considerable patronage that, before the advent of civil service systems based on merit, fell to the disposal of whomever the king selected. The narrow suffrage (probably no more than 250,000 persons in a population of over 6,000,000 had the right to vote) facilitated such influence, as did the inequitable system of representation that favored the aristocratic landholding classes. In some cases medieval constituencies from which population had shifted to rising commercial-industrial centers had become in contemporary eyes "rotten" or "pocket" boroughs with insignificant numbers of voters who could be manipulated by powerful lords or the crown itself.

Even in Great Britain critics decried such practices as violating the theoretical balance of the constitution between the executive and the legislative, but most British politicians brushed the complaints aside as visionary. How else could the government work? To colonists, who did not have to make it work, the practices meant, as Patrick Henry declared to the first Continental Congress, that the mother country "avows, in the face of the world, that bribery is part of her system of government."[15] As long as colonists preferred to remain monarchists and Englishmen, they blamed ministers for imperial policy, not the king. But whomever Americans found at fault, the apparent corruption of British politics explained how a Parliament that had won freedom for Englishmen in the seventeenth century could threaten American liberty in the eighteenth.

Actually, neither ministers nor George III had to resort to bribery to have their way on the American question. Colonial hopes notwithstanding, ministers, king, and a majority of Parliament had been of one mind on imperial affairs for some time. In Parliament there had been a feeling all along that colonists had been avoiding their share of expenses, particularly for their own defense, and that imperial controls needed to be tightened to halt what Britons generally regarded as an abuse. At first, before British emotions became greatly aroused, the government's concern for the effect of colonial boycotts on imperial trade led to repeals of the Stamp Act and the Townshend Duties despite a gnawing worry that yielding to the colonies undermined the mother country's authority. Repeated colonial defiance slowly hardened parliamentary opinion until the famous bull-necked patriotism of the British prevailed. Angered by the Boston Tea Party, Parliament rejected any thought of the economic cost of punitive measures no matter how eloquently a few critics of ministerial policy like Edmund Burke set it forth.[16]

The British majority, of course, did not see themselves as tyrants in the matter. To the contrary, most took as great pride in the vaunted freedom of Englishmen as Americans and conceded in principle that English liberty extended to the colonies. George III, puzzled by criticism from America, once protested that he was "fighting the battle of the legislature" there.[17] The monarch meant that, although his predecessors had often opposed Parliament, he supported its policies and therefore fit the contemporary British definition of a "whig" and a defender of liberty. Strange as it may seem, from one British viewpoint it was the colonists who were enemies of freedom and "tories." The key to Parliament's victory in the Glorious Revolution of 1688, and the whole point of "no taxation without representation," was to deny the crown any revenue except what Parliament appropriated, yet the colonists wanted control of their taxes which some British imagined they might use for the king against Britain's legislature. Though obviously Americans were not taking their stand for the benefit of the crown, such was the confusion of rhetoric and lack of understanding between subjects of the empire.[18]

In the end Thomas Jefferson wrote that an accumulation of little things broke up the empire. Though the examples he listed were constitutional and political, they doubtless stood for a host of other considerations as well. At bottom a clear conflict of interest existed between Parliament and the colonies which colonial leaders recognized immediately in the opening debate on the Stamp Act, but to which most British, not perceiving any danger of their Parliament acting arbitrarily, were less sensitive. If Parliament, in which Americans could not be effectively represented, had the right to tax them, no check stopped the natural temptation to shift financial burdens to the colonies. Worse, as colonists resisted, imperial administrators took measures—the threatened suspension of the New York legislature a few years before and the recent alteration by decree of the structure of Massachusetts's government, for example—that no Briton would have tolerated in his own country. Whatever their intention, the British faced the historic dilemma of imperialists: did rights and customs treasured at home automatically follow the flag overseas? It seemed to Americans that the ministry answered no, implying in the colonists' judgment that the British set a low priority on colonial interests in the empire. The implications of that attitude—economic and financial as well as political and constitutional—resisters could foresee, even though at the moment, as ministerial supporters pointed out, the stakes were only a threepenny tax on tea.[19]

In Virginia Dunmore's part in the crisis reveals many of the attitudes on both sides that led to rebellion. Frustrated after a twenty-year search for advancement at home, first in the army and then in politics (a comment perhaps on his talents), Dunmore had accepted posts overseas to improve his fortune. Although hardly penniless with estates in Scotland earning up to three thousand pounds a year, he eventually had eleven children to support. Despite an intimate friendship with the Earl of Shelburne and a close, although more formal, association over the next decade with Lord Bute and the Duke of Bedford, Dunmore never obtained the post for which he hungered.

The marriage of his wife's sister to Earl Gower, one of Bedford's lieutenants, gave him his opportunity overseas. Gower rose in office under Lord North, the prime minister throughout the seventies, and used his influence to secure appointments for Dunmore, first in 1770 as governor in New York and then within a year in Virginia.[20]

After the troubles began and Virginians thought about it, Dunmore's actions did not surprise them because he was a Scot. Having fought in 1689 and again in uprisings in 1715 and 1745 for the deposed Stuarts, Scots seemed to eighteenth-century Englishmen to have a natural affinity for toryism and tyranny, a prejudice toward Caledonians that colonists shared. Yet in contemporary British terms Dunmore qualified as a whig, that is, he accepted the Glorious Revolution, the supremacy of Parliament, and the accession of the house of Hanover to the British throne. While some of his ancestors, most notably his father, the third earl, in 1745, had supported the ousted Stuarts, the family generally accepted the inevitable and embraced the Act of Union with England under Queen Anne, and an uncle, the second earl, had become one of the principal generals of the Hanoverian monarch George II. Dunmore joined his uncle's regiment as a youth and modeled his political career upon the general's.

In retrospect Virginians said, too, that Dunmore had the mark of a tyrant from the start, that he was arrogant and intemperate, a boor, a drunkard, and a lecher. There is no doubt that the governor had a fiery temper and was often impetuous and incontinent, but most of the judgments are relative; drinking was no novelty in colonial Virginia. Usually the comparison was to Dunmore's immediate predecessor, Lord Botetourt, whose extraordinary charm and social grace inspired the General Assembly to erect a statue to his memory upon his untimely death after only two years in office. Again the judgment is relative. Dunmore was as cultivated as the average nobleman in that age of elegance and brought to the Palace one of the largest libraries in the colonies, many musical instruments, and an art collection noteworthy by contemporary standards. The difference was mainly in attitude and taste. Botetourt was a courtier, according to St. George Tucker of Williamsburg, "a man of parade."[21] Dunmore was an outdoorsman, a military man, who frequently chose the athletic Washington for his companion in the field and at dinner and the theater.

To make a fortune in the colonies Dunmore needed to win over the people, not oppress them, and during his first years in Virginia he succeeded quite well with some and less well with others, a not unusual record. Had it not been for the Revolution, Dunmore would probably have gone down in history as a typical mid-eighteenth-century administrator of little note. The Scot identified his adminis-tration with defense of Virginia's claims in the West, in which he personally invested. As for the constitutional issues, Dunmore off-handedly observed in a speech in the House of Lords shortly before he left for the colonies that "the Americans would soon be quiet, if they were only left to themselves."[22]

At the same time, in the governor's dealings with Virginians, he seemed from the beginning to have been conscious of his station and of the colonists' subordinate position. Informed that it was customary for new governors to call elections upon their arrival, for example, Dunmore explained to the ministry that he consented because "I was told, that it would be pleasing to the people, who are no doubt fond of the exercise of that power, which makes them feel their own con-sequence." He also had a habit of dismissing the legislature, even when they parted amicably, with a homily. Once he told it "to infuse that Spirit of Industry, which alone can make a Country flourish," and another time "to abolish that Spirit of Gaming, which I am afraid but too generally prevails among the People."[23] Later, he resumed his crit-icism of Virginians when events put more bite in his words and fre-quently told British correspondents that Virginians were really quite lazy. Like many of his countrymen in Britain, Dunmore reacted to the Virginians' resistance with some surprise and considerable anger that colonists did not appreciate all that the British had done for them.

Dunmore's overriding concern for opening the West in his early years as governor fitted the predilections of many Virginians. For economy in administration and defense, after the peace in 1763 the ministry issued a proclamation forbidding settlers to cross the Appa-lachian Mountains into the vast area just won from France. Now re-ports circulated that Philadelphia interests who had the ear of the cabinet might obtain an exception to the proclamation and receive a land grant known as Vandalia along the eastern bank of the Ohio River in territory Virginians considered theirs. Since Dunmore's own hopes of speculation made him a Virginian on the matter, he ignored virtually everything his instructions required him to do to enforce the restrictions on western settlement. Reprimands inevitably began to come from Great Britain until at last—ironically, just as the first Vir-ginia Convention was meeting—imperial officials advised the gover-nor of "his Majesty's just Displeasure" and told him that he was on dangerous ground.[24] If other events had not intervened, Dunmore might well have been recalled for being too partial to Virginians.

The dispute over the West also showed that Dunmore was not afraid to settle issues with violence. On a journey to the area around Pittsburgh in the summer of 1773, he encouraged Virginia settlers not to recognize Pennsylvania's authority and fixed upon one of the most aggressive Virginians who had moved into the area, Dr. John Connolly, as his spokesman. During the winter of 1773–1774 Connolly succeeded in capturing Fort Pitt, renaming it Fort Dunmore. The rising hostility of Shawnee Indians in the area, against whom both Virginians and Pennsylvanians retaliated brutally, complicated the situation. Some observers began to wonder whether each side had not provoked the tribe to create a pretext for war among the whites. With the Council's concurrence, in April 1774 Dunmore requested the Virginia legislature to authorize an expedition against the Shawnee and issued a proclamation calling upon the western militia "to repel any insult whatever." The government of Pennsylvania, he declared, was obstructing "his Majesty's Government . . . under my administration." Furthermore, he added—almost as an afterthought— there was "danger of annoyance from the Indians also." Months later Lord Dartmouth wrote back in astonishment, "I must observe to your Lordship that your Proclamation . . . implies too strongly the Necessity of exerting a Military Force, and breathes too much a Spirit of Hostility, that ought not to be encouraged in Matters of Civil Dispute between the Subjects of the same State."[25]

When the burgesses refused the troops he wanted, Dunmore mounted a campaign with western militia. Assuming personal command, he departed from Williamsburg in early July, barely a month after the imperial crisis had forced him to dissolve the legislature and scarcely three weeks before the Virginia Convention was to convene in the colonial capital. The campaign was an overwhelming success, with Colonel Andrew Lewis of Augusta County winning the crucial battle at Point Pleasant at the mouth of the Great Kanawha River in modern West Virginia on October 10. Nine days later Dunmore signed a treaty with Chief Cornstalk who yielded all of the territory south of the Ohio River to Virginia. The governor marched triumphantly back to Williamsburg in early December. "I am just returned from williamsburgh," wrote an officer who accompanied Dunmore to friends in the West, "the news is that all the Country is well pleased with the Governors Expedition."[26]

To crown his laurels, the day before the governor reached the cap-

ital Lady Dunmore gave birth to a daughter, whom the parents chris-
tened Virginia in appreciation of the colony's esteem. Since her arrival in Virginia, the colony's first lady captivated all who met her with
a beauty and charm already renowned in Britain and Europe. The
day after her husband dissolved the assembly in June, the House of
Burgesses had nonetheless proceeded with a ball at the Capitol which
they had been planning in her honor. Now, at another ball that the
governor gave at the Palace on January 19, 1775, the day of his
daughter's christening and the queen's birthday, Dunmore stood at
the pinnacle of his fame. "He is as popular as a Scotsman can be
amongst weak prejudiced people" was the wry comment of a fellow
Scot, the Norfolk merchant James Parker.[27]

Once back in Williamsburg Dunmore hastened to catch up with his
duties and the imperial situation. While in the West, he had dispatched a brief one-page notification of the August Convention
to Lord Dartmouth.[28] Otherwise the governor had sent only routine communications to London that gave insufficient hint of the increasing restlessness in the colony. All through the fall county
committees—more than twenty since the delegates had adjourned—
continued to form to enforce the trade regulations established
by the Convention and reiterated by Congress. A number of persons
had been held up to public censure for violating the Association
or for expressions deemed inimical to the cause. Three or four
counties—Fairfax, Prince William, Spotsylvania, and probably Hanover, too—had each formed an "independent Company of Volunties"
that they equated with the militia although the companies elected
their own officers and were outside the royal governor's command.[29]
As a measure of the Fairfax unit's expected permanence, Washington by midwinter had ordered a uniform from Philadelphia to wear
as the company's commander.

Dunmore summarized all of this activity for Dartmouth in a fifty-
page report dated Christmas Eve 1774. Yet significantly he devoted
four-fifths of the letter to defending his policy in the West and his
machinations against Pennsylvania. Concerning the growing resistance, the governor advised Dartmouth simply to take the Virginians
at their word. They had already closed the courts—he repeated his
view that they hoped to escape payment of their debts to Great Britain—so suspend the entire government, set up a blockade to enforce
the resisters' own ban on British trade, and see who weakened first.
The opposition's apparent strength, Dunmore wrote, sprang from the

fact that the county committees and volunteer companies intimidated people rather than that the dissenters had the support of the majority, whom the earl considered to be wholeheartedly loyal.[30]

Dartmouth thus had little knowledge from his official contact in Virginia of developments in the colony during six crucial months in which the ministry pushed steadfastly ahead with its plans to bring Boston to heel. The government's crucial assumption was that colonies to the south would not aid Massachusetts, allowing the British to confront that colony alone. After learning in July 1774 that Dunmore had dissolved the Virginia legislature for proclaiming a day of fasting, Dartmouth had no hard news from the colony other than the cryptic outline of the Convention's meeting, which he received in October. Not until February 10, 1775, did Dunmore's voluminous report arrive. The secretary was shaken. "The steps which have been pursued in the different Counties of Virginia to carry into execution the Resolutions of the General Congress," he wrote to Dunmore a month later, "are of so extraordinary a Nature, that I am at a loss for words to express the criminality of them, and my Surprise, that, the people should be so infatuated, as tamely to submit to Acts of such Tyranny and Oppression." He had read the letter to Parliament, he told Dunmore, and expected Virginia's trade to be interdicted as was Boston's, just as the governor recommended.[31]

Dunmore failed to follow his own advice to leave punitive action to the navy, however. It was not his nature to be patient. Furthermore, he received two instructions from Dartmouth about checking resistance, one in February and the other in mid-March. The first ordered "the most effectual measures for arresting, detaining, and securing any Gunpowder, or any sort of Arms or Ammunition which may be attempted to be imported into the Province under your Government"; the second directed the prevention of elections for a second Continental Congress. These directives were dispatched to governors generally; in no sense were they intended specifically for Virginia.[32] The ministry clearly did not contemplate military action in all the colonies at once and, not expecting significant trouble outside of Massachusetts, intended its instructions to be preventive rather than confrontational. Dunmore interpreted them in this sense, too, because he confessed to Dartmouth that he had hoped the raid on the magazine in Williamsburg could "have been done privately."[33] Yet apart from these circulars and one other communication in May authorizing Dunmore to reconvene the General Assembly, the earl received no direc-

tions at all until December 1775, as he quite justly and bitterly complained. What he did that spring, he did largely on his own.

Appearances, however, were otherwise. The *Virginia Gazette* had published accounts of the ministry's efforts to halt the munitions traffic
as early as December 8, 1774, and a variety of reports, many inaccurate and some highly inflammatory, emanated from Great Britain
as a result of public discussions there about how to handle the colonies. Often no more than the observations of private citizens, the
opinions expressed made unrealistic assumptions about British capa-
bilities and ignored the effect the comments might have on colonial
feelings—some proposed sending armadas to America and a number
suggested freeing the slaves, for example. Official British plans consequently appeared much better concerted to Americans than they
actually were and to encompass more than just Massachusetts.[34]

The brothers Lee, William and Arthur, provided an important, although by no means exclusive, conduit of these stories to Virginia.
William had settled in London as a merchant and Arthur had been
in Great Britain for over a decade as a seemingly perpetual student,
initially in medicine and then in law. Both associated with a body of
parliamentary dissenters centered in London that was sympathetic to
the colonies, but that had little influence in Parliament because the
British pattern of representation so heavily favored the countryside
over the city. Through these contacts William had been elected a sher-
iff of London in 1773 and alderman two years later. Because the Lees'
connections, and the sources through which Americans received their
information generally, lay mainly among the mercantile, urban classes
in Great Britain, colonists were often misled as to the amount of public support that they could expect in the mother country. At the same
time, rumors about the ministry's plans uncritically reported in the
British press, and as uncritically repeated in the American, gave an
exaggerated view of the extent and efficiency of the ministry's response to colonial resistance.[35]

Dunmore's experience in Virginia serves as a microcosm of the general breakdown in imperial relations. Despite all that the governor
thought he, and by extension the empire, had done for Virginians,
he appeared deeply enmeshed in the Machiavellian scheming. In the
end only Governor Thomas Hutchinson of Massachusetts rivaled the
earl as the most hated British official in North America. Dunmore so
exasperated firebrands like Patrick Henry that other leaders feared

they could not keep Virginia from outracing Congress into rebellion, thereby sacrificing the strength and protection that unity would bring.

As if the coincidence of the magazine raid and the battles of Concord and Lexington were not enough, about the time that word of the fighting in the North reached Virginia in late April the *Virginia Gazette* published excerpts from Dunmore's Christmas Eve letter to Lord Dartmouth. William Lee had been sending copies broadcast to correspondents in Virginia. "Judge whether it may not be proper to publish it," he told his brother Richard Henry, who had remained at home, "the malignancy of it and the wickedness in urging your enemies to persevere in their plans of despotism against America should certainly be exposed."[36] Fortunately for Dunmore, because Dartmouth had read only portions of the report to Parliament, the press had not yet obtained the passages calling for the suspension of Virginia's government and a blockade.

An indication of Virginians' continued high expectations of the empire is their apparently unquestioned assumption that Dunmore ought to have been on their side. They expected the governor to help persuade his countrymen of the need for accommodation by stressing Virginia's resoluteness in defense of its rights and the likelihood that most Americans would stand together against Great Britain. Dunmore's contrary estimation that just a small number of malcontents were the cause of the trouble—an assessment in which he was not alone among royal officials in America—flew so diametrically against what Virginians knew to be the truth that the governor's purpose could only have been malicious. Jefferson expressed the general puzzlement when he observed that "the ministry have been deceived by their officers on this side the water, who (for what purposes I cannot tell) have constantly represented the American opposition as that of a small faction, in which the body of the people took little part." Later, George Mason repeated, "There never was an idler or a falser Notion than that which the British Ministry have imposed upon the Nation 'that this great Revolution has been the Work of a Faction, of a Junto of ambitious Men, against the Sense of the People of America.'"[37]

Whatever the Virginians' anticipation, Dunmore, despite extensive tours of the backcountry, had no comprehension of the extent of disaffection in Virginia. Whatever his motives, the little intelligence that he sent the mother country was simply wrong. It may have been that

his recent popularity clouded his vision or that Virginia leaders protested their loyalty and quieted their more militant followers too well.
It may also have been that Dunmore, like other British of his generation, self-satisfied with the power and glory of the empire and with
their nation's own freedom and the Parliament that had achieved it,
could not take colonial cries of tyranny seriously. Most Britons of that
generation could only conclude that the colonial opposition, despite
American denials, had ulterior motives from the start, to avoid debts
and taxes, for instance, or to gain independence. Appearances did
not coincide with reality on either side.

CHAPTER 2

Britain's Oldest Dominion

T HE oldest British colony in North America, Virginia in the
1770s was also the most populous and the most extensive both
in settled area and in its western claims, which reached beyond the Great Lakes and to the Mississippi River. Geographically the
Chesapeake Bay and four great rivers that flowed into it from the
west, the Potomac, the Rappahannock, the York, and the James, dominated the colony. These water barriers divided the eastern portion of
the colony into broad regions: the Eastern Shore between the Atlantic
Ocean and the bay, which Virginia shared with Maryland, and, from
north to south on the western shore, the Northern Neck, and the
middle and lower peninsulas. To the south and west of the James
beyond the tidal flow lay the Southside. In some cases tides affected
the rivers as much as a hundred miles upstream to a point called the
fall line where a change in the underlying rock formation produced
swirling rapids beyond which oceangoing vessels could not pass. The
fall line divided the Tidewater downstream from the Piedmont to the
west. A hundred miles or so farther on the Blue Ridge Mountains
ran from northeast to southwest, and beyond them lay a great valley
known variously as the Shenandoah Valley, the Valley of Virginia, or
simply the Valley. From Hampton Roads at the mouth of the James
to the Eastern Shore or through the Virginia Capes to open ocean
required most of a day's sail with a favorable wind. Overland from

Williamsburg to Richmond in good weather took more than a day; to the Northern Neck or westward to Charlottesville at the foot of the mountains, about four; and to the Valley, five or more.

Most estimates place the colony's population in the 1770s at around half a million, nearly twice as large as that of either of the nearest challengers, Massachusetts and Pennsylvania. Of the five hundred thousand Virginians, almost 40 percent were slaves. In half of the Tidewater counties and perhaps a third of the Piedmont, a majority of the population was black.

Although the best statistical evidence on the pattern of landholding comes from the closing years of the war and immediately afterward, it seems to reflect a continuation or perhaps intensification of trends under way rather than a sudden shift from the prewar period. At the war's end the typical white Virginia male was a small farmer, yet together, whether as landowners or tenants, small farmers possessed a little less than half of the land in Virginia. Landowners comprised just under 50 percent of the white males while renters made up another 10 to 20 percent. The majority had access to no more than a couple of hundred acres, at most a slave or two, and some cattle. At the other end of the economic spectrum, 10 percent of the white males owned the other half of the land and almost as much of the personal property. The remaining whites were agricultural laborers, free or indentured, with little property and few expectations.[1]

The degree of concentration of land ownership varied among regions. In most of the Tidewater the percentages of landowners (not quite half) and of laborers (about a third) paralleled those in the colony as a whole. But in the Northern Neck, which the crown had granted the Fairfax family as a proprietorship, land had been distributed in the seventeenth and early eighteenth centuries in larger speculative tracts. In some parts after the Revolutionary War as much as 70 percent, the highest figure in Virginia, lay in the hands of a few, and more tenants (20 percent) and laborers (40 percent) lived there than elsewhere. Three-quarters of the whites in the area were landless. Settlement of the Piedmont north of the James River occurred in a spurt during the second quarter of the eighteenth century, produced also by larger grants. As a result, by the end of the Revolution 30 percent of the white population in Powhatan County just west of the fall line owned an average of five hundred acres apiece compared with 20 percent overall, and almost 10 percent had over one thousand. In general, the farther west, the more the small farmer came into his own. More than half of the whites in the Piedmont owned land although the percentage of landless laborers approached that of the Tidewater. About a third of the landowners held no slaves compared with only a tenth of the landholders to the east.[2]

The Valley and the Southside were nearer the frontier stage. Opened about the same time as the Piedmont, the Valley was only half as densely settled by the time of the Revolution. The northern section, which is the lower valley because the Shenandoah flows northward, lay within the Fairfax grant. Large holdings characterized that region, as they did the rest of the proprietorship; small farmers predominated farther south in the upper valley. The southern section and a few scattered areas remote from navigable rivers in the east were the only places in Virginia where subsistence farming lingered.

The majority of Valley settlers were German and Scotch-Irish from Pennsylvania with a significant minority of English background from eastern Virginia. In a total population of around thirty-five thousand, slaves accounted for a little over 10 percent. Hemp, grain, cattle, and horses were the principal products, along with a considerable amount of iron manufactured at such works as Isaac Zane's in Frederick County and Henry Miller's in Augusta. Much of the Valley's early trade had flowed northward along the Great Wagon Road to Philadelphia. Wagon traffic to Alexandria and Fredericksburg from Winchester became possible by the end of the 1740s because the mountains are lower toward the north. Travel through Rockfish Gap from Staunton to Fredericksburg was not feasible until the mid-fifties; through Swift Run Gap not until after the French and Indian War. Alexandria dominated the trade of the northern or lower valley as did Fredericksburg the upper until the 1760s when Richmond captured the burgeoning wheat and flour trade of the region south of Staunton.[3]

The Southside below the James was the region most recently settled. Much of the area is drained by the Roanoke River, which flows southeastward through North Carolina into Albemarle Sound, where it is difficult for deep-sea vessels to go. Not only did Virginia pioneers have no river route to follow as they did in the region north of the James, but there was less of a possibility of establishing a commercial agricultural economy without ready access to world markets. Aside from the Tidewater areas along the James and Appomattox rivers, significant settlement did not begin until mid-century, with predictably less social stratification a single generation later. In Lunenburg County during pre-Revolutionary days, for example, 60 to 70 percent of the whites were landholders, the majority small farmers, but already about half of them owned slaves.[4]

Despite the influx of Scotch-Irish and Germans into the West, over four-fifths of all white Virginians were of English extraction. No more than 5 or 6 percent of the white population followed occupations unrelated to farming, particularly tobacco farming. The broad river system of the Tidewater that permitted oceangoing vessels to sail inland directly to the docks of plantations long discouraged urban growth. Tobacco also did not require the elaborate processing that might have provided a nucleus for large cities, and mechanisms of distribution such as commodity exchanges developed mostly in Europe where the market was. With the opening of the Piedmont, towns like Fredericksburg, Richmond, and Petersburg sprang up at the rapids of streams where goods had to be transshipped, but none had yet attained the size or status of a city. Only three sites incorporated by the legislature could boast of that designation. Jamestown and Williamsburg were essentially governmental entities, and the first, the long-abandoned seventeenth-century capital, had become a ghost town by the 1770s. Norfolk, with a population of about six thousand, alone bore promise of becoming an economic entrepôt for the colony.[5]

In the early 1770s Virginia was exporting annually nearly seventy million pounds of tobacco, which accounted for about 40 percent of the exports to Great Britain from the thirteen colonies combined. For over a hundred years British navigation laws required colonists to ship tobacco only to British or other imperial ports and to buy virtually all their imports from the mother country. So far Virginians had submitted to these controls; apart from allegiance and the need for British help in defense, the mother country's credit and mercantile superiority made acquiescence worth the price. The 1774 Convention, for example, accepted the resulting costs as the colonists' share of the empire's expenses. To offset those costs one resort was to seek economies of scale, explaining in part the rise of great commercial farms or plantations. Larger growers in the eighteenth century functioned as wholesalers, shipping their products to British merchants for sale on consignment in the mother country or on the Continent, and often augmented their cargoes with selective purchases of their smaller neighbors' crops. British correspondents assembled return cargoes of manufactured goods, again on commission, that the planters ordered for their own use or, adding the job of merchants to their role as farmers, for sale in their neighborhoods. Serving in effect as agents in the international marketplace for all tobacco producers, large and small, further enhanced the social and political dominance of the great planters at home.[6]

The Act of Union between England and Scotland in 1707 qualified Scottish merchants as British nationals under the navigation laws, and by the 1770s Scots, led by the great houses of William Cunninghame, John Glassford, and Alexander Speirs in Glasgow, had cornered half or more of the tobacco market. For the most part the Scots did not replace the great planter in the older sections of the colony but proved more adept at handling the increasing production of the Piedmont at a distance from the river highways of the Tidewater. Reversing the pattern of the consignment system, the merchant houses maintained agents or factors in stores around the countryside who purchased tobacco and sold merchandise on the spot, a practice more convenient for small farmers. The system in Virginia centered in Norfolk, where chief factors assembled the necessary quantities of tobacco to fill the holds of company ships quickly and send them home with minimum delay and expense. Not unexpectedly, the Scots' success did not enhance their reputation among Virginians of English descent, especially since restrictive contracts bound many of the factors not to marry in America or otherwise put down roots. Unlike other immigrants, most of them remained aliens among the people who were the source of their obviously quite profitable business.[7]

One aspect of imperial regulation about which Virginians did complain was the enormous debt they owed the mother country. Again figures are inexact, but it is estimated that the total for Virginia, even after Scottish factors sent off massive tobacco shipments as war loomed that may have reduced the debt by as much as a half, easily exceeded one million pounds sterling. The amount nearly equaled that owed by all the rest of the thirteen colonies together. Yet Virginia was one of the richest provinces in British America.

Confusing the issue is the fact that no formal banking system existed in the colonies. All loans were from individual to individual, inextricably mixing credit for private consumption with business investments. Personal extravagance unquestionably contributed to the enormity of the debt, as the number of mansions dotting the Virginia landscape suggests. But commercial farmers in every age have required credit to bridge the gap between planting and selling their crops, and in the case of tobacco the gap was wider than most. British merchants had to finance Virginia growers for as long as two years, one London commentator dolefully observed, before a lender could expect a return.[8] Moreover, the system spawned a different ethic for planters from that of a Puritan or Quaker merchant. While it was incumbent upon the latter to appear to live abstemiously to improve his credit, in a plantation society a grand style afforded the best assurance of solvency.

In addition, the colonies' monetary system proved so inadequate for the volume of trade that even retail transactions produced longstanding debts. No gold or silver mines afforded a ready supply of bullion in British America as they did in parts of Latin America, and what specie came into British colonies through trade with the French and Spanish islands in the Caribbean soon disappeared in remittances to Great Britain. Paper currency, often issued to finance colonial participation in imperial wars, tended to depreciate relative to sterling. To protect British creditors, Parliament severely curtailed emissions. A more widespread solution for the colonists was a sophisticated form of barter in which individuals kept track of obligations on their ledgers until the opportunity arose, sometimes years later, to settle accounts with a reciprocal exchange of goods or services. Everyone owed everyone else. The British debt provided only the outer strand of an intricate and vaster web of indebtedness upon which internal as well as external trade depended entirely.[9]

Because of the marketability and ease of storage of tobacco, Virginia had been able to avoid printing paper money longer than any other mainland province by using the weed itself as currency. Finally the expense of the French and Indian War forced the colony to approve a paper issue in 1755. Generally declining tobacco prices due to the war's disruption of the European market, however, weakened Virginia's economy and depreciated its currency significantly. Lobbying in Parliament by British creditors fearful of losses if sterling debts were paid in the cheaper medium led to the Currency Act of 1764, which banned further issues of paper as legal tender anywhere in the colonies. Coincidentally, revelations upon the death in 1766 of the venerable Speaker of the House of Burgesses, John Robinson, who had held that post for twenty-eight years and who was also treasurer of the colony, worsened the effect of the law in Virginia. Instead of retiring currency when it came into the treasury as taxes as the law directed, Robinson had reissued it in loans to eminent, financially distressed Tidewater planters, speeding depreciation. The scandal deeply divided Robinson's allies and critics within the establishment and provoked serious doubts in all ranks of society about the integrity and justice of the planter elite's governance.[10]

Ironically, it was Virginia's wealth that in large part served to swell its indebtedness beyond that of other colonies. Because mainland America had few products besides tobacco with a guaranteed market in Britain and Europe, the debt seemed good business from a British point of view, and the colony's wealth and obligations grew apace. As the size and value of crops increased, English consignment merchants and Scottish houses freely extended credit in fierce competition with each other. After the French and Indian War, local Virginia merchants had begun to participate in what contemporaries called the "cargo trade," imitating the Scots by importing goods on consignment from English merchants to offer for the purchase of tobacco. In addition, Scottish firms expanded their business by half. The extent of the latter's inroads among smaller producers, especially in the Piedmont, is evident from the fact that by the time of the Revolution Scots held 60 percent of the total British debt. In the case of some companies as much as nine-tenths was for amounts under one hundred pounds, with around thirty pounds the average, the value to a small farmer of about one to two years' crops.[11]

During the 1760s and early 1770s rapid cycles of boom and bust made Virginians more aware of how vulnerable they were because of their dependence on the financial system of Great Britain. A depression in the mother country at the end of the Seven Years' War caused a tightening of credit throughout the empire coinciding with passage of the deflationary currency law of 1764. To the colonists' good fortune, the bad times in Britain magnified the impact of the boycott protesting the Stamp Act. Short crops in the late sixties improved prices again, and the end of nonimportation agreements against the Townshend Acts in 1770 encouraged a rush of imports. In 1772 the boom burst with the collapse of banks in Scotland and London, resulting in another financial crisis for the empire. Record tobacco crops also reversed the upward trend in prices, and, to compound the problem, an issue of paper currency that the Virginia General Assembly had authorized, although not as legal tender, to compensate owners for tobacco destroyed in public warehouses during a flood rapidly depreciated because of extensive counterfeiting. The overall impact proved more detrimental to consignment merchants and Virginia cargo traders than to the Scots. With greater capital and inventories at their disposal, the latter more readily shifted to simple barter in purchasing tobacco. The collapse ended the resurgence in the consignment trade while the Scots increased their share of the tobacco market to about three-fourths for the next year or two.[12]

What effect these economic troubles had upon political developments in Virginia is problematical, for at the time few commentators remarked on the economic aspects of the constitutional debate with Britain. The long resistance of Virginians during and after the Revolutionary War to repayment of the British debt is not directly relevant to the prewar period because after independence such concerns as withholding funds from an enemy and attempting to ensure British compliance with the peace treaty intervened.[13] Contemporaries before the war understood the short-run advantage to debtors of the general resistance to British policy; Dunmore's comments reflect that. But to have decided on rebellion and then independence for primarily personal financial purposes would have required explaining where credit for overseas trade was to come from in the future since the need certainly would continue. From the long-range standpoint the existence of the debts could have become an argument against rebellion—a reason, perhaps, that resisters to British policy did not dwell on the issue.

The thinking of a number of influential opinion makers on the subject of the debts was not consistent with repudiation. The best-known example is the attitude of Jefferson's family. Just after the French and Indian War his father-in-law, John Wayles, remarked, "Luxury and expensive living have gone hand in hand with the increase of Wealth." Although Wayles seldom saw an oriental rug in his youth, "Now nothing are so common as Turkey and Wilton Carpetts."[14] After the Revolution, his son-in-law echoed the sentiment when, having spent years paying off the obligations Wayles bequeathed him, Jefferson lamented how "debts had become hereditary from father to son for many generations."[15] In all the colonies some of the most vocal leaders of the opposition—men like Richard Henry Lee of Virginia, John and Samuel Adams of Massachusetts, and Henry Laurens of South Carolina—found moral as well as political benefits in economic retaliation against the British. Besides applying pressure on the royal government, the restriction of imports to America checked the growth of luxury that these leaders deemed incompatible with a love of liberty and revived handicrafts like the making of homespun, the use of which seemed more virtuous than relying on outside manufactures. In Virginia the answer to the problem of debts that Jefferson, Mason, Lee, and others of this mind preferred was a lower standard of living, not another round of self-gratification by reneging on what was already due.[16]

Actually, changes were occurring in Virginia that promised a way out by diversifying the markets upon which the colonists depended. Although tobacco continued to be the major staple, still accounting for almost five-sixths of the colony's income from exports, more and more Virginians over the past generation had begun to cultivate grain commercially. By the end of the third quarter of the century the province had become the largest colonial producer of corn, exporting well over a half-million bushels a year. It ranked third behind Pennsylvania and New York in the production of wheat, exporting in the form of grain, bread, or flour the equivalent of about four hundred thousand bushels annually—as yet only a third of Pennsylvania's massive output, but four-fifths of New York's.[17]

Behind these figures lay the beginning of a dramatic shift in Virginia's economic base. There had long been a small surplus of foodstuffs for export, which for the most part New Englanders in the West Indian trade had purchased. The change began in the 1730s and 1740s with the settling of new sugar lands in the Caribbean, particularly in the interior of Britain's largest island, Jamaica. By the 1770s the demand for Virginia corn there had increased almost tenfold. About mid-century, too, new markets opened in Spain, Portugal, and the Madeira Islands for New York and Pennsylvania wheat. Demand quadrupled over the next generation. Commercial wheat production for sale to the Middle Colonies spread into northern and western Maryland and the northern section of the Virginia Piedmont. Loudoun and Fauquier counties were heavily committed by the time of their separation from Fairfax and Prince William in 1757 and 1759, and over the next decade and a half the lower and then the upper Valley followed suit. The Eastern Shore and the James River valley remained the colony's centers of corn production, but as tobacco fields wore out, wheat appeared there, too. Wheat also spread into northeastern North Carolina, enabling Norfolk, which tapped that area as well as Virginia, to develop as a center of the wheat trade along with tobacco. Neil Jamieson, chief factor for Glassford and Company, for example, doubled as one of Virginia's leading dealers in grain.[18]

After the Seven Years' War five or six years of exceptionally bad harvests in Italy and the Iberian Peninsula caused a gigantic spurt in demand. In one year, 1768 to 1769, Virginia's exportation of wheat jumped from 170,000 bushels to 392,000. At the same time, increasing population and industrialization forced Great Britain, which had traditionally been a major exporter of grain to Europe, to curtail shipments and even import grain upon occasion. A rising competitor of Philadelphia, New York replaced New England as Virginia's principal customer in the coastwise shipment of wheat. But the shift in trade reflected Virginia's growth, too. Over three-quarters of the vessels in the earlier trade to New England had been from that region and at most a fifth from Virginia; the ratio in the trade to the Middle Colonies was practically the reverse. Although neither Virginia nor Maryland alone yet outstripped Philadelphia, the Chesapeake as a whole displaced the Quaker City as the largest colonial shipbuilding region behind New England. More than a few Virginians were turning to the sea like the Yankees.[19]

These economic changes forged links to sister colonies that were reassuring politically as resistance to Great Britain stepped up. In addition to Washington's fame for his exploits in the French and Indian War and Henry's oratorical renown, Benjamin Harrison, for instance, was known in Philadelphia when he arrived for the first Continental Congress because he had apprenticed his son and namesake to the firm of Willing and Morris in the sixties. Carter Braxton, another Virginian who subsequently became a delegate, had been associated in trade with the Browns of Providence, Rhode Island, and had journeyed to New England himself.[20] Such contacts promoted an awareness of the strength and potential of the American economy that reinforced many Americans' belief in the primary importance of the mainland North American colonies to the empire, particularly after the conquest of Canada. At the outset of the constitutional debate with Great Britain this confidence tended to emphasize rather than loosen imperial ties as Virginians among others turned initially to economic forms of protest on the assumption that Britain could not afford to ignore them. But when it appeared that the British estimate of the colonies' importance in the empire was not the Americans', the same confidence persuaded colonists that they could manage without the mother country if they had to, provided they joined together.

Internally, however, the same economic and geographic growth that provided the energy and self-confidence to confront the empire produced a pluralism that called for internal adjustments as well. In Virginia the established Church of England was losing the allegiance of an increasing proportion of the population. There were large numbers of unchurched, and, although still no more than a fifth of the whites, the membership of dissenting sects had grown dramatically in recent years. Presbyterianism had come to the Valley with the Scotch-Irish and gained believers east of the Blue Ridge during the Great Awakening, the revival that had swept the colonies beginning in the 1740s. The first Virginia presbytery was formed in Hanover County in the Piedmont in 1755. Patrick Henry attributed his eloquence to the oratorical style of the sect's most famous preacher, Samuel Davies. Moravians and other German sectaries and Quakers also settled in the Valley, and a number of the latter lived in the Richmond area. Regular Baptists had been in the northern Piedmont from the 1750s on. More spectacular was the spread of the Separate Baptists from North Carolina into the Southside and the northern Piedmont in the late 1760s and early 1770s. Their membership had risen from virtually none in 1765 to about ten thousand on the eve of the Revolution. This growth rate may have seemed even more explosive to contemporaries because attendance at Baptist gatherings sometimes numbered in the thousands. The Reverend Devereux Jarratt of Dinwiddie County and one or two others who adopted the hortatory style of preaching and emphasis on personal experience of conversion characteristic of the new dissenters brought Wesleyanism (later known as Methodism) to the colony in the 1760s. With missionary reinforcements from Philadelphia in 1772, the Wesleyans, still working within the Anglican church, mounted a revival in the Norfolk–Portsmouth area and the Southside that promised to be as swiftly and as widely successful as the Baptists'.[21]

The evangelicals' success disquieted the establishment and provoked harassment and persecution. Although the Toleration Act passed by Parliament at the time of the Glorious Revolution protected the Presbyterians, the colonial government cracked down on itinerant ministries, a practice popular among New Sides and New Lights, as revivalists of the Great Awakening called themselves. Davies tried to ameliorate the controversy by applying for licenses to preach in specific places as the Toleration Act required, but the issue then became whether he could have a license for more than one site. The real challenge, however, was from the Separate Baptists. Their ministers not only refused to seek permission to preach; they required of themselves no credentials except the fact of their own conversion. Emotional camp meetings that evoked hysterical reactions such as fainting, shrieking, and convulsions injected into the controversy over religion questions of preserving the peace. As a result, between 1768 and 1775 some thirty dissenting preachers and a number of laymen found themselves in jail.

The angry frustration and ungentlemanly violence with which some gentry accosted the evangelicals suggests that more than theology was involved. As the dissenters kept reiterating, the Virginia establishment was not known for the intensity of its religious commitment. By importing puritanism into Virginia, the evangelicals not only defied authority but aggravatingly maligned the life-style of the gentry and the essential character that it imparted to the colony. Their call for repentance and eschewal of temptation in this life stamped the grand manner of the gentry—the fine houses, the balls, the wining and dining, the horse racing, the card playing, the gambling, and, for some preachers, the slaves, in short, the cultivated life that the planter class not only enjoyed but had come to view as embodying the enlightened ideals of the day—as sinful. Anglicans delighted in pointing out that the evangelicals appealed largely to those who did not enjoy such perquisites of wealth and power, that in effect they were making a virtue out of necessity. But poverty could be both a reason for contempt and a cause of social alarm. The threat became more ominous when some evangelicals turned to blacks as brothers and sisters in Christ and eagerly accorded spiritual equality to those who responded.

Unfortunately for the religious establishment its own ranks were in disarray. For over two decades a swelling wave of anticlericalism among churchmen conceded many of their critics' points. Although undoubtedly unfair to some individuals, the general consensus in and out of the Anglican church held the established clergy in low repute. During the 1750s the clergy had been tantalized with the possibility of a windfall when crop failures drove up the price of the sixteen thousand pounds of tobacco that each received annually as his salary. The assembly, however, permitted payments in currency at two pennies a pound, and ministers had mixed results when they challenged the policy in court. In 1763, for example, Patrick Henry made his political debut in the most famous of the Parsons' Causes with a ringing peroration to the jury that resulted in the judgment against the vestry he was defending being limited to one penny. Apart from saving parishes money, the assembly and the gentry as a whole clearly considered the clergy unworthy of the bonus nature had promised them.

Anticlericalism crested in the early 1770s after a group of northern Anglicans proposed the appointment of an American bishop. Although episcopal in form, the Church of England had never transported its hierarchy to the colonies. The reaction to the proposal in New England and the Middle Colonies, where dissenters abounded, was as might be expected. For whigs in particular, bishops—whether Catholic or Anglican—had historically been agents of oppression. More surprising was the response in Virginia where, after a heated exchange in the press, the House of Burgesses voted without dissent to commend opponents of the proposal, and only twelve out of about a hundred clergymen in the colony bothered to attend a convocation to endorse the plan. Four of the twelve, moreover, turned out to be vehemently against the idea. Self-doubt and lack of confidence in the old order appeared on both sides. The establishment was losing its nerve. Proponents of a bishopric asserted that the sorry condition of the clergy necessitated episcopal discipline, while opponents, as in the North, stressed that the political record of the hierarchy hardly argued for importing it to America. The more orthodox opponents acknowledged the incongruity of an establishment repudiating one of its fundamental tenets; the more liberal theologically, including some clergy, saw the inconsistency of contesting the possible oppression of a bishop while enforcing conformity at home. Not all of the questioning of the social and political order came from religious dissenters.

The criticism spilled over to the county courts that lay at the heart of the gentry's control of the colony. Those institutions combined the functions of local court and administrative board and were composed of members of the county elite whom the governor appointed from lists the incumbents supplied, a practice that resulted in seats becoming almost hereditary in some families. The justice dispensed was homespun, for appointment required no training in the law although senior justices, known as justices of the quorum, one of whom had to be present at every session, had considerable on-the-job experience in basic legal processes. Trouble emerged toward the middle of the century as the volume and complexity of business began to exceed the time and capability of unpaid volunteers. Creditors and other plaintiffs complained of the slowness of proceedings—as indeed was probably true, given the number of gentry among the debtors—and dissenters of the bias. Within the courtroom fraternity itself, an increasing number of trained lawyers, some educated in Britain, displayed open contempt for the amateur justices. The professionals demanded such reforms as salaried judges, the licensing of lawyers, and a new layer of assize courts between the county and General courts to make the judiciary more specialized and efficient. Some would have screened jurors to ensure a higher level of intelligence.[22]

But lawyers as a class had as unsavory a reputation in Virginia as bishops. Their reforms seemed self-serving and too susceptible of the favoritism and corruption attributed to their counterparts in Great Britain. The assembly adopted a licensing act in 1748 although it required only a year or so of apprenticeship for compliance. The act also compelled attorneys to choose between practice in the county courts or the General Court in Williamsburg, where only the better trained could survive. The expanding indebtedness of the colony inevitably allied the legal profession with creditors, and an exception to the 1748 law allowing General Court lawyers to practice in local courts near the capital cemented the bond. The hustings court of Williamsburg, which had concurrent jurisdiction over debt cases throughout the colony, and the York County Court became known for the effectiveness of their collections. Many of the most prominent attorneys were associated with the central administration that the Robinson affair so badly besmirched. To compound the image, shortly after Robinson's death, his father-in-law killed a man in a tavern brawl, and when authorities followed custom in capital cases and refused bail, three members of the General Court overrode them to order his release. So blatant an exercise of class privilege generated a torrent of outrage and became the cause célèbre of the decade.[23]

Ironically, it was the coming of the Revolution that redeemed lawyers who, despite their criticism of the establishment, were in most cases part of it. The leadership of attorneys such as Patrick Henry, Peyton Randolph, Robert Carter Nicholas, Edmund Pendleton, Thomas Jefferson, and others against Great Britain brought their profession a reputation for disinterested public service that few had ever associated with it before. Perhaps as a result, a proposal for salaried judges and courts of assize almost passed in 1772. Only a last-minute disagreement over how to bear the cost defeated it.[24]

Complaints notwithstanding, the planter elite still dominated the colony. In fact, from the point of view of actually achieving reform, a significant amount of the criticism, such as the effort to revamp the courts, came from within the establishment. By modern standards eighteenth-century Virginia was a narrowly based oligarchy. About 10 to 12 percent of the white, or 6 to 7 percent of the entire, population had the suffrage. That percentage, however, loomed relatively large

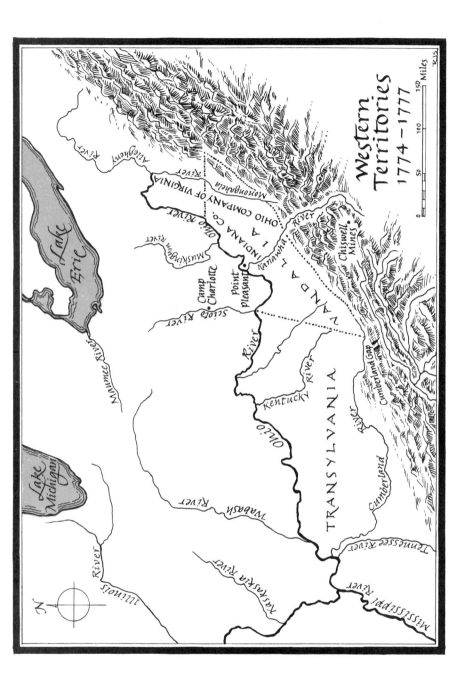

Western
Territories
1774–1777

Lake Erie

Lake Michigan

Allegheny River

Monongahela River

OHIO COMPANY OF VIRGINIA

INDIANA CO.

Muskingum River

Ohio River

Camp Charlotte

Point Pleasant

Scioto River

Kanawha River

Chiswell Mines

VANDALIA

Maumee River

River

Kentucky River

Ohio

River

Cumberland Gap

Cumberland River

TRANSYLVANIA

Wabash River

Tennessee River

Kaskaskia River

Illinois River

Mississippi River

N

0   50   100   150 Miles

within contemporary expectations, which routinely excluded women, blacks, Roman Catholics, non-Christians, and propertyless males from politics. Of those otherwise eligible under these conditions, about three to four times more colonists than British possessed the twenty-five acres "with a house and plantation" required to vote. Inasmuch as tenants for life as well as landowners could participate if they had the necessary acreage, it is estimated that up to 60 percent of the white males over twenty-one years of age held the franchise and that about two-thirds of that number normally exercised their rights.[25]

Politically more limiting for citizens than restraints on the suffrage was the fact that politicians like judges were amateurs, and few even among eligible voters had the wherewithal to indulge in the pastime. Since 1760 only seven men—George Wythe, Robert Carter Nicholas, Richard Bland, Benjamin Harrison, Edmund Pendleton, Richard Henry Lee, and Archibald Cary—had chaired the six standing committees of the House of Burgesses and two-thirds of the thirty or so special committees appointed in a typical session. The names of a dozen other burgesses such as Lewis Burwell, Francis Lightfoot Lee, Patrick Henry, and George Washington, who were nearly as prominent but who had not yet shepherded a standing committee, would complete the roll call of the inner circle. The group comprised roughly one-sixth of the whole house. Most were from the Tidewater. With the Speakers John Robinson and Peyton Randolph, the royal governor, and the twelve members of the Council appointed by the crown, all also from the Tidewater, they ruled Virginia.

Elections for the house were often rollicking affairs. Along with plantation balls, militia musters, fairs, and church services, they afforded an opportunity for a scattered rural population to socialize. Although the law technically forbade treating constituents to entertainment specifically to influence their votes, candidates were expected to be present on election day and to contribute generally to the people's enjoyment. Particularly in more established areas, some legislative careers might be as long as several decades, but others might be abruptly shortened. Landon Carter complained bitterly when he met defeat after many years of service because he had become too aloof—as even he halfway admitted. He chortled a bit later when his son Robert Wormeley Carter also lost even though, in his father's opinion at least, he had abjectly courted popularity. Voters, who as landholders composed a lesser order of the establishment, were not always overawed as a group. Occasionally they invoked their power to remind gentry that there were two sides to deference and that constituents expected paternalistic care from their leaders as their due.[26]

Politics within the House of Burgesses are often hard to discern. The narrowness of the leadership, reinforced by a century of intermarriage among principal families, let Virginia rely on oral communication surprisingly long for a colony its size. To the frustration of modern historians, the elite seldom documented its politics—as opposed to its political theory—on paper. Some alignments are apparent. The votes of burgesses from the Northern Neck often offset those of their colleagues from the Southside because the two areas represented opposite ends of the economic and social spectrum. Patrick Henry, never close to the leadership after speaking out on the Stamp Act too forcefully for their taste during his freshman year, had more of a following in the Southside and among the smaller farmers of the Piedmont generally than in the Tidewater. During the Robinson era burgesses from the Northern Neck, whose constituents' western land speculations the French threatened more than the holdings of others farther south, found colleagues from the lower peninsulas less responsive to defense needs than the Northern Neck representatives liked. The scandal after the Speaker's death perpetuated the split. George Wythe confided to John Adams at the Continental Congress that the animosity the New Englander noted between Richard Henry Lee and his colleagues Carter Braxton and Benjamin Harrison stemmed from Lee having been one of the first to expose Robinson. Ill will from the affair had sprung up among the Williamsburgers Robert Carter Nicholas and John and Peyton Randolph, too. Nicholas, whose scrupulous honesty the revelations shocked, led a successful effort to separate the offices of Speaker and treasurer, to both of which Peyton Randolph aspired. Instead, Nicholas wound up in the latter post himself. The hostility deepened as a result of Nicholas's stalwart Christian orthodoxy and the Randolphs' association with thinkers of a theologically more liberal cast.[27]

But these divisions, as Edmund Pendleton once described them, were "disputes between a few great men."[28] Burgesses, even rough-hewn ones from the West, won election because of their stature as independent country gentlemen in their home communities, not because of their adherence to a political faction at the capital. The opposition to Great Britain was one of the few times colonial Virginia leaders systematically sought ratification of an issue from the elector-

ate. Since burgesses made little or no partisan commitment to obtain
their seats, they could easily be imagined as adhering to the contemporary ideal in both Britain and America—however much it may have
been breached in practice—that each measure before a legislature
should be judged entirely on its merits. Oratory played a crucial role.
The presence or absence of a forceful leader on the floor could reverse the fate of a measure from one day to the next. Some objected
that the East had undue influence in the house because its smaller,
more numerous counties gave it more representatives. The proximity
of the capital also assured better attendance from the area, just as the
duty to advise the governor inevitably gave the Council's membership
an eastern cast. But aside from these geographic complaints, Virginians were generally well pleased with their House of Burgesses. No
one talked of significantly reforming it. By all standards of the day it
was close to being perfect. No wonder its members felt few inhibitions
in being as critical as they were of Parliament.

Whatever the criticism of the Virginia gentry, their leadership of
the colonial opposition to Great Britain on both the local and continental levels enormously enhanced their image. Despite personal divisions and animosities, hardly a leader defected on the issue of
independence. The threat of British policies to the autonomy of the
colony endangered the planter elite's way of life more than any contemporary challenge within. The need for public support for the resistance to Britain and the ensuing war led to internal reforms about
which some Virginia leaders were less enthusiastic than others, but
the enactment of which bolstered their class's reputation for states-
manship. The gentry who ruled the colony for the most part survived
the Revolution, oversaw the transition to a republic, and continued to
govern during the youthful years of the new nation.

CHAPTER 3

The Collapse of Royal Government

B Y May 12, 1775, tempers raised by the raid on the magazine in Williamsburg had subsided enough for Dunmore to bring his family back to the Palace. Soon afterward the "boiled crabs" returned to their ship.[1] About the same time the governor received the only instruction he was to have from the ministry until the end of the year. It authorized him to reconvene the General Assembly to obtain approval of a "conciliatory resolution" that Parliament had adopted at the behest of the prime minister, Lord North. Parliament proposed to forego its claim to tax the colonies if they would undertake to raise sufficient revenue themselves to meet administrative and military needs as determined by Parliament. Dunmore immediately summoned the assembly to meet on June 1. But, as he wrote to the ministry, he was not optimistic about success.[2]

At Dunmore's call word raced through the colony that it was just a trick to seize assembly members. The Williamsburg volunteer company under Captain James Innes immediately proclaimed their readiness to resist the landing of British troops in Virginia or anywhere else on the continent, although they wisely added that they would seek help from the rest of the colony first. Upon receiving the governor's summons, Peyton Randolph relinquished his post as the first president of the Continental Congress to return to his duty as Speaker of the House of Burgesses. When he arrived in Williamsburg

on May 30, volunteers on horseback and afoot escorted him into town
with a fanfare befitting the most distinguished leader of Virginia resistance. That evening townspeople illuminated their houses while the
volunteer company "with many other respectable gentlemen," according to the *Virginia Gazette,* passed "an hour or two in harmony and
cheerfulness" at the Raleigh Tavern. The next morning the Williamsburg company assembled before the Speaker's home to hail Randolph
as "father of your country" and to post a guard at his door.[3]

Despite this defiance Dunmore's opening address to the assembly
on Thursday, June 1, was remarkably conciliatory. One British magazine later observed that "a more humiliating [speech] could not well
be spoken on the part of a Governor."[4] The reaction was ambivalent.
Some burgesses wore hunting shirts, which had become the uniform
of the resistance forces, and carried tomahawks at their sides. Others
like Robert Carter Nicholas, James Mercer, and Robert Wormeley
Carter insisted upon at least discussing Lord North's terms. So concerned were Peyton Randolph and Thomas Jefferson over this newest
threat to continental unity that at the Speaker's request Jefferson put
off going to Philadelphia as Randolph's replacement to help block any
attempt to answer the ministry independently of Congress.[5]

Then no sooner had the assembly been seated than the last hope
of conciliation disappeared. During the weekend a group of young
men broke into the public magazine and were greeted by the shatter-
ing blast of a shotgun that had been cleverly rigged to discharge at
the tripping of a spring. The pellets wounded three, including a well-
liked Yorktown youth, Beverley Dickson.[6] Public outrage at Dunmore
became so great that, when the usually cautious Edmund Pendleton
heard of the incident in Philadelphia, he remarked that assassination
might be in order. If the wounded died, declared Alexander Purdie,
editor of one of the three *Virginia Gazettes* then being published in
Williamsburg, those responsible would deserve "the opprobrious title
of MURDERERS."[7]

Over the next three days the number of incidents multiplied. Monday morning a mob stormed the magazine. Later that day a committee of burgesses visited Dunmore to request the keys of the magazine
so they could investigate the shooting the previous weekend. In the
course of their address the burgesses assured the governor that they
had tried to stop the raid that morning. Dunmore became so infuriated, apparently by what he took to be sheer hypocrisy on the part
of the burgesses, that in a burst of spite he rejected the request on

the foolish ground that, since it was not written and did not identify the petitioners, he could not give the keys to people he did not know. The house immediately halted all other business and replied stiffly that his lordship surely knew to whom he had spoken the day before.[8]

Tension heightened all day Tuesday. Hearing of the trouble in Williamsburg, Captain George Montagu of the *Fowey* inquired if Dunmore needed aid. Quickly the report went out that one hundred marines were coming, and once again James Innes mobilized his company. Two members of the Council, Richard Corbin and Robert Carter, hastened to Dunmore, who told them that he had not asked for troops and would send them back if any came. Unappeased, the House of Burgesses officially requested Innes and his men to remain on guard at the magazine, an act that Dunmore took as the first attempt to usurp his executive authority.[9]

Shortly afterward, Dunmore apologized for the misunderstanding over the keys—he only wanted to be official, he said—and even offered to return the powder, although he could not resist remarking, "The magazine was represented to me as a very insecure Depository, and from Experience, I find it so."[10] He also set a time to meet the assembly on Thursday, June 8. But early that morning the governor abandoned attempts to mitigate the crisis and fled from Williamsburg. About two o'clock, with his family, his aide, Captain Edward Foy, and Foy's wife, Dunmore slipped out of the Palace and made his way to H.M.S. *Magdalen,* which had been waiting for a couple of days in Queen's Creek. Clearly the option of a flight had been held in reserve. Dunmore and his group boarded to the clatter of a thirteen-gun salute. About mid-morning at Yorktown the governor transferred to the *Fowey* to the blast of another honorary salvo.[11]

In his report to London Dunmore explained that in spite of his conciliatory efforts "my house was kept in continual Alarm and threatened every Night with an Assault."[12] Ever since Patrick Henry's attempt to capture the receiver general, Richard Corbin, the governor had become more and more alarmed that he and his family would be held hostage for the well-being of colonial leaders—an obvious preventive measure that had indeed occurred to the other side. The turmoil in town that week and the clear intention of the volunteers to resist any reinforcements sent to Dunmore's aid confirmed fears that the opposition was toying with him. Possibly the earl also learned that on June 8 John Pinkney's *Virginia Gazette* would print the passages of his Christmas Eve letter to Lord Dartmouth in which the governor called for a blockading squadron. It would not have been difficult to surmise what the public reaction would be.[13]

Dunmore's flight brought consternation and anger among the burgesses. Few believed that he really feared for his life, for he had crossed town alone the evening before to visit John Randolph, the attorney general, who testified that the governor had given him no hint of his plans. The appearance in the York River of the sloop H.M.S. *Otter* and the schooner *Arundel,* which had been sent to help him, raised the possibility that the executive's departure was timed to coincide with an invasion. Subsequent information that Governor Josiah Martin of North Carolina had fled from New Bern on May 24 seemed to confirm this supposition. "Lord Dunmore and governor Martin have certainly compared notes," observed Alexander Purdie on printing the news.[14]

For the remaining three weeks of the session the governor refused to leave his ship and the burgesses declined to meet him on board. In the immediate aftermath of Dunmore's flight Jefferson and the Speaker won their way on the question of Lord North's resolution, and Jefferson resumed his journey to Philadelphia. The ministry's offer, the burgesses informed the governor, merely changed the mode of taxation and did not repeal the punitive measures against Massachusetts. Once more the colony's leaders revealed that their overriding concern was for colonial unity. They could not consider the matter apart from Congress, the burgesses declared, "because the proposition . . . involves the interest of all the other Colonies. . . . we . . . should hold ourselves base deserters of that union to which we have acceded, were we to agree on any measures distinct and apart from them."[15]

Retreat proved worse for Dunmore than attack. His flight polarized political opinion in Virginia even more than had his raid on the magazine. Not only might the appearance of the ships in the York River be a harbinger of the fleet Virginians now knew he had summoned. By saying that he had fled for his life, the governor lumped moderates like the treasurer, Robert Carter Nicholas, who had been counseling patience, with firebrands like Patrick Henry, forcing the Nicholases to face the likelihood that Henry was right after all, petitions and soft words had no effect. Fundamentally, Nicholas agreed with the militants that Virginia's liberties needed defending. He had just arranged with John Goodrich, a sea captain and "famous Contraband Man" from Portsmouth, to bring five thousand pounds worth of gunpowder from the West Indies.[16] The disagreement between firebrands and moderates was over pace and style.

Nicholas chaired a committee of burgesses to investigate the reasons for Dunmore's flight, which seemed on the surface to lend credence to the governor's charge that the entire opposition had been planning to turn to violence all along. Ignoring the fact that, upon his return from Congress, Richard Bland had been urging that Dunmore be hanged, the committee questioned every witness they could find whose testimony supported a highly partisan version of events over the past year that emphasized the calm reasonableness of Virginians. It was as if everyone had actually followed the treasurer's advice. The note of wounded innocence that permeates the long resolution attests to the rising despair of the moderates, who were determined that no one would be able to say that Virginians had not tried their best to keep the peace or had been the first to resort to violence. The colony's leaders returned to this theme again and again; even in their final decision for independence they reaffirmed it.[17]

The assembly spent the remaining three weeks of its life trying to persuade Dunmore to return to Williamsburg and resume normal governmental functions, or, if royal authority should fail, to be certain that they could not be blamed. The burgesses carried on the usual routine of legislation, sending papers and messages to Yorktown as if the governor just happened to be temporarily out of town. At one point they even submitted a standard supply request for two thousand stand of arms, five tons of powder, and twenty of lead to restock the public magazine, and another time asked if it would be all right to distribute his collection of arms in the hallway of the Palace to the independent companies! At length Dunmore made the legislators face reality by refusing to sign a bill on which the final settlement of the Indian war depended. Either the assembly ignored the governor's veto and appointed commissioners to conclude the treaty without his consent, thereby consciously usurping executive authority, or fighting would break out again on the frontier.[18]

Eventually, too, people outside the assembly became impatient with the sparring with the governor. The news of his flight brought volunteers to protect Williamsburg from the expected invasion. Soon about two hundred armed men gathered in town. Mostly young, they acted as if on a lark; "We appear rather invited to feast then fight," one observed.[19] The elected officers could not control their troops, and the number of incidents began to increase. When Dunmore refused to let the assembly have the arms in the Palace and a slim majority in the house voted not to seize them, a group of young men led by Theodorick Bland and including James Monroe, Benjamin Harrison, Jr., and the treasurer's son, George Nicholas, broke into the mansion on the afternoon of June 24, just as the legislators met to adjourn. Removing over two hundred pistols and muskets and a number of swords from the front hallway, the raiders carted them to the magazine where Bland issued them to anyone in need of weapons.[20]

Five days later Dunmore said goodbye to Lady Dunmore and their children on board H.M.S. *Magdalen* as they sailed for England. To obtain passage for his family the governor had persuaded Captain Montagu to countermand Admiral Graves's orders sending Lieutenant Collins and the *Magdalen* to Delaware Bay. Dunmore's excuse was that he had to send a dispatch directly to London recounting the events that precipitated his flight. The message was only his second report since the trouble began. The admiral was not impressed by the urgency and threatened to court-martial Montagu.[21]

Lady Dunmore's departure initiated an exodus of several of her husband's most active supporters. The Reverend Thomas Gwatkin, a member of the faculty of the College of William and Mary and tutor of the governor's eldest son, Lord Fincastle, accompanied her and the children on board the *Magdalen*. Four years before the House of Burgesses had officially thanked Gwatkin and a colleague at the college, the Reverend Samuel Henley, for their opposition to the appointment of an Anglican bishop in the colonies. Later, the two became closely identified with Dunmore and were intimidated by armed men who visited their rooms. At the end of April Henley announced his return to England, and now Gwatkin followed. After a relatively short passage of twenty-nine days, Gwatkin and Lieutenant Collins's other passengers, along with the governor's message, arrived safely at Portsmouth, England.[22]

On July 12, two weeks after Lady Dunmore's departure, H.M.S. *Mercury* arrived to relieve the *Fowey*. Dunmore's aide, Captain Foy, took the opportunity of the *Fowey*'s rotation to return with his wife to New York and from there to England. The receiver general's son, Richard Corbin, Jr., accompanied them. The parting of the governor and his subaltern Foy was not happy, and, had Virginians known, they would have enjoyed the irony. To them Foy was cut from the same cloth as his master; if anything, he seemed more arrogant and condescending. Foy had caned a shopkeeper on the streets of Williamsburg and let it be known that it was he who was cited in Tobias Smollett's popular history of England for heroism at the battle of Minden in 1759, which otherwise had been a total disgrace for British arms. As a reward for Foy's services Lord and Lady Dunmore had both tried after the captain's marriage to Hannah Van Horne of New York in 1773 to find him a more suitable post than the one he held in Virginia. When Dunmore's troubles began to multiply, however, the governor decided to keep his assistant at his side. Foy resented Dunmore's change of mind; "I have found . . . that it is not attachment to his interest, and zeal in doing his business, that can recommend a man to his generosity, or even engage him to be Just." More cutting was Foy's remark that "Lord Dunmore's is not a character from which in any difficult times, I should hope for any great advantage . . . at the same time that I should not fail to bear more than my share of all disgrace attending his proceeding." "I am no longer interested in the fate of Lord Dunmore," he wrote as he left.[23]

Within a few more weeks Dunmore lost another supporter, John Randolph, attorney general of Virginia. Educated in England and renowned for his brilliance in law, Randolph was a pillar of the colony's intelligentsia. Fellow violinists and bibliophiles, he and Jefferson were particularly close. Two years before, Randolph had taken a pro-British stand in an exchange of pamphlets with Robert Carter Nicholas. Dunmore, a member of the board of visitors of William and Mary, used his position to have Randolph returned as the college's delegate to the House of Burgesses to ensure that there would be at least one imperial spokesman in that body. The close collaboration between the two officials invited retribution from the populace. Slanderous rumors accused Randolph's daughter, Susan, of being Dunmore's mistress, and the night after the Randolphs left, a mob ransacked their home in Williamsburg. A final, poignant letter from the attorney general to his son, Edmund, an aide to General Washington, begging him to return to Williamsburg to care for the family's interests reveals the anguish felt by families like the Randolphs, Byrds, and Blands, who had members on both sides during the Revolution.[24]

With both the assembly and governor gone, the danger of anarchy in Williamsburg became real. The worst fears of moderates seemed about to come to pass; the leadership could scarcely retain control. Believing that reinforcements for Dunmore hovered just off the Vir-

ginia Capes, Peyton Randolph summoned a town meeting to request
more volunteers. Soon several hundred troops had pitched camp in
Waller's Grove on the eastern edge of the city. The independent companies recognized no authority beyond that of their elected officers
and respective county committees. "Many members are rather disorderly," one soldier wrote home. Eventually the men themselves
chose Charles Scott of Cumberland County as their commander, but
it was said that he "fear[s] to offend."[25] Sleeping on duty, disobedi-
ence, and absence without leave earned expulsion from the service
after the third offense. Shooting a gun without permission, as became
a habit around town to the terror of inhabitants, merited confinement
without food or drink—for two hours! Nor as yet was patriotism a
hardship. "Anderson and Southall's [taverns] entertain elegantly[,] the
first in the best manner by far," wrote George Gilmer of Albemarle
County.[26]

Assaults upon symbols of royal authority became a regular pastime.
On the sixth of July young George Nicholas led a second raid on the
Palace in search of another suspected store of arms and thoroughly
sacked the building before finding the weapons. The next day Dunmore, Montagu, and a small party went on a foolhardy trip to the
governor's farm, Porto Bello, on Queen's Creek, just six miles from
Williamsburg. As they sat with unbelievable equanimity eating dinner
in the farmhouse, they suddenly observed armed men approaching
and barely reached their boat amid a scattering of shots. Later Dunmore read in an intercepted report from Benjamin Harrison to Washington that the attackers only wanted to bring him to the Palace "to
convince him and the world that no injury was intended him."[27] When
H.M.S. *Mercury* arrived on July 12, another detachment rushed from
Williamsburg to repel an invasion and, to the governor's mortification,
paraded boldly along the shore at Yorktown. Shortly afterward troops
raided the Palace a third time, and the last of the governor's servants
who had braved the siege departed. Members of independent companies took up quarters in the mansion, pasturing their horses in
the park to the rear. Other companies had already settled in at the
Capitol.[28]

When the *Fowey* sailed with Foy and his wife about ten days later,
it was learned in Williamsburg that the ship carried £1,200 in royal
revenues from Jacquelin Ambler, a customs collector in Hampton.
Some of the volunteers—who had been looking for a little excitement,
according to one of them—decided to see if any more of the king's

money was lying around. The soldiers haled two prominent Williamsburg merchants, Robert Prentis, clerk for the receiver general, Richard Corbin, and John Blair, who as deputy auditor general kept accounts for Corbin, before a council of officers to swear that they would disburse no government funds without permission. Benjamin Waller, clerk of the Williamsburg Hustings Court, and Lewis Burwell, another customs collector for the James River District, along with two printers, Alexander Purdie and John Dixon, the city's former and present postmasters, had to take the same oath. A detachment rode after Corbin himself to bring him before the council, but soon after they found him, an order to halt arrived from the third session of the Virginia Convention, which had just assembled in Richmond. Although the president of the Convention assured the Williamsburg officers that "no Censure was passed on y'r Conduct," the Convention resolved that such actions "cannot be approved."[29] Chastened, the volunteers sent James Innes to Richmond to apologize and to request specific instructions "lest in our excessive zeal we should precipitate our Countrymen into unnecessary Calamities."[30]

For a while after their rebuff the troops in Williamsburg were content to patrol the peninsula and escort important personages to and from the capital. Then the leadership in Richmond had to step in again when the men seized a shipload of grain that they did not think should be exported although resolutions of both Congress and the Convention sanctioned its shipment. Among the volunteers themselves, George Gilmer and others agreed that the time had come to end the fun and to put the military under better discipline before the men's exuberance really got out of hand.[31]

The task of forming a substitute government began in earnest at the third Virginia Convention. When the delegates assembled in Richmond on July 17, all was confusion. Although Virginia leaders accepted the need to work in concert with Congress, they knew little of its plans until the colony's delegates returned in early August. In June Congress had appointed George Washington its commander in chief and sent him to direct the siege of Boston, where Americans won a great moral victory at the battle of Bunker Hill on June 17. Because the colonists' losses were heavy, Washington sent out a call for reinforcements. In response, Captains Daniel Morgan of Frederick County and Hugh Stephenson of Berkeley marched their rifle companies thirty miles a day to become the first Virginia units to join the

Continental Army. Otherwise Virginians had no communication with
Continental authorities.[32]

"We are of as many different opinions as we are men," one Convention delegate complained, "undoing one day, what we did the day
before."[33] George Mason became so upset by the constant wrangling
that he went to bed for several days. Daily sessions and committee
meetings lasting from seven in the morning until late at night accomplished little. Having adopted one scheme for recruiting an army and
actually opening enlistments, the Convention changed its mind, paid
off the men, and enacted an entirely different program.[34]

Controversy was unending. Old Richard Bland, feeble and half-
blind, had to defend himself for a week before he was acquitted of
charges based on the flimsiest evidence that he was a loyalist. Another
squabble occurred over George Mason's proposal to advance the date
set by Congress for an embargo on the exportation of tobacco and
grain from September 10 to August 5. Mason suspected that Norfolk
merchants were notifying Dunmore of their sailings so that the governor could capture their cargoes and send them to the British army
in Boston. Shippers, particularly from the Eastern Shore and the area
around Hampton Roads, who had based their sailing plans on the
original date fought the change until finally Maryland's refusal to go
along made it useless for Virginia to proceed alone.[35]

The most violent factionalism flared over the election of officers for
the new army. From Philadelphia Patrick Henry announced his candidacy for the colonelcy of the 1st Regiment despite his complete lack
of military experience. His principal rival was Hugh Mercer of Fredericksburg. Mercer was an experienced soldier, but since he had been
exiled to America for participating in the Scottish uprising in 1745,
he suffered because of the prevailing suspicion about Scottish toryism.
Henry's supporters parried the charge of inexperience with the assurance that, since their candidate had sought the post, he must consider himself qualified. The result of the first ballot was forty-one
votes for Mercer and forty for Henry with nine scattered between
Thomas Nelson, Jr., of Yorktown and William Woodford of Caroline
County, both of whom withdrew in Mercer's favor. Henry won on the
next ballot by a small majority. Washington's reaction to the appointment reflected the common dismay of the military: "I think my countrymen made a capital mistake, when they took Henry out of the senate to place him in the field; and pity it is, that he does not see this,
and remove any difficulty by a voluntary resignation."[36]

So intense were the feelings over Henry's selection that Mercer withdrew from the balloting for the 2nd Regiment. The Convention offered that post to Nelson, who conveniently accepted a term in Congress instead. Woodford initially won the election to lead a third regiment that the Convention decided not to fund. He then accepted command of the second.

Eventually the Convention turned to its principal tasks: devising a substitute for royal government and finding the means to defend it. Still insisting that they did so only because Dunmore forced them to, the delegates moved toward assuming full constitutional powers by adopting the procedures of the House of Burgesses. Although legal fastidiousness led the delegates to label their acts "ordinances" rather than statutes, George Mason explained that they wore "the Face of Law" as the "resolves" of previous sessions of the Convention had not.[37] To assure the continuance of local government in as normal a fashion as possible in the absence of the governor, the Convention provided for elections of delegates "to be conducted as Elections for Burgesses."[38] It also regularized county committees by setting their membership at twenty-one, mandating annual elections, and requiring them to "confine themselves within the line of duty prescribed by the continental congress and the general convention, and . . . not assume to themselves any other power or authority whatever."[39]

George Mason left an indelible imprint on these deliberations. The work of a de facto constitutional assembly admirably suited his talents. Concerning the raising of an army, he regarded a militia as "the true natural, and safest Defence of this, or any other free Country," but he conceded the wisdom of having a small core of regulars that citizen reserves could augment when needed.[40] Mason's gravest concern was that in the excitement the Convention would authorize more troops than necessary and bankrupt the colony. James Madison, observing developments from his home in Orange County, anticipated a force of three to four thousand men in addition to the independent companies, "who I suppose will be three times that number."[41] For some months Robert Carter Nicholas had wavered between preaching fear of British retaliation and demanding as many as ten to twenty thousand troops to prevent it. Not until the last minute was Mason able to whittle the number down to the more practicable figure of 1,020.[42]

The Convention provided for three types of military service into which it planned, in Mason's words, to "melt down" the volunteers who had proved so obstreperous.[43] The colony was divided into fifteen districts, each of which was to raise one company of sixty-eight men, who would enlist for one year and compose the two regular regiments. Only the Eastern Shore was exempt because its exposed position necessitated reserving all its men to defend itself. As a concession to Mason's views on the militia, representatives of the county committees in each district appointed the company grade officers, while the Convention selected only the higher ranks.[44]

Fifteen battalions of "minutemen" supported the regular troops. They were to be drawn from the same districts as the regulars. The minutemen were to train immediately for twenty consecutive days and thereafter for twelve days twice annually and were to be ready for instantaneous duty. Mason felt this scheme provided reliable soldiers "in whose Hands the Sword may be safely trusted" without the danger of a coup d'état inherent in a standing army.[45] Finally, as a basic reservoir of men, a militia composed of all free white males between sixteen and fifty years of age was to muster at least eleven times a year. The assembly made the articles of war adopted by Congress applicable to Virginia except, Mason wrote Washington, "that a Court Martial upon Life and Death is more cautiously constituted, and brought nearer to the Principles of the common Law." Specifically, a defendant in a capital case had the right to select the fifteen trial judges from a panel of twenty-four nominated by the commanding officer, and the civil government rather than the commanding general had to approve all sentences of death.[46]

As Mason predicted, financing this program posed a serious problem, especially since the rapidly approaching deadline set by Congress for the cessation of tobacco exports to Great Britain would eliminate Virginia's prime source of revenue until new markets developed. In addition, the Convention inherited the claims of the soldiers from Dunmore's War against the Shawnee. To obtain the necessary funds, the delegates authorized the issuance of £350,000 in paper currency to be redeemed by taxes over a seven-year period beginning in 1777. Mason preached vigorously against the danger of inflation inherent in this delay but because of the poor economic forecast succeeded only in preventing payments from being suspended until 1779.[47]

To superintend its new government the Convention appointed an eleven-man Committee of Safety to control military and civilian matters when the Convention was not in session. Mason found the extent of the committee's authority disturbing, for as a creature of the Convention it wielded considerably more power than had the governor. The committee commanded a permanent army that no royal official ever had, and to meet the needs of the war had the authority to become involved in the economy to an extent unknown before. Besides enforcing the ban on British trade and procuring supplies at home and abroad for the army, the committee had the delegates' sanction to operate cannon works at Fredericksburg and lead mines in Fincastle County as well as subsidize the production of sulfur and saltpeter for gunpowder.[48]

The work of the Convention became more calm and orderly in the final weeks because the arrival of the congressional delegation in early August added weight to the leadership. Also, as Mason crustily remarked, "the Bablers were pretty well silenced" by then.[49] An effort to reconsider Henry's appointment as colonel died without a vote. Carter Braxton, who had sworn to demand a strict accounting of money put up as compensation for the powder Dunmore took from the magazine, moved to accept without debate Henry's report that he had spent the funds to purchase more powder for the colony in Baltimore. In contrast to the month before, elections resulted in tears instead of recriminations. When Bland declined another term in Congress because of his health, the Convention turned to Mason, who pleaded his excuses in such a heartrending address that Speaker Peyton Randolph began to weep. Throughout his career the gout, a large motherless family, and a natural predilection for his library enabled Mason to act the statesman behind the scenes more often than on the stage. But now in escaping Congress, he could not avoid being cast for the Committee of Safety, a role that he relished even less.[50]

The Convention concluded its work on August 26. It had begun a rebellion but hoped that it had not precluded reconciliation. It had been chary of expropriating royal funds as the Williamsburg volunteers wanted, and on the strength of a petition from British merchants in the colony who promised to remain neutral had put off a test oath that Mason proposed to distinguish royalist from rebel. Instead, it adopted and had printed in the *Virginia Gazette* a resolution admonishing county committees and others to treat natives of Great Britain who committed no hostile action "with lenity and friendship."[51] Significantly, when the delegates from Philadelphia brought news of Benjamin Franklin's suggested articles of confederation, on which Congress had taken no action, the report was kept quiet among Convention leaders and forgotten. In its closing declaration the Convention proclaimed "before God and the world, that we do bear faith and true allegiance to his majesty George the third." If, "on the one hand, we are determined to . . . maintain our just rights . . . so, on the other, it is our fixed and unalterable resolution to disband such forces as may be raised in this colony whenever our dangers are removed."[52]

CHAPTER 4

War

IN the waters off Portsmouth Dunmore prepared for war. The process was frustratingly slow. With many colonies in revolt, the royal army had too few reserves scattered too widely about the empire for aid to come very quickly. Besieged in Boston, General Gage and Admiral Graves, to whom Dunmore turned for assistance, were appealing to Great Britain for reinforcements as urgently as the governor importuned them. Having sent the sloop H.M.S. *Otter* and the schooner *Arundel* to Virginia only after he heard a rumor that Dunmore had been taken prisoner, Graves became quite angry when he learned that the governor had diverted the larger *Magdalen* with Lady Dunmore to Great Britain. The best the army could do for Dunmore was to shift a few troops from Florida, and even those Governor Patrick Tonyn released only as other units from the West Indies replaced them. The landing of sixty men of the 14th Regiment from St. Augustine on the last day of July served only to tantalize Dunmore with the prospect of larger contingents to come.[1]

At sea the arrival of the *Otter* balanced the departure of the *Magdalen*, but when H.M.S. *Mercury* replaced the *Fowey*, it proved an inadequate substitute. Instead of the *Fowey*'s cooperative Captain Montagu, who had supported Dunmore in every move, Captain John MacCartney of the *Mercury* soon ignited the governor's combustible temper. MacCartney deemed all Virginians loyal unless proved otherwise. After paying his respects to Dunmore, the captain accepted a dinner invitation from the president of the Council, Thomas Nelson of Yorktown. In a fury over MacCartney's attitude Dunmore wrote to Graves within a week of the *Mercury's* arrival demanding to have its captain removed. When MacCartney and Captain Matthew Squire of the *Otter* refused to harbor escaped slaves without first determining that the masters were criminals whose property was subject to confiscation, the two became minor heroes to Virginians in the Norfolk area. Eventually MacCartney began to play the role Dunmore expected by threatening to bombard Norfolk because a mob roughed up an informer and a local committee intimidated the merchant Andrew Sprowle, in whose house the new troops from Florida were quartered. By then the governor's rage had abated, but it was too late. Graves ordered MacCartney and the *Mercury* back to Boston in September, leaving behind the smaller eighteen-gun sloop *King's Fisher* under Montagu's brother, James. Dunmore's change of heart, and the impossibility of his going to Boston to prosecute the case, resulted in the charges against MacCartney being dropped and a suggestion in the tone of Graves's report to London that the governor had become a bit of a nuisance.[2]

Besides the *King's Fisher* and the *Otter*, Dunmore had impressed two merchantmen, the *William*, reported to have from ten to thirteen guns, on which he first set up his headquarters, and the *Eilbeck*, which was pierced for twenty-two guns but probably never carried more than seven. By December the governor moved his quarters to the latter vessel, renaming it after himself. He also had the use of several tenders attached to the larger naval ships. Armed with swivel guns and a couple of three- or four-pound cannon, the tenders were particularly effective harassing fishing and coastwise vessels plying their trade in Hampton Roads.[3]

Dunmore planned to ensnare Virginia in a massive pincers movement by capitalizing on the friendships he had built in the West. From mid-June to early July his agent, Dr. John Connolly, had been negotiating with Indian chieftains at Pittsburgh to ratify the peace agreements that had resulted from the governor's earlier campaign. Although some westerners had become suspicious of Connolly and petitioned Congress to intervene, Captain James Wood of Winchester, whom the Virginia Convention sent as their observer, reported no danger. The Convention subsequently ratified the terms that Connolly agreed to and passed a resolution of thanks for his services.[4]

This success led Connolly to conclude that he could guarantee the West to Dunmore. Connolly believed that his "superior knowledge of Indian manners and tempers" had subtly swayed the tribesmen to the royalist side despite Congress's inquisitors.[5] Yet Wood found that Connolly had dealt so subtly with at least one chief that the Indian did not know of the trouble in the East until Wood told him. In the continuing conflict over the western border between Virginia and Pennsylvania, the latter's partisans kidnapped Connolly in the middle of the Indian conference. Virginia frontiersmen forcibly rescued him, and he apparently assumed that he could rely on their backing in the imperial quarrel as well. The border dispute did not follow the ideological lines of the confrontation with the mother country, however. By early fall the Convention's supporters established garrisons at the mouth of the Wheeling River and at Point Pleasant, and Captain John Neville of Winchester seized Fort Pitt from both Britain and Pennsylvania for Virginia.[6]

After the Indian conference Connolly set out for Norfolk, using the Convention's commendation as a safe conduct. He reached his destination in early August. Connolly proposed going to Boston with Dunmore's concurrence to obtain General Gage's permission to lead an expedition from Detroit into the Ohio country where he would raise reinforcements among the loyalists and Indians and rendezvous with Dunmore's troops along the Potomac River the next spring. The juncture of the two forces would sever Virginia from the northern colonies and force its early surrender.[7]

The scheme fizzled like a damp fuse. Connolly was able to reach Boston and gain Gage's consent but no troops. Since Washington's army was besieging the Massachusetts capital, the best that Gage could offer was to give Connolly letters asking royal officers at Detroit and the deputy British Indian superintendent at Pittsburgh, Alexander McKee, to aid the plan in every possible way. To make matters worse, Connolly had to return to Virginia by sea because Continental troops invading Canada that winter blocked a more northerly route to Detroit. On the way he stopped at Newport, Rhode Island, where his servant deserted and informed Washington's agents of the plan. Meanwhile, a letter from Connolly to John Gibson, a supposedly loyal supporter in Pittsburgh, alerted Continental authorities in the South. Delayed again by illness in Virginia, Connolly did not set off through Maryland for Pittsburgh in the company of two other loyalists, Dr. J. F. D. Smyth and Allan Cameron, until November 1775. By then the countryside had been warned, and rebel forces took the group prisoner at Hagerstown, Maryland. Incriminating documents found in a secret compartment of Connolly's luggage consigned him to prison for most of the war. Unfortunately for Dunmore, Connolly's plan came to light just as letters to General Gage from John Stuart, the British superintendent for Indian affairs in the southern department, that advocated limited use of Indians in the war were captured. Dunmore stood convicted of raising a "savage enemy" as well as slaves against Virginia.[8]

Open warfare broke out in the Hampton Roads area in September 1775. The first clash occurred as the result of a hurricane that howled through the Tidewater early in the month, providing John Pinkney's *Virginia Gazette* a story of Dunmore tumbling into the water with which to regale its readers. The editor assured the public, however, that "*those who are born to be* h———*d will never be* DROWNED."[9] To the mortification of the British navy, when the skies cleared, the *Mercury*, which had been preparing to leave for Boston, had run aground off Norfolk and one of the *Otter*'s tenders, the *Liberty*, was stranded off Hampton. The British struggled for ten days before they freed the larger ship; they lost the other to the Virginians. Captain Squire of the *Otter*, who was aboard the tender until the last moment, escaped only by jumping into the water and hiding in the woods overnight. Humiliated, he returned with the *Otter* a week later, threatening to bombard Hampton unless reparations were made. One hundred volunteers under James Innes, now a major, hastened from Williamsburg. The Virginians released all of the tender's crew that had been captured except two runaway slaves but refused to return any of its equipment unless Squire gave up Joseph Harris, a Hampton slave who served as the pilot of the *Otter*. The British replied by clamping a tight blockade on Hampton Roads.[10]

As a result of the misadventure Captain Squire was ridiculed in the pages of the Norfolk *Virginia Gazette*, which John Hunter Holt had been publishing since spring. All summer Holt had maintained a rapid fire of epithets and insults at Dunmore and his allies, "not forgetting," one observer reported, "a few anecdotes of the Rebelious principals of L. Dunmores father."[11] Squire now lost patience. His warnings laughed at, on the afternoon of September 30 the naval officer landed a detachment to seize the offender. Luckily for Holt he was able to hide, but the troops carried off his press and two of his workmen to the *Eilbeck*. As a result, Dunmore could commence publication of his own *Virginia Gazette* under the editorship of the Norfolk merchant Hector McAlestor in November. The paper appeared intermittently at least until March. Subsequently the pressmen and their equipment went to help the British army publish newspapers in New York and Philadelphia.[12]

The episode badly injured Norfolk's reputation in the opinion of the rest of the colony since a hundred or more spectators had lined up to watch and made no attempt to stop the soldiers. When the local militia colonel, Matthew Phripp, sounded the alarm, none of the men who responded would go near the British. Phripp resigned his command in anger. Nor did anyone interfere when the soldiers returned a couple of weeks later for more ink and paper. Not all inhabitants of Norfolk were loyalists. When John Schaw, one of Dunmore's commissaries, turned in a resident for wearing a hunting shirt as evidence of rebel sympathies, Schaw barely escaped being tarred and feathered. But once British guns came to bear on the town, men like the printer Holt and Colonel Phripp lost out. Then, to the horror of leaders in Williamsburg, Phripp himself went over to Dunmore although later he cleared his name and was allowed to return when he demonstrated that the British had threatened his family.[13]

Virginia had relatively few active loyalists compared to other colonies. In only two places did significant opposition to the rebels exist. One was the Norfolk–Portsmouth area and, to a lesser extent, the farm country dependent upon it on the Eastern Shore. The other was the southwestern counties where a loyalist uprising occurred later in the war.

In Norfolk and Portsmouth the trouble was mostly ethnic in origin. Longstanding rivalries based on national background merged with the imperial struggle. In fact, the factionalism in pre-Revolutionary Norfolk and Portsmouth grew so divisive that residents seeking compensation from the British Loyalist Commission after the war for losses at the hands of the rebels had to show that the damages resulted from their allegiance to the king and not their involvement in the regional partisan strife.

At the center of the local controversy stood James Parker, a former Scottish factor who became an independent trader and permanent resident of Norfolk and eventually one of the city's wealthiest men. In the late 1760s he and his supporters had provoked violent riots when they inoculated their families against the smallpox. The proce-

dure was new and extremely dangerous. In Norfolk, as almost everywhere else in the colonies, the majority of the population strenuously
objected to its use, and division over the issue quickly hardened along
ethnic lines. Parker became involved in long-drawn-out lawsuits, during the course of which he came to feel that the Virginia courts, and
behind them the colony's establishment, were biased against him.[14]
Although he opposed the Stamp Act and even on the eve of the
Revolution still considered parliamentary taxation of the colonies a
violation of fundamental British liberties, Parker joined Dunmore because he believed the British needed "to convince some of the Great
Men (as they consider themselves) of this country that there is a superior power to which they and all Americans are answerable."[15]

Other loyalists acted from more pragmatic motives. When British
troops came to Virginia, they paid for supplies in specie which American troops did not have. Geography mattered, too, for the Eastern
Shore lay exposed on two sides to British attack and was too far away
for the revolutionaries to defend effectively. Generally Virginia authorities took a tolerant attitude toward loyalists of this ilk. To the
frustration of more impetuous colleagues, especially soldiers in the
field, and of Congress, Virginia leaders only slowly adopted preventive measures to block intercourse with the enemy or force the more
active loyalists into exile. Family ties and former community standing
protected most loyalists from the worst forms of retribution unless
they actually took up arms against the rebellion. Even those who did
could win pardon or parole. Only the most militant such as Parker
and a few others were imprisoned or driven out and told after the
war that "they can never be suffered to come amongst us" again.[16]

With Dunmore in Norfolk the list of the city's wrong-doings length-
ened in the rebels' eyes. Intercepted letters revealed that merchants
anticipating an invasion fleet ordered tens of thousands of pounds
worth of goods to supply it. More damaging, some letter writers
asked influential correspondents in Britain to help them obtain the
posts of Virginia officials they expected to be condemned when
the British suppressed the rebellion. Other letters revealed that the
parent firms of some Norfolk merchants advanced the British
government funds for a southern campaign in the hope of being
compensated from the Virginia estates the invading forces would confiscate. "I intend with many others to . . . spend the Remainder of my
life in a Retirement . . . near to you," wrote one Briton to his brother
in Norfolk.[17] Jefferson put the Virginia reaction quite plainly by para-

phrasing the cry of ancient Romans, "Carthage must be destroyed," in a letter to his friend John Page, "Delenda est Norfolk."[18]

In Williamsburg Patrick Henry and the Committee of Safety had been gathering their own army since the adjournment of the Convention in August. So spirited was the martial ardor in those opening days of the war that, after only a month of recruiting, both regular and minute companies announced the completion of enlistments. By October the committee, which under the chairmanship of Edmund Pendleton had been meeting in Hanover Town on the Pamunkey River, well out of Dunmore's reach, felt secure enough to move its sessions to the colonial capital. Henry established a camp behind the College of William and Mary at the opposite end of town from the volunteers' quarters in Waller's Grove and emptied the Palace and the Capitol of soldiers. Throughout October recruits marched into town until by the end of the month close to two thousand men were bivouacked around the city.[19]

Outfitting the troops posed a major problem because few of the items vital to an army were native products of Virginia. Advertisements in the newspapers urged the people to sell commissaries whatever they had on hand that might be of use. The basic uniform of the Virginia soldier had conveniently come to be the frontiersman's hunting shirt, ideally dyed a dark hue, with some fringe sewn on it. The outfit gave rise among the British to the derisive epithet "shirtmen." Immediately upon its appointment in August, the Committee of Safety had met briefly before it did anything else to name a prominent merchant and planter of King William County, William Aylett, commissary of purchases. Aylett lost no time placing long-term orders in Baltimore and Philadelphia and more immediately began to scrape together what he could find in the small stores around the countryside, run, according to him, mostly by "Wrong headed Scotchmen." On October 12 he opened a supply depot or "publick store" in Williamsburg and soon had the tailors in the area at work sewing tents and coats for Henry's men.[20]

Feeding the army presented less of a problem since Virginia was a rich agricultural province. In fact, the committee could indulge in the luxury of a little politicking by ordering their new commissary of provisions, John Hawkins, a merchant and slave trader of Hanover County, to make his purchases "as diffusive as possible."[21] During October Hawkins ranged through the Piedmont in a wide arc contracting for the delivery of beef, pork, and flour over the next nine months.

The committee completed its tiny logistical force by placing William Finnie of Williamsburg, a veteran of the 2nd Virginia Regiment in the French and Indian War, in charge of armament and transportation. Earlier in the summer Finnie had displaced Dunmore's appointee as keeper of the public magazine in the city, and later when some old cannon used to protect Yorktown in the previous conflict were dragged to Williamsburg, the city fathers recommended him as the proper person to take charge. Apparently neither Finnie nor anyone else in Henry's ranks had much competence as an artillerist, for an army officer later described the armament set up as "horrizontal pointed pieces planted in the streets."[22] The Committee of Safety ordered Finnie to collect whatever additional guns belonging to the public he could find (three hundred was all, he reported) and commissioned him quartermaster general to solve the army's growing need for horses and wagons.[23]

Suddenly Dunmore lashed out at the Virginians' buildup. Buoyed by news that he had been assigned more troops from Florida, he commenced a series of well-planned raids on October 12. Within ten days the British forces eliminated any hope the Virginians had of counteracting Dunmore's naval strength and driving him from the colony in the near future. The Virginians had been moving into hiding the many cannon scattered throughout the Norfolk area that had been left over from privateering ventures during the French and Indian War. Acting on excellent intelligence from loyalists, Dunmore ferreted out the caches and destroyed them. On the first sally he and Captain Samuel Leslie of the 14th Regiment took nineteen guns belonging to a leading rebel, Joseph Hutchings. A few days later the governor sailed up the east branch of the Elizabeth River with a larger detachment, landed, and moved quickly inland to Kemp's Landing, where he just missed capturing the shipment of gunpowder that the Goodrich family had brought in. At Dunmore's approach nearly two hundred militia commanded by Hutchings ran into the woods. The British captured several, including a Convention delegate, William Robinson, and pillaged the settlement at the landing.[24]

Returning to Norfolk on October 18, Dunmore rested only a day before he sent off Lieutenant John Battut with a patrol to search out twenty more cannon in another hideaway a short distance from the city. Similar excursions on the next two days brought the total number of cannon destroyed or taken to seventy-two in addition to many smaller arms and quantities of ball and shot, "which, I believe," Dunmore reported to London, "is all the Military Stores in this neighbourhood that could be of any Service to the Rebels."[25] Captain Leslie took a more pessimistic view in his report, however. He wrote that the quantity of arms destroyed "is a proof that it would require a very large force to subdue this Colony."[26]

After these successes Dunmore turned his attention across the water to Hampton. Captain Squire brought up a squadron of five ships before the town during the night of October 25 but a barricade of sunken vessels in the channel prevented him from approaching close enough to burn the town as he announced he intended to do. Squire landed a party under cover of darkness to raid some houses and take away a slave at Mills Creek. The next day, after a heavy exchange of fire with two companies and some militia under Captains George Nicholas and George Lyne, the British succeeded in burning a farmhouse on Cooper's plantation at the mouth of the Hampton River. That night British sailors finally hacked their way through the barricade, but by then Colonel Woodford had arrived from Williamsburg with a company of riflemen. From the cover of houses along the main street of Hampton the Virginia riflemen poured such heavy fire on the British that they had to withdraw. In close sea-to-shore engagements the accuracy of the riflemen repeatedly proved more than a match for the British navy by preventing the sailors from remaining on deck long enough to fire their guns. Another tender of the *Otter*, the *Hawk*, went aground. In the retreat the Virginians captured ten of its crew and killed its skipper. Dunmore suffered at least one other killed and several wounded. The Virginians had no casualties.[27]

The Committee of Safety, under pressure from Congress to do something about Dunmore, had already laid its plans when the attack on Hampton intervened. The committee halted all traffic to or from Norfolk and Portsmouth and issued orders for the 2nd Regiment to cross the James River and march toward the Southside towns. Ordinarily Patrick Henry as colonel of the 1st Regiment would have been the commander in the field, but the weeks in camp had not diminished concerns about his military inexperience. The complaints were never specified, and possibly with more time Henry might have proved himself. But faced with an immediate decision, the committee dared not risk its meager forces under him. Despite the political risks involved, after several days of discussion, it voted seven to four to send Woodford with the 2nd Regiment and the Culpeper County minutemen against Dunmore, leaving Henry, still nominally in overall command as the senior colonel, with a much reduced force to guard the capital.[28]

The pressure for action notwithstanding, shortages of arms and other supplies kept Woodford in Williamsburg until November 7. Then, just as he began to move his forces across the James River at Jamestown, the *King's Fisher* appeared to cruise up and down the river for a week, preventing further use of the ferry. Woodford marched the rest of his men upriver to Sandy Point, where he crossed after driving off a British tender. By then almost two weeks had passed since Woodford left Williamsburg, long enough for Dunmore to win another victory.[29]

On the night of November 14 Dunmore moved to the vicinity of Great Bridge, where a large force of North Carolinians had been reported. Meanwhile, Joseph Hutchings and Arthur Lawson assembled the Princess Anne militia at Kemp's Landing. About 170 men answered the call. Finding no one at Great Bridge the next day but learning of Hutchings's force, Dunmore marched on with about 100 regulars and 20 loyalists. Although the Virginians had time to set up an ambush, the inexperienced militia gave themselves away by firing too soon and then fled. The Virginians suffered seven dead and eighteen captured, including Hutchings, who, deserted by his men, was made prisoner by one of his own slaves who had joined Dunmore. Lawson and a few others escaped toward the North Carolina border, near which they were later taken in their sleep. The British suffered only one casualty, a grenadier nicked in the knee. Dunmore then moved into Kemp's Landing and continued pillaging where he had left off before.[30]

Flushed with victory, Dunmore seized the occasion to raise the king's standard—an action proclaiming a state of rebellion and requiring all loyal subjects to help suppress it under penalty of law. The governor had already signed the proclamation on November 7 when a third division of reinforcements from the 14th Regiment arrived, but he had refrained from issuing it in the hope of shortly receiving more explicit instructions from the ministry. The acclaim the triumph at Kemp's Landing won from the people of Princess Anne County changed Dunmore's mind. Persuaded that the inhabitants had not rallied to him before out of fear, the governor "determined to run all risques for their support."[31] By then, too, Dunmore had undoubtedly

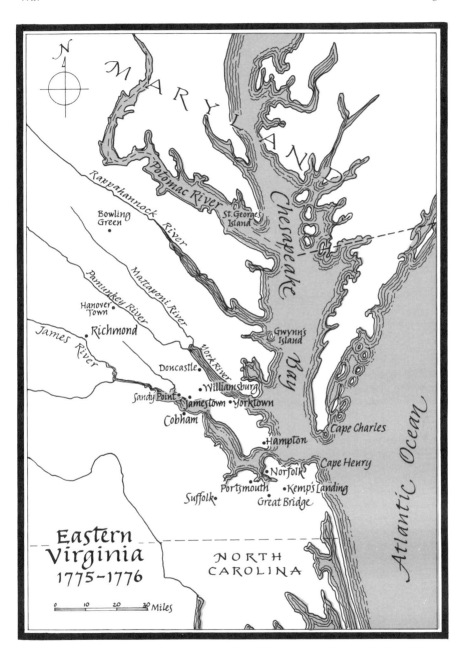

N

MARYLAND

Rappahannock River

Potomac River

Bowling
Green

St. George's
Island

Chesapeake

Mattaponi River

Pamunkey River

Hanover
Town

Richmond

James River

Gwynn's
Island

York River

Doncastle

Bay

Williamsburg

Sandy Point

Jamestown

Yorktown

Cobham

Cape Charles

Hampton

Cape Henry

Norfolk

Portsmouth

Kemp's Landing

Suffolk

Great Bridge

Atlantic Ocean

Eastern
Virginia
1775–1776

NORTH
CAROLINA

0   10   20   30 Miles

learned of the king's own proclamation of rebellion that had appeared in the last issue of the *Virginia Gazette*. But the earl's decree went beyond the monarch's: "And I do hereby farther declare all indented Servants, Negroes, or others (appertaining to Rebels) free, that are able and willing to bear Arms, they joining his Majesty's Troops."[32]

At last Dunmore had done it! He had finally carried out his threat to emancipate the slaves. As an act of war the move was an obvious tactic. Virginians had long regarded the large number of slaves in their midst as the colony's greatest military liability and for most of a year had been fretting over the frequency with which British commentators mentioned enlisting the slaves as a possible weapon against a rebellion. Writing from London a few months before, William Lee even urged freeing the slaves before the British did. Actually, the decree merely summed up Dunmore's policy of several months past that had already enticed blacks to his lines. But it enunciated that policy in final, official form and broadcast it for all to know.[33]

Dunmore's action contained irony for both sides. As British and loyalist publicists happily pointed out, in the Virginians' anger at Dunmore they fell into the position of condemning him for attacking freedom and slavery simultaneously. As for the governor, the declaration had the greatest impact upon those who otherwise had been well disposed toward him. From Williamsburg Archibald Cary reported that "most of the Council" were determined to denounce the proclamation publicly and "from the language of the President [Thomas Nelson] and some others who have been in town—we may expect they will give the deluded publisher a Rowland for his Oliver."[34] The most spectacular reaction came from William Byrd III, who had been quite sympathetic to the governor but now tendered his services to the Convention—a not inconsiderable offer since he had commanded the 2nd Virginia Regiment during the French and Indian War. Virginia leaders turned Byrd down only after careful consideration. In a declaration prepared for the Convention at its next session, Robert Carter Nicholas revealed at once how reluctantly moderates like himself approached rebellion and how central to their position was the right of property, even property in human beings. Dunmore, Nicholas asserted, was the "executioner" of the "system of tyranny adopted by the Ministry and Parliament of Great Britain." The governor had assumed "powers which the king himself cannot exercise," and "if, by his single fiat, he can strip us of our property [that is, slaves] . . . let us bid adieu to every thing valuable in life."[35]

Humanitarian concern was not Dunmore's primary motive. He made no attempt to free the fifty-seven slaves that he left behind when he fled to the *Fowey* and later claimed compensation for them from the British government. The emancipation proclamation carefully included only the slaves of Dunmore's opponents, and then only able-bodied males. In some cases the governor turned back the slaves of tories to their masters when they tried to enlist; others he drafted, however, and some loyalists ordered their slaves into the ranks when they joined Dunmore themselves. Dunmore also had little interest in arranging exchanges for black soldiers when they were captured; Colonel Woodford reported that the governor's negotiator "affected to treat the matter lightly, at last said he supposed we must sell them."[36] On the other hand, there is no basis for the rumor Virginians spread to discourage runaways that Dunmore sold black troops in the West Indies to raise money. Those blacks who were still with him in the end went as free men to New York.[37]

The mere presence of British forces afforded slaves an avenue of escape that they had not had before. The evidence is that even before the magazine affair some blacks interpreted the impending conflict with Great Britain as their opportunity for freedom. Several hundred, including some free blacks who later claimed compensation from the Loyalist Commission for property lost, eventually joined Dunmore's Ethiopian Regiment under the command, ironically, of another of William Byrd III's sons, Thomas, a British army officer. Many of Dunmore's black troops wore on their breasts the defiant motto "Liberty to Slaves" in bitter rebuke to badges proclaiming "Liberty or Death" favored by white Virginians. The number of blacks who enlisted with Dunmore was not large relative to the two hundred thousand blacks in the colony or to the outpouring panic-stricken masters fearfully anticipated, but the blacks who joined the governor played an important part in the struggle. In fact, Dunmore acknowledged that he found it easier to recruit for the Ethiopian Regiment than for the white Queen's Own Loyal Regiment that he was raising simultaneously.[38]

The whites' dread of a black uprising at first greatly exaggerated the threat inherent in Dunmore's proclamation. Many whites calmed their fears with dire counterthreats. The *Virginia Gazette* observed several times that, if black males ran away, they left their women and children at the mercy of "our riflemen from the back country, who never wish to see a negro, and who will pour out their vengence upon them whenever it is desired."[39] Few runaways were actually executed.

To the contrary, in one case from Northampton County the magistrates practically begged the Committee of Safety to reverse the death sentences they had passed on four prisoners. The threat of a black uprising might have been greater had Dunmore had more military success. But by the end of 1775 the Committee of Safety was writing to reassure its counterpart in Maryland that with regard to the slaves "the apprehensions of danger, from that quarter, seem to have subsided."[40] Instead of executing blacks taken in arms the Convention decreed that they should be sold in the West Indies, or sent to the lead mines of Fincastle County or to other public works, and their owners compensated for their loss. The Committee of Safety urged masters to send recaptured runaways inland away from temptation.[41]

Dunmore raised the king's standard on November 15 at Kemp's Landing, although to his chagrin he could not find a national emblem and had to use regimental colors instead. People in the Norfolk–Portsmouth area had been living in terror for fear of the retribution the revolutionaries might wreak upon them. The war preparations in Williamsburg had induced many Norfolk and Portsmouth residents to flee—some estimates ran as high as a third of the population—in anticipation of the Virginians sacking the two towns. A proclamation of the Committee of Safety to the contrary reassured no one; rebels in less official capacities more forthrightly stated their intentions. Many residents who remained put their possessions on vessels in the harbor and slept on board every night. Now crowds cheered Dunmore and his men as they marched back in triumph. The next morning, November 16, over a hundred of the militia who had opposed him in the field took the oath of allegiance, swearing that the rebels had forced them to fight. That afternoon the governor returned to Norfolk where he again erected the standard; two hundred including the mayor and aldermen promptly avowed their loyalty to it. The city leaders provided public entertainment for the victorious troops as they paraded into town, and the price of red cloth for badges to designate the loyalists rose precipitously. It seemed that Dunmore was correct: if only a stand were taken, a small victory won, the people would regain confidence in the government and rally to its support. Within a short time over three thousand whites from Norfolk, Portsmouth, and their environs reportedly took the oath.[42]

Dunmore formally occupied the city of Norfolk on November 23 and put his men to work constructing a ring of fortifications that one observer estimated would have taken 5,000 men and twenty cannon to defend. Obviously the governor expected support soon. The outpouring of loyalists had already provided him with a promising little army. The recent arrival of additional men from the British 14th Regiment brought his force of regulars to 175. Lieutenant Colonel Jacob Ellegood of the local militia led about 600 men to Dunmore's side and was immediately commissioned colonel of the new Queen's Own Loyal Regiment. James Parker became Dunmore's chief engineer, while his partner, Thomas McKnight, took charge of fortifying the city. Neil Jamieson, the principal factor of Glassford & Co., accepted the post of supply agent, and Hector McAlestor the position of paymaster. James Ingram served as chief justice and John Brown as vendue master of Dunmore's admiralty court for the condemnation of prizes taken at sea. The elderly Andrew Sprowle, unofficial leader of the Virginia merchant community for a generation, provided buildings for barracks.[43]

Perhaps the most useful converts Dunmore made were John Goodrich and his sons, John, Jr., William, Bartlett, and Bridger. The elder Goodrich owned a plantation in Isle of Wight County but was known primarily as a smuggler and merchant sea captain in the coastal trade. Although the family had just delivered the shipload of gunpowder that Robert Carter Nicholas had ordered in July, the Goodriches had incurred the Convention's displeasure because they had also landed British goods disguised as Dutch to evade Congress's prohibition of imports from the mother country. Meanwhile Dunmore learned of the powder and with a combination of threats and blandishments won the family to his service.

The Goodriches' knowledge of Tidewater streams made them invaluable for leading foraging expeditions and lightning raids against isolated plantations and ship landings. Obviously fast talkers, they played a double game with the Committee of Safety and the Virginia Convention most of the winter until eventually the rebels captured all five and imprisoned them. Proving equally adept as jailbreakers, the Goodriches escaped one by one to lead a small fleet of loyalist privateers up and down the coast from New Jersey to the Carolinas for the rest of the war. The family retired to England and Bermuda after the peace, perhaps the only loyalists to have made a fortune out of the Revolution.[44]

On November 21, two days before Dunmore began fortifying Norfolk, Woodford was at Cobham when he heard a false rumor that the governor was marching to take Suffolk. Woodford sent Lieutenant Colonel Charles Scott with 215 men racing thirty-five miles in a single day to garrison the town. Woodford's main force reached the town on November 25. The Virginians and the British confronted one another at Great Bridge, where a bridge and causeway formed the only route across the Elizabeth River to Norfolk. Since manning the entrenchments that the British had constructed around Norfolk required many more men than Dunmore presently commanded, he had to keep the Virginians from crossing the river and cutting off the city from the food supplies of Princess Anne and Norfolk counties until reinforcements arrived. On his previous excursion to Great Bridge Dunmore had built a small wooden fort that the Virginians derisively referred to as the "hogpen" and had garrisoned it with about 100 men, half of them black. By November 28 the advanced Virginia detachment under Scott moved into position across the river from the fort and the firing began. Woodford arrived four days later.[45]

The terrain at Great Bridge was ideal for defense. At that point in the river the main channel was lined with wide marshes on both sides. A causeway across which an attacking force could only move five or six abreast ran from the settlement of Great Bridge on the south bank to an island on which there were several houses. The bridge itself spanned the main stream from the island to another causeway opposite where the British fort with two four-pound cannon commanded the approach. Most of the planking on the bridge had been torn up. After pitching camp on the far side of town, the Virginians constructed a barricade at the end of the main street and dug entrenchments along the bank to the west from which riflemen could sweep the bridge. The rebels posted pickets on the island at night but withdrew them at daylight to protect them from British fire.

The stalemate lasted for over a week. The younger officers pushed Woodford, who had the reputation of being overly cautious, to attack, but he declined because he lacked the cannon to reduce the fort and was generally short of ammunition. His plight worsened when loyalists sabotaged Bachelor Mill Dam, preventing his wagons from crossing Deep Creek, the quickest route to Suffolk. Woodford repeatedly wrote to Williamsburg for bullet molds, powder, cannon, and enough blankets to issue each man two as protection against the raw winter weather. Informed that a group of North Carolinians was marching north with cannon, Woodford sent a message urging them to hurry in order to block Dunmore's retreat to the south. One company of Carolinians did arrive on December 3, but they brought no cannon.

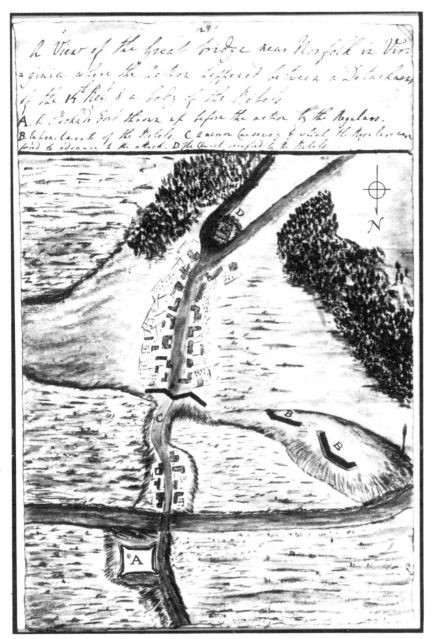

Map of the Battle of Great Bridge. *Courtesy, William L. Clements Library, University of Michigan.*

A View of the Great bridge near Norfolk in Virginia where the action happened between a Detachment of the 14th Reg.t: and a body of Rebels.   A. A Stockade Fort thrown up before the action by the Regulars. B. Entrenchments of the Rebels. C. A narrow Causeway by which the Regulars were forced to advance to the attack. D. The Church occupied by the Rebels.

For several days most of the action occurred at a ford five or six miles downstream from Great Bridge. Both British and Virginians collected boats on the opposite sides of the Elizabeth River and posted detachments to guard them. The day after Scott arrived, a small party of British attacked but were driven off. On December 3 Lieutenant Colonel Edward Stevens and about one hundred Virginians stole across the river a mile or so below the boats to surprise the British but gave themselves away by firing too soon. After a hot skirmish during which they killed two black soldiers and captured two others, Stevens's men withdrew. Three days later Scott tried again with a larger party. Once more the element of surprise was lost when wagoners coming from Norfolk saw the Virginians. The British lost one white and two blacks killed and two more blacks captured, but again the black company frustrated the attack. The Virginians suffered one wounded. Back at Great Bridge the firing was constant every day. The only action was a successful sally on December 4 by a squad of black loyalists who burned five or six houses on the island in the middle of the river to prevent sniping at the British fort.

Despite the advantage of his position, Dunmore broke the deadlock by attacking first. It is not clear why he took the offensive. Woodford heard afterward that an escaped slave told the governor only a couple of hundred Virginians opposed him. Woodford subsequently elaborated the story to suggest that he had sent the man for that purpose. Virginians savored the irony of Dunmore being duped by a runaway black. But since the Virginia troops had camped within sight of the British, more likely Dunmore's reason was as he reported to London, that he had learned of a body of North Carolinians who were one day's march away with cannon that he knew his fort could not withstand.[46]

In retrospect taking the offensive was foolhardy, virtually suicidal. Officers of the 14th Regiment advised against it. They felt that they had been sent to act as bodyguards for Dunmore and found themselves in the position of having to defend Norfolk only because the governor let his judgment be swayed by the pleading of merchants who feared the loss of their property. Yet their commander, Captain Leslie, elected to carry on when he arrived at the fort about three o'clock in the morning of December 9 and discovered the black troops he counted on to create a diversion guarding the ford downstream, too far away to help. Then, because Leslie had let his men rest after their twelve-mile march, he did not attack until just as the drums beat reveille in the Virginia camp, eliminating whatever advantage of surprise he might have had. Both Leslie and Dunmore apparently were too confident that untried rebels, however well positioned, would not stand up to a bayonet charge by disciplined troops. But by the same reasoning the British might have expected to decimate an attack by less well trained men across the bridge even if the attackers were supported by artillery. Wasting time on fortifications around Norfolk he could not maintain, Dunmore too long neglected strengthening the post where a small force might have made a more successful stand.[47]

Leslie had 120 regulars, about 60 loyalists, and some sailors from the fleet plus about 100 men already at the fort. He relaid the planks on the bridge and quickly moved the attacking force across to the island, from which the rebel outposts withdrew after a few shots. According to local legend, the last to leave was a black man named William Flora. Leslie set up cannon on the island and deployed white and black loyalist troops to guard them. Since scattered shots had become commonplace the main body of Virginians was not immediately alarmed and went about the daily routine for several minutes before the cry went up, "Boys, stand to your arms."[48] From the island Captain Charles Fordyce led the regulars onto the causeway toward the Virginia barricade, which 70 or 80 men under Lieutenant Edward Travis defended. The Virginians held their fire until the British almost reached them. The effect was devastating; a participant later wrote, "I then saw the horrers of war in perfection, worse than can be imagin'd; 10 or 12 bullets thro' many; limbs broke in 2 or 3 places; brains turned out. Good God, what a sight!"[49] Captain Fordyce was killed and Lieutenant Battut was wounded just as they reached the barricade.

Falling back to the island, the survivors commenced firing on Woodford's main force as it marched down the street from its camp, but with little effect. The sole Virginia casualty during the entire engagement was a soldier nicked in the finger, just the reverse of the battle at Kemp's Landing. Then the Culpeper minutemen under Lieutenant Colonel Stevens opened fire from the earthworks to the west, driving the British back into their fort. The battle lasted about thirty minutes, during which the 14th Regiment suffered three officers and fourteen men killed, and one officer and forty-eight men wounded. Battut and fifteen others among the wounded were captured. The battle of Great Bridge, Woodford boasted, "was a second

Bunker's Hill affair, in miniature, with this difference, that we kept our post."[50]

To offset rumors that the shirtmen scalped their victims, Woodford made every effort to treat the British with perfect decorum. He buried the heroic Fordyce with full honors and acted so solicitously toward Battut that the latter sent a message to Leslie assuring him that he and the other prisoners were receiving good care. A truce was arranged to allow the British to retrieve their dead. Blacks and other loyalists received harsher treatment. Thirty-three were handcuffed black to white and marched to Williamsburg to be punished.

Dunmore immediately realized that he could not hold Norfolk after the defeat. The British abandoned the "hogpen" that evening and, although some loyalists wanted to make another stand, moved their troops on board ship. Many residents followed. Woodford occupied the fort at Great Bridge the next day when about 250 North Carolina regulars and militia under Colonel Robert Howe joined him. The six cannon the North Carolinians brought turned out to be "honeycombed" and virtually useless, however. Two sound pieces soon arrived from Williamsburg. Woodford was unable to move farther for several days because he had sent all his wagons back to Suffolk and Cabin Point for supplies just before the battle. He also feared that a shipload of Highlanders sighted off Norfolk might be British reinforcements, but a petition for safe conduct soon revealed them to be immigrants bound for the Carolinas. As refugees' stories exposed the extent of Dunmore's losses, Woodford sent the Culpeper minutemen to Kemp's Landing on December 11. After another detachment of North Carolinians and several units from Williamsburg brought his strength to over 1,200, Woodford finally moved into Norfolk on December 14.[51]

The day before, the twenty-eight-gun *Liverpool* under Captain Henry Bellew arrived at the Virginia Capes with the storeship *Maria* carrying three thousand stand of arms. If only he had waited, Dunmore must have lamented. Much of his trouble had come from overoptimistically discounting the physical difficulty of conducting military operations in an empire as vast as Great Britain's. Word of Dunmore's predicament after the magazine affair had reached Lord Dartmouth in late June 1775, and although the minister did not write to his governor for several weeks more, within three days he had ordered arms for him. The ship *Maria* and its cargo were readied in July, and Dartmouth's covering letter to accompany them was dated August 2. But for some reason, perhaps in the general confusion of assembling reinforcements and supplies for the American theater throughout the fall, or perhaps on account of the weather, which delayed some ships endlessly at Cork, Ireland, the *Maria* did not sail for weeks afterward. Two communications from the secretary of state to Dunmore—the first since May—went with the arms: one authorized Dunmore, if he wished, to appoint Richard Corbin acting governor and come home on leave, and the other instructed the earl to share the arms with Governor Martin. Eventually Dunmore sent Martin one thousand stand in February 1776.[52]

Meanwhile, Colonel Woodford almost lost his command, for the crisis over Henry erupted again in Williamsburg. The fourth Virginia Convention had convened in Richmond on December 1 and immediately adjourned to the College of William and Mary in the capital. Since Henry's political strength always lay with the rank-and-file of the Convention rather than with the leaders, he had bided his time until the delegates came back to town before challenging the Committee of Safety's decision to make Woodford the commander in the field. Now, when he received the final insult of having part of his own regiment sent to reinforce Woodford, who was also allowed to have a secretary—the symbol of an independent command—Henry made an issue of his rival's failure to keep the headquarters in Williamsburg informed of his movements. Woodford replied that he was obliged to report to Henry only if neither the committee nor the Convention were in session. Woodford claimed that, during the few days recently when both bodies had adjourned, he thought that Henry was home in Hanover County and so wrote to the committee's chairman, Edmund Pendleton, instead. Unfortunately for Woodford's explanation, Pendleton, too, had been home in Caroline County.[53]

The Committee of Safety's treatment of Henry may well explain why Pendleton fell from first place to fourth in the balloting for committee seats that session. Richard Bland, who also had signed the order against Henry, dropped from fourth to eighth. Two who did not sign, Paul Carrington and James Mercer, moved from sixth to third and from ninth to fifth respectively. But another signer, Dudley Digges, rose more dramatically from seventh place to first. It is impossible to read partisan alignments into these variations. Convention politics were shifting sands that often depended on immediate emotional factors such as the speeches delivered at the moment. Whatever the meaning of the changes in the poll, when the Committee of Safety next met, it chose Pendleton to be its chairman again.[54]

The crisis peaked when a newly elected member of the committee,

Joseph Jones of King William County, told Woodford that he should have reported to Henry. Woodford threatened to resign. The committee deliberated for a week before devising a compromise acceptable to all. Woodford would report his activities to Henry, but would not receive orders directly from Henry unless both the Committee of Safety and the Convention were not in session. As an added mollifier, Henry would have an aide-de-camp. Wiser from experience, however, the committee decided that it would make no nominations to Congress for the appointment of general officers, "lest," Pendleton explained in a personal letter to Woodford, "it should be thought propriety requires our calling or rather recommending our present First Officer to that station."[55]

Henry had one martial accomplishment to his credit: the birth of the Virginia navy. Although the idea of creating a navy had been discussed in the Convention, Henry initiated the action. While he was on a routine inspection of the defenses erected at Hampton to prevent a repetition of the British raid a month before, two large, suspicious-looking merchant ships appeared about fifteen miles out in the Chesapeake Bay. Henry immediately commissioned a local sea captain, James Barron, to man a small vessel with about twenty of Barron's militia company to bring them in. Within ten days Barron and his brother, Richard, had captured nine more prizes and put an end to the freedom with which the British had been harassing Virginia shipping in Hampton Roads. The Convention voted its thanks to the Barrons and placed three armed vessels under James's command. It also authorized the Committee of Safety to form the navy into a separate service.[56]

The rush of events forced the Convention to restore partially the court system that had been in abeyance except for criminal cases for a year and a half. For the moment the Convention itself sat as a prize court to condemn the Barrons' captures, but in view of the prospect that the new navy would seize many more, the delegates established an admiralty court and appointed as judges two young lawyers, John Blair and Edmund Randolph, and a Williamsburg merchant, James Holt. Some disposition, too, had to be made of the eighty-odd prisoners, mostly loyalists, crowding the Williamsburg jail. Again a select committee of the Convention heard the cases, but for the future the delegates ordered each county committee, which in effect was the old county court under a different name, to appoint five of its members as commissioners to try loyalists who bore arms against the colony. Yet again the Convention's self-styled "humane disposition" toward its opponents led it to allow offenders who submitted to the Committee of Safety within two months of the ordinance to be pardoned.[57] Those loyalists who remained adamant in their opposition could be imprisoned if convicted of hostile acts, and the Committee of Safety could "sequester" their estates (that is, hold them in trust until the end of the war). Income from sequestered estates in excess of just debts remained in the colonial treasury. Trials were by jury with appeals permitted to the Committee of Safety. The ordinance also gave the county commissioners jurisdiction over violations of Continental and Virginia trade regulations.[58]

In general, the Convention faced the problem of the loyalists more squarely than had its predecessor, but it still was rather mildly disposed toward them. It rescinded the exemption from military obligation that the earlier session had granted to British merchants in the colony on condition that they remain neutral. Too many had since violated the Continental Association and given aid and information to Dunmore. Now all residents had to serve in the militia or leave the colony. Special committees of the Convention investigated Colonel Woodford's charges of toryism against Charles Robertson, the Edward Hack Moseleys, father and son, Matthew Phripp, John Willoughby, Alexander Campbell, and Cary Mitchell, all distinguished citizens of the Norfolk–Portsmouth area. All were confined to their rooms instead of to jail during the hearings, and all were acquitted. The Convention even seemed at times to be determined not to believe the mounting evidence against the Goodriches.[59]

Aside from the flare-up over Henry, the December Convention behaved in a more tranquil and businesslike manner than had the August session. The housekeeping tasks confronting it set the tone. The military establishment had to be greatly enlarged since it had become clear that the war would last another year. General Washington's requests for support were increasing, and from Great Britain came frightening rumors of an expedition being prepared against the South. After some debate over the number required, the delegates opted for seven new regiments to join the two already in service. The Convention ordered the nine to be stationed two on each of the three Tidewater peninsulas, two in the Southside, and one on the Eastern Shore. One of the nine was to be recruited entirely among the German settlers in the western part of the colony. The Convention designated all the new troops as regular, that is, on the Continental payroll. With the enlistment of seven additional regiments the Convention decided to relieve the minutemen, who were a charge to the colony, of stand-by duty. Henceforth, minutemen had no obligation other than as regular militia although they retained their elite organization among the citizen soldiers for another year. With the exception of the regiment on the Eastern Shore, the Convention increased the size of both the new and the old units to ten companies of sixty-eight men each, thus qualifying them in contemporary terminology as "battalions" although technically the term could be, and was, used interchangeably with "regiment" at the time. In addition, the delegates provided a full panoply of commanders: a major general, two brigadier generals, a quartermaster general, and an adjutant general, each with appropriate deputies, aides, or secretaries.[60]

Congress posed an unexpected obstacle to the plan, however. It refused to accept more than six regiments because of the expense, and worse, sought to exclude the original two because their enlistments were half over, thereby jeopardizing the seniority of those who had fought against Dunmore. The morale of the veterans tumbled, and in the ensuing scramble for positions that Congress would recognize, some rank-and-file came to feel that "the Convention seems very desirous of serving themselves, Cousins or Friends."[61] Convention leaders appealed to the Virginia congressional delegation, which failed to persuade Congress to accept more than six regiments, but succeeded in having the 1st and 2nd regiments included among that number. If every colony could decide by itself how many troops to charge the Continent, Benjamin Harrison pointed out to the Convention, the expense would be limitless.[62]

To round out the delegates' chores, the lengthening war necessitated expanding the Committee of Safety's powers. The Convention reaffirmed the committee's supremacy in military affairs and assigned it greater economic power than any Virginia government had ever enjoyed before by granting it authority to establish public powder mills, let contracts for the manufacture of munitions, and ration saltpeter and sulfur. In addition, to ensure that the county committees wore "the Face of Law," as Mason had previously expressed it, the Convention ordered those counties which because of weather or for some other reason had not held elections as directed by the August session to do so at once and every October thereafter. The Convention authorized county committees to appoint sheriffs, who before the war had been named by the governor from a list submitted by the respective county court. The delegates also provided for the arbitration of debts payable in tobacco, particularly clergymen's salaries, since the laws for public inspection of tobacco had expired. Appointing commissioners to settle accounts arising from Dunmore's Indian campaign caused the Convention the most difficulty. Petitions from western counties charging conflict of interest necessitated rescinding the first appointments and revising the nominating committee several times before John Cabell, John Harvie, and John Neavill could be confirmed.[63]

Gradually the accelerating pace of war compelled the Convention to abandon short-term expedients and to assume greater responsibility for functions of government that the royal authorities had long ceased to exercise. Slowly and pragmatically the course of events drove the delegates toward the point from which they could not return. Finally, on the last day of their session, in response to Dunmore's blockade and depredations around Norfolk, they resolved to open Virginia ports to ships of all nations except Great Britain, Ireland, and the British West Indies and called on Congress to do the same for the entire continent. The effect was to reject the imperial economic system under which the mother country had monopolized the tobacco trade and which Virginians had previously sworn that they had no intention of overturning. The resolution anticipated Congress in a major step toward independence by several months. Yet the delegates continued to remain ambivalent. Their ordinances prescribing the new operations of government carefully left open the possibility of restoring the crown's authority. They extended the Committee of Safety for only one year and permitted it to issue contracts for only six to twelve months at a time. The authority of the counties to appoint sheriffs lasted only until "executive powers of government . . . are restored to their proper channel."[64] Virginians still were not ready to leave the empire.

CHAPTER 5

Independence

THE confrontation between the royal navy and the Virginia shirtmen across the Norfolk waterfront in December 1775 brought the end of rebellion and the beginning of revolution in the colony. At least as much as British assaults, a breakdown of discipline among the rebels fostered violence which, when it had ended, led Virginians finally to see how futile it was to think of returning to their allegiance to the crown. After they had clung to the hope for so long, the shift in opinion occurred relatively rapidly.

On shore, life among the shirtmen in the weeks following the battle of Great Bridge was unpleasant, at least according to the steady stream of complaints directed to the Convention in Williamsburg from the day the American troops entered Norfolk. The weather proved to be unbearable, the food abominable, and since there were so many ships to which loyalists could smuggle supplies, the tours of duty lasted too long. Its glory won, the 2nd Virginia Regiment felt that the time had come for it to go home and for someone else to endure the tedium of garrison duty. Colonel Woodford received numerous requests for leave or for permission to resign, all of which he referred to the Committee of Safety. He also yielded command of the united American forces to Colonel Robert Howe by virtue of the latter's Continental commission.[1]

Discipline suffered as the men took sides over the way the Committee of Safety had treated Patrick Henry. One captain from Henry's command wrote back to his colonel, "We arrived there [at Norfolk] fatigued, dry and hungry, we were neither welcomed, invited to eat or drink, or shown a place to rest our wearied bones."[2] The simmering emotions erupted in the "Boyakin affair," as Edmund Pendleton pronounced it. William Boykin, a lieutenant of Henry's regiment, who had been dispatched to Norfolk, refused to keep his men at the post Woodford assigned to them on the grounds that they were short of food, although they had ample flour and a half-ration of meat per man.[3] Woodford had Boykin court-martialed, but the court acquitted the lieutenant, and when the colonel appealed to the Convention, it supported Boykin. After that, partisans publicly debated the case in the pages of the *Virginia Gazette*.

As for Norfolk's future, the shirtmen made their intentions quite explicit. When frantic residents pleaded that their city be spared, Woodford and Howe issued a proclamation to assuage their immediate fears but left the final decision to the Convention. Both commanders continued to be nervous about the possibility of a surprise landing by the British if they obtained reinforcement. The colonels initially asked the Convention for a massive increase in their forces. Then they realized that an enemy sailing into the Elizabeth River could cut off even a large American force in Norfolk. Howe, Woodford, and most of their officers recommended that Norfolk be abandoned after they made certain that the city would be of no use to the foe.[4]

With hundreds of refugees packed on shipboard, the British found themselves in dire need of fresh provisions which nearby farmers would willingly supply but which the rebels determinedly tried to keep away. When Captain Squire asked "Messrs." Howe and Woodford if he could buy foodstuffs on shore, they answered no, and when Squire asked "Colonels" Howe and Woodford, their reply remained the same.[5] On Christmas Eve, with the *Liverpool, Otter, King's Fisher, Dunmore,* and *William* riding before the town, springs on their anchor lines ready to fire, Captain Bellew again sent a message that he much preferred to purchase the fresh provisions he needed than to take them by force. Howe stalled by referring the request to the Convention with a hint that they might agree since Bellew had been rather decent until then. The Convention had not replied when other events resolved the issue.

Howe also had sought delay by raising the question of a prisoner exchange, which interested the British because of the wounded Lieutenant Battut. Dunmore offered to exchange rank for rank, but Howe refused unless the British recognized the American distinction between regulars, minutemen, and militia. "We can, by no means, submit to place the officers and soldiers of the army, who have been taken in battle, upon a footing with those officers of militia and the peasants, that you have thought proper to deprive of their liberty," Howe argued.[6] A little bewildered, Dunmore observed that Howe's position left militiamen in a "predicament" and wondered why a commander would pay his men "so poor a compliment."[7] Howe replied with a longer description of the several branches in the American service than Dunmore probably cared to have. Howe then gave up the attempt to arrange an exchange and sent Battut to Williamsburg, where he was paroled. Finally, on December 30, Bellew ordered Howe to stop changing the guard in full view of his ships because, as an officer of the crown, it offended him to see rebels parading in public. Howe replied with stiff dignity that his men had orders not to initiate conflict, but the parades would continue and, if Bellew persisted in objecting, would he please give women and children time to leave the city.[8]

When the Americans paraded again on New Year's Day, the British opened fire between three and four o'clock in the afternoon. The cannonading boomed steadily until about ten and then intermittently into the morning. In addition to upholding what Bellew deemed the honor of the crown, the British hoped to destroy the buildings along the shore from which rebel sharpshooters had been sniping, but their plans were not well coordinated. Each ship apparently acted independently. When the firing began, Dunmore sent out a landing party and signaled Bellew to burn a captured shipload of salt. Other ships followed the governor's example and "to shew their Zeal for His Majesty's Service, sent great Numbers of Boats on Shore."[9] A couple of the British landing parties brought field pieces. The fighting and burning continued along the dock area for most of the night until the British withdrew.

On the American side Howe and Woodford initially believed that the attack was the major assault they feared. But once they saw that it was not, they had no objection to the British burning the town. "The wind favoured their design, and we believe the flames will become general," they hopefully reported only a few hours after the bombardment began.[10] The American commanders had just requested permission from the Convention to burn the Thistle Distillery owned by Archibald Campbell and Neil Jamieson as well as Andrew Sprowle's establishment at Gosport across the Elizabeth River, from both of which the British had been obtaining supplies. Without waiting for an answer, Woodford ordered those buildings destroyed as soon as the firing commenced. A counterattack by the British prevented the shirtmen from reducing Robert Tucker's windmill near Portsmouth as well. The next morning, although the British had been repulsed, Howe informed the Committee of Safety that the fire had "now become general and the whole Town will I doubt not be consum'd in a day or two."[11]

For three days the Americans looted and burned their way through Norfolk to the cry "Keep up the Jigg."[12] From Hampton, a soldier described the view in a letter to his mother: "At Night the fire was so great the Clouds above the Town appeared as red and bright as they do in an evening at sun setting."[13] One witness testified later that the soldiers were "drinking Rum and were Crying out let us make hay while the Sun Shines"; another that, when the fires were reported to Howe, the colonel replied that he was too busy to interfere.[14] James Parker's mansion "with marble chimnies and stone steps" and "the best garden in that part of the country" burned among the first.[15] But loyalists were not the only ones who suffered. A witness declared that, when he complained to Howe about rebel properties being burned, the commander told him to stop bothering him. Another witness described shirtmen rekindling the blaze on Joseph Hutchings's wharf when the wind repeatedly blew it out. John Calvert lost seven houses; Thomas Newton nine tenements, ten warehouses, two "elegantly furnished" mansions, and a "well furnished" store.[16] By the time Howe and Woodford finally restored order, Americans had destroyed 863 structures valued at a little under £120,000 in comparison with the British, who had burned 19 worth about £3,000. Earlier Dunmore had razed 32 houses valued at roughly £2,000 to build his fortifications.[17]

Neither Howe nor Woodford ever officially communicated anything of the truth about the burning of Norfolk to the Convention, and, amazing as it may seem, there appears not even to have been a rumor. Everyone automatically assumed that Dunmore was the sole culprit. On January 13 Howe went to Williamsburg to report to the Convention and to be feted, but by all indications said nothing about the cause of the conflagration when he recommended that the rest of

Norfolk be demolished. The Convention and Committee of Safety reluctantly approved the request "since that Town was set on fire by our enemies," while Pendleton wrote privately to Woodford of Dunmore's "horrid work."[18] The first inkling of the truth that the Williamsburg authorities seem to have had was the story in Dunmore's *Gazette* on January 15. Two weeks later the Committee of Safety ordered Howe to investigate, but nothing more was heard until petitions from Norfolk authorities revived the investigation in 1777. At that time the Virginia legislature acknowledged the damage done by rebel troops and provided compensation for any sufferer who was not a loyalist. The official report was not made public until sixty years later, however, and then was buried in a legislative journal from which historians did not unearth it for another hundred years.[19]

Three more skirmishes occurred at Norfolk on January 20 and 21 and on February 1, 1776, when small detachments of British burned three houses that Virginia snipers continued to use and took some tobacco. Eventually Howe completed the destruction of the 416 structures that remained standing and departed on February 6. "We have removed from Norfolk, thank God for that!" he announced, "It is entirely destroyed; thank God for that also!"[20] He left guards of about three hundred men each at Kemp's Landing and Great Bridge as he withdrew to a new base camp at Suffolk.

The burning of Norfolk and the popular impression of what happened made up the minds of many—not just in Virginia—for independence. When Samuel Adams learned of the incident, he wrote to James Warren of Massachusetts, "This will prevail more than a long Train of Reasoning to accomplish a Confederation, and other Matters which I know your heart as well as mine is much set upon."[21] Generally Norfolk was linked in men's minds with Falmouth, as Portland, Maine, was then called, which the British had burned two and one-half months before. The "flaming arguments" that the two ravaged cities provided, Washington remarked in his camp outside Boston, "will not leave numbers at a loss to decide upon the propriety of a separation."[22]

A week or two after the destruction of Norfolk one of the most famous polemical pamphlets in modern history, Thomas Paine's *Common Sense*, appeared in Philadelphia. Traditionally the essay is credited with providing the push that tipped American public opinion toward independence. The author, a recent immigrant from London, where he had been associated with the radical whig opposition, ridiculed the whole notion of monarchy and hereditary distinctions of any sort among persons. Paine's attack completely altered the focus of the constitutional argument from the former American assumption that the British government was essentially sound, though corrupt, to the idea that it was flawed at its core. Republicanism more surely fulfilled the love of freedom in human nature than did monarchy, Paine argued. Rather than half-apologizing for resisting the king as so many colonists had been doing, Paine proclaimed the rebellion "the birthday of a new world."[23] Colonial resistance, he wrote, was setting the pattern of good government for all mankind. *Common Sense* swept the country; as many as 150,000 copies may have been sold.

The extent of the tract's effect in Virginia is uncertain. In his *Notes on Virginia*, written at the end of the war, Thomas Jefferson declared that very few Virginians had seen the pamphlet. John Page had two of the *Virginia Gazettes* then in operation, Alexander Purdie's and John Pinkney's, publish excerpts from *Common Sense* in February, but the selections comprised only a fraction of the original publication, and Pinkney's was scrambled to boot. Otherwise the work was not published in Virginia. On the other hand, copies passed from hand to hand. Landon Carter discussed the pamphlet at John Tayloe's house in mid-February, and Francis Lightfoot Lee sent Tayloe a "parcel" of copies a month later. About then, too, Washington wrote that "by private letters . . . from Virginia, I find 'Common Sense' is working a powerful change there in the minds of many men."[24] Outside the leadership, however, the story of Norfolk probably swayed more Virginians toward independence.

As seemed always to be his lot, help for Dunmore arrived in early February 1776, again after it was too late. The forty-four-gun H.M.S. *Roebuck* under Captain Andrew Snape Hamond with one hundred marines for the governor entered the Chesapeake Bay on February 9. The *Roebuck's* presence may at least have ended the possibility that the first assignment for the newly formed Continental navy would be an attack on Dunmore. Congress had laid plans for a strike about two months before and had brought two pilots from the Chesapeake to Philadelphia to guide the Continental fleet. Delays in the shipyard held up departure until early February, at which time Commodore Ezek Hopkins of Rhode Island decided to sail to the Bahamas instead. Hopkins later claimed that Hamond's arrival caused the change of plan, but there is evidence that the Continental commander had never intended to follow his orders. At any rate, Congress censured Hopkins, in the opinion of John Adams, who defended him, because of an "Anti New England Spirit."[25]

With Captain Hamond's support, Dunmore occupied Tucker's Point, a small promontory jutting into the Elizabeth River from the Portsmouth side. Although some of the buildings had been damaged during the Norfolk fire, the windmill remained standing and Dunmore proceeded to add ovens and wells to relieve the shortage of food and water on board his ships. Barracks were constructed to provide a welcome respite from the overcrowding on shipboard and, with smallpox breaking out, a place where the British could move the sick.[26]

A week after Hamond arrived, General Sir Henry Clinton on H.M.S. *Mercury* accompanied by three transports and several tenders put into the Chesapeake Bay. When he first sighted the incoming ships, Dunmore naturally assumed that they were his long awaited reinforcements. To the governor's "inexpressible mortification" he learned from Clinton that the general was actually on his way to meet Major General Charles, Earl Cornwallis, coming with more troops from England to attack North Carolina.[27] The expedition was in response to the assurances of southern governors to the government in London that loyalists could easily restore royal authority in their provinces if the ministry supported them militarily. Clinton was to strike quickly, establish the loyalists in power, and rejoin the new commander in chief, Lieutenant General Sir William Howe, in time for the main campaign of 1776 in the North. On the strength of Governor Martin's reports and a talk with New York Governor William Tryon, who had formerly served in North Carolina, Clinton expected five or six thousand loyalists to meet him at his destination. The *Mercury* lingered in the Chesapeake Bay only long enough for repairs.[28]

Upon learning the bad news, Dunmore immediately dispatched a letter to let London know what he thought of the plan. He could not imagine how the ministry could prefer "a most insignificant Province" to "the first Colony on the Continent, both for its Riches and power," he declared. Virginia contained a perfect naval base from which to operate against the southern and Middle Colonies. "To see my Government thus totally neglected," he fulminated, "I own is a Mortification I was not prepared to meet with after being imprisoned on board a Ship between eight or Nine Months and now left without a hope of relief either to myself, or the many unhappy friends to Government that are now afloat suffering with me but I have done." He signed in large, bristling characters "DUNMORE."[29]

Clinton's expedition to the South coincided with the last flurry of rumors over possible reconciliation. The king's speech to Parliament in the fall of 1775 had declared the colonies in rebellion, and a subsequent Prohibitory Act withdrew royal protection from America and authorized the detention of American ships. But both statements contained references to an impending appointment of peace commissioners. The prospect of negotiations with Great Britain seriously slowed the momentum toward independence during the spring of 1776, especially in the Middle Colonies. Eventually General Howe, the new British army commander in America, and his brother, Vice Admiral Richard, Viscount Howe, were named the commissioners, but because they had no power to negotiate significant accommodations, nothing came of the appointments.[30]

The reaction in Virginia to the king's announcement of the commission revealed the hopelessness of the situation. Dunmore asked Receiver General Corbin to be the official go-between in the colony and told him, "I catch, with the greatest avidity, at this generous, this humane, this truly noble sentiment."[31] In his account to the ministry, however, Dunmore admitted that he endorsed the idea only because he wanted to have the Virginians refuse to negotiate one more time to be able to pin the blame for the war more squarely upon them.

Corbin took the news of the commission's appointment to the Committee of Safety in hope of obtaining at least a month's truce. At the same time the would-be peacemaker, who was once among the governor's staunchest supporters and was to become acting governor should Dunmore leave Virginia, let it be known that, when he carried his request for a truce to the British fleet, he intended "to give Captain Hammond a true statement of Lord Dunmore's conduct."[32] The committee told Corbin that it would leave all negotiations to Congress, but agreed to let him visit the fleet. When Corbin finally reached the *Roebuck* (virtually every other British vessel he passed rudely forced him to come aboard to show his credentials), Clinton observed of the Committee of Safety's deference to Congress that Parliament would never accept that body as constitutional. For his part, Dunmore rejected Corbin's own suggestion that the governor delegate authority to Thomas Nelson, president of the Council, to call the General Assembly if Dunmore did not want to come ashore to do so himself. James Parker's comment when he heard of the exchange between the two sides summed it up best: "If that is all it is doing nothing."[33]

Clinton's arrival sent another invasion shiver through the colony. In Williamsburg there was particular alarm when it was realized that with most of the troops south of the James River, only three or four hundred were available to defend the city. Upcountry eighteen companies had just been recruited, part of the new regiments authorized by the Convention, and the Committee of Safety hastily ordered them to the capital. But despite Dunmore's pleas to seize the opportunity, Clinton refused to be diverted from his assignment to the south and on February 26 sailed peacefully beyond the Virginia Capes.[34]

A much graver problem for the Committee of Safety arose the night before when Continental commissions for Virginia officers arrived from Philadelphia. When Patrick Henry received his two days later, he read it silently and handed it back to the committee chairman without comment. Henry had been offered only a colonelcy, and, moreover, the Continental commission omitted the key phrase in the Convention's former appointment, "Commander in chief of the forces in Virginia." Pendleton and the committee were blamed for the slight, of course, and a sharp exchange of letters took place in the press. Pendleton insisted that the committee had done nothing to block Henry; it had just not recommended any Virginian to Congress for appointment as general. But given the opinion of Washington, John Adams, and others in Continental circles that Henry should have stayed in the legislative chamber, the lack of official endorsement from his own colony was enough. Instead of the popular hero, Congress appointed the veteran Indian fighter from Augusta County, Andrew Lewis, as Virginia's new brigadier general and named Major General Charles Lee commander in chief in the South.[35]

Henry's resignation brought near mutiny. The next day, according to the *Virginia Gazette*, troops of the 1st Regiment "went into deep mourning" and marched under arms to his quarters, where emotional addresses were exchanged. Although Henry's troops were sorry to see him go, they told him, "We are compelled to applaud your spirited resentment to the most glaring indignity." Later in the day, the regiment's officers honored Henry with a testimonial dinner at the Raleigh Tavern. While they were dining, the men "assembled in a tumultuous manner" at the camp and, resolving never to serve under another commander, demanded their discharges. Henry, who had planned to leave Williamsburg immediately after the banquet, spent the entire night going from barracks to barracks to pacify the soldiers. His eloquence finally persuaded the men at least to complete their terms of service, although most still vowed not to reenlist.[36]

As ineffectual as army discipline was before, Henry's departure left it in shambles. Over ninety officers signed a public testimonial to him as a direct rebuke to the Committee of Safety, whose defenders replied in the press. Henry's critics rallied around Hugh Mercer, who had at last agreed to enter the service as colonel of the new 3rd Regiment and had undertaken to effect "Reform" in the Williamsburg camp. A crisis loomed when George Gibson's rifle company from the district of West Augusta, already known as "Gibson's Lambs" for its tempestuous ways, caused a disturbance. The specifics of the incident are unclear, although about this time the "Lambs" set fire to Lewis Burwell's ferry house where they were stationed and tore up his garden. When Mercer publicly rebuked them for that or some other offense, the "Lambs" demanded a court of inquiry that Pendleton feared would turn into a "second Boyakin affair."[37] Mercer had to apologize publicly to the company. He meant nothing personal, he assured them.[38] After this contretemps, Virginia authorities left the discipline problem for the new Continental commander to handle.

On March 29, 1776, a dark and rainy day, Major General Charles Lee rode into Williamsburg. A native Englishman and a soldier of fortune who had risen in rank and fame through the British, Polish, and Russian services, Lee was a brilliant officer, impulsive and dashing, whose energetic personality was certain to unnerve the methodical administrators of Virginia. He also was an unabashed romantic who fantasized about the glories of republican Rome when men were virtuous, brave, and patriotic, and victorious generals wore sprigs of laurel. "I us'd to regret not being thrown into the World in the glorious third or fourth century of the Romans," Lee once wrote to Patrick Henry, "but now I am thoroughly reconcil'd to my lot: the reveries which have frequently for a while serv'd to tickle my imagination . . . at length bid fair for being realiz'd."[39] Deemed at the moment Congress's most promising military talent, Lee had been sent to take charge of the Canadian front and then was suddenly ordered south when Clinton threatened to invade.

Since Lee could not be certain whether the British would double back to attack Virginia or continue southward to strike at North or South Carolina, he decided to remain in Williamsburg to be able to move quickly in whichever direction he was needed. Lee was appalled at the lack of preparation he found. Recruiting for the new regiments had been completed, but the men remained poorly armed and equipped. Although numerous old cannon barrels lay strewn about the region, the colony had few carpenters who could build carriages on which to mount them. A scarcity of entrenching tools and a dearth of engineers resulted in only laughable excuses for fortifications; "There is not a man or officer in the Army, that knows the difference betwixt a Chevaux de Frise [a log barricade], and a Cabbage Garden," Lee exclaimed.[40] From the general's point of view the Committee of Safety's concepts of strategy were totally negative. On the principle that "as the expense is equal, the security ought to be equal," the committee had scattered the Virginia army along the great rivers of the Tidewater and on the Eastern Shore, rendering offensive action against either Dunmore or Clinton impossible.[41]

"From Pendleton, Bland, the Treasurer & Co. *libera nos Domine*," Lee was shortly writing to friends.[42] John Page and some others in Williamsburg shared this assessment, at least to the extent that they felt the committee was inexcusably lethargic. Pendleton "& Co." saw no need for haste because they considered the major British thrust more likely to be in the North. While the committee's view was for the most part correct, they ignored the possibility of side excursions like Clinton's. To involve Virginia in unwarranted expenditures seemed to them the greater danger in the long run. Ever since Norfolk their primary concern had become to turn the direction, and the expense, of the war over to Congress as quickly as possible. As soon as the Continent's officers arrived, Pendleton quietly slipped away for a well-deserved month of rest in Caroline County.[43]

The leisurely pace Lee found in Williamsburg especially exasperated him because, paradoxically, many in Congress had begun to turn to Virginia for direction. With sentiment for independence slackening in Congress because of rumors of a peace commission, advocates of separation looked for an initiative from outside that body. They believed that the impetus had to come from somewhere other than New England for fear that region's reputation for radicalism might provoke the opposite effect. Because of the enthusiasm for separation in the Virginia delegation in Philadelphia, most hopes for the desired leadership focused on Williamsburg. By November 1775, and perhaps earlier, Jefferson and Richard Henry Lee had accepted the idea of independence; Francis Lightfoot Lee, Nelson, and Wythe followed by at least January or early February, and Harrison no later than mid-March. Of Virginia's seven representatives only Braxton remained opposed until after a stronger continental union could be achieved.[44]

After a few days in Williamsburg, Charles Lee was in despair. "I am sorry to say it," he moaned to Richard Henry Lee in Congress, "but your committee of safety seem to be as desperately and incurably infected with this epidemical malady as the provincial Congress of Maryland, or the quondam assembly of Pennsylvania."[45] Over the next month the general mounted an incessant campaign to prepare the way for a favorable vote on independence at the approaching session of the Virginia Convention. His insistent lobbying to have Virginia take the lead became an important catalyst in the colony's decision to leave the empire.

Militarily the new commander's first step was to scout Dunmore's position and concentrate all the regiments in Williamsburg. He was strict with the troops; the British received a report—greatly exaggerated—that he "flogged them in scores."[46] Lee's engineers, John Stadler and the German Massenbach, set to work entrenching the city, and an advertisement in the *Virginia Gazette* urged wealthy young gentlemen to form a volunteer cavalry corps, the expense of which had kept the Committee of Safety from sponsoring it before. Lee's admiration for the Roman republic led to the idea, which he had earlier discussed with Benjamin Franklin, of arming two companies of the tallest men in each regiment with thirteen-foot spears in the fashion of Roman legions. "It has a fine effect to the eye, and the men in general seemed convinced of the utility of the arrangement," he proudly wrote back to Philadelphia.[47]

The pace of the general's activity alone was enough to bring hornets buzzing about his head. The areas left defenseless when he moved troops to Williamsburg complained to the committee, whose members were also upset because they had just completed arrangements for feeding the troops where they had been stationed. More serious was Lee's cavalier disregard for civilian authority. He took up residence in the Governor's Palace without permission, borrowing a bed, pillow, and some linen from Robert Carter next door. The committee patiently tolerated such indiscretions until the general abruptly appropriated the college for Woodford's sick and injured because the facilities in Suffolk were so poor. At that juncture the committee lectured him: "We . . . are satisfied you are too good a Citizen to repeat such acts of power which though not intended may . . . convey to the people an Idea of our being subjected to an absolute military Government whilst we are straining every nerve in defense of liberty."[48] The Continental commander regained favor with a timely apology, but Richard Henry Lee and others warned him to be careful in the future.

Lee also decided to deal more harshly with the loyalists. The Committee of Safety had generally followed the example set at the last session of the Convention of treating leniently all except those who actually took up arms. In most appeals from county commissions, defendants gained parole. Only a few like Jacob Ellegood, who had been captured trying to escape to the Eastern Shore, were rusticated to inland counties. Lee quickly saw the need for sterner measures to halt the supplies of food and intelligence that Dunmore received daily from the farmers of Nansemond and Princess Anne counties. At a council of war on April 6 Lee recommended the forcible removal of everyone in the area between Great Bridge and the Norfolk coast and the seizure of families of tories to ensure good behavior.[49]

By coincidence, on that same day one of James Barron's cruisers captured a British tender bearing dispatches from London that Dunmore relayed to Governor Robert Eden of Maryland. The affair evoked memories of Connolly's plan to subvert the West, for the courier was a former associate of Connolly from Pittsburgh, a Scot named Alexander Ross, who had outmaneuvered both the Maryland and Virginia committees of safety to reach Dunmore off Norfolk. The royal governor commissioned Ross to raise an Indian force in the West and proceed down the Mississippi River to help block the supply route from New Orleans, but Barron captured Ross as the Scot left Dunmore's fleet and confiscated the incriminating papers. Ross soon escaped and went on to Maryland, where he was again taken, only to be released once more by Congress. This time he succeeded in reaching the Mississippi area.[50]

The more important prize was Governor Eden. Lee had already crossed swords with Eden en route to Virginia. In contrast to Dunmore, the Maryland governor had pursued a frustratingly conciliatory policy in the hope of dividing the opposition. He had succeeded to the extent of winning the temporary protection of the Annapolis Committee of Safety against the less pliable committee in Baltimore. While passing through Baltimore Lee caused an uproar by demanding the arrest of the governor, but to no effect. Now, the captured documents revealed that Eden had been counseling the use of force all along, and, in addition, the letters afforded the first positive intelligence that a large fleet was on the way to meet Clinton for an invasion of the Carolinas "or Virginia."[51] Clearly Eden was as bad as Dunmore, only quieter.

The effect was electric. Within the week the Virginia Committee of Safety approved the recommendation of the council of war to arrest suspected tories. Lee promptly ordered the seizure of several prominent loyalists, including John Agnew, the rector of Suffolk, and Ralph Wormeley, Jr., who had indiscreetly written to John Grymes in response to a plea to assist Dunmore that it was "useless" to join the governor at the moment but that he would do so as soon as there was more chance of victory.[52] On an inspection trip of the front lines near Portsmouth in late April 1776, Lee ordered the destruction of houses and stores belonging to Neil Jamieson, Robert Shedden, Andrew Sprowle, and the Goodriches, conceding as he did so that his methods were "not quite consistent with the regular mode of proceeding." Lee returned to Williamsburg with the further recommendation that the rest of Portsmouth be burned since its inhabitants were "universally" tory.[53] All their blood had been "suck'd out by musketoes," he declared.[54]

At that point, the Committee of Safety's resolve weakened. Under the moderating influence of Pendleton, who returned to his post toward the end of April, it acquitted Agnew and Wormeley and, although Woodford had begun to evacuate the Norfolk area, stayed the order against anyone who could prove that he was friendly. Lee appealed to the Convention, which was just reassembling in Williamsburg, and the delegates reversed the committee. But in the meantime, Woodford reported, the inhabitants had begun spring planting; furthermore, he could not find enough wagons to move the twenty thousand people he estimated would have to be relocated.[55]

By then, Lee was preparing to move on, for he had learned that Clinton was at Cape Fear, North Carolina. The Continental commander left Pendleton a long list of things to do. The regiment on the Eastern Shore should be strengthened and all the livestock there either transported elsewhere or killed to deny them to British raiders. The major rivers had to be fortified at the narrowest points, and a cavalry raised. "Carpenters, Smiths, and Artificers, of every sort" should be drafted into the army because "without a coercive power,

it is difficult in this part of the world to prevail upon 'em to work,"
and the Convention should provide a supplement to the Congressional pay for surgeons because medical practice was "so very lucra-
tive" in Virginia that they would not enlist otherwise.[36] With a parting
reminder to Pendleton to carry out the measures against the loyalists
that the Convention had just reaffirmed, Lee rode out of Williamsburg on May 13 and the whirlwind was over.

The intercepted letters to Governor Eden produced the final argument for independence in Virginia. At last there was concrete evidence that the king intended to wage all-out war. "They had a good
effect here," John Page told Richard Henry Lee, "I think almost every
man, except the Treasurer, is willing to declare for Independency."[37]
During March and April, when home from his duties in Congress,
Jefferson had surveyed opinion around Charlottesville and found
"nine out of ten are for it."[38] Similar reports came from all parts of
the colony. "The people of this Country almost unanimously cry
aloud for Independence," said William Aylett of King William County
in the Tidewater, and a county meeting in Cumberland denounced
the king and instructed the county's delegates to "bid him a good
night forever."[39] So rapid was the swing in public opinion that John
and Samuel Adams, self-appointed floor managers for independence
in Congress, became afraid that Virginia would act before the Middle
Colonies were ready, leaving New England and the South too far
apart geographically for effective government and defense.[60]

The elections for the Convention in the spring of 1776 provided
more excitement than usual in Virginia politics. Heightened interest
in the independence question brought out an abnormally large number of candidates: five in Fauquier County, for example. Yet not all
of the turnover seems to have been a result of the imperial issue. The
number of new faces was in part because several counties had not
sent representatives before and some of the former Convention members who did not return had joined the military. In Richmond County
Francis Lightfoot Lee, who was for separation, thought that he would
have no trouble running from Philadelphia although he had not been
active locally for over a year while in Congress. Nor was Robert
Wormeley Carter, a regular representative from that county and an
opponent of independence, concerned about his chances for reelection. Neither Lee nor Carter made much effort to turn out supporters, and both lost in a light vote. When Lee's managers also placed

his name on the ballot in Lancaster County, he went down to defeat a second time along with Charles Carter of Corotoman, who similarly neglected to campaign.

The Carter family, a pillar of the old order in Virginia, suffered badly. Besides Wormeley Carter and Charles of Corotoman, the latter's cousin, Charles Carter of Ludlowe, failed to be returned in Stafford County. Carter Braxton, who opposed a declaration of independence at that time, lost a confused and disputed contest in King William County but won the resulting by-election in early June. In Charles City County Benjamin Harrison, who had not returned from Congress, and in Fairfax County George Mason, who had been ill recently, also found it more difficult than usual to win although both favored abandoning the empire. Voters in James City County returned the most vociferous opponent of independence, Robert Carter Nicholas, with strict instructions to vote for it although he told them that he would not. Pendleton, who so far had not committed himself on the great issue, also met heavy opposition to his reelection, and then, when the Convention met, Thomas Ludwell Lee seriously contested Pendleton's nomination for the presidency. Still, Pendleton won. Overall, relatively little of the Convention's traditional membership had to be changed to ensure a majority for independence.[61]

The Convention met in the Capitol in Williamsburg on Monday, May 6. Symbolically, forty-five delegates who were also members of the House of Burgesses gathered before the Convention session began to declare the old legislature dead by action of "the king, lords, and commons of Great Britain."[62] The Convention busied itself with routine affairs and with General Lee. Trials of the prominent loyalists Lee had arrested and a lengthy debate on the evacuation of Norfolk and Princess Anne counties consumed the time. Only after Lee finally marched off in the company of the 8th, or "German," Regiment and eleven hundred militiamen on May 13 were the delegates able to turn to the task for which their constituents were waiting.[63]

The debates of the next two days are shrouded in mystery. Only the most meager records survive. As expected, Robert Carter Nicholas made it clear that the instructions of his constituents did not alter his basic opposition to independence. Despite his active participation in the war effort, according to a history written by his son-in-law, Edmund Randolph, the treasurer remained "dubious of the competency of America in so arduous a contest."[64]

More surprising was the hesitancy of Patrick Henry. He did not question the idea of separation, just the timing of the declaration. At the beginning of the session he wondered to General Lee whether Congress should not be more certain of a French alliance first. Henry had grounds for such qualms because, although everyone expected the French to help, only the most tentative contact had been established, and only through Congress's Committee of Secret Correspondence. As informed an observer of Philadelphia affairs as Charles Lee could only reply, "I more than believe, I am almost confident that it has been done."[65] If Congress adopted a declaration of independence before an alliance publicly committed the French to support America, the British might offer to return a portion of France's old North American empire on condition that the French not condone the American rebellion.

As the discussion progressed and Henry found the Convention determined on an immediate declaration, he submitted one of the three draft resolutions placed before the delegates. The other two, one by Meriwether Smith of Essex County and another by an unidentified delegate, possibly Pendleton, unilaterally proclaimed the end of royal government in Virginia. Neither mentioned Congress. Smith also provided for a committee to prepare a new constitution and a declaration of rights, two matters on which the unidentified author was silent.

Henry's draft proposed leaving a declaration of independence to Congress. He enumerated at length the wrongs done America and ended with a typical flourish: "The King of G. B. by a long series of oppressive acts has proved himself the tyrant instead of the protector of his people." As a result, Henry declared, Virginians considered themselves "absolved of our allegiance to the crown of G. B." The great orator nonetheless concluded with uncharacteristic caution by demanding that the formal statement of independence be in the name of all the colonies.[66]

The chore of reconciling the debate fell to Pendleton. He composed the final resolution, which he phrased to satisfy as many in the Convention as possible. From Henry he accepted the need to act in concert with Congress and instructed the Virginia delegates "to propose to that respectable body to declare the United Colonies free and independent states." Pendleton omitted Henry's specific indictment of the king, however, and added a plea to "the SEARCHER OF HEARTS" to witness that earlier protestations of American loyalty to George III had been entirely sincere. The president of the Convention made a further effort to allay Henry's fears by calling upon Congress to form a confederation of states and to arrange alliances with foreign powers.[67] The compromise did not entirely succeed; Henry was not completely persuaded. Although he did not vote against the resolution, immediately after its passage he wrote to John Adams and Richard Henry Lee urging them not to let Congress issue a declaration before obtaining outside aid.[68]

Pendleton drew the remainder of his text from Meriwether Smith. While calling for a confederation, the final draft of the resolution carefully reserved to Virginia the right to determine its own form of government and repeated verbatim Smith's provision for the appointment of a committee to frame a constitution and a declaration of rights. At issue may have been the feeling, expressed by Thomas Paine in *Common Sense* and reiterated in the Convention by Thomas Ludwell Lee, that Congress should dictate one form of government for all the states. The resulting text admirably filled Pendleton's goal of winning broad support, for on May 15, with 112 members present, the resolution passed the Convention without opposition. Even Robert Carter Nicholas did not vote against it in the end.[69]

Although the resolution asked Congress to declare independence, with its passage Virginia independence became a fact. "The exultation here was extreme," Thomas Ludwell Lee reported.[70] A crowd that had gathered outside the Capitol as the final vote approached immediately hauled down the British flag from the cupola and raised the Grand Union flag of Washington's army. Troops paraded and cannon were fired. At a formal celebration the next day, Thursday, General Lewis reviewed his troops at Waller's Grove, and the audience listened to a public reading of the Convention's resolution and to a number of toasts and salutes. The citizenry took up "a handsome collection" to treat the soldiers to refreshments afterward. In the evening there were illuminations and, as the *Virginia Gazette* put it, "other demonstrations of joy."[71] Congress already having designated Friday a day of fasting and prayer, the Convention did not meet but marched as a body to Bruton Parish Church where the Reverend Mr. Thomas Price preached a ringing sermon "to a very crowded audience."[72]

Thomas Nelson rode off directly for Congress with an official copy of the resolution, but was somehow delayed on the road. The *Pennsylvania Evening Post* of Philadelphia published the resolve before he arrived. The effect accomplished everything that those who looked to Virginia for leadership wished. Sentiment for separation had been steadily mounting. Between January and early April, Massachusetts, South Carolina, and Georgia had authorized their delegates in Congress to support measures "for the common good," presumably including independence but without specifically mentioning it.[73] On April 12 North Carolina became the first explicitly to sanction independence, empowering its representatives "to concur with the Delegates of the other Colonies in declaring Independency, and forming foreign alliances," and on May 4 Rhode Island issued instructions that, while not using the word independence, were understood to embrace it.[74] On May 15, the same day that the crucial votes were cast in Williamsburg, John Adams and Richard Henry Lee finally guided through Congress a resolution declaring "that the exercise of every kind of authority under the said crown should be totally suppressed" and advising each colony to establish a new government.[75] At the time many regarded the vote on this motion as Congress's effective decision for independence. But while accepting the necessity of separation, a significant number of members remained hostile to a public declaration, for Henry was not alone in his distrust of France. Virginia's instruction to its representatives to propose a declaration forced the issue, sending delegates scurrying to ask their respective conventions "aye" or "nay."

On Friday, June 7, Richard Henry Lee rose in Congress to offer the fateful resolution: "That these United Colonies are, and of right ought to be, free and independent States." Lee also called for the formation of "foreign Alliances" and the preparation of "a plan of confederation."[76] John Adams seconded Lee's motion. Debate was put off until the next day and then continued on Monday, at which time the committee of the whole recommended that final consideration be postponed for three weeks to give uninstructed delegates time to consult authorities at home. In the meantime, to avoid delay Congress would appoint a committee to prepare the text of a declaration. Congress accepted the compromise seven colonies to five, with New Jersey, New York, Pennsylvania, Delaware, and Maryland voting no. Thomas Jefferson, John Adams, Benjamin Franklin, Roger Sherman of Connecticut, and Robert R. Livingston of New York were named as the drafting committee, but in the end Jefferson did virtually all the work.[77]

The climax in Congress was anticlimactic for Virginians. The debate in Philadelphia on Richard Henry Lee's motion began as scheduled on July 1. Congress adopted the resolution the following day, the actual birthday of the nation. Two days later the delegates accepted Jefferson's draft—with significant modifications—as the official text of the declaration. Most important among the changes, the Georgia and South Carolina members succeeded in eliminating a section condemning slavery and the slave trade in which Jefferson, ignoring the economic reasons for the development of slavery, repeated an idea, already current in Virginia, that the British had forced the institution on the colonies. The two southernmost colonies did not want even so indirect a criticism of the system, however.[78]

The official copy of the declaration that John Hancock mailed to Virginia arrived too late for Alexander Purdie to print in the July 19 *Virginia Gazette*, and Dixon and Hunter scooped him in their edition the next day. The Council ordered the document read publicly at the Capitol, the Palace, and the courthouse in Williamsburg on Thursday, July 25. At four o'clock that afternoon General Lewis mustered all off-duty Continental troops for a grand parade. Cannon and small arms were fired amid the cheers of the crowd, and the newspapers recorded that there were "illuminations in the evening &c., &c."[79] Similar celebrations took place at county court days throughout the young state as the welcome news of the founding of a new nation spread.

CHAPTER 6

"How few . . . have ever enjoyed . . . an election of government"

T HE Virginia Convention lost no time pursuing the logic of its resolution for independence by writing and adopting a new constitution. Although Virginia was in the midst of a war— and, indeed, renewed fighting on one occasion caused a three-week hiatus in the delegates' deliberations—the Convention immediately turned its full attention to filling the void that the end of the monarchy created.

The procedure the Convention followed in framing a constitution was in accord with contemporary ideas of how popular self-government should come about. Eighteenth-century political theorists employed metaphors of covenants and contracts between governors and the governed to describe the process since it seemed reasonable that people would first decide upon the principles under which they wished to be ruled and then arrange for a government to implement those principles. The natural order appeared to be to adopt a declaration of rights first and then a constitution. During the ensuing debates many delegates expressed concerns about how republics work that appear groundless today, but it should be remembered that the Convention had no practical model to emulate since the Roman republic over a millennium and a half before. Not surprising, given the lack of trustworthy examples, the governmental structure upon which the delegates finally agreed encountered difficulty in its operations from the beginning. Yet despite the worries and the inexperience, the main body of delegates—and presumably their constituents—seem to have had more confidence in the local institutions Virginians were accustomed to, and in the people's ability to govern themselves through those institutions, than did many leaders who theorized about the process.

Upon adopting the resolution for independence, the Convention appointed a constitutional committee under the chairmanship of Archibald Cary and, as was the practice in so important a matter, attempted to make the membership as broadly representative as possible. Eventually the Convention assigned over one-quarter of its delegates to the task. When George Mason's gout finally allowed him to take his seat a few days after the vote for independence, he was immediately added. Surveying his colleagues, he opined with his usual testiness that the committee was "according to Custom, overcharged with useless Members" and doubtless would spawn a plan "form'd of hetrogenious, jarring, and unintelligible Ingredients" unless he and a few others of ability took charge.[1]

Again little is known of the ensuing deliberations, and that little depends upon a close textual analysis of a few surviving documents, some of which did not come to the attention of scholars for more than a century. One fact is clear: Mason was the principal author of the Declaration of Rights. Early in the session he placed before the committee a draft containing ten points that he considered "the Basis and Foundation of Government."[2] They were: 1. the equality of all men and their natural right to life, liberty, and property; 2. the responsibility of government to the people; 3. the right of the majority to change the government for due cause; 4. a denial of hereditary privileges; 5. the need for a separation of powers and for frequent elections; 6. government by the consent of the governed; 7. the right of jury trial in criminal cases and freedom from self-incrimination; 8. the necessity of "Justice, Moderation, Temperance, Frugality, and Virtue" in a free society; 9. religious toleration; and 10. a recommendation for jury trials in civil as well as criminal cases.[3]

The committee accepted Mason's propositions in essentially the form he suggested with two significant exceptions. Mason's colleagues subdued his references to the Deity and broadened his proposal for religious toleration by eliminating the last three words in the phrase "unless, under Colour of Religion, any Man disturb the Peace, the Happiness, or Safety of Society, or of Individuals."[4] The committee also recast the wording of Mason's provision for frequent elections in which, either intentionally or through an ambiguity in style, he seemed to call for automatic rotation in office, an idea that some republican theorists of the day espoused. The committee made it clear that while frequent elections were mandatory, incumbents could succeed themselves.[5]

In addition, the committee considerably expanded Mason's basic list. It added eight new articles, of which by his own account Mason contributed five: a guarantee of free elections although with property qualifications for the suffrage; a prohibition against the suspension of laws except by the legislature; a ban on excessive bail or cruel and unusual punishment; freedom of the press; and the subordination of the military to the civil power coupled with a warning of the threat to liberty inherent in a professional standing army. The provisos that others offered forbade general warrants, outlawed ex post facto laws, and prohibited the formation of new states out of Virginia's western lands, as several companies of speculators proposed to do. The one point on which the committee could not reach an agreement was the clause forbidding ex post facto laws, which Thomas Ludwell Lee apparently sponsored. The committee included it in its report with the understanding that it would be amended on the floor of the Convention so as not to exclude such laws when the "safety of the state absolutely requires them."[6]

The committee concluded their deliberations by Friday, May 24, and over that weekend handwritten copies of their recommendations went north in the mail. On Monday Chairman Cary reported the eighteen articles on which the committee had agreed to the Convention. The chamber immediately ordered the report printed by the public printer, Alexander Purdie, for the convenience of its members and set the following Wednesday for the first day of debate. Dixon and Hunter's *Virginia Gazette* published a slightly different text a few days afterward. The Convention did not get to the topic for almost a week, however, and did not approve the final version for almost three. By then the committee's report had circulated widely with the result that for years the eighteen points it contained rather than the sixteen in the final official version were known outside the state as Virginia's pioneering statement of political rights.[7]

The saga of the committee's draft is worth following in view of its long-lasting influence on political thinking. Most likely Jefferson had the committee's version at hand in Philadelphia as he composed similar phrases for the Declaration of Independence since Pennsylvania newspapers published copies during June. Benjamin Franklin used the committee's report as a basis for Pennsylvania's declaration of rights that fall, as did John Adams for Massachusetts's four years later. Of the five other states that adopted declarations of rights in the next decade, the phraseology employed by four—Delaware, Maryland, Vermont, and New Hampshire—suggests that they followed the committee's version rather than that of the Convention. Only North Carolina seems to have had recourse to the latter.[8]

The form in which the declaration became known in Europe departed even farther from the text finally adopted by the Virginia Convention. A serious distortion crept into the wording of Article 10 in the committee's draft as reprinted in the *New York Gazette and Weekly Mercury*. The editor altered the guarantee of a jury trial to "a speedy Trial by an impartial Judge of the vicinage."[9] This corrupt version appeared in late 1776 in John Almon's *The Remembrancer*, a London periodical through which many of the constitutional documents of the Revolution first reached the British reading public. From London the altered text passed via Franklin, by then Congress's representative in France, to his friend, the Duc de La Rochefoucauld, with whom he published translations of the new American state constitutions. Other French editions in turn pirated these translations. By this route the committee's work came directly to influence the Declaration of the Rights of Man and the Citizen, which in the early days of the French Revolution became for Europe what the Declaration of Independence was for America. While serving later as ambassador to France, Jefferson supplied the committee version—though with Article 10 corrected—to his friend Philip Mazzei for publication in 1788.

Stranger still, despite the widespread fame of the Virginia declaration, it was almost impossible to come by a copy of the official text in America for nearly forty years. The Convention published its proceedings and ordinances, of course, but the slim volumes quickly disappeared, as did the pertinent issues of the *Virginia Gazette*. Some years after the war St. George Tucker, professor of law at the College of William and Mary, assembled a set of Revolutionary publications for himself and his sons "with very great Difficulty from several

Friends, and others" and wrote on the copy of the May 1776 proceedings, "There is scarce another Copy to be found in Virginia."[10]
Because the Convention adopted and published the Declaration of
Rights separately from the Virginia constitution, even though the delegates intended the declaration as a foreword to the constitution, subsequent compilations often overlooked the former. The Declaration
of Rights appeared in four Virginia editions in 1784, 1785, 1794, and
1805, but not in the supposedly definitive congressional summary of
state constitutions in 1781 or in any other comprehensive British or
American collection until 1811. The spotty publication record doubtless explains the paradox of a foremost legist, James Wilson of Pennsylvania, arguing in the debate over the ratification of the Federal
Constitution that the United States did not need a bill of rights because pacesetting Virginia did not have one.[11]

The reason for the Convention's three-week delay in adopting the
Declaration of Rights was Dunmore, who suddenly shifted his base
from Tucker's Point near Portsmouth to Gwynn's Island at the mouth
of the Piankatank River. Dunmore had become desperate at his old
post. Smallpox ravaged his ranks, and the Convention's on-again, off-
again campaign against the inhabitants of the Norfolk area drastically
curtailed his food supply. Spies reported that the Virginians had prepared fireships to float down the Elizabeth River into Dunmore's fleet
and in the confusion planned to board as many of the British vessels
as possible. One spy who overheard Major Thomas Parker and other
officers conversing related that, when asked what to do about the tories with Dunmore, Parker replied, "Damn them, Tomahawk them all
and throw them over Board, and give yourself no further trouble
about them."[12] Panic-stricken, Dunmore called for help from Captain
Hamond on the *Roebuck*, who by great fortune was not far from the
Virginia Capes on his way south to join Sir Peter Parker's fleet with
Clinton off South Carolina. Detouring quickly into Hampton Roads,
Hamond saw that, besides the danger from the fireships, if Dunmore
remained at Tucker's Point, the Virginians could trap his ships by
placing cannon downstream. Hamond urged an immediate move to
another site.

Dunmore would have been in trouble without the British navy, for
Hamond had to supply crews for many of the ninety-odd private vessels no one on board knew how to sail. Even so, Hamond had to

scuttle three or four ships "for want of materials to navigate."[13] It took three days to demolish the buildings at Tucker's Point and collect the fleet at the mouth of the Elizabeth River. Then, sailing as if to pass through the Capes, the British suddenly veered north up the Chesapeake Bay and "with more trouble and difficulty than ever I had before experienced," Hamond said, reached Gwynn's Island on May 27.[14]

Unquestionably, Hamond and Dunmore could have found a safer place to go. At the nearest point, the island was just two hundred yards from the mainland across a channel that could be forded at low tide. The two commanders selected the site largely on the recommendation of John Randolph Grymes, who owned land there and reported that the island was "inhabited by many Friends of Government, that it formed an excellent Harbour, had plenty of fresh water on it, and could easily be defended from the Enemy."[15] Hamond described the new base to his superiors as "the best rendezvous of any in Virginia for the fleet," and, as evidence of Dunmore's confidence in the choice, the earl set his men to constructing a windmill and other relatively permanent structures. Because smallpox had left the governor only 150 to 200 regulars plus about 450 volunteers, both black and white, to defend the island's three or four square miles, Hamond had to lend some of his sailors to help with the fortifications.[16]

Hamond and Dunmore still had in mind the possibility that Clinton might stop to reinforce them on the way back to New York from his southern campaign. Off the Carolina coast, Clinton remained undecided what to do. The original plan, which depended upon synchronizing his movements with those of the loyalists in North Carolina and Lord Cornwallis coming from England, had completely fallen through. On February 27, just two weeks after Cornwallis had sailed from Cork, Ireland, impatient North Carolina loyalists challenged the rebels at Moore's Creek and suffered so devastating a defeat that it would have been senseless for Clinton to attempt a landing in the area. Moreover, although Clinton's original orders gave preference to an attack on North Carolina, they had been issued before the high command realized that the waters there were too shallow for his ships. Storms delayed Cornwallis until early May, raising the question whether there was time for the expedition to accomplish its objective in the South without violating Clinton's instructions to rejoin the main

British army under General Howe at New York in time for a summer campaign in the North. A return to Virginia before heading for the rendezvous with Howe might be the only course remaining.[17]

Hamond and Dunmore also counted heavily on being in a better position on Gwynn's Island to tap the reservoir of loyalist sentiment on the Eastern Shore and the Chesapeake Bay islands. The governor had been in contact with Eastern Shore leaders off and on all winter and reestablished communications through a mysterious "gentleman in black."[18] He was especially confident that the recent resolution for independence would generate a groundswell of sentiment for the king. Over the next month the Queen's Own Loyal Regiment gained a couple of hundred recruits, but during the same period lost as many already in the ranks to the pox. H.M.S. *Fowey* brought off Governor Eden from Annapolis, where the Committee of Safety granted his request for a safe conduct to leave, though at the last minute Eden had to depart without his baggage because the *Fowey*'s captain refused to return some indentured servants who fled with the governor.

The sudden move to Gwynn's Island caught Virginia leaders completely by surprise. "I never heard of such a Place before the Enemy reached it," confessed Andrew Lewis.[19] The coincidence of Eden's request for safe passage coming at the same time as the arrival of a captured transport with 217 Scottish Highland troops originally destined for Boston and word that over the winter of 1775–1776 the American invasion of Canada had collapsed because of reinforcements from Great Britain sent another round of invasion nerves throughout Virginia. A concerted attempt by the mother country to end the rebellion seemed to be under way. Hesitating to commit too many troops at Gwynn's Island lest Dunmore was trying to lure him from the Williamsburg area, Lewis just sent Colonel William Daingerfield from Gloucester County and Colonel Hugh Mercer from Fredericksburg to pin the governor down. But because the rebels were without cannon again, the British easily checked them at the water's edge.[20]

The standoff enabled the Convention to turn back to the Declaration of Rights on June 2. Then for several days, Thomas Ludwell Lee informed his brother in Philadelphia, the delegates were "stumbling at the threshold," unable to agree on the first line of Mason's draft "which declares all men to be born equally free and independent." By "a thousand masterly fetches and stratagems," Lee recounted, Robert Carter Nicholas forced the Convention to face the question that muted all such ringing statements of universal right during the American Revolution and for almost a century afterward.[21] Did such pronouncements include the blacks? Did such declarations automatically abolish slavery? Although one of the most idealistic republicans in the state, Lee clearly felt Nicholas's objections to be spurious and the possibility of freeing slaves not a serious enough political issue to waste time debating it.

By the outbreak of the American Revolution, individuals like the Quakers John Woolman and Anthony Benezet were preaching on the moral evil of slavery, and some political leaders like Franklin and Jefferson perceived the glaring inconsistency between Revolutionary rhetoric and the continued existence of black slavery. Critics of slavery were relatively few, however, and readily conceded that they could not retain public confidence or preserve the Continental confederation if they carried their questioning too far. Often, too, their qualms sprang as much from a concern about the effects of slavery on whites as on blacks: the danger of black insurrection or of encouraging arbitrary ways among masters that would undermine the whites' own love of liberty.

The most formidable obstacle opponents of slavery faced was the emphasis Revolutionary ideology placed on the defense of private property. Patriots crying tyranny because Great Britain took money from their pockets without their consent found it difficult to interfere with another's choice of investment. Although St. George Tucker did not attend the May Convention, he recalled what he understood to be the members' intent some years later while serving on the state bench. In a lower court George Wythe, a vociferous critic of slavery, had held that the Declaration of Rights meant all blacks were to be considered free unless proved otherwise. Tucker, also quite outspoken about slavery in Virginia, affirmed the judgment in question but rejected the reasoning, observing that the first clause of the declaration had been "notoriously framed with a cautious eye . . . to embrace the case of free citizens, or aliens only; and not by a side wind to overturn the rights of property."[22] Even in the North where antislavery sentiment led to abolition during and after the war, many emancipation statutes contained gradualist provisions designed to compensate owners and left some black residents of those states enslaved for decades to come.[23]

The outlook of most colonial whites in the Revolutionary generation was overwhelmingly ethnocentric; the necessity of including
blacks in the rights and freedoms they were proclaiming to render
those liberties universal did not occur to them. Later in life, John
Adams confessed as much to St. George Tucker. In answer to an inquiry from the Virginian, who wrote expecting insight into the question of freeing slaves from the Massachusetts man, Adams admitted
that slavery "is a subject to which I have never given any very particular attention."[24] As the war drew to a close, a sympathetic French
observer, St. Jean de Crèvecoeur, caught the ebullience and optimism
of Americans in their moment of triumph with his famous question,
"What then is the American, this new man?" His answer was "an European, or a descendant of an European."[25] White Virginians would
have nodded in agreement almost unanimously. When they protested
that they were Englishmen entitled to all the rights of citizens in the
mother country, most meant it quite literally.

Robert Carter Nicholas compelled the Convention to put on paper
what others were content to accept without saying: blacks were not
Virginians. Once again Edmund Pendleton found the solution to the
Convention's problem by proposing to insert the clause "When they
enter into a state of society" in Mason's statement that people could
not "by any compact deprive or divest their posterity" of their natural
rights.[26] The words derived from the contract theories of government
that had been the cornerstone of British and American political
thought for almost a century. All persons, including blacks, had certain natural rights that they could not alienate but could be forcibly
prevented from enjoying. For this reason people entered covenants
with each other to form societies that would protect those rights, and
then societies contracted with governments to provide external defense and a means of adjudicating internal disputes. Otherwise individuals had to rely solely on their own strength and wits to guard
their liberty. Thus, if blacks were deemed to be outside of American
society, their enslavement would not be nullified by anything the Virginia constitution might say about personal liberty. While the principle of equality remained universal, the blacks' freedom rested entirely upon their own, virtually nonexistent, ability to preserve it. One
can see from this line of reasoning why Virginians were so uneasy
about Dunmore.

The article on religion, too, caused heated debate, although once
more time has obscured the details. Both Mason's draft and the com-

mittee's report proposed only "the fullest toleration" for dissenters, thereby implying no disestablishment of the Anglican church. James Madison, then a freshman delegate from Orange County, where many religious dissenters lived, and a graduate of the Presbyterian college Princeton, objected strongly and jotted down on his printed copy of the committee's report an amendment that provided instead for "full and free exercise" of religion.[27] Madison's proposal constituted one of the most creative contributions of the American Revolution, a major innovation in Western political thought. Previously in Great Britain, where more religious freedom existed than anywhere else in Europe, recognition of the Anglican church as the national religion rendered whatever freedom dissenters enjoyed a mere privilege granted by the state. Madison proposed instead to establish religious liberty as a natural right of all persons for the first time in law.

The ramifications of so unequivocal a statement may not have been as obvious to Madison's contemporaries as to Americans today. A couple of years later, for example, Mason appeared indifferent to the change when he nonchalantly told a friend that his original draft "received few Alterations" in the Convention.[28] Madison had tried to elucidate the implications of his amendment by including a provision forbidding anyone "on account of religion to be invested with peculiar emoluments or privileges." The phrase would have abolished the glebes, or farmlands, that the colonial government supplied for the support of Anglican ministers and would have prevented the new republic from enforcing the collection of tithes or taxes for the use of the church. Madison found, however, that his intention went well beyond the mood of the Convention. Other additions and interlining on Madison's copy of the committee report suggest that he may then have proposed a second amendment. The words "free exercise" remain in the new version but without explicit reference to disestablishment, and the qualifications that Mason placed on the exercise of religious rights—"unless, under colour of religion, any man disturb the peace, the happiness, or safety of society"—were altered to read simply "unless the preservation of equal liberty and the existence of the State are manifestly endangered." Interestingly, the Convention—apparently without appreciating the inconsistency of their refusal to disestablish the church—eliminated even this reservation and proclaimed religious liberty unqualifiedly an absolute right.[29]

Patrick Henry, too, played a key role in the debate. Edmund Randolph, who attended the Convention, credited Henry with composing the article on religion. Henry never claimed authorship, however, and the manuscript record of the Convention indicates that Edmund Pendleton as usual offered the last, and thus possibly the crucial, amendment, although precisely what it contained is unknown. Of greater significance, Randolph reported that because of Henry's recognized sympathy with Presbyterians, he was asked whether the wording of the passage foreshadowed an attack on the Anglican church. Henry flatly denied any such intention and in subsequent years indicated that he considered the religious provisions of the declaration satisfied if the government subsidized all Christian sects instead of just one. Noteworthy, too, are the final words of the paragraph on religion, which Madison as well as Mason approved, admonishing all to practice "Christian Forbearance, love, and charity, towards each other."[30] America as Virginia's founding fathers conceived it was a homogeneous land.

Controversy also flared over the committee's recommendation for the prohibition of ex post facto laws. In a speech on the floor, according to Edmund Randolph, Patrick Henry defended the need for bills of attainder by painting "a terrifying picture of some towering public offender against whom ordinary laws would be impotent" and the Convention rejected the clause.[31] By excluding this article and combining two others on free elections and government by consent of the governed, the delegates wound up with sixteen articles in their final version. Of these Mason was primarily responsible for thirteen and Madison one. The Convention made some stylistic changes and further clarified the committee's insistence that incumbents could run again for office. Finally, on June 12, 1776, the Virginia Convention adopted America's first Declaration of Rights.

The Cary committee had already plunged deep into a discussion of a constitution. Again they commenced with a draft submitted by George Mason, which the committee had printed for its convenience. Recent weeks had also brought a shower of schemes and suggestions from Philadelphia plus a few from persons in Williamsburg. John Adams, Richard Henry Lee, Carter Braxton, and Thomas Jefferson, among others, contributed to the outpouring. Everybody, it seemed, wanted to participate, for everyone regarded one of the great moments of history to be at hand. At Philadelphia John Adams wondered in awe, "How few of the human race have ever enjoyed an opportunity of making an election of government, [any]more than of air, soil, or climate, for themselves or their children!"[32] George Washington expressed the fervent hope that delegates would exercise the greatest care and patience because what they wrought would "render millions happy or miserable."[33] Even the war faded in perspective. Jefferson, in Congress, took time to send three separate drafts of proposed constitutions to the Convention and was beside himself with frustration because he could not be in Williamsburg to help launch the republic correctly.

For one thing, Jefferson questioned the legitimacy of the Convention adopting a constitution. He called upon Edmund Randolph to delay proceedings until another body could be elected solely for that purpose. Although Jefferson may only have been trying to gain time until he could come to Williamsburg, his idea logically followed out of the basic American objection to the British principle of parliamentary supremacy. American thinking slowly evolved toward a distinction between the sovereignty of the people and the authority of even the most popularly elected branch of government. Contemporary political theorists often explained this distinction by invoking the concept of a social covenant through which the people established a society with guarantees of individual freedom before entering a separate political compact with a ruler or rulers to govern according to these dictates. Thus Jefferson argued for a separate constituent body to form a constitution that no mere legislature could set aside in the future without another special expression of popular consent. As a sign of the gradual development of this idea, Jefferson's first draft of a constitution allowed amendments to be enacted merely by the unanimous consent of both houses of the legislature. Not until his second draft did he propose a more difficult process requiring ratification of both the constitution and amendments to it by a majority in two-thirds of Virginia's counties.[34]

Americans came to such conclusions at different times in different places. None of the states that adopted new constitutions in 1776 called a special convention, and only one submitted the result for popular ratification. Three of the first, South Carolina, Virginia, and New Jersey, did not hold special legislative elections for the purpose. In Virginia Henry, Mason, and Pendleton told Randolph that since the issue in the recent elections for the Convention was clearly independence, voters obviously intended the delegates to have the power to choose a substitute for the government they had been elected to abolish. Instructions from several counties to their delegates bore them out. Over the next two years attitudes changed. Seven states sought specific mandates from the electorate to enable their legislative bodies to enact constitutions, and in 1778, when the Massachusetts legislature submitted a proposed constitution to the voters in recognition of the principle of popular sovereignty, the electorate rejected it, in part because the legislature rather than a special convention had written it.[35]

Patriot leaders generally underestimated the republicanism of Virginians, as had Dunmore. Almost all of the proposals for the state's constitution contained provisions that placed less power in the hands of the people than the final result. Even Jefferson in his first draft suggested that the Senate be appointed by the lower house for life. In part, leaders misread public opinion because the debate over independence concentrated so heavily on whether there would be anarchy during the transition between governments. Advocates of independence had obviously identified this as one of the major objections to which they must respond. Naturally loyalists exploited the issue, and doubtless some proponents of a break with Britain had qualms themselves. They had reason enough: the lack of discipline among the volunteers at Williamsburg during the summer of 1775 and then among Woodford's troops at Norfolk, and most recently the dissension in Henry's regiment. Many marveled that trouble had been so confined, thus admitting that they expected it. "That we can no longer do without some fixed form of government, is certain," complained John Augustine Washington, brother of the commanding general; "that we have done as well as we have under our present no-form is astonishing and really not to be accounted for but by Providence."[36] As a counterbalance to such pessimism, supporters of separating from the empire like Richard Henry Lee held "the business of framing government not to be so difficult a thing as most people imagine" and touted John Page's advice to adopt a constitution "as nearly resembling the old one as Circumstances, and the Merit of that Constitution will admit of."[37] To Virginia's leaders the ease with which the colony threw off the yoke of empire came as a bit of a surprise.

With the problem of transition in mind, Richard Henry Lee had approached John Adams the November before to ask how easy he thought it would be to establish a republican government. The ensuing conversation and its aftermath led Adams to become, with Mason and Jefferson, the most influential voice in Virginia's deliberations. Adams replied "a single month is sufficient, without the least convulsion, or even animosity, to accomplish a total revolution" and sketched the form a new government might take.[38] Copies of Adams's suggestions soon found their way to Virginia, and in February Lee prepared a handbill with a seven-point outline based on Adams's proposals which he sent to John Page to have printed. By late March and April, as the pace toward independence accelerated, Adams had become Congress's resident constitutional expert. He supplied ten-page handwritten copies of an expanded model of government to two delegates from North Carolina, one from New Jersey, and George Wythe. When Richard Henry Lee asked again for a copy of the fuller statement, Adams, his writing hand numb, borrowed Wythe's for Lee, who published it under the title *Thoughts on Government.*

The pamphlet was well received in Virginia. Lee saw to it that it reached the right men at the Convention, emphasizing that the "plan, with some variation, would in fact, be nearly the form we have been used to."[39] Patrick Henry responded upon receipt of his copy, "I own my self a Democrat on the plan of our admired friend, J. Adams, whose pamphlet I read with great pleasure," and to the author he wrote in appreciation, "the sentiments are precisely the same I have long since taken up."[40] Most important, the format and wording of the draft Mason submitted to the Convention reveal his close familiarity with one or more versions of Adams's thinking.

Half-apologetically, Adams wrote to his friend James Warren in New England that he had composed his pamphlet with a mind to the supposedly aristocratic temper of the South, recommending an executive veto, for example, which he would not want in Massachusetts. In New England he expected "the *Thoughts on Government* will be . . . not popular enough; in the Southern Colonies . . . too popular."[41] Afterward, to his delight, he found that the Virginia constitution and others in the South were "remarkably popular, more so than I could ever have imagined, even more popular than Thoughts on Government."[42] Lee, too, in his seven-point handbill suggested a veto and septennial terms for the upper house and for all executive officers except the governor who was to be elected annually. Subsequently, he told Charles Lee of his pleasant surprise that the Virginia government turned out to be "very much of the democratic kind."[43]

One of Adams's objectives in publicizing his ideas that spring was to counter Thomas Paine's proposal in *Common Sense* to establish unicameral legislatures, the speakers of which would be the states' executives. Adams confided to his wife, Abigail, that, while he greatly ap-

preciated Paine's ideas on independence, the celebrated author had
"a better Hand at pulling down than building."[44] Although in the end
only two states, Pennsylvania and Vermont, adopted unicameral assemblies, many regarded a single chamber as a more popular form.
Richard Henry Lee used a one-house legislature as the standard by
which to measure how "democratic" a constitution was, although he
never proposed such a body himself.[45] A unicameral branch seemed
closer to the literal meaning of democracy, according to which the
people themselves would gather to enact the laws, an ideal obviously
impossible in a country of any size. Critics pointed out a fallacy in
equating a single chamber with literal democracy, however, namely,
that, once elected, any legislature became "at best, but a species of
aristocracy," as "Democritus," a writer in the *Virginia Gazette*, expressed
it.[46] "A single assembly is liable to all the vices, follies, and frailties of
an individual," explained Adams in *Thoughts on Government*.[47] He advocated a second house as well as a strict separation of the legislative
and executive branches to restrain the abuses to which all governments could succumb.

None of the Virginians who submitted proposals for a constitution
quarreled with Adams on this point. In fact, all improved on him.
Commentators most frequently faulted the colonial Virginia constitution because it dangerously mixed executive, legislative, and judicial
functions in the Council, which had served as an advisory body to the
governor, as the upper house of the legislature, and as the supreme
court of the colony. All of the Virginia plans separated these three
functions, entrusting each to a distinct arm of government. When
Richard Henry Lee introduced such a change in his model of government, he felt obliged to check with Adams and, when the Massachusetts sage acknowledged the wisdom of the amendment, hastened
to report the latter's concurrence to Virginia.[48]

Soon an "Antidote to . . . Thoughts on Government," as Adams
dubbed it, also arrived from Philadelphia.[49] The full title was "An
Address to the Convention of the Colony and Ancient Dominion of
Virginia, on the Subject of Government in general, and recommending a particular Form to their Consideration," which, although signed
anonymously "By a Native of that Colony," contemporaries confidently ascribed to Carter Braxton.[50] The aristocratic tone of the work
made it a subject of general ridicule; "Contemptible little Tract," remarked Richard Henry Lee; "a silly thing," said Patrick Henry.[51] The
pamphlet's eulogy of the British constitution was incredibly badly

timed. The proposal of tenure during good behavior for the governor and life terms for the upper house received no consideration. But
the suggestion clearly posed the basic question for contemporaries in
the debate between aristocracy and republicanism, the seriousness
of which two centuries of stable republican government conceal today: do the common people have the ability to rule themselves?
Eighteenth-century theorists usually taught that the success of republicanism depended on the civic virtue of the populace, by which they
meant selfless commitment to the common good and, to the extent
that public spirit seldom existed without it, private morality. Thomas
Paine assured Americans that 1776 was their time in history precisely
because of their youth as a country uncorrupted by wealth and power.
To preserve that virtue, Jefferson strove throughout his life to keep
America a country of small farmers free from the vices of urban industrial development. In the heady early days of the war, some Americans expressed a euphoric confidence that the elimination of British
corruption had inaugurated a reign of virtue in their land.[52]

Carter Braxton was not one of them. In his mind such idealism
had to assume that citizens would not exercise the rights, especially
that of private property, for which the Revolution supposedly was
being fought. "A disinterested attachment to the public good," he
wrote, "though sometimes possessed by a few individuals, never characterized the mass of the people in any state." Because "men will not
be poor from choice or compulsion, these governments can exist only
in countries where the people are so from necessity." In more bountiful areas citizens "will always claim a right of using and enjoying the
fruits of their honest industry . . . without regarding the whimsical
impropriety of being richer than their neighbours." From this insight,
deduced Braxton, sprang the beauty of the British "mixed" or "balanced" constitution.[53] By intermingling monarchy, aristocracy, and
democracy in the form of the king and the houses of Lords and
Commons, the British institutionalized inevitable social distinctions
and put self-interest to work for the commonwealth. The mixing con-
trolled the worst instincts of the social classes represented by the
three branches by setting them against one another. Granted that the
British constitution had been corrupt, Braxton argued, why not
purge its faults and preserve as much of the principle as possible?

Braxton's question reveals the profound radicalism of the American
Revolution in its own day. Eighteenth-century Americans and their
European admirers viewed the Revolution as one of the great social

upheavals of all time. Yet as we look back across subsequent revolutions like the French, the Russian, and the Chinese, we find the extent of social disturbance comparatively small, in Virginia perhaps less than elsewhere. But Virginians and their allies in other colonies established republics. The impact of that fact is lost today because monarchy is dead unless the ruler is a puppet or a dictator, and legitimacy of descent is essential for neither. In 1776 monarchy, aristocracy, and all forms of hereditary right were very much alive. History afforded few examples of republican government, most of which—Athens, Rome, and most recently Venice and Holland—had succumbed to oligarchical rule. Yet Americans were abandoning for just such a government the one formula that history had so far devised for combining political stability with personal liberty. Even the British, whom Montesquieu and other writers of the Enlightenment deemed a race of political geniuses, had not made republicanism work in Oliver Cromwell's seventeenth-century Commonwealth. A practical man, as Braxton considered himself, had to wonder if the millennium had really come.[54]

In the end the Convention showed that it had its own mind about what of the old way to change. The innovations the Convention adopted centered in the executive branch, in constructing which the delegates overrode the ideas of Adams and Lee and the vigorous oratory of Henry to deny the governor a veto over legislative acts as well as the power to prorogue or adjourn the assembly, which Mason had recommended. The Convention proved to be more liberal than Mason as well by substituting direct election of the Senate for his indirect system of electors. The delegates also opted to hold elections immediately that summer rather than have the Convention appoint the Senate for the first year as again Mason proposed, and rejected his attempt to require estates of one thousand and two thousand pounds respectively for membership in the House of Delegates and Senate. Actually, in this last regard the Convention did no more than continue colonial practice by defining the qualification for office as the same as for the suffrage and ordering that they both should "remain as exercised at present."[55]

In general, the Convention spurned any change that touched the vested interests of those fighting the Revolution. Edmund Randolph reported in his history that "it was tacitly understood that every body and individual came into the Revolution with their rights and was to continue to enjoy them as they existed under the former government."[56] The drafting committee vetoed Mason's effort to abolish representation in the lower house for the corporations of Norfolk and Williamsburg, although the full Convention compromised by providing that a borough should lose its seat if its population over seven years fell below one-half that of the smallest county. The delegates did deny representation to Jamestown and the College of William and Mary. More significant, the committee completely rewrote the passages in Mason's draft pertaining to the appointment of militia officers and justices of the peace and other county officials to perpetuate local control by formally requiring the governor and Council to follow the unwritten practice of colonial days by issuing commissions "upon the recommendation of the respective County Courts."[57]

The final draft of the constitution established a General Assembly consisting of a House of Delegates and a Senate, an executive composed of a governor and Privy Council, and a separate court system. The suffrage for the election of the legislature remained as it had been since 1736; voters must be free, white males over twenty-one who had owned for at least one year in the county in which they voted one hundred acres of unimproved land or twenty-five on which there was a house and plantation, or a lot and house in an incorporated city if they voted there. The Convention adopted a major innovation from Mason's draft requiring representatives to actually reside in the area they represented, reversing the colonial practice of allowing a man to run for office from any county or town in which he owned the requisite property. The evidence suggests, however, that Virginians did not enforce the new provision consistently at first. Otherwise, the constitution provided for each county and the District of West Augusta to elect two delegates annually as had been customary and the corporations of Norfolk and Williamsburg to elect one apiece.[58]

Constructing the Senate presented a knottier problem, for as a republican institution it had to be responsible to the electorate and yet, in order to fit the theory of mixed government, have a constituency different from, and more elite than, that of the lower house. In one of his most ingenious contributions Mason suggested dividing the state into twenty-four districts, in each of which the voters would choose "sub-electors" who would name a senator. The Convention accepted the basic idea but liberalized it to allow the people of the districts to elect the senators directly. Each senator served for four years in staggered terms so that one-quarter of the membership stood for election each year. But the scheme did not really solve the problem, for, once republicanized, the upper house represented the same interests as the lower although in a slightly different fashion. For a decade or more many wondered what role in government the Senate could play, yet no one suggested abandoning the institution. Most just looked for ways to make practice conform to theory. The Virginia constitution designed the upper house to be palpably inferior to the lower, not granting the Senate the power to initiate legislation or amend money bills, limitations on which the House of Delegates insisted. Delegates conceived of the Senate as an aristocracy of talent to temper the delegates' actions with reason and reflection rather than as just a lobby for the wealthy. Surprisingly, after some frustration, the upper chamber took to this function rather well, building a sense of purpose over the years that afforded a sounder justification for being.[59]

The Convention's intentions with regard to the executive were more confusing. The constitution prescribed a vetoless governor who was elected annually by joint ballot of the legislature; who could not serve more than three years successively and thereafter was ineligible to be reelected for four years more; and who could act only with the consent of the Privy Council. In effect, the Convention created a plural executive. As for the Council, the Convention followed Mason's suggestion for a cumbersome system of rotation under which the legislature jointly selected eight councillors who in turn chose two of their own number every third year to be ineligible to serve for the next three years. The Convention modified this scheme to tighten legislative control by having the assembly jointly select the two who would step down, but in the process deleted the provision that this be in rotation, permitting indefinite terms for some. Because the turnover during the war was so rapid anyway, the provision was apparently utilized only twice. The Council annually elected its own president, who doubled as lieutenant governor.[60]

Yet the Convention obviously did not think that the constitution whittled the executive down to nothing. The delegates expected the positions of governor and councillor to retain great prestige and dignity and saw no reason not to expect to recruit candidates comparable in stature to those who served at the top level of colonial government. To smooth the passage to the new system, for example, Richard Henry Lee and Edmund Pendleton wanted to name the secretary of the colony, Thomas Nelson, as governor since as the last president of

the colonial Council he nominally succeeded Dunmore. The Convention, however, chose Patrick Henry, who next to Washington was Virginia's most prestigious citizen, and put Nelson with two other members of the former Council, John Page and John Tayloe, on the new.
Lee also sounded out Robert Carter to see if he would continue to
serve, and the legislature elected another Carter, Charles of Shirley
plantation, but both declined.[61]

Contemporaries had a different perspective on the executive branch
of government from what prevails today. Out of lack of experience
with republican forms, constitution makers did not know what to expect from a popularly chosen governor. Basically, eighteenth-century
republicans thought in terms of reforming the royal version and
hoped ideally to have as little need for an executive as possible. One
radical British writer whose work was highly esteemed in American
republican circles, James Burgh, described the executive's business as
"all a mere routine," and throughout his several drafts of a constitution Jefferson referred to the governor as "the Administrator."[62]
Theories of the separation of powers prescribed the setting of policy
as the legislature's function and implementation the executive's. When
events forced the conclusion that the executive needed more power
than the constitution allowed, the general reaction among the Virginia leadership was to suspend the rules and grant what most
deemed unconstitutional authority—in contemporary terminology, to
create a "dictator." However much the constitution circumscribed the
executive's legitimate scope of action, the potential for abuse remained constant as long as the danger of invasion, tory rebellion, and
other crises required speedy and aggressive response. By implication,
the heaping of constitutional checks and balances on the executive
did not obviate the need for candidates of sterling character. Patrick
Henry misunderstood the honor his colleagues accorded him when
he grumbled that, without at least a veto over legislative actions, the
governorship would be "a mere phantom."[63]

Jefferson had his most significant influence on the formation of the
third branch of government, the court system. Mason suggested separating the General Court from the Council and creating distinct
courts of admiralty and chancery, but otherwise continuing the tradition of a single general or supreme court in addition to the county
courts. To Mason's brief outline the drafting committee added a cryptic suggestion that there be "superior courts" subordinate to the "supreme court." By the time this section of the constitution reached the

Convention floor, Jefferson's proposals had arrived, and the delegates adopted his more detailed provision for a "supreme Court of Appeals" in addition to a "General Court" and the separate courts of admiralty and chancery that Mason recommended. The Convention retained Mason's idea of having the General Assembly jointly elect the judges rather than let the governor appoint them as Jefferson suggested. The delegates on their own also added a prohibition against judicial officers "and all Ministers of the Gospel of every Denomination" sitting in the legislature or on the Privy Council.[64]

The Convention also accepted Jefferson's attempt to resolve the territorial disputes that had plagued Virginia and its neighbors for so long. Following his lead, the final text of the constitution acknowledged the borders granted to Maryland and North Carolina in their colonial charters, reserving for Virginia free navigation of the Potomac River, which was mostly within Maryland's boundaries, and abandoned to Pennsylvania claims to lands around Pittsburgh. At the same time the Convention restated Virginia's claim under its 1609 charter and the peace treaty with France in 1763 to the lands stretching westward from the Appalachian Mountains to the Mississippi River and, to frustrate the increasing interest of land speculators in the area, voided all private claims emanating from direct purchases from Indian tribes not sanctioned by the state. The Convention did not agree to Jefferson's provision that any new "colonies" established in the West "shall be free and independant of this colony and of all the world."[65]

Aside from the sections on the courts and the West, few of Jefferson's proposals found their way into the final text. Jefferson's third and fullest draft arrived late in the session. Had it come earlier sympathizers like Wythe and Madison might have incorporated more. The delegates used the sections of the drafts that touched on topics Mason had not developed as completely, such as the courts and the western borders, or that could be inserted easily into the nearly completed constitution, such as Jefferson's catalog of George III's tyrannies which the Convention adopted as a preamble to explain the need for a new government. Most notably, Jeffersonian proposals that would have significantly altered the established system fell by the roadside: a reduction in property qualifications for the suffrage from one hundred unimproved acres to twenty-five, guarantees of home rule for the West through the creation of new states, full religious freedom as opposed to mere toleration, simplified procedures of naturalization, an end to the importation of slaves, and popular election and annual rotation of sheriffs and coroners.[66]

On June 29 the constitution was at last ready for adoption. The Convention put it into motion by electing Patrick Henry governor with sixty votes to forty-five for Thomas Nelson, the former secretary, and one for John Page. The delegates also elected a Privy Council. Rushing over the next six days to wind up its work, the session provided a major toughening of the laws against tories by enacting that anyone convicted of bearing arms against the republic would be subject to imprisonment for the duration of the war and that the estates of those convicted would be confiscated outright instead of just sequestered. The Convention marked off senatorial districts for elections that summer, adopted new oaths of office, deleted references to the king from the Book of Common Prayer, extended the authority of sheriffs and justices of the peace until the new assembly could meet, adopted a new militia bill, authorized one thousand pounds to refurbish the Palace for the new governor, appointed a board of navy commissioners to supervise the fleet that General Lee had demanded, and, as the final act in this hectic outpouring of legislation, approved a design for the great seal of the commonwealth. With that, the delegates adjourned without waiting to see if the new government would actually work.[67]

Since previously London had almost exclusively handled whole areas of public policy—diplomatic, military, economic—few at the Convention appreciated how much more than just promulgating a constitution it would take to run a government in the midst of war. At his inauguration on July 6, the day after the Convention's adjournment, Patrick Henry was so ill "of a bilious fever" it was feared that he would die at any moment. Yet of the eight privy councillors chosen initially, only five had agreed to serve, and only one replacement had been named before the Convention dissolved. The total was just two more than the minimum needed to designate a lawful successor. Close to a week went by before enough could be rounded up to choose John Page president and lieutenant governor and let Henry retire to Hanover County for the rest of the summer to recuperate.[68]

After Henry's departure, the press of business almost overwhelmed the remaining members of the administration until gradually a tiny bureaucracy evolved. "I am broke in upon again as I have been 15 Times Since I began this scrawl," Page complained at one point to Jefferson. He had not written earlier, he explained, because "the whole Week has slipt away in the hurry of Business, without my being able to spare a single Minute."[69] Daily meetings of the Council ran from 9 or 10 A.M. until past noon (the Committee of Safety used to begin at 8) with hours devoted to official correspondence after that. Two commissioners of public accounts inherited from the Committee of Safety checked vouchers and receipts, but the Council had to issue final orders on the Treasury for payment. There was an endless agenda of warrants to soldiers for tents at £4.10 apiece or to express riders for £16.10 for expenses from Point Pleasant or to the public printer for three blank books and a ream of paper for the commander of a minute battalion. Not until the assembly convened in the fall did the executive secure some relief with the appointment of three public auditors to help with such picayune matters.[70]

Obtaining a quorum remained a constant problem, for with Henry sick and Page in the chair, attendance of all but one of the other councillors was required. The General Assembly in the fall elected six more councillors, but two declined and two others resigned, so that it was early December before a third round of elections finally achieved the Council's full complement. Within days of the inauguration Lieutenant Governor Page set a precedent repeated many times that is surprising for a generation so concerned with constitutional propriety. He filled on his own authority an emergency plea for gunpowder from General Lee. In desperation Page began to convene the Council without a quorum, and although for a time it did not meet if the quorum lacked more than one, eventually a single member was deemed sufficient. Whenever the other councillors were in town, they approved the minutes retroactively. Only when sitting as a court of appeal from the county commissions, as it continued to do until the legislature decided to implement the constitution's provisions for a separate judiciary, did the Council insist upon strict regularity. Later, when Page, too, was absent, Dudley Digges of York County acted as governor by virtue of seniority although the assembly did not sanction the procedure until after he stepped down. Finally, after three years of extemporizing, the board abandoned the effort to function in every case as a plural executive and granted the governor authority to act alone in ordinary administrative matters.[71]

Staffing the government presented another difficulty. With no civil service, like Congress and the other states Virginia had to turn to the private sector, often on a part-time basis, to obtain the skills required. Unfortunately for the patriot cause, contemporaries had little understanding of the meaning of conflict of interest. William Aylett, who at one time was simultaneously Continental deputy commissary general for purchases in Virginia, director of the Public Store or state supply office, and state agent for overseas trade, thought nothing of being a partner in a firm that sold at least one cargo to himself as a government purchaser. As virtuous a republican as John Page blithely told his friend and fellow patriot, St. George Tucker of Williamsburg, to exploit the "vast advantage" of family contacts on the British island of Bermuda to import salt, which was in short supply and sold at an "enormous price here."[72] Inevitably, there were outcries against profiteering and equally indignant protests of innocence—in some cases doubtless sincere—on the grounds that the actions censured were in fact noble sacrifices of time and talent for the cause.

The resulting controversies were some of the most demoralizing the new state and nation had to face, for, despite the confident overlay of republican rhetoric that characterized the Revolution, the incessant sermonizing about public virtue or its lack betrayed an uncertainty over how well Americans could rule themselves. According to contemporary political theory, only if citizens sacrificed private for public interest could a society dispense with the authority and discipline of monarchy or aristocracy. Yet at times even the most optimistic among the revolutionaries had to wonder if Americans had escaped the corruption patriots ascribed to Great Britain by forsaking the empire.

The inefficiency and ineffectiveness of the new state government exasperated contemporaries as they have historians ever since. For whatever reason—distances within the state, natural interferences like winter snows and epidemics, or longstanding habit—government was not easily rushed in Virginia. As Jefferson once told a critical Congress, "The time for complying with a requisition expires frequently before it is discovered that the means provided were defective."[73] Another time he wrote philosophically in answer to an impatient army commander's demand for action, "The Executive . . . sensible that a necessary Work is not to be abandoned because their means are not so energetic as they could wish them and on the contrary that it is their duty to take those means as they find them and to make the most of them for the public good . . . propose to pursue this work, and if they cannot accomplish it in a shorter, they will in a longer time."[74] The danger was that not all republicans were as sanguine as the philosopher, and some came close at times to losing faith in their experiment.

CHAPTER 7

The War Continues

THE most urgent problem in the first days of the new administration was Dunmore, who at the time of Patrick Henry's inauguration still lingered on Gwynn's Island. There, according to one report, "Caterpillar like, . . . he has devoured everything in that place."[1] George Washington and Congress put heavy pressure on the Virginia military to move against the royal governor, for if his small force became the nucleus of a second front, the Continental cause would be in grave jeopardy. At the very least, Dunmore pinned down troops desperately needed elsewhere. The British governor astutely made the same points to his superiors, but they let the opportunity slip and, once Dunmore withdrew, did not send troops to Virginia for most of the rest of Henry's three years as governor.

Until midsummer General Andrew Lewis hesitated to march against Dunmore lest the British double back to attack Williamsburg and the lower peninsula. Lewis had too few troops to cover both fronts. Charles Lee had taken the 8th, or German, Regiment under Colonel John Peter Gabriel Muhlenburg to Charleston, where, despite Lee's complaints of its "disorderly mutinous and dangerous disposition," it participated in the successful defense of Fort Moultrie.[2] Lee also ordered two other Virginia regiments into North Carolina to protect his rear. It took Lewis over a month to find replacements for the troops who left with Lee. Virginia authorities called up thirteen hundred militia. Then Lewis received a second order from Lee, delayed over four weeks in transit, countermanding the dispatch of the two backup units to North Carolina. Fortunately for Lewis, it had taken so long to comply with the original command because the men were scattered and too ill-equipped to march that they were not too far away to recall. Finally, having assembled enough men to guard the capital in his absence, the general, accompanied by a bevy of colonels, rode out of Williamsburg on July 8 at the head of ten companies of the veteran 1st and 2nd regiments for the assault on Dunmore.[3]

When the Virginians reached the shore opposite Gwynn's Island, they found that the British had several hundred men bivouacked in tents at the western end of the island and an artillery battery that James Parker had worked tirelessly for the preceding three days to set up at the channel's narrowest point. Stationed nearby were the *Otter* and several tenders ready to thwart the expected onslaught. On the Virginia side artillery director Dohicky Arundel had brought every piece that could be spared from posts around the Tidewater to assemble a battery of impressive firepower: two eighteen-pounders, two twelve-pounders, five nine-pounders, three six-pounders, and two field pieces. All that remained was for the shirtmen to collect enough rowboats, canoes, and rafts for an amphibious assault.[4]

The next morning Lewis noticed that the *Dunmore* had changed positions with the *Otter* and lay exposed to the two eighteen-pounders that the Virginians had been able to mount unobserved. Without waiting to find more boats, Lewis ordered the gunners to open fire at eight o'clock. Taken completely unaware, the British had no weapon in place large enough to reply adequately. The American gunners hit the *Dunmore* a dozen times, slightly wounding the governor and killing his mate, before the ship could be towed out of range. The vessel survived primarily because the skirmish occurred at ebb tide. When the *Otter* came to the rescue, American shots hulled it, and four tenders in the channel ran aground, three to be burned and one captured. The Virginians burned two more the next day along with a larger ship, the *Logan*. Patriot cannon silenced Parker's battery, in which the largest weapon was a six-pounder, after a little over an hour.

The Virginians' lack of boats saved Dunmore by giving him about forty-eight hours in which to flee before they could reach the island. Having learned that Clinton had finally made up his mind to invest Charleston, thus ending any possibility of his coming to Virginia in the immediate future, and realizing that his own troops were too weakened by the smallpox to make a stand, Dunmore ordered their withdrawal that night. The governor's action caused consternation among the Norfolk refugees, for despite frequent warnings from the military to be ready to move at a moment's notice, many had neglected to store fresh water on board ship and had to leave much valuable gear behind in their scramble to escape. Once again, the navy had to furnish crews. Only about thirty black soldiers too ill to move remained when the Virginians came ashore. The one casualty on their side was Arundel, who in his professional enthusiasm insisted against all advice on firing a wooden mortar with which he had been experimenting and was killed.

Once off Gwynn's Island, Dunmore and Hamond were ready to leave Virginia if they could obtain fresh water. They headed up the Chesapeake Bay to St. George's Island at the mouth of the Potomac River, where they temporarily landed troops to hold off Maryland militia on the mainland. Finding little water there, Dunmore took a few of the warships and some detachments of the 14th and Queen's Own Loyal regiments to forage a hundred miles or so upriver until they secured a supply sufficient for the entire fleet. At George Brent's plantation near Dumfries local militia foolishly dared the British to land and, when the governor's men did, hid in the woods where the approach of the Virginians' own reinforcements so frightened them that they ran themselves "almost to death."[5] Dunmore burned Brent's house in retaliation and was about to do the same to Hugh Mercer's when a change in the wind forced him to return to the main flotilla.

After loading their casks of water on board, Dunmore and Hamond scuttled about twenty unseaworthy vessels. Overall losses were heavy. "A violent bilious intermitting fever, together with a most inveterate scurvy had for these two months past raged with great violence both in the men of war and Transports," Hamond reported.[6] His own *Roebuck* lost thirty seamen. Dunmore's army had left nearly three hundred graves at Tucker's Point and about half that number on Gwynn's Island. On August 4 the British commanders received final confirmation that Clinton, having failed to storm Charleston, was sailing directly back to New York. The next day, Hamond and Dunmore passed through the Virginia Capes themselves. About fifty vessels followed the *Otter* to St. Augustine, a handful went with Governor Eden to England, and the rest turned northward with the British naval commander and the governor for New York, where they arrived on the fourteenth. Dunmore immediately attended "a great formal Dinner" to tell his story to General Howe and others of the British high command.[7]

For almost three years Virginia was of secondary concern in British strategy, which focused instead on Philadelphia, New York City, and the Hudson Valley in an effort to isolate New England, considered by the royal command to be the heart of the rebellion. On July 2, 1776, General William Howe landed on Staten Island, New York, with the vanguard of an army that eventually totaled thirty-four thousand men. Soon calls for reinforcements for the Continental army under General Washington reached Williamsburg and for the first time Virginians began to move into the major theater of war in significant numbers.[8]

In Virginia, discipline continued to be a problem through the summer of 1776, the rigorous regimen of Charles Lee notwithstanding. The number of requests for furloughs embarrassed Andrew Lewis, and courts-martial, frequently of officers, occurred almost daily. A captain and a lieutenant were cashiered and the latter was drummed through Williamsburg for "behaving in a scandalous and infamous manner."[9] Another lieutenant was convicted of refusing to do parade duty because his rifle company had enlisted as light infantry, which usually served only as shock troops and snipers. On another occasion, when red tape delayed their pay, General Lee was informed that units teetered "on the brink of mutiny and general desertion."[10] Soldiers stole from neighboring farms, gambled and rioted, and discharged weapons indiscriminately to the consternation of townspeople. A stray musket ball killed one sergeant in the middle of the camp near the College of William and Mary.

Most serious was the dissension in the 1st and 2nd regiments, among which the Henry affair still rankled. The men of both units announced that they would not reenlist under their current officers when their year expired in September. Colonel Woodford was the primary target of the ill will. He had little control over his own unit, considered to be "the most profane and disorderly of any," and exposed the bickering in its ranks by bringing charges against an officer for "Letter Wrighting."[11] When the two regiments sent a joint message of congratulation on Henry's election as governor, Woodford announced in the *Virginia Gazette* that the address of his men did not reflect the "sentiments of the colonel."[12]

In answer to Congress's call for two regiments to join the main army in early August, General Lewis made a concerted effort to win over the two that should have been his best. He offered additional bounties and personally appealed to the men "to seize the post of Honour" with Washington. In the words of one cynic, the 1st "almost to a man swallowed the bait," but when Woodford called for those of the 2nd who would follow him for another term to step forward, not a man stirred.[13] In the end the 3rd Virginia under Colonel George Weedon marched north with the 1st instead. Shortly afterward Woodford's regiment dissolved, and when Congress promoted Adam Stephen to brigadier general over him, the colonel himself resigned.

By the end of the summer, as almost all of the state's troops departed to the North, a note of panic began to creep into the deliberations of Virginia's leaders. Repeated letters reminded Congress how vulnerable the Tidewater was to attack along its rivers and pointed out that the Virginia executive had no authority to recruit replacements until the assembly convened. An epidemic that swept the lower counties in late summer and fall crippled troops on duty there and noticeably dulled the enthusiasm of others to serve in the area. Increasingly nervous, Lieutenant Governor Page first put the militia on standby alert and then called up minute battalions to garrison Portsmouth and Yorktown. Page ordered cavalry being recruited in accordance with Charles Lee's suggestions to come to Williamsburg as soon as possible and constructed barracks for them in the governor's park north of the Palace.[14]

Fears that the British would attempt another sortie into the South when winter closed operations around New York multiplied. At one point the rumor spread that Dunmore was on his way back with an army. In September the Council insisted that Henry come to the capital even though he had only partially recovered from his illness and subsequently suffered a relapse. Then, upon receipt of Congress's requisition for a second division of three regiments, Lewis ordered the last remaining unit, the 7th, over from Gloucester to guard the governor. After hasty consultation with Generals Lewis and Stephen, Henry and the Council also decided to order the militia of twenty-six counties to march to Williamsburg immediately.[15]

Although the governor and Council acted within their constitutional authority, it seemed to some that they were unduly alarmist since the redcoats were in New York, not the South. Henry's critics went so far as to suggest that he just wanted soldiers around to gratify his vanity, but the most frequent objections stemmed from the expense and the disinclination of upcountrymen to serve in the pestilential Tidewater. Shortly after the House of Delegates met on October 7, it issued a sharp rebuke to the administration by ordering the troops already on the road to turn around and go home. The assembly tried to mollify the executive with a vote of confidence, but to no avail. When the minutemen at Yorktown and Portsmouth also announced that they had been on duty long enough, Dudley Digges wrote a testy note on behalf of his fellow councillors asking what the delegates intended to do about the situation since they did not seem to like anything the executive proposed.[16]

Cries for help from the North continued as Howe took New York and pushed across New Jersey toward Philadelphia in an effort to catch Washington as first-year enlistments expired. The steady loss of strength left the Continental forces increasingly dependent upon the newly arrived Virginians. In Williamsburg Lewis dispatched whatever men he could find. Theodorick Bland's six troops of dragoons departed before they hardly had settled in their new barracks near the Palace. The repeated summonses also undermined George Mason's prized system of minutemen, for Continental recruiters continually cannibalized the units, preventing the least degree of proficiency. At length the legislature overcame its compunction against a standing army and authorized the recruitment of three garrison regiments for duty within the state.[17]

Suddenly, late in the term, after a week of foreboding silence from Philadelphia, a rider brought news that the northern front had collapsed and Congress had fled to Baltimore. The house immediately went into the Committee of the Whole to decide what to do. What transpired in the executive session is unknown. Years later Jefferson, who was not present, accused Henry of trying to become a "Dictator." According to one colorful tradition, Speaker of the Senate Archibald Cary vowed that if Henry ever succeeded, "he shall feel my dagger in his heart before the sunset of that day."[18]

Actually, the ultra whig George Mason offered the resolution that was at the bottom of the controversy. His motion declared that "it is become necessary, for the Preservation of the State, that the usual forms of Government shou'd be suspended, during a limited time, for the more speedy Execution of the most vigorous and effectual Measures, to repel the Invasion of the Enemie."[19] For Mason to advocate such a step reveals the sense of desperation that overtook the delegates as a result of the news of Congress's flight. The next day they accepted the proposal. The Senate attempted to blunt the precedent by amending the statement about suspending the constitution to read simply that "additional powers be given to the Governour and Council," but otherwise did not alter the text.[20]

The powers Mason conferred upon the executive did make Henry a

"Dictator," but like many words in the eighteenth-century republican's lexicon, the term had a meaning different from what it bears today. It referred particularly to the provision in the constitution of the Roman republic for the appointment of a leader with absolute power for a short period of time, usually six months, when invasion threatened. Of course, there was always the chance that the dictator would not give up his power when his term expired.[21]

Mason proposed to let Henry raise whatever number of troops he wanted and send them wherever he wished during the forthcoming legislative recess from December 1776 through May 1777. This expedient would prevent a repetition of the experience the past fall when only Continental troops could be sent to support Washington and no one had the authority to recruit replacements until the assembly reconvened. Henry's power, however, was somewhat more restricted than it would have been in ancient Rome by the requirement that it be exercised "by and with the advice and consent of the Privy Council."[22] The governor immediately began to raise companies of volunteers out of the militia and within days was writing confidently to neighboring states that he could now "act with Vigour and upon a liberal plan" to help them should they be attacked.[23]

The reservations some may have had about Henry's personal motives aside, Virginians had good reason to be disturbed by the assembly's action, regardless of its classical precedents. The creation of a "dictator" bore out the point Jefferson had made the previous spring, that without a special ratifying election, succeeding governments could tinker with the constitution whenever they felt the need. The resolution also indicated that otherwise good republicans had doubts about the viability of popular self-government. When the following months brought no improvement in the military situation, John Banister, a delegate from Chesterfield County, declared in a letter to Theodorick Bland, Jr., that "I am fully convinced the preparations for war and the great business of keeping up supplies of men cannot advantageously be carried on by a popular assembly. . . . Nay, so clear is it from daily experience, that the operations of war should be confided to a few, that I begin to think success is, without the adoption of such a measure, impossible."[24]

By the spring of 1777 the martial ardor of the early months had begun to flag. Hopes for a short struggle had dissipated and Edmund Pendleton lamented that in Virginia as elsewhere on the continent, "The spirit of inlistment is no more!"[25] Congress had raised the minimum length of service to three years, and many feared the smallpox inoculation that Washington insisted upon for all his troops. Nor was the chronic shortage of supplies encouraging. Different forms of militia, state, and Continental service encouraged recruits to shop around and generated resentment when others seemed to have found better terms. Patrick Henry had to abandon his idea of raising independent volunteer companies for local defense because it disrupted regular recruiting, while the Virginia government's willingness to let South Carolina and Georgia recruiters canvass the state led to competitive offers and bounty jumping until the Council rescinded the invitation in March.[26] But despite the difficulties, through the early months of 1777 the old 2nd Virginia, which was being raised anew, and six additional Continental regiments, bringing the total in the Virginia line to fifteen, gradually filled their ranks sufficiently to march north with Andrew Lewis in time for the summer campaign.

How well Virginia contributed to the Continent's manpower is difficult to evaluate; the judgment has to be relative.[27] The state was always badly deficient in meeting its quota (in the spring of 1777, 8,160) as the frantic efforts of its leaders to recruit sufficient numbers demonstrated. Generally Virginia only achieved about 40 to 45 percent of its allotment, although on one occasion the state did attain 75 percent. On the other hand, when Lewis joined Washington in New York in May, his units accounted for over one-third of the main army, and for the next year Virginians always constituted from a fifth to a third of the Continent's forces. After mid-1778, as the numbers from other states increased, Virginia's share declined to 10 to 15 percent, but the total of men enlisted remained roughly the same. In the thirty-one months from Lewis's arrival to the transfer of the Virginia regiments to the southern army at the close of 1779, Virginia maintained an average of around 3,500 men with Washington, its total once rising as high as 6,200 and falling only once below 3,000. Only Massachusetts did better, supplying about half again as many troops on the basis of a somewhat smaller, but more concentrated, white population, geographically nearer the scene of action. It is impossible to determine why individuals did or did not join the army. But given the long-term, professional commitment that Continental service entailed, it may have been that the numbers Virginia produced were about all that a widely dispersed, agricultural society could generate. In the days before mass citizen armies, Virginia's total was respectable for the size of its white population by European standards. Furthermore, in moments of actual invasion, the state proved that it could double the number of men in the field in the form of state troops and militia for one to two months at a time.

Congress urged a draft in 1777, but the Virginia assembly struggled to avoid it as long as possible. "Our people," Jefferson explained to John Adams in May, "even under the monarchical government had learnt to consider it as the last of all oppressions."[28] Instead, the legislature tried to make up deficiencies by offering exemptions from militia duty to any two men who induced a third to join, by sanctioning the enlistment of free blacks and indentured servants with or without their masters' consent, and by holding out the additional attraction of immunity from prosecution for debts up to fifty dollars. Finally, in the case of those counties that did not fill their quotas for the new regiments by August, the assembly reluctantly ordered a draft from the militia, including company grade officers, of those men who in the opinion of the commanders and local J.P.s could "be best spared" for a term of three years. Draftees had the privilege of finding substitutes up to the last minute.[29]

As Jefferson might have predicted, the act provoked resistance. A court had to require a one thousand-pound bond from a member of the legislature from Prince William County to stop him from agitating against it, and officials had difficulty collecting the men after tapping them. Moreover, the policy had a disastrous effect on the recruiting of volunteers. The scramble for substitutes drove the black market price to fifty, seventy, and one hundred dollars over the official twenty-dollar bounty for a three-year enlistment, far beyond the reach of most recruiting officers.[30]

In addition, during the spring of 1777 the assembly ordered the recruitment of a state artillery battalion to supplement the three garrison regiments raised the previous fall. It also tried to capitalize on the number of Frenchmen who had come to America to seek fame and adventure, if not fortune, while their government maintained official neutrality. Congress eventually found the influx embarrassing (although its ambassadors in Paris encouraged it) because many of the immigrants did not possess the talents of which they boasted. To the chagrin of less demanding sponsors, the Continental government began to spurn the proffered services.

Thus Richard Henry Lee, although otherwise a sharp critic of the gullibility of Congress's representatives abroad, repeatedly dunned the reluctant Virginia Council and assembly to appoint one M. Loyauté, "a man of s[c]ience, and not unacquainted with practise," as commander of the state artillery before the country lost his abilities entirely.[31] Lee's assurance that Loyauté would bring with him a team of skilled gunners to train Virginians may not have strengthened the case. Even with Patrick Henry supporting the Frenchman, Washington's recommendation of Thomas Marshall, the father of the future chief justice, won out. The assembly compromised by commissioning Loyauté inspector general. A year later, Loyauté almost caused a mass resignation of the artillery corps by insisting that as inspector general he was in ultimate command. The assembly, apparently under the guidance of Jefferson, who was on the original committee that appointed him, had no choice but to force the French volunteer to resign.[32]

In a similar instance, the Council in 1777 commissioned M. Delaporte DeCrome to enlist a "French Corps" in Williamsburg, but because Virginians proved reluctant to serve under a foreigner, had to let him try to sign up men in the West Indies instead. After nearly a year, Delaporte gave up and returned to test fortune as a private merchant in the Virginia capital.

Fortunately for the patriot cause the British wasted their opportunities during 1777 when American enlistments were in flux. After several false starts, the newly knighted General Howe, having failed to reach Philadelphia by marching across New Jersey the previous fall, decided upon an amphibious assault. Meanwhile, General John Burgoyne with an independent command prepared to invade the Hudson River Valley from Canada. The lack of coordination was prodigious. While Burgoyne moved south from Canada, Howe went the other way. Having dallied for weeks in New Jersey, Howe finally embarked in the midsummer heat for Delaware Bay, where he found the approach to Philadelphia too heavily defended and decided to attack via the Chesapeake Bay.[33]

The British fleet was sighted off the Virginia Capes on August 14, a Thursday. The news spread an "alarm and bustle" through Williamsburg.[34] The governor, who had been ill off and on all year, was in Hanover County, and the Council was adjourned as it had been during most of the summer. On Friday Page called a hasty meeting of as many councillors as were in the vicinity and summoned all the militia east of the mountains to the lower peninsula. Henry returned by Monday, August 18, and the next day commissioned the younger Thomas Nelson of Yorktown brigadier general to command the defense. By the following Thursday six hundred troops were in town, including students from the College of William and Mary, who formed a company under their president, the Reverend James Madison, a cousin of the later United States president. Nelson reviewed his forces on the college green and pronounced himself "much satisfied" with their appearance.[35] The overall response to the emergency was impressive. Some militia marched forty miles in twenty-four hours to reach their posts. At the end of August about four thousand were encamped around Williamsburg and on the peninsula.

By then the British fleet had reached the Head of Elk in Maryland, where Howe disembarked and struck out for Philadelphia. As soon as the enemy's purpose became clear, Henry and the Council ordered a third of the Northern Neck militia into Maryland to support Washington, but overruled Nelson's recommendation to send a larger detachment from the lower peninsula. Once the threat to Virginia diminished, the Council began to send men home, keeping only about fifteen hundred on duty until the empty British transports sailed back to sea at the end of September. Nelson put the time to good use, developing a plan for better organization of the militia and apparently inculcating exemplary military habits in his men, for the citizens of Williamsburg complained that they could not walk about town without being accosted by his sentinels.[36]

Defeated and driven back at Brandywine Creek, Washington was unable to prevent the fall of Philadelphia on September 25. A week later the Americans were again defeated at Germantown, and the 9th Virginia Regiment was decimated. The news that the British had taken Philadelphia "as much frightened the townspeople of Williamsburg as if they had been attacked themselves," Mann Page wrote to the congressional delegation, which by then had fled to York, Pennsylvania.[37] The Council reconsidered Nelson's advice and prepared to send five thousand volunteers north until Washington declined the offer because the troops would arrive too late and there were not enough supplies for them anyway. Washington did accept one thousand militia from the Northern Neck and, as replacement for the lost 9th, the 1st State Regiment under George Gibson, now a colonel, which had set out for Pennsylvania earlier in the summer.[38]

Then, in the midst of despair and gloom, good news! General Burgoyne and his entire army had surrendered at Saratoga! Pushing southward from Canada through upper New York, Burgoyne had counted on aid from Howe if he needed it. Constantly harassed by an American army under General Horatio Gates, in which Daniel Morgan's Virginia riflemen played a vital role, Burgoyne was finally halted and forced to capitulate. Official word reached Williamsburg on October 30. Governor Henry immediately proclaimed a holiday. Officers hastily groomed whatever troops were in town for a parade down Duke of Gloucester Street to the courthouse, where Nelson and other dignitaries reviewed them. The artillery saluted the occasion with thirteen salvos and the infantry fired a feu de joie after which the onlookers gave three huzzahs. The governor ordered a gill of rum for every soldier and freed everyone in the guardhouse except deserters, "who cannot be ranked amongst the friends of the Thirteen United States," declared the *Virginia Gazette*.[39] The celebration lasted well into the evening and featured the illumination of buildings and the ringing of bells. Two weeks later, upon Congress's official proclamation of thanksgiving, the festivities resumed, culminating the second day in a grand ball given by the General Assembly at the Capitol.

Jubilation was premature, however. The winter of 1777–1778 was the time of Valley Forge. In Virginia as elsewhere the efforts to succor Washington proved as ineffective as the year before, though for the opposite reason—the Americans were winning the war. Benjamin Harrison wrote to Robert Morris of a "langour in the minds of the Common People from one end of the Continent to the other," and Mann Page, Jr., told Richard Henry Lee in Congress, "Our people are too desirous of Peace."[40] Because Howe remained ensconced in Philadelphia, the Virginia legislature reluctantly enacted a draft of single men "who have no child" for one year.[41] The statute authorized a bounty of fifteen dollars and permitted draftees to supply substitutes. A provision allowing counties to return deserters apprehended within their borders as part of the locality's quota was politically palatable but militarily self-defeating. The inducement still would not be enough, Edmund Pendleton feared, given the "avarice now in fashion."[42]

As a last-ditch alternative, the delegates adopted Thomas Nelson's plan, which harked back to the old minuteman system, to sign up five thousand militia to serve with Washington for as few as six months. The act called for a ten-dollar bounty. As an added attraction, Baptists and other dissenters could form their own companies, and anyone who volunteered for six months gained exemption from militia duty for the next six. At the same time, the legislature reduced the number of companies in a regiment from ten to eight to distribute the available men as widely as possible.[43]

Nelson's idea did not work and undercut regular recruiting all the more. The scramble for substitutes drove the unofficial price as high as two hundred dollars in wealthier counties. Wherever the draft was resorted to, trouble broke out as before. "It was very generally disagreable to the people, and in some counties occasioned considerable disturbance," wrote Robert Honyman, a Scottish physician living in Hanover County whose diary provides a running account of social conditions during the war years in Virginia.[44] Loudoun County officials told the Council that they could not even hold a draft because of "the violent and riotous behaviour of the People," and there was also resistance in Westmoreland. Even though realists soon halved the goal of 5,000 and the governor and Council ordered the 2nd State Regiment northward to help fill the ranks, Washington reported in the spring that, out of 3,500 new troops Virginia supposedly called up over the winter, only 1,242 ever reached him.[45]

The long awaited treaty with France was signed in February 1778. Official notice of Congress's ratification reached Virginia in May. On hearing the news, the General Assembly scaled down a cavalry troop that it had tentatively authorized from five hundred to three hundred men and abolished the draft. Instead, the legislators escalated the enticements to volunteers. Bounties that soared to thirty dollars for six months and one hundred dollars for three years still fell short of the unofficial rate in some areas. The delegates added fringe benefits: a gill of spirits a day, exemption from poll taxes for periods up to life, full pay for disability, half-pay for widows, various necessities from the Public Store at 1774 prices (this offer was soon retracted), and exemption from militia duty for whole counties until those that had not filled their quotas did so. Only "with great difficulty," John Parke Custis told his stepfather George Washington, did supporters win an extension of the governor's authority to march militia into neighboring states.[46] Authorization for a garrison battalion to man coastal defenses carried the proviso—since similar promises to home guard units had been broken before—that an order to march out of the state would constitute an automatic discharge.

As the royal forces regrouped to defend against a French attack on the West Indies or the British Isles, the blockade of the American coast slackened. In June 1778 a peace commission under the Earl of Carlisle arrived to lure the Americans away from their new ally, but the commission turned out to have no real power to negotiate and Congress sent Carlisle away. A new commander in chief, Sir Henry Clinton, replaced General Howe and shifted the British base from Philadelphia back to New York in early summer, giving rise to speculation that the redcoats intended to withdraw completely from the continent. When Washington sent Colonel James Wood of the 8th Virginia Regiment to press the assembly for more men in the fall, Wood reported that "the whole legislative body were highly pleased, with a thorough persuasion, that the war was at an end" and would do little.[47] As a gesture to the nation's commander, the assembly did authorize an additional six months' pay for veterans who reenlisted, but the legislators also began to make postwar plans. Inasmuch as it had been generally expected all along that the war would eventually have to be paid for with western lands, the delegates set aside territory on the far-distant Green River in Kentucky for bounties "which have been or may be assigned" to volunteers.[48] In the meantime, Washington was forced to reduce the Virginia line from fifteen to eleven regiments since "some of them were not larger than a Company or two."[49]

Wood's mission was prophetic, for he bore a message from Washington conveying his commander's renewed sense of alarm. Because the British had not left New York by the onset of the winter, the general warned, they were obviously not giving up the war. Once General Clinton had time to plan, the royal army would resume the offensive. But distracted by apparent victory, few Virginians listened.

CHAPTER 8

Perfecting the Republic

POLITICS in Virginia went on during the war much as they had in colonial times. The House of Delegates that convened in Williamsburg in October 1776 was the spring Convention under a new name. The constitution provided for its return to ease the transition between regimes. Elections that fall were held only for the Senate. But in these early days of the war there was a new spirit, an excitement and ebullience that quickened pulses, for independence presented opportunities that British rule had barred before. Debates over the formation of an army foreshadowed chances for military advancement, perhaps even for fame and glory, for those who enlisted, and the search for supplies forecast expanded trade and profits for those who wished to pursue them. Land speculators who once had to cope with the idiosyncrasies of imperial administrators looked to more sympathetic hearings nearer home. Religious dissenters prayed for greater freedom of worship, and other reformers hoped to attain their goals at last. Thomas Jefferson in particular, having failed to achieve his constitutional ideas by letter in the spring, was eager to remedy the defects he saw in the fledgling republic. Declining a congressional appointment to serve with Benjamin Franklin and Silas Deane of Connecticut as ambassador to France, he accepted the offer of his old friend, George Wythe, who had been reelected for another term in Philadelphia, to stay in Wythe's home in Williamsburg during the upcoming session of the General Assembly.[1]

A change of a few faces among the Convention delegates who re-convened in the fall greatly altered political alignments from the spring, illustrating again the lack of structure in the legislative politics of the day. Toward the end of the Convention in May, Richard Henry Lee had returned from Congress to put together a coalition with Patrick Henry to reduce the state's congressional delegation from seven members to five. By this stratagem they ignominiously excluded Lee's old antagonists, Benjamin Harrison of Berkeley and Carter Braxton, who were still in Philadelphia. Harrison had left himself open to attack by engineering the appointment of his son-in-law, William Rickman, as chief of the Continental medical service in the South over James McClurg, a local favorite. There was an odor of scandal around Harrison's son, Benjamin, Jr., who as Continental paymaster in Virginia and Robert Morris's agent was charging a 2 percent commission for transferring public funds from Philadelphia. After a "fiery trial," an investigating committee of the Convention that included Henry exonerated young Harrison when it discovered that his fee was small compared to the 12½ percent "sundry avaricious traders" discounted Virginia currency in the North.[2] As for Braxton, his public venture into constitutional theory smacked of toryism, a suspicion, according to William Fleming of Botetourt County, that was exacerbated by indiscreet remarks of his wife, the daughter of the loyalist receiver general, Richard Corbin. Now with Lee back in Philadelphia and Henry in the governor's chair, their opponents had the floor.

Indignantly rejecting an offer of a seat on the Council in order to defend himself in the House of Delegates, the elder Harrison won unanimous absolution with a "very Spirited Speech" at the opening of the fall session.[3] With only five dissenting votes, the combined chambers changed the Convention's stand and reelected him to Congress in place of Jefferson. Braxton, too, according to his own account, humbled Lee with his eloquence. Together with Jefferson, Braxton received a unanimous vote of thanks for his service in Philadelphia and emerged as one of the most influential members of the chamber.

In contrast to the Lee–Harrison–Braxton feud, Jefferson's campaign to new-model Virginia, although of far-reaching consequences for the future of republicanism, often had the air of a friendly contest among gentlemen. Before the assembly convened, he exchanged learned letters with Pendleton, of whose agility in devising legislative hamstrings for his plans Jefferson later boasted in awe, over whether to reestablish the free land tenure of early Anglo-Saxon England. Jef-

ferson favorably contrasted English land law before the Norman Conquest in 1066 with the system of his own day, which Jefferson traced
to the aristocratic feudalism of the later "Dark Ages." Pendleton's in-
stinctive reaction was that a new law would produce a maze of conflicting property rights unless it was retroactive, and the Speaker did
not bother to mention the arguments against that possibility. Had
men learned nothing since the days of the Anglo-Saxons, he inquired.[4]

To Pendleton and others such as Robert Carter Nicholas and Carter
Braxton it sufficed to substitute republican forms for the monarchy
without otherwise altering the political habits of Virginians. After all,
they had gone to war to protect a style of government with which
they were well satisfied. More extensive changes, Braxton wrote to his
uncle Landon Carter during the session, were "Chimerical Schemes."
Promising to elaborate later "under Cover of a Bottle of wine and a
good Pipe of Tobacco," he declared, "I own upon a familiar Acquaintance with many Men said to possess unbounded knowledge and upon
summing up the result of their Schemes and Ideas, I am of the Opinion that in general they injure more than they benefit Mankind and
that more Safety is to be found in the ways of the Man of sound
reason and good Judgment, than in the wild flights of these fanciful
Genius's."[5]

Jefferson, on the other hand, believed it necessary to go beyond
mere governmental reform to eradicate "every fibre . . . of antient or
future aristocracy" in order to lay "a foundation . . . truly republican."[6] He repeatedly introduced measures to eliminate the privileged
position of special interests—the first families, the church, the speculators—and to open up opportunities for ordinary citizens. Yet again
eighteenth-century rhetoric can be misleading, for Jefferson's goal was
not as thoroughly egalitarian as his language might imply today. Although he argued that small, independent farmers or "husbandmen"
were "the chosen people of God" and the only dependable republicans, they ought nonetheless to be ruled by their betters.[7] The essential question in Jefferson's mind was whether rulers would come from
the "aristocracy of virtue and talent, which nature has wisely provided
for the direction . . . of society" or from an "aristocracy of wealth,"
which could be "of more harm and danger, than benefit" to the
nation.[8]

Jefferson quickly guided through the first assembly the repeal of
one vestige of medieval England, the entailing of estates, and laid the

groundwork for the demise of another, primogeniture, a decade later. Pendleton endeavored to make the reform of entail voluntary by inserting a subtle change in language, but Jefferson caught the trick in time. Few bemoaned the passing of these archaic institutions. Freezing lands and slaves within a family proved so troublesome when fields became exhausted that for years a steadily increasing procession of private bills docking tails had filed through the legislature, and the guarantee of the bulk of an estate to the eldest male heir applied only if a landholder died intestate, as few wealthy men did. The reforms thus had little practical social effect. The real impact lay in the elimination of a code that, however often breached, extolled the ideal of a landed aristocracy. Jefferson preferred the small family farm as a model, especially for the empire opening to the West.[9]

The problem of the western lands afforded Jefferson an excellent opportunity in the first session of the legislature to implement his ideals. The issue was urgent, for if Virginia did not exercise authority and meet its responsibilities in the area, the state risked losing its vast claims beyond the Appalachian Mountains to other contenders. About a thousand settlers had already followed Daniel Boone through the Cumberland Gap into Kentucky where they lived virtually without government in the westernmost reaches of what was technically Fincastle County, a region almost as big as the rest of Virginia together. A comparable number had gone with John Sevier into Tennessee. Many westerners allied with the North Carolina speculator Richard Henderson, who was importuning Congress to recognize the lands between the Cumberland and Kentucky rivers as a new state named Transylvania. Dissatisfaction with Henderson's sales policies, however, prompted settlers at Harrodsburg to petition the Virginia Convention in June 1776 to organize Kentucky as a separate county and accept George Rogers Clark and John Gabriel Jones as their delegates. Arriving in Williamsburg in the summer after the Convention had adjourned, Clark first asked for five hundred pounds of gunpowder for defense against Indians in the Ohio Valley whom the British at Detroit were inciting to war. When the Council hesitated for fear it did not have the constitutional right to grant his request, Clark pointedly observed "that if a Cuntrey was not worth protecting it was not worth Claiming," and they quickly found the authority.[10]

Another threat to Virginia's claims came from Philadelphia where speculators who had been lobbying in London to find ways around the

Proclamation of 1763 shifted their attention as soon as independence was declared. The interests associated with the Wharton brothers, Samuel and Thomas, whose mantle had fallen to Robert Morris and whose efforts to establish the colony of Vandalia Benjamin Franklin had long espoused in Great Britain, now rallied around the Indiana Company to preserve their claims (despite the company's name) in present-day West Virginia. Another Pennsylvania group led by the Gratz family formed the Illinois and Wabash companies to assert rights to lands beyond the Ohio River in modern Illinois and Indiana.[11]

The dispute had national constitutional ramifications. The colonial charters of six states, including Pennsylvania, specified definite western boundaries while the charters of seven, including Virginia, allowed them to extend their claims to the Mississippi River. Only if the landless states could secure title to the West for Congress would they share in that rich domain. After independence John Dickinson, who represented the landless state of Delaware, drafted articles of confederation for Congress. His proposal awarded the West to the Continental government, but the other states with western claims—Massachusetts, Connecticut, New York, North and South Carolina, and Georgia—joined Virginia in striking the provision from the final document. For four years the landless state of Maryland refused to ratify the amended articles unless Congress regained jurisdiction over the West on the grounds that the Continental government needed the revenue from land sales to pay for the war. Marylanders also pointed out that, since Virginia's claim—the most extensive of all—stretched to the Mississippi on the west and the Great Lakes on the north, to recognize it would allow one state to dominate the continent and threaten the union. Many contemporaries doubted Maryland's altruism, however, for, if Virginia sustained its claims, Maryland speculators, among whom was the governor, Thomas Johnson, an associate of the Illinois–Wabash group, lost theirs.[12] The Virginia Convention, at Jefferson's suggestion, had included an article in the state's constitution voiding any claim on the frontier derived from Indian purchases (such as those depended upon by all out-of-state claimants) unless Virginia gave its sanction.

In the fall of 1776 the House of Delegates refused to seat Clark and Jones because, coming from Kentucky, they did not represent a county as the constitution required, but the legislature immediately resolved that a new county ought to be formed. In general, there was little resistance in the fall session to petitions for the creation of new counties.

The District of West Augusta also asked to be elevated to county status, and Cumberland and Pittsylvania counties each requested to be divided in two. The differences between the handling of the four cases is instructive. The house referred the Cumberland and Pittsylvania petitions in routine fashion to the Committee on Propositions and Grievances, from which Carter Braxton reported bills in the usual form that had little difficulty securing passage. The West Augusta petition involved larger political considerations because boundary negotiations with Pennsylvania had stalled. Like the Harrodsburg request, West Augusta's case went before the committee of the whole house sitting as the Committee on the State of the Country. Robert Carter Nicholas shortly reported a bill dividing West Augusta into three counties, Ohio, Monongalia, and Yohogania, the last almost entirely in modern Pennsylvania. Nicholas coupled the bill with a stern resolution condemning any attempt to set up independent governments within Virginia's borders. Both bill and resolution quickly passed the two chambers.[13]

The fortunes of the petition to divide Fincastle were much more complex. The issue precipitated the most intricate parliamentary maneuvering of the fall 1776 session. Although many details of the battle are lost in the secrecy of executive committee meetings, what is known is rewarding to follow because it affords a classic illustration of how personalities dominated assembly politics in that day.

Carter Braxton reported the initial bill from a subcommittee of the Committee on the State of the Country organizing western Fincastle beyond the Cumberland Gap as Kentucky County. To this bill Richard Henderson, in town to look after his interests, offered no objection since in an address to the assembly he had already renounced any idea of secession and acknowledged Virginia's sovereignty. His goal was to protect the Transylvania Company's title to the land.[14]

Jefferson challenged Braxton's bill by corralling sufficient votes to recommit it for amendment to another subcommittee chaired by himself. Jefferson offered four changes: two were perfecting amendments, and a third tapped patriotic sentiment by altering the name of the old county, now reduced to the area east of the Cumberland Gap, from Fincastle, the title of Lord Dunmore's eldest son, to Washington. The last amendment was fundamental. It allowed inhabitants to vote if they possessed the usual property qualifications "altho' no legal title in the land shall have been conveyed to such possessor."[15] This provision also appeared in the West Augusta bill, where it occasioned no problem. In fact, when the house passed the West Augusta bill and sent it to the Senate, the upper chamber added the words "and enjoy all other privileges of freeholders," which the House of Delegates readily accepted.[16]

Jefferson's wording actually continued a privilege the Convention had extended to both Fincastle and West Augusta in August 1775 pending settlement of the confused land titles there. The result was to give preemptive title to squatters, thus encouraging settlement of the area before the speculators' claims could be confirmed. Braxton's attempt to delete the privilege from the original draft of the Kentucky bill squared exactly with Henderson's policy of yielding political control to Virginia but retaining title to the land for his company. As for Braxton's motives, in his recent pamphlet he had insisted that Virginia keep its western lands for "payment of the vast burden of taxes we shall incur by this war."[17] With this point secured through Henderson's acknowledgment of Virginia's rule, Braxton presumably saw no need to eliminate the speculators themselves.

Jefferson guided the amended bill to the stage of actually being engrossed for final passage. Then, on the eve of victory, he unwisely left Williamsburg for a long weekend and allowed Braxton to regain the initiative. As a sign of the nearly even balance between the contending factions, the house permitted Braxton to continue consideration of a duplicate bill in the Committee on Propositions and Grievances. At Jefferson's departure Braxton succeeded in postponing final consideration of his rival's amendments in favor of his own second unaltered bill.

The pendulum swung back when Jefferson returned and shortly afterward Braxton left town for a week. Jefferson then gained control of his opponent's committee. The struggle at that point went behind closed doors for a month until Braxton had to leave again. Jefferson moved quickly. He transferred all of his amendments to Braxton's duplicate bill, added a proviso for another county, Montgomery, to create a parallel to the three in the West Augusta bill, and obtained final approval of the house. Once again thinking his work done, Jefferson obtained permission from the house to go home for the remainder of the session. Five days later he was back. The Senate insisted on three amendments of which the house would accept only one. What the changes were is not certain. At some point in the proceedings, perhaps here, Jefferson had to abandon a condemnation of Henderson by name and a prohibition against private surveys in the West. Whatever produced the stalemate with the Senate, with Jefferson present the upper chamber finally yielded.[18]

When Jefferson came back the second time to the assembly, he found another cherished project in trouble, the disestablishment of the Anglican church. The religious disturbances of the previous decade and the encouragement of the Declaration of Rights ensured that the first legislature would face the issue. Petitions from dissenting groups, mostly in counties outside the Tidewater, whose disproportionate representation among the delegates proved decisive, flooded the session. "Although the majority of our citizens were dissenters," Jefferson declared with some exaggeration, "a majority of the legislature were churchmen." He recalled "the severest contests in which I have ever been engaged." Again committee room doors conceal much of the drama.[19]

Early in the session Jefferson wrote down as his objectives the disestablishment of the Anglican church, the repeal of the taxes levied to support the church, and the reversion of the glebe lands to the state at the death or resignation of incumbent ministers. Because the church had used the power of taxation to purchase the glebes, dissenters considered them public property. After a month of deliberation a special Committee on Religion chaired by Carter Braxton became so ensnarled in controversy that the Committee on the State of the Country superseded it on November 9 before the Braxton committee filed a report. Ten days later—during one of Braxton's absences—the house approved compromise resolutions calling for the repeal of legislation punishing heresy and blasphemy or requiring church attendance, as Jefferson proposed, but instead of forthrightly endorsing disestablishment as the delegate from Albemarle wished, merely recommending the exemption of dissenters from the obligation to support the church. Despite Baptist objections, the compromise sanctioned continued licensing of clergy, a guarantee of present salaries to incumbent clergy, and confirmation of the glebe lands to the church. The house directed a committee on which Jefferson and Madison as well as Braxton and Robert Carter Nicholas sat to bring in a bill accordingly.

The committee reported on November 30, the day after Jefferson first departed. In a well-coordinated maneuver the committee prevailed on the house to adopt another set of resolutions rescinding virtually all of its earlier instructions, allowing the committee to submit a bill it had already drafted that contained little more than the exemption for dissenters. On the floor—perhaps after Jefferson's return—George Mason, who joined the session late himself, succeeded in reinstating a clause repealing all acts of religious conformity except the one that established the church in Virginia, thus rescuing much of what the reformers had hoped to obtain from the November 19 resolutions.[20] The assembly adopted the amended bill.

It is clear from both the November 19 resolutions and the committee's bill that the economic effects of disestablishment weighed heavily in determining the response of church supporters to the issue. As long as the financial responsibility of the church continued as in the colonial period, the more dissenters who gained exemption from the tithe, the greater the assessment each remaining church member might have to pay. Not only would the loss of the glebes seriously curtail the church's ability to meet contractual obligations already incurred to ministers and others. The church, in addition, had responsibility under colonial law for the care of the poor, and the assembly did not create a substitute system of public poor commissioners until 1785. The compromise that the November 19 resolutions attempted left the glebes to the church and allowed vestries to continue taxing dissenters as well as church members for clerical salaries already negotiated. The committee bill went farther, allowing vestries to continue imposing such levies for the care of the poor "as they have hitherto by Law been accustomed to make."[21] Moreover, the committee referred favorably to instituting a general assessment for all Christian religions although it refrained from submitting legislation for the purpose until public opinion could be sounded. Finally, the committee legislated specifically that levies on church members should never be greater than if dissenters had not received exemptions. Ironically, this guarantee did not satisfy Nicholas, and he became the person who effectively achieved Jefferson's end by offering an amendment to ensure absolutely that no churchman's taxes would increase. Nicholas moved suspension of assessments on all persons for a year until the general levy could be enacted, thus temporarily rendering church support entirely voluntary. The legislature extended the suspension in each of the succeeding two years.

Although in 1777 Jefferson drafted a bill for religious freedom that would have disestablished the church once and for all, he did not find the moment propitious to seek its passage until June 1779. Originally Jefferson had supported the dissenters' view that glebes should revert to the state at the end of the incumbent minister's term, but to gain whatever moderate Anglican backing he could, in his draft bill he accepted the compromise allocating to the church "in all times to come" the lands it held at the time of independence.[22] When the delegates once more postponed consideration, someone, most likely Jefferson, had the bill printed privately and distributed through the state during the summer, presumably to rally support and reintroduce it in the fall. However the test of public opinion turned out, the bill was not resubmitted.

Instead, the house in the fall of 1779 took up a bill for a general assessment for all Christian sects, an idea that won away a number of dissenters who had originally favored the bill for religious freedom. Although the general assessment bill survived a preliminary decision by three votes, the house ultimately defeated it.[23]

Taking advantage of the momentum of this victory, George Mason put forth two bills again extending the compromise on the glebes that Jefferson had sanctioned but asking for less in return. Rather than total disestablishment, Mason's first bill merely made permanent the suspension of public support for the Anglican church that the assembly had been enacting year to year since Nicholas's motion in 1776. The second bill reiterated Jefferson's proposal to guarantee glebes to the church. The first bill passed, the second did not. The delegates clearly were not ready to go beyond the arrangement that had been in effect since independence.

Mason's phraseology in these bills affords added insight into his thinking on the religious question. The preamble to the first bill illustrates the extent to which, from an Anglican point of view, the obstacles to total disestablishment were economic. A loyal and active churchman, Mason explained that the bill would jolt his coreligionists into devising "proper Measures, among themselves" to provide for their church.[24] Perhaps because critics asked why the state should concern itself about church members in this fashion, the assembly deleted the preamble from the final text. Mason's second bill added to Jefferson's proposal regarding the glebes a section enabling individual vestries to remove ministers who were "disaffected to the Commonwealth, of immoral Characters, or inattentive to the Duties of their Function" during the period before the church could be reorganized. Mason did not explain why special procedures other than those available to everyone through the courts were justified.[25] The author of the Virginia Declaration of Rights insisted less on a total separation of church and state in his definition of religious liberty than his friend from Monticello in his. The legislature in the end did not adopt Jefferson's famous bill until 1786.

To round out the new government in 1776, Jefferson also wanted an independent judiciary, the complete construction of which—like his religious reforms—took several years. The Convention had already incorporated the basic outline of his plan for the courts into the constitution, but had not implemented the provisions. The need to hold criminal trials soon pressed for further action. The old General Court had held criminal sessions until October 1775, but thereafter the Convention and the Committee of Safety confined themselves to appeals from county commissions involving loyalists. Some citizens also complained that closing the courts forestalled debt collection by Virginia creditors as well as British. The counterargument—which undoubtedly some advanced with ulterior motives—remained nonetheless true: to reopen the courts for Virginians meant that British, too, might sue, and, after all, it was the British navy that was choking off trade, the only effective method of repaying foreign debts. So strong was the concern over the British instituting litigation that, when Jefferson hastened back to the assembly to salvage his many projects, he was forced to introduce a bill that suspended executions for debt until trade became normal. Virginians could thus enjoy the advantages of reopening the courts without fear of ruin, his preamble explained. Most delegates remained skeptical and postponed consideration of the bills for establishing a General Court, a High Court of Chancery, and a Court of Appeals.[26]

The only judiciary bill that the assembly accepted during the fall 1776 session was one placing the Convention's Court of Admiralty, which had been functioning for almost a year, on a formal footing. Two of the three judges then sitting, William Holt and Bernard Moore, continued on the bench. Richard Cary became the new member. The same reason that motivated the Convention to revive the admiralty court while keeping the other courts in abeyance—the number of maritime captures to be condemned—sped the bill through both houses in just twelve days. As for criminal trials, the assembly decided to forego for a while longer the luxury of the separation of powers that the constitution prescribed and instead appointed the five senior members of the Council as commissioners of oyer and terminer to clear the jails periodically.

On the county level, the new government followed the Convention's precedent of causing as little disruption as possible. The governor and Council had been reconfirming commissions of incumbent justices and sheriffs whenever feasible, and the assembly told county courts that still had vacancies to nominate candidates immediately. The assembly also ordered those courts that had not been doing so right along to commence registering deeds again. Even where there had been a hiatus in registrations, the legislature decreed that all deeds drawn since 1774, if properly witnessed and if recorded within the next eight months, should "be as effectual . . . as if such deeds had been recorded within the times respectively prescribed by law."[27]

Independence also allowed the rebel government for the first time to deal forthrightly with treason and subversion. The assembly defined the first as the bearing of arms against the new republic or giving "aid and comfort" to its enemies. The assembly carefully included in its decree, however, a provision adopted in England after the Glorious Revolution requiring two witnesses or a voluntary confession for conviction. For the first time, too, any "word" as well as "open deed, or act" in behalf of the king became a crime punishable by a fine of up to twenty thousand pounds and five years' imprisonment.[28] A joint resolution of the house and Senate accused merchants in particular of "seducing and corrupting the minds of the people . . . and giving intelligence to the enemy," and invoked the Statute Staple of Edward III to give loyalist traders forty days after January 1, 1777, to leave the commonwealth if they would not switch their allegiance.[29] Originally passed in 1353 to induce foreigners to trade in England, the Statute Staple guaranteed aliens adequate notice should war break out with their sovereigns. Now it was applied to force loyal Britishers to leave Virginia. The following spring the assembly similarly gave all free males over sixteen until October 10, 1777, to swear allegiance to the state. Although only merchants had to depart, other recusants were to be disarmed (yet they still had to attend militia drills) and their names published. They could not hold office, serve on juries, sue in court, or buy land—crippling restrictions in a plantation economy.

Under these pressures the number of departures announced in the *Virginia Gazette* remained high through the first half of 1777. The authorities apparently were firm but understanding in enforcing the expulsions. A number of merchants, for example, purchased the *Albion*, which was under construction at South Quay on the Blackwater River, to take them home to Britain. They received several extensions when the work took longer than expected. Then a British cruiser captured the ship on its way from South Quay through Albemarle Sound and up the coast to the James River, but Henry and the assembly arranged with the British captain to let the vessel complete its mission. The *Albion* finally sailed for Great Britain on June 15, 1777. Despite the stricter measures that the assembly adopted after independence, the Virginians' attitude toward loyalists remained relatively tolerant. The people who were ousted, Benjamin Harrison explained, were not "looked on as banished" but as casualties of war, and, except for a few who "committed

. . . depradations" will, "I have no doubt . . . be suffered to return" when
the danger ceased.[30]

Politics during the second and third years of Virginia's independence
followed the pattern of the first. In the spring of 1777 Benjamin Harrison nearly turned the tables on Richard Henry Lee by revealing that
Lee had forced his tenants to pay their rents in tobacco or specie rather
than paper currency in order to avoid a loss through depreciation. Harrison charged that Lee thereby contributed to public distrust of Virginia
currency, which was declining in value rapidly enough as it was. The
accusation was all the more damning because of Lee's incessant denunciation in both Congress and Virginia of lagging patriotism in others.
Once again those who had the floor prevailed, and Lee failed of reelection to Congress. John Banister, although he allowed that he was
"not very fond of that gentleman," protested that Lee had not been
given a hearing, and a stinging letter from Francis Lightfoot Lee and
Mann Page, Jr., demanded permission to resign from Congress since a
man's reputation might be blackened if he remained away.[31]

Racing back from Philadelphia to defend himself, Lee had his chance
to cast a spell. Whatever one thought of the delegates' "consistency and
uniformity of opinion" in heeding Lee's excuses, Banister remarked,
"no defense was ever made with more graceful eloquence, more manly
firmness, equalness of temper, serenity, calmness and judgment, than
this very accomplished speaker displayed on this occasion."[32] Relying on
eloquence more than logic, Lee admitted that he had altered the leases
for fear of inflation, but argued that at the time very little paper money
had been issued to depreciate. Besides, he charged, his enemies only
wanted him out of Philadelphia so they could get on with their schemes
to rob the public. The legislature immediately voted him back to Congress, this time in place of Mason, who again declined to serve because
of illness, and subsequent attempts to revive the question of the rents
died on the floor.

Lee's case was not the only time that session when the legislature did
not evince "consistency." When Edmund Pendleton had to step down as
Speaker at the beginning of the term because of an injury, the delegates
replaced one of the most persistent opponents of Jefferson's reforms
with one of Jefferson's staunchest allies, George Wythe. Nonetheless,
Wythe "declared from the Chair that he considered his appointment as
Vicarious only" and promised to retire in favor of Pendleton as soon as
the latter recovered.[33] So, too, after eliminating Mann Page, Jr., from

the congressional delegation in the same vote that dropped Lee—probably because Page had befriended Lee—the delegates decided to reinstate him in place of Lee's accuser, Benjamin Harrison, who had resigned. When Page in turn declined, to Pendleton's delight the assembly substituted another of Lee's critics, John Banister, whom the former Speaker had been trying to have elected for some time.

The squabble between Harrison and Lee in Virginia took on national and international implications as a backdrop to the Silas Deane affair, a complex, cloak-and-dagger imbroglio that revolved around the military aid France surreptitiously extended to the colonies before declaring open war against its archenemy Great Britain. When a French agent, the playwright Caron de Beaumarchais, author of *The Marriage of Figaro* and *The Barber of Seville*, contacted Arthur Lee in London early in 1776, Lee reported to Congress that the French intended to extend outright gifts of munitions to the colonists. Beaumarchais, however, acted as if the bogus company set up to handle the aid and protect French neutrality was truly private—it had some private investors, it should be noted—and demanded that Congress pay. When Silas Deane, the new ambassador to Paris, agreed—whether because he felt that the colonies could not afford to argue with Beaumarchais or because he himself was conniving with the Frenchman has never been satisfactorily determined—Lee was outraged and charged Deane with duplicity.[34]

The quarrel quickly ballooned to include most of the American merchant community trading overseas, for Robert Morris, the commercial baron of Philadelphia, supported Deane. Both sides gave their opponents ample ammunition. Morris and Deane kept up their connections in England for speculative purposes, secretaries of both Deane and Arthur Lee turned out to be British spies, and another of Lee's was charged with counterfeiting and toryism. Ships and cargoes mysteriously shuttled back and forth between public and private accounts, allegedly to confuse the enemy, but likely congressional auditors as well. Nor did the Lees appear as innocent as Caesar's wife, for their candidate to succeed Deane as the American commercial representative in Paris was brother William, who transferred his business from London to Nantes when the war broke out. The anti-Morris faction in Congress ultimately forced Deane's recall, but Continental politics were left in a maelstrom. Although the major storms occurred in Philadelphia, waves rolled to and from Virginia, where Carter Braxton emerged as the chief defender of the Morris entourage. On his return from France, Arthur Lee immediately went to press and traced the antecedents of the local political division over the issue of Deane all the way back to the Robinson affair.[35]

By the fall of 1777 the state's worsening financial situation distracted legislators from reform. Until then, Virginia had managed by issuing paper currency, £946,492 in all, considerably more than its revenue for the period, £91,246. Such deficits were acceptable as long as Virginians could hope that the war would not be long and peace would come before the inflation became too great. But with that probability receding, Washington, Lee, Pendleton, and others began to correspond about where additional revenue might be found, and as in the case of so many other wartime needs, the delegates tended to look to the team of Mason and Jefferson for the answer.[36] The two embodied their solution in two bills. The authorship of the first, a bill fundamentally altering Virginia's tax structure, is uncertain, although Mason had sketched out the basic outline in conversations earlier. The second, a proposal to sell western lands for revenue, was unquestionably the work of Mason in tandem with Jefferson.

The effort to change the tax structure proved highly controversial. Previously Virginia had levied only custom duties, real estate and excise taxes, and a poll tax on "tithables," that is, on all free males and slaves of either sex above sixteen years of age. Although the levy on land and slaves constituted a tax on wealth, contemporaries generally took strong exception to the idea of citizens sharing public expenses "in proportion to their property," as Jefferson testified the sponsors intended. Only after two months and "much Altercation and long debate," Edmund Pendleton recounted, did the assembly agree to augment the old levies with a tax of ½ of 1 percent on the value of personal property, including slaves, along with a miscellany of new fees. Such an assessment "being disgusting where it has been tried," Pendleton explained, the legislature took "much care to make it as Palatable as possible, by confining it to the Capital Articles of Property so as to prevent Rumaging of Houses." The tax on tithables continued but only on free males over twenty-one since the new system taxed slaves ad valorem as property. Other features included a 10 percent tax on interest and annuities, 5 percent on cash on hand over £5 a person, and ½ of 1 percent on "all salaries, and . . . the neat income of all offices of profit" other than military.[37] Confident that the state would be solvent at last, the legislators authorized the issuance of another $1,700,000 in paper currency in the final paragraph of the act.

The state had difficulty enforcing the new taxes from the beginning. Assessors could not agree whether the values of items should be in terms of sterling or the state's depreciated currency, or whether to consider as market prices those obtainable at normal or forced sales. Not only did the people become "much dissatisfied" with the wide variations in individual tax bills, the legislature stated the next year, but the levy did not bring in sufficient revenue. Consequently, the assembly raised the rate on personal property to 1½ percent in 1778 and required assessors in each county to "consult together and form some general mode which they shall pursue in Rating the several articles of Taxation."[38] Jefferson proposed a more sophisticated method of determining average values, but the legislators probably thought that it was too complicated.

To Mason, however, the most promising source of revenue was the state's western lands, which ultimately did prove to be Virginia's salvation from its war debt. He and Jefferson introduced a bill to open a land office, the details of which suggest that they also saw one more opportunity to ensure equal access to the new lands for the individual pioneer along with the inevitable speculator. In the process, too, Mason hoped to settle the claims of the Ohio Company, for which he had been treasurer and principal lobbyist for a quarter-century. The bill provided for opening a land office under a "register" whom the legislature would elect annually by joint ballot, established procedures for soldiers to claim their bounties in the West, and set up out of the revenue from land sales a "sinking fund, in aid of Annual Taxes, to discharge the Public Debt." The proposed legislation also continued the colonial headright system by which whoever paid the fare of an immigrant other than a slave across the ocean could obtain title to fifty acres, offered seventy-five acres "to encourage Marriage and Population" to each native citizen who resided at least one year in Virginia after marrying, prescribed a simple method for the sale of lands at the county level that favored small purchasers, and in a magnanimous gesture offered states with insufficient land reserves the opportunity to pay off Continental bounties within Virginia at ten dollars a hundred acres.[39]

The legislative journal tells only the briefest story of the bill's fate. After Mason first secured adoption of a general resolution sanctioning the creation of a land office and the idea of using western lands to retire the public debt, he was able to move the bill through several stages on the house floor until it suddenly stalled and the legislature tabled it.[40]

The legislators also blocked a second bill, which Mason most likely wrote and which had Jefferson's sanction. It would have established guidelines for the settlement of conflicting land titles in the West by guaranteeing claims obtained under traditional procedures such as headrights, treasury rights, and military bounties, while seeking, as Jefferson later explained, "to remove out of the way the great and numerous orders of council to the Ohio co. Loyal co. Misissipi co. Vandalia co. Indiana co. &c." unless those companies had already surveyed their grants.[41] Under this last exception Mason hoped to salvage the claims of the Ohio Company, which had surveyed two hundred thousand of its five hundred thousand-acre grant. The question was whether the company's surveyors had acted legally since, while holding licenses from the College of William and Mary as the law required, they had neglected to obtain approval of local authorities. The legislature eventually said no.

Mason's second bill further granted preemption rights for up to two thousand acres to settlers who had not been able to follow normal procedures for filing claims because of the war and required land companies to sell at the price that they had been advertising when the settlers moved onto their land even though buyers had not been able to conclude the sale before prices rose. Most surprising because the expedient violated the right of jury trial to which Mason and Jefferson were supposedly committed was a provision to appoint a four-man commission whose "Judgement, when rendered, shall be final" to resolve disputes.[42] But all Mason could manage out of these proposals was a standoff resolution on the very last day of the session in January 1778 reaffirming the wisdom of selling western lands to pay the public debt, freezing all claims until a land office could be opened, and calling on the speculating companies to present their cases at the next session of the General Assembly.

The reason for the failure of these bills can only be surmised. Representatives of the Transylvania and Indiana companies attended the session, for Richard Henderson succeeded in reviving, if not his company's original pretensions, at least a claim for compensation, and agents of the Indiana Company presented a petition. Possibly, too, Mason appeared less than altruistic since his bills protected headrights in which he was speculating heavily as well as provided a loophole for the claims of the Ohio Company.

The assembly passed as a separate act a year later the section of the land office bill by which Mason and Jefferson sought to end the stalemate over ratifying the Articles of Confederation. Virginia offered to set aside land from its holdings to help landless states pay their military bounties, but the state's generosity was to no avail. Maryland's adamant refusal to ratify the articles unless the Continent received title to the West left Congress without a constitutional basis for most of the war.[43]

In the fall of 1777 the assembly decided to include the loyalists in the effort to bolster the state's faltering finances. In November Congress had recommended outright confiscation of tory property, but Jefferson turned aside the suggestion with the argument that, unless the British began to seize American property within their control, Virginia ought to abide by international law and not confiscate theirs. So many influential Virginians had valuable holdings in the mother country that few were yet ready to endorse confiscation of tory property except in the case of persons convicted of bearing arms against the state. Jefferson argued, however, that the state ought not to "strengthen the hands of our enemies during the continuance of the present war, by remitting to them the profits or proceeds of such estates or the interest or principal of . . . debts."[44] He accordingly proposed that the state sequester loyalists' estates and invest the income after expenses in Continental loan office certificates. Title to both estates and certificates remained with the owners, who could recover them at the assembly's discretion after the war. In the interim Congress had the use of the funds. Debtors could also satisfy sterling debts by using paper money to buy loan certificates in their creditors' names in the amount owed.

Jefferson hoped to achieve several goals at once. His Sequestration Act maintained a vestige of legitimacy while recognizing the political fact that Virginians did not want the British and their loyalist allies to gain economically during the war. Jefferson also sought to retire the state's currency and offset continuing depreciation by capitalizing on the desire of debtors to escape their obligations as cheaply as possible. Amazingly, few Virginians took advantage of the opportunity. Although an estimated 35,000 were indebted to the British, only 307 individuals and companies, including Jefferson himself, whose payment of £2,666 in currency constituted one of the largest, paid a total of £272,544 in paper worth £12,035 in sterling into the Loan Office before the act was repealed in 1780. Despite the evidence of the ledgers, Jefferson and Edmund Randolph both thought at the time that "great sums of money were paid in by debtors."[45] Why so few took advantage of the act is unclear. Perhaps many felt that they would not have to pay in any case. In fact, a major reason for ever honoring the debts was to protect American credit ratings if trade with Great Britain resumed after the war. Anyone with that objective in mind may have concluded that the British most likely would not recognize such payments, as indeed in the peace negotiations they did not.

The Sequestration Act finally quieted the fear in the assembly that reopening the courts would aid the collection of British debts. But another problem, the result of an unusual alliance between Pendleton and Jefferson, lay in wait. As submitted, the bill for a General Court contained a section written by Pendleton that revived the long-standing argument over interjecting assize, or circuit, courts between the county courts and the highest bench. In addition to presiding over twice-yearly sessions of the General Court in Williamsburg, its judges would ride individual circuits around the state to hear cases that otherwise would have to come to the capital. Unless a party to a case appealed from the circuit to the General Court, participants would avoid a long journey that for some, especially in the West, amounted virtually to denial of justice.

The seeming liberality of the plan notwithstanding, a coalition of "County court clerks and attorneys, magistrates and Debtors," as one advocate of circuit courts identified them, rose to quash it.[46] Although Jefferson had decided not to include the prewar requirement that lawyers choose between practice in the General Court or in county courts, the bill would extend the influence of the professional elite in the capital throughout the state. The issue became one of the few during the war to require roll call votes and reveals yet another cleavage in Virginia politics that crisscrossed the others. Madison and Mason sided with Jefferson as might have been expected, but so did Pendleton, Braxton, Benjamin Harrison of Brandon, Charles Carter of Stafford, and William Fitzhugh. Opposed were Patrick Henry and the planter-merchant Meriwether Smith, who did not normally ally himself with Henry. Robert Carter Nicholas, Benjamin Harrison of Berkeley, and Charles Henry Harrison also opposed the bill. Jefferson and Pendleton won in two house votes on the bill by narrow margins of six and two, and Pendleton honestly admitted that his plan for assize courts survived only because they were interlocked with the General Court. The Senate, however, struck them from the bill by a majority of one. For a while, the bill's sponsors in the house considered postponing establishment of the General Court unless they could restore the assize courts, but eventually decided that the need to reopen the higher court took precedence.

Shortly afterward, Jefferson changed his mind about distinguishing between practice in the General Court and in the counties. Only in the former, he explained, did "men of science" in the law practice. If the legislature allowed county lawyers to do business before the General Court, clients would retain the attorneys they used in the lower courts when they appealed their cases to the capital. The better trained lawyers specializing in General Court practice would not have enough cases to earn a living unless the assembly restored their prewar monopoly before the superior tribunal. Without such regulation, Jefferson concluded, "insects" from the counties would have all.[47] His change of heart did not survive a second reading, however. Madison brought the matter up again in the mid-eighties and momentarily succeeded in pushing the act through, only to have the legislature almost immediately repeal it. County establishments in Virginia were not easily dislodged.

The legislature readily approved Jefferson's bill for a separate three-judge High Court of Chancery during the 1777 session. Jefferson claimed later that he had to fend off Pendleton's attempt to make voluntary the bill's innovative provision for jury trials in matters of fact, which chancery procedure had not permitted before. Had Pendleton prevailed, Jefferson pointed out, the practical effect would have been to block the use of juries since to request one amounted to telling the judge that the petitioner did not trust him. In the same session, the legislature again postponed Jefferson's bill for a Court of Appeals to take over the former appellate functions of the king's Privy Council, perhaps because the delegates concluded no appeals would materialize for a while.[48]

The year 1778 was the time of "languor" of which Benjamin Harrison complained. Because rumors of peace and a return to normality had captured people's attention after the battle of Saratoga, Mason and Jefferson marked time in their campaign for major reform. Mason did not attend the assembly at all in the spring, although he had promised fellow members of the Ohio Company that he would pursue their claims for western land. His absence left the legislators at a loss after the intensity of their activity the previous year. John Augustine Washington early predicted that "it will be a short session, unless Col. Mason, who is not yet got down, should carve out more business for them than they have yet thought of." Perhaps because sparse attendance favored the nearby Tidewater, Benjamin Harrison "greatly outvoted" Jefferson for the speakership of the lower house.[49] Richard Henry Lee also suffered a setback. As a result of continuing controversy over whether congressional delegates should serve even three years in a row as the law permitted, Lee had been reelected in January only for the period May through August 1778, which would have completed his second year. In

May Lee won another full one-year term to begin in August but fell in the balloting to next to the last place. Henry took the ranking as an affront and told Lee that it sprang from "that rancorous Malice that has so long followed you."[50]

In the spring 1778 session Virginia became one of the first governments in the modern world to abolish the slave trade. The bill, which in all likelihood Jefferson composed although the evidence is not conclusive, had been before the assembly since the spring of 1777 and had suffered considerable modification in the interim. Amendments eliminated an implication in the original wording that the legislature intended some day to restrict slavery even more, as well as a provision permitting manumission. As adopted, the statute simply declared that all slaves thereafter imported into the state would become free, but carefully excluded from the act's provision slaves brought in by owners merely passing through with their slaves or by newcomers planning to settle permanently in Virginia. The bill also excluded slaves Virginians inherited or obtained from outside the state by marriage. Only the commercial slave trade was forbidden, but for a time of "languor" that was an accomplishment.[51]

Quorums as usual formed slowly in the fall of 1778. Again the assembly did not really settle down to business until Mason appeared more than six weeks after the date appointed for the session to commence. Jefferson arrived even later. The body's work that session consisted largely of wrapping up matters that had been debated for some time. Besides strengthening the embargo, the representatives accepted Mason's proposal to follow the recommendation of Congress and ban distillation of grain as a conservation measure. They also extended the prohibitions he had proposed against speculation in imported clothing needed by the army. At long last, too, they completed the task of reopening the courts by accepting Jefferson's plan for a Court of Appeals composed of judges of the admiralty, chancery, and General courts sitting in review of each other's decisions. In the name of restoring prewar conditions as soon as possible, the assembly reestablished the colonial system of public inspection of tobacco for export at public warehouses along the major waterways.[52]

The debate over final settlement of the Transylvania Company's claims to Virginia's western lands dominated the fall 1778 legislative meeting. "A great part of the present session has been taken up in considering the grants made by the Cherokees to Henderson and Company," Washington's observer James Wood reported to headquarters.

Henderson presented his petition to a joint session of the assembly on October 29, smoothing the way by acknowledging Virginia's political jurisdiction over the area and asking merely that he and his partners receive compensation. On October 30 Thomas Burke of North Carolina delivered "a great speech"—in Henderson's estimation at least—defending the company's title.[53] The assembly responded by once more invalidating all claims based on Indian treaties not recognized by Virginia but awarded Henderson eight hundred thousand acres. A series of maneuvers in which Jefferson may have had a hand whittled down the amount to two hundred thousand acres located on the Green River in Kentucky, so far away that the area could not be opened for settlement for another twenty years.

As a capstone to his reforms, Jefferson had moved in 1776 for the appointment of a committee to conduct a revisal of Virginia law. Soon after adjournment that year a committee consisting of himself, Pendleton, Wythe, Mason, and Thomas Ludwell Lee met in Fredericksburg to decide on general philosophy and to parcel out assignments. Surprisingly, Jefferson found himself arguing against Lee and the usually cautious Speaker, both of whom wanted to write an entirely new code patterned after the one Sir William Blackstone recently completed for England. The other three argued that they did not have time for so comprehensive a project, which moreover would further complicate the law until repeated judicial decisions ironed out every nuance of language. Jefferson preferred merely to simplify the often overly elaborate and redundant phraseology of the current law without altering the vocabulary already familiar to the courts. Lee died shortly after the meeting and Mason excused himself because he was not a lawyer, leaving the work to the other three, who labored over two years before submitting their report to the legislature.[54]

Jefferson and Wythe finally presented the revisal in the form of 126 separate bills in the spring of 1779. The legislature had previously enacted or adopted during that session about two dozen that applied to Jefferson's design for government or pertained to the war effort. The vast majority the delegates put aside until after the peace treaty. In 1785, when Jefferson had gone abroad as ambassador to France, Madison loyally reintroduced all that were still relevant, 118, again including some already law. For two years he badgered the assembly to consider the revisions one by one until in the end the body accepted about two-thirds of the original number.[55]

While the revisal codified Jefferson's reforms, it produced no more of a social revolution than had the bills individually. "I considered 4," Jefferson later wrote, "as forming a system by which every fibre would be eradicated of antient or future aristocracy; and a foundation laid for a government truly republican. The repeal of the laws of entail . . . The abolition of primogeniture . . . The restoration of the rights of conscience . . . and . . . the bill for a general education." Jefferson overestimated the practical effect of the first two regarding estates. The last, his educational scheme, would have been profoundly innovative: primary schools for all free male and female children, grammar schools for the abler among them "calculated for the common purposes of life," and college for the truly talented, all at public expense. Jefferson's object was to guarantee that those "whom nature hath endowed with genius and virtue . . . should be called to that charge without regard to wealth, birth or other accidental condition or circumstance."[56] But only the provisions for primary schools were ever adopted—because of the cost, some said—although not all Virginians may have agreed with Jefferson that true republicanism meant the rule of an intellectual elite. The real achievement of the revisal and of Jefferson's reforms lay in the intellectual rather than the social realm, as the third item, Jefferson's bill for religious freedom, testified. That document's adulation of the individual and the integrity of the human mind secured for its author a place in the first rank of liberal thinkers. It came at the right time and in the right place; it spoke for the eighteenth century.

Along with such monuments to human reason, the revisal also included Jefferson's bill on capital crimes as if to prove that the great, too, can stumble. While the bill's provision for quartering, gibbeting, castration, and other mutilations reflected contemporary practice inherited from harsher ages, the failure to propose reforms already discussed in Europe, and indeed the step backward in accepting the Mosaic principle of "an eye for an eye, a tooth for a tooth," proved too illiberal for the legislature which ultimately rejected the proposed draft. The bill embarrassed Madison when he reintroduced it after the war, and Jefferson himself later wondered "how this last revolting principle came to obtain our approbation."[57]

The revisal also brought out in detail for the first time Jefferson's ideas on slavery. He offered a bill to complement the abolition of the slave trade the year before, for which he was probably responsible, by providing that slavery would never expand beyond its present extent in Virginia and creating conditions under which it would likely decline. Besides decreeing that all slaves newly entering the state in the future would become free after five years, the bill declared that no one would ever be a slave in Virginia who was not a slave when the bill passed or was not a descendant of a woman who was. The bill also established procedures for manumission, thus introducing the possibility of a constantly shrinking number of slaves. The drawback was that free blacks and white women who bore children by black men and their offspring had to leave the state within a year or be outlawed. Jefferson later explained that, had public opinion seemed amenable, he had amendments ready to declare free any child born of slave parents after a given date and to provide for training such children at public expense in "tillage, arts or sciences, according to their geniuses" before requiring them to leave the commonwealth. When Madison resubmitted the unamended bill in 1785, the legislature proved more liberal than the bill's author by enacting the measure without the mandate that free blacks had to go into exile. Because Jefferson believed blacks to be intellectually inferior to whites, and because he feared the "deep rooted prejudices entertained by whites" and the "ten thousand recollections, by the blacks, of the injuries they have sustained," he remained convinced for the remainder of his life that only colonization of free blacks outside the settled parts of America offered a practical alternative to slavery.[58]

Finally, in the revisal of the laws Jefferson tried for a third time to reform county government by eliminating the colonial practice of binding governors to accept incumbent justices' nominations for appointment of their successors. Instead, Jefferson proposed that each county elect three "Aldermen" who would serve as justices and also submit to the governor nominations for as many others as would be necessary to provide one justice for every fifty militiamen in the county. The legislature once more ignored the idea.[59] This final rebuff points up again that the attraction for contemporaries of Jefferson's contributions to the Revolution lay in the intellectual rather than the social realm. Virginians gradually heeded his teaching on the constitutional intricacies of republicanism, but shunned his proposals that would have fundamentally altered class relationships. At independence, Virginians like other Americans did not have to be persuaded that all government officers ought to depend in some fashion on the consent of the people. Virginians already had sufficient experience with popular self-government to be convinced of that principle. Jefferson led his compatriots beyond the mere abolition of monarchy, however, to educate them on the essential distinction between constitutions and statutes; on the need for the meticulous separation of powers and relentless consistency with regard to religious and other individual freedoms; in short, on the myriad ramifications of which a people had to be aware if even popular government were not to be oppressive. At first, some found it difficult to understand his concern, to see how a society that had nurtured them to be republicans could be oppressive for others, like dissenting Protestants, Catholics, Jews, and the poor. But then, with regard to blacks, not even Jefferson was sensitive to every implication.

CHAPTER 9

The Economy in War

HAVING treated itself to a new constitution, Virginia matched it with a new economy. The basis for the change was the economic development of the preceding generation, but the war catapulted Virginians in the direction they had been stepping gingerly before. Independence ended the colony's almost total dependence on Great Britain for manufactures and transatlantic shipping. Virtually overnight substitutes had to be found for British consignment merchants and factors who had previously monopolized the continent's most salable product, tobacco. As successive campaigns depleted supplies in the northern theater, the colony's burgeoning foodstuff trade increasingly became the mainstay of armies stationed around the nation. Virginians began to dream of commercial empires that once had been the preserve of Boston, New York, and Philadelphia.

The war offered Virginians an opportunity of fulfilling a promise that they had been making themselves ever since the founding of the colony: to diversify and escape the unending cycle of luxury and debt of a one-crop economy. The challenge especially stirred the amateur scientist in the model eighteenth-century planter, and suggestions for projects of varying practicality rained upon the government from every side. Might not the calamine crystals so common around the state be used to manufacture brass for cannon from the veins of cop-

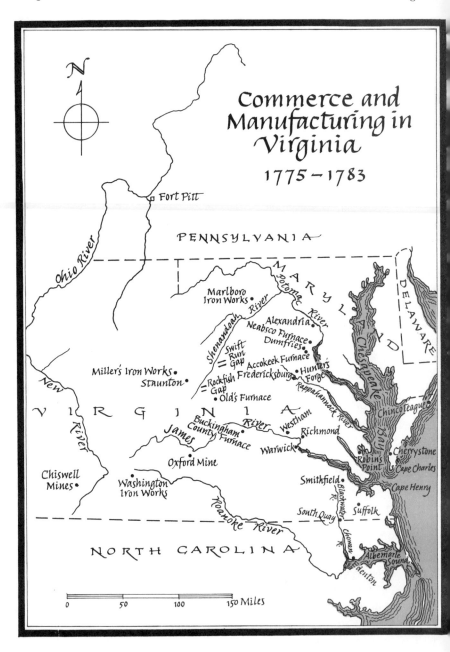

Commerce and Manufacturing in Virginia 1775–1783

per that David Jameson had discovered at Yorktown, asked Lieutenant Governor Page. Virginia planters repeatedly assured Congress that the sweepings of Virginia tobacco sheds afforded a virtually limitless source of saltpeter. Purdie's *Virginia Gazette* estimated that two hundred thousand pounds of nitrates could be extracted annually from just a few of the largest plantations. The Isle of Wight County committee offered a reward for the first five thousand pounds of explosive produced, and the Convention guaranteed a premium for up to two thousand. Cumberland County set a more realistic goal of fifty. Experimenters poured over encyclopedias for instructions, and Congress sent a specialist, Jacob Rubsamen, to help.[1]

With his usual impatience, John Page flayed the legislature for its skepticism toward such projects and for months sputtered to friends about the way Edmund Pendleton dismissed one of his pet schemes, a powder mill invented by Benjamin Bucktrout of Williamsburg, as a "Bauble."[2] On the Northern Neck Charles Carter of Stafford advertised lessons in the use of a process for extracting saltpeter that his father had dabbled in earlier, while a syndicate led by Archibald Cary, Richard and Theodorick Bland, John Banister, and Rubsamen actually operated half a dozen mills along the Appomattox and James rivers for a number of years. By early 1776 their mills produced two hundred pounds a day. Charles Lynch had considerable success in Bedford County, where he discovered natural deposits, and others made attempts on a smaller scale. But in the long run the total output was meager. Discoveries of sulfur and nitrates in the West proved unfruitful because of the distance, although they rendered frontier areas self-sufficient. Like the rest of the colonies, Virginia depended for most of its gunpowder upon shipments from the West Indies and Europe.[3]

Most pressing was the need for salt to feed cattle and to preserve meat and fish. Almost all of Virginia's prewar supply came from Great Britain or the West Indies. The salt licks in the West were too far from populated areas for easy transportation, and Parliament allowed importation from southern Europe, whose product was deemed the best, only to the northern colonies in order to encourage the fishing trade. At the earliest sign of trouble with the mother country the Convention had authorized subsidies to James Tait of Northampton County for experiments in producing salt by boiling seawater. A year later Tait had no salt to show for the money. With Dunmore diligently destroying all the salt that he could find during the spring and summer of 1776, the situation became critical. The price rose from one to fifteen shillings a bushel. Armed bands in search of the precious commodity raided storehouses in Henrico and Hanover counties. To forestall hoarding the Convention allowed dealers to charge whatever the market would bear and sought permission from Congress to export foodstuffs in exchange for salt from Bermuda. Dr. George Gilmer consoled one company of recruits with the thought that the shortage would improve their physical fitness: "Salt flesh and gravy,—compare the unaccustomed to these and see who are the most robust and hearty."[4]

The spring Convention in 1776 had authorized the erection of ten public saltworks to evaporate seawater by the sun. Necessity and the persuasiveness of Richard Henry Lee overcame the Speaker's initial preference for grants to private operators that would be less of a drain on the treasury. Construction took much longer than expected, and, as Pendleton feared, costs rose. An unusually rainy summer demonstrated the need for extra-large iron pans and heavy brick fireplaces to boil the water instead of relying solely on the sun. Of the ten works projected, only seven were ever attempted, and only four completed. The one in York County turned out to be useless because the sandy soil absorbed the water. The works in Isle of Wight County could be reached only at high tide, and the builders in Northumberland County dug the pits so deep that rain continually flooded them. The most successful, at Robin's Point in Gloucester County, eventually had nine pans ranging in capacity up to eighteen hundred gallons in operation. By late 1778 the Gloucester works had produced over eight hundred bushels compared to about five hundred for all the rest. After three years of effort the state found it cheaper to abandon these attempts and rely entirely upon imports from France, Bermuda, and the West Indies for its needs.[5]

Wool and cotton cards to prepare fiber for spinning became standard items in orders from abroad. For much of the war, according to Jefferson, the civilian population produced enough textiles to satisfy its own needs. The wool, linen, and hemp cloth, however, was "very coarse, unsightly and unpleasant," although the cotton bore "some comparison" with that of Europe.[6] At Nomini Hall Robert Carter sent to New Jersey for a man who could set up stocking looms on the plantation. George Mason tracked down another who had worked in the sailcloth factories of Hull, England, and wrote to friends to help him locate someone who knew about the new spinning machine "introduced a few years ago from Russia."[7] Landon Carter offered to finance anyone who would come to teach weaving in his neighborhood. Merchants in Fredericksburg brought weavers from Philadelphia to run a "Cotton and Linen Manufactory," and in Richmond Archibald Cary, who had one ropewalk at Warwick in Chesterfield County, established another.[8]

In Williamsburg Robert Carter Nicholas and other enterprising citizens formed a Manufacturing Society that built a "factory" at Capitol Landing on Queen's Creek to produce all kinds of textiles, although they principally made linen. The society wrote to France for skilled workmen but had to be content with local children apprenticed for five years plus assorted hired hands. As soon as the Public Store commenced operations, it distributed cloth and leather for local tailors and shoemakers to convert into uniforms. Housewives and young ladies of the town patriotically sewed shirts for the soldiers. As the demands of war increased, the state opened a "Public Taylors Shop" in the capital and a "Country Shop," or shoe manufactory, and a tanyard at Warwick in Chesterfield County.[9]

Virginia was more fortunate in the production of lead. Some years before, Colonel John Chiswell had discovered the only mines of significance in the colonies near the present site of Austinville in Wythe County. At the outbreak of the war the new government took them over and within a year had a steadily increasing supply of the vital metal flowing to the colonial armies. To create a work force in the wilderness the state commuted sentences of criminals to three years of hard labor and sent out slaves recaptured from the British in lieu of transporting them to the West Indies. Other slaves were purchased or hired. Under the management first of James Callaway, who operated the Washington Iron Works in present Franklin County, and later of Charles Lynch, who went into partnership with Rubsamen, the mines became one of the most important material assets of the Continental cause.[10]

The state's most impressive achievement occurred in iron manufacture, in which it had long experience going back to the opening of Governor Spotswood's mines at Germanna fifty years before. By the Revolution more than a half-dozen active furnaces produced thousands of tons of iron annually. As the contest with Dunmore intensified in 1775, the Convention moved to utilize this capacity by establishing a center of small arms manufacture at Fredericksburg and allocating over five thousand pounds in currency for a public factory under the direction of two local merchant-planters, Fielding Lewis and Charles Dick. The state also encouraged James Hunter, whose forge in nearby Falmouth a British customs officer described a few years earlier as "the greatest Iron Works that is upon the Continent, which manufactures one and half Tons of Pig Iron, into Barrs p day," to develop slitting, plating, and wire mills and a steel furnace to produce arms, entrenching tools, anchors, and camp utensils.[11]

The two operations worked together as a unit, government orders often being placed on an either-or basis. At peak production the public works turned out a hundred stand of arms a month that the director boasted were superior to most imports, and repaired many more. The state adopted the quality of Hunter's muskets as the standard for all others. Late in the war James Mercer wrote to Jefferson, "I need not [tell] you that it is from Mr. Hunter's works that every Camp kettle has been supplyed . . . in this State and to the Southward this year past, that all the Anchors for this State and Maryland and some for the Continent have been produced . . . and that without the assistance of the Bar Iron made there even the planters hereabouts and to the Southward . . . wou'd not be able to make Bread to eat [in their mills and ovens]."[12]

For heavier ordnance the 1776 Convention ordered the construction of a public foundry at Westham outside Richmond. Initially John Ballendine, who had been trying to dig a canal around the falls of the Potomac for ten years, and John Reveley, an associate of Hunter, asked to build it under a subsidy, but the delegates decided upon state control. Perhaps because Ballendine's previous engineering efforts had earned him the reputation of being a laggard, Reveley alone became manager of the foundry. But Ballendine remained on the fringe of the operation since he held rights for a canal around Richmond on land essential to the new works. The government granted the two entrepreneurs a total of seventy-five hundred pounds for a new blast furnace in Buckingham County to supply the foundry, and although Ballendine agreed to finish the canal on which the boring mill depended with only minor public assistance, the state eventually had to contribute over twenty-five hundred pounds. To no surprise of his critics, Ballendine's diversion dam collapsed in the first spring runoff.[13]

Construction of the furnace took until the summer of 1778, and not until the succeeding March did the foundry begin casting iron ball. The following August completion of the canal allowed Reveley to begin boring twenty four-pounders. By then the legislature had lost all patience with Ballendine and condemned part of his land for an arms laboratory in which to prove the cannon from the foundry. Jefferson proposed letting the French firm of Penet, Windel et Cie. take over both canal and foundry, but the French government refused to let skilled workmen leave the realm. Through it all, Reveley toiled away, managing to keep up a steady production until the British destroyed his plant in 1781, the last year of fighting in Virginia.[14]

The state also obtained cannon from Isaac Zane, who operated the Marlboro Mine in Frederick County, and for a few years the government subsidized two other small arms factories in Berkeley and Loudoun counties. Zane's cast iron had a formidable reputation. The pans he made for the saltworks were said to be unbreakable. David Ross's Oxford Mine in Bedford County enjoyed the same prestige, and when Ballendine's Buckingham mine failed to meet all Reveley's needs, Ross became the principal supplier of the foundry. Hunter, on the other hand, depended upon Maryland ore. In the Tidewater only John Tayloe's Neabsco Mine in Prince William County still operated. Hunter received permission to reopen the old Accokeek Mine in Stafford County, but Tidewater ore proved not to be the best for forging. Robert Carter, a part owner of the Baltimore Iron Works, committed his portion of its production to Hunter although not without difficulty because of Virginia embargoes on the grain that the terms of the partnership required him to send for the workers' food in Maryland. In all, Jefferson reported in 1781 that the five ironworks mentioned, along with John Old's in Albemarle and John Miller's in Augusta counties, annually produced nine hundred tons of bar iron and thirty-three hundred of pig.[15]

But Virginia could not alter its economy overnight. Except in areas such as iron and lead production where the state had natural endowments, the industrial seedlings withered after a year or two. Fault finding and ill will resulted, for to enthusiasts failure seemed the result of incompetence, selfishness, and lack of patriotism. Others questioned the wisdom of encouraging industrialization and economic might. "Corruption of morals in the mass of cultivators is a phenomenon of which no age or nation has furnished an example," Jefferson wrote in the midst of Virginia's worst shortages. "Let our workshops remain in Europe. It is better to carry provisions and materials there,

than bring . . . [the workshops] to the provisions and materials, and
with them their manners and principles."[16] For the time being at least
the laws of economics gave Jefferson his wish.

The prospects for changing Virginia's economy appeared better at
sea, but it took time to develop the contacts and services for which Virginia had largely relied on Great Britain and the northern colonies before. The Goodriches' betrayal delayed efforts to open a West Indian
trade, and by the time the state's new government took office the supply
situation had become desperate. Stores scraped together in the early
days of the war ran out along with the first enlistments. "I believe there
is not a pocket handkerchief in all Virginia," Benjamin Harrison reported to Philadelphia in the spring of 1776.[17]
    Not until March of that year had the Committee of Safety reestab-
lished touch with Richard Harrison and Abraham Van Bibber, agents in
Martinique and St. Eustatius respectively for Lux & Bowly of Baltimore, with whom the Goodriches had dealt. For a while the state depended on private blockade runners who kept up with the demand for
gunpowder but little else. In March Captain Eliezer Callender brought
in fifteen thousand pounds for Fielding Lewis who operated a small
squadron of coastal vessels. In August Captain John Pasteur landed nine
thousand more concealed in barrels of limes at Hampton, and Harrison
and Van Bibber managed to transport sixteen thousand pounds to the
Eastern Shore, which Lux & Bowly sold to Virginia. By the next winter
French coastwise vessels from the Caribbean arrived regularly in the
Chesapeake Bay, principally bringing salt. The toll of the blockade was
high—Callender, for example, was lost during the summer—and,
worse, the small size of vessels capable of running it severely limited
cargoes.[18]
    To test their luck in another direction, in May 1776 the Committee of
Safety sent George Gibson and William Linn down the Mississippi River
to New Orleans, where with the help of Robert Morris's agent, Oliver
Pollock, they secured over nine thousand pounds of gunpowder from
the Spanish. It took Linn until the spring of 1777 to bring the bulk of
the purchase back up the Mississippi and Ohio rivers to Wheeling in
western Virginia; Gibson, whom the Spanish governor, Bernardo de
Gálvez, temporarily arrested to placate the British, had arrived with a
smaller load via the Atlantic coast the previous October. Summing up
the first months of the new government's operations, the irrepressible
Page reported to George Washington, "If we had Blankets and Clothes

for our Troops with a few 2000 good muskets and a few good heavy Cannon with some Field Pieces—I should defy the Enemy for we have a very good Stock of Powder." [19]

In the fall of 1776 the Council devised a scheme for the state itself to enter the West Indian trade with seven small vessels borrowed from the navy. To operate the commercial fleet, they named William Aylett state agent, expanding his duties at the Public Store to include the procurement of supplies as well as their disbursement. State authorities pushed construction of two armed galleys to defend Ocracoke Inlet, an old pirates' den in North Carolina that was an ideal haven for blockade runners, and ordered fortifications built at Cherrystone (later Cheriton, Northampton County) and Chincoteague on the Eastern Shore and beacons at Cape Henry to warn of British ships in the Chesapeake Bay. Delays to obtain legislative approval and assemble cargoes kept the first vessel, the schooner *Revenge,* in port until November 1776. The others followed slowly, the seventh, the sloop *Liberty,* not clearing for St. Eustatius until spring. In the meantime, the 4th, 5th, 6th, and 9th regiments moved northward almost entirely without arms or adequate clothing. [20]

Complications in the Council's scheme developed when Van Bibber and Harrison reported a glut on the West Indian flour market and recommended indigo instead. Aylett dispatched a flotilla of minuscule pilot boats to Charleston, where the Council sent St. George Tucker to exchange the flour for eight tons of indigo. A shipment of arms reached Virginia on board the tiny *Molly* in April 1777, for which the appreciative Council voted Captain John Pasteur and his crew a handsome bonus. The diminutive *Nicholson* followed; then the price of indigo tumbled, too. [21]

A dramatic sequel to the indigo project marked the end of Van Bibber's agency in St. Eustatius. Although the Dutch authorities normally winked at contraband trade, they needed a scapegoat at the moment for diplomatic reasons. Their opportunity came with the arrival of the boat *Jenny* under Captain George Ralls, whom a committee of the House of Delegates subsequently branded "a man of very indifferent character, and much addicted to drinking." [22] Ralls was more intent upon privateering than indigo. He boasted of his plans in local taverns, and when he finally seized a British ship as it left the harbor, Ralls hove to the *Jenny* and its prize for a little celebration. H.M.S. *Seaford* easily surprised the ships and discovered a compromising letter from Van Bibber cautioning Ralls to secrecy if the American carried out his plan. Technically a Dutch

neutral, Van Bibber found himself charged with treason and imprisoned in Fort Orange, from which he escaped a few months later, billing
Virginia for the necessary bribes. Ralls went in chains to Great Britain,
but somehow managed to return to America to sail and be captured
again.[23]

The Council quickly replaced Van Bibber and through 1777 stretched
a network of agents over the Caribbean: John Ball in St. Eustatius,
Thomas Webb in Curaçao, Richard Harrison in Martinique, Raleigh
Colston in Santo Domingo, and Thomas Bretman in Surinam. Private
commission merchants for whom the government was just another customer, these men often provided valuable service by risking their own
credit for the state, as they would for any client, until shipments of tobacco arrived. On the other hand, they exacted full recompense. If they
held public money on account and had nothing to ship that the state
had ordered, they might place the funds temporarily at the service of
another customer. Rather than let a state-owned ship sail half-empty
because they had no public cargo ready, they might add a private consignment to fill the hold. Misunderstandings became rampant, and the
thought of auditing such transactions foolhardy. Eventually the Council
fired Harrison for using state vessels too freely to ship his own goods.
Colston, a former apprentice at Tarpley, Thompson & Co. of Williamsburg and a law student of George Wythe, made an admittedly "easy
Fortune" in the state's service at Cap François in the West Indies. Yet he
found his own patriotism much "grieved" in negotiations with the crew
of the sloop *Liberty*—"a sett of unfeeling animals," he declared—when
their spokesman told him, "Country here or Country there, damn my
Eyes and limbs but I'll serve them that give the best wages."[24]

Virginia also encountered heavy competition for the nation's major
source of foreign exchange, tobacco, from a bevy of congressional buyers and private entrepreneurs. Before the ink of the Declaration of Independence had dried, Americans contracted to supply the Farmers
General, the syndicate of French merchants whose management of the
royal monopoly of tobacco sales in their country made them the largest
single purchasers of that commodity in the world. At the center of this
activity was the long-established Philadelphia firm of Willing and Morris, which had connections in Virginia from the prewar flour trade
through Jenifer and Hooe of Alexandria and Inglis and Long of
Norfolk.[25]

Early in the spring of 1776 Morris appointed his former apprentice,

Benjamin Harrison, Jr., Continental paymaster in Virginia to oversee Morris's public affairs in the state. At the same time young Harrison acted as the leading purchaser of tobacco in Virginia for Willing and Morris's private account. Besides Harrison, Morris's contacts in the state included John Hatley Norton of Yorktown, who had managed Virginia affairs for his family's firm in London, then formed a partnership with Samuel Beall of Williamsburg. With appropriate letters of introduction, Beall sailed to France, where he concluded a business alliance with Ambassador Silas Deane and opened a trade with the Delaps of Bordeaux and Clifford and Teysset of Amsterdam, two of Morris's principal correspondents in Europe.[26] While serving in Congress during the spring of 1776, Carter Braxton obtained a similar commission from Morris to buy for the Continent. In addition, Braxton engaged to purchase tobacco privately for Morris and entered into an agreement with John Merckle of Amsterdam, who was in America looking for business, to ship tobacco to him in exchange for ten thousand pounds in goods. Braxton conceded to Morris that his multiple roles might lead to "a Difficulty and some Delicacy in my Situation."[27]

Jenifer and Hooe, young Harrison, Norton, and Braxton bought tobacco for Morris independently of each other through the winter of 1776–1777 and drove the price up from under twenty to over thirty shillings a hundredweight. Heavy purchases by Robert Pleasant, whom the elder Harrison identified to Morris as representing "the Tory quakers in your Town," contributed to the rise.[28] The next spring planters who had sold to Braxton at a lower price refused to deliver, and after haggling, he wrote off their contracts, charging the loss to his Continental quota rather than his own. Eventually Richard Henry Lee demanded a congressional investigation, but Morris had foreseen the danger and had had Braxton prepare documents to clear himself by showing that he had patriotically signed the contracts for Congress first while the price was low, and only later for himself after it had begun to rise. Congress therefore had to bear the loss of the earlier contracts.[29]

During the winter of 1776–1777 Braxton also clashed with William Aylett when Braxton began to fill an order from Morris for ten thousand barrels of flour to supply packet ships that he and Morris planned to keep sailing between Boston and Virginia. Simultaneously Aylett received orders to stockpile twenty to thirty thousand barrels for the Continent. In the ensuing scramble Aylett denounced Morris and Braxton to Congress as forestallers. Richard Henry Lee exacted an apology from Morris, who promised to sell the flour below the market price. Although

Lee understood that Morris would sell at the original cost of twelve shillings a barrel, before Lee could get in touch with Aylett, Braxton on Morris's order imposed the "moderate" markup of 25 percent for "various little etceteras."[30]

To set Aylett straight, Braxton sent the state agent an indignant epistle on the spirit of capitalism. No one had ever told him that private trade was improper, Braxton wrote. If it was, let the legislature say so and "I shall have a rule for my Government." Otherwise, Aylett must accept the frustrations of which he constantly complained as part of his job and not imply that they resulted from a tory conspiracy. "It will naturally happen that you and all the Mercts in this Country will have different parts to act and you must expect some Interference, for they will endeavour to purchase to derive a profit even if they knew you wanted the Article, and this you must impute to that first motive in the human Soul a Love for Self."[31] St. George Tucker's brother, Thomas Ludwell Tucker, agreed. "It is just that every Person shou'd get what Price he fairly can," he explained when the legislature investigated the family's salt business, "but it ought not to be enhanced by Artifice."[32]

Needless to say, Aylett's own policies as head of the Public Store did not escape attack. The legislature expected him to cover costs. He carried equipment on his books as if he sold rather than issued it, although in most instances the allotments the Convention granted the military units offset the charges. Disputes usually involved Aylett's markup because it included such hard to determine factors as the difference in the risk accompanying voyages from the West Indies compared with overland trips from Philadelphia. Sharp increases within short periods reflected separate shipments, and howls of outrage greeted rises of up to 450 percent to compensate for lost cargoes. Two fruitless investigations by the legislature merely elicited protests from Aylett that he was doing his best. The state agent also quite candidly explained the terms under which he worked: "I see no reason why I should move in a Sphere truly laborious, and out of the Road of Military legislative or Executive fame, without a reward adequate to the private Sacrifice of Interest it occasions me to make." Consequently, Aylett wanted an increase in salary and commissions on all services he performed other than his basic obligation to provide supplies for Continental troops recruited in Virginia.[33]

In a letter to Joseph Hughes of Edenton, North Carolina, who had called him a "damned rascal," Aylett recounted the kind of trials he had to endure. Aylett denied Hughes's claim that Virginia merchants would say the same of the agent. "I know to whom you are referring," Aylett wrote, "to wit, Wells Cowper [of Suffolk] . . . for obliging him to take to himself eight Hogsheads of Tobacco Rottens that he Bot. for this Commonwealth. . . . Norton and Beall, Braxton, and Phripp have been displeased with me, for opposing them in their schemes of forestalling and engrossing, but these gentlemen . . . have never presumed to say more, than they thought I was over Zealous in the publick interest, and that I should injure myself with individuals and get no thanks for it, in which I believe they are right."[34]

Undaunted by the disappointment of the indigo project, the Council in 1777 embarked on an ambitious plan to establish direct trade with the European continent. They had experimented with the idea the previous fall when they helped George Mason and John Dalton of Alexandria send off a cargo of tobacco to Hival and Sons of Dunkerque on an old brigantine, *The Adventure*. The real opportunity came the next spring when two associates of Silas Deane, Pierre Penet and Emanuel de Pliarne of Nantes, who were in America negotiating a contract with Congress, concluded an arrangement with Virginia as well. Aylett immediately unloaded two ships already scheduled to carry flour and provisions to the West Indies and readied four more. When Penet returned to France, de Pliarne came to Virginia to load a seventh, the *Custis*, in conjunction with Mason and Dalton on the Potomac.

The results never equaled expectations. Two of the vessels fell victims of the blockade, and one proved unfit for sea. Of the four that completed the round trip, the French partners detained the brig *Liberty* for months in European waters as a privateer. Two others also suffered excessive delays with the result that only the *Congress* returned in time to be of any help that year. When it arrived back in December 1777, the commissary immediately hustled its cargo of fifteen hundred blankets, twelve hundred pairs of stockings, and other clothing to Washington's frostbitten soldiers at Valley Forge. Only the *Liberty* ever made a second trip to France. Fearing that not enough tobacco would reach France in time to pay for all the goods that were needed, the Council sent John King, a Petersburg merchant, to arrange a backup loan for the state. He signed a second agreement with Penet's associates, James Gruel et Cie., who dispatched one more cargo to the West Indies for Virginia on board *La Chavigny*.[35]

Few vessels slipped through the blockade to the Chesapeake during 1777. A private ship from Nantes with fifteen hundred stand of arms and thirty thousand pounds of powder arrived in March. Seven months later the brig *Roultrac* came with a shipment for Norton and Beall from John Bondfield of Bordeaux, another correspondent of Robert Morris, and in November one of Beaumarchais's ships with more clothing reached Portsmouth. As the British slowly tightened their noose, Congress began to advise its agents in France to route shipments through northern ports which could be "entered with so much more safety than the Southern."[36] By year's end the royal navy choked off the bay completely. According to the diarist Robert Honyman, "not a single vessel comes into the Capes."[37] As a result of the blockade, the governor and Council decided to abandon the European trade entirely to the neutral French and to accept an alternative plan proposed by a new councillor, Bolling Starke of Dinwiddie County. The executive ordered the state agent to sell the Virginia fleet as each vessel next sailed to Nantes (only the *Liberty* ever went again) and convey the return cargoes in French bottoms to Cap François in the West Indies. For its part, the state agreed to provide six fast pilot boats for the dash through the blockade to the North Carolina coast. In Virginia the appointment of assistant state agents on each major river decentralized tobacco purchases. The agents sent the tobacco overland to North Carolina via Smithfield, Suffolk, and South Quay. By this time the Council had learned that Penet's associates, Gruel et Cie., had an unsavory reputation in their homeland and seized upon the new plan as an excuse to transfer the state's agency in France from Penet to William Lee. Lee negotiated a contract under the new policy with John Bondfield and William Haywood of Nantes, who shipped three cargoes of dry goods early in 1778 before open warfare between France and Great Britain ended French neutrality as a useful cover. By dissolving his partnership with Gruel and coming to plead his case in Virginia, Penet eventually managed to win reappointment as coagent with Lee, but succeeded in dispatching only two shiploads of tobacco to France for his new firm, Penet, D'Acosta Frères et Cie.[38]

The winter of 1777–1778 was the time of Valley Forge. The most bountiful harvest in years in Virginia proved no help for the troops with Washington, who received a tablespoon of vinegar and a half-gill of rice for Thanksgiving dinner. Two years of campaigning in the mid-Atlantic region had diminished local stocks, and with Howe in Philadelphia, the populace hesitated to sell the Americans what little remained. When the Continental commissariat tried to bring supplies from farther afield, its organization completely collapsed. The fault lay largely with Congress since it had ignored urgent appeals for stricter regulation until well into 1777, delaying, for example, the appointment of a quartermaster general to coordinate transportation until the height of the crisis. As deputy Continental commissary general for Virginia, William Aylett had difficulty finding out how many rations to furnish or what accounting methods to employ. At one point Aylett learned only from an advertisement in the *Virginia Gazette* that another agent at Dumfries was duplicating his issues to troops marching north. Congress finally ordered a reorganization during the summer of 1777, too late for the changes to function smoothly that year.[39]

Under the new plan Congress divided the Continental commissary into two divisions, issuing and purchasing. Aylett became deputy commissary general for purchases in the southern department in June, but not until the end of the year could he put aside his state responsibilities. His young assistant, William Armistead of New Kent County, then took over the Virginia Public Store, and Thomas Smith, a Gloucester County merchant connected with the Gratz family enterprises of Pennsylvania before the war, succeeded Aylett as state agent. The Continental reorganization prompted a similar revision of the state commissariat. On two occasions during the summer the Council for some reason put off renewing the contract with John Hawkins, who had been Virginia's principal supplier since the beginning of the war—Hawkins may have been trying to retire, although there also appears to have been some problem about his prices. In September the executive substituted salaried officials on annual appointments, naming two small Williamsburg merchants, William Eaton and John Pierce, issuing and purchasing commissaries respectively. Along with John Brown, who began as their assistant but later supplanted them for a while, Eaton and Pierce operated the state commissariat under a variety of formats for the remainder of the war.[40]

The changes provided little comfort to Washington, who in desperation finally bypassed the Continental commissariat in the early months of 1778 and appealed directly to governors from New Jersey south to North Carolina for help. Ignoring Aylett, Henry sent out Abraham and Thomas Hite and James Barbour as special agents. They tracked down over ten thousand head of beef cattle and hogs in the mountains of Virginia, an area that the deputy commissary had supposedly scoured. Then to resuscitate the state's entire system, the governor prevailed upon his old friend Hawkins, whom everyone regarded as a wizard in rooting out supplies, to reenter public service. Unfortunately, the man died within days of agreeing to the governor's request. Hawkins's partner, Richard Morris, stepped forward instead to serve as commissary in an ad hoc capacity for the rest of the year and by the summer of 1778 was regularly herding cattle northward. Miffed, Aylett ungraciously remarked that he was "Glad to hear Hawkins is at last paying his debt" at the news of the latter's death.[41] Aylett threatened to resign, especially after a Continental auditor whom the deputy commissary had not met before publicly quizzed him on the street in Williamsburg, but at length Aylett overcame his feelings and stayed at his post another year.

The General Assembly that met in Williamsburg from October 1777 to January 1778 seemed paralyzed in the face of these repeated crises. Despite Howe's invasion, or perhaps because of it, the delegates took over a week—from October 20 to 30—to muster a quorum, and attendance remained a daily problem throughout the session. By the time George Mason arrived on November 14, word had preceded him that, in the area of supplies as well as taxes, he was bringing the answer to the state's problems. Mason's proposals again showed that his whiggism did not preclude flexing the state's muscle when required. The assembly shortly adopted a bill that Mason largely composed empowering commissioners to confiscate any clothing "proper for the use of the army" if speculators purchased it for resale after it had been landed in this country.[42] The act permitted only the original importers to offer the goods for sale. The assembly attempted to keep the act secret to prevent merchants from hiding their goods. As a result, the authorities seized several wagonloads of cloth belonging to a surprised Carter Braxton who had been briskly shipping materials between Petersburg and Baltimore to take maximum advantage of the two markets. In Williamsburg John Hatley Norton had a narrow escape. According to subsequent testimony, Norton inveigled the text of the act out of workers in Alexander Purdie's shop, where it was being printed over the weekend, and, having discovered the exemption for original importers, had documents ready to show that he had imported every item in his store when a befuddled commissioner arrived the next week.[43]

Mason also initiated companion statutes that clamped an embargo on the exportation of beef, pork, and bacon from Virginia except for military purposes. The legislation permitted J.P.s to confiscate supplies in excess of a family's immediate needs if the owner refused to sell to a commissary "at moderate prices."[44] Mason most likely also prepared the bill authorizing the seizure of salt at the fixed price of five pounds a bushel, which both houses enacted in just a single day toward the end of the session, reflecting the seriousness of the emergency by then.

Rebuilding the state's supply system, which had so completely disintegrated over the winter, held first priority in 1778. Richard Morris stayed on as special agent for the Continental commissary until December of that year, by which time Aylett was able to take over successfully again. Meanwhile, the new state agent, Thomas Smith, worked closely with the newly elected councillor, Bolling Starke, to open routes outflanking the British blockade. Smith developed overland routes across the Eastern Shore and via Suffolk and South Quay to Albemarle Sound in North Carolina. The first soon failed. Smith's assistant had trouble finding boats to ferry tobacco across the bay, and private merchants attempting to use the same route forced up the price of the vessels that were available. Smith largely gave up the effort early in the summer of 1778 although he occasionally shipped cargoes to the Eastern Shore in 1779 when British warships patrolled the bay.[45]

The second route proved more practical. Suffolk soon developed into a boom town as the terminus of a wagon trail to South Quay near the North Carolina border. From there the route followed the Chowan River to Edenton, North Carolina, where the state stationed its small fleet of blockade runners. Smith's letters reveal him to have been a volatile, feisty fellow whose attempts to coordinate operations so far from headquarters in Williamsburg brought a hail of denunciations on his subordinates. Once when he learned that a captain had not sailed on schedule he shot back, "I received yours with perfect astonishment! the *Congress* gone! your Vessel returned! no Hands, God help us! what is to be done in such an unfortunate Situation!"[46] Another time Smith told Archibald Richardson, a long-suffering assistant at Suffolk, that Richardson's reports "contain such a catalogue of disagreeable circumstances as is enough to put a Man out of his mind. Gracious God what can be done in such a scene of trouble and perplexity." Richardson told Smith to come down himself, but the latter replied that he already had to do "more than any one Man in Virginia could attend to."[47] To another correspondent Smith wrote sarcastically at one point, "How in the name of Common sense the States Tobacco happens to be in worse order than any private property is strange to me."[48] By fall Smith could hardly wait to abandon the North Carolina route and, as the blockade eased in the Chesapeake Bay, phased out state activities in Suffolk by the end of 1778 although the town continued to serve as a major entrepôt for private shippers for some time longer.

With so many buyers in the field, speculation became rife and inflation endemic. Besides Smith, Morris, and Aylett, Duncan Rose of Petersburg bought on contract for the Virginia regiments in the Continental line, and then there were the private purchasers. During March, for example, Michael Gratz of Philadelphia came to Williamsburg to arrange a shipment of tobacco to S. and J. Delap of Bordeaux. Farmers withheld supplies to capitalize on price advances, sometimes forcing government purchasers to confiscate each other's collections in order to fill individual quotas. "The Spirit of Traffic prevails so much amongst us, and the Demon of Avarice is . . . let loose upon us," John Page exclaimed to Richard Henry Lee, and once Thomas Smith exploded, "I have such a dislike to the Speculating Gentry that I have sometimes as Cruel thoughts as ever Caligula had."[49] Henry and the Council even authorized the state to offer slaves as a form of exchange more tempting to hoarders than Virginia's depreciating currency. Smith had trouble just finding agents to act for him. When Fielding Lewis of Fredericksburg declined because of his health and recommended Yates and Payne instead, they excused themselves because "the buying of Tobacco, formerly no very difficult task to those who had been sometime established in the business, as the Planters either came to their Stores, or were to be met with at stated times and places, has now got into quite a different channel—You must look for them at the back County Courts, Musters or go to their Houses, and then probably fail in persuading to sell at any price."[50]

Nor did relaxation of the blockade bring foreign supplies as rapidly as some expected. French merchants waited to see if there would be peace, which might bring a flood of British goods into America, or an alliance with Spain, which might open the tobacco of its colonies to them. Such speculation kept markets jittery through the year. Finally, on May 28, 1778, the most important of the ships to reach Virginia as a result of the controversial deal between Silas Deane and Beaumarchais, the fifty-four-gun *Le Fier Roderique* and the forty-gun *Lyon,* dropped anchor at Yorktown. In keeping with Beaumarchais's insistence on the private character of his company, the supercargoes, Pierre Chevallie and Lazarus de Francy, offered their goods at public sale, obtaining an exchange rate from the state, which bought the entire cargo, of six shillings on the livre. A year and a half earlier Aylett had calculated the rate to be about 1⅓ shillings per livre. Virginia filled the two vessels with two thousand hogsheads (about two million pounds) of tobacco over the summer and still owed £161,603.13 in state currency, or about £32,000 sterling, for which Beaumarchais's agents allowed a loan at 6 percent interest. The state recovered some of this cost when the Continent bought what it wanted and the commissary sold the remnants of the cargo at public auction. Collecting so much tobacco at Yorktown and then at Alexandria, where the *Lyon* moved for additional cargo, so taxed the state's logistical system that all other operations came to a standstill during June, July, and August. There also were minor trials, such as the riot among sailors at Yorktown that resulted in the shooting of a Frenchman. Nonetheless, the *Fier Roderique* sailed in time to be back in France by October, and its companion followed a little later.[51]

Then, on the heels of the massive purchases of tobacco for Beaumarchais came orders from Congress for twenty thousand barrels of flour to feed the French fleet under Admiral d'Estaing, which arrived off Delaware Bay in early July. Congress explicitly instructed the new commissary general, Jeremiah Wadsworth of Connecticut, to obtain the grain in the South since prices were so high in the North. When Wadsworth and his assistant, Ephraim Blaine, toured Maryland and Virginia in August, however, they discovered to their dismay that the worst rains in memory had brought savage attacks of the Hessian fly that devastated crops, in startling contrast to the amplitude that had blessed Virginia the year before. Continental purchasers bought everything available, and prices zoomed upward. The fall 1778 assembly tried to help by progressively tightening the embargo on private exports of grain, first allowing seizure of hoarded stocks and, finally, in an emergency statute that Mason drafted, banning violators "for ever" from trading in Virginia.[52] Still, some hoarders loaded vessels and simply waited at anchor for the embargo to lift, while others evaded the law by posing as government purchasers. In December Congress ordered yet another eighteen thousand barrels which Aylett—amazingly—was able to supply, but then he warned Continental authorities not to expect any more since prices had become "extortionate."[53]

Hardly, too, had Beaumarchais's vessels been loaded when Congress ordered Robert Morris to prepare a tobacco convoy for its own agents in France. Morris entrusted the assignment to Braxton, by whose name the fleet came to be known. To add to the fervor Silas Deane's brother Simeon simultaneously arrived in Virginia to set up operations to meet the family's obligations overseas. The Braxton fleet finally sailed at the end of October, barely escaping H.M.S. *Perseus* lying in wait outside the Capes. By then the price of tobacco, which had been about thirty shillings a hundredweight during 1777 and around three pounds earlier in 1778, reached five pounds in the fall and doubled again by early 1779.[54]

Since previous attempts to purchase goods in Europe with direct shipments of tobacco had fallen well short of their goals, the state launched a campaign over the winter of 1778–1779 to borrow one million or more pounds sterling from European countries. The governor and Council planned to ship the goods purchased with the loans via Holland and the Dutch West Indies inasmuch as the French no longer afforded a safe neutral cover. To implement the scheme Henry and the Council instructed the former commercial agent, Thomas Smith, to go to Holland, Germany, Sweden, and anywhere else that promised success and place initial orders of up to fifty thousand pounds sterling.[55]

The decision to seek European financing reflected a general confidence in the wake of the French alliance that foreign assistance would be available for the asking. In addition to Smith's assignment, William Lee set out in optimistic pursuit of a two million-livre grant from France, and when Pierre Penet announced his return to Europe, the state commissioned him to borrow up to one hundred thousand pounds sterling from Switzerland. The most dashing Virginia agent was Philip Mazzei, an Italian wine merchant who migrated in 1773 to Virginia, where he became a close friend of Jefferson and undertook to introduce wine-making to the state at the plantation Colle in Albemarle County. In April 1779 Patrick Henry authorized Mazzei to seek up to nine hundred thousand pounds sterling at a maximum interest rate of 5 percent from his native Tuscany, or from Genoa, Spain, or anywhere else except Switzerland.

Nothing came of these plans. The British captured Smith in June 1779 on board the *Fanny*, a ship consigned to Penet, D'Acosta et Cie., and by the time Smith obtained his release and prepared to embark again in the fall, the governor and Council abruptly canceled the scheme, probably because the Virginia economy continued to decline so badly. Pierre Penet did not reach France until March 1780 when he consulted Benjamin Franklin and discovered, as had William Lee, that the ambassador vigorously opposed individual states seeking loans from the French government for fear that the states would interfere with Congress's efforts. Mazzei sailed in June 1779 on board the *Jonathan Smith*, also consigned to Penet's firm, but one of the Goodriches captured it and brought it to New York. The winemaker persuaded the British to let him continue to Cork, Ireland, where he secured passage for France, arriving in November 1779. After that date Mazzei had no contact with Virginia until August 1781 when a large accumulation of mail caught up with him in Florence and he read that the governor and Council had abandoned the project almost two years before.

The outcome of Virginia's attempts to finance the Revolution cannot be surprising. Previous colonial wars had required deficit financing, and most of the matériel for those conflicts had come from abroad. Virginians had a major asset in tobacco, and many believed that they could greatly enhance their profit by recapturing the costs that had previously gone to British middlemen. To the Virginians' dismay, they found it vastly more difficult than they expected either to arrange for the distribution of their crops overseas or to develop domestic manufactures to lessen the state's dependence on imports. More serious for the war effort, the initial enthusiasm with which they had undertaken the experiments slowly dissipated as the projects atrophied and the economy deteriorated.

CHAPTER 10

The War in the West

OR sheer adventure, some of the most thrilling exploits of the
war for Virginians occurred in the campaign in the West. After
a few months of uneasy peace following Dunmore's failure to
win over western settlers for the crown, the British adopted the strategy that the French had employed against them for almost a century.
Operating from bases along the Great Lakes and the Gulf of Mexico,
royal agents organized the Indian tribes of the Ohio country and the
old Southwest to keep Americans from expanding across the Appalachian Mountains. With the main Continental armies engaged
primarily in the Northeast during the early years of the war, Virginia and other southern states were left to defend themselves on the
frontier, and they met the challenge with a remarkable display of
cooperation and organization. Authorities had noticeably less difficulty recruiting troops for the conquest and defense of the West than
for reinforcement of Washington in the North.

After John Connolly's plan collapsed in the fall of 1775, James
Wood, whom the Convention had sent to investigate, went on an extensive tour of the Ohio country to invite Indian leaders who had not
participated in Connolly's conference during the summer to another
meeting at Pittsburgh in October. Both Congress and Virginia appointed commissioners for the new round of deliberations, with
Thomas Walker of Virginia serving as chairman and Arthur St. Clair

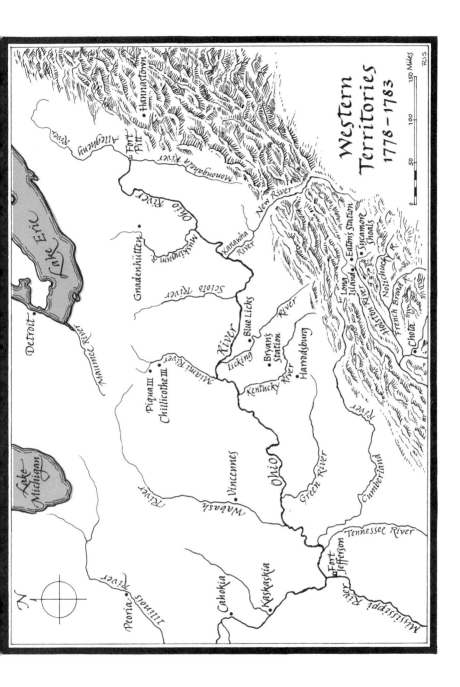

Western Territories 1778–1783

0 50 100 150 Miles

RJS

of Pennsylvania as secretary. After meeting from October 7 to 19, Cornstalk and other chiefs reaffirmed the agreement they had made at the conclusion of Dunmore's War, exactly one year before to the day, not to molest white settlements south of the Ohio River provided the whites left the Indians alone to the north.[1]

To the south of Virginia, Americans suspected John Stuart, the superintendent of Indian affairs for the southern department, of being the master architect behind a plan to raise the Indians against the colonists. During the preceding spring rebels had forced him to flee from Charleston to Savannah and then to St. Augustine. Actually at the time, rather than being a warmonger, Stuart counseled British leaders to keep the Indians neutral for fear that a wholesale uprising would drive potential loyalists into the rebel ranks. When Stuart's superiors finally elected to enlist Indians in the loyalist cause, he dispatched his brother and deputy superintendent, Henry, with a shipment of ammunition for the Overhill Cherokee in the spring of 1776. Henry's standing orders remained to secure the Indians' aid in "distressing the Rebels" without stirring "an indiscriminate attack" that would alienate the king's supporters as well.[2] The Stuarts' efforts to fine tune the responses of their Indian allies failed because the Indians were no more ready to surrender their lands to tories than to whigs while the prospect of a loyalist-led retreat to the east in order to pacify the tribesmen attracted few settlers, whatever their political persuasion.

At a May 1776 conference in the Indian town of Chota in modern Tennessee, Henry Stuart and Alexander Cameron, the permanent British representative to the Cherokee, found a group of younger Indians led by Chief Dragging Canoe determined to take advantage of the upheaval among the whites. The Indians' resolve was strengthened by the timely arrival of Cornstalk and other ambassadors from tribes north of the Ohio River with pledges of aid. Dragging Canoe's ire centered on the Watauga settlements in western North Carolina, which he claimed with some justice had been established by fraud beyond the boundary set for white settlement in the Proclamation of 1763. The British agents persuaded the Indians to delay their attack until authorities could offer the Watauga settlers alternative lands in the lower Mississippi River Valley in return for continued allegiance to the king. As the Indians predicted, the offer only put the settlers "on their Guard," for, although the Watauga inhabitants pledged loyalty to the crown, they refused to move and clearly were buying time to prepare their defense.[3] Finally, the belligerent defiance of the Fincastle County Committee of Safety "so exasperated" the Indians, the British agents reported, that "all our Rhetorick could no longer diswade them from taking up the Hatchet."[4]

With the support of British forces at St. Augustine, Pensacola, and Mobile, the Cherokee attacked all along the frontier from Georgia to Virginia during the summer of 1776. In the northern sector they raided Eaton's Station near Long Island in the Holston River on July 20 and the next day struck at Watauga Fort near Sycamore Shoals, North Carolina. The colonists drove off the initial attacks, but the Indians besieged Watauga for two weeks before Lieutenant Colonel William Russell of Fincastle County, whom the Virginia Convention had sent with six companies of rangers to patrol the area, relieved the fort. Most colonists agreed with Adam Stephen's call for quick retaliation to "make such an impression . . . as will Strike terror into the most distant Indian Nations."[5] Jefferson advised that the Cherokee "be driven beyond the Missisipi" to show "the invariable consequence of their beginning a war" because "our contest with Britain is too serious and too great to permit any possibility of avocation from the Indians."[6]

A flurry of letters from General Lee at his headquarters in Charleston orchestrated a superbly coordinated counterattack by the four southeastern states. In all, an overawing total of six thousand men massed for the assault. Clearly, the colonial militia was well designed for Indian warfare. At Lee's first summons the Virginia Council (meeting without a quorum) ordered a minuteman battalion under Andrew Lewis's brother, Colonel Charles Lewis of Augusta County, to reinforce Russell. Ten days later, on August 1, the Council superseded Lewis with Colonel William Christian of Fincastle County, Patrick Henry's brother-in-law and successor as commander of the 1st Regiment. Whether politics were involved is unclear, but Lieutenant Governor Page took care to report that the change was "by the request of Col. Russell and the Consent of Col. Lewis."[7] The new commander took charge of a combined Virginia–North Carolina force of almost two thousand men.

By October Christian had moved his army down the French Broad River in modern North Carolina and ravaged the Overhill Cherokee towns along the upper Tennessee River. Two columns farther south had already devastated the towns and crops of the Lower and Middle Cherokee. Finding to his surprise that the Overhill tribes offered little resistance, Christian demanded the surrender of Henry Stuart, Cameron, and Dragging Canoe, for whose scalps he posted bounties of one hundred pounds apiece, as ransom for the towns. He relented, however, when most of the Indians sued for peace, and he destroyed only those towns loyal to Dragging Canoe. Christian then pulled back into winter quarters at Fort Patrick Henry, which Russell had built on Long Island. Since boundary lines in the region remained vague, the Virginians assumed that the fort lay within their own state's borders.[8]

Negotiations with the Indians continued through the winter. By May, Christian had concluded preliminaries and, before finally signing the agreement with the Indians, brought forty "gentlemen and ladies of the Cherokee nation," as the *Virginia Gazette* described them, including the chiefs Oucanastota and Little Carpenter, to Williamsburg on a goodwill visit. The governor and Council received the party and gave them presents, and the guests "favoured the publick with a dance on the green in front of the palace."[9] But as a measure of the Virginians' lingering hostility despite the Indians' friendly gesture, Henry had to order a military guard for the delegation because of rumors of an assassination attempt.

On July 20, 1777, the first anniversary of the outbreak of the Indian war in Virginia, Cherokee chiefs met with representatives of that state and North Carolina at Long Island to pledge their neutrality in the struggle with Great Britain and to cede all their lands east of the Blue Ridge and north of the Nolichucky River. Georgia and South Carolina concluded a treaty with the southern tribes at Dewitt's Corner, South Carolina. The terms Virginia won brought the Cumberland Gap under the state's control, a major objective of Governor Henry, who had already planned a road to the West although the survey would not be complete for two more years. Ominously, some Overhill Cherokee under Chief Dragging Canoe refused to sign the treaty and withdrew to Chickamauga in modern Georgia to wait their chance again.[10]

After the Cherokees' defeat, the scene shifted northward as each side prepared for the next round. Because British efforts in the following months concentrated on winning support of New York tribes for the ill-fated Burgoyne, Major Henry Hamilton, the royal governor of Detroit, could not mount an attack against Pittsburgh as he ardently desired. Hamilton did manage to deploy enough Indians to terrorize the frontier and keep it in a state of frequent siege. Although evidence suggests that the governor may have been among the more restrained of the Indian leaders in the area, he won the hateful sobriquet among the settlers of the "Hair Buyer General."[11]

The Americans took little defensive action at first. The principal congressional agent in Pittsburgh, George Morgan, opposed any campaign that might stir up the Indians any more than they already were unless the Americans could take Detroit. As the raids continued, a clamor arose among frontiersmen against Morgan, and a call went out for a congressional investigation of his suspected toryism. Virginians also suspected that, as a Pennsylvanian and a member of the Indiana Company, Morgan had little desire to fight for territory that Virginia claimed.

Virginia interest in the West had grown considerably since Gibson and Linn had traveled to New Orleans to purchase gunpowder for the state. That expedition greatly broadened people's awareness of the area's geography and the possibilities of trade with the Spanish. Merchants, land speculators, and the new governor of Louisiana, Bernardo de Gálvez, were all intrigued with the idea of establishing communication via the Mississippi, but it was the state's military commander at Harrodsburg, George Rogers Clark, who came up with a plan for significant Virginia involvement in the West. Immediately upon William Linn's return in April 1777, Clark sent Linn's brother Benjamin and Samuel Moore to spy on the British garrison at Kaskaskia in modern Illinois. Their report indicated that the region north of the Ohio was a military vacuum because the British had withdrawn their forces to reinforce Detroit. They described the French-Canadian population as disaffected toward the British and observed that a naturalized French civilian, Phillippe de Rastel, Chevalier de Rocheblave, held the reins of local government. Clark set out for Williamsburg with this information, arriving early in November 1777, ostensibly to settle accounts with the treasury.[12]

At the Virginia capital officials handled the matter with utmost secrecy to avoid alerting the British and raised some interesting constitutional questions in the process. As soon as Clark arrived, he explained his plan to "a few Gentlemen" who "communicated it to the Governour." If he could win over the French in Illinois and "shew them that I ment to protect rather than treat them as a Conquered People. . . . It might probably have so great an effect on their Country men at Detroyet, (they already disliked their Master,) that it would be an easy prey for me." To take Detroit in this fashion, Clark estimated, would require only five hundred men, whereas "it was a general oppinion that it would take several thousand" to attack the main British base directly.[13] Henry and the others responded enthusiastically, but first they had to obtain legislative approval without letting more than a few delegates know what was going on. In the meantime, Clark finished his business with the treasury and went to his father's home in Caroline County until early December.

Clark returned to Williamsburg on December 10. That day the House of Delegates in the Committee of the Whole adopted a resolution permitting the governor and Council to employ the militia "on any expedition which may be undertaken by . . . congress . . . against any of our western Enemies" and granting the power of arrest within Virginia to any commissioners Congress appointed to investigate Morgan—a not too subtle reminder of Virginia's claim to the Pittsburgh area.[14] The whole emphasis of the resolve was to provide for Kentucky's defense in the face of Morgan's inactivity. Although the house appointed a committee consisting of George Mason, John Banister, Edmund Pendleton, Benjamin Harrison, and Thomas Bullitt to bring in a bill, Mason chiefly composed the measure. The committee's draft added to the house's original resolutions the clause "and also that the Governor with advice of the privy council at any time within nine months after the passing of this act, may empower a number of volunteers not exceeding six hundred to march against and attack any of our said enemies, and may appoint the proper officers and give the necessary Orders for the Expedition."[15] The bill passed easily although "but a few in the House knew the real intent of it," Clark said.[16]

On the same day, December 10, 1777, Clark briefed the Council about his plans under tight security, no mention of the meeting appearing in the minutes. The governor and five members attended. Then, "being desired by the Governour to stay some time in Town," Clark subsequently related, "I wated with impatience."[17] A three-week delay ensued until the legislature adopted the necessary bill on December 22 and the holidays were over. Finally, on January 2, Henry and the Council recalled Clark to give him his orders. He received two sets of instructions: one to be made public directing him to enlist seven companies of fifty men each for three months to defend Kentucky; the other authorizing him to lead them into Illinois. "So warmly Ingaged in the sucksess" of the operation were the governor and his advisers, Clark later recalled, "that I had very little trouble in geting matters adjusted"; once given command, "I then got every request granted."[18] Specifically, he obtained promises of bounties for his men. George Mason, Speaker George Wythe, and Thomas Jefferson signed a letter assuring Clark that each of his men would receive at least three hundred acres out of whatever lands they conquered from the Indians. Although the assembly was then in session, the three could not seek its approval without breaking secrecy, but they told Clark "we think you may safely confide" in the legislators' "Justice and Generosity."[19] They were wrong. When the time came, the assembly allowed only two hundred acres. The troops had to reenlist to earn the other one hundred.

The Council also ordered Clark to build a fort near the confluence of the Ohio and Mississippi rivers to protect the route to New Orleans, a project in which Governors Henry and Jefferson both took an active interest. Three days before Clark left Williamsburg, Henry dispatched Colonel David Rogers, who had connections with Thomas Bentley, a Kaskaskia trader, to pick up more supplies in New Orleans for Virginia and explore further the possibilities of trade.[20]

The unusual speed and energy the state leaders exhibited on this occasion paid off. At about the same time the congressional Committee of Commerce in Philadelphia, which Robert Morris chaired, decided to send Captain James Willing, the brother of Morris's partner Thomas Willing, to duplicate the feat of Virginia's Gibson and Linn and open trade to New Orleans in the name of the Continent. But Congress delayed further planning until the summer of 1778. Then, informed that the Continent was contemplating an attack on Detroit, the Virginia Council could honestly reply without revealing its own plans that in view of the late season and the shortage of supplies, they were "of Opinion that the Expedition is utterly impracticable."[21] By the time the Continental general, Lachlan McIntosh, was ready to set out from Pittsburgh in October 1778, he considered only a limited excursion against hostile tribes nearby to be feasible.

The subterfuge to conceal Clark's plans backfired when he began recruiting. Although officially he called for enlistments to defend Kentucky, some suspected the true purpose. County officials prevented Captain Leonard Helms from raising men in Fauquier County because "no such service was known of by the assembly" until he sent for a letter of authorization from the governor.[22] Helms and Captain Joseph Bowman in Frederick County lost two-thirds of their recruits through desertion as word of the expedition's real goal began to trickle down. Similarly, fewer than a quarter of the two hundred men Clark expected Major William Smith and Captain Thomas Dillard to bring from the settlements on the Holston River in North Carolina arrived. At Pittsburgh the Continental commander, General Edward Hand, willingly cooperated with Clark although he had no authority from Congress. But Pennsylvanians tried hard to keep anyone from enlisting in the service of Virginia, and many expressed sentiment for George Morgan's point of view, let the few people in Kentucky come back rather than leave more settled areas defenseless to protect them.[23]

In June Clark collected the various units on an island at the falls of the Ohio near present-day Cincinnati to prevent the troops from escaping when he finally told them that they were going to Illinois. Despite Clark's precautions and his orders to kill any deserter who refused to return, Captain Dillard and most of his company forded the river and fled. The rest of "the Soldiery in Genl. Debated on the subject but determined to follow their Officers," Clark wrote in his memoir. Left with only about 175 men, Clark decided that he could not attack Vincennes, the strongest of the French towns, as he had planned, and settled on Kaskaskia instead. Then, on June 24, 1778, just as the tiny expedition set out, an 80 to 90 percent eclipse of the sun occurred, "which," Clark wryly observed, "caused Various conjectures among the superstitious."[24]

Fortunately for Clark, his intelligence about Kaskaskia from over twelve months before remained accurate. Hunters he met on the way confirmed the earlier information and especially strengthened the Virginia leader's supposition that the French inhabitants disliked Americans only because they feared them as near-barbarians, or "Big Knives" as the Indians aptly nicknamed them, rather than because of loyalty to the British. Moving without baggage "in the Indean mode," Clark landed his men across from and a little below the mouth of the Tennessee River and went overland to avoid being seen by lookouts along the Ohio's banks.[25] For a while the troops lost their way until the guide found the trail again when Clark threatened to kill him if he did not. The column reached Kaskaskia on the evening of July 4. In spite of all efforts at secrecy, rumors of Clark's movements had circulated in Kaskaskia a few days before. The French militia mobilized but disbanded when no one appeared. Catching the town entirely by surprise, the Virginians took it without resistance.

Clark adopted a stern policy, commanding his men not to talk to inhabitants and ordering the people to stay in their houses under penalty of being shot. He arrested the commander, de Rocheblave, and stationed a guard over Mme. de Rocheblave as well as the wife of a prominent merchant suspected of British sympathies whom Clark wanted to intimidate. The physical appearance of the Virginians had the impact intended: "As we had left our Cloath at the River we were almost naked and torn by the Bushes and Bryers," Clark explained.[26] When the town priest and a few elders finally gathered courage to beg for the safety of the women and children, Clark at last revealed that the French king had signed an alliance with America and offered the Kaskaskians a chance to become American citizens.

Clark achieved the result that he wished. The French militia volunteered to go with Captain Bowman to talk their friends and relatives at Cahokia into surrendering. That town capitulated on July 6, also without a shot being fired. When the Virginians continued their policy of leniency—setting up elected governments in the two towns, for example—Father Joseph Gibault offered to persuade the residents of Vincennes also to give up. Clark agreed to let the priest go unaccompanied except by a few of Gibault's own compatriots—among whom the Americans planted a spy, however—and after an absence of about two weeks, "which," Clark admitted, "caused great anciety in me," the party arrived back about August 1 with the "Joyfull News" that their mission had been accomplished.[27] Only the Chevalier de Rocheblave held out, at times becoming so violent in his denunciations of the Americans and the inhabitants who cooperated with them that Clark had to imprison the Frenchman for his own safety. Stationing Captain Helms with a small detachment at Vincennes and Bowman at Cahokia, Clark sent Captain John Montgomery to convey de Rocheblave to Williamsburg along with the good news of the American victories and a plea for reinforcements.

Considering himself seriously overextended, Clark resorted to bluff. He spread the word that he commanded only a small reconnaissance unit from a main army still at the falls of the Ohio (he had actually left a few "Invalids" and camp followers to establish a base there) and that an even larger force from Pittsburgh would soon reinforce him. Apparently the ruse worked, for over the next two months many Indians of the vicinity came into Kaskaskia and renounced their alliance with the British.[28]

Montgomery reached Williamsburg about the middle of November 1778, at which time Patrick Henry at last confessed to Congress—and probably for the first time to the assembly as well—that "the Executive power of this State having been impressed with a strong apprehension of incursions on their frontier . . . and supposing the danger would be greatly obviated by an enterprise against . . . that country . . . sent a detachment . . . on that service some time last spring." The governor reported with pleasure that Clark's success "equalled the most sanguine expectations."[29] The assembly quickly voted a resolution extolling

Clark's contribution "to the common cause of America, as well as to this Commonwealth in particular," and within two weeks organized a government for all the area "on the western side of the Ohio . . . adjacent to the river Mississippi," designating it Illinois County.[30] Henry appointed Clark military commander and Colonel John Todd of Kentucky county lieutenant. The governor sent Clark copies of the Virginia constitution and Declaration of Rights to help persuade the Illinois inhabitants of Virginia's good intentions and enlist their support for an attack on Detroit. Meanwhile, the governor and Council directed Montgomery to raise five new companies of reinforcements. Henry wrote privately to Clark that because the land office had not yet opened, Virginia authorities could not grant Clark and his men the land bounties that had been promised, but the governor assured Clark that "I shall not forget you."[31]

Yet even as Virginians rejoiced, Henry Hamilton marched to counterattack. Setting out from Detroit on October 6 with about sixty militiamen and seventy Indians, the British leader rallied the tribes along his way that remained loyal and was able to swell his ranks to about five hundred by the time the force reached Vincennes. Slowed by snow, freezing rivers, high winds, and innumerable stops to cement Indian alliances, the British took seventy-one days to cover six hundred miles. Hamilton was within three days of Vincennes before Helms learned of his approach. The British captured the scouts that the Virginian sent out and invested Vincennes on December 17 before Helms could prepare. Most of the fifty-odd French militiamen who had enlisted with Helms deserted, and since only twenty-one of his own garrison remained, the Virginia commander surrendered without a struggle the same day.[32]

Word of Helms's capitulation at Vincennes soon reached Kaskaskia. Panic swept through the town at the rumor that Hamilton and an army of five hundred were just a few miles away. Finally, on January 29, 1779, Francis Vigo, a merchant in the employ of Spanish authorities at St. Louis, arrived with the information that Hamilton had decided not to attack Kaskaskia but to winter at Vincennes with a garrison of only eighty men, fifty of them French. The British commander had sent his Indian allies off on raiding parties with instructions to return in the spring. Clark concluded that without reinforcements the Virginians and their French supporters would be unable to withstand the combined forces that Hamilton could muster the next year. Clark's decision to attack at once typified the daring that characterized the entire expedition:

"I am Resolved . . . to Risque the whole on a Single Battle," he wrote to Governor Henry.[33]

Clark set off on February 5 with about 130 men including French volunteers. In order to move across country as rapidly as possible, Clark sent his artillery and an additional 50 men by boat with orders to meet him on the Wabash River, but the vessel did not reach the rendezvous before the campaign ended. "Through Increditable difficulties far surpassing any thing any of us had ever experienced," Clark reported, he and his men marched 180 miles to Vincennes, a feat possible only because the weather had turned relatively mild for that season.[34] The thaw flooded many of the rivers that the troops had to ford; the Wabash was five miles wide at the point where they crossed. At last, on February 23, 1779, the Americans arrived at Vincennes, taking the British completely unaware. Hamilton's men were engaged in sports outside the fort when the enemy appeared. When the British hastily withdrew to Fort Sackville, the French inhabitants of the town came over to the Virginians. Stores of powder that the French had hidden from the British proved invaluable to Clark since his support vessel had not arrived and most of the supply his men had taken with them had been ruined crossing swollen rivers.

Clark's memoir makes clear again that he prided himself on being able to manipulate the enemy, although his psychological tactics may not have influenced the outcome in this instance as much as at Kaskaskia. As dusk fell, Clark maneuvered his troops around the fort to create the illusion of overwhelming force until darkness allowed Virginia riflemen to creep close enough to shoot into embrasures and prevent the British gunners from firing. According to Clark's description, the fighting remained brisk for the next twenty-four hours, yet only one Virginian and seven British were wounded. Throughout, despite the fact that Clark wrote his account after the fact, the American commander seems to have been supremely confident, probably because the intelligence from the townspeople predicted that most of the French still with the British would eventually desert. Clark even let a British scouting party sneak back into the fort to be certain that he captured them all.

On the evening of the twenty-fourth Hamilton proposed terms that included a three-day truce prior to the actual surrender, causing Clark to wonder if reinforcements were coming. Clark rejected the offer and demanded unconditional surrender because "I wanted a sufficient excuse to put all the Indians and partisans to death." Hamilton asked, "Why will you force me to dishonour myself when you cannot acquire more honour by it?" Clark recalled later that he had responded, "Could I look on you Sir as a Gentleman I would do [so] to the utmost of my power, but on you Sir who have embrued your hands in the blood of our women and children, Honor, my country, everything calls on me alloud for Vengeance."[35]

To keep up the pressure, Clark ordered several Indian prisoners tomahawked to death before the main gate of the fort during the parley with Hamilton. As Clark anticipated, the remaining Indians blamed the British for not protecting their comrades rather than the Virginians for executing them. Clark's men also captured François Maisonville, one of the French partisans with Hamilton. The Virginians first used Maisonville as a shield behind which they could fire without fear of the British shooting back, and then partially scalped him—according to Hamilton at Clark's direct order. In his memoir Clark simply said matter-of-factly that it was others who were "so Inhumane" but noted that they did Maisonville "no other damage."[36]

Actually, the terror Clark induced may have had a reverse effect by convincing the British they might as well fight to the end. Hamilton broke off discussions when Clark insisted upon unconditional surrender. At that, the Virginians modified their demands, Clark conceding that despite the British commander's reputation, "almost every man had conceived a very favourable opinion of Govr. Hamilton."[37] The Virginians finally agreed to allow the British to keep their arms and to permit the three-day period for the prisoners to settle their local affairs that Hamilton had requested, but Clark insisted that the surrender should take place before rather than after the truce. The terms made no mention of parole for Hamilton, however. Although the British signed the capitulation late on February 24, the Virginians delayed the actual surrender until ten o'clock the next morning because they wanted to be certain that they did not overlook any prisoners in the dark.

As the savagery with which Clark conducted the negotiations reveals, the feeling against Hamilton and the leaders of the French partisans, Major Jehu Hay, Captain William La Mothe, and Maisonville, was extreme. Contrary to the terms of surrender, Clark prepared to cast them in chains but then relented. On several occasions the Virginians would have murdered the captives had they not fled to Clark's tent for protection. When Clark sent twenty-seven of the most important prisoners under guard to Williamsburg on March 8, he predicted that none would arrive alive, the animosity among the frontiersmen was so strong. "In this we found he had told us the truth, being often threatened upon the march and waylaid at different times," Hamilton later reported to his superiors, but the British commander praised the escort who "behaved very well, protected us and hunted for us else we must have starved for our rations were long since expended."[38]

The prisoners reached Chesterfield County, Virginia, just as Jefferson began his first term as governor, and the new executive ordered La Mothe and the "Hair Buyer General" brought immediately to the capital in irons. The two arrived on June 17, 1779, Virginia's most impressive war trophies to date. Hamilton wrote in his account that "a considerable Mob gather'd about us, which accompanied us to jail."[39] The rest of the prisoners arrived shortly afterward. The state confined the leaders among the prisoners in chains, forbidding them to converse with outsiders and denying them any means of correspondence. The winter of 1779–1780 was one of the severest on record, and the Williamsburg jail seldom had enough heat. The poor diet resulted in Hamilton growing so thin that he could slip his hands in and out of the irons. The bulk of the prisoners moved to King William County in December; Hamilton and Hay went to Chesterfield in August 1780. One by one the prisoners found exchanges except Hamilton and Hay, who stubbornly refused the terms of parole the Virginians offered because the terms so strictly limited their right of correspondence. They felt that any malicious informer could easily remand them to prison in disgrace for breaching their honor. Jefferson pointed out that the British used essentially the same form for Americans in New York. Finally, in October 1780, the two sides reached accommodation, and Hamilton and Hay accepted a parole to arrange their exchange in New York, which they accomplished the following spring.

The British severely censured Jefferson for his treatment of Hamilton, and had the Virginia governor been captured, he undoubtedly would have suffered accordingly. Today the evidence upon which the Virginia authorities acted is open to challenge, particularly the testimony of a disreputable Indian trader, John Dodge, who had his own reasons for hating Hamilton and pledged to see that the British prisoners "will all be hanged without redemption."[40] The most damaging evidence against the captives was the proclamation that Hamilton issued after he recaptured Vincennes to entice the other former French towns to surrender. When the document is read today, it does not substantiate the charge of "Hair Buyer," at least if one assumes that an Indian war at the time was likely for the Indians' own reasons. Virginians, of course, did not. Jefferson declared that, although the British governor's proc-

lamation "does not in express terms threaten vengeance, blood and Mas-
sacre, yet it . . . gives in detail the horrid Catalogue of savage nations,
extending from south to North, whom he had leagued with himself to
wage combined war on our frontiers: and it is well known that that war
could of course be made up of blood, and general Massacres of Men
Women and Children."[41] Virginians conveniently overlooked the atroc-
ities perpetrated on the frontier by their own side during the war.

For the next eighteen months Clark maintained control of the Northwest with similar hairbreadth escapades plus an ample ration of good
luck despite an almost total lack of support from the East. Until the
spring of 1780 he clung to a slim hope of mounting an attack on Detroit.
Then a second round of bills for fifty thousand dollars from suppliers
in Havana for the expedition against Kaskaskia and Vincennes came as
a shock to the governor and Council, who already owed Oliver Pollock
in New Orleans sixty-five thousand. The executive immediately rescinded Clark's authority to order supplies independently and directed
him to forget Detroit. Mysteriously, strategy and economics coincided.
A thousand miles away, Clark had assessed the situation realistically and
decided on his own to withdraw from north of the Ohio River to the
fort that Governors Henry and Jefferson had been pressing him to build
where the Ohio joined the Mississippi.[42]

In the meantime, the British revamped their strategy to open a new
theater in the South and simultaneously attempted to recoup their losses
of the previous year in the West. From Michilimackinac and Chicago a
large force of about nine hundred British and Indians set out in May
1780 to capture St. Louis and drive the Spanish back down the Mississippi River. A second force of about eleven hundred, many of them
Indians whom Hamilton's successor, Major Arent Schuyler de Peyster,
spent eighty-four hundred pounds sterling in gifts recruiting, left
Detroit to attack the forts along the Ohio. A precipitous decline in pro-
American sentiment among the French settlers of the region encouraged the British. The Virginians had first duped the French into believing that the state's currency was equal in value to specie, and then, when
the French discovered otherwise, impressed the settlers' provisions.[43]

Clark's initiative and daring again enabled him to carry the campaign.
In mid-April he established Fort Jefferson about five miles below where
the Ohio and Mississippi meet, and by persuading Lieutenant Governor
Todd to exceed his authority and grant settlers four hundred acres
apiece, attracted a number of families to establish the town of Clarksville

nearby. Clark thus was in position to block the British expedition when it attacked Cahokia and St. Louis on May 26. Warned of the enemy's approach, the Spanish at St. Louis put up such resistance that, with the added danger of Clark's proximity, the British attackers broke off and retreated northward. Clark immediately organized a punitive force of about 350 men from among the Spanish and French and sent them off in pursuit under Colonel John Montgomery. The expedition pushed as far as the Indian towns at Peoria, which Montgomery burned before retiring.[44]

Knowing that Clark was far away on the Mississippi, Colonel Henry Bird in command of the second British column hastened southward from Detroit. But after reducing Rudelle's and Martin's stations on the Licking River in northern Kentucky, Bird learned that a Virginia relief column under Colonel George Slaughter had arrived at the falls of the Ohio. Fearing that the reinforcements might hold him up until Clark's return, Bird decided to withdraw to Detroit and be satisfied with the number of prisoners he had already taken. When Clark heard of Bird's movements early in July, he and a couple of companions disguised as Indians left Illinois and raced back through the wilderness. After a narrow escape from capture and adventurous crossings of the swollen Tennessee and Kentucky rivers on log rafts bound with grapevines, the three reached Harrodsburg, Kentucky, where Clark raised over a thousand men for a counterattack.

The expedition crossed the Ohio on August 1. Clark later discovered from a prisoner that dissident Frenchmen had given the Shawnee about ten days' notice of his intentions. The Indians moved their women and children to safety and with the aid of the tory leader, Simon Girty, fortified the town of Piqua. The Indians abandoned their major settlement at Chillicothe, knowing that it would be destroyed. As soon as Clark's forces reached Piqua on August 8 the battle began. Although at one point the Indians outmaneuvered the Virginians, Clark eventually drove them off with heavy losses. But lack of supplies prevented him from carrying out Governor Jefferson's explicit directions: "The end proposed should be their extermination, or their removal beyond the lakes or Illinois river" since "the same world will scarcely do for them and us."[45] Nonetheless, the destruction of the two towns and of approximately eight hundred acres of corn crippled the Shawnee sufficiently to prevent further military activity on their part during 1780.

On the southern frontier Alexander Cameron, the British agent among the Cherokee, had convinced Chief Dragging Canoe and his followers that it was again time to strike since renewed British activity under General Cornwallis in South Carolina and Georgia had drawn away almost all of the militia. A battle with loyalist forces at King's Mountain in October 1780, however, resulted in a victory for the Americans, and John Sevier and his men returned before the Indians had hardly gone on the warpath. Sending word to Virginia for help, Sevier set off with a party of about 250 North Carolinians. They met a band of Indians at Boyd's Creek on the French Broad River on December 8 and inflicted heavy losses while suffering only one casualty themselves. Arthur Campbell of Washington County joined Sevier later in December with 400 Virginians. After that, the combined force met no serious resistance. When the Indians sued for peace, Campbell put them off a few days, he reported to Jefferson, because he wanted "to distress the whole, as much as possible, by destroying their habitations and Provisions." Chota and ten other towns "besides some small ones, and several scattering settlements" were eradicated, in all, "upwards of One thousand Houses, and not less than fifty thousand Bushels of Corn, and large quantities of other kinds of Provisions." The enemy lost twenty-nine dead and seventeen prisoners; the frontiersmen suffered only three casualties. Finally, on New Year's Day 1781, the invaders decided to go home, "no other object of importance being in view."[46] By aggressiveness and good fortune the frontier's defenders had made the entire West north and south of the Ohio River for the moment secure.

From that high point American fortunes in the West began to recede. Although innocent of malfeasance himself, Clark proved not to be a good administrator. Complaints multiplied about the abuses of his appointees, particularly John Dodge, the Indian agent in Illinois. Having initially won over the French population from the British, Clark's subordinates were driving them back to the enemy and rekindling royalist hopes of reclaiming the region. Increasing British activity in the coastal areas of the South entirely occupied authorities there with local defense, leaving Clark to his own continuously diminishing resources. Although many of the setbacks Clark suffered were beyond his control, repeated misfortunes turned the commander from a hero into a pathetic figure in the eyes of eastern leaders.

For a while after Jefferson became governor, he displayed the same zeal for Clark's enterprises that he had on the eve of the first expedition. Early in 1781 Jefferson called the commander to the capital for consultations about another assault on Detroit. If successful, the governor explained, the campaign would "quiet . . . our frontiers . . . form a barrier against . . . the British Province of Canada and add to the Empire of liberty an extensive and fertile Country."[47] The Indian fighter's charisma was disappearing, however. Militia widely refused to join the new expedition because of the growing disaffection with Clark's administration, and with the British obviously preparing to take advantage of the malaise, the Continental commander at Fort Pitt, Colonel Daniel Brodhead, who was jealous of Clark, had the reason he needed to allocate fewer men and supplies than a full-scale campaign required.

By the summer of 1781, too, the garrison at Fort Jefferson on the Mississippi River had to abandon its post for want of supplies. Except for a few troops at Vincennes, the westernmost point of Virginia's authority thereafter was Fort Nelson at the falls of the Ohio. A council of war in September advised Clark to abandon any thought of an excursion against the British and pull back still farther to the mouth of the Kentucky River. "My chain appears to have run out," the western commander wrote despondently to Richmond.[48] The House of Delegates agreed with the defensive strategy recommended by the council of war and ordered the construction of additional forts along the river to the east of the falls with a couple of gunboats stationed at each. Regarding resources, Clark's instructions may have contained the understatement of the war: "You will very probably ask how the Business required to be done can be carried on without Money. The answer indeed is difficult." Borrow what you can locally, he was told.[49]

The initiative shifted dramatically in 1782. In March Pennsylvania militia under Colonel David Williamson senselessly massacred a peaceful community of Christian Delaware Indians at Gnadenhütten about one hundred miles west of Pittsburgh. According to a newspaper report, the frontiersmen "killed and scalped upwards of ninety (but few making their escape), about forty of which were warriors, the rest old men, women, and children." Although Virginia's governor at the time, Benjamin Harrison, spoke for many when he condemned the event as a "most shocking and cruel murder," both he and congressional authorities heeded the warning of General William Irvine, Brodhead's successor at Pittsburgh, that any attempt to prosecute the culprits "may be attended with disagreeable consequences."[50] Nonetheless, vengeance came swiftly. About two months later, the Indians overran another expedition for which Williamson served as second in command and, although Williamson himself escaped, the victors hideously tortured to death the commander, William Crawford, and a number of others as the loyalist leaders, Simon Girty and Alexander McKee, looked on.[51]

The British went on the offensive for the rest of the summer of 1782.

The commander at Detroit, Major de Peyster, directed the assault. He had the assistance of a number of well-known tories who had gathered ready for revenge: Dunmore's agent, Dr. John Connolly, Colonel Hamilton's former aide, William La Mothe, and the one-time commander in Illinois, Phillippe de Rocheblave, all of whom had been exchanged. Indian raids penetrated as far as Hannastown (near modern Greensburg), thirty miles east of Pittsburgh. The British Captains William Caldwell and Alexander McKee assembled the largest single body of Indians marshaled during the war, over eleven hundred, and by early August had advanced as far as Wheeling. Yet once again, despite the numbers, the awe with which British and Indians regarded Clark frustrated the undertaking. When the first of the gunboats that the assembly had ordered appeared on the Ohio at the mouth of the Miami River in late July, a new round of rumors that Clark was on the move convinced de Peyster to suspend the attack. Unwilling to lose the opportunity completely, a splinter group of about three hundred under Girty, Caldwell, and McKee headed for Kentucky instead.[52]

By mid-August the raiders were south of the Ohio River at Blue Licks, Kentucky, where a much smaller force of frontiersmen under Daniel Boone and other local leaders foolhardily attacked the British without waiting for the reinforcements Benjamin Logan was leading from Lexington. "We Marched in order to gain great applause with our men," one of the survivors subsequently admitted.[53] Trapped on a peninsula formed by a loop in the Licking River, over a third of the Kentuckians, between sixty and seventy, a significant proportion of the region's leadership at the time, were killed in about five minutes. By the end of September William Christian reported to Governor Harrison that "numbers of People are now on the Road, moving out."[54]

Many blamed the area's lack of defense on Clark because he had "become a Sot; perhaps something worse." Harrison furiously upbraided him for not building the forts that the legislature had ordered and, since Clark's last letter to his superiors had been written in May, accused the commander of deliberately concealing his lack of progress from eastern officials. Apologizing because "it is disagreeable to me to make inquirey in this Way," the executive wrote to William Fleming and others in the West to ask if Clark was "so addicted to liquor as to be incapable of Attending to his Duty."[55]

Clark angrily responded to the governor. He attributed the rumors of his drinking to his personal enemies John Donelson and Arthur Campbell, who Clark charged wanted to secede from Virginia and form a separate state in Kentucky and Tennessee. Then the western commander lashed out. Marching forth with over a thousand men on November 3, he reached the Shawnee town of Chillicothe on the tenth. Although most of the Indians had time to escape, the frontiersmen quickly reduced Chillicothe and four other towns, along with the British trading post at the portage of the Miami River, to ashes. "The Quantity of provisions destroyed far surpassed any Idea we had of their Stores of that kind," Clark reported to Harrison.[56] Receiving no further challenge, the Americans returned to Lexington, Kentucky, by the eighteenth.

Clark found the investigating commission that the legislature had appointed to look into the alleged abuses in the West awaiting him. Hearings over the next several months exonerated the commander of personal peculation, but left the impression that he could have watched his associates more closely.[57] Clark resigned in an angry exchange with Harrison, charging again that a "Numerous Clan of Partizans or pretended Proprietors [with claims in the West] residing in Philadelphia" had prejudiced the governor against him and "put it out of my power to save the Country."[58] At first Harrison tried to mollify the western leader by approving—hesitantly, to be sure, for the state had no money—Clark's recommendation for another preventive war since trouble with the Indians would not end "until we shall . . . be Reduced to the necessity of convincing them that we are always able to crush them at pleasure." But by the time Clark reached the Virginia capital in the spring of 1783 to fashion a new plan, the governor had changed his mind. Perfunctorily thanking Clark for conquering the West for Virginia, Harrison told him to "consider yourself as out of Command."[59]

One of the most romantic and heroic chapters in the Revolutionary annals ended in bitterness, recriminations, and disgrace for some of its leading participants. In terms of the objectives of Clark and the Virginia politicians who laid the initial plans, the western campaign was not a success. Militarily, Virginia failed to sustain its claims north of the Ohio River. Congress did no better, however, and in terms of overall strategy, Clark and his associates with a minimum commitment of resources kept the British and Indians in the West sufficiently off balance to prevent them from mounting a campaign that could distract American armies in the East. Sevier, the Campbells, and their compatriots had similar success on the southern frontier. The British resurgence in the West at the end of the Revolution failed to achieve all of its objectives and was too late to affect the war's outcome.

CHAPTER 11

British Strategy Shifts Southward

THE war returned to eastern Virginia on May 8, 1779, less than a month before the end of Patrick Henry's third term as governor. Late on that day, a Saturday, a flotilla of twenty-eight ships led by the sixty-four-gun H.M.S. *Raisonable* and the forty-four-gun *Rainbow* under Commodore Sir George Collier entered the Virginia Capes and anchored off Willoughby's Point near Norfolk. A few weeks earlier Collier, one of the ablest British officers in the war, had assumed temporary command of the royal naval forces in the North American theater in the interval between the departure of Rear Admiral James Gambier and the arrival of Vice Admiral Marriot Arbuthnot. With energy that was not characteristic of either his predecessor or successor, Collier talked the usually cautious supreme commander, Henry Clinton, into authorizing a surprise assault in the Chesapeake. Although Clinton was desperate for reinforcements from Great Britain, he let Collier have eighteen hundred men under Major General Edward Mathew for the enterprise. The strategy was to distract the Americans by launching a "desultory expedition" in the South, as Clinton put it, and then hurry back to surprise Washington and the main American army at King's Ferry and West Point in New York.[1]

"Desultory" or not, the expedition was a brilliant success. Leaving the *Raisonable* to blockade Hampton because he did not trust its greater draft in the tidal waters, Collier entered the Elizabeth River on board the *Rainbow*. On the afternoon of May 10 he and Mathew personally led an amphibious assault on Fort Nelson which guarded Portsmouth. According to British engineers who later dismantled it, the fort was amazingly well built. Its fourteen-foot parapets were as thick as they were high and contained forty-eight gun embrasures. At the moment, however, fewer than one hundred men manned it, and the Virginia commander, Major Thomas Matthews, abandoned the post the next day. The British quickly occupied Portsmouth and Gosport, whose shipyard Collier pronounced "the *most considerable* in America," and crossed the river to Norfolk.[2] Before retreating, the Virginians burned the twenty-eight-gun *Virginia*, which was just about to be launched, and two French merchantmen, one of which was loaded with over one thousand hogsheads of tobacco belonging to Silas Deane. Six other vessels in various stages of construction on the stocks, including two frigates commissioned by Congress, fell to the invaders.

Without a moment's loss, Collier and Mathew followed up their advantage before the Virginians could recover. A half-dozen smaller ships pursued the vessels that had fled up the South Branch of the Elizabeth River, where the British burned or captured twenty-two. Major Matthews had to destroy the quantity of powder he tried to salvage from the fort and retreat precipitously into North Carolina. Because Matthews had to march all the way around the Great Dismal Swamp to return to Virginia, it was several days before Williamsburg authorities learned precisely what had happened at Portsmouth. Meanwhile, a detachment of Royal Highlanders raided Kemp's Landing where they uncovered another cache of arms and stores.

A second spear of the British attack struck Suffolk, which had mushroomed over the past year into a major supply center. The British caused extremely heavy damage. The occupying force burned virtually the entire town, destroying many thousand barrels of tobacco, salt provisions, and naval stores. In a twist of fate, because the town had been a Scottish trading center before the war, loyalists whose warehouses the state had expropriated suffered some of the severest losses. From Suffolk the British planned to go on to Smithfield but fell back toward Portsmouth when they heard that a large force of militia was approaching. In all, the British suffered only two men wounded.[3]

Just as some of the bloodiest fighting in the North occurred when patriot and loyalist troops confronted each other, the raid was Virginia's introduction to the brutality of civil war. Virginians who had endured the misery of defeat had been waiting their opportunity. Although the assembly had provided for reestablishing local government and reregistering titles in Norfolk and had compensated whigs for their losses, little rebuilding had taken place. A number of inhabitants had constructed "small huts" on their lots, but even a year and a half after Collier's raid American intelligence reports listed only "about 15 Houses built up again."[4] Marauders who had held out after Dunmore's departure and were driven in desperation over the fine line dividing military action from crime periodically terrorized whigs and tories alike. The most notorious was Josiah Phillips whom the authorities finally caught and hanged with a number of his band at the end of 1778. Among those who fled with Dunmore, James Parker, George Blair, and others had been planning revenge for at least six months, briefing the British on the Virginia leadership and the state's geography. Mathew later said that he was "greatly indebted for the success that ensued" to Parker, who came along as a guide, and Blair had led the way to Suffolk.[5] The elder Goodrich and at least one of his sons, Bridger, accompanied the expedition as privateers. Little wonder that Virginia officials banned Parker, Blair, and the Goodriches from the state after the war.

The ferocity of the attack on Suffolk, and the plundering of the privateers led by H.M.S. *Otter,* which Collier sent to sweep the upper bay, produced a flurry of atrocity stories. One lady "shewed . . . her torn fingers from whence [the British] had taken her rings," and there were tales of women carried off to British ships and of sailors with their eyes put out, or strangled. Collier admitted that despite his orders "some little irregularities happened," but blamed them on the fact that "the privateers had no idea of order or discipline." He distributed to civilians as compensation some captured salt that was "useless to the fleet."[6] Subsequent, and cooler, testimony indicated that several Frenchmen in Portsmouth supervising the loading of Silas Deane's tobacco had indeed been murdered. Deane's brother Simeon escaped in the confusion of the night, but about thirty of his party went as prisoners to Long Island. Although Silas joined Simeon in Williamsburg the following winter, the Deane family's Virginia enterprises never recovered from the loss. Eventually—as undoubtedly the Lees had always expected—a disheartened Silas turned tory and on a trip to France slipped across the Channel to England.

The Collier–Mathew raid sent a paroxysm of fear through Virginia, where many assumed that Hampton, Yorktown, and Williamsburg were next, and into North Carolina, where New Bern seemed the most likely target. At the first news of the invasion on May 8 Thomas Smith began to evacuate the Public Store and sent two sacks to the Capitol to pack the "publick papers."[7] Governor Henry immediately issued a limited call-up of local militia, but because of the delay in intelligence from Portsmouth did not order a full mobilization until May 14. Henry subsequently suffered severe criticism for this sluggishness. The assembly and other authorities came in for their share of the censure for Virginia's lack of preparation, but with less than a month to go in an otherwise successful term as governor, Henry bore the heaviest blame for the overconfidence into which all Virginians had slipped.

Most commentators agreed that, once summoned, the militia responded with unexpected alacrity until by May 18 or 19—even allowing for exaggeration—a thousand or more had mustered in the Yorktown–Williamsburg area with a like number at both Hampton and Smithfield. Once more in command, Thomas Nelson had to keep his troops scattered because he did not know the British intentions. Worse, the militia had weapons enough for only every third or fourth man. The volunteer cavalry responded especially well. The student company at the College of William and Mary rode swiftly to Smithfield, and the corps under the general's brother, Hugh Nelson, received compliments for its performance. The House of Delegates summoned Theodorick Bland's Continental dragoons from their station at Winchester—an action that Governor Henry took as a rebuke because the state had to rely on outside aid—and asked General Charles Scott, a Continental officer recruiting in Virginia, to place eight hundred new enlistees at the state's service. The house gratefully voted Scott five hundred dollars and a new horse for his help.[8]

State leaders were confident that the outpouring of militia forced the British to embark from Portsmouth on May 24, but actually the royal troops paid scant attention to the Virginians' activities. Because of the enthusiastic reception by local inhabitants, Collier hurried off a plea to Clinton to establish a permanent base at Portsmouth and tried to prevail upon Mathew at least to wait for the reply. The army leader refused to deviate from the original conception of the expedition as merely a raid and insisted on returning to New York by the first of June. Clinton's answer just pointed out that as the commanders on the scene the decision was entirely theirs, but they bore complete responsibility for the consequences, too.[9]

Disappointed, Collier loaded seventeen of the prize ships with as much of the captured stores as they could hold. Ninety tories, including forty-four women and children, who had been waiting to be rescued for years, came aboard, among them the Reverend John Agnew's wife and a survivor of Dunmore's campaigns who had been hiding in the swamps since the ex-governor fled. There were also 518 blacks who had come into the British lines. The British collected the stores that could not be moved—"five thousand loads of fine seasoned oak knees for shipbuilding; an infinite quantity of plank, masts, cordage," Collier reported—at the shipyard in Gosport and burned them. "The conflagration in the night appeared grand beyond description," wrote the British commander, his sailor's soul anguished by the waste, "a very melancholy" sight.[10] In all, the expedition captured or destroyed 137 vessels and stores valued at two million pounds, prompting the House of Delegates to insist upon reparations in the event of peace talks and Congress to urge the burning of British cities in retaliation. When the main fleet departed, three privateers under Bridger Goodrich remained behind and destroyed the tobacco warehouses at Wicomico. Patrick Henry issued a proclamation threatening vengeance on tories if the attacks did not cease. They did not. And when Congress sent two frigates to chase the privateers, the *Rainbow* and the *Solebay* returned to plague traffic in the Chesapeake Bay throughout the summer.[11]

The invasion shocked the assembly into realizing the worth of Washington's warning the previous fall that the war was not yet over and brought home to the Virginia legislators the seriousness of the manpower shortage. The legislators had no practical remedy, however. In addition to Thomas Nelson, whom it appointed major general, the assembly called for the commissioning of two brigadier generals and the enlistment of 4,560 men in eight battalions with full retinues of fifers and drummers, surgeons, and supply officers. Two of the battalions were to serve in the West for nine months, the other six in the East for the duration of the raid plus one month. The legislature also ordered recruitment of a troop of cavalry. This grandiose scheme led one army pundit to remark that "our legislature on most things relative to military matters run into this error of passing acts that are not . . . calculated for execution."[12] Nothing resulted from the plan. When the assembly had time for second thoughts, it decided instead to raise four regiments out of the militia, two in the East and two in the West, for the defense of Virginia, Maryland, North Carolina, and western Pennsylvania, but without the array of generals. The bounty for enlistment until December 1781 rose to £750, but instead of being paid directly by the state, each taxpayer in the militia district from which a recruit came was to be assessed for the purpose.

Once Collier departed on May 24, the General Assembly turned to the election of Thomas Jefferson to the first of two consecutive terms as governor. There was a contest for the post. The invasion alerted Virginians to difficult days ahead, and some legislators may have wanted a candidate with more administrative or military experience than Jefferson had. On the first ballot John Page, who as lieutenant governor for three years had often been Virginia's chief administrator during Henry's frequent absences from the capital, received thirty-eight votes, General Nelson, the militia commander, thirty-two, and Jefferson, fifty-five. The legislators eliminated Nelson on the second ballot, in which most of his supporters voted for Page. Enough shifted to Jefferson, however, to elect him by the narrow margin of sixty-seven to sixty-one. Page, who had been Jefferson's close friend since college, was embarrassed and hastily sent off an apologetic letter assuring Jefferson of his continued affection. Friends had entered his name, Page said, but he did not explain why he had not withdrawn.[13]

The problem of defense occupied the government for the remainder of the year. Despite initial satisfaction with the performance of the militia during the invasion, later reports called for some updating of the basic militia law of 1776. The record of the debate is unclear, but the statute that emerged suggests that the operation of the militia system had broken down in some areas. The act increased fines for officers and enlisted men who got drunk at musters, missed meetings entirely, or refused to march when ordered, and for bystanders who "interrupt, molest, or insult" the men on duty.[14]

Despite the political liabilities, the assembly had to reinstate the draft to fill the Continental quota. To lessen the political impact and increase volunteer enlistments if possible, the state offered, in addition to increased bounties, one hundred acres of land, pensions for widows and disabled veterans, exemption from taxes during service, and, once again, supplies at fixed prices from the Public Store. Because of the political ramifications, the most significant decision was to allow officers who served until the end of the war half-pay for life. The idea of pensions for a favored few troubled many people because they associated the practice with the corruption they complained about in British politics. Opponents in Congress and in other states fiercely resisted the pressure from the officer corps for such a provision. Threatened with mass resignations of officers in 1778, Congress finally gave in and granted half-pay for seven years, extending the privilege to life in 1780. After the war, however, Congress commuted all such pensions to full pay for five years.

But the Virginia recruiters' greatest handicap in 1779 must have been the astounding news that the state was running out of liquor! The prohibition on distillation of spirits that Mason had initiated to save grain was the cause. The assembly had to cut the usual ration of a gill of liquor a day per man until the delegates could repeal the restriction and restore supplies to normal.

A few days before the legislature adjourned on Christmas Eve—an earlier date than usual—a message arrived from the French ambassador in Philadelphia, the Chevalier de La Luzerne, warning the captains of the seventy-four-gun *La Fendant* and *Le Fier Roderique,* which were wintering in Yorktown, that a British fleet sailing out of New York harbor might be headed for the Chesapeake Bay. The news climaxed more than a month of rumors generated by General Clinton's preparations for an attack on Charleston, South Carolina. This time the British activity presaged more than a "desultory expedition." Stalled in the North by the defeat at Saratoga and the stationing of a French fleet at Newport, Rhode Island, the British commander had decided to open a second front in the South where intelligence reports of loyalist support promised more success than he had heretofore achieved.

Mindful of the criticism of Patrick Henry for not responding with more alacrity to the last invasion, his successor had already ordered the Board of War to prepare a detailed plan of defense in early November. The governor and the Council at that time had implemented all of the board's recommendations except its most urgent request, the immediate appointment of a commanding general. The board considered the appointment imperative since as civilians they felt "Illy calculated" to direct operations.[15] Jefferson and the Council did not believe that they had the authority to install a general, however, until an actual invasion occurred.

The executive was thus ready to spring into action at the latest intelligence from La Luzerne. Although observing that the enemy might attack anywhere along Virginia's broad rivers, the war board nonetheless recommended concentrating defensive measures at Yorktown where the French ships were moored and at Portsmouth where the British had struck before. The governor and Council agreed and had Mason sponsor a concurring resolution in the assembly to cover their political flanks. The governor mobilized one-third of the militia on the lower and middle peninsulas to guard the banks of the York River, and made similar provisions to strengthen Portsmouth and the guard for British prisoners housed near Charlottesville, another possible target.[16]

Jefferson was a model of efficiency. He drew up a checklist of things to do: Captain Barron was to position lookout boats and establish express riders to bring word of any sightings; Colonel Charles Porterfield of the State Garrison Regiment was to move the prisoners in Williamsburg to King William County Courthouse; Quartermaster General Finnie was to supply wagons to move arms at Jamestown to safety; General Charles Scott, who was still in the state recruiting for the Continent, was asked to delay marching men away; and so on. On December 28, General Nelson, who returned to service, his brother Hugh, colonel of a cavalry troop stationed at Yorktown, and Colonel Thomas Marshall of the artillery regiment held a council of war with the Marquis de Vaudreuil, commander of *La Fendant*. The result augured poorly for allied cooperation. Although the marquis reiterated several times that he was at their service, the state's representatives found Vaudreuil and his officers so "inclinable to construe Advice into insult" that they ended the conference with just a mutual promise to defend Yorktown.[17] Fortunately, the British sailed southward, and Jefferson canceled the alert after about two weeks. *La Fendant* sailed for Martinique in January.

Although the British bypassed Virginia soil, Clinton's campaign in the South brought disaster to the state. Almost the entire Virginia Continental line was lost at Charleston. As soon as the British set sail from New York, Congress ordered General William Woodford to lead the Virginia regiments, whom George Washington considered the best trained in the army at the time, from the Continental camp at Morristown, New Jersey, to South Carolina. Bad weather delayed Woodford in Philadelphia until mid-January. He reached Fredericksburg, Virginia, in time to celebrate Washington's birthday, which had already become a national holiday, and then moved on to Petersburg. The regiments remained in Virginia another month to allow their artillery and baggage to catch up and to replace men lost because of expiring enlistments and "a *general dislike of the southern service*."[18] At length, Woodford marched out of

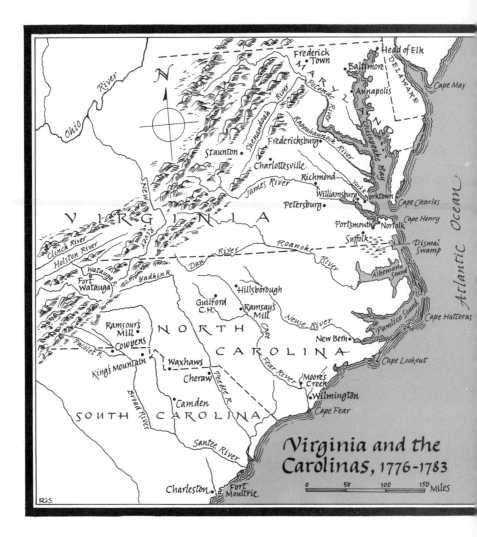

Virginia and the Carolinas, 1776-1783

Petersburg on March 8 with about seven hundred troops. Prodded by General Benjamin Lincoln's incessant pleas to hurry, the Virginians covered the five hundred miles to Charleston in thirty days. General Charles Scott joined Woodford with the recruits he had been raising, and Jefferson sent Colonel Porterfield with over four hundred volunteers from the state line, although they did not reach the city in time.

Woodford's army entered Charleston on the evening of April 7 to the cheers of the garrison, and the city's bells pealed into the night in celebration. But the relief column could not reverse the situation. A week before the Virginians arrived, Clinton, who had been massing ten thousand men before the city since February, sealed off all routes except the one the Virginians took along the east bank of the Cooper River and across the river by ferry. On April 8 the navy under Admiral Arbuthnot forced its way into Charleston harbor, and six days later the British closed the Cooper River route as well. Trapped and short of supplies, an American council of war on April 19 and 20 agreed to seek a negotiated surrender. Clinton refused and began the bombardment on May 9. Three days later Lincoln unconditionally surrendered the garrison of fifty-five hundred men. On May 29 Lieutenant Colonel Banastre Tarleton and the British cavalry virtually annihilated most of the remaining Virginia line on their way to Charleston under Colonel Abraham Buford—about four hundred men—at Waxhaws, South Carolina. The British massacred many Virginians after they surrendered.[19]

News of the capitulation of Charleston took twenty-four days to reach Virginia, where the absence of any word during the entire month of May had generated another bout of near panic. The assembly ignored the tradition that militia did not serve outside the state and ordered twenty-five hundred citizen-soldiers to South Carolina. The legislature also provided for a new troop of fifty cavalry. According to Honyman, the order to the militia "met with great opposition in the assembly," and he predicted that "they will not get one half of them out to S. Carolina."[20] An equally alarming plea from North Carolina for help revealed that state had no arms for its militia. The governor sent ten thousand stand, and on May 24 the assembly adopted a petition to Congress, which George Mason likely composed, asking for replacements and pointedly observing that militia alone could not halt the British drive. With increasing apprehension, the assembly the same day ordered the governor and Council to be ready to call up another five thousand men. It also granted the executive power to impress any horses and wagons needed to facilitate the movement across the state of fourteen hundred

Delaware and Maryland troops under Baron de Kalb, who had just arrived in Petersburg on the way to South Carolina. Finally, on June 5 came official confirmation of Charleston's fate.

Congress wasted little time rebuilding the southern army and, against the advice of Washington, who preferred Nathanael Greene, appointed Horatio Gates, the victor of Saratoga, to command it. Congress assigned the fourteen hundred Delaware and Maryland Continentals under de Kalb to Gates, and asked Virginia and North Carolina to augment the number of militia that they had in the field—in Virginia's case to five thousand with three thousand more ready for instant service. Strong opposition continued to sending militia out of state—Honyman commented on "violent mutinies" in several counties—but it was either go or serve eight months with the regulars. By mid-July General Gates reported that about fourteen hundred of the twenty-five hundred militia that Virginia had previously ordered to Charleston had joined him at Hillsborough, North Carolina.[21]

Despite its earlier inclination to mobilize large numbers of militia, the General Assembly decided not to call up more than the twenty-five hundred already summoned and instead to enlist first five thousand, then in the end only three thousand, men until December 1781 to fill the state's chronic deficiency in its Continental quota. The resulting bill was the product of many hands, including Mason's and Richard Henry Lee's, and took over two weeks to be perfected. The assembly did not finally enact it until the end of the session.[22]

The statute continued the trend begun in 1779 of shifting the burden of providing bounties to the counties. Each locality could add as much as it desired from local taxes to a basic state grant of one thousand pounds of tobacco. As a backup, the assembly reinstituted the draft, which the legislators had eliminated in the optimism of the year before, affording counties all the more incentive to raise the bounty. Heavier and heavier levies fell on the counties as offers for service soared as high as six thousand pounds of tobacco. David Jameson observed to Madison, "Who will run the risk of being drafted if he can by taxing his Neighbours procure a Man"?[23]

After the fall of Charleston, Clinton divided his command and returned with about three thousand men to New York, leaving General Cornwallis to mop up in the South. Continental authorities immediately sought to reinstitute the flow of Virginia troops and supplies to the North on the assumption that it would again become the major theater. But Jefferson forcefully argued that with an enemy army continuing in the South, Virginia's troops should remain there, for "Georgia and S. Carolina are not to be counted as any thing in their present state" and North Carolina "contains but a tenth of the American militia."[24] Reluctantly Congress agreed and committed Virginia's resources to the southern army. Gates assumed command in the South on July 25, 1780, and ignoring the advice of de Kalb and other officers, ordered a rapid advance toward Camden, South Carolina, two days later. The advisers demurred because the route Gates chose led the army, already desperately short of supplies, through tory countryside where food stocks were known to be scarce. A more circuitous route, on the other hand, would have forewarned the British. Living mostly on green corn and peaches, a diet that proved physically debilitating, the troops bordered on mutiny when they reached Camden on the evening of August 15. By then, Gates had about 900 regulars under de Kalb and 120 Continental cavalry, about 100 troops from the Virginia State Garrison Regiment under Colonel Porterfield, and 2,800 Virginia and North Carolina militia under Generals Edward Stevens and Richard Caswell. Gates apparently did not know that Cornwallis had moved up his main force, about 2,200 British regulars, to confront the Americans. Another disaster resulted. Besides feeding the men a meal of corn and molasses just before they marched, Gates attempted a night approach with troops who had never drilled together. When he finally attacked the British the next morning, the poorly trained militia whom he concentrated on his left flank broke at the first encounter. As Jefferson described the debacle from the reports he received, the troops "ran like a torrent and bore all before them."[25] The regulars positioned on the American right were surrounded, de Kalb and Porterfield fell mortally wounded, and about two-thirds of the Continentals were lost. Gates covered the two hundred miles to Hillsborough in three and a half days, but only about 700 of his original force survived to follow him.

Fortunately for American morale, the string of disasters ended a few weeks later. When Cornwallis moved northward through Georgia and South Carolina, he sent Lieutenant Colonel Banastre Tarleton and Major Patrick Ferguson to terrorize the country on his western flank. The fighting between loyalist and whig guerrillas in the southern backcountry was some of the most vicious in the war; seldom did either side give quarter. When Ferguson led over one thousand loyalists into the mountains in pursuit of patriot refugees, threatening to devastate any settlement that harbored them, John Sevier and Isaac Shelby summoned the frontiersmen of Virginia and the Carolinas to rendezvous at

Sycamore Shoals, North Carolina, in late September. About four hundred Virginians joined a combined force eventually totaling fourteen hundred over which Colonel William Campbell assumed command. Because many were mounted, the army moved swiftly and caught Ferguson at King's Mountain, South Carolina, where the rebels annihilated his force on October 7. Ferguson was killed, and the patriots executed a number of tories with him after they surrendered.[26]

The British soon gave Virginians a foretaste of their plans for the South when Major General Alexander Leslie at the head of an invasion force of over twenty-two hundred men sailed into the Chesapeake Bay on October 20, 1780. A small fleet commanded by Commodore George Gayton consisting of three naval ships, the *Romulus* of forty-four guns, the *Blonde* of thirty-two, and the *Delight* of sixteen, along with one of the Goodriches' privateers and several smaller craft, escorted Leslie. James Parker, Hector McAlestor, and other tories from the Norfolk area were on board. The British divided their force, landing the next day at Portsmouth and two days later at Newport News and Hampton. Cavalry swept out to take Kemp's Landing and Great Bridge to the southeast of Portsmouth and moved northwest of Newport News about halfway to Williamsburg.

According to Leslie's instructions from the British commander in chief, General Clinton, the excursion was to provide "a diversion in favor of Lieutenant General Earl Cornwallis."[27] The latter had been beseeching Clinton to assist in his invasion of the Carolinas by distracting American defenders to the north. The best way, Clinton concluded, was for Leslie to establish a post at Portsmouth from which he could raid the major American supply depots at Richmond and Petersburg. Any effort of the rebels to rebuild their army in the South would depend upon men and materials flowing through those towns. It might even be possible for Leslie to push as far inland as Taylor's Ferry on the Roanoke River, via which reinforcements and stores crossed to Gates in North Carolina and from which Leslie would be in position to join forces with Cornwallis.[28]

The tactic fell far short of the brilliant success of the Collier–Mathew expedition in 1779. Ordered to support Cornwallis, Leslie was uncertain what the earl wanted him to do, or even where Cornwallis was at the moment, and so moved cautiously while a packet boat sped to Charleston to find out. A report that the Virginians had fortified narrow stretches of the James River upstream and had raised a "formidable militia" to defend them apparently duped the British for a while.[29] Leslie also could not find pilots to help navigate the James River, and the general unfriendliness of the local populace whom he had expected to be more tory in their sympathies put him off. Suffice it to say, the British commander found ample excuse not to move with the alacrity that had characterized the earlier invasion.

The Virginians had been expecting the attack because of early warnings from Washington's headquarters about British preparations in New York harbor. Jefferson had instructed William Eaton, the state commissary, to seize any supplies that might be of use to the enemy in the counties adjacent to Portsmouth. Aware of the strategic importance of Portsmouth, Gates had sent his chief engineer, John Christian Senf, a professional soldier from Scandinavia and a colonel in the South Carolina line, to coordinate the town's defense. Senf helped guide the American response when the British attacked.[30]

As soon as Leslie's forces landed, Jefferson issued a call for ten thousand militia, but reduced the number to six thousand once the authorities ascertained the enemy's strength. Working from a carefully prepared plan, Jefferson strove to orchestrate the state's reaction precisely so as to divert as little as possible from Virginia's support for the southern army. He summoned troops to defend Portsmouth from counties closest to the town and left men available in counties nearer to North Carolina should Gates need them. Because the British had numerous cavalry, the governor delayed the departure to the south of Colonel Robert Lawson's five hundred volunteer horsemen and prevailed upon Congress to assign Lighthorse Harry Lee's Continental troop to Virginia. Lee did not arrive until December, however. The militia gathered in two divisions, one at Pagan Creek near Smithfield under Generals John Peter Gabriel Muhlenberg and George Weedon, and the other on the lower peninsula under Thomas Nelson.[31]

The recent reduction of the Continental line, which left many officers without assignment in Virginia, for once provided the militia with experienced leaders. On the other hand, militiamen were not used to the regulars' discipline. Edmund Pendleton said that Caroline County men would be reluctant to serve again because of "forced Marches and too *Strict* Attention to Order, not being allowed to break their Ranks, tho' to avoid Deep Ponds of water or to drink."[32] Otherwise, observers were generally pleased with the way the militia turned out, except that the dearth of arms could have been crippling had fighting taken place. One company commander from Brunswick County wrote politely to the governor to report that he had only fifteen weapons for 225 men and asked, "should Be glad you would please to inform me in what manner We are to Be accuterd as I do not think it prudent to March any lower [down-river toward Portsmouth] with out arms."[33]

For the sake of defense, Jefferson also had to end one of the most pleasant chapters of the war for him. The Convention Army composed of the British and German prisoners captured at Saratoga had been camped near Charlottesville since early 1779. From Saratoga the five thousand-odd captives had been marched to camp just north of Boston where they remained until November 1778. Then, when the arrival of Admiral d'Estaing's fleet strained the local economy, the prisoners were sent seven hundred miles through severe winter weather to Virginia, where they arrived early the next year.[34]

The main body of the captives, who after exchanges and escapes numbered about twenty-eight hundred, lived in barracks at Ivy Creek northwest of Charlottesville. Initially Continental troops under Colonel Theodorick Bland and later state cavalry under Colonel James Wood guarded them. The assignment was good duty, because to obscure the state's economic plight, standing orders called for both captives and guards to be "very liberally and sumptuously supplied."[35] In addition, the prisoners supplemented their diet by planting crops and raising stock. A steady supply of specie from Europe which the men spent for extras benefited the local economy. At least one ship arrived under a flag of truce with new clothes, wine, and other amenities.

The Virginia government allowed officers of the Convention Army on parole to rent private quarters throughout the Charlottesville area. The British commander, Major General William Phillips, established himself at Blenheim, Edward Carter's plantation, and the German leader, Friedrich Adolph von Riedesel, Baron of Eisenbach, accompanied by the baroness and their three daughters, occupied Colle, the home of Jefferson's Italian friend, Philip Mazzei, who had returned to Europe that summer on state business. Both commanders had been quickly assimilated into planter society. They dined with the Jeffersons, and during the summer Phillips ventured an amateur theatrical production, the traditional entertainment of a plantation weekend.[36]

At times Jefferson became rhapsodic over the captives. When critics alleged that the state could not afford the prisoners, he retorted indignantly that the captives helped the economy. Furthermore, "The environs of the barracks are delightful. The ground cleared, laid off into hundreds of gardens each inclosed in it's separate paling, these well prepared, and exhibiting a fine appearance. General Riedezel alone paid out upwards of 200£ in garden seeds for the German troops only. . . . Their poultry, pigeons, and other preparations of that kind present to the mind an idea of a company of farmers rather than of a camp of soldiers."[37] The governor granted the officers passes for vacations at mineral springs farther west and to pick up supplies in Richmond and Hampton, apparently unmindful of warnings from fellow Virginians about letting the enemy wander around the state gathering intelligence wherever they could. For Jefferson the experience illustrated how gentlemen ought to wage war. Then, at Cornwallis's approach, the philosopher awoke from his reverie.

Besides the danger from the advancing British, tory conspiracies unearthed in the southwest of the state with disturbing frequency posed another threat that might liberate the Convention Army. At the time the history of the southwestern frontier belonged as much to that of North Carolina as of Virginia. The French and Indian War had prevented significant settlement until the mid-1760s, when a rapid influx occurred into the upper New River Valley near modern Blacksburg, where Colonel William Preston led the whigs, and the upper Holston River Valley near modern Abingdon, where Colonels Arthur and William Campbell held sway. Throughout the war, reports, especially from Montgomery County where Preston lived, raised the possibility that half or more of the population might be supporters of the king.[38]

The loyalists took encouragement from the extent of royalist sentiment in North Carolina, where it centered among Highland Scots who had fled the grinding poverty of their homeland in increasing numbers after the Seven Years' War. Through the mid-1770s several hundred landed at Wilmington each year and spread inland to the west–central portion of the colony along the Cape Fear and Yadkin river valleys. Scottish names appear on both sides of the struggle, and from the records it is impossible to distinguish one group from the other. According to local lore, older settlers were whigs while more recent, less well assimilated arrivals, some of them refugees from New York and other colonies, tended to be tory. By 1778 marauding tory bands appeared in nearby southwestern Virginia, and the next year Carolina loyalists from the Yadkin River Valley joined sympathizers on the New and Holston rivers in an attempt to seize Chiswell Mines and capture Preston. Not entirely trusting the county court or militia in his own area, Preston called for aid from the Campbells, who had already hanged a number of tories in Washington County, and together they fended off the threat.

In the spring of 1780 advance agents for Cornwallis recruited throughout the region but gave strict instructions for tories not to rise until the British arrived. Disregarding the advice, a number of exuberant loyalists gathered at Ramsour's Mill, North Carolina, where they suffered a devastating defeat in June. "This I trust will put an end to Toryism in this Country," Arthur Campbell predicted.[39] Still, a tory band threatened Chiswell Mines throughout the summer, and the Campbells had to come to the rescue once more. The threat in the Southwest was not resolved until the battle of King's Mountain, where numbers from the Virginia–North Carolina border fought on both sides.

The unrest spread through Montgomery, Botetourt, Bedford, Washington, Pittsylvania, and Henry counties, and perhaps, Jefferson feared, as far east as Culpeper. Since convictions were difficult to obtain under the law on treason, to meet the threat the legislature in the spring of 1780 defined a variety of acts as lesser crimes, including to "wish health, prosperity, or success to the king of Great Britain," and authorities initiated prosecutions.[40] Local patriots had more direct ways of dealing with suspects, and "to lynch," immortalizing Charles Lynch, the whig commander at Chiswell Mines, came into the language. Among lesser offenders, Preston reported, "some have been whipped and others, against whom little can be made appear, have enlisted to serve in the Continental Army. . . . Some of the Capital offenders have dissappeared whose personal Property . . . the Soldiers . . . insist on being sold and divided as Plunder to which the Officers have submitted, otherwise it would be almost impossible to get men on these pressing Occasions."[41] Tory prisoners taken at King's Mountain, whom Gates sent to be imprisoned in Montgomery County under the mistaken impression that it was solidly whig territory, complicated the problem. Jefferson objected strenuously to Gates's order and said that he was going to keep the prisoners moving northward until Congress decided what else to do with them.

Within a week of Leslie's invasion Jefferson ordered James Wood to move the Convention troops to Fort Frederick in Maryland, warning him to be careful lest the British land a detachment at Alexandria to intercept him. Other problems developed. Jefferson learned that Frederick did not have enough barracks and that Wood had too few troops to escort all of the Convention Army at once. The governor scaled down his order to include only the eight hundred British among the prisoners; the Germans, numbering fifteen hundred, he thought were less likely to join Cornwallis. In fact, the governor told Wood that he could let the Germans living around the countryside stay where they were rather than recall them to camp. Governor Thomas Sims Lee of Maryland announced that his state could only afford to support a part of the prisoners, so Congress ordered Virginia to supply half their provisions. Jefferson responded that he considered Virginia "now acquitted as to them."[42] Finally, on November 20, Wood had the British contingent on the road, and they arrived in Maryland early in December.

About a week after his initial landing, Leslie withdrew his troops from the Newport News–Hampton side of the James River and fanned out to take Suffolk on the southwest. Holding control of vital creeks and swamp passes, the British were in a strong position. All signs indicated that they planned to stay awhile. Loyalists who had come back with them from New York resettled in their former homes, and as if preparing for land operations, the British impressed as many horses and wagons as they could find. Then the packet ship returned from Charleston with orders that completely reversed the British plans. Because of the American victory at King's Mountain, Cornwallis told Leslie to forget the idea of a joint invasion of North Carolina for the moment and move directly to Charleston.[43]

The British precipitantly abandoned Portsmouth during the night of November 15–16. Debating whether to attempt one last raid up the James River, Leslie hovered around its mouth for another week before finally putting out to sea on the evening of the twenty-second. Hoping to use the fortifications that he had begun around the city later, he did not destroy them and left undamaged several vessels the Virginians found on the shipyard stocks. Leslie's departure left several hundred blacks who had fled to the British lines stranded because there was no room for them in the fleet.

Consistent with his precision planning, Jefferson immediately began to dismantle the defense he had erected and move as many men as were well enough equipped to North Carolina. Despite the dark clouds over the southern front and possibly insurmountable obstacles to rebuilding the southern army, the mood of the Virginia administration reflected a feeling of quiet satisfaction. The state's record of response to alarms over the past year had been good and seemed to be improving. As in the case of Collier, Virginians believed Leslie retreated because of the defenses he encountered rather than the British army's changing strategy.[44]

Five weeks later the king's men returned, this time under the command of Brigadier General Benedict Arnold, the former American commander at West Point, New York, who had attempted to betray his post to the British just a few months before. Although the Americans discovered the plot and executed Major John André, the British officer serving as go-between, Arnold escaped, to be rewarded with a royal army command. Still convinced that a pincer movement to interdict supplies flowing to the South was the proper plan, Clinton sent Arnold to complete Leslie's assignment and ordered Cornwallis not to divert him "without absolute necessity."[45]

The newest invasion caught Virginia authorities entirely by surprise, and in startling contrast to previous responses, contemporaries widely considered the state's reaction to have "disgraced our Country."[46] Both Continental and Virginia intelligence broke down disastrously. Washington's information about British movements arrived noticeably less promptly than before. Although the commander in chief warned Jefferson in early December that the British were preparing another fleet, Continental and Virginia authorities assumed that in view of the season the ships would go to South Carolina. On December 23 Washington learned that the British vessels had dropped down to Sandy Hook three days before. But confused reports suggested the fleet had delayed sailing, and over the next week Washington merely apprised various commanders, including Jefferson to whom he wrote on the twenty-seventh, of the situation in routine correspondence. Not until January 2 did the American commander discover that the ships had actually sailed on the twenty-first. He wrote immediately, but neither notice reached Virginia before Arnold's fleet.[47]

When Arnold entered the Chesapeake Bay on December 30, a Hampton merchant, Jacob Wray, alerted General Nelson. Jefferson received the report the next day, a Sunday. Although Washington's warning about the British fleet's movements earlier in the month had alerted Jefferson, the governor could not be certain of the incoming vessels' hostile intent and hesitated to summon the militia on account of the many alarms that had occurred of late. Whether due to Jefferson's neglect or the impossibility of the task—there were chronic complaints about express riders—an elaborate system of messengers that the governor had established during the summer failed. Confirmation of the ships' hostile activity did not reach Jefferson until 10 A.M. on Tuesday. By that time "the first Intelligence had become totally disbelieved," he admitted.[48] More than two days had been lost, and Arnold was at Jamestown.

Although almost one-third of Arnold's troops—about six hundred— were still at sea on board three transports that had been blown off course, on the water Arnold had strength: the forty-four-gun *Charon*, four frigates, the familiar *Fowey*, three sloops, two brigs, and sixteen other ships. As a result, the British leader decided to keep the Virginians off balance by sailing right up the James River without stopping first at Portsmouth. The gods, too, favored the British, for the wind blew steadily upriver until Arnold accomplished his mission and then steadily downstream for his return.[49]

Pandemonium broke out in Richmond and Petersburg, the two most likely objects of Arnold's attention. Upon hearing that the British were at Hood's Landing, St. George Tucker fled inland with his wife and week-old son from their home at Matoax near Petersburg on January 5. Tucker then went back to help the elder Theodorick Bland escape from his plantation nearby. Others did the same. One witness said that "the alarm was so great and sudden, that almost every person in the neighbourhood was endeavouring to put some of his Property in a state of safety by removing it."[50]

For two days the governor had been directing the carting of stores and public records across the James River to Manchester. Some took his directions "to throw them across the river" literally, for Jefferson subsequently found many "in a heap near the shore."[51] When the general panic set in, however, the governor fled from the city with his family in the early morning hours of January 5, an action occasioning charges of cowardice that plagued him throughout his political career. Actually, Jefferson seems merely to have led his family to a place of safety and then to have returned later in the day to direct operations at Manchester.

Arnold landed about eight hundred men at the Byrd plantation at Westover and marched to Richmond, which he entered completely unopposed just after noon on January 5. The British stayed for about twenty-four hours, but "the people who remained . . . say they were most visibly disappointed in finding we had removed almost every thing out of their reach, which had been effected in 19. hours," Jefferson bragged.[52] The boast is justified if the destruction of the Westham foundry, which the British put out of operation for the rest of the war, is ignored. The Virginians recovered five field pieces that the British had dumped into the river at the foundry, as well as five tons of gunpowder, which incredibly state craftsmen reprocessed. The invaders destroyed a good deal of private property, mostly tobacco in warehouses, but of public property, which Jefferson obviously considered virtually his sole responsibility, only 300 stand of arms, 120 sides of leather, some tools, and a small amount of miscellaneous clothing. The British burned just two public storehouses and a craft shop but three or four private buildings. The records of the Council and the state auditors for the previous two years, which a wagoner had mistakenly taken to the foundry instead of across the James River, also disappeared. Ironically, the public records left in place survived although "totally deranged and dissorted" by the enemy. "In truth we have escaped to a miracle," Jefferson exclaimed.[53]

Arnold did not attempt to cross the river and destroy the supplies at Manchester though only a few militia guarded them. He fell back to Westover and Berkeley, the nearby home of Benjamin Harrison. Because of Harrison's position in the rebel government, the British damaged Berkeley heavily and freed the slaves. A party of British went up the Appomattox River, but militia under General William Smallwood prevented them from capturing any tobacco ships there. The British left Westover on January 10 and moved down the James River, raiding as they went. At Hood's Landing the redcoats met a militia force under George Rogers Clark, who had been in Richmond for consultations with the governor, and lost seventeen dead and thirteen wounded before driving the Americans off with a bayonet charge. Arnold's men seized sixty hogsheads of tobacco at Cobham and plundered Smithfield as well. Finally, on January 19, the British set up winter quarters at Portsmouth.[54]

The Virginia militia responded lethargically compared to their record against Leslie in November, although the lateness of the summons explains some of the laggardness. Only about two hundred had appeared by the time Arnold entered Richmond on January 5, and on January 10 Jefferson complained that the troops continued to appear "very slowly." But the twelfth brought word that "large Numbers of men are hourly Crowding" into Petersburg.[55] Still, the state could provide arms for fewer than half of them. By the time Arnold returned to Portsmouth, about thirty-seven hundred Virginia troops had reported at three sites: at Fredericksburg to guard Hunter's ironworks; at Williamsburg; and at Cabin Point on the south side of the James River.

Critics, both local and in Congress, sharply chastised Jefferson and the Virginia government for the ease with which Arnold took the state capital. Jefferson went to great lengths to assemble documents and testimony from participants to justify his actions, and Madison tried to explain to persons in Philadelphia who did not know Virginia geography how the rivers allowed an enemy to raid deep into the interior with impunity. Yet even Madison sarcastically remarked when he learned of the first resistance, "I am glad to hear that Arnold has been at last fired at."[56]

Shortly after the British retired to Portsmouth, news of one of the most remarkable American victories of the war helped ease the sting of defeat by Arnold. At Cowpens, South Carolina, the Virginia general Daniel Morgan with a force composed largely of militia destroyed the much feared legion of Banastre Tarleton. The victory extirpated the shame of the Virginia militia at Camden. Since General Nathanael Greene had assumed the leadership of the southern army from the defeated Gates in December 1780, the new commander had been trying to avoid a pitched battle with Cornwallis for which Greene considered his force woefully inadequate, but at the same time to avoid further eroding American morale by appearing to retreat before the enemy. Greene divided his army in two, placing one-half under Morgan on the Pacolet River to the west and the other under General Isaac Huger of South Carolina and himself at Cheraw Hill to the east. Should the British pursue one wing, the other would be in position to raid in the British rear. Cornwallis countered by dividing his army into three. Leaving Leslie to hold Camden, he sent Tarleton after Morgan and led the main army after Greene.[57]

Retreating a short distance from his campsite on the Pacolet, Morgan turned to face Tarleton at Cowpens on January 17. The forces had equal numbers, about ten or eleven hundred men on a side, but the British had more experience. When criticized for selecting a site that afforded few impediments to the charge of the dreaded British cavalry and from which the river blocked the possibility of retreat, Morgan claimed that he chose the location to keep the militia from running. He also may have just decided to fight and did not care where. Morgan's battle plan was masterful, and he prepared his troops well psychologically. He placed the rawest militia with a few riflemen in front. After a brief exchange of fire that inflicted significant damage on the British, the militia moved in good order off the field to their left under cover of American cavalry Morgan concealed behind a hill. The British rushed on to the second American line made up of Continental troops and more experienced militia. By the time the British reached the Americans, the royal troops had fallen into disorder. Suddenly the American cavalry appeared and struck the British right flank while the militia from the front line, who had marched all the way around the American rear, attacked on the left. The rout was complete. British casualties included over two hundred killed and six hundred captured. Morgan could write with pride that he had given Tarleton "a devil of a whiping."[58]

Then the race for the Virginia border began. Greene planned to lure the British farther and farther from their base of supply at Charleston, and Cornwallis—"maddened" by defeat, Virginians liked to say— played into his hands by destroying most of the British baggage in order to move more rapidly.[59] Success depended on the Americans staying out of Cornwallis's reach but not so far away that he would become discouraged and end his pursuit. For several weeks Greene had been preparing the route for retreat, scouting fords and arranging for boats on the many rivers that were daily swelling from the spring thaw. Morgan's rear guard had several close calls as they crossed a stream only minutes before the British arrived at the other bank. The two divisions of the American army reunited at Guilford Courthouse, North Carolina, on February 6 and after another week of cat-and-mouse tactics with Cornwallis safely crossed the Dan River into Virginia on February 14.

That same day the sixty-four-gun French warship *Eveille* and two frigates of thirty-six guns each under Captain Arnaud de Gardeur de Tilly arrived in the Chesapeake Bay to blockade Arnold at Portsmouth. George Washington and the Virginia delegation in Congress had been urging the French commander in chief, Comte de Rochambeau, to send a detachment from the fleet in Newport, Rhode Island, to help against Arnold. The opportunity came when a severe storm late in January seriously damaged the British squadron in New York, which until then had checkmated the French. On Tilly's arrival, however, Arnold withdrew his ships up the Elizabeth River, where the larger French ships could not follow. Fearing that he might in turn be trapped by British reinforcements, Tilly remained in Virginia only six days, although during that time he managed to capture eight of the privateers harassing the bay.

Tilly's departure deeply disappointed Virginians. As invasions of the state increased in number, they considered Congress inexcusably dilatory in coming to their defense even though—in their opinion—Virginia had never hesitated, when Congress asked, to send aid to Washington in the North and to Lincoln and Greene in the South. Tilly's presence temporarily reassured Virginians that assistance was on the way. His departure revived their doubts.[60]

CHAPTER 12

Reform and Taxes

ONLY gradually did Virginians come to appreciate the full significance of the change in British strategy. Collier's traumatic assault taught Virginians never to succumb again to overconfidence as they had after the battle of Saratoga. But between the appearance of the British in the spring of 1779 and the fall of Charleston in May 1780, months of relative military calm produced one of the busiest legislative sessions of the war. The period also marked the high point of efforts to improve the republic. Jefferson's shift from the assembly to the executive gave him new leverage with which to achieve reforms that had eluded him before. At the same time, in the legislature, George Mason struggled to complete other changes while desperately searching for better ways to fund the war.

Skyrocketing inflation posed the major problem for the General Assembly in the spring of 1779. Indeed, tobacco appeared almost stable because its price had risen only 50 percent since winter. Salt, which had cost eight to ten pounds a pound a few months before, soared to twenty-five pounds a pound in Richmond for the best quality. The price had been between fifteen and twenty shillings a pound in 1776. Bacon had gone from six or seven pence four years before to over ten shillings a pound; sugar from two shillings in 1776 to over twenty a pound; and rum from one pound a gallon to over eight. Inflation, not British guns, seemed the greater threat to America.[1]

Bickering and contention on every side signified sagging morale. Profiteering merchants became popular scapegoats, Robert Morris in particular. Newspapers described how irate citizens in Albany, New York City, and Philadelphia held mass meetings to regulate prices, and in Williamsburg "publick spirited inhabitants"—"as contradistinguished from the tumultuous proceedings of a mob," the *Virginia Gazette* carefully explained—followed suit.[2] For two days the citizens met in heated sessions with the rector of Bruton Parish, the Reverend Robert Andrews, in the chair. They adopted regulations forbidding the movement of goods out of the city except for government purchases and appointed a committee of fifteen, including several merchants, to enforce prices at a set percentage of sterling cost. Assuming a 200 percent markup "to give the importer and retailer a living profit," the meetings fixed the price at 16⅔ times that cost, the lowest rate of exchange between sterling and currency that participants could hope for.[3] James City, York, Warwick, and Elizabeth City counties added their agreement, but the movement petered out beyond the lower peninsula. "Most sensible men," Honyman wrote in his diary, "look upon the whole affair as impracticable and of bad tendency, as producing confusion, dissention, and dissatisfaction." Besides, "the people are too much engrossed by their hopes and schemes of making money, let it be of what value it will, to listen to such remonstrances."[4]

Antimercantile feeling flared up in the assembly during congressional elections when the delegates required their representatives in Philadelphia to take an oath not to engage in trade while in office. The immediate target was Meriwether Smith, the merchant-planter of Essex County, who for the moment bore the brunt of popular animosity against the Morris faction, for whom everything seemed to be going badly in recent months. Congress held hearings throughout the winter on Silas Deane's activities in Paris and referred to Virginia for prosecution as piracy a complaint about the seizure of a neutral Portuguese ship, *Our Lady of Mt. Carmel and St. Anthony,* by a privateer that Carter Braxton partly owned. The state attorney general, Edmund Randolph, declined to pursue the case. Then, on board the *Willis,* one of the four ships that Braxton lost during the spring, the British found a letter that the Virginian had foolishly written to John Ross, Morris's agent in Nantes, in which Braxton questioned the advantage of the French alliance and proposed a partnership to import British goods into America. The compromising paragraphs soon appeared in James Rivington's *Royal Gazette* in New York, which patriot editors eagerly copied elsewhere. A similar proposal from John Hatley Norton of Yorktown, mailed on the same ship, escaped attention.[5]

The constant quarreling in Congress and the press disgusted and worried observers. Richard Parker, Richard Henry Lee's agent in Virginia, had increasing difficulty placing Lee's letters to the editor in any of the Virginia newspapers. "The printers have advertised they will not publish any Controversial pieces but for a very high Price," he reported.[6] Pendleton, who sympathized with Braxton, had to admit that Rivington's exposé was damaging and feared "the Enemy will think these disputes . . . of more consequence than they really are, and be induced to hold out yet a little longer."[7] George Washington went right to the point when he wrote to Mason criticizing "the fatal policy too prevalent in most of the states, of employing their ablest Men at home." "C[ongress] is rent by party," he continued. "Much business of a trifling nature and personal concernment withdraws their attention from matters of great national moment. . . . Do not from a mistaken opinion that we are about to set down under our own Vine and our own fig tree let our hitherto noble struggle end in ignominy."[8]

Although the Virginia assembly responded to such criticism by rescinding its prohibition against congressional delegates serving simultaneously in the state legislature, the resulting election in 1779 brought no improvement from Mason's point of view. "Some of our best Men have refused to go, and others will not risque their Reputation with Men in whom they can't confide," he told Richard Henry Lee, who had to retire because of the three-year limitation. Among those elected, Mason approved of only Gabriel Jones and Patrick Henry, although, as he expected, the latter did not serve; as for the rest of the delegation—Meriwether Smith, Cyrus Griffin, William Fleming, Edmund Randolph, and James Mercer—Mason grumbled, "we never had so bad [a] one."[9] Smith resigned in November when the antimercantile oath became effective, protesting that he was being deprived "of the Rights and privileges of a free Citizen."[10] Apparently Cyrus Griffin, whom the legislation also affected, conformed since he continued to serve. A year later Smith brought himself to accept another term.

The legislature tried to solve the inflation in the spring of 1779 by facing up determinedly to three topics that it had been skirting for years: sale of western lands, reform of the tax system, and confiscation of loyalist estates. The delegates finally took up the bills to open a land office and establish guidelines for settling western land claims that Jefferson and Mason had introduced a year and a half before. When the assembly put off consideration in January 1778, Mason had immediately laid plans to follow up the issue in the next session, but for some reason failed to attend. Nor did either sponsor pursue the measures in the fall term. At last in April 1779 Mason wrote Jefferson that he had revised the bills to repair "some Omissions, and Difficultys in the Execution" and felt that "it will be best to push these Laws in the next Session. They have been too long delayed already, to the great Loss of the Public; and the Confusion among the People in the back Country."[11]

The bills did not reach the floor of the house until after Jefferson had left the chamber. The land office bill omitted the sponsors' earlier proposals for continuing the historic headright system, for granting free land to newlyweds, and for establishing a decentralized procedure of patenting lands that would have been more convenient for small purchasers. Instead, the bill provided for a 5 percent margin of error for surveyors and a complex method for challenging surveys that favored larger grantees. Plaintiffs had to pay costs if they lost. The speculators clearly had gained along this front. It would seem that Jefferson and Mason had suffered a major defeat.[12]

Strangely, Mason was not bothered. He recounted to Richard Henry Lee how he had shepherded the two bills through the House of Delegates "with a good deal of Labour," especially through "our Butcher's Shambles, the Committee of the Whole House," where he expected them to be "mutilated mangled and chop'd to Peices." But when the struggle had ended, Mason pronounced himself well satisfied. The final legislation, he said, followed "Principles of sound policy and Justice." Mason especially bubbled with pleasure over the fact that, although the bills abolished headrights for the future, they guaranteed old claims in which he had been investing, claims that "Friend B[raxto]n, and some others did everything they cou'd to invalidate."[13] Within three weeks of enactment, Mason filed headright claims for 62,800 acres.

The worsening economic situation may have forced Mason and Jefferson to focus their priorities more sharply. While the need for revenue perhaps lessened sympathy for the speculating interests who had blocked passage before, the state's financial plight also exposed the inconsistency of selling land for revenue and continuing the headright system. In fact, since Mason never indicated that he had suffered even a minor loss in the course of the debate, he may have eliminated these provisions himself before submitting the bills. Jefferson just commented in a matter-of-fact tone to the state's congressional delegation that the two measures with some others "I hope will put our finances into a better way."[14]

The bill for settling land claims on the frontier passed with its salient features unchanged. Jefferson and Mason scored a crucial victory. The act validated headrights, treasury rights, and military bounties for colonial troops issued before 1778 but, unless the tracts had already been legally surveyed, canceled the large grants to speculating companies that the colonial Council had authorized. The statute confirmed preemption rights at a new price of forty pounds currency per one hundred acres, although only for up to one thousand acres instead of the two thousand that Mason had recommended. The act also set a more restrictive deadline than Mason wanted by requiring the completion of all surveys for claims under these provisions within twelve months. Subsequent legislation twice extended the deadline, first for an extra year and then for several months more. The legislature also retained the provision that land companies had to sell to settlers at the price at which they originally offered the land even if the sale was delayed and inflation occurred in the meantime. Finally, the assembly slightly modified Mason's controversial procedure for adjudicating title disputes by increasing the number of commissioners and permitting limited appeals to the courts. These changes probably corrected the "Difficultys in Execution" that Mason said he found in the bill.[15]

The bills eliminated about half of the land companies left over from colonial days. Only the Loyal and Greenbriar companies, which had surveyed their grants before hostilities broke out, sustained their claims, some two million Kentucky acres in all. As for the Ohio Company, although Mason argued that its claim complied with the terms of the act, the assembly did not even allow it a courtesy hearing. The minimum of complaint in Mason's correspondence, however, suggests that the outcome may not have been unexpected.

The test of the new policy came in the hearing the legislature granted the Indiana Company, known to contemporaries as the "suffering traders" because its hopes rested on claims purchased from traders who had endured losses at the hands of the Indians during the French and Indian War. By the Treaty of Fort Stanwix, New York, in 1768, the Shawnee had agreed to compensate the traders who had lost property with lands in modern West Virginia that overlapped the Ohio Company's claim. In drafting the Virginia constitution, Mason and Jefferson had taken pains to ensure that any claim relying solely on an Indian treaty would remain invalid unless the Virginia General Assembly specifically recognized it. Now, before the delegates could open a land office and secure a revenue for the state, they had to decide whether to acknowledge the "suffering traders'" claims.

The hearing began Monday, June 7, 1779. Through the following Wednesday, the house sat as a Committee of the Whole with the Senate in attendance to listen to the Indiana Company's appeal. William Trent of New Jersey, the company's administrative head, attended, and Thomas Walker, a member of the company who represented the government of Virginia at the Fort Stanwix conference, testified. Despite the arguments, the assembly rejected the company's petition. Unofficial reports indicate that Mason most compellingly reminded the legislators that to recognize the claim of a Philadelphia-based company would strengthen the claims of other states and of Congress to the West. Carter Braxton, who otherwise favored the "suffering traders," had already called for a Virginia monopoly of the western lands. A similar opinion may explain why, on the question of whether to allow compensation such as had been given the Transylvania Company, Speaker Benjamin Harrison broke his usual alliance with Philadelphia interests to cast a tie-breaking vote against the company.

The assembly intended the state, and the state alone, to realize an income from Virginia's vast western inheritance as soon as possible. When Brigadier General Woodford expressed the fear, which George Washington and other army leaders also voiced, that opening the West would drain away potential recruits, Edmund Pendleton told him that it was too late to worry since the state had already recognized the right of preemption. On the contrary, he wrote, if the state did not act swiftly to sell its land, all would soon be "ingrossed by Settlers and none left for Sale; which I beleive was the most powerful motive" of the legislature in the actions it took.[16]

As the second step of the program to raise more money, the assembly turned to another revision of the tax system, for which the legislators still had not found a workable formula. Despite amendments in the previous session admonishing assessors to "consult" and agree upon standard valuations, Pendleton reported that many still considered the system "horrid" because "the inequality of Assessments particularly in choice slaves, differing from £70. to £1590," meant that "one man would pay 21s and another £22.10. for the like property." Debate on the subject in the House of Delegates became "violently agitated," he recorded, observing cynically that there were as many conflicting opinions on what to do as variations in the assessments.[17]

To remedy these ailments in the tax law, the assembly turned to a suggestion of Jefferson which Mason did not like but which he allowed was at least better than the existing system. Mason gave top priority to pushing some form of bill through in time for that year. The new statute ordered assessors to value property in terms of currency rather than specie and as if it were on sale "in moderate quantities according to the usual course of things" rather than at a forced sale.[18] To promote consistency, the assembly required assessors to calculate average assessments for the different kinds of lands in each county. The legislature also adopted Jefferson's idea to restore the poll tax on slaves and thus avoid continued wrangling over comparative value. As a gauge of the rising inflation, when Jefferson first made the suggestion in 1778, he proposed a per capita levy of fifteen shillings; the assembly decided on five pounds a year later.

In an effort to mitigate the erosive effect of inflation on state income, the representatives adopted a five-year levy payable in certain commodities, which became known as the "specific tax." Beginning in March 1780, one bushel of wheat, or two of corn, rye, or barley, or ten pecks of oats, fifteen pounds of hemp, or twenty-eight pounds of tobacco were due for every man, free or slave, and every female slave above sixteen years of age. Two commissioners collected the specific tax in each county. The assembly expected most payments to be in tobacco or corn.[19]

For the third part of the revenue package, Mason and Jefferson worked together like a well-drilled team to fashion a policy that would abandon the subterfuge of sequestering loyalist estates and provide for forthright confiscation and sale. But in order to determine who was a tory, the state first had to define who was a citizen, for which purpose Mason introduced a bill Jefferson had prepared as part of the revisal of the laws.

The subject of citizenship had a close connection with the issue of religious freedom. In 1776 Edmund Pendleton had introduced a bill entitled "Naturalization of Foreign Protestts," which Jefferson succeeded in amending in the Committee of the Whole to read simply "for the Naturalization of Foreigners." Jefferson's notes on the debate reveal that at the time he specifically had in mind citizenship for Jews, although the wording, of course, included all others as well. The parliamentary act of 1740 permitting Jews to be naturalized as British subjects did not apply in Virginia, and Jefferson hoped to fill the void. He also appended a clause providing for a bonus of twenty dollars and fifty acres of free land to encourage immigration. The bill and the amendments were postponed in that session and never reintroduced.[20]

The bill that Mason submitted in 1779 was more positive in approach and more comprehensive. Besides native Virginians and persons resident in the state for at least two years before passage of the bill, it extended citizenship to all whites who took an oath of allegiance before a court and certified their intention to live in Virginia. Although Jefferson had suggested a residence requirement of seven years in his draft constitution, the 1779 bill specified none. The bill also recognized the "natural" right of expatriation—which few other nations acknowledged for over a century—by providing a procedure for renouncing citizenship. In addition, the bill granted reciprocity to "free white inhabitants" of other states in the union, and, in the same spirit of confederation, allowed extradition of criminals to other states and declared forfeited the Virginia estates of persons a sister state attainted. Interestingly, the legislature omitted these three provisions for interstate cooperation in the reenactment of the statute in 1786.[21]

Given the exigencies of the moment, Jefferson's bill passed easily under the expert guidance of Mason, although one observer noted with concern how many "warm advocates" the tories had in the legislature.[22] The assembly excluded "alien enemies" from the act's final provisions and paid more attention to the rights of the individual in defining the conditions for denaturalization than Jefferson had. The legislators eliminated a clause permitting the state to assume that a person had renounced his or her citizenship upon joining the service of another country, or another state of the union, and declared instead that an individual could give up allegiance only through formal court action.

John Harvie of Albemarle County introduced Jefferson's bill "concerning Escheats and Forfeitures from British subjects," and the governor took time to sit in the audience while the house debated. The preamble reveals Jefferson's uneasiness over a policy of confiscation by dwelling too long on the necessities of war and blaming the bill itself on the king for making British and Americans "aliens and enemies" to one another. Jefferson also argued somewhat hypocritically that it was better for owners to have their estates seized while prices were high in case they were ever able to recover the money under procedures prescribed in the bill. The bill authorized county officials to confiscate and sell the estates of anyone who was out of the country at the time of the battles of Lexington and Concord and had not returned or otherwise manifested loyalty to the United States or who fled Virginia before the assembly had defined the terms of allegiance in the fall of 1776. A typically Jeffersonian touch was the provision that the sales be in parcels of no more than four hundred acres each. Another act extended the provisions for confiscation to include the slaves and movable property of tories as well. The state eventually realized a little over three million pounds in currency under the act, a modest contribution but one that at least offset the additional one million pounds in paper money the assembly authorized in that session.[23]

The barrage of bills in the spring of 1779 wore George Mason down physically; he was "fatigued, beyond Measure, by the Share which Necessity obliges me to bear in the public Business, since Mr. Jefferson . . . has left the House." Early in the session, Mason suffered a severe attack of the gout and continued to feel so ill that he requested leave of the house to remain seated when addressing it. To prolong his discomfort, the legislature in his opinion wasted time on "Trifles and Whims."[24] With many bills still in committee toward the middle of June, Mason became concerned that the delegates had become too "inattentive, tired, and restless to get away" to complete their work. He and Lieutenant Governor Page accordingly concocted "a little Piece of Generalship" to keep them at the task. Page arranged for an order withholding pay certificates until adjournment instead of issuing them as the session progressed. "Some of the Fellows threat'ned, and kick'd, and strugled; but can't loosen the Knot," Mason told Richard Henry Lee with amusement. "We shou'd not have had a House now" but for Page's action, he said.[25]

The "Trifles and Whims" of which Mason complained included a bill to move the state capital to Richmond. The author, Jefferson, along with many others, assigned the change much higher priority than Mason. But Mason and other influential Tidewater men like Pendleton objected mainly to the cost of such a shift during war; "I have Hopes it will be rejected, or at least the expensive part of it altered, or prolonged, in the Senate," Mason wrote, and in large part the legislature did eliminate the costlier portions.[26] Despite Mason's indifference to the issue, the debate over changing the capital was almost as divisive as that over the land bills. There had been repeated efforts for a generation to move the seat of government from Williamsburg as settlement pushed farther west and the city became increasingly distant from the population center of the colony. Jefferson, who had not liked the town in his college days, first submitted a bill to select a new site in 1776 at which time the house defeated the suggestion by a vote of thirty-eight to sixty-one. But most people recognized that Williamsburg's time was limited. By 1779 supporters of a move had an upper hand in the assembly, and the recent invasion strengthened their argument by exposing the capital's vulnerability. Jefferson's notes for a speech on the bill indicate that, besides the city's geographic drawbacks, he feared Williamsburg would not attain the architectural splendor that he deemed appropriate for the capital of a new republic because it was not a trading center; "Wmsbgh. nevr. cn. b. grt.—100 y. xprce. [experience]," he had scribbled down.[27]

Jefferson wrote the draft from which he worked on the same piece of paper that he had used three years earlier. Revisions that from internal evidence could only have been written in 1779 called for "magnificent Buildings," a capitol and courthouse "which . . . shall be built in a handsome manner with walls of Brick, and Porticos," a "state house" with twelve "apartments" for executive offices, and "a palace for the use of the Govr."[28] Jefferson soon realized that his enthusiasm had run away with him for he amended this section to eliminate the grandiose language in which he first expressed his architectural dreams. The assembly further altered the draft to assure doubters that for the moment government buildings in the new capital need only be "temporary" and, in the act for the confiscation of loyalist estates, provided an added economy by reserving forfeited lands in Richmond for public use. For a time the house seemed on the verge of defeating the bill again when supporters divided over whether to locate the capital in Richmond, Fredericksburg, Charlottesville, or Staunton, but finally Richmond prevailed. The legislature made its final decision; an attempt to reconsider a few months later failed on a rare roll call vote, forty to forty-five.

Despite the relative weakness of the Virginia executive, Jefferson discovered that the gubernatorial office had ways to attain objectives that had evaded him while an assemblyman. Following tradition, the board of visitors of the College of William and Mary elected the governor a member a few months after his inauguration. The college's destitution because of the war prepared the way for change. An annual income of over three thousand pounds had fallen to a few hundred. For more than a decade, the faculty and the board of visitors, with ample prodding from outside critics, had been debating whether to broaden the curriculum beyond the heavily classical emphasis of a sectarian institution. Many felt that the college could not expand its offerings in higher education as long as it had to run a grammar school and an Indian school as well. Jefferson had his own answers to these problems, and he could expect the support of fellow members of the board of visitors like John Page, Edmund Randolph, and Thomas Nelson, Jr.[29]

At this stage in Jefferson's thinking about an educational system for Virginia, he intended the College of William and Mary to become the state university and included in the revisal of the laws a measure to convert the college from an Anglican to a public institution. The bill provided state funding and abolished the two professorships of divinity. In their stead the draft proposed chairs in more secular subjects: law, mathematics, medicine, modern languages, and history. The last included both "ecclesiastical" and "civil" topics. Jefferson's plan retained the chairs in moral philosophy and natural philosophy (that is, natural science) and renamed the chair of humanity, by which contemporaries normally meant Greek and Latin, the chair of ancient languages. Since the classics would be taught in the lower grades if the state adopted Jefferson's ideas for that level of education, the term "ancient languages" included, should someone capable of teaching them all be found, Hebrew, which the divinity professor had offered before, Chaldee, Syriac, Moese Gothic, Anglo-Saxon, and old Icelandic. Just as had happened in his debate with Pendleton over the comparative virtues of Anglo-Saxon and Norman law, Jefferson's sense of practicality gave way here to his infatuation with the Germanic heritage of the English people, a knowledge of which he considered as important an ingredient in republican education as familiarity with the classics. Since Jefferson's plan provided for primary and secondary education in localities throughout the state, his bill for William and Mary abolished the college's grammar school and, in place of The Brafferton, or Indian school, recommended that the college establish missions among the tribes.

The college bill languished during the spring session of the 1779 assembly. Jefferson blamed the dissenting churches who feared that the American successor to the Anglican church, the Protestant Episcopal church, would continue to dominate the college. Its president at the moment, for example, was the Reverend James Madison, a leading Anglican cleric who supported the Revolution. Samuel Stanhope Smith, rector of Hampden-Sydney Academy, which the Hanover Presbytery had founded in Prince Edward County on the eve of independence, offered Jefferson his personal support for the proposed reforms because he believed in the principles of liberal education. Smith warned, however, that it would be difficult "to persuade a very considerable part

of the state that that institution can ever be delivered form the influence
of party."[30]

Frustrated in the assembly, Jefferson and his supporters on the board
of visitors achieved most of the reforms administratively by leaving va-
cant some old positions and redefining the duties of others. Although
the charter of 1693 called for only seven faculty members including the
president and Jefferson planned to have eight, the discrepancy caused
no immediate problem since during the war the college could barely
afford five. By not filling the mastership of the Indian school and the
two divinity posts and discharging John Bracken as head of the grammar school, the visitors made room to appoint George Wythe to teach
law, Dr. James McClurg medicine, the Reverend Robert Andrews, formerly chaplain to the 2nd Virginia and the State Artillery regiments,
"Moral philosophy, the laws of nature and of nations, and of the fine
arts," and Charles Bellini modern languages. Bellini, a recent immigrant
from Italy, had come to help Jefferson's friend, Philip Mazzei, introduce
winemaking to Virginia. The visitors reappointed only one member of
the prewar faculty, President Madison, to teach both natural philosophy
and mathematics. The board also economized by reducing salaries and
scholarships and contracting with townspeople for food service in order
to abolish commons.

William and Mary did not realize the promise of Jefferson's innovative changes in the curriculum, particularly the treatment of professional studies as subjects of academic inquiry; the weight of sectarianism
and toryism bore down too heavily. Five of the pre-Revolutionary
faculty had been vociferous loyalists: Thomas Gwatkin and Samuel
Henley fled to England, and the visitors removed President John Camm,
John Dixon, and Emanuel Jones after independence. Only the Reverend James Madison and John Bracken became patriots. Moreover, during the previous generation, the faculty had acquired a reputation of
being extremely contentious—among themselves, with the visitors, and
in colonial politics. Jefferson's bill consequently called for the assembly
to elect three chancellors from among the state judiciary to serve as ar-
biters in academic disputes with the power to dismiss faculty members,
if necessary. Jefferson's overall plan for a statewide educational system
would have placed college admissions, long a source of controversy between faculty and visitors, in the hands of a single governing board for
the state. The college's reputation for dissension and toryism, however,
had left republican Virginians unwilling to provide it with either funds
or students. Jefferson's bill again failed when delegate James Madison

reintroduced the revisal of the laws in the mid-1780s, and Jefferson eventually turned his attention to building a completely new state university in Charlottesville nearer his home, leaving William and Mary a private, but more secular, institution until the twentieth century.

Jefferson also oversaw a major reorganization of the state administration that he had planned before leaving the legislature. Although Jefferson prepared the bills as part of the revisal of the laws, the assembly took up the pertinent measures separately early in the spring 1779 session. The proposed format continued a trend since the establishment of the government of shifting to subordinates the more technical or voluminous aspects of administration from the direct supervision of the governor and Council. In the spring of 1776 the Committee of Safety had established five commissioners of the navy to look after an area with which planters normally had little acquaintance, and in December of that year the Council had separated commercial shipping from the navy's responsibility and assigned it to a commercial agent. The governor and Council, for their part, retained primary control of military supplies and personnel, and generally worked more closely with the commercial agent than with the navy.

By 1779 the volume of both trade and military affairs had become so heavy that Jefferson proposed adding several pairs of hands to supplement the Council. A Board of Trade, none of whose three members might engage in commerce during his tenure of office, replaced the commercial agent, while the naval board added two members to its previous three to become a Board of War to oversee military affairs on land and sea. Under the Board of War's supervision, a single commissioner became responsible for the navy. Watching from the High Court of Chancery, to which the legislature had appointed him a year before, Edmund Pendleton was skeptical of the new arrangement. "The Assembly have established a board of War," he drily observed, "but for what purpose I know not, as I think the Governor and Council have not so much to do, but they might have superintended two Regiments, which are to be compleated, and are all the Force we are to have." Pendleton allowed that the Board of Trade might be more "useful."[31]

As if to refute Pendleton, the growth of the war board's duties seemed beyond control. The enabling legislation initially charged it to manage "all matters and things within the department of war" and specifically to perform periodic inspections of military stores around the state and oversee the commissioner of the navy.[32] But even while debating the bill, the assembly added a new position for the board to supervise, the commissary of prisoners. About the same time Congress instructed all states to appoint sub-clothiers general to distribute among the Confederation's members a surplus created because the French sent more clothes than the Continent could use. The assembly appointed John Peyton and divided the former post of commissary of stores in two. By the end of the year, county commissioners of the specific tax also reported to the board along with the quartermaster general and purveyors of the state hospitals. Eventually, too, the board appointed one of its members, Colonel William Nelson, as commissary of military stores to undertake the quarterly tours of state warehouses and storage places that the original legislation had instructed all the board members to carry out in rotation.

Whether the new system relieved the executive of any burden is doubtful; indeed, it may have increased the load. The war board itself had little authority; it chiefly kept the books for the governor and Council and offered advice. The law required the governor to countersign all of the board's decisions, even whether to let captains of artillery draw riding boots from the Public Store when a change in Continental regulations mandated that they be mounted. First the Board of War and then the governor and Council reviewed purchase orders from the clothier general, a process that makes understandable why the Council finally decided to let the governor sign for it in routine matters.

The Board of War defended the bureaucratic complexity as necessary to "prevent a vast Degree of embezzlement, fraud and confusion, which we are apprehensive have been too prevalent in some of our public departments."[33] But the innovations did not promote efficiency. Several months after its formation the war board had to admit that it did not know what effect a promotion of one artillery officer would have on others because it did not have a roster of the corps. Another time it asked General Nelson to come to Williamsburg for a few days to help give "proper dispatch" to its directions since "when an Order leaves our Office it is seldom executed with the necessary Expedition."[34]

Establishment of the war board also meant one more level of government to be plagued by the problem of a quorum. The original appointees included James Innes as chairman, James Barron, who with Innes had served on the old naval board, William Nelson, the militia commander's younger brother, Colonel Robert Lawson of Prince William County, an active army officer, and Samuel Griffin of Williamsburg. The latter two resigned within a few months, Lawson with the comment that he only accepted the post because he feared no one else would serve and the board would never begin to function. Apparently the scarcity of applicants continued, for in its fall session the assembly appointed only one replacement, George Lyne, and reduced the quorum to two.[35]

Problems of staffing also mushroomed into a constitutional crisis that aggravated the already strained relations between Page and Jefferson. The original statute allotted the Board of War only one clerk, whereas it allowed the Board of Trade several. As work accumulated, Chairman Innes requested another, which Page as lieutenant governor approved in Jefferson's absence. Jefferson later complained in a sharply worded letter to the assembly that Page should not have allowed an increase in staff without legislative approval. Innes defended Page and remarked that "the feelings of my heart are sensibly affected by this official altercation, which I fear . . . may become a personal one." The situation remained tense until the legislature granted the new position.[36]

In trade, the decision in the last months of Patrick Henry's term to send the commercial agent Thomas Smith to Europe to handle purchases in person facilitated the reorganization. In Smith's place as state agent the executive appointed his assistant, Benjamin Day, who, being younger and less well established as a merchant, could more appropriately report to the new Board of Trade instead of directly to the Council. Like the war board, the Board of Trade acted as a record keeping and advisory appendage of the Council. The commercial board did not have the personnel problems of its counterpart, for the law allowed a sufficient number of clerks, and the original members, Chairman Jacquelin Ambler, a merchant and customs collector from Yorktown, Duncan Rose, a Petersburg merchant, and Thomas Whiting, a wealthy merchant from Gloucester County who had served on the old naval board since the beginning of the war, remained through the Board of Trade's lifetime. Technically the governor and Council had to approve the board's every action.[37]

In general, Jefferson endeavored to delegate as much of the administrative burden as he could to subordinate agencies. The governor repeatedly told the Board of Trade that he just wanted to give routine approval for their recommendations on tobacco purchases, and he abruptly reprimanded the Board of Auditors for sending him a matter that he thought they should handle themselves. Eventually Jefferson met resistance from lower-ranking administrators who did not want to assume such responsibility. Twice when the Council became confused about the proper channel of command and assigned the Board of Trade duties that normally fell elsewhere, the board pointedly replied that they would carry out the instruction as a favor to the executive. Finally, when the governor and Council told them to use their own discretion in filling the Board of War's requests for supplies, they responded by quoting the original statute to the effect that they needed "the advice of the Council."[38]

When assembly members returned in the fall of 1779, they found a less demanding agenda than in the spring, but the overwhelming problem of depreciating currency remained. Once more Mason provided a main item of the session's agenda, a scheme reputed to be capable of realizing five million pounds in currency for the state. Mason hoped to induce wealthy individuals to loan the government amounts of one thousand pounds or more, first by guaranteeing annual payments of 5 percent interest from a special levy earmarked for that purpose, and, second, by insuring the interest payments against depreciation. To pay the interest Mason proposed an additional specific tax of thirty pounds of tobacco on all tithables except free whites between the ages of sixteen and twenty-one to be paid every August for eleven years beginning in 1780. At the last moment, however, a rider to the bill postponed collection for the first year until December, an action that could not have reassured potential investors. To offset depreciation, Mason proposed that a grand jury of the General Court establish the interest in terms of tobacco each year. Initially, the statute set the ratio at thirty pounds per hundredweight, double the price of the preceding June.[39]

Mason also guided the assembly toward a general increase in taxes. Under his direction, the legislature sought to fill the most recent Continental requisition for $2,500,000 by enacting a new three-pound poll tax on all free males and white servants over twenty-one, a four-pound levy on all slaves, additional taxes on carriages and liquors, and a 2½ percent excise on the sale of imported goods within the state, all due the following spring. In addition, since the state had been frequently delinquent in meeting Congress's requests, the act set aside in a general fund for fulfilling the state's obligations to the Continent £1,500,000 currency from the proceeds of forfeited estates (more than twice the actual rate of return) and £600,000 from the specific tax due in March 1780. Then, in case anyone had any money left, the delegates increased the property tax to 2 percent and added new impositions on cattle and ordinaries to finance the state government for the coming year.[40]

The battle over the western land claims resumed in the fall of 1779. William Trent and George Morgan of the Indiana Company had carried their case to Congress, and, after a vigorous debate in which company sympathizers heavily outnumbered the Virginia delegation, the Continental legislature passed a resolution demanding that Virginia postpone opening a land office. Within hours of learning of Congress's action, the Virginia assembly unanimously adopted a counter resolution, which Mason most likely wrote, calling for the preparation of a remonstrance "firmly asserting the Rights of this Commonwealth."[41] Actually, Congress had worded its statement warily to encourage compromise, and Trent was willing to negotiate. He told the Virginia delegation and notified Edmund Randolph, whom he had commissioned to represent the Indiana Company in Williamsburg, that he would settle for compensation like Richard Henderson. Presumably Meriwether Smith brought the same message in October when he returned to testify on the company's case for two days before an executive session of the house. Undoubtedly Smith repeated the congressional delegation's warning not to expect "Justice" in Philadelphia since "the prejudice of Congress against Virginia on account of the Land office is now so great."[42]

To Mason, the issues bulked larger than the claims of one company. When he drafted the remonstrance the House of Delegates requested, he composed such an uncompromising statement of Virginia sovereignty that it effectively silenced the state's opponents in Congress for months to come. Mason correctly pointed out that, since Maryland had not ratified the Articles of Confederation, the United States technically did not exist and Congress had no authority. The Virginia assembly had made the same point during the previous session by formally ratifying the treaty with France to legitimate Congress's signing. No one could gainsay this legalistic fact.[43]

Yet despite its intransigence, the remonstrance amounted to an offer to bargain. Virginia wanted the articles ratified; it also wanted to put the western lands to the best use for the state. But Virginians increasingly defined this interest broadly; "There is," after all, "more land than can be settled for ages," Patrick Henry once boasted to the Spanish governor of New Orleans.[44] Most important, Virginians like Mason, Braxton, and Jefferson, whatever their disagreement over speculation by citizens of the state, agreed that they wanted to keep nonresident speculators out. As soon as Mason heard of Maryland's refusal to ratify the Articles of Confederation, he had warned Richard Henry Lee that behind it stood the Illinois–Wabash Company, which had even vaster claims north of the Ohio River than did the Indiana Company to the south. Mason repeated this observation in the remonstrance, slyly recalling for readers that the Illinois–Wabash Company originally included as partners "the Earl of

Dunmore and other Subjects of the British King." Mason reminded
Congress that Virginia had already offered to share its land with less
fortunate states to help pay their soldiers' bounties, and that for military
reasons it had just prohibited settlement north of the Ohio River.[45] In
other words, Virginia literally had room for negotiation. But until Congress agreed to an accommodation, Virginia remained an independent
nation.

Other assembly actions that fall revealed the intensifying pressures of
the war. The legislature revived prohibitions against forestalling and engrossing, extended embargoes on meat and grain, and threatened anyone exporting salt without permission with a fine of forty pounds a
bushel. Among the penalties the delegates placed a carrot by offering to
allow exportation of one hogshead of tobacco duty free for every five
bushels of salt imported. The assembly also tried to end the immorality
that so many complained about, such as the horse race for a purse of
thirty thousand pounds and the gaming table reserved for bets of five
hundred dollars or more that Edmund Pendleton discovered to his horror in Caroline County. The legislature responded by limiting wagers to
five pounds, branding anyone convicted of a violation "an infamous
gambler," and banning violators from all public affairs. At Mason's suggestion, the session also increased fines on "tippling houses."[46] Speaker
of the Senate Archibald Cary cynically remarked on the appropriateness
of these measures since assemblymen did their share of the tippling and
the gambling. Mason submitted another bill ostensibly designed to cure
the age-old Virginia habit of piling up debts by requiring merchants to
request payment within six months of a sale or forfeit their claims. Edmund Randolph said that Virginians thought the act would impel Great
Britain to seek an early peace to prevent its merchants from losing their
debts, but Mason could hardly have been so naive.[47] More likely, he had
local engrossers in mind.

Jefferson's election to the governorship in June 1779 afforded a second chance to achieve more of the reforms he had come from Philadelphia to effect three years before. But the moment passed with little accomplished. Except among a handful like himself, the initial enthusiasm
for changing the world, or at least the republic, waned. The war was
lasting much longer than anyone had imagined. Shortages, inflation,
militia duty, and rampant self-interest sapped morale. The conflict entered a new phase just as Congress's and the state's capacity to continue
came increasingly into doubt. By 1780 the question became how long
Virginians and other Americans could hang on. Longer-range concerns
necessarily fell lower down the scale of priorities.

CHAPTER 13

"Barely sufficient to keep us joging along"

T HE weather during the winter of 1779–1780 forecast the trials ahead for the patriot cause. The worst cold wave in generations began early in December and continued unabated until the first of February. President Madison of William and Mary reported to the American Philosophical Society in Philadelphia, a clearinghouse for scientific information at the time, that between January 7 and 23 the temperature rose above freezing on only three occasions. Honyman said that he knew people whose "Mercury sunk into the Bulb of the Thermometer."[1] By the middle of January rivers in the Tidewater had frozen so that wagons could cross the James at Warwick and Burwell's Landing, the York at Yorktown, and the Potomac at Hooe's Ferry. The cold finally broke in mid-February but returned intermittently into spring, thus at least slowing the thaw and moderating the flooding. Honyman observed snow on the ground in Hanover County in mid-April.

Because of prodigiously inflating costs, the public establishment steadily constricted throughout the year. Even as Jefferson designed expanded boards of war and trade, at another level he hawked for sale to North Carolina two naval galleys in Ocracoke Sound until he learned that the bottom of one had already fallen out. The Board of Trade closed its shipyard at Cumberland because it had only six vessels left, and the assembly further eliminated three of the navy's five ships and six of the remaining eight galleys. A legislative committee found that "a train of supernumerary officers, and dependents, are continued in the service without necessity" and that at one post "17,500 rations per month, have been issued . . . and only 10,800 of it for the use of the troops."[2] The committee particularly recommended abolition of the state military hospital at Williamsburg and reassignment of the staff to regional hospitals under the Board of War's new inspector of stores and provisions rather than the medical director general. In conveying this decision to the latter, Dr. James McClurg, the Board of War hinted that he ought to sue.

The move of the state capital to Richmond in April 1780 provided an opportunity to eliminate the boards of war and trade as well. The war board simply disintegrated toward the end. Innes and Barron did their duty through April 7, the day on which Williamsburg officially ceased to be the capital, but no record exists that any of the board went to Richmond. The governor and Council assumed the war board's functions for a while until the commander of the State Garrison Regiment, George Muter, took over about the middle of June. On the Board of Trade only the chairman, Jacquelin Ambler, was in Richmond in May. As a result of this state of affairs, the assembly in June replaced Jefferson's system of boards with three commissioners, one each for war, the navy, and trade. The legislature confirmed Muter in his position and placed James Maxwell of Norfolk, a member of the old naval board, in charge of the navy. The commissary of stores, William Armistead, with considerable help from the governor, temporarily took over control of trade until David Ross was permanently installed as commissioner in December.[3]

The move to Richmond naturally created more confusion than usual in the government. Although Jefferson laid meticulous plans to move the Palace furniture and public records, as late as March 25 no one had given thought to whether the Public Store and commissary should go. The government officially ceased operations completely on April 7 and did not resume until April 24, but Jefferson conducted business in Richmond on the twelfth. Although the Council met without a quorum six days later, it could not legally convene for another month. John Page resigned rather than commute. Two other councillors left about the same time—although one at least for reasons other than the move—and a third did not come to Richmond in May, leaving barely enough members for a quorum until the legislature convened. David Jameson attended out of a sense of duty, but being used to salty breezes, complained of the fog and "the thin putrid state of the Air" at the new site.[4] The two auditors of four years' standing, Thomas Everard and James Cocke, also resigned. Benjamin Waller, judge of the admiralty court, absolutely refused to leave Williamsburg, so the assembly granted leave for the court to meet in the former capital as long as he was on it. The Council finally pushed the governor into ordering the Public Store and the sub-clothier to come to Richmond in July, but the quartermaster general remained in Williamsburg until the end of the year.

In Richmond the consensus was that, while the town might have the potential of magnificence that Jefferson envisioned, it had a long way to go. One of the governor's slaves, Isaac, later recalled "not more than two brick houses in the town" at the time.[5] As one of the worst winters on record lingered into spring, state officials constantly complained of inadequate accommodations. The possibility throughout the fall 1779 session that the legislature might reverse its decision to move had delayed any construction. Not until after the assembly met in its new home did it finally decide that the permanent public buildings would be on Shockoe Hill. New arrivals in many cases simply ousted previous inhabitants, many of them "Caledonians." Jacquelin Ambler's family, according to his daughter, took over quarters that "one of these hardy Scots had thought proper to vacate."[6] As for the governor, he rented a small wooden house from a relative. To compound the new capital's difficulties, the United States Post Office refused to recognize the change in location and continued to deliver official correspondence to Williamsburg for most of the year. Then, when winter came again, the legislature discovered that it had left its heating stove behind and had to send someone to try to recover it.

In June 1780 word of the fall of Charleston jolted the delegates into considering a proposal from Congress for a drastic revision of the Continental supply and financial systems since the existing ones had collapsed. Congress had experimented with a new method for raising supplies in a few states toward the end of 1779 and in February 1780 decided to extend it to all. Instead of requisitioning funds from the states and purchasing materials itself, Congress began to request the commodities it needed directly from the states. The advantage, of course, was that the states had the power to obtain the goods through specific taxes or even seize them if necessary. The scheme also ended the ruinous competition between state and Continental buyers that contributed so greatly to inflation.[7]

George Mason moved to implement the plan by introducing a bill for a Provision Law in the Virginia assembly on June 6. The statute the legislators adopted four days later called for the appointment of commissioners in each county with authority until December 1780 to compel the sale at fixed prices of any meat, grain, flour, biscuit, liquor, and salt that a family or tavern keeper might have over and above actual needs. Payment was to be in certificates that could be redeemed in six months at 6 percent interest or submitted in payment of taxes.[8]

Virginia's congressional assessment for 1780 was the largest of all the states': 47,000 hundredweight of beef, 1,278 barrels of flour, 10,700 bushels of salt, 400 tons of hay, 200,000 bushels of corn, 6,000 hogsheads of tobacco, and 100,000 gallons of rum. Congress later added 60,000 pounds of pork and 29,700 bushels of grain for animals to the list. The poor harvest of 1779 prevented meeting the July 1 deadline for the first installment, and Jefferson reported pessimistically that in fulfilling Congress's demands, Mason's confiscation law would be the state's "ultimate dependence."[9] But by September the governor announced that most of the pork had been secured and the first of the corn was in.

On March 18, 1780, Congress instituted the second phase of the plan, a scheme to slash the national debt from two hundred million dollars to five million with one stroke by revaluing outstanding Continental currency at 40:1 in specie. At the same time Congress hoped to provide a new source of revenue by calling upon the states to retire through taxation fifteen million dollars each month for thirteen months. As the existing bills came in, they would be replaced at the rate of 40:1 divided two-fifths to Congress and three-fifths to the state turning in the old money. If all went according to plan, ten million dollars worth of new currency would be issued, creating five million in new funds (and new debt). Presumably the division with the states would keep them from adding new currency of their own. To prevent the new issue from depreciating, Congress approved an interest rate of 5 percent payable in bills of exchange drawn on hard money accounts in Europe and ordered the entire issue to be redeemed within six years through special taxes exclusively for that purpose.[10]

Unfortunately for the nation, the two parts of Congress's plan proved incompatible. The scarcer funds became, the more the Continental army resorted to impressments and the more public opinion demanded that the certificates given for impressments be accepted for taxes. Allowing such payments, in Jefferson's word, "anticipated" taxes.[11] As levies increasingly brought in certificates, less old currency came in, less new money went out, and the state received less new income. Only $31,000,000 of the old currency had been redeemed and $620,000 of the new released by the spring of 1781, at which time the old currency attained a market value of 150:1 in specie and ceased to circulate.

Opposition to the second stage of the congressional plan came overwhelmingly from the South. Only one delegate from north of Delaware failed to vote for it; virtually all from Delaware southward who voted opposed it. Virginia's sole representative in Philadelphia at the moment was Cyrus Griffin, who opposed the bill; two days later James Madison, who favored it, took his seat. But once Congress adopted the plan, Griffin urged compliance, "for without unanimity upon these important points our confederation will break to pieces."[12]

Opponents feared that the plan would depress prices in the agricultural South and raise taxes to redeem currency that had already gravitated to the more mercantile North. Patrick Henry's oratorical pyrotechnics in the Virginia assembly on June 6 led to the defeat of the fiscal plan on two roll call votes, twenty-five to fifty-nine and twenty-eight to fifty-three, despite the fact that George Mason and Richard Henry Lee acted as floor managers for the affirmative. Henry even had the support of Carter Braxton and Speaker Harrison. The alternative that Henry endorsed was to redeem the national debt in ten years (extended on the floor to fifteen), thus moderating the rate of both deflation and tax increases. Henry suggested that Virginia meet the immediate crisis by raising the specific tax instead of imposing a levy in desperately scarce currency or specie. He also expounded on the sanctity of contracts, which revaluation would violate, a principal objection to the new scheme in Congress as well. Proponents argued that devaluation was one way to ensure that the war debt would fall relatively equally on all. Everyone understood from the beginning, Edmund Randolph insisted, that the currency's *"real,* not its nominal value would be the standard" at the end of the war.[13] Mason had already instituted procedures for establishing a sliding scale of depreciation in the loan plan he submitted the previous fall. Henry left the assembly for the rest of the session on June 7, the day after the vote on the plan. Thereafter, the maneuvering only occasionally surfaces in the record. The ways and means committee, which the house instructed to prepare a bill based on Henry's proposals and of which Mason was a member, never reported. Instead, the Committee of the Whole House on the State of the Commonwealth brought forth a resolution about two weeks later calling upon Virginia to "concur with

a majority of the United States" in support of the plan.[14] From the wording of both the resolution and the final assembly bill, congressional supporters apparently argued that Virginia could not afford to isolate itself
from the union by not accepting revaluation but agreed that the state
ought not to do so until a majority of the other states acceded. The
assembly also provided for the retirement of all outstanding issues of
state currency at the same time as the Continental.

The vote on the committee's bill, fifty-two to thirty-four, virtually reversed the previous tally. Of those delegates who had voted before, Mason and Lee won twelve converts with only one defection from their own
ranks. But a more dramatic illustration of the way alignments fluctuated
in the assembly is the almost 40 percent turnover between the members
present for the first vote and the second. About two-thirds of those absent the second time had favored Henry's side earlier; of the newcomers,
nearly the same proportion supported Mason and Lee. The bill passed
in a small Senate, eight to five. Subsequent divisions on related motions
in the lower house remained extremely close; in one case the plan "escaped by two voices only," according to Jefferson.[15]

To finance the measure the legislators enacted new taxes: $2\frac{1}{2}$ percent
on the specie value of property in 1781, reduced to 1 percent for five
years after that, plus a battery of excise taxes. The assembly repealed all
other property levies except the specific tax. Because of the uncertainty
over implementation of the congressional plan, Mason sponsored a bill
for the emission of another two million dollars in state money, similarly
valued against old currency at 40:1, but because the new state money
was acceptable only for taxes specifically designed to redeem it, people
proved less willing than usual to use it. Meanwhile, the governor pressed
the Virginia delegates in Congress to report the action of other states
on Congress's refinancing as promptly as possible so that he could pro-
claim Virginia's adherence before opponents had a chance in the
next assembly to repeal it. His proclamation ultimately was dated
August 28.[16]

Opponents nonetheless had their way in the fall. The state's inability
to issue significant amounts of the new currency because of the influx
of impressment certificates forced the assembly to authorize an additional printing of ten million dollars in state paper and postpone redemption until after 1785. Even Jefferson and Richard Henry Lee admitted that they could conceive of no alternative. Benjamin Harrison
appended an amendment declaring both the new congressional issue
and the two million the last session emitted legal tender in payment of

any tax. Congress's original plan envisioned not accepting the new Continental currency for taxes until all the bills from previous issues had been withdrawn, and the assembly initially had hoped to limit acceptance of the two million-dollar issue to the taxes designed to redeem it. Joseph Jones and Edmund Pendleton considered the congressional 40-to-1 plan "in great measure defeated" by the Speaker's action.[17]

The assembly turned again to private loans to remedy the deficiency in the state's cash flow. In May Congress learned that the French fleet had at last sailed and, in anticipation of added expenses when it arrived, imposed an extraordinary requisition on the states of $10,000,000 payable in thirty days. The Virginia assembly moved swiftly to raise the state's share of $1,953,000. Since the deadline Congress set for payment fell long before the year's taxes were due, the ways and means committee proposed that the legislators themselves and "gentlemen in the country and towns adjacent" to Richmond advance the necessary sum until December.[18] The assembly guaranteed repayment in constant dollars at 6 percent interest and allowed lenders to apply the loans to their taxes. Apparently persons around Richmond still had more liquid assets than the bad times would suggest, for on June 30 Jefferson sent Congress $1,430,239⅔ with the promise that the remaining half million would soon follow.

By the time the assembly adjourned in mid-July it had earned a reputation for disputation, a reflection of the unnerving crisis. Delegates demanded roll call votes on six occasions during the session. Possibly because he lost on half of them, Mason was more sour than usual about his colleagues and decided to retire after the next session. Undated notes in his papers on the need to revise the electoral process may be from this period. Mason described recent assemblies as "filled with Men . . . unequal of the Office" because "unfortunately Elections are now so little attended to, that a factious bawling Fellow, who will make a Noise four or five miles round him, and prevail upon his party to attend, may carry an Election against a Man of ten times his Weight and Influence."[19] Assuming that an attentive public would not allow such mistakes to occur, Mason proposed heavy fines for voters who did not come to the polls, as had Jefferson in a bill prepared for the revisal of the laws, but in neither case to any avail.

Honyman agreed about the quality of representation. The unusual interest generated by inflation and taxes in the 1780 elections, he said, tempted candidates to make "fair promises of altering things for the better" with the result that "many of those chosen are men of mean abilities and no rank." Others had different reasons to complain. John Parke Custis, who supported Congress's currency revaluation, judged the imposts the legislature enacted to support the plan "excessive" but hoped "industry and Frugality" would tide people over.[20] The poll tax on slaves that the assembly had revived at Jefferson's behest the year before especially incensed eastern planters because they felt it bore unfairly on them, the largest slaveholders in the state. Meanwhile, Theodorick Bland flailed away at the policy of having counties provide recruiting bounties because it put taxation "in the hands of the very lowest class of people."[21] The one policy that evoked no criticism seems to have been the requirement that all assemblymen take an oath that they were not secretly tories.

With no defensive force between Virginia and Cornwallis, the state's leaders plunged into rebuilding the southern army a second time. While the consensus appears to have been that the state could readily call up another five thousand men, it had weapons for only about half that number. In the campaign that culminated in the battle of Camden, the state had to supply a large quantity of arms for both its own and North Carolina militia, all of which had been lost in the defeat. There remained scarcely three thousand stand in Virginia, and when Jefferson wrote to Washington for help, the general replied with regret because recent imports of weapons from France had been less than expected. At least, Jefferson commented in response to reports of desertions, the loss of the men would take away "the necessity of answering the question how they shall be armed?"[22]

Supplies of other matériel fell short as well. The troops at Camden had had no tents, and the problem persisted as another winter approached. As for munitions, Jefferson said that he knew of just a few reams of cartridge paper in the entire state, and the government's only cartridge boxes had arrived in the lower Chesapeake Bay on board ship from Baltimore as Leslie sailed in. Worst of all, the two million dollars that the assembly had issued in the spring was exhausted by September 1. When Gates sharply reminded Jefferson that he wanted only fully equipped troops, the governor retorted in that case he would get none; to another complaint about units arriving in North Carolina poorly clad, Jefferson quipped that the men "will be as warm in their present cloathing at Hillsborough as at Chesterfield Court House" where they had mustered.[23] Although Virginia succeeded in sending about five hundred newly recruited regulars and a slightly larger number of militia to the front by early November 1780, General Edward Stevens found them "in a most Pitifull condition. Many of them cant Hide their nakedness, and scarce a Blankett among them."[24] A week or two later Stevens had acquired some "tolerable Musketts" for them and Jefferson had turned up some tents, but for the rest of the year army leaders complained that men arrived in camp "altogether unfit for further service" because of a lack of clothing and equipment.[25]

Everyone naturally looked to the legislature for help in the fall of 1780, but it was almost a month late assembling and had to reduce its quorum to fifty to remain in session. Even then the sergeant-at-arms had to arrest forty-five members one day and compel them to attend to meet the new minimum. Besides the British invasion, an epidemic, possibly of influenza, swept the eastern portion of the state, encouraging both militiamen and legislators to stay home. Joseph Jones, who had recently returned from Congress disgusted at the pettiness he found there, became equally upset with his fellow assemblymen. He willingly excused those who came from exposed coastal regions or from the distant West, but he saw no justification for representatives of "the interior part of the State" not to be on time.[26] That they might have been concerned about the ease with which Leslie could have struck at Richmond seems not to have moved him.

The assembly continued to struggle with a poor image throughout the fall session. When a weary Jefferson announced that he was thinking of resigning, George Mason implored him to stay "at least 'til after the next general Election; for I really dread the Choice which the present Assembly may make."[27] It did not help that Mason, who had decided to retire from the assembly at the end of 1780 in any event, did not make it to his last session because of another flare-up of the gout. Jefferson tried to supply some of the leadership the absent Mason might have afforded by having General Nathanael Greene address the assembly on his way to his new command. The governor more than likely composed the detailed list of army needs that Greene presented the delegates, and Jefferson spurred the legislators on to their work with the warning that Leslie's departure from Virginia would only be temporary and "seems yet to call for an increase rather than abatement of military preparation."[28]

The assembly attacked the supply problem by continuing the Provision Law for another year and extending the principle of the specific tax to clothing, beef, and wagons. The delegates authorized the governor to begin seizing beef and salt immediately and to open negotiations with North Carolina to obtain pork on which that state had placed an embargo. Jefferson called Richard Morris back into service to take charge.

The debate over inducements to encourage three thousand additional enlistments became divisive. Early in the session the delegates voted overwhelmingly to use the draft only as a last resort however high bounties rose. The legislature finally set the rate at eight thousand dollars for three years and twelve thousand for the duration of the war. The furor came when the assembly fattened the last offer by adding three hundred acres of land and "a healthy sound negro, between the ages of ten and thirty years" or sixty pounds in gold or silver.[29] The debate centered not on whether to adopt the measure—most felt that it would be quite effective—but how to obtain the slaves for it. The original bill provided for the impressment of slaves at fixed prices from owners of twenty or more. As Joseph Jones described the alignment to Madison, "the Negro holders in general . . . clamour agt. the project . . . but you know the great part of our House are not of that Class."[30] Madison to his credit responded that it seemed "more consonant to the principles of liberty" to free the blacks and enlist them. His remark elicited a revealing rejoinder from Jones. Madison's suggestion was not "politic," Jones declared. While freedom for blacks was "a great and desireable object," it had to be extended gradually lest it "draw off immediately such a number of the best labourers for the Culture of the Earth as to ruin individuals, distress the State and perhaps the continent when all that can be now raised by their assistance is but barely sufficient to keep us joging along."[31] As it developed, Jones's prediction was wrong; the slaveholders won the debate since the final statute charged the cost of the bounty in slaves to the property tax which bore equally on all.

Another manpower problem arose in the navy. Privateers effectively choked off the Chesapeake Bay during most of 1780. Although the enemy vessels were relatively small, the remaining elements of the state's navy, the brig *Jefferson* and the boats *Liberty* and *Patriot,* had little success against them until mid-August when Commodore James Barron captured five raiders in the vicinity of Tangier Island. Shortly afterward, the governor of Maryland announced that Baltimore merchants would outfit two brigs and three barges to assist that state's two public vessels in sweeping the bay and invited Virginians to join. The only way Barron could recruit enough men for the cruise, however, was to convert the usual bounty and clothing ration into a cash payment that brought the pay to ten dollars a day. He warned the governor that volunteers enlisted in this way—"mere landsmen," Jefferson termed them—would be un-dependable in battle.[32] Jefferson also had hoped to overhaul the ship *Thetis* and the two Eastern Shore galleys *Accomac* and *Diligence* for service in the bay, but after Barron's experience doubted that he could ever find enough men to man them.

The assembly responded by adopting the hated British practice of impressment, under which royal press gangs had abducted men on board commercial vessels or portside to fill out naval crews. The assembly authorized Virginia captains to take 20 percent of the sailors on any non-naval vessel except those in the service of Maryland or North Carolina or on vessels already loaded and bound from port. For the future, the legislature required county courts to apprentice at least half of the orphans in their care to the sea. The delegates then felt able to sanction the moderate increase in the fleet that Jefferson recommended. The navy recommissioned the galley *Lewis* and the ship *Thetis*, and Jefferson ordered two new galleys patterned on a model that had caught his imagination in Philadelphia. Otherwise the assembly reiterated its previous directive that the remaining state vessels be sold.[33]

When the delegates tallied the cost of their programs, it was staggering. Joseph Jones predicted that the bills already due "will soon exhaust the new emission [of ten million dollars] which will be gone as soon and as fast as they can make it." Congress seemed to be letting "the whole burthen of the Southern Army . . . fall on this State."[34] As a result, the assembly accepted Patrick Henry's proposal to send a special emissary to General Washington and Congress to extract more aid from the Continent, or, at the very least, to see if Congress would put pressure on Spain and France to help recapture South Carolina and Georgia. The current delegation—one of whom, Jones, was present in the chamber—took the decision as a rebuff although the pretext was that the delegates already had enough to do in Congress without having to travel to consult with Washington as well.

Linked to Henry's proposal was another rescinding instructions to Virginia's congressional delegation not to vote for any agreement with Spain that did not permit Americans free navigation of the Mississippi River, which Spanish control of New Orleans cut off at its mouth. Georgia and South Carolina had recently requested Congress not to insist on this condition in order to hasten Spain's intervention against the British invasion of the South, in effect bartering the future interests of the West for the immediate needs of the East. One of the two Virginia representatives then present in Philadelphia, Theodorick Bland, who was a partisan of Richard Henry Lee, recommended that the assembly agree; the other, James Madison, did not. Apparently Madison reasoned that the concession would unnecessarily yield a vital point when recent dispatches from John Jay, the United States minister in Madrid, hinted that Spain was about to allow Americans the use of the river. The assembly found Bland's argument more persuasive and voted to remove the section on navigation of the Mississippi from the congressional delegation's instructions.[35]

The choice of an envoy to present Virginia's needs to Washington and Congress precipitated another confrontation between Richard Henry Lee and Benjamin Harrison, adding to the interminable wrangling of the session. Although the delegates made their decision to send a special representative on December 2, they could not agree on a candidate until the twenty-seventh. Harrison and Lee each received forty votes in a joint session of the assembly. As Speaker, Harrison had the tie-breaking vote but could not cast it in his own behalf. There the issue remained until "after much debate and perplexity" Lee withdrew, by which time Harrison was so angry that he almost declined the assignment.[36]

The delegates' smoldering resentment of Congress ironically led to their most nationalistic decision: cession of the state's western claims to the Continent. Virginia could hardly expect to receive military aid against the British if it denied Congress the most promising means of paying for it. A break had come in this controversial issue earlier in the year when New York abandoned its claims, next to Virginia's the most extensive. By summer Mason concluded that he had enough votes in the assembly to propose a cession of the lands north of the Ohio River to the Continent if Congress would guarantee the state's title to the remainder. With his retirement imminent, Mason decided to bring about "this last piece of service to the American union, before I quit."[37]

As a first step, Mason moved to end the long-festering border dispute with Pennsylvania. In August 1779 President Madison of William and Mary and another member of the faculty had met in Baltimore with a Pennsylvania team led by the noted astronomer David Rittenhouse to negotiate a settlement. They agreed to extend the Mason and Dixon Line, which divided Pennsylvania from Maryland, due west to a point five degrees of latitude from the Delaware River, and then run the border due north instead of following a sinuous line paralleling the course of the Delaware River in the East, as the Pennsylvania charter literally required. Virginia thus yielded its claim to the Pittsburgh region and retained a narrow panhandle on the south side of the Ohio River which

Mason deemed "of little value" and suggested giving to Congress. All in all, Mason thought that the Pennsylvania representatives "overmatched" the Virginians in the conference.[38] Pennsylvania's speedy ratification of the arrangement suggests that its legislators, too, thought they had the better of the bargain.

In Virginia, solid opposition from the West forced appointment of another committee composed entirely of representatives from the disputed area to "inquire in what manner the rights of this Commonwealth and of its citizens will be affected."[39] Meanwhile, the Virginia land office opened a branch in the region, provoking a barrage of protests from Pennsylvania and Congress to which Governor Jefferson replied with lawyerly obfuscation. Virginia's courts welcomed any Pennsylvanian who felt aggrieved, he said. Finally, on June 23, 1780, Mason, having "labored the ratification . . . as heartily as I ever did any subject in my life," was "able to carry it only by a small majority." The saving proviso was that Pennsylvania recognize the titles already recorded and not tax Virginians in the area until the end of 1780. Overlooking "some unwarrantable claims," the Pennsylvania legislature quickly acquiesced in the added conditions "to promote peace and harmony with a Sister State."[40] Five years, much bitterness, and many confrontations lay ahead before surveyors ran the actual boundary.

Soon afterward, Mason sent the Virginia delegation in Congress a full explanation of the state's requirements for giving up its northwest territory. Congress would have to organize the area into at least two states, reimburse Virginia for George Rogers Clark's expenses in conquering the region, confirm French residents in their property and protect them against the British, reserve one hundred fifty thousand acres for bounties to Clark's men, award Clark personally seven and a half square miles at the falls of the Ohio, guarantee Virginia additional lands should the section set aside for bounties on the Cumberland River prove insufficient, and declare previous purchases of lands in the area by Indian treaty to be "void and of no effect." Congressional opposition bridled most at the last stipulation, but from it Virginia would not retreat. As Mason explained, it was "the general Opinion here that many Members of Congress have been privately admitted into the Indiana, Vandalia and other Companys; which is conceived to be as effectual Bribery, as if they had received a round sum in Guineas." Without this condition, he continued, Virginia's objective in ceding the lands of helping to finance the war would be defeated, for "the most valuable Part wou'd be converted to private Purposes."[41]

During the spring of 1780 Congress had tendered its own gesture of goodwill by voting while the Maryland delegates were absent to guarantee the rights of all states to their territory, in effect recognizing Virginia's claims to Kentucky. It had then appointed a committee, on which Joseph Jones sat, whose report put the onus "upon those States which can remove the Embarrassment respecting the Western Country [by] a liberal Surrender of . . . their territorial Claims, since they cannot be preserved entire without endangering the Stability of the general Confederacy."[42]

On September 6, the day Congress adopted the report, Jones and Madison submitted a resolution based on Mason's requirements. Over the next month Congress tentatively agreed to absorb Clark's expenses, but balked at confirming the remainder of Virginia's territorial claims and invalidating Indian purchases. Ultimately, the Continental legislature rejected the entire resolution, six states to four, with two divided and Delaware absent. Because Jones had left for home, Bland and John Walker overrode Madison to his "chagrin" and cast Virginia's own vote against accepting the state's terms of cession. Although Madison first thought of attacking his colleagues in the General Assembly for their vote, "on cooler reflection" he decided it would serve his unionist sentiments better to cite their vote as an illustration that not all opponents of Virginia's terms of cession were in league with the speculators. He urged Jones to point out to the assembly that some in Congress considered Virginia's conditions redundant because the creation of a national public domain implied a pledge by Congress to see that the land would not all be subordinated to private interest. Madison himself appeared to find some merit in this view. Nonetheless, when the speculators continued to machinate, Madison accepted the need for control. Although "I do not believe there is any serious design in Congress to gratify the avidity of land mongers . . . the best security for their virtue in this respect will be to keep it out of their power."[43]

The record tells little about the debate over the issue in the fall 1780 session of the General Assembly. Before the legislature convened, Jefferson predicted success, and despite the lack of progress as the meetings wore on, Joseph Jones remained optimistic. But Mason never appeared, and Jones left the assembly early in December when his family fell ill. Without Mason to discipline them, the legislators wasted time on other issues and did not turn to the question of cession until the last two days of the term. The House of Delegates went into the Committee of the Whole to consider Congress's September 6 resolution on New Year's Day. Simultaneously the intelligence arrived that a British fleet under

Benedict Arnold had appeared in the Chesapeake Bay. The news hastened discussion, and on January 2, 1781, the delegates adopted a resolution offering to cede Virginia's northwest territory on essentially the conditions that Mason had dictated. The Senate quickly concurred, permitting both chambers to scurry to safety.[44]

With some last-minute assistance from Arnold, Mason finally accomplished the "last bit of service" he could do for the "American union" in the assembly. When Congress eventually accepted it, the cession added cement to the bonds of nationhood. It made available to the Continent the principal means by which the central government could pay for the war and ensured that Congress rather than a few states would direct the advance of settlement westward.

Arnold's mission to disrupt Virginia's logistics succeeded better than he knew. The swiftness of his attack prevented Jefferson from executing many of the fall assembly's directives. Notice of the statute for supplying clothes, beef, and wagons went out so late that the expiration date, February 1, was upon counties before they learned of the law. Jefferson told officials to enforce the statute anyway, assuring them that the next assembly would absolve them retroactively. The absence of so many militia from their counties prevented implementation of the recruiting act, and as soon as Arnold was quiet, Jefferson tried to rotate calls among counties so that at some point the men in each would be free of militia duty long enough to enlist them for the regular service.[45]

Already it seemed to the militia that they were serving as long as if they had regularly enlisted. Ordinarily county lieutenants staggered terms of service. But the frequency of calls and the fact that six years of regular enlistments cut deeply into the number of men eligible meant that those remaining were summoned for new tours of duty almost as soon as they returned from the one before. "A spirit of disquietude prevails among the poorer Class, whose Corporeal Labours are necessary to sustain their families," Colonel James Innes cautioned the governor, while Edmund Pendleton warned that "our crops, of corn particularly, will be much Injured by the large Number of Militia already in Service."[46] Commander after commander advised Jefferson not to rely on their men much longer because they might mutiny at any moment.

Then, to cap the state's problems, the money supply ran out again. Just three weeks after the last session of the assembly, the state treasurer, George Brooke, notified Jefferson that the demands pending at his office "exceed the sum I was empowered to Emit."[47]

Jefferson accordingly called a special session of the legislature for March 1, and, with unprecedented attentiveness to duty, the House of Delegates formed a quorum just one day late. The house unanimously elected Richard Henry Lee Speaker in place of Benjamin Harrison, who had gone to Philadelphia on special assignment. The three-point agenda that Jefferson presented—extension of the Provision Law, recruitment, and money—promised, he thought, a short meeting, but the querulous mood of the delegates, reflecting the sullenness of a public weighed down by militia duty, high taxes, impressments, and the threat from Arnold, prolonged the session to three weeks.[48]

The delegates immediately appointed Patrick Henry, John Taylor of Caroline, and John Tyler to draft a remonstrance "in the most pressing terms calling the Aid of the United States to Support a due part of the Ruinous Burden under which this State at present labours."[49] The text, which Taylor probably drafted, bitterly recounted with some hyperbole the willing contributions of Virginians earlier in the war when the fighting was mostly in the North and listed the heavy obligations the state still bore while others availed "themselves of resolutions of Congress, by which they get rid of their State paper at the expense of the Union." Virginians "demand" help, the petition concluded; let "the consequences be on the heads of those who refuse them."[50] The committee never submitted the draft to the house because a few days later Benjamin Harrison returned from Philadelphia with word that Washington was at last sending the Marquis de Lafayette with twelve hundred New England and New Jersey troops to help.

Despite this comforting news, the delegates remained contentious throughout the session. Each item on Jefferson's agenda engendered controversy, although it would seem that two at least required only simple extensions of existing statutes. The delegates debated at length a militia bill, the details of which are not in the record, but which presumably spoke to Jefferson's request for more effective means of compelling men to report for duty and discouraging desertion, and finally defeated the measure on the third reading, twenty-seven to thirty-two. Instead, the assembly called for a full report at its next session to determine what changes really needed to be made.[51]

The delegates found more acceptable for the moment yet another version of the minutemen in order to be able to respond more rapidly to invasion. Continental officers wanted forty-two hundred men on call for a year at a time, a series of redoubts at the mouths of strategic rivers, and a parallel series of magazines a short distance inland to form a second line of defense. A committee chaired by Patrick Henry preferred a simpler plan that Alexander Spotswood proposed to enlist fourteen hundred volunteers who would meet frequently for training and receive half-pay when not in the field. The house added a bonus of two thousand dollars for each enlistee and appointed Spotswood a brigadier general to lead them.[52]

The issue of supplies provoked an inordinately long debate over a bill to "remedy the inconveniences arising from the interruption" of the acts for requisitioning clothes, beef, and wagons, and for recruiting the state's Continental quota.[53] The house considered the "remedy" in the Committee of the Whole for several days, reported it out, recommitted it to the committee, reported it out again, passed it, the Senate amended it, and the house ultimately accepted the amendments on the next to the last day of the session. The text of the final statute suggests that the controversy raged over an attempt to control the prices assessed for impressments. Because of "great abuses," the act forbade collectors to allow more than the prices stated in the Provision Law for items taken.[54] Horses commandeered for Nathanael Greene presented a special problem since assessments sometimes ran to thirty-five thousand pounds an animal. Jefferson suggested having publicly supported commissioners submit the evaluations rather than private citizens as the law currently required, but before he could prevent it, the assembly plunged ahead and set a maximum price of five thousand pounds for a horse. Greene immediately protested that the ceiling "amounts . . . to a prohibition."[55]

The third item, money, also provoked a confrontation, this time between the two chambers. A house bill that provided for printing a new issue of currency included the usual paragraphs designating the new money as legal tender and authorizing the punishment of counterfeiters. The Senate objected that these latter sections did not pertain in a strict sense to the appropriation of funds and consequently did not fall under the constitutional prohibition against the Senate initiating or amending a money bill. The upper chamber had raised this objection in the previous session but had withdrawn the complaint in order not to delay legislation. This time the Senate insisted on its interpretation of the constitution despite the emergency and won. After a "free conference" between the chambers, two bills emerged, one authorizing the emission of ten million dollars more in paper money, or up to fifteen million if circumstances required, to be redeemed by the end of 1792, and the other embodying the provisions regarding legal tender and counterfeiting.[56]

Although Jefferson had tactfully hinted that he was "not apprehending that the Assembly, when convened at so unusual a season, will propose to go on general business," some members thought otherwise.[57] Toward the end of the session an unidentified delegate suddenly submitted a motion to move the capital once more, although exactly where the record does not reveal. The house speedily defeated the proposal thirty-three to forty. Another motion immediately followed that would have required the recording of the ayes and nays at the request of any two members of the house so voters could distinguish "virtuous conduct" from "vicious, weak or wicked conduct." The chamber rejected that idea without a division.[58]

A struggle also loomed over whether to select Arthur Lee or Benjamin Harrison for Congress in a by-election, but the assembly put off the choice until the regular session.[59] Controversy cropped up, too, over what might appear to have been a minor matter, the effort to exchange Colonel William Roscoe Wilson Curle of Elizabeth City County, who had been captured during a British raid on Newport News and Hampton just as the special session got under way. Overnight the local establishment on the lower peninsula launched a campaign to obtain an exchange, describing Curle as "the very life and soul of his county."[60] There had been no exchanges for some time, however, because Arnold had added more restrictive language to the oath normally given for parole than American officers would subscribe to. He had also been using the parole system to gain a tactical advantage by seizing civilians before they were called to militia duty and putting them on oath not to serve. In Curle's case the question seems to have been whether seeking an exception constituted special privilege since others had been imprisoned longer waiting for the dispute with Arnold to be resolved. The wrangle produced two failed attempts to reconcile differences between the house and Senate. Ultimately, the arrival of a new British commander, Major General William Phillips, settled the matter. Having been liberally treated himself while a prisoner in Virginia, Phillips consented to limit the issuance of paroles to "those American Prisoners of War who . . . have been taken in Arms" and leave civilians alone.[61] Two days later Curle was in Richmond, presumably without having sworn the offending words of Arnold's oath. A quarrel between Phillips and the Continental commander, Baron von Steuben, however, soon shut down exchanges again.

The special session finally ended on March 22, apparently able to agree easily on only two matters: an extension of time for filing preemption rights in the West and the presentation of "a Horse, with furniture and a Sword" to General Morgan for his victory at Cowpens.[62]

The efforts of the special session notwithstanding, both the state and Continental supply systems in Virginia rapidly disintegrated. Congress's new policy of decentralization had effectively merged the two, for the Provision Law became the principal mode of supplying both. The two gradually fell under the supervision of John Brown, commissary of the Provision Law and commissary general of Virginia. The Continental deputy commissary general for purchases in the southern department, Robert Forsythe, left to join Greene after his duties in the state became "a nullity."[63] Logistically, the weakness of the new arrangement became apparent when the number of Continental troops in the state began to increase because Brown had no authority to call upon other states to help Virginia feed them.

Worst of all, Brown and another key bureaucrat, commissioner of war George Muter, were simply incompetent. Their continuance in office seriously reflects on Jefferson's capacity as an administrator. Steuben ultimately appealed over the governor's head to have Muter fired. The general charged that "the Ordinance, Ammunition, Bombs, Shells, and Cannon Balls" of the state were in a "disorderly situation," and the ensuing investigation found "a considerable number of Muskets wanting repair" and "Cannon belonging to this State . . . rendered useless by not being mounted on Carriages." "In short," the assembly concluded, "the whole Business of the War Office appears to be entirely deranged," and "the present Commissioner of the War Office is not qualified to fill that important Office and ought to be discharged therefrom."[64] Colonel William Davies replaced Muter for the remainder of the war.

As for Brown, a study later documented that, however scarce provisions were, Virginians received credit at best for "a fiftieth part of what they supplied in fact" because no one systematically recorded their contributions. The new commissioner Davies put the matter quite bluntly: "Mr. Brown does not know where the public Stores are lodged, what they consist of, or what quantitys are collected."[65] The Council eventually ordered a formal hearing, but summer came before Davies could get to it, for besides his own work he had to fill in for William Armistead who, he charged, had "abandoned" the Public Store.[66] When at last Davies convened a panel, Brown resigned before it could meet. "I congratulate my Country . . . upon the riddance," the commissioner declared.[67] Brown's able assistant, John Pierce, assumed responsibility for state purchasing and joined Davies in calling for the appointment of a new Continental deputy commissary general for purchases in Virginia, but the suggestion was not heeded before the war ended. Just as Virginia faced the war's greatest challenge, the state's administration began to fall apart.

CHAPTER 14

Defeat

THE Marquis de Lafayette arrived in Yorktown on March 14, just two days after Harrison reported Washington's decision to send help against Arnold. The French in Rhode Island also promised to send a stronger support fleet than Tilly's. Because the French vessels had not yet arrived and the Chesapeake states could not supply enough boats to convoy his force safely down the bay, the marquis had left his troops at Annapolis and Head of Elk in Maryland and come on alone. Jefferson, who had learned of Lafayette's orders as early as February 28 but to ensure security said nothing to the assembly, had ordered out more militia and, without giving away the secret, asked the legislature for power to impress boats and crews as a prelude to blockading Portsmouth. Unaware of the significance of the request, the assembly took a week to grant the authority. The governor, however, had not waited and began the impressments the day before his petition reached the House of Delegates.[1]

Along with the supply system in confusion, Lafayette found little coordination between the Virginia leadership and the southern army. General Greene relentlessly dunned the state for the men and matériel he needed to stop running and fight the British. To Greene's way of thinking, Jefferson let Arnold divert Virginia's attention from the main target to the south. Washington, too, cautioned Jefferson against being distracted by local problems, but at the same time wisely ad-

monished Greene that "while there is an Enemy in the heart of the
Country you can neither expect Men or supplies from it in that full
and regular manner in which they ought to be given."[2] Washington
predicted that Lafayette's arrival would change the situation. In contrast to General Gates, who had briefed Jefferson regularly on his
movements, Greene kept correspondence with the governor to a minimum. Jefferson sent Major Charles Magill to Greene's headquarters
to obtain better intelligence since, as the governor wrote to Greene,
"the multiplicity of your business . . . must forbid me to hope for a
very frequent communication." Greene replied that security prevented
him from telling Magill any "facts in time to make them important,"
but promised to keep the major informed of whatever "immediately
concerns the policy of Virginia."[3]

   Not surprisingly, the pressure from southern headquarters began
to raise fundamental questions of federal-state relations and civilian
control of the military. Greene's position was clear: "Civil polity must
accomodate itself to the emergency of war, or the people submit to
the power of the enemy. There is no other alternative." Congress had
to decide "whether the militia or state troops shall be under the orders of the Continental officers or not," the general declared. Otherwise, "no officer can be safe in his measures: nor can the war be
prosecuted upon a general scale."[4] As might have been expected, state
officials generally took an opposing stand. Moreover, the potential for
conflict in Virginia was heightened by the fact that two totally dissim-
ilar personalities held the chief military and civilian posts in the state.
When Greene passed through Richmond the previous November, he
had left behind a Prussian volunteer, Major General Baron von Steuben, to expedite the flow of men and supplies to the southern army.
A well-trained professional, Steuben busily set about organizing the
Old Dominion more efficiently than it had ever been before in order
to meet the challenge. As Steuben perceived the assignment, his task
was "tormenting the Governor" for whatever Greene requested.[5]

   Relations between Virginia officials and the baron soon became official and cold; then occasionally very hot indeed. The state of affairs
in Virginia must have driven a precise military mind like Steuben's to
distraction. "The Baron," an aide confided to Greene after a few
months, "had rather Obey in an Army, than Command in Virginia."[6]
Jefferson's friend, John Walker, whom the governor had assigned as
liaison to the general at the latter's request, sympathized with the baron's predicament. After one Germanic outburst, Walker told Jefferson

that "the difficulties and embarrasments . . . have perhaps transported him beyond the bounds of moderation; but were you acquainted with them all, you would make great allowances," although "I well know your situation is not less disagreable."[7]

One of many sources of irritation was the effort to fortify Hood's Point on the James River, where the narrow channel created a natural site at which to check British raids. Virginia authorities already had moved cannon to the spot when the general arrived in November, and when Jefferson asked for advice, Steuben had the chief engineer, Christian Senf, prepare a plan for a sixty-man redoubt. The governor submitted the scheme to the legislature, but the assembly had taken no action when Arnold forced its adjournment. As the British fleet sailed up the James, the ships approached Hood's with extreme caution, but to the amazement of the British, they found the post "totally abandoned when they landed."[8]

When even after Arnold returned down the river in mid-January and settled in Portsmouth, construction did not progress on the fortification, Steuben again upbraided the governor because "the Work could have been half finished."[9] Jefferson and the Council decided they lacked the authority to impress slaves or call out neighboring militia to perform the labor, causing Steuben to fulminate to Washington that "the Executive Power is so confined that the Governor has it not in his power to procure me 40 negroes to work at Hoods."[10] Jefferson tried to hire slaves from local planters but with little success and canceled an offer to allow local militia time off from their next tour of duty if they worked at Hood's because another invasion intervened and the army needed them as soldiers. One had to be patient, Jefferson counseled the baron. "We can only be answerable for the orders we give, and not for their execution. If they are disobeyed from obstinacy of spirit or want of coercion in the laws it is not our fault."[11]

Steuben alienated his officers as much as the civil authorities. Although respected for his talent in training militia, the Prussian's haughtiness precluded real popularity. Once he summoned supernumerary officers in the state to Petersburg for reassignment and kept them waiting for a week. He ran afoul of the sensitivity to minuscule distinctions in rank to which the Virginia officer corps had become addicted when he restored General John Peter Gabriel Muhlenberg to full seniority despite a break in service even though Muhlenberg had resigned over a similar slight two years before. Colonel William

Davies, Steuben's hand-picked candidate to succeed George Muter as commissioner of war, led a delegation of Virginia field officers who warned the baron that "confusion, disgust, and resignations . . . followed such irregularities."[12] Then a similarly trivial incident, "the black affair at Westover," captured the entire attention of many in the high command just as they should have been planning an attack on Arnold.[13]

In mid-February the watch at Sandy Point on the James River apprehended a boat flying a flag of truce. Although the use of such flags was common during wartime in the eighteenth century, the commander, Lieutenant Charles Hare of H.M.S. *Swift* at Portsmouth, raised suspicions by attempting to pass at night and not heaving to when challenged until fired upon and boarded. It developed that Arnold had sent Hare to Westover to advise Mary Willing Byrd, the widow of William Byrd III and the cousin of Arnold's wife, that the British would soon restore the slaves they had taken during the recent raid. The governor, however, had forbidden precisely such returns because Arnold used them to reward tory sympathizers like Mary Byrd while keeping the slaves of whigs. The militiamen decided to hold Lieutenant Hare pending further orders.[14]

Then Hare's guards discovered him burning evidence that allegedly incriminated Mary Byrd. As a result, the commander at Sandy Point, Major George Turberville, searched Westover early one morning before Mrs. Byrd and two of her daughters had risen from bed (a "Liberty that Savages would have blushed at," the outraged plantation mistress complained to Steuben).[15] Jefferson and Steuben both tried to minimize the entire incident. The governor referred Byrd's dealing with the enemy to the attorney general for prosecution and ordered Hare released for fear that Arnold, who had written menacingly that "I wish not to be forced into acts of severity, at which the humane heart must recoil," might retaliate.[16] But James Innes, temporarily in command of the Virginia forces, refused to free Hare. A physical giant, Innes had never been known to kowtow to authority, as Jefferson had already discovered. Infuriated, Steuben demanded that Jefferson make Innes obey, prompting the governor to ask how a civilian could control an officer if the army could not. Emotions flared for a time—Turberville, for example, challenged the baron to a duel and had to resign—but the authorities quieted the crisis by postponing Mary Byrd's trial indefinitely and letting Hare return to Portsmouth once they ascertained that he could convey no intelligence of importance.

For most of March state and army officials strained to prepare for the assault against Arnold. Jefferson remained confident that the number of men required would be provided "though not quite so early as had been proposed," and when Lafayette apologized for having to leave his troops behind, the governor assured him that the "Delays at the head of Elk will not produce any inconvenience." But Steuben, stung by the fact that Lafayette outranked him and would assume command, became more impatient than ever to have everything ready before the marquis's force arrived in order to snatch back some of the glory that he felt had been denied him.[17]

The plan was to amass twenty-two hundred Virginia militia before Portsmouth and send eight hundred more to join twelve hundred North Carolinians under General Isaac Gregory near Great Bridge to block Arnold's escape to the south. As the troops gathered, shortages of arms and ammunition revealed the full extent of Muter's inadequacy. For three weeks Jefferson issued repeated calls, juggled quotas, and alternated counties from which he summoned troops to compensate for greater deficiencies in militia returns than the most pessimistic had expected. Eventually the required number of troops assembled, but the pressures overcame Steuben. The frustration of months erupted in a series of letters to the governor and others in which the baron declared that he had been disgraced and blamed Jefferson for the humiliation: "On the Assurances I received from Government . . . I had the Weakness to write Genl. Washington and Marquis De la fayette that every thing was ready for the expedition; my Credulity, however, is punished at the expence of my honor."[18] Steuben's denunciation of Jefferson was so intemperate that even the baron later thought of apologizing, though there is no evidence that he did.

The arrival in the Chesapeake Bay on Tuesday, March 20, of twelve British warships, the vanguard of a fleet under Admiral Arbuthnot escorting General Phillips with relief for Arnold, put an end to any thought of attacking Portsmouth. On the twenty-sixth about twenty more vessels appeared bearing over two thousand British reinforcements. Admiral Destouches had sailed from Newport, Rhode Island, to support Lafayette, and Arbuthnot, who had succeeded in repairing the damages suffered in the great storm, followed from New York with a slightly superior force. The two fleets had met off the Virginia Capes on the sixteenth, and although the French claimed a small victory, the British continued on to the Chesapeake Bay while Destouches returned to his base in Rhode Island for repairs. Although Lafayette did not know precisely where Destouches had sailed, he knew that the opportunity had been lost. He immediately rejoined his troops in Maryland after expressing his regret to Jefferson "that so much trouble, so many Expenses Have Been the only Result of our Enterprise."[19]

Despite the doomsayers, the allies had come close. Arbuthnot wrote the Admiralty that the relief force found Arnold "prest for provisions as well as by the formidable combination against him."[20] The Virginians had mobilized over three thousand militia, and by impressing four vessels to add to the *Tempest,* the *Jefferson,* and two galleys of the regular navy, had readied a small flotilla for an attack on the city.

Before Lafayette left, he endorsed Steuben's suggestion to avoid wasting all this effort by letting the baron lead two thousand of the militia to help Greene in North Carolina. Speaker Lee and General Weedon added their support for the idea. Steuben reasoned that if the Americans moved vigorously against Cornwallis, Phillips would have to abandon Virginia to assist the earl. Steuben thought that Destouches had probably gone on to Cape Fear after the engagement off the Virginia Capes and that quite likely Phillips already planned to follow, or, if not, would do so as soon as the Virginians moved southward. Jefferson and the Council considered the plan too risky, however, especially since half of all the armament in the state would have to accompany the detachment to North Carolina. Instead, the executive called up two thousand new militia for Greene from southwestern and western counties where settlers more likely had their own arms. To Steuben the decision was the final rebuff, and he announced that he would join Greene as soon as possible. General Weedon grumbled that the executive "have not an Idea beyond Local Security."[21] Although Weedon felt less certain than Steuben about the unlikelihood of danger from Phillips, he and other Virginia military leaders agreed that it would be wiser for the state to keep the fighting elsewhere if it could.

About the first of April, Phillips sent a flotilla of six vessels with twelve to eighteen guns each and a half-dozen smaller craft to block the passage of Lafayette's troops at the Potomac River and harass the area. The expedition terrorized the region for over two weeks and caused a ripple effect statewide because militia summoned to defend Alexandria, Dumfries, and Hunter's ironworks at Fredericksburg had to be kept out of the normal rotation, disrupting defenses everywhere.[22] Aside from the capture at Alexandria one night of a small tender and sixteen of its crew, the superior mobility of the British allowed them to ravage with impunity. They burned numerous houses, took a large quantity of tobacco from warehouses at Cedar Point, Maryland, and released numbers of slaves, including twenty-five from a plantation of Robert Carter and "several" from Chotank, which George Washington owned. The episode embarrassed the American commander in chief because his cousin Lund Washington ransomed the plantation buildings by offering provisions to the raiders. The general chastised Lund for dealing "with a parcel of plundering Scoundrels" and setting an example that "may become a subject for animadversion."[23]

Once the opportunity to expel Arnold evaporated, the chronic problems with the militia intensified. Besides the western troops sent to Greene, Steuben's defense plan called for two thousand more to be stationed under Muhlenberg near Portsmouth to harass the British should they march from the town and eight hundred under Nelson on the lower peninsula north of the James River should the enemy move there by water. Jefferson and the Council realized that such a demand would stretch the tolerance of the populace to a breaking point. "Being very unwilling to harrass the Militia more than shall be absolutely unavoidable," the executive urged county lieutenants to send those who had been derelict in their duty in previous calls before summoning "the better part of the County" who had served before.[24] Still, there were rumblings in Charlotte, Northumberland, Lancaster, Botetourt, Loudoun, and Fauquier counties, and riots against recruiting and the impressment of beef and wagons in Augusta, Rockbridge, Northampton, Accomack, and Hampshire. When the Hampshire County lieutenant reported that his attempt to control the mob "proved inefectual by reason of their having a superiour force," Jefferson advised him not to confront the rioters head-on, "but when they shall have dispersed to go and take them out of their Beds, singly and without Noise."[25]

Jefferson's efforts to rotate duty calls and quiet complaints collapsed when, with the sudden appearance of the British sailing up the James River on April 18, he had to call out every militiaman in the surrounding counties. The raid was swift-moving and destructive. A British force under Colonel John Simcoe landed at Burwell's Landing on April 20, compelled James Innes and his militia to retire from Williamsburg, scouted Yorktown, and then rode on to the Chickahominy River shipyard, where they burned the *Thetis,* which was still on the stocks. Two days later the enemy sailed upriver again. Panic swept through Richmond at the prospect of another visit from Arnold, and Jefferson ordered the public records moved in preparation for the government's departure. Bolling Starke, the newly appointed state auditor, lugged records around the countryside for several days before he found a private home where he could squirrel them away. Richmond was practically denuded of public and private property by the time the British occupied it.[26]

For a while Jefferson and Steuben did not know where either Phillips or Innes was. Both Steuben and the governor thought there might be time to put the unfinished works at Hood's in defensible condition. Then Phillips appeared offshore on the twenty-third. Steuben ordered Innes to the north bank of the James across from Hood's to check the British, not knowing that Innes, encumbered with twenty wagons of supplies and one hundred sick from the military hospital at Williamsburg, had veered away from the James and crossed the Pamunkey River. The British hovered off Westover on the twenty-fourth, prolonging the suspense in Richmond. Within British councils, Simcoe argued for an attack on the capital, but Phillips favored an attempt to capture the supplies stockpiled in Petersburg first. On April 24 the British landed at City Point at the confluence of the Appomattox and James rivers, finally signaling their intention to leave Richmond alone for the while.

The British, twenty-three hundred strong, met Steuben and Muhlenberg with one thousand militia at Blandford about a mile east of Petersburg late in the afternoon of April 25. The Americans stubbornly resisted for a couple of hours before the British artillery drove them across the Appomattox River. The retreating forces succeeded in destroying Pocahontas Bridge behind them to prevent pursuit and fell back in good order to Chesterfield County Courthouse. The militia earned wide acclaim for their performance on this occasion. "This little affair shows plainly the militia will fight," declared John Banister, who had fled from his home Battersea nearby.[27]

Steuben and Jefferson raced to move the state supplies stored around Petersburg inland to Point of Fork, where the Rivanna River flows into the James. But the state commissary, John Brown, had not carried out orders to prepare a roster of wagons that could be impressed in an emergency and not enough could be found. "Pray is there no means of bringing to punishment some of those people who abuse the public by neglecting the duties incumbent upon them?" exclaimed Greene's quartermaster, Edward Carrington, when he heard of Brown's negligence. Presumably the Virginians made some headway, because Steuben solemnly reported to Washington that "not the least article fell into the Enemy's hands" at either Petersburg or Chesterfield County Courthouse, although he may have been referring only to Continental matériel for which he was directly responsible.[28]

Phillips treated the captured town generously. Banister reported that the British commander gave strict orders not to harm the property of Theodorick Bland out of gratitude for the kindness of Bland's son while commanding the guard over the Convention troops. Phillips announced that, if townspeople moved their tobacco outside for the solders to burn, he would spare their buildings and, according to Banister, destroyed four thousand hogsheads and some ships along the river bank but only one warehouse, and that inadvertently. Phillips then rode with part of his force to Chesterfield County Courthouse, which had been Steuben's headquarters and a staging area for reinforcements moving south, and burned the barracks and three hundred barrels of flour and other stores there.[29]

Meanwhile, Arnold led another column back to Osborne's on the James River, where the Virginians had gathered a number of merchant vessels under the protection of the navy. Steuben's orders had been for the navy to attack the British ships at City Point, but the Council stayed the order and wisely told the commissioner of the navy, James Maxwell, "to go down and examine our strength and that of the enemy" first. The Virginia fleet was dangerously undermanned; the number of crewmen totaled 78 whereas the full complement should have been 590. Two of the nine naval ships had neither arms nor crews. Commissioner Maxwell, moreover, had gone off looking for a supply of cartridge paper and "some other stores."[30]

As a result, the fleet lay clustered at Osborne's when the enemy closed in. Yet, although the British surprised the Virginians, the battle on April 27 raged evenly until a shot severed the mooring cable of the largest ship, the *Tempest*, and it drifted into an exposed position. The *Tempest*'s crew abandoned ship, and those on the other vessels panicked. The entire Virginia navy, nine ships in all, was lost; the *Jefferson* and some others scuttled, the remainder captured. The British also took twelve private vessels with two thousand hogsheads of tobacco among their cargoes.[31]

Once Phillips rejoined Arnold the combined force turned upriver toward Richmond and on April 30 arrived at Manchester, which Lafayette's troops had reached the evening before, well in advance of British expectations. Although only nine hundred in number and without artillery, which Lafayette had left behind in order to move more quickly, the Americans occupied strong positions. Phillips also knew that Steuben's militia was on the way. The British consequently fell back to Osborne's after destroying about twelve hundred hogsheads of tobacco. Reports filtering in to Lafayette told how Phillips "flew into a violent passion and swore vengence" at being thwarted.[32] Undaunted, the mar-

quis and Steuben celebrated by holding a review parade in a field outside Richmond. The British moved to Bermuda Hundred where they
obtained fresh provisions and embarked for the trip downstream on
May 2. Along the way they destroyed whatever horses and cattle they
could not use. But the greatest loss to planters en route was in slaves,
who, according to the diarist Honyman, "flocked to the Enemy from all
quarters even from very remote parts." [33]

      Farther south, Cornwallis had made a momentous decision. After fail-
ing to catch Greene in the race to the Dan River, he had gone into camp
at Hillsborough, North Carolina, while the Americans moved around
the northern part of the state waiting for reinforcements. By March 15
Greene had finally collected about forty-five hundred men, including
seventeen hundred militia from Virginia, and decided to take a stand at
Guilford Courthouse. The American forces outnumbered the British
over two to one and occupied an advantageous site. To attack, the enemy
had to approach through cleared areas and in some places uphill.
Greene employed a variant of Morgan's tactic at Cowpens by placing the
rawest militia in the first line, asking them to fire at least twice before
fleeing, and stationing riflemen behind them to ensure that they did.
The battle was one of the hardest fought in the war, with notable heroism and military skill on both sides. Toward the end Greene had a
chance to overwhelm the British, but chose to withdraw to husband his
army which had been rebuilt with such difficulty. Cornwallis remained
in possession of the field at the cost of over 25 percent of his men. The
army of four thousand with which he had left Charleston ten weeks
before had shrunk to under fifteen hundred. [34]

      After resting a couple of days, Cornwallis began to retreat toward
Cape Fear and the sea, reaching Wilmington on April 7. Greene, who
after the battle camped at Ramsey's Mill, marched to the south toward
South Carolina and Georgia, which Cornwallis's southeasterly retreat
left exposed to the Americans. Contrary to the expectations of Greene
and his subordinates in Virginia, Cornwallis decided not to pursue the
rebel army. One reason was that, if the British moved overland, they
would probably be too late to assist Lord Rawdon, who commanded
British forces in the deep South, and a more rapid return to Charleston
by water Cornwallis deemed too humiliating a withdrawal. Instead,
when Cornwallis learned that Phillips had entered the Chesapeake Bay,
the earl elected to march north and invade Virginia. He observed that,
while he left South Carolina and Georgia open to Greene, Greene left
Virginia open to him. [35]

In Virginia people had already begun to move back into Petersburg as Phillips's force headed down the James River. Suddenly the British were back. Cornwallis's orders to rendezvous with him in Petersburg reached Phillips just as his fleet passed Burwell's Landing. Phillips's troops landed at Brandon on May 7 and marched into Petersburg the following night. Meanwhile, Lafayette moved to Bottom's Bridge on the Chickahominy River, expecting that a position central to Fredericksburg, Williamsburg, and Richmond would enable him to check the enemy's greater mobility along the Tidewater's rivers. Phillips's change of direction brought Lafayette back to Richmond, but from there the French commander dared move no closer to the British than Osborne's.

The British reappearance dealt another severe blow to Petersburg. Once more Banister had to flee. The last time he had lost eleven of his slaves; now the British took the rest. He expected the destruction of his flour mills next. The British also captured a state wagon train with six thousand yards of cloth and a ton of lead, which David Ross had ordered to Point of Fork but had not been able to find enough wagons to move before the British arrived a second time.[36]

Seven days after reentering Petersburg, Phillips died of a "fever" on May 15, and Arnold resumed command until Cornwallis arrived with the fifteen hundred men remaining in his army on May 20. With a precision of timing that only coincidence could achieve, an additional fifteen hundred reinforcements from Clinton entered the bay on the twenty-first, bringing the total British force in Virginia to about seven thousand.[37]

Cornwallis wasted no time. On May 23 the cavalry commander Banastre Tarleton gave Virginia an example of the reasons for his fearsome reputation. The British colonel staged a lightning raid on Chesterfield County Courthouse in a driving rainstorm that prevented the Virginians from firing their weapons and captured the militia on guard there. The next day the British marched out of Petersburg and began crossing the James River at Westover. Because Cornwallis had to act under the orders that Clinton had issued to Phillips for Virginia until the commander in chief altered them, the earl wrote to Clinton from Westover reiterating his opinion that Virginia was the key to the war and urging that it be turned into a major theater. Cornwallis calculated that he would receive Clinton's reply in about a month, during which he would have time for some "desultory" action in line with the old instructions to disrupt Virginia's recruiting and supplies.[38] He sent General Leslie to reinforce Portsmouth and set out himself after Lafayette.

The marquis could not oppose the British, for he had only nine hundred Continentals and about fifteen hundred militia who kept coming and going. Since February Brigadier General "Mad Anthony" Wayne had orders to march south with part of the Pennsylvania Continental Line, but difficulties in recruiting and obtaining supplies held up his departure. Then, early in May, Wayne's troops mutinied over pay. The seemingly inexplicable delay led to rumors and bitterness among Virginians. Many suspected that Wayne did not want to serve under Lafayette or that Pennsylvanians impeded the march saying that "Virginia was too grand—let her be humbled by the Enemy, and such like."[39] When Cornwallis appeared, Lafayette wrote to Wayne to hurry, but the Pennsylvanian replied that he could not be in Virginia until well into June.

As Cornwallis approached, Lafayette abandoned Richmond and withdrew in a northwesterly direction, endeavoring always to remain between the British and the route that Wayne would have to take. The marquis camped between Allen's Creek and Gold Mine Creek on the South Anna River on the night of May 27 as the British crossed the Chickahominy River at Bottom's Bridge. Lafayette sent orders ahead to Weedon to evacuate Hunter's Forge and prepare the militia to defend Fredericksburg. By May 30 Cornwallis was at Hanover County Courthouse on the North Anna; Lafayette reached Mattaponi Church the next day. Although Weedon could do little to protect Fredericksburg, the Virginians had removed most of the military stores and Cornwallis saw no advantage in attacking. By then, Lafayette had crossed the Rapidan at Ely's Ford, and Cornwallis decided to abandon the pursuit of the Frenchman since the marquis's northerly route left the western sections of the state defenseless against the British.[40]

Virginia was extremely vulnerable in the West. The governor and Council had moved most of the state's stores to Point of Fork, assuming the location to be relatively secure from British attack because of the distance from a tidal stream. War Commissioner Davies saw the fallacy of this thinking when the British began rounding up every horse they could find. On May 12 he warned Steuben that "if these stores are lost, the whole wealth of the state in its present situation can never replace them" and urged the baron to move closer than the Convention Army's former barracks in Albemarle County, which Steuben had taken over for his recruits after the British burned the buildings at Chesterfield County Courthouse.[41] The legislature also had adjourned to Charlottesville—far from harm, the members thought—as soon as Cornwallis had entered the state.

Despite recriminations among the state's leaders afterward as to who should bear the most blame for the gravest threat to Virginia thus far in the war, none perceived the danger very quickly. Jefferson and his executive staff reached Charlottesville on May 21, and as late as the twenty-fifth the governor directed a shipment of clothing from Philadelphia to Point of Fork. The next day he was out on the road with Davies and the state agent, David Ross, trying to move stores away from the storage site as quickly as possible. It took until the twenty-eighth for the legislators to form a quorum, however, and Jefferson waited to confer with them before deciding to transport the supplies to old Albemarle County Courthouse.[42]

At the barracks near Charlottesville, Steuben learned on May 28 that Lafayette had evacuated Richmond and marched northward, leaving the baron to defend Point of Fork. Earlier in the month, before Greene knew that Cornwallis had marched north, the American commander had ordered Steuben south, and then the British intercepted Greene's attempt to countermand the order. Not until June 12 did Steuben find out that his orders had been changed and he was to remain in Virginia. Yet the delay hardly excuses the baron's lack of aggressiveness. Clearly uneasy about removing his troops from the state, Steuben had written on May 26 to remind Greene that Cornwallis had shifted his strategy since Greene had issued the initial order, and two days later, Steuben suggested to Lafayette that it might be "prudent to await another letter" from Greene before marching.[43] Yet Steuben also announced that he would not rescind Greene's order on his own authority and that, if Lafayette did not countermand Greene's directions, Steuben and the recruits would go to South Carolina.

Lafayette had become concerned about the possibility of Steuben leaving the state once the import of Cornwallis's movements became clear. But embarrassed because at twenty-three he commanded a Prussian veteran over twice his age, Lafayette did not interfere. The Frenchman may also have wondered if perhaps the German had not overstayed his welcome in Virginia. Lafayette did not grasp any more quickly than most others in Virginia that a major shift in strategy had occurred as a result of Cornwallis's march into the state. While Lafayette perceived the danger to the stores in the West on the twenty-sixth—about the same time as Jefferson did—the marquis did not begin to modify his assumption that South Carolina rather than Virginia was the central theater of war until after a message from Greene arrived on May 31.[44]

The time lag in the patriot leaders' thinking is understandable in view of the lack of detailed news from farther south. Although Greene had

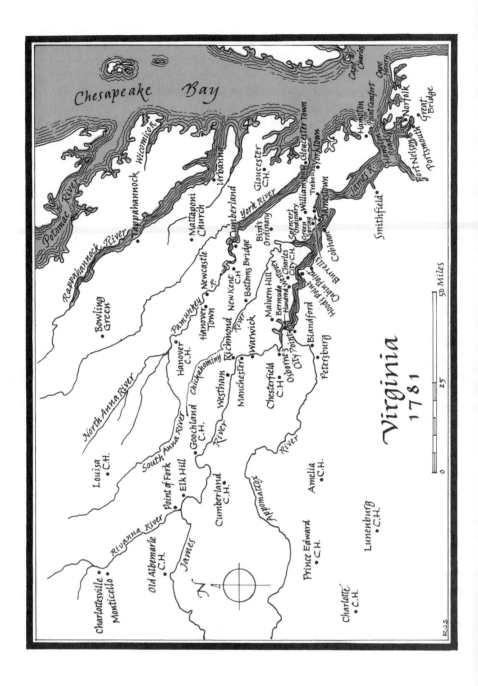

Chesapeake Bay

Potomac River

Rappahannock River

Wicomico R.

Tappahannock

Mattaponi Church

Bowling Green

North Anna River

Louisa C.H.

South Anna River

Point of Fork

Elk Hill

Pamunkey

Hanover C.H.

Newcastle Town

Goochland C.H.

Chickahominy River

Westham

Richmond

Manchester

Cumberland C.H.

Appomattox River

Rivanna River

Charlottesville
Monticello

Old Albemarle C.H.

James

Prince Edward C.H.

Charlotte C.H.

Amelia C.H.

Lunenburg C.H.

Chesterfield C.H.

Osborne's
City Point

Warwick

Bottoms Bridge

New Kent C.H.

Cumberland

Urbanna

York River

Gloucester C.H.

Byrd's Ordinary

Bermuda Hundred
Westover
Charles City C.H.

Malvern Hill

Blandford

Petersburg

Hoods Point

Cabin Point

Burrells

Spencer's Ordinary

Green Spring

Williamsburg

Trebell

Jamestown

Gloucester Town

Yorktown

Cobham

James R.

Smithfield

Hampton
Hampton Roads
Point Comfort

Fort Nelson
Portsmouth

Norfolk

Great Bridge

Cape Charles

Cape Henry

N

Virginia
1781

0   25   50 Miles

R~S

already forced the British back to the gates of Charleston, only rumors of the first of his gains, Lord Rawdon's abandonment of Camden on May 10, had reached Virginia so far. Not until he received Greene's letter on May 31 did the marquis learn officially of the British evacuation of Camden and the fall of Fort Motte, Orangeburg, and Fort Granby as well. That communication, which Greene had dispatched on the sixteenth, also informed the marquis of Steuben's new orders. Until then, Lafayette saw his mission as secondary to Greene's. "Nothing can attract my sight from the supplies and reinforcements destined to General Greene's army," the marquis informed Washington before Cornwallis arrived.[45] Lafayette promised Washington not to keep Wayne long before sending him to the South, and even in early June still expected the Pennsylvanian to move on to join Greene. Little wonder that Lafayette did not challenge the order to Steuben to do so, too.

By a few hours it was Jefferson who first acted on the assumption that Virginia had become the main theater of war. On May 28 he wrote to Washington that it would be necessary for the commander in chief to come to the state himself. The next day the House of Delegates adopted a resolution demanding that no more men or supplies be sent from Virginia. Two days later Lafayette received Greene's orders to the same effect.[46]

About the same time that Greene's letter arrived Cornwallis decided that he had chased Lafayette far enough and ordered Colonels Simcoe and Tarleton to lead a two-pronged raid into the West, one column against Point of Fork and the other to capture the governor and legislature at Charlottesville. Simcoe's force consisted of his loyalist legion, the Queen's Rangers, which at the moment could only muster three hundred men—"near fifty . . . absolutely barefooted," he complained—and two hundred of the 71st Highlanders.[47] Tarleton had 70 mounted infantrymen and his dragoons, numbering 180, whom he had recruited anew since Cowpens. The commanders drove their forces relentlessly, taking advantage of some of the finest horseflesh in Virginia which they had commandeered, and, to prevent word of their movements from preceding them, kept prisoner anyone they met along the road.

At Point of Fork Steuben received a report of the British advance on the night of June 3, but discounted it because it was vague and returned to the task of removing the stores. His recruits by that time had shrunk to 420, to which had been added 250 militia under General Robert Lawson. Early the next morning an officer of the Continental dragoons, Major Richard Call, rode into camp with positive intelligence of the enemy, from whom he had barely escaped, moving in two columns through Goochland and Louisa counties. Fearing that one column would cross the Rivanna River upstream to trap him within the fork—as, indeed, was Tarleton's secondary objective—Steuben immediately crossed the James to the south. By noon on June 4 Simcoe reached the northern bank. Knowing that his men had carelessly left canoes on the opposite shore, Steuben withdrew that night a considerable distance farther south—from seven to thirty miles, depending on the source and how strongly the author felt that the baron should have stayed to fight. The next morning Steuben wrote to Governor Abner Nash of North Carolina that "in the present situation of affairs here and by orders from General Greene to me, I find it expedient to march" southward and asked for provisions for his men.[48] Left behind, Simcoe later recorded, were twenty-five hundred stand of arms, "a large quantity" of gunpowder and shot, over sixty casks of saltpeter, sulfur, rum, and brandy, "a great variety of small stores, necessary for the equipment of cavalry and infantry," a thirteen-inch mortar, five brass howitzers, and four brass nine-pounders. Simcoe also burned one hundred fifty barrels of gunpowder and much tobacco in warehouses along the James River. Local inhabitants plundered other stores.[49]

It is more likely that Simcoe outfoxed Steuben than that the baron lacked courage as some detractors alleged. In memoirs written for publication and perhaps embellished for effect, Simcoe said that, thinking his forces outnumbered, he had tried to trick the Americans into believing that he had more men than he did. Simcoe described how he dispersed the "women and baggage" around the hillside (although why the British had either on a midnight ride, the colonel did not explain) as if he planned to establish a large encampment. In another published account Lighthorse Harry Lee reported that Simcoe had lighted campfires all over the hill during the night to perpetuate the illusion of a superior force. Simcoe did not entirely fool Steuben, who correctly estimated the enemy to be between four and five hundred men. But Steuben did assume Simcoe's troops to be a portion of the main British army, a conclusion Simcoe encouraged by marching the 71st Highlanders in their red coats to the river bank and keeping his legion, who wore green, out of sight. Simcoe also fired a single shot from a little three-pounder, the only cannon he had, to frighten the enemy into thinking he had artillery. Steuben acknowledged the effectiveness of the ruse when he described how fifty men guarding the landing had run away at the shot and could be induced to come back only "with much persuasion and threats." The episode showed the caliber of the troops he had to work with, the baron said.[50]

From the reports Lafayette received—admittedly garbled—the marquis thought that Steuben could have held out for twenty-four hours, by which time all the stores might have been safely removed. General Lawson, who was at Point of Fork, thought so, too. Steuben, as might have been expected, blamed the state officials. He had no confidence, the baron said, that whatever he did, the matériel could have been saved. When he had generously helped Colonel Davies earlier move supplies from Point of Fork, the "business was very illy executed by the State Officers."[51]

The baron clearly was in no mood to undertake unusual heroics for the sake of Virginia. He pointed out that no Continental stores had been lost at Point of Fork and obviously found satisfaction in reiterating how he had wisely scattered Continental supplies at Prince Edward, Charlotte, and Halifax county courthouses instead of concentrating them in one place. The baron rubbed the point in by noting that, before leaving Point of Fork, he had further dispersed as many state stores as possible "in such a manner that only part could fall into the Enemies Hands in any Rout they could take." Given these circumstances, the general declared, he "thought it absurd to be making a Bravado with a small number of bad Troops against such a force whilst the Marquis being near a 100 Miles off could make no diversion."[52]

Meanwhile, the second prong of the British attack under Banastre Tarleton struck Charlottesville. The British almost succeeded in capturing the entire Virginia government, which had gone leisurely about its business with no anticipation of the impending danger. Although Jefferson's term legally ended on Saturday, June 2, no one seemed concerned about such a nicety. The assembly nonchalantly postponed the election of a successor until Monday, and Jefferson spent part of the weekend on official correspondence he could not legally sign.[53]

Late Sunday night in Louisa County, Captain John Jouett, Jr., saw Tarleton's legionnaires ride by. Taking a shortcut, Jouett managed to reach Jefferson's home at Monticello just before daybreak and warn the governor of their approach. Jouett then rode on to Charlottesville to alert the legislators. Still, the alarm seems not to have been great although Jefferson's accounts of the affair, based on a diary that has since disappeared, were written later when he was trying to offset political charges that he had panicked. Archibald Cary and Benjamin Harrison, speakers of the Senate and the house, and some other legislators who were guests at Monticello, rode into town and then, "so incredulous were some of us," said Harrison, had difficulty persuading the assembly to adjourn before the British came.[54] Jefferson sent off his family but remained behind to gather some state papers. At a second warning that the enemy had arrived at the foot of the hill on which Monticello stands, Jefferson snatched up the remaining papers—he later apologized because he upset the order—and fled into the woods of Carter's Mountain through which the British could not follow. Catching up with his family, he took them to a friend's home in Amherst County. Tarleton's men arrived at Monticello minutes after the quarry had flown.

With Jefferson's flight Virginia's fortunes reached the lowest point of the war. For over a week the legitimacy of the executive remained in doubt, although not entirely as a result of Tarleton's raid. Theoretically, the president of the Council as lieutenant governor should have acted in Jefferson's stead, but Dudley Digges, who had held that position for the past year, had resigned when Jefferson moved the government to Charlottesville, and the Council never managed to form a quorum to elect another. Digges's resignation created the third vacancy on the board since the special session of the legislature. The next in seniority after Digges was David Jameson, who had been present at the last Council meeting in Richmond but did not come to Charlottesville until July. After Jameson came William Fleming, who had not been present at a meeting since April. Jefferson wrote to him and Andrew Lewis, who also had been absent since April, to be certain that they attended in Charlottesville in order to avoid just such a crisis. Only George Webb followed the governor from Richmond and only he appeared on May 24, the day appointed for the legislature to reassemble. Fleming finally arrived on the thirtieth, and, after the raid, found himself the sole representative of the executive in Staunton until Webb showed up on June 12.[55]

Fleming did not officially become acting governor. When acknowledging communications from him in his executive capacity, the delegates referred to him as "a Member of the Privy Council," and Fleming himself doubted his authority to call out the militia.[56] In the first days of exile in Staunton, the Speaker of the house also issued directives that normally would have come from the executive. Later the assembly felt it necessary to adopt a resolution indemnifying Fleming for stepping in as governor.

By June 7 enough of the lower house—in the act of adjournment in

Charlottesville, the members had wisely reduced the quorum to forty—reached Staunton to reconvene the chamber, but the Senate remained unformed for several days more. Benjamin Harrison implied in a letter to Joseph Jones that some officials had asked Jefferson to continue as governor although whether they did so before the flight or afterward is not clear. (Jefferson did return briefly to Monticello, but his home is over fifty miles from Staunton.) The former governor had apparently declined on the ground that without a Senate the selection would be illegal. The legislature, of course, could have passed an indemnity like the one for Fleming, but Jefferson had been waiting for almost a year to be rid of the office and, despite all pleas, clearly felt no obligation to circumvent the letter of the law to perpetuate what unquestionably would have continued to be a thankless chore. In the disruption of the moment he could have done little that another could not, except perhaps exercise greater moral influence. Jefferson obviously thought that he had done his share; let someone else take a turn.[57]

As if to belie the prevailing panic, the House of Delegates coolly set the election of Jefferson's successor for five days after it met, probably to let the Senate assemble, and spent the interval debating the nature of the office. Although no mention appears in the official journal, shortly after the delegates gathered, George Nicholas moved to appoint "a Dictator . . . in this Commonwealth who should have the power of disposing of the lives and fortunes of the Citizens thereof without being subject to account."[58] Nicholas proposed either Washington or Greene. Patrick Henry supported the motion and tried to avoid any delay over semantics by arguing that it mattered little what title the person bore so long as he had the powers required. Jefferson later said that the motion lost by a thin margin of six. The retiring governor long harbored deep resentment toward his predecessor for attempting to overthrow the constitution—or so Jefferson believed—to serve Henry's ambition. Whatever the intention, the demand for an all-powerful leader spread. While the legislators debated in Staunton, in the Tidewater at the other end of the state Richard Henry Lee simultaneously launched a salvo of letters to Philadelphia urging that Congress send Washington as a dictator to take over Virginia.

On June 12 the legislature finally elected Thomas Nelson to succeed Jefferson. On the same day, just as the latter's friends prepared to submit a resolution commending him, George Nicholas moved "that at the next session of Assembly an inquiry be made into the conduct of the Executive of this State for the last twelve months."[59] Archibald Cary said that, once the motion was before the house, Jefferson's friends seconded it to give the former governor a chance to exculpate himself. The legislature also called for an inquiry into Steuben's defeat at Point of Fork. The feeling against the baron had intensified because Steuben seemed to be lingering in North Carolina in defiance of Greene's direct orders to help defend Virginia. Indeed, some members of the Council, including the general's former aide, John Walker, wanted the baron hanged. Few knew at the time that Steuben did not learn of the change in Greene's orders until the day of Nelson's election. As for the new governor, at the moment he was with Lafayette and did not reach Staunton to be sworn in until the evening of the eighteenth. After a two-week hiatus, Virginia again had a leader.

Under the pressure of its worst defeat in the war, Virginia went the farthest yet in a whirlwind of legislation over the next five days toward acknowledging the need for a vastly stronger authority both in Philadelphia and at home. To the cession the previous January of the state's western lands to the Continent, the assembly added an agreement to let Congress levy a 5 percent duty on imports, the cornerstone of Robert Morris's new financial program. The effect, if all the states concurred, would be for the first time to give the central government a source of income independent of the states. In general, the delegates granted advocates of strong government most of what they had been seeking during the previous two sessions. Although still requiring Nelson to have the consent of the Council, the assembly authorized the governor to call out the entire militia whenever he wished and to send it wherever he chose; to impress equipment, slaves, horses, wagons, vessels, and "all other necessaries as may be wanted"; to imprison without recourse to the courts "any person and persons whatsoever"; to banish suspected tories under pain of death; to extend by decree any act relating to recruiting and impressment that should expire; and to create courts of oyer and terminer with all the powers of the General Court in criminal matters whenever he deemed it wise.[60] The legislature also imposed martial law within twenty miles of any American or British army; ended the requirement that militiamen be court-martialed only by militia officers; ordered delinquents from militia service to serve six months as regulars in the Continental service; and, since militiamen constantly absconded with the arms issued them, decreed death for any who did so. In addition, the assembly granted the commissioner of war powers over other agencies of government that for practical purposes rendered him a prime minister for war. To obtain soldiers the legislators raised the bounty to ten thousand dollars for a two-year enlistment and, recognizing the collapse of Congress's attempt to stabilize the currency, suspended the exchange of old Continental money for the new issue of 1780. Instead, the representatives authorized a new printing of twenty million dollars in state paper. The efforts at financial reform of the previous year had come to naught.[61]

The Virginians' fortunes had totally collapsed. Simcoe and Tarleton's raid left the government in shambles. The state's supply system had fallen into disarray. Militarily, Cornwallis appeared to be in complete control. The legislature took the first steps toward recovery, but at a cost that many considered to entail abandonment of the Revolution's ideals. The assembly ceded the power of taxation to a legislature in Philadelphia that critics considered almost as remote from the people as the one in London, and, while heeding Patrick Henry's advice not to use the term, the delegates created a "dictator" more powerful than the one they had fashioned in 1776.

CHAPTER 15

Victory

OVING up in support of Simcoe and Tarleton, Cornwallis
and the main British army reached Elk Hill near Point of
Fork on June 7 and remained in camp there for the next
six days. Once his pursuer turned away, Lafayette headed southward
from the Rapidan River toward the South Anna, in the vicinity of
which General Wayne with nearly eight hundred Pennsylvanians finally joined him on June 10. Wayne's arrival persuaded Cornwallis
not to send Tarleton after Steuben or to raid the remaining American
stores at old Albemarle County Courthouse. Besides, it was time to
find out what Clinton had decided.[1]

Cornwallis marched eastward at a leisurely pace while Lafayette,
now in command of almost four thousand troops, pressed closer to
the British than he had dared before. The marquis wrote to Washington of "the retreat of the ennemy," and Virginians generally interpreted the British movement in that light.[2] Cornwallis, however, ignored Lafayette's effort to lure him into battle because it did not
conform to his plan. The British commander had intended no more
than a month in "desultory" action and was timing his return to the
Tidewater to coincide with the anticipated arrival of Clinton's reply to
Cornwallis's latest proposal on strategy.

Clinton's initial reaction when he learned that his subordinate had
gone to Virginia was amazement: "My wonder at this move of Lord

Cornwallis will never cease."[3] The commander in chief's instructions when he left Cornwallis in charge of the southern theater after the fall of Charleston had presumed that Cornwallis would conquer the area in steps, progressively consolidating each section, and that British forces in the South would operate mainly from bases along the coast to ensure contact with the navy. The army's trump card had always been the greater mobility it enjoyed because of the British navy's normal superiority at sea. In Clinton's mind the earlier assaults on the Chesapeake region, which he approved of, had been to intercept the movement of supplies to Greene and relieve the pressure on Cornwallis, not to establish a major front. Clinton imagined an extensive campaign in the Chesapeake only as a prelude to an attack on the mid-Atlantic states, which he intended to invade once he obtained sufficient reinforcements. To Clinton the key to victory was New York and its environs, not the South.

Clinton immediately saw that if Franco-American forces gained temporary naval superiority in the Chesapeake Bay, a British army in Virginia could easily be lost. He wrote to Cornwallis that "had it been possible for Your Lordship . . . to have intimated the probability of your intention to form a junction with General Phillips, I should certainly have endeavored to have stopped you." The commander in chief considered his subordinate's strategy "dangerous to our interests in the southern colonies." But faced with a fait accompli, Clinton left the question of what to do next "totally to Your Lordship to decide upon, until you either hear from me or we meet."[4]

Plaguing British strategy at this critical moment was the ill will between Clinton and the naval commander Arbuthnot, and between Clinton and Cornwallis. The previous fall Clinton had notified the cabinet that he could not continue unless the admiral was replaced. As conservative and slow-moving as Clinton was, he found the admiral, who was nearing seventy, the epitome of negativeness and lethargy. The two hardly communicated. Indeed, about this time Arbuthnot went on a six-day cruise without telling Clinton, leaving New York harbor wide open to attack by the French fleet based in Newport, Rhode Island.

An inability to get along with fellow commanders had characterized Clinton's career, however, and the ministry was becoming tired of his complaining. Moreover, Lord George Germain agreed with Cornwallis that victory lay in the Chesapeake. As a result, the ministry hinted that they would not be unhappy if Clinton resigned to make room for Cornwallis. Once the earl became aware that he had the favor of the cabinet, his differences of opinion with Clinton turned into open hostility. He had not consulted the commander in chief on the decision to chase Greene deep into North Carolina and, after a report describing the loss at Cowpens in January 1781, wrote to his superior only once again before he reached Wilmington on April 10. Clinton received that communiqué on the twenty-second and did not get the next, which was dated April 23 and announced the move to Virginia on the very eve of the march, until four weeks later. For almost five months Clinton depended more on accounts in rebel newspapers than his subordinate's reports to know what was happening in the South.[5]

The ministry, too, had its problems, for practically all of Europe joined the fray. The entrance of France into the war in 1778 had been followed by that of Spain in 1779, although not as a formal ally of the United States. The next year Russia, Denmark, and Sweden formed a League of Armed Neutrality to prevent Great Britain from interfering with their trade with France. The Dutch were about to join the league, but the British declared war on them because Dutch intercourse with the French and Americans had become so flagrant.

So many enemies gravely taxed Britain's vaunted naval superiority. Besides America and the West Indies, fronts opened against the Dutch in the North Sea and South Africa and against the Spanish at Gibraltar and Minorca, while a Franco-Spanish Combined Fleet of forty-nine ships of the line cruised off the English Channel. When the French unexpectedly went on the offensive in the Carnatic in India, the first lord of the Admiralty, the Earl of Sandwich, bluntly declared that that theater had priority. The best they could do, the ministry told Clinton, would be to send Rear Admiral Robert Digby with three additional ships of the line. But Digby had to wait for the return of the Channel fleet which had gone to relieve Gibraltar before three ships became available, and then they had to reprovision. Digby finally sailed in mid-July. Earlier in the spring, Admiral de Grasse had gathered an armada at Brest. The size of the French fleet precluded secrecy. But with so many potential targets the British could not be certain where the French might go, and because the British hesitated to reduce the home fleet by detaching vessels for patrol, they could not maintain an adequate watch on de Grasse's movements. As a result, the French fleet slipped out of port unobserved and had almost reached the West Indies before the British knew.

Hardly had Clinton dispatched his first response to Cornwallis's request for a change in orders, when he learned from an intercepted letter that Washington and Rochambeau had met in Wethersfield, Connecticut, on May 22 and 23. The allies, Clinton read, planned to unite Rochambeau's forces with Washington's and move on New York to blunt the British offensive in the South by forcing Clinton to recall troops for his own defense. Rochambeau told Washington at the conference of de Grasse's departure from France with twenty ships of the line and the French admiral's intention to assist operations on the North American mainland after stopping briefly in the West Indies. Clinton by then already knew about de Grasse's departure and could surmise the rest, but neither side knew precisely where along the Atlantic coast the French fleet would appear.[6]

Clinton immediately sent Cornwallis revised instructions, calling three thousand men back to New York. By assuming that Cornwallis had sustained virtually no losses during the campaign in the South, Clinton overestimated the number at his subordinate's command, and by discounting the Virginia militia underestimated Lafayette's strength by half. The commander in chief concluded that Cornwallis had more than enough men to check the marquis. At the same time Clinton calculated that Washington and Rochambeau together had twenty thousand troops (they actually had about ten thousand) against whom he could muster just over half the number he assumed they had. Clinton directed Cornwallis to find an easily defensible site (he suggested Williamsburg and Yorktown) from which raiding parties could be dispatched to keep Virginians off balance. The earl could then relinquish almost half his army to help protect New York City.

Cornwallis reached Richmond on June 16. Lafayette followed as far as Allen's Creek, about twenty miles northwest of the state capital, where Baron von Steuben finally joined the main American army the next day. Remaining less than three days in Richmond, Cornwallis crossed the Chickahominy River at Bottom's Bridge and headed toward Williamsburg at a leisurely pace.

Their confidence bolstered by Steuben's reinforcements, Lafayette and Wayne pressed closer to the British in the hope of ambushing the rear guard under Simcoe. Cornwallis reached Williamsburg on June 25. The next day advance detachments of American dragoons and mounted infantry under Colonel Richard Butler and Major William McPherson caught up with Simcoe at Spencer's Ordinary about five miles from the city. In spirited fighting the Americans forced the outnumbered British back until Cornwallis moved up reinforcements. The Americans gained an important psychological victory, although Lafayette exaggerated the outcome. He reported to Washington that the British suffered over one hundred fifty casualties, but British records reveal that the royal forces captured at least thirty-one Americans and lost ten British killed and thirty-three wounded.

On June 25 Cornwallis received Clinton's second set of orders recalling half of the British army in Virginia to New York. (Clinton's first set grudgingly conceding Cornwallis autonomy in the Chesapeake had not yet arrived.) The earl had no choice except to obey, but his resentment showed in his acknowledgment a few days later. Cornwallis announced that with the troops remaining he could not establish a base at Williamsburg and Yorktown as Clinton suggested because the British would have to occupy Gloucester Point across the York River to protect ships moored at Yorktown. The alternative as Cornwallis saw it was to move to Portsmouth, although the earl admitted that he probably could not hold that position any more easily. Clinton's decision not to conquer Virginia, Cornwallis declared, meant the end of the entire southern campaign because the British failure to suppress Greene earlier had demonstrated the hopelessness of trying to subdue the South while Virginia served as a depot for men and matériel. Cornwallis derived some satisfaction from the fact that by assuming an American threat to New York the new instructions also ruled out the attack on the mid-Atlantic states that Clinton wanted. In fact, the earl concluded, the situation was so serious all along the East Coast that instead of trying "to hold a sickly, defensive post in this bay, which will always be exposed to a sudden French attack," it would be wiser for the British to withdraw completely from the Chesapeake and return to Charleston to defend that city against the assault that Cornwallis now expected Greene to mount.[7]

Cornwallis also took solace from a small defeat that he inflicted on Lafayette before abandoning the lower peninsula to the Americans. Counting on the marquis's overconfidence because the British appeared to be retreating, Cornwallis prepared an ambush. On July 4 he moved his army to Jamestown while Lafayette celebrated American independence with a review parade and a dinner for his officers at Tyree's plantation, twenty miles away. The next day Cornwallis began to transport his heavy equipment across the James River, but instead of leaving behind only a rear guard, he kept most of his troops on the northern bank. On July 6 Lafayette ordered General Wayne to pursue with about five hundred men, and at Green Spring the impetuous Pennsylvanian attacked across unfavorable terrain directly in front of the main British army, which was concealed in a woods. The rout would have been worse had dusk not prevented the British from sending out cavalry to cut down survivors. Instead, their frustrations vented, the British continued their withdrawal across the river, allowing the marquis to persuade himself that he had again compelled them to retreat. Lafayette told General Greene and Governor Nelson that the enemy suffered twice as many casualties as he had, whereas the reverse was true.

On July 8 Cornwallis was at Cobham in Surry County, where he received another change in orders from Clinton. The troops recalled to New York were still to go, but they were to assist in an attack on Philadelphia en route. Rochambeau had joined forces with Washington outside New York City by the end of June, and Clinton wanted to mount a diversion. He could attack the French fleet at Newport, which Rochambeau's departure had left without the protection of land batteries, or he could strike at the Quaker City, Clinton's favorite target. Unfortunately for the British, in either case Clinton still had to rely on Arbuthnot, for whom no replacement had as yet appeared. Clinton had written to Admiral Sir George Rodney to come from the West Indies, but Rodney was ill and by the time Clinton's letter arrived had gone home to nurse his health. Rear Admiral Thomas Graves finally did assume command of the fleet in New York, but by then circumstances forced a change in plans once more.

Cornwallis had the troops scheduled to go to New York ready to embark from Portsmouth when a fourth set of instructions from Clinton arrived on July 20 countermanding their recall. Clinton had been horror-stricken when he learned that Cornwallis was abandoning the lower peninsula for Portsmouth, which both the earl and Phillips had previously represented as indefensible with the troops on hand. To remedy the situation Clinton ordered Cornwallis to fortify Old Point Comfort at Hampton and establish an outpost at Yorktown to check an attack from that direction. Intimating that he thought Cornwallis exaggerated British needs in Virginia, the commander in chief nonetheless told the earl to keep as many men as Cornwallis felt would be necessary. Cornwallis, in turn, was furious that Clinton found the British could spare a whole army from the defense of New York to maintain a garrison in Virginia but not to launch an offensive. As for the implication that Cornwallis had violated orders by moving to

Portsmouth, it should be noted that stylistically Clinton's orders were seldom incontrovertible. In this instance, he had placed parentheses around his recommendation that Williamsburg and Yorktown be defended as if the suggestion were a casual observation. On the other hand, the resentfulness with which Cornwallis acknowledged Clinton's instructions may well have left the earl prepared to find any idea of his commander unworkable no matter what it was.[8]

The British engineers soon discovered that the soil at Old Point Comfort would not sustain the heavy fortifications necessary to protect the fleet and that the anchorage would not accommodate deep-draft vessels. Cornwallis decided to abandon Portsmouth and return to Yorktown as Clinton had originally proposed. This time, of course, the British would have enough troops to occupy Gloucester Point as well. Because the French could bottle up Cornwallis's ships in the York River and his troops would have no convenient land routes for escape, the earl made it clear that he chose the location only because Clinton insisted upon having a deepwater base in the Chesapeake. Given that injunction, Cornwallis declared, Yorktown was the only spot that would do. The British landed at Gloucester Point on the evening of August 1 and in the heat of summer began to prepare their defenses at Yorktown the next morning.[9]

Cornwallis's movements puzzled Lafayette. When the British crossed the James River, the marquis divided his forces even though they had shrunk considerably because many militia and volunteer "men of fortune," as Lafayette called them, had gone home. "You might as well stop the flood tide as to stop militia whose times are out," he observed.[10] Bivouacking the main body of twenty-two hundred at Malvern Hill about halfway between Williamsburg and Richmond, he dispatched Wayne's Pennsylvanians, now reduced through desertions and sickness to five hundred, to follow Cornwallis in case the British should attempt another raid. To augment Wayne's force Lafayette added an equal number of riflemen under General Daniel Morgan and three hundred new Virginia recruits. As Cornwallis moved toward Portsmouth, the earl sent Tarleton after rebel supplies in Amelia County, but the stores had been moved and no significant fighting occurred. The Americans captured one of Tarleton's troopers and from him learned of the orders recalling a large part of the British force to New York. Lafayette also succeeded in placing among Cornwallis's servants a black spy who adopted the name James Lafayette. Although this agent was not privy to all British planning, he kept Lafayette informed of much that went on within Cornwallis's headquarters throughout the summer.

On the strength of the new information Lafayette alerted the troops south of the James River to be ready to attack Portsmouth. But generally the intelligence confirmed the marquis's supposition that the principal fighting would soon shift elsewhere. He had already laid plans for Wayne and the Pennsylvanians to reinforce Greene and, assuring Washington that militarily Virginia was "in a state of languor," requested a transfer to a theater that offered a greater chance for military glory. Lafayette even suggested that Baron von Steuben, whom the marquis had recently severely criticized, could take over in Virginia; "a prudent officer would do our business here, and the Baron is prudent to the utmost." The one baffling aspect of the situation, Lafayette told his commander in chief, was that, although the British had loaded their transports and the wind was right, they did not sail.[11]

When the British finally did move, to Lafayette's wonder they turned up the Chesapeake Bay instead of out to sea. He immediately assumed that they were heading for Baltimore and, ordering Wayne to follow, set out for that city. Hardly had Lafayette reached Richmond before he learned that the enemy had landed at Yorktown. Marching back, Lafayette went into camp first at Newcastle on the Pamunkey River and then at New Kent County Courthouse, from which he could move his troops on either side of the York River. The marquis felt compelled to apologize to Washington for the resulting confusion in his reports. "You must not wonder, my dear General, that there has been a fluctuation in my intelligences. I am positive the British Councils have also been fluctuating."[12]

About the time that Cornwallis moved to Yorktown, Lafayette received a broad hint from Washington that led him to reconsider his desire for reassignment. "I shall shortly have occasion to communicate matters of very great importance to you," the commander wrote, "so much so, that I shall send a confidential Officer on purpose to you. You will in the mean time endeavour to draw together as respectable a Body of Continental troops as you possibly can and take every measure to augment your Cavalry."[13] Ever since the American commander in chief had learned that de Grasse would sail to the North American mainland later in the summer, Washington had been thinking of using the French fleet primarily against New York. But from the beginning the Chesapeake remained a possible alternative. The choice, Washington maintained, was de Grasse's, whichever destination would be more suitable for him.

As time went on, the chances of success against New York looked less promising, especially if Cornwallis reinforced Clinton, as Washington continued to expect on the basis of the latest intelligence from Lafayette. Furthermore, Rochambeau had never been as enthusiastic about besieging New York as Washington. When the French general reported the results of the Wethersfield conference to de Grasse in May, he practically told the admiral to go to the Chesapeake: "There are two places for an offensive against the enemy: the Chesapeake and New York. In view of the southwest winds and the distressed state of Virginia, you will probably prefer Chesapeake Bay, and it is there that we think you can render the greatest service, besides which it will only take you two days to come from there to New York."[14] The question was finally settled on August 14 when Washington learned that de Grasse had fixed on the Chesapeake. At practically the same moment Washington also heard from Lafayette of Cornwallis's shift to Yorktown. Five days later, on August 19, the allied armies before New York decamped and began the march to Virginia.

The British in turn completely misread the French and American maneuvers. "I cannot well ascertain Mr. Washington's real intentions by this move of his army," Sir Henry Clinton confessed.[15] When the British commander learned on August 2 that Cornwallis had gone to Yorktown, he immediately penned a long epistle to the earl recounting the succession of orders he had issued over the spring to prove that the decision was entirely Cornwallis's. The latter replied at almost equal length that it was not. As yet neither foresaw any pressing danger. None of the British leaders dreamed that de Grasse would denude the French West Indies of all naval defense in order to sail his entire fleet to the North American coast. When the British admiral in the Caribbean, Sir George Rodney, made arrangements to return home to England for his health, he assumed that de Grasse would sail north with only a portion of his force and left the British second in command, Rear Admiral Samuel Hood, only fourteen ships of the line, exactly half de Grasse's strength, with which to follow the French. Rodney also apparently neglected to inform Hood or Admiral Graves, who was in charge of British naval forces in New York, of intelligence that indicated the French would go to the Chesapeake; or if he did, Hood and Graves did not act upon it by attempting to block access to the bay.

Neither Graves nor Clinton was prepared mentally or militarily for de Grasse's approach. Although Graves knew that the enemy might come from the West Indies, he had gone on a month-long cruise off Boston as if the major threat of French reinforcements lay in the north and did not return until mid-August. Only then did he belatedly receive intelligence of de Grasse's sailing, although not of the French fleet's numbers. Just a few days prior to Graves's return, the reinforcements for which Clinton had been waiting before mounting an attack on Newport, Rhode Island, arrived, and plans went into motion again for an assault that might have kept the French squadron stationed there under the Comte de Barras from joining de Grasse. But preparations moved so slowly that the French squadron slipped away before the British were ready.[16]

Although Clinton received an increasing number of intelligence reports to the contrary, he continued to assume that de Grasse would bring only a few capital ships which Hood's fleet would offset. The departure of Rochambeau and Washington from New York puzzled him. Assuming that they did not have the necessary naval support to go to Virginia, he guessed that the combined armies would head for Morristown, New Jersey, from which they could more easily send detachments to reinforce Lafayette than from New York. Hood, who reconnoitered the Chesapeake Bay on August 25 and found no enemy, reached New York on August 28. As confident as Clinton that de Grasse had only a small squadron, Hood prevailed upon Graves to sail on the thirty-first to meet the French.

De Grasse's fleet raised the Virginia Capes on August 30 and, to Cornwallis's dismay, soon anchored in Hampton Roads. The French lost little time moving their transports up to Jamestown, where the Marquis de Saint Simon began to disembark the three thousand soldiers under his command on September 2. Shortly news of the approach of the combined British fleet caused de Grasse to take his ships to sea again, and for the first time the British admirals realized what had happened. Cornwallis's report reached Clinton at just about the same moment.

On September 5 the French and British fleets fought an inconclusive action outside the Virginia Capes, then for a week maneuvered against one another with no result. Meanwhile, de Barras entered the Chesapeake Bay from Newport, raising the total number of French ships of

the line to thirty-six, nearly double the nineteen the British had. Faced
with these odds, Graves and Hood withdrew to New York on September 13.

Virginians hardly knew what was happening before the new campaign broke upon them. Lafayette learned of de Grasse's decision only nine days before the French appeared in the Chesapeake Bay. The state was not ready. The government had remained badly disorganized in the wake of the raids in June. Once the British began falling back to the east, the government had moved briefly to Charlottesville and, on July 3, returned to Richmond. Then, for almost two weeks, the new governor had disappeared, presumably having fallen ill along the way. Commissioner of War William Davies complained that "nobody here knows where the Governor is, nor have we heard the least tittle from him since he left Charlottesville."[17] Not until July 16 did Nelson finally show up at the capital.

Other departments, particularly the treasury with the press for printing more money, did not return to Richmond until well into August. As Lafayette tried to carry out Washington's instructions to gather men and supplies, he encountered more than the usual difficulties. County lieutenants on their own authority, he said, reduced the service obligations of the militia "against the law established by their Representatives," and county commissioners, "as they think no one will ever punish them," were "very remiss in their duty" and "indifferent to the suffering of the army." Threats of "the severest punishments" promised the only solution.[18]

Within the executive, John Walker, who had been elected to the Council in June, declined to serve (he apparently transferred to Lafayette's staff), and William Fleming did not return to Richmond, putting the quorum in constant jeopardy. Nelson and the remaining councillors worked hard through mid-August to resuscitate the administration. Then once again Nelson became ill on the way from Richmond to Lafayette's camp and dropped from sight a second time. For over a week the Council thought that he was with the army, and Lafayette that he was in Richmond. Communications went astray, and the disposition of troops that Lafayette ordered as the last British forces withdrew from Portsmouth never occurred. About the same time, another councillor, Samuel Hardy, also took ill, and for five days the Council had no quorum and did not meet until, with the French offshore, Lieutenant Governor David Jameson decided to hold sessions anyway.[19]

Feuds also broke out between state and Continental officers. When Major Richard Claiborne, Continental deputy quartermaster general for Virginia, fell ill in July, he appointed Captain Berryman Green as his substitute. Green proved a stickler for procedure and refused to accept orders from Governor Nelson unless they were relayed through Lafayette. Nelson snapped that "by Punctilios the Army is likely to go without Provisions," but complied rather than waste time arguing. Green's superior, Major Claiborne, bristled, too, when he requested another six million pounds in credit and the Council asked to see his books before they advanced it. "I beg Leave to inform them," he retorted to Nelson, "that . . . I can render my accounts to one person, that is the Quarter Master General." When Nelson rebuked him for being testy, Claiborne conceded half-apologetically that he might have "written in a more easy stile," but did not abandon his position.[20]

Deeper animosity flared between General Wayne and the governor. Impatient with the state suppliers, Wayne took care of his own men by seizing a store of shoes and some cloth that Davies had deposited in Chesterfield County. The commissioner of war protested, and Nelson wrote angrily to Lafayette that such action "is not to be tolerated where civil Government is established." He also added mysteriously that he had heard of "other Excesses."[21] The fiery Pennsylvanian retorted that his honor had been besmirched and threatened to lead his men from the state if they could not have the shoes they needed to fight. Lafayette attempted to mediate by having Wayne issue some shoes to the most needy and return the rest. As for Davies, the marquis reminded him that the Pennsylvanians had come to help Virginia and that their long march had "left the poor fellows almost naked." Other than the shoes in contention, the Frenchman observed, the supplies Virginia had provided the Pennsylvanians were "inconsiderable."[22] Lafayette offered to replace the shoes from his own stores if the Virginians insisted, but let them know that Washington had already designated those supplies for other purposes.

To the commander in chief himself Lafayette confided how serious he felt the confrontation to be. It was best to move Wayne's men out of Virginia, he thought. "The Pennsylvanians and Virginians have never agreed but at the present time, it is worse then ever," Lafayette explained. "Every day the troops remain here adds to the danger." Without Washington's knowledge, the marquis had invoked the general's authority to send the Pennsylvanians to join General Greene. Remarking in an intriguing observation that "the mode of making war and procuring

supplies in Carolina is better adapted" to the Pennsylvanians' ways "than
the management we must have with the Virginians," Lafayette asked his
commander to back him up. Washington, however, had already issued
orders for Wayne to remain in Virginia for the buildup against Cornwallis and responded that, since the issue was "of a very disagreeable
nature and must be handled delicately," he would settle it himself.[23]

As the extent of the administrative breakdown became apparent, the
governor and a few aides, assisted by the vast powers the assembly
granted in June, reacted with unusual vigor and relative efficiency. Nelson returned to Richmond on September 2 and proclaimed an embargo
on the exportation of provisions. The governor, the new commissary
general John Pierce, and the members of the Council present in Richmond commenced a letter writing campaign to agents around the state
in an effort to revitalize the supply system that had atrophied under
Brown. Among others, David Ross left off from his duties as commercial
agent to search for beef and flour around Petersburg, William Armistead came back to the Public Store, Benjamin Day, Ross's predecessor
as state agent, offered his assistance, and the governor called upon old
standbys like Richard Morris to return. With surprising alacrity,
the remnants of the logistical bureaucracy mobilized to meet the
emergency.[24]

The fact that the water level in Tidewater streams at that time of year
dropped too low to operate grist mills presented a particularly pressing
problem. Flour had to be brought from the interior. Utilizing the governor's new powers, Nelson authorized impressment of "any grain, in
or out of the straw, Mills, waggons, carts, Horses or negroes" that might
be necessary.[25] If mills upstream from those seized by the government
interfered with the flow of water, they had to shut down, and if commissaries met resistance, they could call out the militia. To encourage
cooperation the Council offered farmers a hedge against inflation by
permitting the redemption of commissary certificates at the rate of depreciation on the date of redemption rather than of issue. The Council
also offered exemptions from militia duty for any who contributed supplies. "In short," the councillors reported to Nelson, "every thing we
could think of, that would give a spring to this momentous concern we
have endeavour'd to set in motion."[26]

State agents had more success the farther from the coast they foraged,
for when Virginia authorities could not supply them, the French began
to buy their own provisions in the Tidewater with gold. Loyalist sympathizers in some areas seized the chance to be disruptive by urging

farmers not to thresh their grain unless they could sell to the French. Nelson reacted by rounding up suspected loyalists, including his old friends the Wormeleys, father and son, and his brother-in-law, Phillip Grymes. But the governor could not end the trouble so easily, for months of depreciation and inflation made the promise of payment in specie too alluring. Nelson's own aide, St. George Tucker, used his position to alert his wife to the coming of de Grasse's agents so that she could withhold provisions from state commissaries until the French arrived. Eventually Nelson overcame the difficulty by inducing the French to buy locally only through a single representative of the state, a post the governor assigned to Richard Morris.[27]

By mid-September Pierce could report to the Council that "things are now in such a train as to keep the Army properly supplied with both meat and Bread," although there would never be a surfeit. The commissioner of war told the governor that "from every information I can obtain, it appears that the people are using their endeavors to have their grain manufactured for the army, tho' there does not appear the same willingness to furnish their waggons and teams."[28] Nelson's whirlwind activity had put the supply system back into operation again.

Nelson's rejuvenation of executive authority imposed a heavy cost on the constitution. The governor remained with the Council in Richmond only four days before leaving for Lafayette's camp as commander in chief of the state forces. Never again did Nelson attend the board as chief executive. Although both the lieutenant governor and the commissioner of war begged the governor to return since only a "shadow of a Executive" was left, Nelson refused on the ground that at Richmond he could not care for the army's needs as quickly as at camp. However inconvenient his absence, the militia commander said, it could not be helped, for if the current operations failed, "we shall have but the Shadow of a Government, if even that; whereas if they succeed, the Hands of Government will be stronger and will be more respectable than ever."[29]

Nelson's departure left the Council with no hope of obtaining a quorum since both Andrew Lewis and Samuel Hardy could not attend because of their health. But the Council had worked without a quorum before. The physical distance between the two parts of the executive posed the greater difficulty on this occasion inasmuch as the governor could not seek the board's advice as the constitution enjoined and move with the speed he desired. For its part, the Council acquiesced in the situation by qualifying its orders with the proviso "unless the Governor shall have given other instructions on this head."[30] Nelson explained his actions with an argument from expediency at which strict constitutionalists must have blanched: "I think the trust my country has repos'd in me demands that I should stretch my powers to their utmost extent, regardless of the censures of the inconsiderate or any other evil that may result to myself from such a step."[31] The governor then ordered impressments to begin.

In the capital, the remaining members of the Council conducted business as best they could. On one occasion when Jacquelin Ambler alone was present, he proclaimed the governor's summons for a legislative session without waiting for his colleagues, and at other times he appointed sheriffs for Prince Edward and Augusta counties on his own authority. As usual, the Council was more punctilious about a quorum in matters with judicial overtones. But in the case of the Reverend John Lyon of the Eastern Shore, who had been convicted of tory activities, the requisite number of votes to send him to an inland county had to be obtained by mail since both Lieutenant Governor Jameson and Nelson had gone with the army to Yorktown. Not until the fighting ended in Virginia and the legislature elected a new governor did the executive again function in a regular manner. The assembly impeached Nelson for his forceful exercise of gubernatorial authority at the next sitting of the legislature, the same session at which the delegates tried Jefferson for administering the office in exactly the opposite way.[32]

Late on the afternoon of Friday, September 14, Washington, Rochambeau, and another French general, François-Jean, Chevalier de Chastellux, rode into Williamsburg. They had left the allied army at Baltimore and Head of Elk in the hope that shipping could be found to transport the troops and save a tedious journey overland. En route Washington and his party rested for two days at Mount Vernon, which the American commander had not seen for over six years. As the three generals entered the old colonial capital, Lafayette, although ill with a fever, rushed out to greet the commander in chief and embraced him, according to St. George Tucker, "with an ardour not easily described." French and American troops hastily lined up for a salute. That evening the officers attended a grand dinner, highlighted by a French band playing a popular tune from André Gentry's contemporary opera *Lucille*. The party broke up around ten o'clock, one observer recorded, "after mutual congratulations and the greatest expression of joy."[33] But undoubtedly Washington found the greatest pleasure that night in the news that de

Grasse had chased the British fleet away and that de Barras had arrived with Rochambeau's siege guns and heavy equipment from Rhode Island.

Washington immediately requested a council of war with de Grasse. The American leader and Rochambeau met the admiral on board the massive French flagship, the 110-gun *Ville de Paris*, on September 18. The French naval commander agreed to remain in Virginia waters through the end of October, two weeks longer than he had originally intended, and offered to supply up to two thousand men in addition to those already ashore. The conference lasted only a few hours, but heavy winds prevented Washington's party from returning to Williamsburg for another four days. Then, they were hardly back when they heard a rumor that Admiral Digby had finally reached New York with ten ships of the line (he actually had three). Because ten would have made the naval strength of the British and French fleets more nearly equal, de Grasse announced that he would have to put to sea in order to be in a better position for battle. In considerable alarm, Washington rushed Lafayette and one of Rochambeau's subordinates, Baron Ludwig von Closen, out to the fleet to dissuade the French from such a move. However, by the time the envoys climbed aboard the *Ville de Paris*, de Grasse and his officers had changed their minds and decided to stay.

The French navy supplied ships to bring Washington's and Rochambeau's troops from Maryland. Units soon began arriving at College Landing, and others came to Jamestown and to Burwell's and Tredell's landings on the James River. Contrary winds continued to impede movement up the river and kept some soldiers on board ship for fourteen days. By September 26, however, General Lincoln and Baron de Vioménil, who had been left in charge of the movement, reached Williamsburg with the last contingents. Two days later the army set out on the last leg of its journey to Yorktown.[34]

Although the net slowly tightened, it took a while before Cornwallis realized the seriousness of his position, and he did not act as aggressively to save himself as might have been expected. British intelligence did not correctly assess the strength of the combined Franco-American forces until several days after de Grasse appeared in the bay. Then, the news on September 5 that the French had sailed out to sea again preserved the hope that a relief expedition was on the way. Cornwallis let pass the opportunity of either attacking Saint Simon's forces as they disembarked or Lafayette's before Saint Simon's joined up with them. The British were also dilatory in fortifying Yorktown though even their mistaken estimate of the forces they confronted should have been reason enough to prepare battlements. The explanation is simply that Cornwallis had no inkling of Washington's and Rochambeau's approach until September 8. Indeed, until Clinton wrote the letter that Cornwallis received on that day, the commander in chief had been advising his lieutenant that the allied forces would not march south.[35]

Once Washington's and Rochambeau's destination became known, the British realized that, if they were to escape by land, they had to do so before the Franco-American army arrived. Tarleton in particular argued that to do nothing spelled defeat. Cornwallis sent the cavalry leader to reconnoiter the French and American position at Williamsburg and serendipitously obtained an accurate return of the enemy's forces from a loyalist. The British developed a plan to attack Williamsburg under cover of darkness, using the many ravines around the city to avoid the defenders' artillery fire. Then another letter from Clinton holding out the possibility of reinforcements, especially if Admiral Digby came as expected, arrived on September 14 and restored the mood of inactivity. Although Cornwallis learned of Graves's and Hood's defeat three days later, the chance that Digby and Clinton might appear continued to be a strong inducement for simply waiting while the allies completed their deployment before Yorktown.

Two other considerations weighed in Cornwallis's final decision not to move. One was the question whether the cost of an attempt to escape would be too great. He would have to abandon the ships in the York River and all his equipment as well as the sick and wounded and the loyalists and escaped slaves who had joined him. Even if he made the sacrifice, Cornwallis had no certainty that the remaining elements of his force would survive since the enemy, many of whom were as well trained as the British, outnumbered them eight to five. The disgrace of having virtually to destroy his army in order to save it would end his military career.

The other consideration was less frightening. If Cornwallis could not be rescued and had to surrender, the blame would fall on Clinton. Just as the commander in chief had been trying to avoid criticism for the southern campaign, Cornwallis had prepared his brief to show that Clinton had caused the debacle at Yorktown. Cornwallis wrote cagily to New York explaining why, despite the British setback off the Virginia Capes and the weakness of his fortifications, he had decided to risk a siege. "If I had no hopes of relief, I would rather risk an action than defend my half-finished works. But, as you say, Admiral Digby is hourly expected and promise every exertion to assist me, I do not think myself justifiable in putting the fate of the war on so desperate an attempt." At the same time the earl warned Clinton, "If you cannot relieve me very soon, you must be prepared to hear the worst."[36] The burden now rested entirely on the commander in chief.

Clinton tried to find a way to save his subordinate, but to no avail. For a while he hoped that Cornwallis would escape and solve the problem for him. He also thought of diversions. He sent Arnold to raid New London, where the refusal of loyalist troops to accept the defenders' surrender evoked more charges of British barbarism. Clinton repeatedly advanced the idea of attacking Philadelphia, although he could hardly have expected such an effort to have deterred Washington from the impending conquest of Cornwallis. Graves's report of the action off the Virginia Capes came on September 17, and two days later the battered fleet returned. Nonetheless, Admiral Hood and the royal governor of New York, Major General James Robertson, pressed for an attempt to land reinforcements at Yorktown despite the risk. Like Tarleton, they argued that any action would be better than none.

On September 24 Admiral Digby finally arrived with three ships of the line. Two others came from the West Indies, and two that had been in dock for repairs returned to their station, bringing the total available, once the British refitted the ships just back from Virginia, to twenty-five. Graves hesitantly agreed to be ready to sail on October 5. The British planned to take advantage of the strong tides in the Chesapeake Bay and slip into the York River with five thousand troops before the French could turn at anchor and bring their guns to bear. How the British would get out again, no one knew. Each council of war raised new doubts because if the fleet was trapped along with Cornwallis, not just the mainland colonies but the West Indies and Canada, too, would fall. With individual captains apparently in no hurry to complete repairs, the departure had to be repeatedly postponed until October 17.[37]

The allied armies moved into position before Yorktown on September 29 and set up camp about two miles from town without opposition. The terrain strongly favored the defenders. To the northwest stretched the marshlands of Yorktown Creek which could be crossed only along the river bank where the road connecting Williamsburg and Yorktown ran. There the British had thrown up a large redoubt supported by naval ships anchored nearby. Wormeley Creek and a mill pond precluded easy

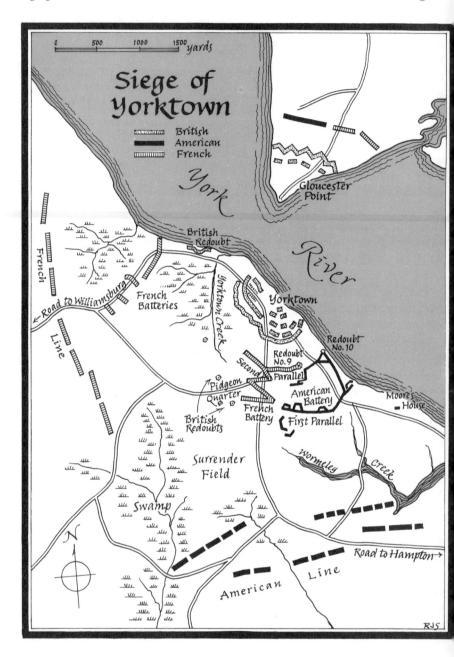

access to Yorktown from the south. Between the headwaters of York-town and Wormeley creeks south of town lay a half-mile of high ground known as Pigeon Quarter, which belonged to Governor Nelson. Here the road from Hampton ran, and Cornwallis had constructed three re-doubts as his outermost line of defense.[38]

On the night of the twenty-ninth, to Washington's amazement, the British fell back from the outer perimeter. The American commander first thought that the enemy was retreating across the river. But Corn-wallis had just received Clinton's initial promise to sail to the rescue in six days. Under other circumstances the earl might have fought to hold the outer posts and gain time for rescuers to come, but in view of the nearness of Clinton's planned arrival, the effort seemed unnecessary. Buoyed by the encouragement from New York, Cornwallis for the mo-ment remained entirely confident and wrote to Clinton as the British withdrew to the inner lines that "there was but one wish throughout the whole army, which was that the enemy would advance."[39]

Having effortlessly breached the natural defenses of Yorktown, Wash-ington laid plans for a siege in classic European style. He had successive parallels of trenches dug in zigzag fashion to bring the attackers closer and closer to the town without exposing them to the defenders' fire. Because Yorktown Creek left too little room to the northwest of the town for a pattern of trenches, the first excavation stretched southeastward from Pigeon Quarter north of Wormeley Creek about six to eight hun-dred yards from the British defenses. For the moment, the allies occu-pied the outer redoubts the British had abandoned, but could not pro-ceed farther until the last of Rochambeau's artillery, which had just been landed at Trebell's Landing on the James River, could be dragged across the peninsula. While waiting, the troops manufactured gabions, which were baskets filled with dirt, and tied bundles of brush called fascines to protect fatigue details from enemy fire as the digging progressed.

The first fighting of the siege broke out across the river. In August Cornwallis had assigned Simcoe to fortify Gloucester Point to control the crossing and prevent the enemy from mounting artillery within range of Yorktown and the ships in the river. Although Simcoe did not display his usual verve as a commander because of poor health, the Brit-ish established a strong position with seven hundred men and nineteen guns.[40] The fifteen hundred Virginia militia under General Weedon who opposed them proved insufficient to keep the British from foraging widely in the area. Admiral de Grasse declined to send vessels up the river to sever communications between the British posts as Washington repeatedly requested for fear the French ships would be too exposed. Nothing impeded the flow of provisions across to Yorktown throughout September.

When the allies marched on Yorktown toward the end of the month, Washington sent the Marquis de Choisy with 1,400 men, including the Duc de Lauzun's lancers, to reinforce Weedon and assume command. Cornwallis countered on October 2 by transferring Tarleton and 230 of his legion across the river since, after the British withdrew to their inner lines, the cavalry did not have sufficient room around Yorktown to maneuver effectively. Because of Simcoe's worsening illness, Tarleton took charge and, hoping to surprise the French and Americans before they realized his legion had arrived, led out a foray in force the next day. Returning with a quantity of corn, Tarleton ran into de Choisy's force as it moved up to invest the British works. After a hard skirmish between the opposing cavalry during which Tarleton barely escaped capture, the British troopers fell back to the protection of their infantry. When the foot soldiers' fire in turn drove off the pursuing French, Tarleton counterattacked, but was halted—to everyone's surprise —by Virginia militia under Lieutenant Colonel John Mercer. De Choisy then tightly encircled the British position and put an end to foraging.

By October 6 the French artillery had been brought up before Yorktown, and construction of the first trenches began. Since abandoning the outer redoubts, the British had been shelling the allied lines day and night at five- to fifteen-minute intervals. To divert the British guns, Washington had Saint Simon simultaneously construct an entrenchment from which the French could bombard the British redoubt on the Williamsburg road and the ships in the river beyond. A French deserter may have given the British information about Saint Simon's activity that intensified their attention in that direction. The weather also helped, for rain on the night of the sixth kept British gunners from seeing clearly. The firing concentrated toward the northwest, just as Washington hoped. To the southeast, by morning his men had thrown up an embankment over a mile long reaching to the river. Under cover of the entrenchment the allies moved their artillery into position during the next two days.

At three o'clock on the afternoon of October 9 the first allied batteries went into action. Over the next twenty-four hours more and more guns commenced firing until fifty-two cannon, many sixteen- and twenty-four-pounders, were booming. One American found the sight "beautifully tremendous" as "shot and shel [went] over our heads in a continual blaze." But those in Yorktown had a different experience. A German soldier said that "we could find no refuge in or out of town. The people fled to the waterside and hid in hastily contrived shelters on the banks, but many of them were killed by bursting bombs." Another described how "one saw men lying nearly everywhere who were mortally wounded and whose heads, arms, and legs had been shot off."[41]

A brief truce on the tenth allowed the governor's uncle, the sixty-five-year-old retired secretary of the colony, Thomas Nelson, to come over to the allied lines. The British, he reported, were "dispirited" but affected to "have no apprehensions of the Garrison's falling." Then the firing began again. The shelling destroyed the secretary's house, where Cornwallis had his headquarters, and forced the general to seek refuge in a "grotto" in the garden.[42] The headquarters staff moved their meetings to a cave on the river bank. Offshore, H.M.S. *Charon*, endeavoring to silence Saint Simon's battery, was hit and burned.

By the night of October 11, British defenses had been softened sufficiently for Washington to order a second line of trenches running northeasterly from the western end of the first parallel. The French and Americans expected Cornwallis to order a sortie to stop them and puzzled over why none occurred. Washington planned the operation so well and the bombardment and sickness had so weakened the British that Cornwallis decided that he did not have the strength to penetrate the trench diggers' defenses. The French and Americans, the earl stated, "not only secured their flanks but proceeded in every respect with the utmost regularity and caution" as they advanced.[43]

During the next three days and nights the allies pushed the second parallel toward Redoubts No. Nine and Ten, which stood outside the British lines to protect Yorktown's left flank. The French and Americans had to take these outworks before the combined armies could launch a direct assault on the British. While the digging progressed, Washington directed as much firepower as possible at the two redoubts, and when the troops completed the new trench to within three hundred yards of their objective, the soldiers constructed an epaulement or bunker to shelter preparations for the attack. Both French and Americans shared the honor. Washington assigned Baron de Vioménil to take Redoubt No. Nine, and Lafayette, No. Ten. Under Lafayette, Alexander Hamilton, who had recently transferred from Washington's headquarters staff to see more action in the field, demanded and received the right to lead the charge on the grounds of seniority.

As the hour for the assault approached, Washington ordered Saint

Simon in the northwestern sector and de Choisy at Gloucester Point to
create diversions. Then, at approximately 7 P.M. on October 14, two
raiding parties of about four hundred men each crept out of the epaulement. They moved forward unobserved until the miners and sappers
could begin to clear away the fraise work and abatis—sharpened stakes
and tangled trunks of trees—that guarded the breastworks. When the
British discovered the attackers, a brief exchange of fire and a hand-to-
hand struggle with bayonets broke out, but the defenders, outnumbered
two or three to one, soon perceived the folly of resisting to the end. The
allies spent the remainder of the night extending the trenches and in-
corporating the captured redoubts into the second parallel.

Allied gunners could enfilade the British lines from the captured
posts. The time had come for whatever final desperate action the British
could muster. Before dawn on October 16 a party of about 350 redcoats
broke through an unfinished section of the allied line and, moving along
the trenches, surprised an artillery unit, killing or injuring seventeen
and spiking six cannon. The guns were soon repaired. Washington dismissed the effort as "small and ineffectual," and Cornwallis agreed; the
sortie, he said, "proved of little public advantage."[44]

That night Cornwallis decided to abandon his equipment and supplies, move as many men as possible to Gloucester, and attempt to march
northward. Since the British could only find sixteen boats, it would require three trips to accommodate everyone. The ferrying commenced
at ten o'clock, and one load of thirteen hundred troops crossed safely.
But just as the second division began to embark, a violent squall blew all
the craft downstream, including a few that had already been loaded.
Once Cornwallis could recover his boats the next morning he ordered
back the troops who had reached Gloucester because he realized that
Washington would immediately attack when he saw that the enemy was
divided. By the time the troops returned from Gloucester, the French
and Americans had all their artillery in position on the second parallel
within easy range of the river, precluding another British effort to cross.

According to some estimates, the allies had over one hundred cannon
in action. The British, on the other hand, had barely one hundred mortar shells remaining. "Our works . . . were going to ruin" under the can-
nonade and "were in many parts very assailable in the forenoon," Cornwallis explained to Clinton. "I thought it would have been wanton and
inhuman to the last degree to sacrifice the lives of this small body of
gallant soldiers . . . by exposing them to an assault."[45] A little before ten
o'clock on the morning of October 17—the fourth anniversary of Bur-

goyne's capitulation—a drummer beat the parley on the breastwork and an officer appeared with a flag of truce and Cornwallis's offer to surrender. The same day the British fleet under Graves and Digby set sail from New York to save him.

Just as the battle had followed classic European formulas for siege warfare, the process of surrender conformed to gentlemanly rituals. Arranging the formal ceremony took over seventy-two hours though there was no serious debate over terms. Cannonading continued sporadically on the seventeenth until Washington received more precisely defined proposals from Cornwallis in the late afternoon. The American commander agreed in some measure to most of the British requests, refusing only to let the British troops be paroled and to settle the fate of civilian captives whom he considered the civil government's responsibility. The next day at Augustine Moore's home behind the allied lines representatives of the armies labored until nearly midnight without completing the official documents because of the number of fine points the British brought up. The negotiators signed the final agreement shortly before noon on the morning of the nineteenth.[46]

The surrender ceremony constituted an elaborate pageant and a dramatic advertisement for the new nation. Beginning at 2 P.M., the British marched out between parallel lines of American and French soldiers for half a mile to a field where they laid down their arms, their banners furled and their musicians forbidden by the terms of surrender to play American or French tunes. At the opening of the ceremonies the principal figures maneuvered as if in a round of chess. Pleading indisposition, Cornwallis sent his second-in-command, Brigadier Charles O'Hara, to lead the British troops. O'Hara first attempted to surrender to the French, but Rochambeau declined. Washington then countered by designating his second-in-command, Benjamin Lincoln, as his stand-in. Afterward Washington invited O'Hara to dinner, where the brigadier impressed even the French, known for their own savoir faire, with the poise and equanimity of a British officer. Then, the amenities over, Washington dispatched the report that Congress and the country had been waiting for—he had won.

CHAPTER 16

"The most painful suspense with regard to events in Europe"

ALTHOUGH in retrospect the battle of Yorktown ended the war for Americans, Virginia and the other United States had to wait another seventeen months for a treaty of peace. Despite mounting sentiment in Britain against continuing the struggle, it required a number of additional defeats in the West Indies, India, and, nearer home, Minorca before the king and his ministers would brook negotiations. After discussions finally began many issues besides those pertaining to North America had to be settled. For example, Spain, an ally of France although not of the United States, hoped to recover Gibraltar, which it had lost to Great Britain earlier in the century. Then the tide turned; the French suffered a major defeat in the Caribbean, and Gibraltar did not fall.

In Virginia, despite a de facto truce in the East, bitter fighting continued for well over a year in the West, and no letup occurred at sea. Privateers roamed practically at will off the coast and in the Chesapeake Bay. Most trying for Virginians, as for all Americans, they seldom knew what was happening. At best, news from Europe reached their shores two months after the event, and the secrecy of diplomacy seldom provided a solid fact to report. Congress itself had difficulty keeping informed. After nearly a year of patient waiting, James Madison at his post in Philadelphia, where he had access to the best intelligence available, burst out in frustration, "We are still left by our Ministers in the most painful suspense with regard to events in Europe."[1]

After the capitulation at Yorktown, few of the major participants lingered long in Virginia. Washington and de Grasse waited to see whether the British relief fleet under Admiral Graves would attack. The British ships reached the Virginia Capes on October 28 and departed on the afternoon of the thirtieth without an engagement. Four days later, November 3, Cornwallis, who accepted parole, sailed for New York, and all of the Americans except the Virginia, Pennsylvania, and Maryland units returned up the Chesapeake Bay by transport. The next day the remaining American regiments began marching southward to join General Greene, while de Grasse, ignoring Washington's hopeful observation that the allies still had time to strike at Charleston, departed for the Caribbean. On November 5, the American commander rode off for the North.[2]

Seventy-two hundred forty-one captives, British and German, remained behind plus an undetermined number of sailors from the supporting vessels. About 250 of the vanquished had escaped on the sloop *Bonetta,* in which the surrender terms allowed Cornwallis to send dispatches and "such soldiers as he may think proper" to his commander in chief in New York. According to Colonel Simcoe, the British packed on board "as many of the Rangers, and of the other corps, deserters from the enemy, as she could possibly hold."[3] A good many escaped blacks also went, Governor Nelson suspected, but Washington had promised not to inspect the vessel before it sailed. Had the Rangers remained they would undoubtedly have created a treacherous problem, for public opinion probably would not have allowed Washington to treat the tories who followed Simcoe as legitimate prisoners of war.

Governor Nelson began moving the prisoners the day after the signing of the surrender and completed the task by the twenty-ninth. Half went to the prison camp at Winchester, the others to Frederick Town in Maryland. About seventeen hundred sick remained for a couple of weeks in Gloucester to recover before joining their fellows. Virginia had difficulty coping with such numbers. The militia guarding them occasionally spread panic among local inhabitants by leaving their charges unattended. From Winchester came constant complaints that the prisoners caused disturbances, and farmers refused to supply them with food. By resorting to impressment, the administration so outraged public opinion that the legislature ordered it to stop. Virginia simply could not afford to maintain so many prisoners, the state's delegates informed Congress. Yet when Congress ordered all the prisoners to Maryland in December, the counties surrounding Winchester protested vigorously that their business would be injured. The governor and Council replied curtly: "If they are loosers by it it is their own doings."[4] Meanwhile, Washington opened negotiations for a general exchange of prisoners, especially the Americans taken at Charleston, but because the British had captured no one equivalent in rank to Cornwallis, talks bogged down over that question and others for months to come.

After the Americans and British departed, the French set about destroying the fortifications in Yorktown and those Arnold had built in Portsmouth. About mid-November Rochambeau's troops moved into winter quarters at Williamsburg with detachments at Yorktown, Gloucester, Hampton, and West Point. The winter of 1781–1782 proved extraordinarily mild, and from the journals of French officers, all appeared to enjoy themselves as much as anyone doing garrison duty on the outskirts of civilization could. Local Virginians, at least those of the wealthier classes, seem from the same accounts to have eagerly and pleasantly discharged their duties as hosts with dances, cockfights, horse races, hunts, and similar events. Congress decreed a holiday on December 15 to celebrate the victory at Yorktown. Rochambeau had a Te Deum mass sung in Williamsburg and gave a dinner and ball that evening, of which Baron von Closen noted in his diary, "Everyone very much pleased with it."[5]

A wing of the main college building that the French took over for a hospital and the old governor's mansion, which the Americans used for their wounded, burned during the winter. But overall Williamsburg residents had few complaints about the army of occupation. When the French at last announced their departure the following June, their hosts expressed genuine regret, not only because of the defense the French afforded, but because the visitors had been model guests whose discipline and deportment the Virginians universally lauded. The major portion of the French army marched out of Williamsburg between July 1 and 4, 1782, in weather so hot that the troops began their daily treks at 1 A.M. to avoid the worst. Six months later the army arrived in Boston, where it embarked for the long voyage home.[6]

The only dissonance in the chorus of praise for the French concerned their refusal to return the slaves they had captured. From among the blacks Cornwallis had left behind, according to one French officer, the visiting army "garnered a veritable harvest of domesticks. Those among us who had no servant were happy to find one so cheap."[7] Virginia officials protested to Rochambeau until they were wearied out. In most cases Virginians registering claims had no proof of ownership to counter the blacks' assertions of freedom—an idea, one administrator bluntly informed Rochambeau, the French had "inculcated into them to serve the purpose of detention." In a final effort before the French left, Benjamin Harrison disingenuously proposed on behalf of the state that, if the allies would simply leave all the blacks with him, he would "make it my Business" to sort them out and return them to their masters. Rochambeau naturally refused since there had been blacks with his army all along. "You saw the French army when it came here," Harrison wrote to Washington to refute that argument, "when You see it again You will be able to determine whether the Charge is just or not."[8]

The legislature was more dilatory than usual convening for the fall 1781 session in Richmond. Originally scheduled for October 1, the meeting had been postponed because of the impending battle at Yorktown. Then Governor Nelson's decree setting a new date, which he signed on the battlefield, took nine days in transit and did not reach the Council in the capital until October 26, just eleven days before the appointed time. Although the Council rushed copies around the state, a quorum did not materialize until November 19, and then only after the sergeant at arms borrowed horses and riders from the state quartermaster to bring delinquents in. Rampant absenteeism—twice reaching almost 50 percent—forced the delegates to reduce the quorum to sixty and then to fifty-five members. Still the quartermaster had to send out riders once more to collect errant delegates.[9] Nelson, who fell ill again, went to Offley Hoo, his plantation in Hanover County, and never returned to Richmond as governor. The Council, with no more than half of its membership available for duty, limped along without a quorum. As soon as the General Assembly met, Nelson submitted his resignation although no one bothered officially to tell the Council for most of a week. Finally, on the last day of November, the legislature filled the vacancies on the Council and chose the Speaker of the House of Delegates, Benjamin Harrison, as Nelson's successor over John Page and Richard Henry Lee.[10]

The legislature proved inflexibly economy-minded that session, for, as Harrison chanted in a litany that ran throughout his correspondence, "We have not a Shilling in the Treasury"; "we have but 4/ [shillings] in the Treasury"; "not one shilling has been obtained."[11] The assembly cut back the western regiments, the three state regiments, the State Garrison Regiment, the artillery regiment, and the hospital service and reduced the navy, such as it was, to a single lookout boat, the *Liberty*, plus four new row galleys to be built for defense against privateers. As compensation to the troops discharged, the delegates made up arrears in back pay since 1777 with certificates redeemable in gold in 1785, but rejected Patrick Henry's more costly proposal to put officers on half-pay for life. The legislators dismissed the paymasters general of the army and navy—obviously surplus positions—and pared down the number of state quartermasters and commissioners in proportion to the decline in the number of troops. Harrison terminated Philip Mazzei's appointment as the state's agent in Europe and closed the state ropewalk in Chesterfield County, which was in need of repair, and the state tannery as well. When Colonel Arthur Campbell of Washington County requested assistance against the Indians, the governor told him that the state had no money and "the Executive therefore recommend to the Citizens on our Frontiers to use every means in their Power for preserving a good Understanding with the Savage Tribes."[12]

There remained the gnawing possibility that the state was letting down its guard prematurely. As part of the buildup to support Cornwallis and reestablish prewar governments in the South, Lord Dunmore had arrived in Charleston at the head of a well-equipped detachment of loyalists. When the loss at Yorktown thwarted the original plan Dunmore shifted to New York, where he spent the winter of 1781–1782 advocating enlistment of a black army to invade the southern backcountry from West Florida. Although the threat of a black invasion could hardly be taken seriously after Cornwallis's defeat—a Richmond newspaper called Dunmore's carrying-on "a laughable circumstance"—the former royal governor remained a reminder of the uncertainty that would continue until the signing of a formal peace.[13] About midwinter a communiqué from Greene warned of the possibility of four thousand British reinforcements landing in Charleston and called for two thousand Virginia militia to defend Georgia and

South Carolina. The bogey of dictatorship reemerged when William Lee in Brussels alerted Virginians that Benedict Arnold might be outfitting another expedition for an assault on the South. Richard Henry Lee secured assembly approval for an eleven-man junto to map out defense because of "the experience of the inefficacy of a multitude to perform with accuracy or dispatch." Upon reconsideration, however, his colleagues demurred.[14]

What might have been the most dramatic issue of the fall 1781 session, the impeachment of Jefferson, died with hardly a whimper. The episode embittered the former governor and temporarily drove him from politics. A by-election in Albemarle County allowed Jefferson to obtain a seat in the House of Delegates about three weeks after the session began, but he participated only minimally in the house's business, remaining just long enough for his case to be heard. When the time came, not even George Nicholas, who had moved the original impeachment and served on the investigating committee, appeared to testify. Jefferson, who had been preparing for that moment for months, insisted on taking the floor anyway to read Nicholas's charges and reply to each in turn. The house on December 12 thanked him without dissent for his "impartial, upright, and attentive administration."[15] The Senate offered a few amendments to eliminate any reference even to the need for an inquiry, to which the lower chamber agreed on December 19. On the same day Jefferson declined election to Congress which the assembly was eager to thrust on him, and two days later, patently impatient to flee the political scene, obtained permission to be absent for the rest of the session. When the legislature tried again to elect him in the spring of 1782, he once more excused himself because of his wife's serious illness and because of the "wound" of his impeachment which, he melodramatically told friends, could "only be cured by the all-healing grave."[16]

By the time of Jefferson's hearing the delegates' wrath had shifted instead to Thomas Nelson for his aggressiveness in turning up supplies for the Franco-American armies. With the fighting over, the soldier-governor's reputation had plummeted catastrophically. Edmund Pendleton ascribed Nelson's resignation less to illness than to his being "vexed to se[e] his great Popularity so suddenly change into general execration."[17] The main impetus for the attack in the legislature came from George Mason. Although retired from the House of Delegates, Mason composed a long petition on behalf of inhabitants of Prince William County about half-way through the session.

The petition accused Nelson of violating the constitution by authorizing impressments without the consent of the Council as the law required and placing no restrictions on the seizures "other than the arbitrary Will and Pleasure of the Persons" in charge, often "military Sergeants, and common Soldiers."[18] Mason had been concerned about abuses in impressment since his friend Jefferson's administration, but had refrained from pushing the issue before. Under Nelson, however, Mason found the abuses so excessive that he compared them to the oppressions of King Charles I whom the English beheaded and King James II whose subjects had driven him from the throne.

The complaint that Nelson had cost both the state and individuals money probably agitated more people than Mason's concern about constitutional propriety. In an effort to equalize the distribution of supplies between the armies, the former governor had persuaded the French, who alone had gold to spend, to buy through state agents who had to rely on impressment. The policy discouraged an influx of specie that would have checked inflation, Mason explained, but to hear others, the governor aggrieved them more by preventing them from making a profit. Moreover, Nelson had given away supplies to troops from other states too freely, Mason charged. Mason claimed that he knew of at least one Pennsylvania cavalry unit that had not been equipped at home but sent directly to Virginia for outfitting.[19]

On December 22 an ailing Nelson requested the delegates to "indulge me with half an hour today." They immediately went into the Committee of the Whole to hear him. Presumably he pleaded the necessities of war. He may have argued, as he did later, "that those exertions were crowned with success."[20] Other governors had obtained Council approval retroactively, and among the incumbent councillors, David Jameson for one indicated that he would have consented to Nelson's policies had he the chance. In the end, according to Pendleton, Nelson's detractors became convinced "that what he did wrong was imputable to a mistake in his Judgment and not from a corrupt heart."[21] The house immediately resolved without dissent to forgive the ex-governor and passed an act of indemnity that Arthur Lee prepared. Nonetheless, the delegates also discharged a committee considering renewal of the extraordinary powers previously granted to the executive, thereby revoking them, and enacted a bill that Lee submitted limiting the power of impressment to periods of actual invasion and permitting J.P.s to imprison anyone attempting to exercise it otherwise.

Benjamin Harrison deeply resented that he had to bear the brunt of the legislature's pique at the executive because of Nelson. The governor no longer had the authority to impress, Nelson's successor reminded anyone who asked for supplies; the legislature had rendered Virginia's leader "the poorest and the most impotent Executive perhaps in the world." When Thomas Newton resigned as a commissioner of the navy, Harrison felt mortified because the delegates transferred naval affairs to a three-man board directly responsible to the assembly. Responding later to an inquiry from the Speaker about the navy, Harrison sarcastically told him to ask the board, who "will be ready I make no doubt to explain."[22]

Over the next year the wartime bureaucracy withered away as the campaign for economy went on. First went various assistants, the commercial agent, and the commissary of military stores, and when Davies resigned a little later, the post of war commissioner as well. All of the discontinued offices' work devolved upon the governor and Council and the one remaining agency, the quartermaster. Although the Council gained a third clerk, Harrison's lament shortly afterward echoed John Page's during the first weeks of the republic: "The eternal interruptions I meet with by being under the necessity of hearing every Man that has Business . . . with me . . . are such as often to take up my Time for several Hours in the Day."[23] Government in Virginia had turned full circle.

Politics after the war differed little from before, although contemporaries often thought that they perceived a change. Observers who said that they saw a difference usually meant that other people no longer knew their place. Benjamin Day, for instance, whom the Revolution had raised from a fledgling assistant in the state supply office to state agent in charge of virtually all the commonwealth's purchases, once burst out, "Why Sir, a Cobbler of the lowest Rank, whose daily Bread formerly depended on his Industry, and Character, now lays his Awl aside, reads the Papers, and talks learnedly on the Subject of Trade and Navigation."[24] After the peace, in a passage often quoted by historians, the preacher Devereux Jarratt told with obvious distaste how as a humble youth (that is, compared to the great planters, for his father left a farm and one hundred pounds of personal property) he had looked on the "gentle folks, as being of a superior order" and run away when he saw a "periwig" coming. Now, he declared, "in our high republican times, there is more leveling than ought to be . . . and . . . want of proper distinction, between the various orders of the people."[25]

The Revolution brought great changes in the public administration of Virginia. In terms of number and variety of responsibilities and problems to be met and the number of personnel required to meet them, the colony had been comparatively simple to govern. Suddenly, besides county positions, the executive council, and the lower house of assembly which continued as before, there were a governorship, senatorships, judgeships, a host of military and administrative posts, and an entire tier of officialdom at the Continental level to be filled. The war brought many more into public life than ever before, and while demobilization eliminated most of the new offices, it could not erase the experience.

Yet the two pinnacles of political power in Virginia, the county courts and the House of Delegates, came through the Revolution virtually unaltered. Jefferson and others of similar mind had no success modifying the oligarchical structure of local government, and during the decade following the war the legislature's satisfaction with the status quo continued. In the mid-eighties Madison reintroduced his friend's proposal to license attorneys and establish assize courts to curb local jurisdictions and sought again to restrict practice in the higher courts to professional lawyers. Madison scored a temporary victory, but before the act went into effect opponents succeeded in repealing it.[26]

The House of Delegates differed little in structure and politics from the former House of Burgesses. Although Peyton Randolph, Pendleton, Jefferson, and Mason had left the stage, Patrick Henry and Richard Henry Lee dominated still. Partisan alignments remained fluid, allowing maximum advantage to charismatic orators such as they. The only discernible consistency in voting patterns continued to be the old antagonism between the Southside and the Northern Neck, possibly now as much a function of the two leaders' contending personalities as the two areas' different characteristics. A critic noted one change, however. Neither of the current leaders had the ability of his predecessors to see an issue through. The "two great Commanders make excellent harrangues," he wrote, but they "want executive Officers or shd. be more so themselves. . . . a Pendleton and Jefferson wod. be valuable acquisitions."[27]

One of the two issues that most occupied the delegates while they awaited peace, putting the economy in order, evoked remarkable agreement. A majority regularly supported the same massive deflation of depreciated currency on the state level as Congress pursued on the national. After Yorktown, the legislature quickly abolished paper money as legal tender effective immediately in December 1781 except for the payment of taxes to redeem it. Mason, who addressed the question in his petition against Nelson, which he utilized as a tract for the times, explained that legal tender laws, although originally enacted to counter depreciation, had the opposite effect. Not only "men in desperate Circumstances, and Speculators of all Denominations," but those paragons of republican virtue, "the Planters and Farmers," welcomed a decline in the value of money in order to meet their obligations in a cheaper medium.[28]

The scale of depreciation that the delegates adopted, which ranged from 1½:1 in January 1777 to 1,000:1 four years later for all contracts not specifically calling for payment in specie or commodities, amounted to almost total repudiation. All currency had to be exchanged by October 1, 1782, at 1,000:1 for certificates redeemable in gold in 1790 with annual interest guaranteed by a first claim on the land tax or—the more promising alternative—by warrants on western lands that the legislature held back from Congress for the purpose. The superior courts that had been suspended during the invasion also reopened, although suits could not proceed for recovery of judgments on wartime debts until December 1783. Later the legislature advanced the date to March of the same year. Critics of a hard-money policy led by Henry focused on continuing commodity payments and successively postponing tax deadlines. Only once in the years 1781–1783, and then half-heartedly, did proponents of an easier money policy attempt to reenact the legal tender laws.[29]

The other issue that dominated the legislators' attention, the state's relations with Congress, provided more colorful fireworks. Resentment of the slowness with which northern states seemed to have come to Virginia's aid during Cornwallis's invasion blossomed into a conviction that Virginia had done more than any other state to win final victory. The attitude completely reversed the ardent support for the union that had characterized the commonwealth since early in the Revolution. "Our people still retain their opinions of the importance of this State, its superiority in the Union, and the very great exertions and advances it has made [for the war effort]," wrote a correspondent to James Madison. "Their views are generally local, not seeing the necessity or propriety [o]f general measures now the War is over."[30] Eventually, the suspicion of central authority converted Virginia into one of the most Antifederalist states in the campaign for ratification of the federal Constitution later in the decade.

Virginians confidently believed that Congress owed a heavy debt to them—"at least one million pounds," Joseph Jones reported to Madison.[31] Although a member of Congress, Jones frequently attended the legislature in Richmond during these years and sent a running account of assembly affairs to his fellow congressman in Philadelphia. Jones and Madison emerged as the union's strongest advocates in Virginia while Lee and Henry found hostility to Congress one of the few points upon which they could agree. Not until after almost a decade of negotiations did Virginians accept that they owed one hundred thousand dollars to the Continental government, in great measure because the commissary general, John Brown, had neglected to record many deliveries to Continental forces. In the meantime, Virginians bristled at incessant demands from the Continent's superintendent of finance, Robert Morris, for payment. The correspondence between Governor Harrison and his old friend over the issue became barely civil. The superintendent's "Stile," Harrison informed him, was "illy suited to the character of the writer or to that of the Supreme magistrate of any one of the United States, and savours much more of that passion and ignorance you so obligingly attribute to me, than that calmness and decency ever the Characteristic of the great Minister."[32]

Virginians also considered Congress to be trifling with them in regard to western lands. Although the cession in 1781 had finally induced Maryland to ratify the Articles of Confederation and legitimate the government that had been directing the war, most members of the House of Delegates regarded the Continent as generally ungrateful and on a couple of occasions came close to retracting the offer. When a congressional committee recommended in November 1781 that Congress accept New York's cession but reject Virginia's unless the latter resubmitted it "free from any Conditions and restrictions whatever," even Madison advised his fellows that they had "ample justification for revoking or at least suspending their Act of Cession."[33]

Continued suspicion of many congressmen's personal involvement in the Continent's claim to the West led Arthur Lee in April 1782 to offer "a purifying declaration" requiring every member of the national legislature to "declare upon his honour, whether he is . . . interested . . . in the claims of . . . companies, which have petitioned against the territorial rights of any one of the states." The resolution was "evaded by three days chicane," Lee wrote to Samuel Adams.[34] Attorney General Randolph thought that the assembly might repeal the cession on this occasion, too, but the legislature contented itself with appointing another committee under his chairmanship to restate its position.

The deterioration of the Continent's finances ultimately led to a compromise in June 1783. Congress tacitly agreed to Virginia's demands not to recognize claims prior to the date of cession provided Virginia reenacted the cession without legal conditions. In Virginia, Henry seized the occasion to make another attempt to withhold more lands north of the Ohio River for military bounties, but Madison, Jones, and their allies convinced the assembly in December 1783 to comply with the congressional proposal. On March 3, 1784, Congress at long last accepted Virginia's second, unconditional cession of the Northwest Territory. The Continental legislature shortly afterward adopted the first of three land ordinances that established a mechanism for the evolution of the area to equality with the thirteen original states. Had Britain devised a comparable means for its colonies to attain full citizenship within the empire, the Revolution might have been averted.[35]

Although victorious on the issue of the western cession, the unionists went down to defeat on the question of Robert Morris's impost.[36] Under the pressure of Cornwallis in the summer of 1781, Virginia had agreed to the plan. Later, when the fighting ceased and doubts about the enhanced authority of the central government arose, the legislature amended its permission to require the prior consent of all the other states. Then, when news arrived in early December 1782 that the Rhode Island assembly had unanimously rejected the scheme, Richard Henry Lee whisked through in just three days a bill to rescind even conditional assent. The earlier assembly, Lee argued, had acted "without thought; and amidst the alarms of war." Better the "evil" of the central government having to depend on unenforceable annual assessments on the states than to grant it a taxing power that "would render congress, too remote from the controuling influence of separate states."[37] In the fall of 1783 the delegates reversed themselves again and accepted Congress's amendment letting the states appoint the impost collectors and limiting the grant of authority to twenty-five years. Then, New York exercised its veto. Robert Morris left the superintendency in disgust, and some unionists in Virginia and elsewhere began to ask whether the solution might be to call a constitutional convention to endow Congress with the powers that they believed it needed.[38]

The Virginia assembly's most arresting action during the immediate postwar years, enactment of a statute permitting masters to manumit slaves, evoked no public debate. For most of the century manumission had required the consent of the governor and Council who had authority to agree only if the slave performed "meritorious services."[39] As a result, only a couple of thousand free blacks out of a total of about two hundred thousand lived in Virginia by the time of the Revolution. An

earlier attempt to liberalize the law after the war broke out had failed.
Now, religious rather than constitutional scruples led to the change.
When Quakers and Methodists decided in the 1770s to have their members free their slaves and campaigned to have others do the same, the
law of manumission defeated them. Intense lobbying in 1782 by three
Quakers, George Dillwyn, Warner Mifflin, and John Parrish, finally persuaded the assembly to let masters free slaves by will or by filing a deed
with the county court. About ten thousand gained freedom over the
next decade. From the ease of passage, the act must have appeared relatively innocuous at first; assemblymen probably considered it more an
acknowledgment of the religious rights of whites than of the natural
rights of blacks. Two or three years later opposition appeared in petitions from the new tobacco growing areas of south-central Virginia. The
continued efforts of the Methodist preachers, Francis Asbury and
Thomas Coke, to move beyond manumission to emancipation aroused
planters who objected to the bad example they considered that freedmen set for their remaining slaves. Restrictions over the next twenty
years gradually narrowed the range of the statute until finally in 1806
the requirement that freedmen move out of state or face resale into
bondage effectively nullified it. On the question of slavery, Virginia was
not ready for change.[40]

In Paris, the American negotiators finally ended the months-long
stalemate that the conflicting interests of the belligerents had occasioned
by breaking with their French ally and settling the United States' differences with Great Britain separately. Benjamin Franklin, John Adams,
John Jay, and Henry Laurens (Jefferson, the fifth appointee, could not
reach Paris in time) signed preliminary articles of peace on November
30, 1782, with the provision, as a gesture to the alliance, that the agreement not go into effect until Britain concluded peace with France. The
diplomats fulfilled that requirement in January.

The first word of the preliminary understanding between Britain and
the United States came to Virginia on February 15, 1783, when the *Virginia Gazette, or, the American Advertiser* in Richmond reported the king's
speech to Parliament announcing that he had agreed to the American
colonies becoming "free and independent states."[41] The official text of
the preliminary treaty reached the Virginia capital a month later on
March 19. Because James Hayes, the editor of the *Gazette,* had already
set most of that week's issue in type, he could only provide an outline of
the terms with a warning of their tentative nature. The state government delayed a public celebration in the capital until Saturday, March

29, when news of the treaty between Britain and France arrived. According to the press, "the agreeable and important intelligence of *Peace Liberty* and *Independence* being secured to this country ... was announced by repeated discharges of cannon ... and in the evening a general illumination took place."[42] A month later, at a public reading of Congress's proclamation of the cessation of hostilities, the cannons boomed again. Harrison issued a proclamation for the state on April 21, 1783, the eighth anniversary of Dunmore's raid on the magazine in Williamsburg.

"The preliminary Articles," George Mason wrote to Arthur Lee, "are, upon the whole, as favourable as America, in her present Situation, has a Right to expect." Madison considered the treaty's provisions "extremely liberal," and Pendleton agreed: "I think the peace upon the whole a very liberal one ... never was so Important a Revolution as Ours, so cheaply, and in so short a time purchased." Particularly in the West, "the boundaries of the United States [along the Mississippi River and the Great Lakes] are fixed in a most satisfactory manner," editor Hayes commented upon publishing the first brief summary of the treaty. With regard to Detroit and other posts in the far Northwest, George Rogers Clark for one expressed understandable pleasure at gaining at the bargaining table what he had been unable to win in the field.[43]

The Virginians' only reservation about the peace terms concerned the provisions for payment of British debts and restitution of loyalist property. The first "does not set well on the stomachs of people in general here," Pendleton informed Madison, but the second, he thought, "is touched so gently, as to produce no effect." Legally, since the Continental government under the Articles of Confederation had no authority to compel the states to comply, Congress had only promised to recommend that the states open their courts for the British to collect debts and recover property. When some Virginians began to ask "what have we been fighting for," Mason emphatically replied, "surely not to avoid our just Debts" and commenced a letter-writing campaign to Patrick Henry and others in the legislature to convince them not to interfere with these provisions of the treaty.[44] Mason reflected the economic views of planters who planned to continue exporting tobacco and wanted to reestablish their credit abroad. A substantial number of Virginians less involved in international trade—and probably less well off economically—for whom Henry served as advocate saw the issue as increasing their own and the state's current financial burdens for the benefit of recent enemies. Upon receiving the General Assembly's resolution calling on Virginia delegates to oppose such provisions in the final settlement, Congress directed its negotiators to try to amend the preliminary articles, but the new instructions came too late.

The preliminary articles also provided that the British would not take "any Negroes and other Property of the American inhabitants" when they evacuated their remaining posts in America, a point for which a strong lobby from the regions of the state that Cornwallis raided had been anxiously contending.[45] Over the year persistent rumors described General Sir Guy Carleton, the British commander in chief, as favorably disposed to returning slaves still in British possession, and Congress and the states began compiling lists of their losses to present to him. Then came the shock. Carleton notified Washington in May 1783 that he considered the blacks within his lines no longer American "property" under terms of the treaty. Since they had joined the British in response to promises of freedom, Carleton could not believe that in agreeing to the treaty the ministry intended "violating their faith to the negroes."[46] When the British finally evacuated New York City, approximately three thousand blacks went with them. Virginia seized upon Carleton's action as sufficient warrant to block the collection of British debts in the state's courts, and the British government took Virginia's stand as reason not to give up several forts along the Canadian border that the mother country had agreed to turn over. The result was a diplomatic entanglement not unwound until John Jay negotiated another treaty for the new federal government in 1794, although the blacks still remained free and their masters uncompensated.

Through most of 1783 American negotiators pressed for modification of these and other aspects of the preliminary articles, and particularly for a companion commercial treaty allowing Americans to continue trading with the British empire. Otherwise, British recognition of United States independence classified Americans as foreigners under the terms of the Navigation Acts and prevented the former colonists from returning to their accustomed markets. In Britain a succession of ministries came under intense criticism for having already given away too much in the treaty without at least a quid pro quo from France, if not from the United States. Many British felt, too, that the loyalists had been forgotten and mistreated. The British government refused to accept any further change in the treaty in favor of the Americans, and, after many frustrating sessions and much bitterness, the negotiators incorporated the preliminary articles directly into the definitive treaty. The final signing took place in Paris on September 3, 1783. The war at last had ended.[47]

Notes

Works frequently cited in the notes have been identified by the following abbreviations:

American Archives	Peter Force, comp. *American Archives...*, 4th Series, 6 vols. Washington, D. C., 1837–1846. 5th Series, 3 vols. Washington, D. C., 1848–1853.
Bland Papers	Charles Campbell, ed. *The Bland Papers: Being a Selection from the Manuscripts of Colonel Theodorick Bland, Jr., of Prince George County, Virginia.* 2 vols. Petersburg, Va., 1840–1843.
Calendar of Virginia State Papers	Wm. P. Palmer et al., eds. *Calendar of Virginia State Papers and Other Manuscripts Preserved in the Capitol at Richmond.* 3 vols. Richmond, Va., 1875–1883.
Clark Papers, 1771–1781, 1781–1784	James Alton James, ed. *George Rogers Clark Papers, 1771–1781, 1781–1784.* Illinois State Historical Library, *Collections,* VIII, XIX (Springfield, Ill., 1912, 1926).
Henry	William Wirt Henry. *Patrick Henry: Life, Correspondence and Speeches.* 3 vols. New York, 1891.

History of Virginia	Edmund Randolph. *History of Virginia*. Ed. Arthur H. Shaffer. Charlottesville, Va., 1970.
Honyman Diary	Robert Honyman Diary, 1776–1782. Library of Congress and Henry Huntington Library, San Marino, Calif.
Journals of Burgesses, 1770–1772, 1773–1776	John Pendleton Kennedy, ed. *Journals of the House of Burgesses of Virginia, 1770–1772, 1773–1776*. Richmond, Va., 1905.
Journals of the Continental Congress	Worthington Chauncey Ford, ed. *Journals of the Continental Congress, 1774–1789. Edited from the Original Records in the Library of Congress.* 34 vols. Washington, D. C., 1904–1937.
Journals of the Council	H. R. McIlwaine and Wilmer L. Hall, eds. *Journals of the Council of the State of Virginia.* 3 vols. Richmond, Va., 1931–1952.
Lee Papers	*The Lee Papers.* New-York Historical Society, *Collections*, IV–VII (New York, 1872–1875).
Letters and Papers of Pendleton	David John Mays, ed. *The Letters and Papers of Edmund Pendleton, 1734–1803.* 2 vols. Charlottesville, Va., 1967.
Letters of R. H. Lee	James Curtis Ballagh, ed. *The Letters of Richard Henry Lee.* 2 vols. New York, 1911–1914.
Official Letters of Governors	H. R. McIlwaine, ed. *Official Letters of the Governors of the State of Virginia.* 3 vols. Richmond, Va., 1926–1929.
Papers of Jefferson	Julian P. Boyd et al., eds. *The Papers of Thomas Jefferson.* Princeton, N. J., 1950–.
Papers of Madison	William T. Hutchinson and William M. E. Rachal, eds. *The Papers of James Madison.* Chicago, 1962–.
Papers of Mason	Robert A. Rutland, ed. *The Papers of George Mason, 1725–1792.* 3 vols. Chapel Hill, N. C., 1970.
Papers of the Continental Congress	1774–1789. Microfilm, Library of Congress.
Pendleton	David John Mays. *Edmund Pendleton, 1721–1803: A Biography.* 2 vols. Cambridge, Mass., 1952.

SLM	*Southern Literary Messenger.* N.S., XXVII (1858).
Statutes	William Waller Hening, ed. *The Statutes at Large; Being a Collection of All the Laws of Virginia, from the First Session of the Legislature, in the Year 1619.* 13 vols. New York, Philadelphia, and Richmond, Va., 1819–1823.
"Virginia Commerce"	Robert Walter Coakley. "Virginia Commerce During the American Revolution." Ph.D. dissertation, University of Virginia, 1949.
Writings of Washington	John C. Fitzpatrick, ed. *The Writings of George Washington from the Original Manuscript Sources, 1745–1799.* 39 vols. Washington, D. C., 1931–1944.

Prologue. THE MAGAZINE.

1. Descriptions of the magazine incident in this and following paragraphs are from Purdie's *Virginia Gazette* (Williamsburg), Apr. 21, 1775, supplement; Dixon and Hunter's *Va. Gaz.* (Williamsburg), Apr. 22, 1775; H.M.S. *Magdalen's* log, Apr. 20, 1775, Adm. 51/3894, pt. IV; and Lord Dunmore to Lord Dartmouth, May 1, 1775, C.O. 5/1373, fols. 60–68, Public Record Office. References to Public Record Office material, unless otherwise noted, are to the Virginia Colonial Records Project microfilm, Foundation Library, Colonial Williamsburg Foundation, Williamsburg, Va. See also *History of Virginia*, pp. 219–220; and "Report of the committee on the causes of the late disturbances," *Journals of Burgesses, 1773–1776*, pp. 213–237.

2. Hints of the circular letters are in the *Va. Gaz.* (Purdie), Dec. 8, 1774, supp.; and *ibid.* (Dixon and Hunter), Jan. 14, 1775. Dunmore acknowledged receipt of the circulars to Dartmouth, Feb. 7 and 14, 1775, C.O. 5/1353, fols. 87–88, 103–110.

3. Mar. 23, 1775, William J. Van Schreeven and Robert L. Scribner, comps., ed. Robert L. Scribner, *Revolutionary Virginia. The Road to Independence.* Vol. II: *The Committees and the Second Convention, 1773–1775. A Documentary Record* (Charlottesville, Va., 1975), p. 366.

4. Proclamation, Mar. 28, 1775, *American Archives*, 4th Ser., II, p. 236; Edmund Pendleton to George Washington, Apr. 21, 1775, *Letters and Papers of Pendleton*, I, p. 102.

5. Dunmore to Dartmouth, May 1, 1775, C.O. 5/1373, fols. 63–68. See also *Va. Gaz.* (Purdie), Apr. 21, 1775, supp.

6. Dunmore to Dartmouth, May 1, 1775, C.O. 5/1373, fols. 63–68. For concern over slave unrest, see Robert Donald to Patrick Hunter, Apr. 18, 1775,

Buchanan and Milliken v. *Robert Donald,* U. S. Circuit Court, Virginia District, Ended Cases, 1794, Virginia State Library, Richmond, Va.; *Letters and Papers of Pendleton,* I, p. 102; and Edward Stabler to Isaac Pemberton, May 16, 1775, Pemberton Papers, XXVII, p. 144, Historical Society of Pennsylvania, Philadelphia, microfilm, Foundation Lib.

7. "Report on the causes of the late disturbances," *Journals of Burgesses, 1773–1776,* pp. 231–237.

8. Peyton Randolph to Mann Page, Jr., Lewis Willis, and Benjamin Grymes, Jr., Apr. 27, 1775, Lee Family Papers, Alderman Library, University of Virginia, Charlottesville, Va., microfilm, Foundation Lib. See also *Va. Gaz.* (Purdie), Apr. 28, 1775, supp.; and *ibid.* (Dixon and Hunter), Apr. 29, 1775, supp.

9. Gloucester, Henrico, Amelia, New Kent, Cumberland, and Loudoun County and Norfolk Committee resolutions, *American Archives,* 4th Ser., II, pp. 387, 395, 476–478, 502–504, 710; Landon Carter to the Independent Company of Richmond County, Apr. 28, 1775, Carter Family Correspondence, 1775–1797, Alderman Lib.; Richard Henry Lee to L. Carter, Apr. 24, 1775, *Letters of R. H. Lee,* I, pp. 132–134; Dunmore to Dartmouth, May 15, 1775, C.O. 5/1373, fol. 68.

10. *Pendleton,* II, p. 14; *American Archives,* 4th Ser., II, pp. 442–443, 710–711; Douglas Southall Freeman, *George Washington: A Biography,* Vol. III: *Planter and Patriot* (New York, 1951), p. 412n; Washington to Albemarle County Independent Company, May 3, 1775, R. A. Brock, ed., "Papers Military and Political, 1775–1778, of George Gilmer, M.D., of 'Pen Park,' Albemarle County, Va." (Virginia Historical Society, *Collections,* N.S., VI [Richmond, Va., 1887]), p. 81; James Madison to William Bradford, May 9, 1775, *Papers of Madison,* I, pp. 144–145.

11. *Va. Gaz.* (Purdie), May 12, 1775. See also *ibid.* (Dixon and Hunter), May 13, 1775; Edward Miles Riley, ed., *The Journal of John Harrower: An Indentured Servant in the Colony of Virginia, 1773–1776* (Williamsburg, Va., 1963), p. 94; and Michael Wallace to Gustavus B. Wallace, May 14, 1775, Wallace Papers, Alderman Lib. Wallace described the conference as lasting three days, but this description conflicts with the date of the council's statement. See also Alexander Spotswood to Washington, Apr. 30, 1775, *American Archives,* 4th Ser., II, pp. 447–448.

12. Albemarle County Committee minutes, May 31, 1775, "Papers of Gilmer," p. 84; E. C. Branchi, trans., "Memoirs of the Life and Voyages of Doctor Philip Mazzei," *William and Mary Quarterly,* 2nd Ser., IX (1929), pp. 172–173. Written in 1810, Mazzei's account is very confused, but he referred specifically to Henry's address.

13. Descriptions of Henry's march in this and following paragraphs are from Charles Dabney to William Wirt, Dec. 21, 1805, Nathaniel Pope to Wirt, June 23, 1806, Patrick Henry Papers, Library of Congress, microfilm, Foundation Lib.; John Daly Burk, *The History of Virginia from Its First Settlement to the Present Day,* IV (Petersburg, Va., 1816), pp. 12n, 13n, which is based on participants' accounts; Hanover County Committee resolutions, May 9, 1775, *American*

Archives, 4th Ser., II, pp. 540–541; Pinkney's *Va. Gaz.* (Williamsburg), May 4, 1775; *ibid.* (Purdie), May 5, 1775; *ibid.* (Dixon and Hunter), May 6, 1775; James Parker to Charles Steuart, May 6, 1775, MS 5029, fol. 49, Charles Steuart Papers, National Library of Scotland, Edinburgh, microfilm, Foundation Lib.; Dunmore to Dartmouth, May 1 and 15, 1775, C.O. 5/1373, fols. 63–68; *Papers of Madison*, I, p. 147n; and Richard Caswell to his son, May 11, 1775, Richard Caswell Papers, P.C. 375.1, North Carolina Department of Archives and History, Raleigh, N. C., microfilm, Foundation Lib.

14. Dunmore to Dartmouth, May 1, 1775, C.O. 5/1373, fols. 63–68; *Va. Gaz.* (Purdie), May 19, 1775.

15. William Reynolds to John Norton & Sons, May 16, 1775, William Reynolds Letter Book, Lib. Cong.; Betsy Ambler Carrington to Nancy Ambler Fisher, Mar. 1809, Eliza Jacquelin Ambler Papers, Foundation Lib.

16. Patrick Henry to Robert Carter Nicholas, May 4, 1775, *American Archives*, 4th Ser., II, p. 541. See also Dunmore's proclamation of Henry's outlawry, *ibid.*, p. 516; R. C. Nicholas to Burwell Bassett, May 8, 1775, Bassett Papers, Lib. Cong.; and Emory G. Evans, *Thomas Nelson of Yorktown: Revolutionary Virginian* (Williamsburg, Va., 1975), p. 47.

17. Pendleton to Joseph Chew, June 15, 1775, *Letters and Papers of Pendleton*, I, p. 110.

18. Pendleton to William Woodford, May 30, 1775, *ibid.*, p. 103. See also Henry to Francis Lightfoot Lee, May 8, 1775, *Henry*, I, pp. 287–289; and Madison to Bradford, May 9, 1775, *Papers of Madison*, I, p. 145.

Chapter 1. "THE MALIGNANCY . . . AND THE WICKEDNESS . . . IN THEIR PLANS OF DESPOTISM"

1. Edmund S. Morgan and Helen M. Morgan, *The Stamp Act Crisis: Prologue to Revolution* (Chapel Hill, N. C., 1953), pp. 38–39, 155, 159–160, 172–173, 177n.

2. *Pendleton*, I, pp. 249–261; "Virginia Nonimportation Resolutions, 1769," *Papers of Jefferson*, I, pp. 27–31.

3. *Papers of Jefferson*, I, pp. 105–112, quotation on p. 108.

4. George M. Curtis III, "The Role of the Courts in the Making of the Revolution in Virginia," in James Kirby Martin, ed., *Dimensions of Nation Making: Essays on Colonial and Revolutionary America* (Madison, Wis., 1976), pp. 121–146; Frank L. Dewey, "The Fee Bill Crisis of 1774: Thomas Jefferson's Opinion" (unpublished MS, Williamsburg, Va., 1982); *Pendleton*, I, pp. 244–248; "Opinion on the Power of the General Court to Establish Fees," *Letters and Papers of Pendleton*, I, pp. 82–85, Pendleton to Ralph Wormeley, Jr., June 28, 1774, *ibid.*, pp. 96–98; R. H. Lee to Samuel Adams, Apr. 24, May 8, June 23, 1774, R. H. Lee to [L.

Carter], Apr. 25, 1774, R. H. Lee to Arthur Lee, June 26, 1774, *R. H. Lee Letters,* I, pp. 106–117; Gilbert Chinard, ed., *The Commonplace Book of Thomas Jefferson: A Repertory of His Ideas on Government* (Baltimore, Md., 1926), pp. 193–201.

5. Van Schreeven, comp., ed. Scribner, *Revolutionary Virginia.* Vol. I: *Forming Thunderheads and the First Convention, 1763–1774: A Documentary Record* (Charlottesville, Va., 1973), pp. 109–168, quotation on p. 111; Merrill Jensen, *The Founding of a Nation: A History of the American Revolution, 1763–1776* (New York, 1968), pp. 453–460.

6. Van Schreeven and Scribner, comps., ed. Scribner, *Revolutionary Virginia,* II: *Committees and the Second Convention,* pp. 87, 89–93.

7. Van Schreeven, comp., ed. Scribner, *Revolutionary Virginia,* I: *Forming Thunderheads,* pp. 87, 89–93, 96, 122, 133, 135, 150, 161.

8. *Ibid.,* pp. 238–239.

9. *Journals of the Continental Congress,* I, p. 39. See also Jensen, *Founding of a Nation,* pp. 483–507.

10. Bernard Bailyn, *The Ideological Origins of the American Revolution* (Cambridge, Mass., 1967); Van Schreeven, comp., ed. Scribner, *Revolutionary Virginia,* I: *Forming Thunderheads,* p. 347.

11. Charles de Secondat, Baron de Montesquieu, *The Spirit of the Laws,* trans. Thomas Nugent (Chicago, 1952), Bk. XI, chap. 6; Paul Merrill Spurlin, *Montesquieu in America, 1760–1801* (University, Ala., 1940).

12. H. Trevor Colbourn, *The Lamp of Experience: Whig History and the Intellectual Origins of the American Revolution* (Chapel Hill, N. C., 1965).

13. Bailyn, *Ideological Origins;* Stella F. Duff, "The Case Against the King: The *Virginia Gazettes* Indict George III," *WMQ,* 3rd Ser., VI (1949), pp. 383–397.

14. The description of constitutional ideas in this and following paragraphs is based on Lewis Namier, *England in the Age of the American Revolution,* 2nd ed. (New York, 1961); Richard Pares, *King George III and the Politicians* (Oxford, 1953); Bailyn, *Ideological Origins;* Caroline Robbins, *The Eighteenth-Century Commonwealthman: Studies in the Transmission, Development and Circumstance of English Liberal Thought from the Restoration of Charles II until the War with the Thirteen Colonies* (Cambridge, Mass., 1959); and Isaac Kramnick, *Bolingbroke and His Circle: The Politics of Nostalgia in the Age of Walpole* (Cambridge, Mass., 1968). For the suffrage, see Lewis Namier, *The Structure of Politics at the Accession of George III,* 2nd ed. (London, 1957), pp. 65, 81.

15. *Henry,* I, p. 234.

16. Bernard Donoughue, *British Politics and the American Revolution: The Path*

to War, 1773–75 (New York, 1964), chap. 3; Pares, *George III and the Politicians,* pp. 68, 90–91.

17. Pares, *George III and the Politicians,* p. 50.

18. Namier, *England in the Age of the American Revolution,* p. 42.

19. Morgan and Morgan, *Stamp Act Crisis,* pp. 71–87; Jensen, *Founding of a Nation,* pp. 225–228, 453–460.

20. The best account of Dunmore's governorships is Percy Burdelle Caley, "Dunmore: Colonial Governor of New York and Virginia, 1770–1782" (Ph.D. diss., University of Pittsburgh, 1939). For Dunmore's income, see Dunmore Papers, microfilm, Earl Gregg Swem Library, College of William and Mary, Williamsburg, Va., originals owned by the Earl of Dunmore; and Jane Carson, "Lady Dunmore in Virginia" (research report, n.d., Foundation Lib.). For the description of Dunmore's early career in this and following paragraphs, see John E. Selby, *Dunmore* (Williamsburg, Va., 1977).

21. "Notes of Judge St. George Tucker [on William Wirt's Life of Patrick Henry]," *WMQ,* 1st Ser., XXII (1913–1914), p. 252. See also *Dictionary of American Biography,* s.v. "Botetourt, Norborne Berkeley, Baron de." For criticism of Dunmore, see Louise B. Dunbar, "The Royal Governors in the Middle and Southern Colonies on the Eve of the Revolution: A Study in Imperial Personnel," in *The Era of the American Revolution: Studies Inscribed to Evarts Boutell Greene* (New York, 1939), pp. 241–242; and A. Lee to R. H. Lee, Dec. 6, 1774, Lee-Ludwell Papers, Virginia Historical Society, Richmond, Va.

22. William Strahan to David Hall, Jan. 11, 1770, *Pennsylvania Magazine of History and Biography,* XI (1887), p. 224.

23. Dunmore to Hillsborough, Oct. 15, 1771, Caley, "Dunmore," p. 110; *Journals of Burgesses, 1770–1772,* p. 317; *Journals of Burgesses, 1773–1776,* p. 36. See also Dunmore to Dartmouth, Dec. 24, 1774, C.O. 5/1373, fols. 43–44.

24. Dartmouth to Dunmore, Sept. 8, 1774, C.O. 5/1352, fols. 116–120. See also Caley, "Dunmore," pp. 149, 152, 159, 193, 204–205; Jack M. Sosin, *The Revolutionary Frontier, 1763–1783* (New York, 1967), pp. 9–15; and Thomas Perkins Abernethy, *Western Lands and the American Revolution* (New York, 1937), pp. 40–58.

25. *American Archives,* 4th Ser., I, p. 283; Dartmouth to Dunmore, July 6, 1774, C.O. 5/1352, fol. 178. See also Caley, "Dunmore," pp. 182–183, 236–322; and Sosin, *Revolutionary Frontier,* pp. 84–87.

26. Maj. Angus MacDonald to William Harrod, Jan. 8, 1775, Reuben Gold Thwaites and Louise Phelps Kellogg, eds., *Documentary History of Dunmore's War, 1774* (Madison, Wis., 1905), pp. 395–396. See also Caley, "Dunmore," pp. 272, 293–365, 386, 400; and Virgil A. Lewis, *History of the Battle of Point Pleasant* (Charleston, W. Va., 1909).

27. Parker to Steuart, Jan. 27, 1775, MS 5029, fol. 14, Steuart Papers. See also Carson, "Lady Dunmore"; and Caley, "Dunmore," pp. 397, 428. Lady Dunmore and nine of her ten children arrived in Virginia in Feb. 1774 after Dunmore decided that they could endure the climate. The tenth and youngest child was still too small to travel.

28. Caley, "Dunmore," p. 391; Dunmore to Dartmouth, Aug. 14, 1774, C.O. 5/1352, fols. 147–148.

29. Fairfax County Militia Association, Sept. 21, 1774, Fairfax County Militia Plan [Feb. 6, 1775], *Papers of Mason*, I, pp. 211, 215. See also Dunmore to Dartmouth, June 4, 6, 9, 20, Oct. 16, 1774, C.O. 5/1352, fols. 92–93, 108–110, 121–123, 139–140, C.O. 5/1353, fols. 1–2. Dartmouth received the first two on July 11, the second two on Sept. 21, 1774, and the fifth on Jan. 5 [or 15], 1775. *Pendleton*, II, pp. 5, 31–32; Spotsylvania and Fairfax County committees, Dec. 15, 1774, Jan. 17, 1775, Van Schreeven and Scribner, comps., ed. Scribner, *Revolutionary Virginia*, II: *Committees and the Second Convention*, pp. 197, 242; William Minor to Washington, Mar. 7, 1775, *Writings of Washington*, V, pp. 132–133.

30. Dunmore to Dartmouth, Dec. 24, 1774 (received Feb. 10, 1775), C.O. 5/1353, fols. 7–39.

31. Dartmouth to Dunmore, Mar. 3, 1775, C.O. 5/1353, fol. 85 (acknowledged May 15, 1775). See also Dunmore to Dartmouth, May 29 (received July 4, 1774), Aug. 14, 1774 (received Oct. 8, 1774), and Dartmouth to Dunmore, July 6, Dec. 24, 1774 (received Feb. 10, 1775), C.O. 5/1352, fols. 81–82, 88–91, 147–148, C.O. 5/1353, fols. 7–39.

32. Dartmouth to American governors, Oct. 19, 1774, *American Archives*, 4th Ser., I, p. 881, acknowledged in Dunmore to Dartmouth, Feb. 7, 1775, C.O. 5/1353, fols. 87–88. Dunmore acknowledged the circular letter of Jan. 14, 1775, on Mar. 14, 1775, C.O. 5/1353, fols. 103–110. In contrast to the circular instructions Dunmore received, Gen. Thomas Gage in Boston received direct marching orders that led to the battles of Concord and Lexington. See also John Richard Alden, "Why the March to Concord?" *American Historical Review*, XLIX (1943–1944), pp. 446–454.

33. Dunmore to Dartmouth, May 1, 1775, C.O. 5/1353, fol. 63. Dunmore acknowledged Dartmouth's letter of Apr. 5, 1775, on May 15, 1775, C.O. 5/1353, fols. 141–144, and indicated that those of July 5 and 12 and Aug. 2, 1775, had arrived by Dec. 20, 1775. See Dunmore to Dartmouth, postscript, Feb. 18, 1776, C.O. 5/1353, fols. 333–334. The letter from Dartmouth of May 30, 1775, which Dunmore acknowledged on Sept. 24, 1775, concerned the West, C.O. 5/1353, fols. 135–136, 254.

34. *Va. Gaz.* (Purdie), Dec. 8, 1774, supp. A good example is A. Lee to R. H. Lee, Dec. 6, 1774, Lee-Ludwell Papers. See Caroline Robbins, "The Strenuous Whig: Thomas Hollis of Lincoln's Inn," *WMQ*, 3rd Ser., VII (1950), pp. 406–453.

35. *DAB*, s.v. "Lee, Arthur," and "Lee, William"; Colin Bonwick, *English Radicals and the American Revolution* (Chapel Hill, N. C., 1977). For an illustration, see Gen. William Draper and the effect of his writings, *Dictionary of National Biography*, s.v. "Draper, William." See also Caley, "Dunmore," p. 78; Jack P. Greene, ed., *The Diary of Colonel Landon Carter of Sabine Hall, 1752–1778*, II (Charlottesville, Va., 1965), p. 812; and [William Draper], *The Thoughts of a Traveller upon our American Disputes* (London, 1774). The Lib. Cong. copy was Arthur Lee's. A. Lee to R. H. Lee, Dec. 6, 1774, Lee-Ludwell Papers; William Lee to R. H. Lee, Sept. 10, 1774, Worthington Chauncey Ford, ed., *Letters of William Lee, 1766–1783*, I (Brooklyn, N. Y., 1891), p. 89; Madison to Bradford, Nov. 26, 1774, Bradford to Madison, Jan. 4, July 10, 1775, *Papers of Madison*, I, pp. 129, 132, 157n; Address to Ld. Dunmore, June 19, 1775, *Journals of Burgesses, 1773–1776*, pp. 256–257.

36. W. Lee to R. H. Lee, Feb. 25, 1775, W. Lee to R. C. Nicholas, Mar. 6, 1775, Ford, ed., *Letters of W. Lee*, I, pp. 127, 139–140. See also *Va. Gaz.* (Pinkney), Apr. 28, 1775; *ibid.* (Purdie), Apr. 28, 1775; and *ibid.* (Dixon and Hunter), Apr. 29, 1775.

37. Thomas Jefferson to John Randolph, Aug. 25, 1775, *Papers of Jefferson*, I, p. 241; George Mason to [Mr. Brent?], Oct. 2, 1778, *Papers of Mason*, I, p. 435. See also Rawleigh Downman to Samuel Athawes, July 10, 1775, Joseph Ball Letter Book, Lib. Cong.; and Madison to Bradford, June 19, 1775, *Papers of Madison*, I, p. 153.

Chapter 2. BRITAIN'S OLDEST DOMINION

1. Evarts B. Greene and Virginia D. Harrington, *American Population Before the Federal Census of 1790* (New York, 1936), pp. 141–142; Stella H. Sutherland, *Population Distribution in Colonial America* (New York, 1936), pp. xii, 202; Robert V. Wells, *The Population of the British Colonies in America before 1776: A Survey of Census Data* (Princeton, N. J., 1975), p. 284; Robert McColley, *Slavery and Jeffersonian Virginia* (Urbana, Ill., 1964), p. 141; Aubrey C. Land, "Economic Behavior in a Planting Society: The Eighteenth-Century Chesapeake," *Journal of Southern History*, XXXIII (1967), pp. 471–473; Jackson Turner Main, *The Social Structure of Revolutionary America* (Princeton, N. J., 1965), p. 65; Main, "The Distribution of Property in Post-Revolutionary Virginia," *Mississippi Valley Historical Review*, XLI (1954–1955), pp. 243–246, 248n, 249.

2. Main, "Distribution of Property," pp. 244, 246, 248n, 253; Douglas Southall Freeman, *George Washington: A Biography*. Vol. I: *Young Washington* (New York, 1948), chap. 1; Richard L. Morton, *Colonial Virginia*. Vol. II: *Westward Expansion and Prelude to Revolution, 1710–1763* (Chapel Hill, N. C., 1960), chaps. 13–14.

3. Morton, *Colonial Virginia*, II, chaps. 13, 15; Main, *Social Structure*, pp. 50–52; Main, "Distribution of Property," pp. 243, 256; Land, "Economic Behavior," pp. 471–472; Robert D. Mitchell, *Commercialism and Frontier: Perspectives on*

the Early Shenandoah Valley (Charlottesville, Va., 1977), pp. 149–157, 187–188, 204, 223–229, 238; Freeman H. Hart, *The Valley of Virginia in the American Revolution, 1763–1789* (Chapel Hill, N. C., 1942), pp. 7–14.

4. Main, *Social Structure,* pp. 46–47; Richard R. Beeman, "Social Change and Cultural Conflict in Virginia: Lunenburg County, 1746 to 1774," *WMQ,* 3rd Ser., XXXV (1978), pp. 464–466.

5. Main, *Social Structure,* p. 66; Sutherland, *Population Distribution,* pp. 199, 206.

6. Jacob M. Price, "The Economic Growth of the Chesapeake and the European Market, 1697–1775," *Journal of Economic History,* XXIV (1964), pp. 496–497; Van Schreeven, comp., ed. Scribner, *Revolutionary Virginia,* I: *Forming Thunderheads,* p. 237. See also Thomas Jefferson, *A Summary View of the Rights of British America* (1774), in Paul Leicester Ford, ed., *The Works of Thomas Jefferson* (New York, 1904–1905), II, pp. 65–66, 68–91.

7. Jacob M. Price, "The Rise of Glasgow in the Chesapeake Tobacco Trade, 1707–1775," *WMQ,* 3rd Ser., XI (1954), pp. 179–199.

8. Jacob M. Price, *Capital and Credit in British Overseas Trade: The View from the Chesapeake, 1700–1776* (Cambridge, Mass., 1980), pp. 6–10; James F. Shepherd and Gary M. Walton, *Shipping, Maritime Trade, and the Economic Development of Colonial North America* (Cambridge, 1972), p. 132n; William Knox, *The Interest of the Merchants and Manufacturers of Great Britain in the Present Contest with the Colonies* (1774), in Richard B. Sheridan, "The British Credit Crisis of 1772 and the American Colonies," *JEH,* XX (1960), p. 163.

9. Land, "Economic Behavior," pp. 469–485; Mitchell, *Commercialism and Frontier,* p. 116.

10. Jacob M. Price, *France and the Chesapeake: A History of the French Tobacco Monopoly, 1674–1791, and of Its Relationship to the British and American Tobacco Trades,* I (Ann Arbor, Mich., 1973), pp. 672–673; Joseph Albert Ernst, *Money and Politics in America, 1755–1775: A Study in the Currency Act of 1764 and the Political Economy of Revolution* (Chapel Hill, N. C., 1973), chaps. 3, 6; *Pendleton,* I, chap. 11.

11. Price, *Capital and Credit,* pp. 6, 9, 127–128; Sheridan, "British Credit Crisis of 1772," pp. 178ff.

12. Sheridan, "British Credit Crisis of 1772," pp. 169, 178, 183; Price, *Capital and Credit,* pp. 127–129, 132–135.

13. Emory G. Evans, "Planter Indebtedness and the Coming of the Revolution in Virginia," *WMQ,* 3rd Ser., XIX (1962), pp. 511–533; Evans, "Private Indebtedness and the Revolution in Virginia, 1776 to 1796," *ibid.,* XXVIII (1971), pp. 349–374.

14. John Wayles to Farrell & Jones, Aug. 30, 1766, Price, *Capital and Credit*, p. 18; Gordon S. Wood, "Rhetoric and Reality in the American Revolution," *WMQ*, 3rd Ser., XXIII (1966), pp. 27–32.

15. Answers to Demeusnier's Additional Queries [ca. Jan.–Feb. 1786], Price, *Capital and Credit*, p. 6.

16. Edmund S. Morgan, "The Puritan Ethic and the American Revolution," *WMQ*, 3rd Ser., XXIV (1967), pp. 3–43.

17. David C. Klingaman, *Colonial Virginia's Coastwise and Grain Trade* (New York, 1975), pp. 47, 100; Klingaman, "The Significance of Grain in the Development of the Tobacco Colonies," *JEH*, XXIX (1969), p. 270; Harold B. Gill, Jr., "Wheat Culture in Colonial Virginia," *Agricultural History*, LII (1978), pp. 382–383.

18. Paul G. E. Clemens, *The Atlantic Economy and Colonial Maryland's Eastern Shore: From Tobacco to Grain* (Ithaca, N. Y., 1980), chap. 6; Klingaman, *Colonial Virginia's Coastwise and Grain Trade*, pp. 88–95, 100, 129, 145; Mitchell, *Commercialism and Frontier*, pp. 187–188; Lewis Cecil Gray, *History of Agriculture in the Southern United States to 1860*, I (Washington, D. C., 1933), chap. 7; Gaspar J. Saladino, "The Maryland and Virginia Wheat Trade from Its Beginnings to the American Revolution" (M.A. thesis, University of Wisconsin, 1960), pp. 26, 29–31.

19. Saladino, "Maryland and Virginia Wheat Trade," chap. 5; Klingaman, *Colonial Virginia's Coastwise and Grain Trade*, pp. 49, 58; Joseph A. Goldenberg, *Shipbuilding in Colonial America* (Charlottesville, Va., 1976), pp. 119–120.

20. Nicholas Brown to Carter Braxton, Sept. 1763, Braxton to Nicholas Brown & Co., Oct. 16, 1763, Elizabeth Donnan, *Documents Illustrative of the History of the Slave Trade to America*, III (Washington, D. C., 1932), pp. 194–195; William Palfrey to Braxton, Dec. 14, 1767, Palfrey Papers, Houghton Library, Harvard University, Cambridge, Mass.

21. For the discussion of religious issues in this and following paragraphs, see especially Rhys Isaac, *The Transformation of Virginia, 1740–1790* (Chapel Hill, N. C., 1982), chap. 9; Isaac, "Religion and Authority: Problems of the Anglican Establishment in Virginia in the Era of the Great Awakening and the Parsons' Cause," *WMQ*, 3rd Ser., XXX (1973), pp. 3–36; Isaac, "Evangelical Revolt: The Nature of the Baptists' Challenge to the Traditional Order in Virginia, 1765 to 1775," *ibid.*, XXXI (1974), pp. 345–368; and Isaac, "Preachers and Patriots: Popular Culture and the Revolution in Virginia," in Alfred F. Young, ed., *The American Revolution: Explorations in the History of American Radicalism* (De Kalb, Ill., 1976), pp. 125–156. See also Wesley M. Gewehr, *The Great Awakening in Virginia, 1740–1790* (Durham, N. C., 1930); H. J. Eckenrode, *Separation of Church and State in Virginia: A Study in the Development of the Revolution* (Richmond, Va., 1910); Morton, *Colonial Virginia*, II, chap. 16; and Carl Bridenbaugh, *Mitre and Sceptre: Transatlantic Faiths, Ideas, Personalities, and Politics, 1689–1775* (New York, 1962), pp. 316–323.

22. Charles S. Sydnor, *Gentlemen Freeholders: Political Practices in Washington's Virginia* (Chapel Hill, N. C., 1952); A. G. Roeber, *Faithful Magistrates and Republican Lawyers: Creators of Virginia Legal Culture, 1680–1810* (Chapel Hill, N. C., 1981), pp. 76–77, 119, 135, 137–147, and chap. 4.

23. Roeber, *Faithful Magistrates*, pp. 121, 131, 149–153; *Statutes*, IV, p. 542; Calvin B. Coulter, "The Virginia Merchant" (Ph.D. diss., Princeton University, 1944), pp. 239–240; Carl Bridenbaugh, "Violence and Virtue in Virginia, 1766: or, The Importance of the Trivial," Massachusetts Historical Society, *Proceedings*, LXXVI (1964), pp. 3–29.

24. Roeber, *Faithful Magistrates*, pp. 145–146, 153–156.

25. Sydnor, *Gentlemen Freeholders*, pp. 35–36. See also Lucille Griffith, *The Virginia House of Burgesses, 1750–1774* (University, Ala., 1968), pp. 55–60. The figures given are extrapolations of Griffith's, pp. 58–59. Robert E. Brown and B. Katherine Brown, *Virginia 1705–1786: Democracy or Aristocracy?* (East Lansing, Mich., 1964), pp. 128–129, 144–145.

26. Sydnor, *Gentlemen Freeholders*, pp. 89–90; Jack P. Greene, *The Quest for Power: The Lower Houses of Assembly in the Southern Royal Colonies, 1689–1776* (Chapel Hill, N. C., 1963), pp. 462–474; Isaac, "Preachers and Patriots," pp. 134–137; Greene, ed., *Diary of Landon Carter*, II, pp. 1008–1009.

27. Jackson T. Main, "Sections and Politics in Virginia, 1781–1787," *WMQ*, 3rd Ser., XII (1955), pp. 96–112; Main, *Political Parties before the Constitution* (Chapel Hill, N. C., 1973), pp. 244–249; Marc Egnal, "The Origins of the Revolution in Virginia: A Reinterpretation," *WMQ*, 3rd Ser., XXXVII (1980), pp. 401–428; Isaac, *Transformation of Virginia*, chap. 10.

28. Pendleton to Bradford, Apr. 1, 1779, *Letters and Papers of Pendleton*, I, p. 278.

Chapter 3. THE COLLAPSE OF ROYAL GOVERNMENT

1. *Va. Gaz.* (Dixon and Hunter), May 13, 1775.

2. Dartmouth to Dunmore, Apr. 5, 1775, C.O. 5/1353, fols. 101–102; Dunmore to Dartmouth, May 15, 1775, C.O. 5/1373, fol. 68; *Va. Gaz.* (Purdie), May 19, 1775.

3. *Va. Gaz.* (Purdie), June 2, 1775, supp.; *ibid.* (Dixon and Hunter), June 3, 1775.

4. *Gentleman's Magazine*, XLV (1775), p. 345. See also *Journals of Burgesses, 1773–1776*, pp. 114–115.

5. Dumas Malone, *Jefferson and His Time*. Vol. I: *Jefferson the Virginian* (Bos-

ton, 1948), pp. 199–200; *Papers of Jefferson*, X, p. 371; Thomas Jefferson, "Auto-biography," in Ford, ed., *Works of Jefferson*, I, pp. 16–17; Dunmore to Dartmouth, June 25–27, 1775, C.O. 5/1373, fols. 72–84.

6. *Va. Gaz.* (Purdie), June 9, 1775, supp., dated the episode June 5; *ibid.* (Dixon and Hunter), June 10, 1775, and *ibid.* (Pinkney), June 8, 1775, dated it June 3. There were two incidents which Purdie confused. See Report of the committee to inspect the magazine and Address of the House of Burgesses to Ld. Dunmore, *American Archives*, 4th Ser., II, pp. 1207–1208, 1228–1229, al-though the exact date of the first incident is not clear in these. Dunmore to Dartmouth, June 25–27, 1775, C.O. 5/1373, fols. 72–84, dated it Sunday, June 4. See also Parker to Steuart, June 12, 1775, MS 5029, fol. 62, Steuart Papers.

7. *Va. Gaz.* (Purdie), June 9, 1775, supp.; Pendleton to Chew, June 15, 1775, *Letters and Papers of Pendleton*, I, pp. 112–113.

8. Dunmore to Dartmouth, June 25–27, 1775, C.O. 5/1373, fols. 72–84; *Journals of Burgesses, 1773–1776*, pp. 193–194, 201, 260.

9. *Journals of Burgesses, 1773–1776*, pp. 198, 214; Dunmore to Dartmouth, June 25–27, 1775, C.O. 5/1373, fols. 72–84; *Va. Gaz.* (Pinkney), June 8, 1775; *ibid.* (Purdie), June 9, 1775; *ibid.* (Dixon and Hunter), June 10, 1775.

10. *Journals of Burgesses, 1773–1776*, p. 194.

11. *Ibid.*, p. 202; *Va. Gaz.* (Purdie), June 9, 1775; *ibid.* (Dixon and Hunter), June 10, 1775; H.M.S. *Magdalen*'s log, June 6–8, 1775, Adm. 51/3894, pt. IV.

12. Dunmore to Dartmouth, June 25–27, 1775, C.O. 5/1373, fols. 72–84.

13. *Va. Gaz.* (Pinkney), June 8, 1775; *ibid.* (Dixon and Hunter), June 10, 1775; *ibid.* (Purdie), June 9, 1775.

14. *Va. Gaz.* (Purdie), July 22, 1775. See also *ibid.*, June 9, 1775, supp.; Capt. George Montagu to Adm. Samuel Graves, June 17, 1775, Adm. 1/485, fols. 289–290; A Williamsburg merchant to Wilson, Kilmarnock, June 12, 1775, in Loudoun to Dartmouth, July 17, 1775, C.O. 5/154, fol. 197; Madison to Bradford, June 19, 1775, *Papers of Madison*, I, pp. 152–153; Robert McCluer Calhoon, *The Loyalists in Revolutionary America, 1760–1781* (New York, 1973), p. 442; and *Journals of Burgesses, 1773–1776*, pp. 206–207, 237, 259.

15. Resolution, June 12, 1775, *Journals of Burgesses, 1773–1776*, pp. 219–221, quotation on p. 220. See also *ibid.*, pp. 278–286; and Dunmore to Dartmouth, June 25–27, 1775, C.O. 5/1373, fols. 72–84.

16. R. H. Lee to [F. L. Lee], May 21, 1775, *Letters of R. H. Lee*, I, pp. 138–139. See also Deposition of William Goodrich in Dunmore to Dartmouth, Dec. 6, 1775–Feb. 13, 1776, C.O. 5/1353, fol. 352; and George M. Curtis III, "The Goodrich Family and the Revolution in Virginia, 1774–1776," *Virginia Magazine*

338 Notes to Pages 45–47

of History and Biography, LXXXIV (1976), pp. 49–74. For the discussion of the burgesses' response to Dunmore in this and following paragraphs, see Enclosure #13 in Dunmore to Dartmouth, June 25–27, 1775, C.O. 5/1373, fols. 72–84; and *Journals of Burgesses, 1773–1776,* pp. 231–237, 241, 248, 253–262.

17. Resolutions of the Virginia Convention Calling upon Congress for a Declaration of Independence, *Letters and Papers of Pendleton,* I, p. 178.

18. *Journals of Burgesses, 1773–1776,* pp. 250, 273–274, 279–283.

19. George Gilmer to Jefferson, July 26 or 27, 1775, *Papers of Jefferson,* I, p. 237.

20. Parker to Steuart, June 24, 1775, MS 5029, fol. 66, Steuart Papers; *Bland Papers,* I, p. xxiii.

21. *Va. Gaz.* (Dixon and Hunter), July 1, 1775; H.M.S. *Magdalen*'s log, June 28–29, 1775, Adm. 51/3894, pt. IV; Graves to Philip Stephens [secretary to the Admiralty], June 16, July 16, 1775, Adm. 1/485, fols. 216, 271–276; Graves to Dunmore, July 28, 1775, Montagu to Dunmore, Aug. 9, 1775, *Aspinwall Papers* (Mass. Hist. Soc., *Collections,* 4th Ser., Pt. II, XL [Boston, 1871]), pp. 751–752, 754–756.

22. H.M.S. *Magdalen*'s muster book, June 29, July 28, 1775, Adm. 36/8478, fols. 86, 90; Bridenbaugh, *Mitre and Sceptre,* pp. 317–322; *Va. Gaz.* (Purdie), Apr. 28, May 4, 1775; *ibid.* (Pinkney), June 15, 1775; *ibid.* (Dixon and Hunter), Oct. 14, 1775; Dunmore to Dartmouth, June 6, 1774, C.O. 5/1352, fols. 108–110; E. Alfred Jones, "Two Professors of William and Mary College," *WMQ,* 1st Ser., XXVI (1917–1918), pp. 221–231.

23. Capt. Edward Foy to Ralph Wormeley, Jr. [July 8–14, 1775], Ralph Wormeley, Jr., Papers, Alderman Lib. For Foy's biography, see Marvin L. Brown, Jr., trans., *Baroness von Riedesel and the American Revolution: Journal and Correspondence of a Tour of Duty, 1776–1783* (Chapel Hill, N. C., 1965), pp. 11n, 156, 159, 172, 174; *History of Virginia,* pp. 196, 214; Louise Hall Tharp, *The Baroness and the General* (Boston, 1962), pp. 35, 421n; William L. Stone, trans., *Letters of Brunswick and Hessian Officers During the American Revolution* (Albany, N. Y., 1891), p. 74 and n.; Tobias Smollett, *The History of England,* V (Edinburgh, 1818), pp. 97n, 98; Dunmore to Dartmouth, May 25, 1773, Lady Dunmore to Dartmouth, Aug. 10, 1773, Dunmore to Dartmouth, Apr. 2, 1774, Lady Gower to Dartmouth, May 30, 1775, *The Manuscripts of the Earl of Dartmouth* (Historical Manuscripts Commission, *Fourteenth Report,* Appendix, Part X [London, 1895]), II, pp. 152, 165, 207, 305; Caley, "Dunmore," p. 881; and Dunmore to Dartmouth, July 12, 1775, Dec. 6, 1775–Feb. 13, 1776, C.O. 5/1353, fols. 228, 321.

24. *DAB,* s.v. "Randolph, John"; Jefferson to J. Randolph, Aug. 25, Nov. 29, 1775, J. Randolph to Jefferson, Aug. 31, 1775, *Papers of Jefferson,* I, pp. 240–243, 268–270; Earl Gregg Swem, ed., *Virginia and the Revolution: Two Pamphlets* (New York, 1919); Parker to Steuart, May 19, 1773, MS 5028, fols. 75–76,

Steuart Papers; John Coles to Rebecca Coles, Aug. 26, 1775, Carter-Smith Family Papers, Alderman Lib., photostat, Foundation Lib.; J. Randolph to E. Randolph, Aug. 12, 1775, Gage Papers, 1763–1775, CXXXIII, Willliam L. Clements Library, University of Michigan, Ann Arbor, Mich., microfilm, Foundation Lib.; *Va. Gaz.* (Pinkney), Oct. 19, 1775; Holt's *Virginia Gazette, or the Norfolk Intelligencer,* Aug. 23, 1775; Dunmore to Dartmouth, Sept. 24, 1775, C.O. 5/1353, fol. 249.

25. Gilmer to Jefferson, July 26 or 27, 1775, *Papers of Jefferson,* I, p. 237. See also *Va. Gaz.* (Purdie), June 30, 1775, supp., July 14, 1775, supp.; *ibid.* (Dixon and Hunter), July 8, 1775; and Parker to Steuart, July 14, 1775, MS 5029, fol. 73, Steuart Papers.

26. Gilmer to Jefferson, July 26 or 27, 1775, *Papers of Jefferson,* I, p. 237. See also resolutions adopted by the officers at Williamsburg, July 18, 1775, "Papers of Gilmer," pp. 92–93; and *Va. Gaz.* (Purdie), Sept. 14, 1775.

27. Benjamin Harrison to Washington, July 21, 1775, Dunmore's *Virginia Gazette* (Norfolk), Nov. 25, 1775. See also *Va. Gaz.* (Pinkney), July 6, 1775; *ibid.* (Dixon and Hunter), July 8, 1775; and Dunmore to Dartmouth, July 12, 1775, C.O. 5/1353, fol. 228.

28. C.O. 5/1353, fol. 228; *Va. Gaz.* (Purdie), July 14, 1775; J. Coles to R. Coles, Aug. 26, 1775, Carter-Smith Family Papers.

29. P. Randolph to officers at Williamsburg, July 28, 1775, Convention resolution, July 28, 1775, "Papers of Gilmer," pp. 107–108. See also *ibid.,* pp. 94–110; *Va. Gaz.* (Dixon and Hunter), July 29, 1775; Gilmer to Jefferson, July 26 or 27, 1775, *Papers of Jefferson,* I, p. 237; and Richard Corbin to Dunmore, July 31, 1775, enclosed in Dunmore to Dartmouth, Sept. 24, 1775, C.O. 5/1353, fol. 291.

30. [Officers of the Volunteer Companies, now in Williamsburg] to the President and Gentlemen of the Convention [Aug. 1, 1775], "Papers of Gilmer," p. 109.

31. *The Proceedings of the Convention of Delegates . . . Held at Richmond . . . the 17th of July, 1775* (Williamsburg, Va. [1775]), p. 26; Gilmer to Jefferson, July 26 or 27, 1775, *Papers of Jefferson,* I, p. 237.

32. Jensen, *Founding of a Nation,* p. 611. News of Bunker Hill was in the *Va. Gaz.* (Dixon and Hunter), July 8, 1775. See also Don Higginbotham, *Daniel Morgan: Revolutionary Rifleman* (Chapel Hill, N. C., 1961), p. 24.

33. Robert Wormeley Carter to L. Carter, Aug. 5, 1775, *Pendleton,* II, p. 358.

34. Mason to Martin Cockburn, July 24, Aug. 5, 1775, Mason to Washington, Oct. 14, 1775, *Papers of Mason,* I, pp. 241, 246, 255; *Proceedings of the Convention, July 1775,* pp. 19, 30, 42.

35. *Proceedings of the Convention, July 1775*, pp. 8, 9–10, 13, 15, 17–19, 22; Nonimportation resolution [July 24, 1775], *Papers of Mason*, I, pp. 242–243; *Va. Gaz.* (Dixon and Hunter), July 22, 1775; *Va. Gaz., or Norfolk Intelligencer*, July 5, 1775; Reynolds to George Goosley, July 28, 1775, Reynolds Letter Book; Montagu to Graves, June 17, 1775, Adm. 1/485, fols. 289–299.

36. Washington to Joseph Reed, Mar. 7, 1776, *Writings of Washington*, IV, p. 381. See also *Proceedings of the Convention, July 1775*, pp. 20–21; W. Maury to St. George Tucker, Aug. 24, 1775, and Archibald Campbell to Tucker, Aug. 26, 1775, Tucker-Coleman Collection, Swem Lib.

37. Mason to Cockburn, Aug. 22, 1775, *Papers of Mason*, I, p. 252. See also Mason to Washington, Oct. 14, 1775, *ibid.*, p. 255; and *Proceedings of the Convention, July 1775*, p. 5.

38. R. W. Carter to L. Carter, July 29, 1775, Carter Family Papers, 1659–1787, Alderman Lib., microfilm, Foundation Lib. See also *Statutes*, IX, pp. 53–57.

39. *Statutes*, IX, pp. 57–60, quotation on p. 59.

40. Mason to Cockburn, Aug. 5, 1775, *Papers of Mason*, I, pp. 245–246.

41. Madison to Bradford, July 28, 1775, *Papers of Madison*, I, p. 160.

42. Mason to Cockburn, Aug. 5, 1775, Mason to Washington, Oct. 14, 1775, *Papers of Mason*, I, pp. 245–246, 255–257; *Pendleton*, II, p. 7.

43. Mason to Cockburn, July 24, 1775, *Papers of Mason*, I, p. 241.

44. *Ibid.; Statutes*, IX, pp. 9–35.

45. Mason to Washington, Oct. 14, 1775, *Papers of Mason*, I, pp. 255–256.

46. *Ibid.* See also *Statutes*, IX, pp. 41, 48.

47. *Statutes*, IX, pp. 61–71; Mason to Washington, Oct. 14, 1775, *Papers of Mason*, I, p. 256.

48. Mason to Cockburn, July 24, 1775, *Papers of Mason*, I, p. 241; *Statutes*, IX, pp. 49–53, 71–73.

49. Mason to Washington, Oct. 14, 1775, *Papers of Mason*, I, p. 255. See also *Proceedings of the Convention, July 1775*, pp. 23, 25.

50. *Proceedings of the Convention, July 1775*, p. 25; R. W. Carter to L. Carter, Aug. 10, 1775, Carter Family Papers; *Proceedings of the Convention, July 1775*, pp. 27, 28, 33; Mason to Cockburn, Aug. 22, 1775, *Papers of Mason*, I, p. 250.

51. *Va. Gaz.* (Purdie), Aug. 31, 1775. See also Ordinance for Establishing a

General Test Oath [Aug. 19, 1775], Mason to Cockburn, Aug. 22, 1775, and Resolution concerning Peaceable British Subjects Resident in Virginia [Aug. 25, 1775], *Papers of Mason*, I, pp. 246–249, 251, 253.

52. *Proceedings of the Convention, July 1775*, p. 59. See also Jefferson's Annotated Copy of Franklin's Proposed Articles of Confederation [June–July 1775], *Papers of Jefferson*, I, pp. 171–182; Merrill Jensen, *The Articles of Confederation: An Interpretation of the Social-Constitutional History of the American Revolution, 1774–1781* (Madison, Wis., 1940), p. 84; Examination of William Robertson, enclosed in Dunmore to Dartmouth, Oct. 22, 1775, C.O. 5/1353, fol. 312; and Virginia Committee of Safety to Va. Delegates in Congress, Nov. 11, 1775, *Letters and Papers of Pendleton*, I, p. 129.

Chapter 4. WAR

1. Gage to Dartmouth, May 15, 1775, Gage to Dunmore, May 15, 1775, Clarence Edwin Carter, comp. and ed., *The Correspondence of General Thomas Gage . . . 1763–1775*, I (New Haven, Conn., 1931), p. 399; Graves to Stephens, May 15, 18, 19, June 16, 1775, Adm. 1/485, fols. 172, 177–178, 182, 216–220; Dunmore to Gov. Patrick Tonyn, Aug. 29, 1775, Tonyn to Dunmore, Sept. 15, 1775, C.O. 5/555, fols. 348, 371; *Va. Gaz.* (Dixon and Hunter), Aug. 5, 1775.

2. "Papers of Gilmer," p. 89; Dunmore to Graves, July 17, 1775, Montagu to Graves, Aug. 7, 1775, Graves to Stephens, Aug. 17, Oct. 9, 1775, Dunmore to Graves, Sept. 12, 1775, C.O. 5/122, nos. 15b, 15e, 15g, 35ee; *Va. Gaz.* (Dixon and Hunter), Aug. 5, Sept. 2, 1775; *ibid.* (Pinkney), Sept. 21, 1775; Capt. John Macartney to mayor of Norfolk, Aug. 12, 1775, Norfolk Borough Committee resolution, Aug. 28, 1775, *American Archives*, 4th Ser., III, pp. 92–96, 444; Graves to Dunmore, Aug. 7, 1775, Adm. 1/485, fol. 324.

3. Petitions for payment for ships *Dunmore* and *William*, T. 1/527, fols. 295–296, 457–462, T. 1/535, fols. 3–5; Parker to Steuart, July 19, 1775, MS 5029, fol. 77, Steuart Papers; *Va. Gaz.* (Holt), Aug. 23, 1775; John Goodrich, Jr., to Matthew Phripp [ca. Aug. 14, 1775], *VMHB*, XV (1907–1908), p. 148; James Gilchrist to S. G. Tucker, Sept. 14, 1775, Tucker-Coleman Collection.

4. For the description of Connolly's activities in this and following paragraphs, see "Correspondence of Dr. John Connolly, May–Aug. 1775," "Virginia Legislative Papers," *VMHB*, XIV (1906–1907), pp. 58–78; *Journals of Burgesses, 1773–1776*, p. 230; *Proceedings of the Convention, July 1775*, p. 10; and James Wood to P. Randolph, July 9, 1775, Reuben Gold Thwaites and Louise Phelps Kellogg, eds., *The Revolution on the Upper Ohio, 1775–1777* (Madison, Wis., 1908), pp. 35–37.

5. "A Narrative of the Transactions, Imprisonment, and Sufferings of John Connolly, an American Loyalist and Lieut. Col. in His Majesty's Service," *PMHB*, XII (1888), pp. 315–316.

6. Journal, July 10, 1775, Thwaites and Kellogg, eds., *Revolution on the*

Upper Ohio, pp. 40–41; Minutes of Treaty at Fort Dunmore, June 19, 1775, *VMHB,* XIV (1906–1907), p. 61; Abernethy, *Western Lands and the Revolution,* p. 141; *Statutes,* IX, p. 18; "Narrative of Connolly," pp. 317–321.

7. "Narrative of Connolly," pp. 321–324; Thwaites and Kellogg, eds., *Revolution on the Upper Ohio,* pp. 140–142; John Connolly to John Gibson, Aug. 9, 1775, Frederick County, Md., committee to president of Congress, Nov. 24, 1775, *American Archives,* 4th Ser., III, pp. 72, 1660; Dunmore to Dartmouth, Dec. 6, 1775–Feb. 13, 1776, C.O. 5/1353, fol. 331.

8. Gage to Dartmouth, Sept. 23, 1775, C.O. 5/92, fol. 281; "Narrative of Connolly," pp. 408–417; Deposition of William Cowley, Oct. 12, 1775, examination of John Connolly, Nov. 23, 1775, *American Archives,* 4th Ser., III, pp. 1047, 1660–1661; *The Proceedings of the Convention of Delegates Held at . . . Richmond . . . the 1st of December, 1775* (Williamsburg, Va. [1776]), p. 11.

9. *Va. Gaz.* (Pinkney), Sept. 14, 1775.

10. *Ibid.,* Sept. 9, 1775; *ibid.* (Dixon and Hunter), Sept. 9, 23, 1775; *ibid.* (Purdie), Sept. 13, 21, 1775; Dunmore to Dartmouth, Oct. 5, 1775, C.O. 5/1353, fols. 300–302.

11. Parker to Steuart, Oct. 2, 1775, MS 5029, fol. 106, Steuart Papers. See also Clarence S. Brigham, comp., *History and Bibliography of American Newspapers, 1690–1820,* II (Worcester, Mass., 1947), pp. 1129–1130; and Arthur M. Schlesinger, *Prelude To Independence: The Newspaper War on Britain, 1764–1776* (New York, 1958), pp. 53, 55–56, 239.

12. *Va. Gaz.* (Purdie), Sept. 15, Oct. 6, 1775, Apr. 26, 1776, supp.; Dunmore to Dartmouth, Oct. 5, 1775, C.O. 5/1353, fols. 300–302; Fred S. Siebert, "The Confiscated Revolutionary Press," *Journalism Quarterly,* XIII (1936), pp. 179–181.

13. For events in, and attitudes toward, Norfolk, see Alexander Gordon to Campbell, Oct. 2, 1775, C.O. 5/1353, fols. 307–308; *Proceedings of the Convention, December 1775,* pp. 62–63; Parker to Steuart, Oct. 9 [or 19], 1775, MS 5029, fol. 112, Steuart Papers; R. H. Lee to Washington, Oct. 22, 1775, *Letters of R. H. Lee,* I, pp. 152–153; [A. Lee?] to R. H. Lee, Sept. 22, 1775, Chalmers Collection, New York Public Library, New York, N. Y., microfilm, Foundation Lib.; *Va. Gaz., or Norfolk Intelligencer,* Aug. 9, 16, 1775; Dunmore to Dartmouth, Oct. 5, 1775, C.O. 5/1353, fols. 305–306; Pendleton to Va. delegates in Congress, Oct. 28, 1775, *Letters and Papers of Pendleton,* I, p. 125; *Proceedings of the Convention, December 1775,* pp. 62–63; Neil Jamieson to Glassford, Gordon & Co., Nov. 17, 1775, Jamieson to Edward Payne, Nov. 20, 1775, Jamieson to James Anderson, Nov. 28, 1775, Papers of the Continental Congress, reel 65, item 51, I, pp. 393–395, 405, 421; and R. C. Nicholas to Va. Delegates in Congress, Dec. 12, 1775, *Papers of Jefferson,* I, p. 271.

14. Parker to Steuart, May 6, 1768, Patrick Henderson, "Smallpox and Pa-

triotism: The Norfolk Riots, 1768–1769," *VMHB*, LXXIII (1965), p. 417. See also Brent Tarter, ed., *The Order Book and Related Papers of the Common Hall of the Borough of Norfolk, Virginia, 1736–1798* (Richmond, Va., 1979), pp. 145, 154, 158; and claims of Mary Rothery and William Orange of Norfolk, A.O. 12/54, fols. 35, 176.

15. Parker to Steuart, June 1, 1773, Henderson, "Smallpox and Patriotism," p. 423. See also Parker to Steuart, June 7, 1774, MS 5028, fol. 206ff., Steuart Papers; and Capt. J. Morgan to Gov. Fauquier, Apr. 5, 1766, *WMQ*, 1st Ser., XXI (1912–1913), p. 165.

16. Harrison to another governor, Oct. 17, 1783, *The History of America in Documents: Original Autograph Letters, Manuscripts, and Source Materials*, Pt. 2 (New York, 1950), p. 12. Emory G. Evans called this reference to my attention. See also James Ingram to Steuart, May 31, 1783, MS 5033, fol. 69, Steuart Papers.

17. Archibald Ingram to J. Ingram, Aug. 30, 1775, *VMHB*, XIV (1906–1907), pp. 129–130. See also James Brown to William Brown, Nov. 7, 21, 1775, Robert Shedden to John Shedden, Nov. 9, 20, 1775, R. Shedden to Andrew Lynn, Nov. 21, 1775, and Archibald Brown to James Woddrop, Nov. 21, 1775, *ibid.*, pp. 131, 248–250, 255–256, 383–384.

18. Jefferson to John Page, Oct. 31, 1775, *ibid.*, p. 251.

19. Minutes of the Committee of Safety, Aug. 26, 1775, *American Archives*, 4th Ser., III, p. 435; *Va. Gaz.* (Dixon and Hunter), Sept. 23, 1775; *ibid.* (Purdie), Sept. 29, 1775; Pendleton to R. H. Lee, Oct. 15, 1775, *Letters and Papers of Pendleton*, I, p. 121.

20. William Aylett to Committee of Safety, n.d., "Correspondence of Col. William Aylett, Commissary General of Virginia," *Tyler's Quarterly Historical and Genealogical Magazine*, I (1920), p. 146. See also Pendleton to Commissary of Purchases, Sept. 1, 1775, *Letters and Papers of Pendleton*, I, p. 118; Public Store Day Book, Oct. 12, 13, 17, 23, 28, 1775, Records of the Public Store in Williamsburg, 1775–1780, Va. State Lib., microfilm, Foundation Lib.; and *Va. Gaz.* (Dixon and Hunter), Sept. 23, 30, 1775.

21. *Va. Gaz.* (Dixon and Hunter), Sept. 30, 1775.

22. Woodford to Pendleton, Dec. 10, 1775, "The Letters of Col. William Woodford, Col. Robert Howe and Gen. Charles Lee to Edmund Pendleton," *Richmond College Historical Papers*, I (1915), pp. 116–117. See also *Va. Gaz.* (Dixon and Hunter), Sept. 16, 1775.

23. *Va. Gaz.* (Purdie), Sept. 29, 1775; *Proceedings of the Convention, December 1775*, p. 31; *The Proceedings of the Convention of Delegates Held at . . . Williamsburg . . . The 6th of May, 1776* (Williamsburg, Va. [1776]), p. 42.

24. Capt. Samuel Leslie to Gen. Sir Wm. Howe, Nov. 1 [postscript Nov. 26],

1775, *American Archives*, 4th Ser., III, pp. 1716–1717; Parker to Steuart, Oct. 9, 1775, MS 5029, fol. 112, Steuart Papers; Dunmore to Dartmouth, Oct. 22, 1775, C.O. 5/1353, fols. 310–311.

25. C.O. 5/1353, fols. 310–311.

26. Leslie to Howe, Nov. 1 [postscript Nov. 26], 1775, *American Archives*, 4th Ser., III, p. 1716.

27. *Proceedings of the Convention, May 1776*, pp. 136–137; J. Page to Jefferson, Nov. 11, 1775, *Papers of Jefferson*, I, pp. 256–259; *Va. Gaz.* (Pinkney), Nov. 2, 1775; *ibid.* (Purdie), Oct. 27, supp., Nov. 3, 1775.

28. *Va. Gaz.* (Purdie), Nov. 3, 1775; Hugh Blair Grigsby, *The Virginia Convention of 1776* (Richmond, Va., 1855), pp. 52n–53n; Pendleton to Woodford, Oct. 24, 1775, Pendleton to Henry, Oct. 25, 1775, *Letters and Papers of Pendleton*, I, pp. 122–123, 124.

29. Pendleton to Henry, Nov. 6, 1775, *Letters and Papers of Pendleton*, I, pp. 125–126; Page to Jefferson, Nov. 11, 1775, *Papers of Jefferson*, I, p. 258; *Va. Gaz.* (Purdie), Nov. 17, 24, 1775, supp.

30. Leslie to Howe, Nov. 1 [postscript Nov. 26], 1775, *American Archives*, 4th Ser., III, p. 1717; R. C. Nicholas to Va. Delegates in Congress, Nov. 25, 1775, *Papers of Jefferson*, I, p. 267; Pendleton to R. H. Lee, Nov. 27, 1775, *Letters and Papers of Pendleton*, I, pp. 132–133; Dunmore to Dartmouth, Dec. 6, 1775–Feb. 13, 1776, C.O. 5/1353, fol. 322; *Va. Gaz.* (Dunmore), Nov. 25, 1775; Dunmore to Dartmouth, Dec. 6, 1775–Feb. 13, 1776, C.O. 5/1353, fol. 339.

31. Dunmore to Dartmouth, Dec. 6, 1775–Feb. 13, 1776, C.O. 5/1353, fols. 321–322.

32. *Va. Gaz.* (Purdie), Nov. 10, 1775; Francis Berkeley, ed., *Dunmore's Proclamation of Emancipation* (Charlottesville, Va., 1941).

33. Caley, "Dunmore," pp. 118–121; Madison to Bradford, Nov. 26, 1774, *Papers of Madison*, I, pp. 129–130; Robert Beverley to William Fitzhugh, July 20, 1775, Robert Beverley Letter Book, 1761–1793, Lib. Cong.; W. Lee to R. H. Lee, Feb. 25, 1775, W. Lee to R. C. Nicholas, Mar. 6, 1775, Ford, ed., *Letters of W. Lee*, I, pp. 130, 144.

34. Archibald Cary to R. H. Lee, Dec. 24, 1775, Lee Family Papers, Alderman Lib. The allusion is to Charlemagne's legendary knights, Roland and Oliver, and suggests "a blow for a blow." For a discussion of how Jefferson and Congress wrestled with the irony, see Garry Wills, *Inventing America: Jefferson's Declaration of Independence* (New York, 1978), pp. 64–75.

35. *Proceedings of the Convention, December 1775*, pp. 11–12. See also Cary to R. H. Lee, Dec. 24, 1775, Lee Family Papers, Alderman Lib.; William Byrd III

to Ralph Wormeley, Oct. 4, 1775, endorsement, Ralph Wormeley Papers; and Greene, ed., *Diary of Landon Carter,* II, p. 989.

36. Woodford to Pendleton, Dec. 30, 1775, "Letters of Woodford, Howe and Lee," pp. 144–146. See also Dunmore's loyalist claim, July 9, 1784, claim of Penelope D'Ende, A.O. 12/54, fols. 89, 127; *Journal of the House of Delegates of Virginia. Anno Domine 1776* (Williamsburg, Va., 1776), p. 71; and *Va. Gaz.* (Purdie), Nov. 30, 1775.

37. *Va. Gaz.* (Purdie), Dec. 15, 1775; Pendleton to Jefferson, Nov. 16, 1775, *Papers of Jefferson,* I, p. 261; Richard Kidder Meade to Theodorick Bland, Dec. 18, 1775, Jacob Morris to Bland, July 17, 1783, *Bland Papers,* I, p. 39, II, pp. 111–112.

38. For officers of the Ethiopian Regiment, see T. 1/580, fols. 113–114. See also loyalist claim of Peter Anderson, ca. Sept. 1, 1783, A.O. 12/99, fol. 356; Madison to Bradford, Nov. 26, 1774, *Papers of Madison,* I, pp. 129–130; *Pendleton,* II, p. 56; and Dunmore to Ld. George Germain, Mar. 30, 1776, C.O. 5/1353, fol. 377.

39. *Va. Gaz.* (Purdie), Nov. 17, 30, 1775. See also *ibid.* (Dixon and Hunter), Nov. 25, 1775.

40. Edmund Pendleton et al. to Matthew Tilghman et al., Dec. 29, 1775, *American Archives,* 4th Ser., IV, p. 576. See also Benjamin Quarles, *The Negro in the American Revolution* (Chapel Hill, N. C., 1961), pp. 25–26; and Northampton County committee to Committee of Safety, Apr. 23, 1776, *VMHB,* XV (1907–1908), pp. 406–407.

41. *American Archives,* 4th Ser., VI, p. 1553; *Journal of the House of Delegates, 1776,* p. 13; *Proceedings of the Convention, December 1775,* p. 18; Journals of the Committee of Safety, Feb. 12, 1776, *Journals of the Council,* II, p. 141.

42. *Pendleton,* II, pp. 57–59; William Maxwell, "My Mother" [Helen Read], *Lower Norfolk County Virginia Antiquary,* II (1899), pp. 133–134; *Va. Gaz.* (Dunmore), Nov. 11, 1775; Dunmore to Dartmouth, Dec. 6, 1775–Feb. 13, 1776, C.O. 5/1353, fols. 322, 339.

43. C.O. 5/1353, fols. 321–324; Leslie to Howe, postscript, Nov. 26, 1775, monthly returns of the 14th Regiment, *American Archives,* 4th Ser., III, p. 1717, IV, pp. 349–350; James Parker and Thomas MacKnight, memorials to the Loyalist Commission, 1784, No. 16 misc., Parker Family Papers, Liverpool Library, Liverpool, Eng., microfilm, Foundation Lib.; MacKnight to Dr. MacKnight, Dec. 26, 1775, Misc. MSS, Clements Lib.; Dunmore to Dartmouth, Feb. 20, 1776, C.O. 5/1353, fol. 353; Statement of Ld. Dunmore's account, Nov. 1, 1775–May 2, 1777, T. 1/566, fols. 283–290; *Va. Gaz.* (Purdie), Apr. 26, 1776, supp.; Woodford to Pendleton, Dec. 19, 1775, Robert Howe to Pendleton, Dec. 12, 1775, "Letters of Woodford, Howe and Lee," pp. 134–139; Parker to Foy [June 2, 1773], enclosed in Parker to Steuart, June 1–2, 1773, MS 5028, fol. 82, Steuart Papers.

44. Campbell to Steuart, Apr. 30, 1783, MS 5033, fol. 57, Steuart Papers; Curtis, "Goodrich Family," pp. 49–74.

45. For the description of the battle of Great Bridge in this and following paragraphs, see Woodford to Pendleton, Nov. 26, Dec. 4, 5, 7, 1775, "Letters of Woodford, Howe and Lee," pp. 104–114; Leslie to Gage, Dec. 1, 1775, Col. Scott to Capt. Southall, Dec. 4, 1775, *American Archives*, 4th Ser., IV, pp. 171–172, 183; *History of Virginia*, p. 230; and *Va. Gaz.* (Purdie), Nov. 24, supp., Dec. 9, 1775.

46. *Va. Gaz.* (Purdie), Dec. 15, 1775; Dunmore to Dartmouth, Dec. 6, 1775–Feb. 13, 1776, C.O. 5/1353, fol. 323; "Cassius," *Bland Papers*, I, p. 39.

47. Further descriptions of the battle are in Dunmore to Dartmouth, Dec. 6, 1775–Feb. 13, 1776, return of the 14th Regiment, Jan. 11, 1776, C.O. 5/1353, fols. 323, 362; "J.D." to the Earl of Dumfries, Jan. 14, 1776, C.O. 5/40, fols. 124–127; *Va. Gaz.* (Pinkney), Dec. 20, 1775; Woodford to Pendleton, Dec. 9, 10, 1775, Woodford to Va. Convention, Dec. 10, 12, 1775, "Letters of Woodford, Howe and Lee," pp. 115–122; Meade to Bland, Dec. 18, 1775, *Bland Papers*, I, pp. 38–39; Luther P. Jackson, "Virginia Negro Soldiers and Seamen in the American Revolution," *Journal of Negro History*, XXVII (1942), p. 273; Maj. Spotswood to a friend, Dec. 9, 1775, and a midshipman of H.M.S. *Otter* to [?], Dec. 9, 1775, *American Archives*, 4th Ser., IV, pp. 224, 540.

48. Spotswood to a friend, Dec. 9, 1775, *American Archives*, 4th Ser., IV, p. 224.

49. Meade to Bland, Dec. 18, 1775, *Bland Papers*, I, pp. 38–39.

50. Woodford to Va. Convention, Dec. 9, 1775, "Letters of Woodford, Howe and Lee," pp. 119–120.

51. Woodford to Pendleton, Dec. 10, 11, 14, 1775, Woodford to Va. Convention, Dec. 19, 1775, R. Howe to Va. Convention, Dec. 13, 1775, *ibid.*, pp. 116–128; Scott to Southall, Dec. 12, 1775, *Va. Gaz.* (Purdie), Dec. 16, 1775; Morning report, Dec. 17, 1775, *American Archives*, 4th Ser., IV, p. 294.

52. R. Howe to Va. Convention, Dec. 13, 1775, *American Archives*, 4th Ser., IV, p. 251; Dartmouth to Gage, July 1, 1775, Carter, ed., *Correspondence of Gage*, II, p. 201; Minutes of the Surveyor-General of the Board of Ordnance, July 11, 1775, W.O. 47/86, pp. 7, 10, 11; Dartmouth to Dunmore, Aug. 2, 1775, C.O. 5/1353, fols. 225–226; MacKnight to Loyalist Commission, 1784, Dunmore to Ld. North, May 29, 1777, No. 16 misc., Parker Family Papers.

53. *Proceedings of the Convention, December 1775*, pp. 1–2, 5; Henry to Woodford, Dec. 6, 1775, Woodford to Henry, Dec. 7, 1775, William Wirt, *The Life of Patrick Henry*, 7th ed. (New York, 1834), pp. 186–188; *Pendleton*, II, p. 68; Pendleton to Jefferson, Nov. 16, 1775, *Papers of Jefferson*, I, pp. 260–261.

54. *Proceedings of the Convention, December 1775*, pp. 1, 18, 21.

55. Pendleton to Woodford, Dec. 24, 1775, *Letters and Papers of Pendleton*, I, pp. 140–143 and n., quotation on p. 141; Joseph Jones to Woodford, Dec. 13, 1775, *Henry*, I, pp. 341–342.

56. *Proceedings of the Convention, December 1775*, p. 40; Va. Committee of Safety to Md. Committee of Safety, Dec. 29, 1775, *American Archives*, 4th Ser., IV, p. 577; Jones to Woodford, Dec. 13, 1775, Henry to Pendleton, Dec. 19, 23, 1775, *Henry*, I, p. 341, III, pp. 3–5; *Statutes*, IX, p. 83.

57. *Statutes*, IX, p. 101.

58. *Ibid.*, pp. 101–107; *Proceedings of the Convention, December 1775*, pp. 65–66, 91, 98–100.

59. *Proceedings of the Convention, December 1775*, pp. 15, 26–28, 56–58, 62–63, 89–91, 94–95; Curtis, "Goodrich Family," pp. 61–64.

60. *Statutes*, IX, pp. 75–92, 198.

61. Leven Powell to Sally Powell, Dec. 31, 1775, Robert C. Powell, ed., *A Biographical Sketch of Col. Leven Powell, Including His Correspondence During the Revolutionary War* (Alexandria, Va., 1877), pp. 21–23. See also *Va. Gaz.* (Dixon and Hunter), Mar. 16, 1776.

62. Harrison to Jefferson, Feb. 13, 1776, Edmund C. Burnett, ed., *Letters of Members of the Continental Congress* (Washington, D. C., 1921–1936), I, p. 347; *Journals of the Continental Congress*, IV, p. 132; *Proceedings of the Convention, December 1775*, pp. 78–79.

63. *Proceedings of the Convention, December 1775*, pp. 7, 34, 75, 97; *Statutes*, IX, pp. 92–101.

64. *Statutes*, IX, p. 93. See also *ibid.*, p. 95; and *Proceedings of the Convention, December 1775*, p. 104.

Chapter 5. INDEPENDENCE

1. Woodford to Pendleton, Dec. 19, 22, 1775, "Letters of Woodford, Howe and Lee," pp. 134–137; Scott to Southall, Dec. 17, 1775, *American Archives*, 4th Ser., IV, p. 292.

2. Capt. Ballard to Henry, Dec. 20, 1775, *Henry*, I, p. 337n.

3. Pendleton to Woodford, Mar. 16, 1776, *Letters and Papers of Pendleton*, II, p. 92. See also Pendleton to Woodford, Jan. 5, 1776, *ibid.*, I, p. 147; *Va. Gaz.* (Dixon and Hunter), Jan. 20, 1776; *ibid.* (Pinkney), Jan. 20, 1776; *ibid.* (Purdie), Feb. 2, 1776; and Woodford to Pendleton, Dec. 26, 1775, "Letters of Woodford, Howe and Lee," pp. 140–143.

4. Woodford and R. Howe to Mayor of Norfolk, n.d., Woodford and R. Howe to Pendleton, Dec. 16, 1775, Woodford to Pendleton, Dec. 22, 1775, R. Howe to Pendleton, Dec. 22, 1775, "Letters of Woodford, Howe and Lee," pp. 129, 131–132, 136–139.

5. Woodford to Pendleton, Dec. 17, 1775, *American Archives*, 4th Ser., IV, pp. 292–293.

6. R. Howe to Dunmore, Dec. 25, 1775, *ibid.*, p. 474. See also R. Howe to Pendleton, Dec. 25, 28, 1775, Dunmore to R. Howe, Dec. 25, 1775, *ibid.*, pp. 452–453, 474; Dunmore to Dartmouth, Dec. 6, 1775–Feb. 13, 1776, and Henry Bellew to R. Howe, Dec. 24, 1775, C.O. 5/1353, fols. 326, 344.

7. Dunmore to R. Howe, Dec. 26, 1775, *American Archives*, 4th Ser., IV, p. 474.

8. R. Howe to Dunmore, Dec. 27, 1775, *ibid.*, pp. 474–475; Woodford to Pendleton, Dec. 30, 1775, "Letters of Woodford, Howe and Lee," pp. 144–146; *Va. Gaz.* (Purdie), Jan. 5, 1776, supp.; Bellew to R. Howe, R. Howe to Bellew, Dec. 30, 1775, C.O. 5/1353, fol. 345.

9. Dunmore to Dartmouth, Dec. 6, 1775–Feb. 13, 1776, C.O. 5/1353, fol. 326. See also Woodford to Col. Elliott, Jan. 4, 1776, and *Va. Gaz.* (Dunmore), Jan. 15, 1776, *American Archives*, 4th Ser., IV, pp. 539, 540–541.

10. R. Howe and Woodford to Va. Convention, Jan. 1, 1776, "Letters of Woodford, Howe and Lee," p. 147.

11. R. Howe to Pendleton, Jan. 2, 1776, *ibid.*, p. 149. See also Woodford to Pendleton, Dec. 30, 1775, Jan. 5, 1776, *ibid.*, pp. 144–146, 150–152.

12. James Leitch's deposition, No. 11, Auditor's Item 177, Va. State Lib.

13. William Campbell to Margaret Campbell, Jan. 15, 1776, Campbell-Preston Papers, Lib. Cong., microfilm, Foundation Lib.

14. Robert Tolbot's deposition, Oct. 4, 1782, Princess Anne County Petitions, Va. State Lib.; John Roger's deposition, No. 3, Auditor's Item 177.

15. James Parker's memorial to the Loyalist Commission, Mar. 9, 1784, PA-16.36, Parker Family Papers.

16. Losses from the British: Norfolk, Va. State Lib. See also William Ivey's deposition, No. 10, Auditor's Item 177; and Caleb Herbert's deposition, Oct. 2, 1792, Princess Anne Co. Petitions.

17. Report of the committee to investigate the burning of Norfolk, 1776, *Journal of the House of Delegates . . . 1835–1836* (Richmond, Va., 1835), Document 43, p. 16.

18. Committee of Safety, resolution, Jan. 16, 1776, Pendleton to Woodford, Jan. 16, 1776, Burk, *History of Virginia,* IV, pp. 110–111 and n. See also Greene, ed., *Diary of Landon Carter,* II, p. 968; Honyman Diary, Jan. 21, 1776; Annie Christian to Annie Fleming, Jan. 14, 1776, Misc. MSS, Va. Hist. Soc.; William Cabell Diary, Jan. 23, 1776, W. H. Cabell Papers, Va. State Lib.; and *Proceedings of the Convention, December 1775,* pp. 86–87.

19. *Va. Gaz.* (Dunmore), Jan. 15, 1776, *American Archives,* 4th Ser., IV, pp. 540–541; Order of Committee of Safety, Jan. 31, 1776, "Virginia Legislative Papers," p. 252; Petition of the mayor of Norfolk, Nov. 17, 1776, Norfolk County Petitions, Va. State Lib.; *Pendleton,* II, pp. 82–83; *Journal of the House of Delegates, 1835–1836,* Document 43.

20. R. Howe to Woodford, Feb. 9, 1776, Burk, *History of Virginia,* IV, p. 111. See also *Journal of the House of Delegates, 1835–1836,* Document 43; and *Va. Gaz.* (Purdie), Jan. 26, Feb. 9, 1776.

21. S. Adams to James Warren, Jan. 7, 1776, *Warren-Adams Letters* (Mass. Hist. Soc., *Colls.,* LXXII [Boston, 1917]), I, p. 200.

22. Washington to Reed, Jan. 31, 1776, *Writings of Washington,* IV, p. 297. See also J. Page to Woodford, Jan. 2, 1776, Burk, *History of Virginia,* IV, p. 110n; and J. Page to R. H. Lee, Feb. 3, 1776, Lee Family Papers, Alderman Lib.

23. For the most recent discussion of Paine's impact, see Eric Foner, *Tom Paine and Revolutionary America* (New York, 1976), chap. 3, quotation on p. 78.

24. F. L. Lee to L. Carter, Mar. 18, 1776, John H. Hazelton, *The Declaration of Independence: Its History* (New York, 1906), pp. 93–94; Washington to Reed, Apr. 1, 1776, *Writings of Washington,* IV, p. 455. See also Thomas Jefferson, *Notes on the State of Virginia,* ed. William Peden (Chapel Hill, N. C., 1955), p. 122; J. Page to R. H. Lee, Feb. 3, 1776, Lee Family Papers, Alderman Lib.; *Va. Gaz.* (Purdie), Feb. 2, 1776; *ibid.* (Pinkney), Feb. 3, 1776; and Greene, ed., *Diary of Landon Carter,* II, pp. 986–987.

25. J. Adams, Autobiography, Aug. 12, 1776, in William James Morgan, ed., *Naval Documents of The American Revolution,* VI (Washington, D. C., 1972), p. 157. See also Thomas Jefferson's Notes on Hopkins's Defense, Aug. 12, 1776, Journal of the Continental Congress, Aug. 16, 1776, *ibid.,* pp. 195–198, 209; and R. H. Lee to [A. Lee], July 6, 1783, *Letters of R. H. Lee,* II, pp. 285–286.

26. Account of A. S. Hamond's part in The American Revolution (1775–1777), Feb. 12–27, 1776, A. S. Hamond Naval Papers, 1766–1825, roll I, Alderman Lib., microfilm, Foundation Lib.

27. Dunmore to Dartmouth, Dec. 6, 1775–Feb. 13, 1776, C.O. 5/1353, fol. 334.

28. Eric Robson, "The Expedition to the Southern Colonies, 1775–1776,"

English Historical Review, LXVI (1951), pp. 535–560; William B. Willcox, ed., *The American Rebellion: Sir Henry Clinton's Narrative of His Campaigns, 1775–1782, with an Appendix of Original Documents* (New Haven, Conn., 1954), pp. 24–28.

29. Dunmore to Dartmouth, Dec. 6, 1775–Feb. 13, 1776, C.O. 5/1353, fol. 334.

30. John Richard Alden, *The American Revolution, 1775–1783* (New York, 1954), pp. 95–96.

31. Dunmore to Corbin, Jan. 22, 1776, *Va. Gaz.* (Purdie), Mar. 1, 1776.

32. J. Page to R. H. Lee, Feb. 20, 1776, *American Archives,* 4th Ser., IV, p. 1208. See also Greene, ed., *Diary of Landon Carter,* II, pp. 988–989; Committee of Safety to Corbin, Feb. 19, 1776, *Va. Gaz.* (Purdie), Mar. 1, 1776; and Dunmore to Dartmouth, Dec. 6, 1775–Feb. 13, 1776, C.O. 5/1353, fol. 333.

33. Parker to Steuart, Feb. 21, 1776, MS 5029, fol. 149, Steuart Papers. See also *American Archives,* 4th Ser., IV, pp. 1210, 1506–1507; and L. Powell to S. Powell, Feb. 24, 1776, Leven Powell Letters, Alderman Lib.

34. *Va. Gaz.* (Dixon and Hunter), Mar. 2, 9, 1776.

35. *Ibid.,* Mar. 30, 1776; *ibid.* (Purdie), Mar. 1, 15, 22, 1776; Pendleton to Woodford, Mar. 16, 1776, *Letters and Papers of Pendleton,* I, pp. 158–159; John Adams to Abigail Adams, Feb. 13, 1776, L. H. Butterfield et al., eds., *Adams Family Correspondence* (Cambridge, Mass., 1963–1973), I, p. 347; Reed to Washington, Mar. 15, 1776, *American Archives,* 4th Ser., V, pp. 234–235; *Journals of the Continental Congress,* IV, p. 181.

36. *Va. Gaz.* (Purdie), Mar. 1, 1776.

37. Pendleton to Woodford, Mar. 16, 1776, *Letters and Papers of Pendleton,* I, p. 159. See also John T. Goolrick, *The Life of General Hugh Mercer* (New York, 1906), pp. 44–45; *Journal of the House of Delegates of . . . Virginia; Begun on the Third Day of May . . . 1779* (Richmond, Va., 1827), pp. 41–42; *Va. Gaz.* (Dixon and Hunter), Mar. 30, 1776; and *ibid.* (Purdie), Mar. 22, 1776.

38. *Va. Gaz.* (Purdie), Apr. 5, 1776.

39. Charles Lee to Henry, July 29, 1776, *Lee Papers,* II, p. 177. See also John Richard Alden, *General Charles Lee: Traitor or Patriot?* (Baton Rouge, La., 1951); and *Va. Gaz.* (Dixon and Hunter), Mar. 30, 1776.

40. C. Lee to John Hancock, May 7, 1776, *Lee Papers,* I, p. 480.

41. C. Lee to Washington, Apr. 5, 1776, *ibid.,* p. 377. See also C. Lee to R. H. Lee, Apr. 5, 1776, *ibid.,* pp. 379–380.

42. C. Lee to Washington, Apr. 5, 1776, *ibid.*, p. 377.

43. James McClurg to Jefferson, Apr. 6, 1776, J. Page to Jefferson, Apr. 26, 1776, *Papers of Jefferson*, I, pp. 286–289.

44. Jefferson to J. Randolph, Nov. 29, 1775, *ibid.*, pp. 268–270; Alden, *General Charles Lee*, pp. 116–117; J. Adams to R. H. Lee, Nov. 15, 1775, J. Adams to John Taylor, Apr. 9, 1814, Charles Francis Adams, ed., *The Works of John Adams* (Boston, 1856–1865), IV, pp. 185–187, X, p. 95; Evans, *Nelson*, p. 112; F. L. Lee to L. Carter, Jan. 22, 1776, photostat, Foundation Lib., original owned by Dr. Joseph E. Fields, Williamsburg, Va.

45. C. Lee to R. H. Lee, Apr. 5, 1776, *Lee Papers*, I, pp. 379–380.

46. Alexander Speirs to [William] Molleson, Aug. 25, 1776, C.O. 5/154, fols. 418–421. See also Lt. Col. Frank Eppes to C. Lee, Mar. 31, 1776, *Lee Papers*, I, pp. 365–366.

47. C. Lee to R. H. Lee, Apr. 12, 1776, *Lee Papers*, I, p. 417. See also R. H. Lee to C. Lee, Apr. 1, 1776, *ibid.*, pp. 367–368; *Va. Gaz.* (Dixon and Hunter), Apr. 20, 1776; J. Page to R. H. Lee, Apr. 12, 1776, *SLM*, p. 255; and J. Page to Jefferson, Apr. 26, 1776, *Papers of Jefferson*, I, pp. 288–290.

48. Pendleton to C. Lee, Apr. 25, 1776, *Lee Papers*, I, pp. 451–452. See also Robert Morris to Gen. Gates, Apr. 6, 1776, Committee of Safety to C. Lee, Apr. 10, 1776, J. Page to C. Lee, Apr. 28, 1776, Pendleton to C. Lee, May 2, 1776, C. Lee to R. Morris, May 2, 1776, R. H. Lee to C. Lee, May 11, 1776, *ibid.*, pp. 388, 403–405, 455–456, 463–464, 467, II, pp. 24–26; J. Page to R. H. Lee, Apr. 20, 1776, *Pendleton*, II, p. 94; and Robert Carter to C. Lee, Apr. 22, 1776, Robert Carter Letter Books, 1772–1785, III, p. 17, Duke University Library, Durham, N. C., microfilm, Foundation Lib.

49. Proceedings at a Council of Officers, Apr. 6, 1776, C. Lee to the president of the Committee of Safety, Apr. 8, 1776, *Lee Papers*, I, pp. 387, 393–394.

50. J. Page to Maryland Committee of Safety, Apr. 12, 1776, Maryland Committee of Safety to Maryland congressional delegates, Apr. 17, 1776, Col. Smallwood to Maryland Committee of Safety, Apr. 18, 1776, *American Archives*, 4th Ser., V, pp. 928, 960, 969; Memorial of Alexander Ross to Commissioners of the Treasury, Apr. 14, 1779, T. 1/549, fols. 192–193; *Va. Gaz.* (Purdie), Apr. 12, 1776.

51. *Va. Gaz.* (Purdie), Apr. 12, 1776; Alden, *General Charles Lee*, p. 108.

52. R. Wormeley, Jr., to John Grymes, Apr. 4, 1776, *Va. Gaz.* (Purdie), Apr. 26, 1776, supp. See also *ibid.*, May 3, 1776; Committee of Safety to C. Lee, Apr. 10, 1776, and C. Lee to Col. Muhlenburg, Apr. 23, 1776, *Lee Papers*, I, pp. 404, 444–445.

53. C. Lee to Pendleton, May 4, 1776, *Lee Papers*, I, pp. 467–469. See also *Va. Gaz.* (Purdie), Apr. 26, 1776.

54. C. Lee to Henry, May 7, 1776, *Lee Papers*, II, pp. 1–3.

55. Woodford to Committee of Safety, May 16, 1776, Misc. MSS, Hist. Soc. Pa.; J. Page to C. Lee, Apr. 28, 1776, Resolve of the Committee of Safety, May 3, 1776, *Lee Papers*, I, pp. 455–457, 464–465.

56. C. Lee to Pendleton, May 9, 1776, *Lee Papers*, II, pp. 15–16. See also C. Lee to R. H. Lee, Apr. 12, 1776, C. Lee to President of Congress, Apr. 19, 1776, *ibid.*, pp. 417, 433–434; Otway Byrd to W. Byrd III, May 6, 1776, "Letters of the Byrd Family," *VMHB*, XXXIX (1931), p. 226; Journal of the Committee of Safety, Feb. 8, Mar. 14, June 12, 1776, *Journals of the Council*, II, pp. 408, 453, I, p. 17; Alden, *General Charles Lee*, pp. 119–120; and John Augustine Washington to R. H. Lee, May 18, 1776, *SLM*, p. 330.

57. J. Page to R. H. Lee, Apr. 12, 1776, *SLM*, p. 255.

58. Jefferson to Thomas Nelson, May 16, 1776, *Papers of Jefferson*, I, p. 292.

59. Aylett to R. H. Lee, Apr. 20, 1776, *SLM*, p. 326; Minutes of the Cumberland County meeting, Apr. 22, 1776, *WMQ*, 1st Ser., II (1893–1894), pp. 252–255.

60. J. Adams to Warren, Apr. 20, 1776, *Warren-Adams Letters*, I, pp. 230–232; S. Adams to Samuel Cooper, Apr. 30, 1776, *WMQ*, 1st Ser., XIX (1910–1911), p. 249; Elbridge Gerry to Warren, May 1, 1776, *American Archives*, 4th Ser., V, p. 1163.

61. Robert Brent to R. H. Lee, Apr. 28, 1776, Lee Family Papers, Alderman Lib.; Pendleton to R. H. Lee, Apr. 8, 1776, Address to Virginia Convention of 1776 [May 6, 1776], *Letters and Papers of Pendleton*, I, pp. 175–176; Apr. 1, 1776, Robert Wormeley Carter Diary, 1776, Swem Lib., microfilm, Foundation Lib.; Greene, ed., *Diary of Landon Carter*, II, pp. 1008–1009, 1013; Josiah Parker to L. Carter, Apr. 14, 1776, Landon Carter Papers; McClurg to Jefferson, Apr. 6, 1776, *Papers of Jefferson*, I, p. 287; *Proceedings of the Convention, May 1776*, p. 5; Disputed election of William Aylett, Papers of the Committee on Privileges and Elections, *Papers of Madison*, I, pp. 165–169; *Va. Gaz.* (Purdie), Apr. 26, 1776.

62. *Va. Gaz.* (Purdie), May 10, 1776.

63. *Proceedings of the Convention, May 1776*, pp. 5–30.

64. *History of Virginia*, p. 251. Randolph attended the Convention as a representative of the College of William and Mary.

65. C. Lee to Henry, May 7, 1776, *Lee Papers*, II, p. 1.

66. *Henry*, I, pp. 394–396, quotation on p. 394; *Letters and Papers of Pendleton*, I, p. 179n.

67. Resolutions of the Virginia Convention Calling upon Congress for a Declaration of Independence, *Letters and Papers of Pendleton*, I, pp. 178–179; *Pendleton*, II, pp. 108–110.

68. Henry to J. Adams, May 20, 1776, Henry to R. H. Lee, May 20, 1776, *Henry*, I, pp. 410–413.

69. *History of Virginia*, p. 251; *Proceedings of the Convention, May 1776*, pp. 31–33; Thomas Ludwell Lee to R. H. Lee, May 18, 1776, J. A. Washington to R. H. Lee, May 18, 1776, *SLM*, pp. 324–325, 330.

70. T. L. Lee to R. H. Lee, May 18, 1776, *SLM*, pp. 324–325.

71. *Va. Gaz.* (Purdie), May 17, 1776.

72. *Ibid.* (Dixon and Hunter), May 18, 1776; T. L. Lee to R. H. Lee, May 18, 1776, *SLM*, pp. 324–325.

73. Hazelton, *Declaration of Independence*, p. 90. See also *ibid.*, pp. 87–88; R. H. Lee to C. Lee, May 27, 1776, R. H. Lee to T. L. Lee, May 28, 1776, *Letters of R. H. Lee*, I, pp. 195–196; and *Pennsylvania Evening Post* (Philadelphia), May 28, 1776.

74. Apr. 12, 1776, *American Archives*, 4th Ser., V, p. 860. See also Hazelton, *Declaration of Independence*, pp. 55–56.

75. Edmund Cody Burnett, *The Continental Congress* (New York, 1941), p. 158.

76. *Ibid.*, p. 171.

77. *Ibid.*, pp. 171–174.

78. Hazelton, *Declaration of Independence*, pp. 166–178; *Papers of Jefferson*, I, pp. 338, 357, 426; McColley, *Slavery and Jeffersonian Virginia*, pp. 116–117.

79. *Va. Gaz.* (Dixon and Hunter), July 29, 1776. See also *ibid.*, July 30, Aug. 10, 1776; *ibid.* (Purdie), July 19, 26, 1776; Hazelton, *Declaration of Independence*, p. 240; and *Journals of the Council*, I, p. 83.

Chapter 6. "HOW FEW . . . HAVE EVER ENJOYED . . . AN ELECTION OF GOVERNMENT"

1. Mason to R. H. Lee, May 18, 1776, *Papers of Mason*, I, p. 271.

2. *Ibid.*, p. 276.

3. *Ibid.*, pp. 276–278.

4. *Ibid.*, pp. 278, 284–285.

5. *Ibid.*, pp. 277, 283.

6. *Ibid.*, p. 278. See also Irving Brant, *James Madison, The Virginia Revolutionist* (New York, 1941), p. 237.

7. The discussion of the distribution of the Virginia Declaration of Rights in this and following paragraphs is based on R. Carter Pittman, *VMHB*, LXVIII (1960), pp. 109–111; Gilbert Chinard, "Notes on the French Translations of the 'Forms of Government or Constitutions of the Several United States' 1778 and 1783," American Philosophical Society, *Year Book 1943* (Philadelphia, 1944), pp. 88–106; Durand Echeverria, "French Publications of the Declaration of Independence and the American Constitutions, 1776–1783," *Papers of the Bibliographical Society of America*, XLVII (1953), pp. 313–338; and Brant, *Madison the Revolutionist*, p. 428.

8. *Pa. Evening Post*, June 6, 1776; Francis N. Thorpe, comp., *The Federal and State Constitutions, Colonial Charters, and Other Organic Laws of the States, Territories, and Colonies Now or Heretofore Forming the United States of America* (Washington, D. C., 1909), I, pp. 562–568, III, pp. 1681–1701, IV, pp. 2451–2453, V, pp. 2787–2798, VI, pp. 3737–3749.

9. *New York Gazette, and Weekly Mercury* (New York, N. Y.), June 17, 1776.

10. S. G. Tucker's copy is in the Tucker-Coleman Collection.

11. Chinard, "Notes on French Translations of the Constitutions," pp. 105–106; John Bach McMaster and Frederick D. Stone, eds., *Pennsylvania and the Federal Constitution, 1787–1788* (Philadelphia, 1888), pp. 252–253.

12. Information of spy, May 3, 1776, C.O. 5/1353, fol. 383.

13. Account of Hamond, May 26, 1776. See also *ibid.*, May 22, 25, 1776; and Capt. Hamond to Adm. Shuldham, Nov. 28, 1776, Adm. 1/487, fol. 294.

14. Hamond to Shuldham, Nov. 28, 1776, Adm. 1/487, fol. 294.

15. Account of Hamond, May 25, 1776. See also Dunmore to Germain, June 26, 1776, C.O. 5/1353, fol. 385; Deposition of William Barry, June 11, 1776, *American Archives*, 4th Ser., VI, pp. 810–811; and Hamond to Shuldham, Nov. 28, 1776, Adm. 1/487, fol. 294.

16. Hamond to Sir Peter Parker, June 10, 1776, Letter Book, Hamond Naval Papers, roll 2. See also *Va. Gaz.* (Dixon and Hunter), June 1, 1776.

17. Christopher Ward, *The War of the Revolution*, ed. John Richard Alden (New York, 1952), pp. 662–664; Robson, "Expedition to Southern Colonies," pp. 535–560.

18. Deposition of John Emmes, June 21, 1776, *American Archives,* 4th Ser., VI, p. 1008. See also Montagu to Gov. Robert Eden, June 23, 1776, Maryland Convention, resolution, June 24, 1776, Montagu to Convention, June 25, 1776, *ibid.,* pp. 1034, 1044–1045, 1046; and Dunmore to Germain, June 26, 1776, C.O. 5/1353, fol. 385.

19. Andrew Lewis to C. Lee, May 27, 1776, *Lee Papers,* II, pp. 42–45.

20. Lewis to C. Lee, June 12, 1776, *ibid.,* pp. 62–65; *Va. Gaz.* (Dixon and Hunter), June 1, 22, 1776; *Proceedings of the Convention, May 1776,* pp. 150–151; Caley, "Dunmore," pp. 817–818; Arthur Campbell to Fincastle County Committee of Safety, May 28, 1776, Richard Barksdale Harwell, ed., *The Committees of Safety of Westmoreland and Fincastle: Proceedings of the County Committees, 1774–1776* (Richmond, Va., 1956), p. 108.

21. T. L. Lee to R. H. Lee, June 1, 1776, *SLM,* p. 325; *History of Virginia,* p. 253.

22. *Hudgins* v. *Wrights* (1806), Helen T. Catterall, ed., *Judicial Cases concerning American Slavery and the Negro. Cases from the Courts of England, Virginia, West Virginia, and Kentucky,* I (Washington, D. C., 1926), p. 112.

23. Winthrop D. Jordan, *White Over Black: American Attitudes Toward the Negro, 1550–1812* (Chapel Hill, N. C., 1968), pp. 350–351, 429–435; Leon F. Litwack, *North of Slavery: The Negro in the Free States, 1790–1860* (Chicago, 1961), p. 1; Donald L. Robinson, *Slavery in the Structure of American Politics, 1765–1820* (New York, 1971), pp. 71–88, 478, n. 72; Arthur Zilversmit, *The First Emancipation: The Abolition of Slavery in the North* (Chicago, 1967), pp. 199–200, 226–229.

24. J. Adams to Jeremy Belknap, Mar. 21, 1795, "Letters and Documents Relating to Slavery in Massachusetts" (Mass. Hist. Soc., *Colls.,* 5th Ser., III [Boston, 1877]), p. 401.

25. J. Hector St. John Crèvecoeur, *Letters from an American Farmer* (London, 1782), p. 43.

26. *Pendleton,* II, pp. 121–122.

27. *Papers of Madison,* I, pp. 172–174; Brant, *Madison the Revolutionist,* pp. 245–250.

28. Mason to [Brent?], Oct. 2, 1778, *Papers of Mason,* I, p. 434.

29. *Papers of Madison,* I, pp. 173–175.

30. *Ibid.;* Brant, *Madison the Revolutionist,* pp. 241–242, 247, 430, n. 16; *History of Virginia,* p. 254.

31. *History of Virginia*, p. 255. See also *Papers of Mason*, I, pp. 287–291.

32. John Adams, *Thoughts on Government* (1776), in Adams, ed., *Works of John Adams*, IV, p. 200. See also *Papers of Mason*, I, pp. 299–304.

33. Washington to J. A. Washington, May 31, 1776, *Writings of Washington*, V, p. 92.

34. *History of Virginia*, p. 251; Brant, *Madison the Revolutionist*, p. 252; *Papers of Jefferson*, I, pp. 345, 354.

35. Allan Nevins, *The American States During and After the Revolution, 1775–1789* (New York, 1924), pp. 128–129, 176–177; *History of Virginia*, p. 252; Charlotte County Committee, Apr. 23, 1776, *Va. Gaz.* (Purdie), May 10, 1776; Buckingham County Committee [May 1776], *American Archives*, 4th Ser., V, pp. 1206–1207; *Proceedings of the Convention, May 1776*, p. 21.

36. J. A. Washington to R. H. Lee, Apr. 22, 1776, *SLM*, pp. 328–329. See also *Papers of Jefferson*, I, p. 341.

37. R. H. Lee to [Henry], Apr. 20, 1776, *Letters of R. H. Lee*, I, p. 179; Page to Jefferson, Apr. 26, 1776, *Papers of Jefferson*, I, p. 288.

38. J. Adams to R. H. Lee, Nov. 15, 1776, The Adams Papers, microfilm, reel 345, Mass. Hist. Soc. See also John E. Selby, "Richard Henry Lee, John Adams, and the Virginia Constitution of 1776," *VMHB*, LXXXIV (1976), pp. 387–400.

39. R. H. Lee to R. C. Nicholas, Apr. 30, 1776, *Letters of R. H. Lee*, I, p. 184.

40. Henry to R. H. Lee, May 20, 1776, Henry to J. Adams, May 20, 1776, *Henry*, I, pp. 411, 412. See also *Papers of Jefferson*, I, p. 337n.

41. J. Adams to Warren, May 12, 1776, *Warren-Adams Letters*, I, pp. 242–243.

42. J. Adams to A. Adams, July 10, 1776, Butterfield et al., eds., *Adams Family Correspondence*, II, p. 42.

43. R. H. Lee to C. Lee, June 29, 1776, *Lee Papers*, II, pp. 97–99. See also Selby, "Lee, Adams, and the Virginia Constitution," p. 390.

44. J. Adams to A. Adams, Mar. 19, 1776, Butterfield et al., eds., *Adams Family Correspondence*, I, p. 363. See also Thomas Paine, *Common Sense* (1776), in Moncure Conway, ed., *The Writings of Thomas Paine*, I (New York, 1894), pp. 97–98.

45. R. H. Lee to C. Lee, June 29, 1776, *Lee Papers*, II, pp. 97–98.

46. *Va. Gaz.* (Purdie), June 7, 1776.

47. Adams, ed., *Works of John Adams,* IV, p. 195.

48. R. H. Lee to Henry, Apr. 20, 1776, *Henry,* I, p. 381; R. H. Lee to [Pendleton], May 12, 1776, *Letters of R. H. Lee,* I, pp. 190–191.

49. J. Adams to Warren, May 12, 1776, *Warren-Adams Letters,* I, pp. 242–243.

50. [Carter Braxton], *An Address to the Convention of the Colony and Ancient Dominion of Virginia, on the Subject of Government in general, and recommending a particular Form to their Consideration* (Philadelphia, 1776); Henry to J. Adams, May 20, 1776, *Henry,* I, pp. 412–413.

51. R. H. Lee to [Pendleton], May 12, 1776, *Letters of R. H. Lee,* I, pp. 190–191; *Henry,* I, pp. 412–413.

52. Gordon Wood, *The Creation of the American Republic, 1776–1787* (Chapel Hill, N. C., 1969), pp. 66–70, 91–124.

53. [Braxton], *Address to the Convention,* pp. 15–17. See also *ibid.,* pp. 11–12.

54. *Ibid.,* pp. 17–18; Bailyn, *Ideological Origins,* pp. 63–66, 287–288; Colbourn, *Lamp of Experience,* pp. 101–102.

55. *Papers of Jefferson,* I, p. 380. See also *ibid.,* pp. 366–368, 379–381; Adams, *Thoughts on Government,* in Adams, ed., *Works of John Adams,* IV, p. 197; Selby, "Lee, Adams, and the Virginia Constitution," p. 390; and *History of Virginia,* p. 255.

56. *History of Virginia,* p. 256.

57. *Papers of Jefferson,* I, p. 382. See also *ibid.,* pp. 366–369, 371–372, 379.

58. *Ibid.,* pp. 366, 379; *Statutes,* VIII, p. 305; Julius F. Prufer, "Franchise in Virginia From Jefferson through the Constitution of 1829," *WMQ,* 2nd Ser., VII (1927), pp. 256–259.

59. Jackson Turner Main, *The Upper House in Revolutionary America, 1763–1788* (Madison, Wis., 1967), pp. 124–132, 241; *Papers of Jefferson,* I, pp. 366, 379–380.

60. *Papers of Jefferson,* I, pp. 367, 381, 385n. The House of Delegates itself was apparently confused about the procedure, for in May 1777 it "reelected" the incumbents except Meriwether Smith. *Va. Gaz.* (Dixon and Hunter), May 30, 1777. It removed Thomas Walker and Benjamin Waller in 1779. *Journal of the House of Delegates, May 1779,* p. 62.

61. R. H. Lee to R. C. Nicholas, Apr. 30, 1776, R. H. Lee to [Pendleton], May 12, 1776, *Letters of R. H. Lee,* I, pp. 184, 190–191; *Henry,* I, p. 446; *Proceedings of the Convention, May 1776,* p. 168; Charles Carter to Fitzhugh, July 3, 1776,

VMHB, XVII (1909), p. 257; R. Carter to R. H. Lee, June 14, 1776, Robert Carter Letter Book, III, pp. 34–35.

62. J[ames] B[urgh], *Political Disquisitions: or, An Enquiry into Public Errors, Defects, and Abuses etc.* (London, 1774), II, no. ix, p. 97; *Papers of Jefferson*, I, pp. 341, 349, 359.

63. *Henry*, I, p. 438; Namier, *Structure of Politics*, pp. 1–2; Pares, *George III and the Politicians*, pp. 1–5; *Papers of Mason*, I, pp. 303n–304n.

64. *Papers of Jefferson*, I, pp. 343, 351–352, 361–362, 367, 371, 381–382.

65. *Ibid.*, p. 363. See also *ibid.*, pp. 344, 352–353, 362, 383.

66. *Ibid.*, pp. 337–338, 347, 358, 361, 363, 367, 379–383, 385, nn. 3, 16, 19.

67. *Proceedings of the Convention, May 1776*, pp. 168–185; *Papers of Mason*, I, pp. 313–314; *Statutes*, IX, pp. 119–122, 126–132, 135–143, 149–151.

68. J. Page to C. Lee, July 12, 1776, *Lee Papers*, II, pp. 131–136; *Journals of the Council*, I, pp. 67–68; *Proceedings of the Convention, May 1776*, pp. 168, 172, 174–175, 185; E. Randolph to Washington, Oct. 11, 1776, *American Archives*, 5th Scr., II, pp. 987–988; C. Carter to Fitzhugh, July 3, 1776, *VMHB*, XVII (1909), p. 257; *Henry*, I, pp. 451–452; J. Page to Jefferson, July 6, 1776, *Papers of Jefferson*, I, pp. 454–455.

69. J. Page to Jefferson, July 6, 1776, *Papers of Jefferson*, I, pp. 454–455. See also *ibid.*, VI, pp. 640–641.

70. Henry to Pendleton, Dec. 6, 1776, *Henry*, I, pp. 474–475; *Statutes*, IX, pp. 245–247; Journals of the Committee of Safety, *Journals of the Council*, I, pp. 1–66.

71. *Journals of the Council*, I, pp. 72, 76, 129, 188, 216–223, 225, 233; *Journal of the House of Delegates, 1776*, pp. 6–8, 223, 39, 81; John Tayloe to E. Randolph, Oct. 9, 1776, *VMHB*, XVII (1909), pp. 369–373; J. Page to C. Lee, July 12, 1776, *Lee Papers*, II, pp. 131–136; Executive Council to Jefferson, Nov. 13, 1779, *Papers of Jefferson*, III, pp. 183–184. Emory G. Evans, "Executive Leadership in Virginia, 1776–1781: Henry, Jefferson, and Nelson," in Ronald Hoffman and Peter J. Albert, eds., *Sovereign States in an Age of Uncertainty* (Charlottesville, Va., 1981), pp. 185–225, discusses the administrative evolution.

72. J. Page to S. G. Tucker, Sept. 28, 1776, Tucker-Coleman Collection. See also Susie M. Ames, "A Typical Virginia Business Man of the Revolutionary Era: Nathaniel Littleton Savage and his Account Book," *Journal of Economic and Business History*, III (1930–1931), pp. 407–423. For the general problem, see E. James Ferguson, *The Power of the Purse: A History of American Public Finance,*

1776–1790 (Chapel Hill, N. C., 1961), chap. 5. Aylett worried about the conflict. Aylett to [R. H. Lee], Nov. 26, 1776, State Agent's Loose Papers, 1795, Correspondence, William Aylett, 1775–1777, Va. State Lib., microfilm, Foundation Lib.

73. Jefferson to Samuel Huntington, July 27, 1780, *Papers of Jefferson*, III, p. 512.

74. Jefferson to Baron von Steuben, Feb. 12, 1781, *ibid.*, IV, pp. 593–594.

Chapter 7. THE WAR CONTINUES

1. R. H. Lee to [C. Lee], July 6, 1776, *Letters of R. H. Lee*, I, p. 206.

2. C. Lee to Pendleton, May 24, 1776, *Lee Papers*, II, pp. 34–35. See also C. Lee to Washington, July 1, 1776, *ibid.*, p. 102.

3. C. Lee to Lewis, June 6, 1776, Lewis to C. Lee, June 21, 1776, J. Page to Lee, July 12, 1776, *ibid.*, pp. 55, 62–65, 131–136; Lewis to Congress, June 18, 1776, *American Archives*, 4th Ser., VI, p. 948; J. Page to Jefferson, July 6, 1776, *Papers of Jefferson*, I, pp. 454–455; David Griffith to L. Powell, July 6, 1776, Powell, ed., *Biographical Sketch of Powell*, pp. 66–68.

4. For the description of the battle of Gwynn's Island in this and following paragraphs, see George Johnston, Jr., to L. Powell, July 13, 1776, Powell, ed., *Biographical Sketch of Powell*, pp. 36–37; J. Page to C. Lee, July 12, 1776, Adam Stephen to C. Lee, July 13, 1776, *Lee Papers*, II, pp. 131–136, 136–139; *Va. Gaz.* (Dixon and Hunter), July 20, 1776; James Parker's Journal, July 8–10, 1776, Parker Family Papers; Dunmore to Germain, July 31, 1776, C.O. 5/1353, fol. 393; Account of Hamond, July 8–11, 1776; Hamond to Shuldham, Nov. 28, 1776, Adm. 1/487, fol. 294; and J. Page to Jefferson, July 6, 20, 1776, *Papers of Jefferson*, I, pp. 454–455, 468–469.

5. Stephen to Jefferson, July 29, 1776, *Papers of Jefferson*, I, p. 481. See also Pendleton to Jefferson, July 29, 1776, *ibid.*, p. 480; Account of Hamond, July 23, 25, 1776; and Dunmore to Germain, July 31, 1776, C.O. 5/1353, fol. 393.

6. Account of Hamond, after July 29, 1776.

7. Edward H. Tatum, Jr., ed., *The American Journals of Ambrose Serle, Secretary of Lord Howe, 1776–1778* (San Marino, Calif., 1940), pp. 63–64. See also Account of Hamond, Aug. 4–5, 14, 1776; Hamond to Dunmore [Aug. 8, 1776], *Aspinwall Papers*, pp. 788–789; Hamond to Shuldham, Nov. 28, 1776, Adm. 1/487, fol. 294; Dunmore to Germain, July 31, postscript, Aug. 4, 1776, C.O. 5/1353, fols. 393–397; and Howe to Dartmouth, Aug. 15, 1776, Dartmouth MSS, II, p. 423.

8. Alden, *South in the Revolution,* p. 90; Lewis to Hancock, Aug. 3, Sept. 30, 1776, Papers of the Continental Congress, reel 178, item 159, pp. 242, 254; Hancock to Lewis, Sept. 3, 1776, *American Archives,* 5th Ser., II, pp. 135–136.

9. *Va. Gaz.* (Purdie), July 19, 1776. See also Charles Campbell, ed., *The Orderly Book of Andrew Lewis, from March 18th, 1776, to August 28th, 1776* (Richmond, Va., 1860), pp. 25, 49, 52, 55–56, 58, 61, 63, 67.

10. C. Lee to Benjamin Harrison, Jr., July 28, 1776, *Lee Papers,* II, p. 175. See also C. Lee to Henry, July 29, 1776, *ibid.,* p. 178; and Campbell, ed., *Orderly Book of Lewis,* pp. 41, 47, 51, 52, 58, 60, 72.

11. Campbell, ed., *Orderly Book of Lewis,* p. 58; Griffith to L. Powell, June 16, 1776, Powell Letters; R. H. Lee to [S. Adams], July 6, 1776, *Letters of R. H. Lee,* I, p. 207.

12. *Va. Gaz.* (Purdie), Aug. 9, 1776. See also George M'Intosh to L. Powell, July 7, 1776, "The Leven Powell Correspondence, 1775–1787," *John P. Branch Historical Papers of Randolph-Macon College,* No. 1 (1901), pp. 117–118.

13. Johnston to L. Powell, Aug. 6, 1776, Powell Letters. See also *Va. Gaz.* (Purdie), Aug. 9, 1776; Pendleton to Woodford, Oct. 11, 1776, *Letters and Papers of Pendleton,* I, pp. 202–203; and Lewis to Hancock, Aug. 3, 1776, Papers of the Continental Congress, reel 178, item 159, p. 242.

14. Lewis to Hancock, Aug. 3, Sept. 20, 1776, Papers of the Continental Congress, reel 178, item 159, pp. 242, 254; *Journals of the Council,* I, pp. 115, 153, 168, 175; Broadside, Aug. 20, 1776, Va. Misc. MSS, Lib. Cong.; J. Page to Hancock, July 20, Aug. 3, 1776, E. Randolph to Washington, Oct. 11, 1776, *American Archives,* 5th Ser., I, pp. 465, 736, II, pp. 987–988.

15. Hancock to the assemblies of the southern states, Nov. 15, 1776, Aylett to R. H. Lee, Nov. 30, 1776, *American Archives,* 5th Ser., III, pp. 697, 913–914; *Journals of the Council,* I, pp. 154, 173, 176; *Va. Gaz.* (Dixon and Hunter), Sept. 21, 1776; *Henry,* I, p. 491.

16. Jefferson to Pendleton, Aug. 13, 1776, *Papers of Jefferson,* I, p. 493; *Journal of the House of Delegates, 1776,* p. 8; Charles Lewis to Henry, Oct. 14, 1776, Dudley Digges to Pendleton, Nov. 16, 1776, *VMHB,* XVII (1909), pp. 58–59, 381–383; L. Carter to Washington, Oct. 13, 1776, *American Archives,* 5th Ser., II, pp. 1303–1307.

17. Henry to Hancock, Dec. 6, 1776, A. Lewis to Hancock, Dec. 21, 1776, *American Archives,* 5th Ser., III, pp. 1092, 1329; *Va. Gaz.* (Purdie), Dec. 20, 1776; *Statutes,* IX, pp. 192, 198; Alden, *American Revolution,* pp. 97–111.

18. *Henry,* I, pp. 505–506. See also *Va. Gaz.* (Dixon and Hunter), Dec. 20, 1776; and *Journal of the House of Delegates, 1776,* pp. 107–108.

19. *Papers of Mason,* I, p. 326.

20. *Ibid.*, p. 327n.

21. *History of Virginia*, p. 281.

22. *Papers of Mason*, I, p. 326.

23. Henry to [governor of North Carolina?], Dec. 23, 1776, Misc. MSS, Hist. Soc. Pa. See also *American Archives*, 5th Ser., III, pp. 1425–1426; and *Va. Gaz.* (Purdie), Dec. 27, 1776.

24. John Banister to Bland, June 10, 1777, *Bland Papers*, I, p. 56. See also Malone, *Jefferson the Virginian*, pp. 305, 360–362.

25. Pendleton to Woodford, May 15, 1777, *Letters and Papers of Pendleton*, I, p. 209.

26. Henry to R. H. Lee, Mar. 28, 1777, *Official Letters of Governors*, I, p. 129; R. H. Lee to Jefferson, May 20, 1777, *Papers of Jefferson*, II, p. 20; Honyman Diary, Jan. 6, Mar. 4, 1777; *Va. Gaz.* (Dixon and Hunter), June 15, 1776; *ibid.* (Purdie), Feb. 14, 28, Mar. 28, 1777, supp.

27. For the discussion in this and the following paragraph, see *Va. Gaz.* (Purdie), Feb. 14, 21, Mar. 14, 1777; Aylett to Hancock, Apr. 18, 1777, Papers of the Continental Congress, reel 90, I, p. 77; Banister to Bland, Mar. 27, 1777, *Bland Papers*, I, p. 51; General Return of the 12 Virginia regiments in camp, May 17, 1777, Executive Papers, Box 2, Va. State Lib.; *Statutes*, IX, p. 338; and Charles H. Lesser, ed., *The Sinews of Independence: Monthly Strength Reports of the Continental Army* (Chicago, 1976).

28. Jefferson to J. Adams, May 16, 1777, *Papers of Jefferson*, II, p. 18.

29. *Statutes*, IX, pp. 275–280.

30. Honyman Diary, Aug. 29, 1777; Prince William County Court, Oct. 6, 1777, Executive Communications, Box 1, Va. State Lib.; Jones to Washington, Aug. 11, 1777, Worthington C. Ford, ed., *Letters of Joseph Jones of Virginia, 1777–1787* (Washington, D. C., 1889), p. 1; Granville Smith to L. Powell, Aug. 28, 1777, "Leven Powell Correspondence," p. 125; Cole Digges to Bland, Sept. 16, 1777, *Bland Papers*, I, p. 69; *Va. Gaz.* (Dixon and Hunter), Sept. 26, 1777; *ibid.* (Purdie), Oct. 3, 1777.

31. R. H. Lee to Henry, Oct. 8, 1777, *Letters of R. H. Lee*, I, pp. 326–327. See also R. H. Lee to Henry, Nov. 24, 1777, Virginia Delegates in Congress to Henry, Nov. 27, 1777, R. H. Lee to Henry, Jan. 7, 1778, *ibid.*, pp. 364, 367–369 and n., 376–378; and J. Page to R. H. Lee, Nov. 9, 1777, Lee Family Papers, Alderman Lib.

32. *Journals of the Council*, I, p. 389, II, p. 167; J. Page to R. H. Lee, Oct. 17, 1777, M. Page to R. H. Lee, May 21, 1778, *SLM*, pp. 257–258, 261–262; R. H.

Lee to Jefferson, May 11, 1778, *Papers of Jefferson*, II, pp. 177–178; Henry to R. H. Lee, Dec. 18, 1777, *Henry*, III, p. 133.

33. Alden, *American Revolution*, pp. 112–122.

34. *Va. Gaz.* (Purdie), Aug. 22, 1777. See also *ibid.*, Aug. 15, 1777.

35. *Ibid.*, Aug. 22, 1777. See also *ibid.* (Dixon and Hunter), Aug. 22, 1777; *Journals of the Council*, I, pp. 463–470; and Honyman Diary, Sept. 2, 1777.

36. Honyman Diary, Sept. 21, Oct. 1, 1777; Henry to Berkeley County Lieutenant, Aug. 30, 1777, Morristown National Historical Park, Morristown, N. J., microfilm, Foundation Lib.; Evans, *Nelson*, pp. 67–68; *Va. Gaz.* (Purdie), Sept. 26, 1777; *Journals of the Council*, I, p. 490; M. Page to R. H. Lee, Oct. 14, 1777, *SLM*, p. 261.

37. *SLM*, p. 261. See also Alden, *American Revolution*, pp. 122–126.

38. *Journals of the Council*, II, pp. 1, 5; Evans, *Nelson*, pp. 67–68; M. Page to R. H. Lee, Oct. 14, 1777, *SLM*, p. 261; *Statutes*, IX, p. 338; Honyman Diary, July 13, 1777; Washington to Nelson, Sept. 27, 1777, Washington to commander of Va. militia, Sept. 27, 1777, *Writings of Washington*, IX, pp. 271, 273–274.

39. *Va. Gaz.* (Dixon and Hunter), Oct. 31, 1777. See also *ibid.* (Purdie), Nov. 21, 1777; Alden, *American Revolution*, pp. 128–149; and Evans, *Nelson*, p. 70.

40. Harrison, Sr., to R. Morris, June 8, 1778, Morristown Natl. Hist. Park; M. Page to R. H. Lee, May 21, 1778, *SLM*, pp. 261–262. See also J. Page to W. Lee, Mar. 12, 1778, Misc. MSS, Va. Hist. Soc.; Banister to S. G. Tucker, Apr. 23, 1778, Tucker-Coleman Collection; Henry to R. H. Lee, May 15, 1778, Lee Family Papers, Alderman Lib.; and Jefferson to R. H. Lee, Aug. 30, 1778, *Papers of Jefferson*, II, p. 210.

41. *Statutes*, IX, pp. 337–349, quotation on p. 339.

42. Pendleton to Washington, Dec. 22, 1776, *Letters and Papers of Pendleton*, I, pp. 276–277.

43. *Statutes*, IX, pp. 337–349; George Weedon to R. H. Lee, Feb. 1, 1778, Lee Family Papers, Alderman Lib.; Washington to T. Nelson, Feb. 6, 1778, Washington to R. H. Lee, Feb. 15, 1778, *Writings of Washington*, X, pp. 432, 466.

44. Honyman Diary, Feb. 22, 1778. See also Harrison, Sr., to R. Morris, Feb. 19, 1778, Stan V. Henkels, ed., *The Confidential Correspondence of Robert Morris* (Philadelphia, 1917), pp. 17–18.

45. *Journals of the Council*, II, pp. 93–94; James Parker's Journal, May 1, 1778, Parker Family Papers; F. L. Lee to R. H. Lee, June 25, 1778, *SLM*, p. 259. But see Pendleton to Woodford, Feb. 15, 1778, *Letters and Papers of Pendleton*, I,

pp. 250–251; R. H. Lee to [S. Adams], Mar. 1, 1778, *Letters of R. H. Lee*, I, pp. 390–391; and Washington to R. H. Lee, May 25, 1778, *Writings of Washington*, IX, p. 452.

46. John Parke Custis to Washington, July 15, 1778, Edward G. W. Butler Papers, 1778–1780, Duke University Lib. See also *Va. Gaz.* (Dixon and Hunter), May 15, 1778; M. Page to R. H. Lee, May 21, 1778, F. L. Lee to R. H. Lee, June 25, 1778, *SLM*, pp. 259, 261–262; and *Statutes*, IX, pp. 445–456, 458, 580–581, 588–592.

47. Wood to Washington, Nov. 12, 1778, Kate Mason Rowland, *The Life of George Mason, 1725–1792* (New York, 1892), I, p. 306.

48. Resolutions Recommending Additional Land Bounties for Troops Serving with the Virginia Regiments, Dec. 19, 1778, *Papers of Mason*, I, p. 465; *Statutes*, IX, pp. 566–567, 580–581.

49. Washington to Henry, Oct. 7, 1778, *Writings of Washington*, XIII, p. 46. See also Wood to Washington, Nov. 12, 1778, Rowland, *Mason*, I, pp. 306–307.

Chapter 8. PERFECTING THE REPUBLIC

1. Malone, *Jefferson the Virginian*, p. 245; George Wythe to Jefferson, Oct. 28, 1776, *Papers of Jefferson*, I, p. 585.

2. Harrison, Jr., to R. Morris, June 7, 1776, Clarence L. Ver Steeg, *Robert Morris: Revolutionary Financier* (Philadelphia, 1954), p. 209n; *Proceedings of the Convention, May 1776*, p. 175. See also E. Randolph to Jefferson, June 23, 1776, Pendleton to Jefferson, July 22, 1776, William Fleming to Jefferson, July 27, 1776, *Papers of Jefferson*, I, pp. 407, 472, 475; L. H. Butterfield et al., eds., *Diary and Autobiography of John Adams*, III (Cambridge, Mass., 1961), pp. 367–368; and *Pendleton*, I, chap. 11, Appendix II.

3. Pendleton to Woodford, Oct. 11, 1776, *Letters and Papers of Pendleton*, I, p. 203. See also E. Randolph to Washington, Oct. 11, 1776, *American Archives*, 5th Ser., II, pp. 987, 988; and Braxton to L. Carter, Oct. 16, 1776, John Carter Matthews, "Richard Henry Lee and the American Revolution" (Ph.D. diss., University of Virginia, 1939), I, pp. 197–198.

4. Jefferson, "Autobiography," in Ford, ed., *Works of Jefferson*, I, p. 59; Pendleton to Jefferson, Aug. 3, 10, 26, 1776, Jefferson to Pendleton, Aug. 13, 26, 1776, *Papers of Jefferson*, I, pp. 484, 488, 503, 491, 507.

5. Braxton to L. Carter, Dec. 19, 1776, Dearborn Collection, Houghton Lib.

6. Jefferson, "Autobiography," in Ford, ed., *Works of Jefferson*, I, p. 77.

7. Jefferson, *Notes on Virginia*, ed. Peden, p. 165.

8. Jefferson, "Autobiography," in Ford, ed., *Works of Jefferson*, I, p. 58.

9. Malone, *Jefferson the Virginian*, pp. 252–257; *Papers of Jefferson*, II, p. 393n; C. Ray Keim, "Primogeniture and Entail in Colonial Virginia," *WMQ*, 3rd Ser., XXV (1968), pp. 545–586.

10. George Rogers Clark to John Brown [1791], *Clark Papers, 1771–1781*, p. 213. See also *ibid.*, pp. 11–13, 18–19, 208–210; and Abernethy, *Western Lands and the Revolution*, pp. 123–135.

11. Abernethy, *Western Lands and the Revolution*, pp. 40–58, 116–122, 142–148, 238–239.

12. *Papers of Jefferson*, I, pp. 344, 352–353, 362–363, 383; Jensen, *Articles of Confederation*, pp. 116–125, 138–139, 150–160.

13. See *Journal of the House of Delegates, 1776*, for Fincastle Co., pp. 4, 8–9, Pittsylvania Co., pp. 5, 11, 14, 16, West Augusta Co., pp. 26, 31, 34–35, 43, and Cumberland Co., pp. 40, 49, 53, 66, 75, 80, 82. See also *Journal of the Senate Anno Domini 1777* (Williamsburg, Va., 1777), p. 19; and *Statutes*, IX, p. 322.

14. *Journal of the House of Delegates, 1776*, p. 13; Clark to Brown [1791], *Clark Papers, 1771–1781*, p. 214; *Papers of Jefferson*, I, pp. 565–566, 569–571.

15. *Papers of Jefferson*, I, p. 571.

16. *Journal of the House of Delegates, 1776*, p. 43. See also *Statutes*, IX, pp. 58–59; Abernethy, *Western Lands and the Revolution*, pp. 190, 218; Proclamation of the Transylvania Company proprietors, June 26, 1776, *Calendar of Virginia State Papers*, I, pp. 271–272; and *Proceedings of the Convention, July 1775*, p. 48.

17. Braxton, *Address to the Convention*, *American Archives*, 4th Ser., VI, p. 754.

18. *Papers of Jefferson*, I, pp. 566–569. For Braxton's and Jefferson's absences, see *Journal of the House of Delegates, 1776*, pp. 18, 26, 56, 71, 75, 82.

19. Jefferson, "Autobiography," in Ford, ed., *Works of Jefferson*, I, pp. 62–63; Pendleton, II, pp. 133–137.

20. *Papers of Jefferson*, I, pp. 525–535.

21. *Ibid.*, p. 532. See also *ibid.*, p. 534; and *Statutes*, IX, pp. 312, 387–388, 469, 578–579, X, pp. 111, 197–198.

22. *Papers of Mason*, II, p. 590. See also *ibid.*, pp. 553–554.

23. Pendleton to Woodford, Nov. 1, 1779, *Letters and Papers of Pendleton*, I, p. 303. See also *Papers of Jefferson*, II, pp. 547n–548n; *Journal of the House of*

Delegates, October 1779, pp. 24, 96; and Jefferson, "Autobiography," in Ford, ed., *Works of Jefferson*, I, p. 54.

24. *Papers of Mason*, II, p. 553. See also Rowland, *Mason*, II, p. 199.

25. *Papers of Mason*, II, pp. 590–592, quotation on p. 590. See also *Papers of Jefferson*, I, pp. 530–531, II, pp. 553–555.

26. *Papers of Jefferson*, I, pp. 605–607, 657–658; *Statutes*, IX, pp. 101–107, 130–132; George Lafong's advertisement, *Va. Gaz.* (Dixon and Hunter), May 11, 1776, *ibid.*, Apr. 12, 1776; William Dawson's advertisement, *ibid.* (Purdie), Apr. 11, 1777, *ibid.*, June 15, Oct. 27, 1777; R. H. Lee to W. Lee, June 30, 1777, Brock Collection, Box 3, Henry L. Huntington Library, San Marino, Calif., microfilm, Foundation Lib.

27. *Statutes*, IX, p. 215. See also *ibid.*, pp. 169, 172, 218, 306; Thomas Adams to Robert Withers, Apr. 6, 1775, *VMHB*, XXIII (1915), pp. 64–65; *Journal of the House of Delegates, 1776*, pp. 100–101; and *Papers of Jefferson*, I, p. 649n.

28. *Statutes*, IX, pp. 168, 170.

29. *Journal of the House of Delegates, 1776*, p. 139. See also *Statutes*, IX, pp. 281–283.

30. Harrison to another governor, Oct. 17, 1783, *History of America in Documents*, Pt. II, p. 12. See also *Va. Gaz.* (Dixon and Hunter), May 9, 23, June 20, 1777; *Journals of the Council*, I, pp. 333, 360, 373, 404, 413, 420, 430; and Henry to Wythe, May 27, 1777, "Patrick Henry and the Deportation of the Royalists," *Tyler's Quarterly*, IV (1922–1923), pp. 128–129.

31. Banister to Bland, June 10, 1777, *Bland Papers*, I, pp. 57–58. See also Joseph Blackwell to R. H. Lee, Jan. 16, 1777, F. L. Lee and M. Page, Jr., to Wythe, June 10, 1777, Matthews, "Richard Henry Lee," pp. 207, 208; Pendleton to Woodford, May 29, 1777, *Letters and Papers of Pendleton*, I, pp. 212–213; and James Lovell to William Whipple, July 7, 1777, Burnett, ed., *Letters of the Continental Congress*, II, pp. 402–403.

32. Banister to Bland, June 10, 1777, *Bland Papers*, I, pp. 57–58. See also R. H. Lee to [Henry], May 26, 1777, *Letters of R. H. Lee*, I, pp. 298–300; Mason to Wythe, June 14, 1777, *Papers of Mason*, I, p. 346n; M. Page to R. H. Lee, Oct. 27, 1777, and Wythe to R. H. Lee, Nov. 6, 1777, Lee Papers, 1769–1789, Amer. Phil. Soc., microfilm, Foundation Lib.

33. Pendleton to Woodford, May 15, 1777, *Letters and Papers of Pendleton*, I, p. 209. See also Pendleton to Woodford, May 29, Nov. 29, 1777, *ibid.*, pp. 212–213, 240.

34. For the discussion of the Lee-Deane affair in this and following paragraphs, see Thomas P. Abernethy, "Commercial Activities of Silas Deane in France," *AHR*, XXXIX (1933–1934), pp. 477–485; Abernethy, "The Origins of

the Franklin-Lee Imbroglio," *North Carolina Historical Review*, XV (1938), pp. 41–52; Abernethy, *Western Lands and the Revolution*, pp. 180–187, 205–215, 230–232, 239, 275; Elizabeth S. Kite, *Beaumarchais and the War of American Independence* (Boston, 1918); and John C. Miller, *Triumph of Freedom, 1775–1783* (Boston, 1948), pp. 357–377.

35. J. Page to R. H. Lee, Mar. 19, 1779, Lee Family Papers, Alderman Lib.; *Va. Gaz.* (Dixon and Hunter), Oct. 9, 23, 1779.

36. Isaac Samuel Harrell, *Loyalism in Virginia: Chapters in the Economic History of the Revolution* (Philadelphia, 1926), p. 80; *Papers of Mason*, I, pp. 375n–378n.

37. Pendleton to Woodford, Jan. 16, 31, 1776, *Letters and Papers of Pendleton*, I, p. 246; *Statutes*, IX, pp. 349–368, quotation on p. 350. See also Jefferson, *Notes on Virginia*, ed. Peden, p. 137.

38. [Walter] Jones to [R. H. Lee], June 29, 1778, Lee Family Papers, Alderman Lib.; *Papers of Jefferson*, II, pp. 217–224, quotation on p. 219. See also *ibid.*, pp. 186–188, 223.

39. *Papers of Jefferson*, II, pp. 133–167; *Papers of Mason*, I, pp. 399–409.

40. *Papers of Mason*, I, pp. 378–379.

41. Notes on my title to 485. acres of land surveyed for me Mar. 27, 1788, *Papers of Jefferson*, II, p. 138; Kenneth P. Bailey, *The Ohio Company of Virginia and the Westward Movement, 1748–1792: A Chapter in the History of the Colonial Frontier* (Glendale, Ill., 1939), pp. 278–279.

42. *Papers of Mason*, I, p. 419. See also *ibid.*, pp. 414–422, 424–425.

43. *Papers of Jefferson*, II, pp. 111–112, 120–121, 148–149.

44. *Ibid.*, pp. 168–171, quotation on p. 168. See also *ibid.*, p. 280.

45. Jefferson, *Notes on Virginia*, ed. Peden, p. 156. See also *History of Virginia*, p. 277; Evans, "Private Indebtedness," pp. 349–374; and Evans, *Nelson*, pp. 84–85.

46. Archibald Stuart to Jefferson, Oct. 17, 1785, *Papers of Jefferson*, VIII, p. 646. See also *ibid.*, I, pp. 606–607, 621–644; *Journal of the House of Delegates of . . . Virginia, Begun . . . the Twentieth Day of October . . . 1777* (Richmond, Va., 1827), pp. 98–99; *Papers of Madison*, VIII, p. 443, n. 3; and Pendleton to Woodford, Jan. 2, 31, 1778, *Letters and Papers of Pendleton*, I, pp. 240, 247.

47. Jefferson to Wythe, Mar. 1, 1779, *Papers of Jefferson*, II, p. 235. See also *History of Virginia*, p. 267; and *Papers of Madison*, VIII, p. 446, n. 3.

48. Jefferson, "Autobiography," in Ford, ed., *Works of Jefferson*, I, pp. 59–60. See also *ibid.*, p. 609n.

49. J. A. Washington to R. H. Lee, May 26, 1778, *SLM*, p. 331; M. Page, Jr., to R. H. Lee, May 15, 1778, *ibid.*, p. 261. See also M. Page, Jr., to R. H. Lee, May 28, 1778, Lee Family Papers, Alderman Lib.; *Journal of the House of Delegates of . . . Virginia; Begun . . . the Fourth Day of May . . . 1778* (Richmond, Va., 1827), pp. 3–4; and *Journal of the Senate* [May 4–June 1, 1778] (Williamsburg, Va., 1778), p. 5.

50. Henry to R. H. Lee, June 18, 1778, Lee Papers, Amer. Phil. Soc. See also *Journal of the House of Delegates, October 1777*, p. 131; *Journal of the House of Delegates, May 1778*, p. 27; and F. L. Lee to R. H. Lee, June 25, 1778, *SLM*, p. 259.

51. *Statutes*, IX, pp. 471–472; James Curtis Ballagh, *A History of Slavery in Virginia* (Baltimore, Md., 1902), p. 23; Bill to Prevent the Importation of Slaves, *Papers of Jefferson*, II, pp. 22–24.

52. *Papers of Jefferson*, II, p. 22; *Papers of Mason*, I, pp. 452, 458–459; *Statutes*, IX, pp. 476–477, 482–525, 581–583, X, pp. 89–92.

53. Wood to Washington, Nov. 12, 1778, Rowland, *Mason*, I, p. 306; Henderson to John Williams, Oct. 30, 1778, *Papers of Jefferson*, II, p. 66n. See also *ibid.*, pp. 64–66; William Stewart Lester, *The Transylvania Company* (Spencer, Ind., 1935), pp. 232–243; and *Statutes*, IX, pp. 571–572.

54. *Papers of Jefferson*, II, pp. 305n–324n; *Pendleton*, II, pp. 138–143.

55. *Papers of Jefferson*, II, pp. 317n, 321n–324n.

56. Jefferson, "Autobiography," in Ford, ed., *Works of Jefferson*, I, pp. 75, 77–78; Bill No. 79, *Papers of Jefferson*, II, p. 527.

57. Jefferson, "Autobiography," in Ford, ed., *Works of Jefferson*, I, p. 69. See also *Papers of Jefferson*, II, pp. 505n–506n.

58. Jefferson, *Notes on Virginia*, ed. Peden, pp. 137–138. See also *Papers of Jefferson*, II, pp. 472n–473n. The 1785 statute, however, contained a loophole that might have revived a trade in slaves by allowing planters to bring blacks they owned in other states into Virginia.

59. Bill No. 95, *Papers of Jefferson*, II, pp. 578–581, 582n.

Chapter 9. THE ECONOMY IN WAR

1. *Va. Gaz.* (Purdie), Feb. 23, Dec. 13, 1775; *ibid.* (Dixon and Hunter), Mar. 23, 1775; *Statutes*, IX, p. 72; *Journals of the Continental Congress*, III, pp. 345–346, 511; Cary to Dr. Bland, Dec. 21, 1775, Brock Collection, Misc. file, Box 1777–1781; J. Page to R. H. Lee, Feb. 27, 1777, *SLM*, p. 256.

2. J. Page to R. H. Lee, Feb. 19, 1776, *SLM*, p. 255. See also J. Page to Jefferson, Apr. 26, 1776, *Papers of Jefferson*, I, pp. 288–289.

3. Gilmer to Jefferson, July 26 or 27, 1775, Charles Lynch to Jefferson, Nov. 20, 1775, Lynch to Va. Delegates in Congress, Nov. 20, 1775, *Papers of Jefferson*, I, pp. 237, 261–262, 262–264; Jacob Rubsamen to Bland, Aug. 2, 1782, *Bland Papers*, II, pp. 82–92; *American Archives*, 4th Ser., IV, p. 911; *Va. Gaz.* (Purdie), Mar. 8, 1776; Donald E. F. Reynolds, "Ammunition Supply in Revolutionary Virginia," *VMHB*, LXX (1965), pp. 56–77; Greene, ed., *Diary of Landon Carter*, II, pp. 960–961, 971.

4. Speech [after Oct. 22, 1775], "Papers of Gilmer," pp. 119–120. See also Arthur Pierce Middleton, *Tobacco Coast: A Maritime History of Chesapeake Bay in the Colonial Era* (Newport News, Va., 1953), pp. 207–208; *Pendleton*, II, pp. 47–48; Van Schreeven and Scribner, comps., ed. Scribner, *Revolutionary Virginia*, II: *Committees and the Second Convention*, p. 382; *Proceedings of the Convention, December 1775*, p. 7; *Va. Gaz.* (Purdie), Dec. 6, 1775; Dunmore to Dartmouth, Dec. 6, 1775–Feb. 13, 1776, C.O. 5/1353, fols. 325, 332; and Virginia Committee of Safety to Va. Delegates in Congress, Nov. 11, 1775, *Letters and Papers of Pendleton*, I, p. 127.

5. Pendleton to R. H. Lee, Apr. 20, 1776, *Letters and Papers of Pendleton*, I, p. 164; *Statutes*, IX, p. 123; R. H. Lee to Nicholas, Apr. 30, 1776, R. H. Lee to Henry, Aug. 30, 1776, *Letters of R. H. Lee*, I, pp. 184, 213–214; Richard Parker to R. H. Lee, Dec. 5, 1776, T. L. Lee to R. H. Lee, Sept. 9, 1777, *SLM*, pp. 326–327; *Journal of the House of Delegates of . . . Virginia; Begun . . . the Fifth Day of October . . . 1778* (Richmond, Va., 1827), p. 122; *Journal of the House of Delegates, May 1779*, pp. 65, 67; *Va. Gaz.* (Dixon and Nicolson) (Williamsburg), July 10, Nov. 27, 1779; "Virginia Commerce," p. 316.

6. Jefferson, *Notes on Virginia*, ed. Peden, p. 164.

7. Mason to Henry, Apr. 6, 1777, *Papers of Mason*, I, p. 336. See also R. Carter to John Dick, Sept. 18, 1775, Robert Carter Letter Book, III, p. 31.

8. *Va. Gaz.* (Purdie), Mar. 28, 1777; *ibid.* (Dixon and Hunter), Feb. 12, 1779; Charles Yates to William Harwood, Nov. 14, 1775, Charles Yates Letter Book, 1773–1783, Alderman Lib.

9. *Va. Gaz.* (Dixon and Hunter), Dec. 13, 1776, Apr. 25, May 16, 1777; *ibid.* (Dixon and Nicolson), Oct. 9, 1779; William Pasteur to W. Lee, Feb. 16, 177[8], Arthur Lee MSS, Box IV, p. 46, Houghton Lib.; Mary R. M. Goodwin, "Clothing and Accoutrements of the Officers and Soldiers of the Virginia Forces, 1775–1780. From the Records of the Public Store at Williamsburg" (unpubl. research report, CWF, 1962), pp. 51, 147n, 151, 203; Public Store Day Book, June 27, Aug. 8, 1778, Nov. 1779; Charles Thomas to Board of Trade, Nov. 17, 1779, Brock Collection; *Journals of the Council*, II, p. 410.

10. *Journals of the Council*, II, pp. 42, 411; *Virginia: A Guide to the Old Dominion*, Writers' Program of the W.P.A. in the State of Virginia (New York, 1941),

pp. 477–478; *Pendleton*, I, pp. 202–205; *Statutes*, IX, pp. 73, 237–238; Quarles, *Negro in the Revolution*, p. 99; T. L. Lee to R. H. Lee, May 18, 1776, *SLM*, pp. 324–325; Henry to Va. delegates, Oct. 19, 1776, *American Archives*, 5th Ser., II, pp. 986–987; Capt. Onslow to Gen. Howe, Mar. 27, 1778, Adm. 1/488, fol. 221.

11. Williams to Commissioners of Customs at Boston, Mar. 7, 1770, T. 1/476, fols. 126–127. See also Kathleen Bruce, *Virginia Iron Manufacture in the Slave Era* (New York, 1931), pp. 1–79; *Statutes*, IX, p. 70; and *American Archives*, 4th Ser., III, pp. 429–430.

12. James Mercer to Jefferson, Apr. 14, 1781, *Papers of Jefferson*, V, pp. 446–447; "Fredericksburg in Revolutionary Days, Part III," *WMQ*, 1st Ser., XXVII (1918–1919), pp. 248–253; *Official Letters of Governors*, I, pp. 30, 166–167, II, p. 343; *Proceedings of the Convention, May 1776*, p. 83.

13. *Proceedings of the Convention, May 1776*, pp. 34–35, 50–51; R. H. Lee to Jefferson, Nov. 3, 1776, Cary to Jefferson, July 22, 1779, Jefferson to Harrison, Oct. 30, 1779, *Papers of Jefferson*, I, p. 591, III, pp. 43–44, 125–131.

14. Bill for Establishing a Manufactory of Arms, *Papers of Jefferson*, III, pp. 131–147; Peter Penet to Jefferson, May 20, 1780, *ibid.*, pp. 383–385; John Reveley to Board of Trade, Aug. 16, 1779, Brock Collection; Robert Johnson, "Government Regulation of Business Enterprise in Virginia, 1750–1820" (Ph.D. diss., University of Minnesota, 1958), pp. 320–321; Bruce, *Virginia Iron Manufacture*, pp. 42–60.

15. Bruce, *Virginia Iron Manufacture*, pp. 20–21; Naval Commissioners to Isaac Zane, May 8, June 11, 1777, Navy Board Letter Book 1776–1777, Va. State Lib.; R. Carter to Clement Brooke, Mar. 15, 1777, Robert Carter Letter Book, III, p. 97; "Fredericksburg in Revolutionary Days, Part I, Appendix 4," pp. 82–93; *Statutes*, IX, pp. 303–305; *Journals of the Council*, I, pp. 258, 297, 388, 495, II, pp. 63, 469.

16. *Journals of the Council*, II, pp. 164–165.

17. Harrison, Sr., to R. Morris [May 1776], "Virginia Commerce," p. 299.

18. Abraham Van Bibber to Virginia Committee of Safety, Mar. 11, 1776, Van Bibber to Va. Convention, Mar. 23, 1776, Van Bibber to William Lux, Mar. 28, 1776, *VMHB*, XV (1907–1908), pp. 156–157, 292, 288–289; Van Bibber and Richard Harrison to Va. Committee of Safety, July 25–Aug. 15, 1776, *ibid.*, XVI (1908–1909), pp. 163–170; M. Page, Jr., to brother, Mar. 4, 1778, Morristown Natl. Hist. Park; *Journals of the Council*, I, pp. 107, 114, 129, II, p. 496; Committee of Safety Ledger, 1775–1776, p. 54, Va. State Lib.; Honyman Diary, Dec. 4, 1776, Jan. 16, 1777; George Bryan to Samuel Bryan, Jan. 26, 1777, Burton Alva Konkle, *George Bryan and the Constitution of Pennsylvania, 1731–1791* (Philadelphia, 1922), p. 133n.

19. J. Page to Washington, Dec. 20, 1776, Emmet Collection, N. Y. Pub. Lib. See also Abernethy, *Western Lands and the Revolution*, p. 197; and James Alton

James, *Oliver Pollock: The Life and Times of an Unknown Patriot* (New York, 1937), pp. 61, 69–70.

20. "Virginia Commerce," pp. 230–238; *Journals of the Council*, I, pp. 3, 119, 246, 296, 350; Aylett to [?], Nov. 26, 1776, Correspondence, Aylett; Nov. 23, 1776, Mar. 8, 1777, Tobacco Invoice Book, 1776–1779, Va. State Lib.

21. Jan.–Mar. 1777, Tobacco Invoice Book, passim; *Journals of the Council*, I, pp. 324, 349, 357, 399–400; Van Bibber and Harrison to Maryland Committee of Safety, Oct. 20, 1776, *American Archives*, 5th Ser., I, pp. 1134–1135; Van Bibber and Harrison to Aylett, Apr. 19, 1777, Correspondence, Aylett.

22. Robert Armistead Stewart, *The History of Virginia's Navy of the Revolution* (Richmond, Va., 1934), p. 32.

23. *Ibid.*, chap. 3.

24. Raleigh Colston to Aylett, Oct. 24, 1777, "Correspondence of Aylett," pp. 152–153. See also Van Bibber and Harrison to Aylett, Apr. 2, 1777, *ibid.*, pp. 99–103; Recollections of his family by Raleigh Colston of Honeywood, Berkeley County [Mar. 1812], Family Bible, Jones Memorial Library, Lynchburg, Va., typescript, Foundation Lib.; "Virginia Commerce," p. 240; War Office Letter Book, May 3, 1779, War Office Papers, 1779–1803, Va. State Lib.; Thomas Smith to Thomas Bretman, Dec. 15, 1778, and T. Smith to R. Harrison, Aug. 29, Nov. 13, 1778, Thomas Smith Letter Book, December 26, 1777–November 7, 1778, Va. State Lib., microfilm, Foundation Lib.

25. Ver Steeg, *Robert Morris*, pp. 3–5, 28–29.

26. *Journals of the Continental Congress*, IV, p. 151; "Virginia Commerce," pp. 132–133, 199–200, 315–316; *Va. Gaz.* (Purdie), Aug. 1, 1777; Samuel Beall to Silas Deane, June, Aug. 5, 1776, Norton & Beall to S. Deane, Mar. 7, Apr. 1777, *The Deane Papers: Correspondence between Silas Deane, His Brothers, and their Business and Political Associates, 1771–1795* (Connecticut Historical Society, *Collections*, XXIII [Hartford, Conn., 1930]), pp. 20, 34, 78, 85; Frances Norton Mason, ed., *John Norton & Sons, Merchants of London and Virginia: Being the Papers from their Counting House for the Years 1750 to 1795* (Richmond, Va., 1937), p. 459; Curtis, "Goodrich Family," p. 55n. Norton imported powder for the Committee of Safety and compromised the elder Norton by drawing a bill of exchange on the family's London firm to pay for the Goodriches' 1775 shipment.

27. Braxton to R. Morris, July 16, 1777, in R. Morris to Henrico County Court auditors, No. 3 [June 17, 1785?], p. 9, Carter Braxton Business Papers, Hist. Soc. Pa. See also Braxton to Isaac Governor, Sept. 28, 1777, C.O. 5/126, fols. 243–246.

28. Harrison, Sr., to R. Morris, Jan. 8, 1777, "Letters to Robert Morris, 1775–1782" (N.-Y. Hist. Soc., *Colls.*, XI [New York, 1878]), p. 408. See also R. Morris to the Secret Committee, Feb. 19, 1777, Ver Steeg, *Robert Morris*, p. 21.

29. R. Morris to Braxton, Jan. 6, 1777, Braxton to R. Morris, Feb. 26, May 7, 1777, in R. Morris's answer for Henrico County Court auditors to Braxton's account No. 3 [May 21, 1785?], pp. 5–6, Braxton's answer to R. Morris's answer of May 21, 1785 [June 17, 1785?], R. Morris to Braxton, Mar. 18, Apr. 17, June 10, 1777, and Braxton to R. Morris, Apr. 5, 1777, in R. Morris to Henrico County Court auditors, No. 3 [after June 17, 1785], pp. 8–11, Braxton Business Papers; Cabell Diary [Nov. 28, 1778]; *Journals of the Continental Congress,* XII, pp. 12–16; R. H. Lee to [Henry Laurens], June 6, 13, 1779, *Letters of R. H. Lee,* II, pp. 61–64, 70–72.

30. Aylett to Hancock, June 29, 1777, Papers of the Continental Congress, reel 90, I, p. 99. See also Aylett to Hancock, Apr. 13, 18, 1777, *ibid.,* pp. 73, 77; Henry to R. H. Lee, Mar. 28, 1777, *Official Letters of Governors,* I, p. 129; Braxton to Aylett, Apr. 7, 1777, "Virginia Commerce," p. 322; and R. H. Lee to Henry, Apr. 15, 1777, *Letters of R. H. Lee,* I, pp. 273–274.

31. Braxton to Aylett, Apr. 7, 1777, Correspondence, Aylett.

32. Thomas Ludwell Tucker to S. G. Tucker, Nov. 20, 1777, Tucker-Coleman Collection.

33. Aylett to Jonathan Trumbull, June 22, 1777, Papers of the Continental Congress, reel 90, XXII, p. 261. See also *Journals of the Council,* I, pp. 394, 462; Aylett's memorial to Convention, June 7, 1776, *American Archives,* 4th Ser., VI, pp. 1553–1554; *Journal of the House of Delegates of . . . Virginia, Begun . . . the Fifth Day of May . . . 1777* (Richmond, Va., 1827), p. 52; and *Journal of the House of Delegates, October 1777,* pp. 55, 114.

34. Aylett to Joseph Hughes, June 10, 1778, Papers of the Continental Congress, reel 90, I, p. 207. See also the exchange between Aylett and "Agricola," *Va. Gaz.* (Dixon and Nicolson), Nov. 13, 1778, Dec. 11, 1779, Feb. 5, 1780.

35. *Journals of the Council,* I, pp. 168, 199, 204, 370, 398, 454, II, p. 43; "Virginia Commerce," pp. 238–251; Tobacco Invoice Book; Mason to Aylett, June 8, 1777, *Papers of Mason,* I, pp. 343–345; Pendleton to Woodford, Nov. 29, 1777, *Letters and Papers of Pendleton,* I, p. 238; William Finnie to Board of War, Dec. 5, 1777, Papers of the Continental Congress, reel 195, IX, p. 125; W. Lee to Henry, Sept. 30, 1777, Va. Misc. MSS, Lib. Cong.; J. Gruel & Co. to Aylett, Oct. 11, 1777, Pliarne Penet & Co. to Aylett, Oct. 17, 1777, *Tyler's Quarterly,* I (1920), pp. 151–152; Account of William Aylett with Gruel & Co., June 26, 1778, Papers of Penet, Dacosta Frères & Co. (June 1777–1795), State Agent's Loose Papers, Box 5, Va. State Lib.

36. Committee of Secret Correspondence to Commissioners in France [Feb. 17, 1777], *Letters of R. H. Lee,* I, p. 259. See also Contract between William Aylett and Peter Bonalque, Oct. 28, 1777, Papers of Penet, Dacosta Frères & Co.; John Bondfield to Norton & Beall, Apr. 18, 1778, H.C.A. 32/493; *Va. Gaz.* (Purdie), Mar. 21, 1777, supp.; T. Nelson to Washington, Nov. 21, 1777, *Writings of Washington,* X, p. 146; and Honyman Diary, Jan. 21, 1778.

37. Honyman Diary, Nov. 2, 1777.

38. Bolling Starke instructions, n.d., Correspondence, Aylett; "Virginia Commerce," pp. 159 and n., 246–251, 265, 272; Council to T. Smith, Nov. 29, 1777, T. Smith to Fielding Lewis, Mar. 3, 1778, T. Smith to Thomas Starke, Mar. 13, 1778, T. Smith Letter Book, pp. 4–5, 18, 21; T. Smith to John Bowdoin, Mar. 3, 1778, *Calendar of Virginia State Papers*, I, p. 298; W. Lee to Jefferson, Sept. 24, 1779, *Papers of Jefferson*, III, pp. 90–93; Mar. 9, May 14, 1779, Tobacco Invoice Book; Receipt Book, Thomas Smith, December 24, 1777–March 17, 1779, Records of the State Agent, Williamsburg, 1777–1780, Va. State Lib., microfilm, Foundation Lib.

39. Alden, *American Revolution*, pp. 188–189, 197–198; Honyman Diary, Sept. 21, 1777; Joseph Plumb Martin, *Private Yankee Doodle, Being a Narrative of Some of the Adventures, Dangers and Sufferings of a Revolutionary Soldier*, ed. George F. Scheer (Boston, 1962), p. 100; Victor Leroy Johnson, *The Administration of the American Commissariat During the Revolutionary War* (Philadelphia, 1941), pp. 74, 81–85, 96; Aylett to Hancock, Feb. 21, Apr. 12, 1777, Papers of the Continental Congress, reel 90, I, pp. 59, 73; *Va. Gaz.* (Dixon and Hunter), Feb. 21, 1777.

40. Johnson, *Administration of the American Commissariat*, p. 74; *Journals of the Council*, I, pp. 494, 497, 498, II, pp. 11, 40, III, p. 358.

41. Aylett to James Hunter, Jr., June 5, 1778, Calendar of Hunter Family Manuscripts, 1704–1779, Alderman Lib., microfilm, Foundation Lib. See also Aylett to Laurens, June 5, 10, 1778, Papers of the Continental Congress, reel 90, I, pp. 181, 195; Washington to inhabitants of New Jersey, Pennsylvania, Maryland, and Virginia, Feb. 18, 1778, Washington to Henry, Feb. 19, 1778, *Writings of Washington*, X, pp. 480, 483–485; *Journals of the Council*, II, pp. 66, 107, 114, 139; Henry to R. H. Lee, Apr. 7, 1778, *Official Letters of Governors*, I, p. 260; receipt to Walker Maury, Sept. 4, 1778, statement of debit, Nov. 2, 1778, and [Richard Morris] to [Maury], Dec. 10, 1778, Richard Morris Papers, 1776–1778, Alderman Lib.

42. *Statutes*, IX, p. 376. See also *Papers of Mason*, I, pp. 352–357, 372–373.

43. Braxton to Jonathan Hudson, Dec. 12, 1777, John Carter Brown Library, Providence, R. I.; *Journal of the House of Delegates, October 1777*, pp. 82–83.

44. *Papers of Mason*, I, pp. 359–362, quotation on p. 360. See also *ibid.*, pp. 374–375.

45. [Richard Morris] to [Maury], Dec. 10, 1778, Richard Morris Papers; "Virginia Commerce," pp. 159–161, 272; Honble. B. Starke, Esq. Instructions [1777], Correspondence, Aylett; T. Smith to Bowdoin, Mar. 3, 1778, *Calendar of Virginia State Papers*, I, p. 298; T. Smith to Moses Tandy, June 26, 1778, T. Smith Letter Book.

46. T. Smith to Capt. Buckler, Jan. 30, 1779, T. Smith Letter Book. See also "Virginia Commerce," p. 159 and n.

47. T. Smith to Archibald Richardson, June 22, 1778, T. Smith Letter Book.

48. T. Smith to Christopher Calvert, June 22, 1778, *ibid.* See also "Virginia Commerce," pp. 160–161.

49. J. Page to R. H. Lee, Feb. 17, 1778, Revolutionary Papers (Letters to Richard Henry, Arthur, and William Lee), 1750–1824, Alderman Lib.; T. Smith to Benjamin Day, Oct. 9, 1778, T. Smith Letter Book. See also *Journals of the Council*, II, pp. 89, 124; Michael Gratz to S. & J. Delap, Mar. 30, 1778, H.C.A. 32/493; George Slaughter's affidavit, May 28, 1778, Papers of the Continental Congress, reel 90, I, p. 193; and Robert Allison to Hunter, June 21, 1778, Calendar of Hunter Family MSS.

50. Mar. 30, 1778, State Agent's Loose Papers, Correspondence, Thomas Smith, January–May 1778, Box 2, Va. State Lib., microfilm, Foundation Lib. See also F. Lewis to T. Smith, Mar. 14, 1778, *ibid.;* and *Journals of the Council*, II, p. 143.

51. Pendleton to R. H. Lee, June 13, 1778, Lee Family Papers, Alderman Lib.; Elliot & Davis to T. Smith, Mar. 12, 1778, R. Harrison to T. Smith, Mar. 6, 1778, Correspondence, T. Smith, Box 2; John Bondfield to Thomas Jett, Apr. 10, 1778, H.C.A. 32/493; "Virginia Commerce," pp. 222, 260; Public Store Day Book, Feb. 24, 1777, Aug. 5, 14, 29, Sept. 17, 1778; State Agent Day Book, Oct. 14, 1778; June–Aug. 1778, Tobacco Invoice Book; *Journals of the Council*, II, pp. 146, 149, 180–181, 183; *Va. Gaz.* (Purdie), Aug. 21, 1778; Caron de Beaumarchais to Lazarus de Francy [fall 1778], Kite, *Beaumarchais*, II, p. 197.

52. *Papers of Mason*, I, pp. 459–464, quotation on p. 464; *Statutes*, IX, pp. 474, 530, 584; Honyman Diary, July 10, Aug. 21, Sept. 29, 1778. See also Johnson, *Administration of the American Commissariat*, pp. 138–156.

53. Chalomer & White to Jeremiah Wadsworth, Apr. 20, 1779, Johnson, *Administration of the American Commissariat*, p. 156. See also *ibid.*, p. 147; and R. H. Lee to Aylett, Feb. 10, 1779, Lee Family Papers, Alderman Lib.

54. *Journals of the Continental Congress*, II, p. 740n; H.M.S. *Perseus* log, Nov. 7, 1778, Adm. 52/1908, Pt. III; Day to T. Smith, Sept. 14, 1778, Correspondence, T. Smith, Box 3; "Virginia Commerce," p. 277.

55. For the discussion in this and following paragraphs, see Henry to T. Smith, Mar. 15, 1779, Mazzei's instructions, Apr. 22, 1779, Penet's instructions, May 22, 1779, War Office Letter Book, Nov. 1779–Mar. 1780 [2nd section], Va. State Lib. microfilm, reel 264; T. Smith to Day, Feb. 26, 1779, T. Smith Letter Book; Contract between the State of Virginia and Peter Penet, Windel & Co., July 22, 1779, W. Lee to Jefferson, Sept. 24, 1779, Board of Trade to Jefferson, Oct. 29, 1779, Jefferson to Harrison, Oct. 30, 1779, Penet to Jefferson, Mar. 17, May 20, Nov. 22, 1780, and Philip Mazzei to Jefferson, Nov. 27, 1779, Mar. 4, 19, 1780, Aug. 8, 1781, *Papers of Jefferson*, III, pp. 49, 90–93, 123, 125–130, 315, 382, IV, pp. 144–147, III, pp. 201–203, 310–312, 319, VI, pp. 114–115.

Chapter 10. THE WAR IN THE WEST

1. Stephen to R. H. Lee, Sept. 23, 1775, *American Archives*, 4th Ser., III, pp. 776–777; James Wood's Diary, Thwaites and Kellogg, eds., *Revolution on the Upper Ohio*, pp. 34–67, 82–127; Abernethy, *Western Lands and the Revolution*, p. 141.

2. John Stuart to Henry Stuart, Oct. 24, 1775, Philip M. Hamer, "John Stuart's Indian Policy During the Early Months of the American Revolution," *MVHR*, XVII (1930–1931), p. 361.

3. H. Stuart to J. Stuart, Aug. 25, 1776, William L. Saunders, ed., *The Colonial Records of North Carolina*, X (Raleigh, N. C., 1890), p. 774. See also John P. Brown, *Old Frontiers: The Story of the Cherokee Indians from Earliest Times to the Date of Their Removal to the West, 1838* (Kingsport, Tenn., 1938), pp. 137–138.

4. Alexander Cameron to J. Stuart, July 9, 1776, Hamer, "Stuart's Indian Policy," p. 366. See also H. Stuart to J. Stuart, Aug. 25, 1776, Saunders, ed., *Colonial Records of North Carolina*, X, pp. 769, 781–782; *Proceedings of the Convention, 1776*, pp. 88–89; *Va. Gaz.* (Purdie), June 7, 1776; and *Lee Papers*, II, pp. 28–30.

5. Stephen to Jefferson, July 29, 1776, *Papers of Jefferson*, I, pp. 480–481. See also W. Fleming to Jefferson, June 15, 1776, *ibid.*, p. 386; *Va. Gaz.* (Dixon and Hunter), Aug. 3, 10, 17, 1776; and John Richard Alden, *The South in the Revolution, 1763–1789* (Baton Rouge, La., 1957), pp. 270–273.

6. Jefferson to Pendleton, Aug. 13, 1776, *Papers of Jefferson*, I, p. 494.

7. J. Page to C. Lee, Aug. 13, 1776, *Lee Papers*, II, pp. 214–216. See also C. Lee to Pendleton, July 7, 20, 1776, C. Lee to President of the Congress of North Carolina, July 7, 1776, *ibid.*, pp. 127–128, 152–153, 129; *Journals of the Council*, I, pp. 82, 103–104; and Alden, *South in the Revolution*, pp. 272–273.

8. Reports from the West are in *VMHB*, XVII (1909), pp. 52–64; *Va. Gaz.* (Dixon and Hunter), Nov. 1, 15, 1776; *ibid.* (Purdie), Nov. 29, 1776; and Brown, *Old Frontiers*, pp. 160–161.

9. *Va. Gaz.* (Dixon and Hunter), May 30, 1777. See also *ibid.* (Purdie), May 30, 1777; and *Journals of the Council*, I, pp. 317, 416, 419, 421.

10. Abernethy, *Western Lands and the Revolution*, p. 190; Philip M. Rice, "Internal Improvements in Virginia, 1775–1860" (Ph.D. diss., University of North Carolina, 1948), p. 40n; Alden, *South in the Revolution*, p. 273.

11. Clark to Henry, Feb. 3, 1779, *Clark Papers, 1771–1781*, p. 97. See also Sosin, *Revolutionary Frontier*, p. 92.

12. Clark to [Henry], 1777, *Clark Papers, 1771–1781*, pp. 30–31; Clark to J. Brown, 1791, *ibid.*, p. 218.

13. Clark to Mason, Nov. 19, 1779, *Papers of Mason,* II, pp. 555–556.

14. *Ibid.,* I, p. 398. See also Clark's Diary, Nov. 3, 22, Dec. 10, 1777, *Clark Papers, 1771–1781,* pp. 26–27.

15. *Papers of Mason,* I, pp. 398–399.

16. Clark to Mason, Nov. 19, 1779, *ibid.,* II, p. 556.

17. *Ibid.* See also *Journals of the Council,* II, p. 44.

18. *Clark Papers, 1771–1781,* p. 219. See also *ibid.,* pp. 34–36; Clark to Mason, Nov. 19, 1779, *Papers of Mason,* II, p. 556, *ibid.,* I, p. 399n; and *Journals of the Council,* II, p. 56.

19. Wythe, Mason, and Jefferson to Clark, Jan. 3, 1778, *Papers of Mason,* I, p. 410. See also *Statutes,* X, pp. 26–27.

20. Abernethy, *Western Lands and the Revolution,* pp. 193–199; Sosin, *Revolutionary Frontier,* pp. 116–120; *Clark Papers, 1771–1781,* p. 35; Clark to Jefferson, Sept. 23, 1779, *Papers of Jefferson,* III, p. 88. See also *ibid.,* pp. 161n, 279n.

21. *Journals of the Council,* II, pp. 161–162. See also Abernethy, *Western Lands and the Revolution,* pp. 196–197; Sosin, *Revolutionary Frontier,* p. 116; and *Clark Papers, 1771–1781,* pp. xlviii–1.

22. *Clark Papers, 1771–1781,* p. 220.

23. *Ibid.,* pp. 219–224; Abernethy, *Western Lands and the Revolution,* pp. 190–191; Max Savelle, *George Morgan: Colony Builder* (New York, 1932), p. 179.

24. *Clark Papers, 1771–1781,* p. 222. See also *ibid.,* p. lxi.

25. *Ibid.,* p. 224. See also *ibid.,* pp. 225–228.

26. *Ibid.,* p. 229.

27. *Ibid.,* p. 239.

28. *Ibid.,* pp. 239–242, quotation on p. 242.

29. Henry to the Va. delegates, Nov. 16, 1778, *ibid.,* p. 72.

30. Resolution of Virginia House of Delegates, Nov. 23, 1778, *ibid.,* p. 74; *Statutes,* IX, pp. 552–553, quotation on p. 552.

31. Henry to Clark, Dec. 12, 1778, *Clark Papers, 1771–1781,* pp. 75–76. See also Virginia Council to Clark, Dec. 12, 1778, Virginia Council to John Montgomery, Dec. 12, 1778, and Virginia Council to John Todd, Dec. 12, 1778, *ibid.,* pp. 78–87.

32. Henry Hamilton's report, July 6, 1781, Leonard Helm to Clark, Dec. 17, 1778, *ibid.*, pp. 176–181, 89–91.

33. Clark to Henry, Feb. 3, 1779, *ibid.*, p. 98. For the general account, see *ibid.*, pp. 261–268.

34. *Ibid.*, p. 270. See also *ibid.*, p. lxxvi.

35. Clark to Mason, Nov. 19, 1779, *ibid.*, pp. 144, 167. For the general story, see *ibid.*, pp. 268–290.

36. *Ibid.*, p. 283. See also Hamilton's report, *ibid.*, pp. 189–190; and Clark to Mason, Nov. 19, 1779, *Papers of Mason*, II, pp. 579–580.

37. *Clark Papers, 1771–1781*, p. 289. See also Hamilton's report, *ibid.*, pp. 190–194.

38. Hamilton's report, *ibid.*, p. 196. See also *ibid.*, pp. 193–196.

39. *Ibid.*, p. 197. See also *ibid.*, pp. 198–207; and Jefferson to William Phillips, July 22, 1779, *Papers of Jefferson*, III, p. 45.

40. John Dodge to Philip Boyle, July 13, 1779, *Papers of Jefferson*, II, p. 295n.

41. Jefferson to Phillips, July 22, 1779, *ibid.*, III, p. 47. See also Order of Virginia Council Placing Henry Hamilton and Others in Arms, June 16, 1779, *ibid.*, II, pp. 292–294; and Hamilton to the people of Illinois, Dec. 29, 1778, *Clark Papers, 1771–1781*, pp. 95–96.

42. Clark to Todd, Mar. 1780, *Clark Papers, 1771–1781*, pp. 404–406; Jefferson to Bernardo de Gálvez, Nov. 8, 1779, Jefferson to Board of Trade, Jan. 26, 1780, Jefferson to Washington, Feb. 10, 1780, Washington to Jefferson, Mar. 5, 1780, Jefferson to Clark, Mar. 19, 1780, Jefferson to Todd, Mar. 19, 1780, *Papers of Jefferson*, III, pp. 167–170, 270–271, 291–292, 312, 316–317, 319–321.

43. Inhabitants of Vincennes to governor of Virginia, June 30, 1781, *Clark Papers, 1771–1781*, pp. 430–433. See also James A. James, *The Life of George Rogers Clark* (Chicago, 1928), pp. 196–210.

44. Clark to Todd, Mar. 1780, Clark to Dodge, Apr. 20, 1780, Todd to Jefferson, June 2, 1780, Jefferson to Speaker of House of Delegates, June 14, 1780, *Clark Papers, 1771–1781*, pp. 404–406, 417–418, 422–423, 427–428.

45. Jefferson to Clark, Jan. 1, 1780, *Papers of Jefferson*, III, p. 259. For the general story, see Clark to Jefferson, Aug. 22, 1780, *ibid.*, pp. 560–561; James, *Life of Clark*, pp. 207–213; and Henry Wilson, account of campaign against the Shawnee, n.d., *Clark Papers, 1771–1781*, pp. 476–484.

46. Campbell to Jefferson, Jan. 15, 1781, *Papers of Jefferson*, IV, pp. 359–363, quotations on pp. 361–362. See also Brown, *Old Frontiers*, pp. 191–196.

47. Jefferson to Clark, Dec. 25, 1780, *Papers of Jefferson*, IV, pp. 237–238.

48. Clark to Nelson, Oct. 1, 1781, *Clark Papers, 1771–1781*, pp. 606–607. See also Robert George to George Slaughter, Feb. 15, 1781, Montgomery to Nelson, Aug. 10, 1781, minutes, Sept. 6–7, 1781, *ibid.*, pp. 506–507, 585–586, 596–603; Todd to Nelson, Oct. 21, 1781, plan for Kentucky defense, Dec. 11, 1781, and order for organizing western troops, Jan. 18, 1782, *Clark Papers, 1781–1784*, pp. 8–10, 15–17, 30.

49. Harrison to Clark, Dec. 20, 1781, *Clark Papers, 1781–1784*, p. 20.

50. *Pennsylvania Packet* (Philadelphia), Apr. 16, 1782; William Irvine to William Moore, May 9, 1782, C. W. Butterfield, ed., *Washington-Irvine Correspondence* (Madison, Wis., 1882), pp. 102n, 242; Harrison to [John] Duval, [William] Crawford, and [John] Evans, Apr. 30, 1782, Harrison to Evans, Aug. 13, 1782, *Official Letters of Governors*, III, p. 200. See also John Heckewelder, *A Narrative of the Mission of the United Brethren among the Delaware and Mohegan Indians; from Its Commencement in the Year 1740 to the Close of the Year 1808* (Philadelphia, 1820), pp. 301–325.

51. John Turney to Arent de Peyster, June 7, 1782, William Caldwell to de Peyster, June 11, 1782, David Williamson to Irvine, June 13, 1782, John Rose to Irvine, June 13, 1782, de Peyster to Thomas Brown, July 18, 1782, Butterfield, ed., *Washington-Irvine Correspondence*, pp. 128n, 366–378 and n.

52. Clark to Harrison, Mar. 5, May 2, 1782, Harrison to House of Delegates, May 6, 1782, gentleman in Quebec to friend in Edinburgh, July 17, 1782, Jacob Pyatt to Clark, Aug. 4, 1782, *Clark Papers, 1781–1784*, pp. 44–45, 63–66, 78, 86. See also *ibid.*, pp. xliii–xliv; Council minutes, Nov. 9, Dec. 8, 10, 11, 1781, de Peyster to Alexander McKee, Apr. 3, 1782, Frederick Haldimand to [?], Apr. 21, 1782, William Lamothe to de Peyster, Apr. 24, 1782, Haldimand to de Peyster, Apr. 28, 1782, "The Haldimand Papers, 1762–1782," Michigan Pioneer and Historical Society, *Collections*, X (1888), pp. 538–546, 565–567, 569–572; Irvine to Washington, Feb. 7, July 11, 1782, Irvine to Benjamin Lincoln, July 1, 1782, and Michael Huffnagle to Moore [July 14], 1782, Butterfield, ed., *Washington-Irvine Correspondence*, pp. 90–91, 128, 174–176, 251n.

53. Hugh McGary to Benjamin Logan, Aug. 28, 1782, *Clark Papers, 1781–1784*, p. 92.

54. William Christian to Harrison, Sept. 28, 1782, *ibid.*, p. 119. See also Logan to Harrison, Aug. 31, 1782, and Clark to Harrison, Oct. 18, 1782, *ibid.*, pp. 102, 135.

55. Arthur Campbell to William Davies, Oct. 3, 1782, Harrison to Joseph Crockett, Oct. 16, 1782, Harrison to W. Fleming, Oct. 16, 1782, *ibid.*, pp. 122, 131–133. See also Harrison to Clark, Oct. 17, 1782, *ibid.*, pp. 133–135.

56. Clark to Harrison, Nov. 27, 1782, *ibid.*, p. 157. See also Clark to Harrison, Nov. 30, 1782, *ibid.*, p. 164; and Abernethy, *Western Lands and the Revolution*, pp. 264–267.

57. James Monroe to Clark, Jan. 5, 1783, Western Commissioners to Harrison, Mar. 9, 1783, journal, June 14, 28, 1783, *Clark Papers, 1781–1784,* pp. 178–180, 215, 393, 401–403; James, *Life of Clark,* p. 417.

58. Clark to Harrison, Mar. 8, 1783, *Clark Papers, 1781–1784,* p. 214. See also Clark to Harrison, Oct. 22, 1782, and Harrison to Clark, Dec. 19, 1782, *ibid.,* pp. 140, 171.

59. Clark to Harrison, May 22, 1783, Harrison to Clark, July 2, 1783, *ibid.,* pp. 237, 245. See also Harrison to Clark, Apr. 9, 1783, *ibid.,* pp. 221–224.

Chapter 11. BRITISH STRATEGY SHIFTS SOUTHWARD

1. Sir Henry Clinton's narrative is in Willcox, ed., *American Rebellion,* p. 122. For the description of the expedition in this and following paragraphs, see Henry to John Jay, May 11, 1779, *Papers of Madison,* I, pp. 282–283; Henry to Jay, May 12, 1779, Henry to R. H. Lee, May 19, 1779, *Henry,* III, p. 240, II, p. 30; "Biographical Memoir of Sir George Collier, Knt., Vice-Admiral of the Blue," *The Naval Chronicle for 1814: Containing a General and Biographical History of the Royal Navy of the United Kingdom,* XXXII (1814), pp. 360–367; Sir George Collier to Clinton, May 16, 1779, Sir Henry Clinton Papers, 1776–1779, Clements Lib., microfilm, Foundation Lib.; Collier to Philip Stevens, May 17, 1779, Edward Mathew to Clinton, May 16, 24, 1779, John Almon, ed., *The Remembrancer, or Impartial Repository of Public Events,* VIII (London, 1779), pt. II, pp. 290–297; and Ward, *War of the Revolution,* ed. Alden, II, p. 867.

2. "Biographical Memoir of Collier," p. 366. See also *Journal of the House of Delegates of . . . Virginia; Begun . . . the Twenty-first Day of October . . . 1782* (Richmond, Va., 1828), p. 31; "Virginia Commerce," p. 331; Pendleton to Woodford, June 21, 1779, *Letters and Papers of Pendleton,* I, p. 290; and Henry to Gov. Thomas Johnson, May 11, 1779, Hubert S. Smith Collection, 1777–1782, Clements Lib.

3. Claim of James Gibson, Sam Donaldson, Douglas Hamilton, Mar. 2, 1784, A.O. 13/96, pt. 1, fol. 24. See also Memorial, 1786, MS 5034, fol. 155, Steuart Papers; claim of John and George Sparling, William Bolden, John Lawrence [1784], A.O. 12/74, fol. 212; and *Va. Gaz.* (Dixon and Nicolson), May 15, 1779.

4. John Christian Senf to Gates, Oct. 12, 1780, Walter Clark, ed., *The State Records of North Carolina,* XIV (Winston-Salem, N. C., 1896), p. 690. See also Thomas J. Wertenbaker, *Norfolk: Historic Southern Port* (Durham, N. C., 1931), pp. 68–70; *Va. Gaz.* (Purdie), Mar. 6, June 12, 1778; and *Statutes,* IX, p. 231.

5. Mathew to Earl of Shelburne, Sept. 14, 1783, No. 16 misc., Parker Family Papers. See also George Blair's loyalist claim, A.O., 12/56, fol. 186; Blair to Steuart, Apr. 25, 1786, MS 5034, fol. 147, Steuart Papers; Parker to Steuart, May 3, 1779, No. 16 misc., fol. 5, Parker Family Papers; John Goodrich to Clin-

ton, Nov. 2, 1778, Parker to Mathew, Nov. 30, 1778, Hector McAlestor's Plan for occupying Virginia [1778–1779], Clinton Papers; prize case of the *John*, June 25, 1779, H.C.A. 32/382, folder 15; Pendleton to Woodford, May 31, 1779, *Letters and Papers of Pendleton*, I, p. 289; and Adele Hast, *Loyalism in Revolutionary Virginia: The Norfolk Area and the Eastern Shore* (Ann Arbor, Mich., 1982), pp. 91–106.

6. *Va. Gaz.* (Dixon and Nicolson), May 15, 1779; "Biographical Memoir of Collier," pp. 360–367. See also Whit Hill to Thomas Burke [ca. May 1779], Clark, ed., *State Records of North Carolina*, XIV, p. 3; Henry's proclamation, May 14, 1779, *Official Letters of Governors*, I, p. 370; William Fleming to Nancy Fleming, May 20, 1779, Fleming-Christian Letters, Grigsby Papers, Misc. MSS Collections, Va. Hist. Soc.; Jefferson to Huntington, Oct. 24, 1779, *Papers of Jefferson*, III, pp. 113–114; Simeon Deane to Josiah Buck, Apr. 1780, Silas Deane to Simeon Deane, June 20, 1780, *Deane Papers*, pp. 150–155; *DAB*, s.v. "Deane, Silas"; and "Virginia Commerce," p. 331.

7. Public Store Day Book, Nov. 24, 1779. See also Finnie to Col. H. Hollingsworth, May 12, 1779, Nathanael Greene Papers, Amer. Phil. Soc.; and New Bern committee to Gov. Caswell, May 19, 1779, Clark, ed., *State Records of North Carolina*, XIV, pp. 85–86.

8. Evans, *Nelson*, pp. 81–82; Henry's proclamation, May 14, 1779, *Official Letters of Governors*, I, p. 370; Henry to R. H. Lee, May 19, 1779, *Henry*, II, p. 30; Robert Forsyth to Nathanael Greene, May 19, 1779, Greene Papers; Joseph Hewes to Caswell, May 23, 1779, John Tazewell to Burke, June 4, 1779, Clark, ed., *State Records of North Carolina*, XIV, pp. 94–95, 308–309; Thomas Marshall to Henry, May 26, 1779, *Va. Gaz.* (Dixon and Nicolson), May 29, 1779. See also *ibid.*, June 5, 1779; S. G. Tucker to Bland, June 6, 1779, *Bland Papers*, II, p. 11; and Pendleton to Woodford, July 26, 1779, *Letters and Papers of Pendleton*, II, p. 293.

9. Pendleton to Woodford, May 31, 1779, *Letters and Papers of Pendleton*, II, p. 289; *Va. Gaz.* (Dixon and Nicolson), May 29, 1779; Tazewell to Burke, June 4, 1779, Clark, ed., *State Records of North Carolina*, XIV, pp. 308–309; Clinton to Mathew, May 20, 1779, Willcox, ed., *American Rebellion*, pp. 406–407; Mathew to Clinton, May 24, 1779, *Almon's Remembrancer* (1779), pt. II, pp. 296–297; Collier to Germain, June 15, 1779, Germain Papers, 1768–1782, Clements Lib., microfilm, Foundation Lib.

10. "Biographical Memoir of Collier," pp. 360–367. See also Collier to Stephens, June 13, 1779, *Almon's Remembrancer* (1779), pt. II, p. 299; return of persons who came off from Virginia with General Mathew in the Fleet on the 24th of May 1779, British Headquarters Papers microfilm, N. 10235, Clements Lib., microfilm, Foundation Lib.; and John Agnew's claim, 1784, S.O. 12/56, fols. 402–425.

11. Mason to R. H. Lee, June 19, 1779, *Papers of Mason*, II, p. 523; Jefferson to Jay, June 19, 1779, *Papers of Jefferson*, III, p. 5; prize case of the *Hatteras Shoals*, June 30, 1779, prize case of the *Pateline*, Aug. 17, Sept. 8, 1779, H.C.A. 32/428,

bundles d and f; Honyman Diary, June 28, 1779; Marine Committee to Benjamin Franklin [July 19, 1779], Burnett, ed., *Letters of the Continental Congress,* IV, pp. 328–329; *Papers of Madison,* I, p. 284, n. 4.

12. Porterfield to Woodford, May 28, 1779, *Manuscripts,* XVII, No. 3 (1965), p. 30. See also *Statutes,* X, pp. 18–21, 28–29, 32–34.

13. Pendleton to Woodford, Apr. 26, 1779, *Letters and Papers of Pendleton,* I, p. 280; J. Page to Jefferson, June 2, 1779, *Papers of Jefferson,* II, p. 278 and n.

14. *Statutes,* X, pp. 83–85. See also *ibid.,* pp. 19, 23–27, 112; Porterfield to Woodford, May 28, 1779, *Manuscripts,* p. 30; and Miller, *Triumph of Freedom,* pp. 497–499.

15. Board of War to Jefferson, Nov. 16, 1779, *Papers of Jefferson,* III, p. 191. See also R. H. Lee to Jefferson, Oct. 13, Dec. 1, 1779, Washington to Jefferson, Dec. 11, 25, 1779, Jefferson to Board of War, Nov. 18, 1779, Jefferson to Harrison, Dec. 23, 1779, *ibid.,* pp. 105–106, 210, 217, 243, 193–194, 241; La Luzerne to governor of Maryland, Dec. 12, 1779, W. H. Browne et al., eds., *Archives of Maryland,* XLIII (Baltimore, Md., 1924), p. 383; and Ministère des Affaires Étrangères, *Les Combattants Français de la Guerre Américaine, 1778–1783* (Paris, 1903), p. 76.

16. Board of War to Jefferson, Dec. 23, 1779, Jefferson to Board of War, Dec. 23, 1779, *Papers of Jefferson,* III, pp. 238–239; *Papers of Mason,* II, pp. 613–616.

17. [T. Nelson, Hugh Nelson, and Marshall to Jefferson, between Dec. 28 and 31, 1779], War Office Letter Book. See also Board of War to Capt. Barron, Dec. 23, 1779, Board of War to Porterfield, Dec. 24, 1779, *ibid.;* Notes on Threatened British Invasion [Dec. 1779], Jefferson to James Innes, Dec. 28, 1779, Jefferson to Bland, Jan. 16, 1780, *Papers of Jefferson,* III, pp. 252–253, 246–248, 263; and Simeon Deane to Buck, Apr. 17, 1780, *Deane Papers,* p. 152.

18. Woodford to Washington, Mar. 8, 1780, Mrs. Catesby Willis Stewart, *The Life of Brigadier General William Woodford of the American Revolution,* II (Richmond, Va., 1973), pp. 1154–1156. See also Woodford to Washington, Apr. 9, 1780, *ibid.,* pp. 1164–1166; *Va. Gaz.* (Dixon and Nicolson), Feb. 26, 1780; Henry Young to Greene, Feb. 18, 1780, Greene Papers; Jefferson to Washington, Feb. 17, 1780, Board of War to Porterfield, Mar. 29, 1780, and Jefferson to [William Galvan], May 28, 1780, *Papers of Jefferson,* III, pp. 296–297, 337–338, 401.

19. Jefferson to Washington, June 11, 1780, *Papers of Jefferson,* III, p. 433; Stewart, *Life of Woodford,* II, pp. 1154–1167; Alden, *South in the Revolution,* pp. 239–241; Ward, *War of the Revolution,* ed. Alden, II, p. 705.

20. Honyman Diary, May 29, 1780. See also *Statutes,* X, pp. 221–226; *Journal of the House of Delegates of . . . Virginia; Begun . . . the First Day of May . . . 1780*

(Richmond, Va., 1827), pp. 4, 11, 20, 35; David Jameson to Madison, May 21, 1780, *Papers of Madison,* II, pp. 28–31; Jefferson to Galvan, May 28, 1780, Abner Nash to Jefferson, May 30, 1780, *Papers of Jefferson,* III, pp. 401, 403 and n.; and Address of the General Assembly of Virginia to the Continental Congress, May 24, 1780, *Papers of Mason,* II, pp. 623–624.

21. Gates to Jefferson, July 19, 1780, *Papers of Jefferson,* III, p. 496.

22. Jefferson to Committee of Congress at Headquarters, July 2, 1780, Jefferson to J. Page, July 12, 1780, Jefferson to Madison, July 26, 1780, Jefferson to Huntington, July 27, 1780, *ibid.,* pp. 476, 485, 506–507, 508–513; *Papers of Mason,* II, pp. 637–638.

23. Jameson to Madison, Aug. 13, 1780, *Papers of Madison,* II, p. 58. See also *Statutes,* X, pp. 257–262; and Honyman Diary, July 16, 1780.

24. Jefferson to the Committee of Congress at Headquarters, July 22, 1780, Jefferson to Madison, July 26, 1780, *Papers of Jefferson,* III, pp. 500, 507. See also Jefferson to Washington, July 2, 1780, Jefferson to Committee of Congress at Headquarters, July 2, 22, 1780, Jefferson to J. Page, July 12, 1780, Jefferson to John Mathews, Sept. 2, 1780, Committee of Congress at Headquarters to Jefferson, July 23, 1780, *ibid.,* pp. 478, 476, 500, 485, 585, 502; and *Journals of the Continental Congress,* XVII, pp. 524, 599.

25. Jefferson to Washington, Sept. 5, 1780, *Papers of Jefferson,* III, pp. 595–596. For the description of the battles, see Alden, *South in the Revolution,* pp. 244–246; Ward, *War of the Revolution,* ed. Alden, II, pp. 722–733; and Robert Porterfield to Jefferson, Feb. 1, 1781, *Papers of Jefferson,* IV, p. 497.

26. Alden, *South in the Revolution,* pp. 249–250.

27. Clinton to Maj. Gen. Alexander Leslie, Oct. 12, 1780, Willcox, ed., *American Rebellion,* p. 467. See also Innes to Jefferson [Oct. 21, 1780], T. Nelson to Jefferson, Oct. 21, 1780, Jefferson to Huntington, Nov. 3, 1780, *Papers of Jefferson,* IV, pp. 55–57, 54, 92–93; Parker, statement regarding Leslie expedition, Oct. 1780, Parker Family Papers; McAlestor's loyalist claim, Jan. 28, 1784, A.O. 13/91, folder M.1, fols. 146–160; and John Cramond's loyalist claim, Mar. 18, 1784, A.O. 13/97, fol. 417.

28. Clinton's Narrative, Cornwallis to Clinton, Aug. 6, Clinton to Leslie, Nov. 2, 1780, Willcox, ed., *American Rebellion,* pp. 221, 448–449, 472.

29. Leslie to Clinton, Nov. 4, 1780, *ibid.,* p. 472. See also Leslie to Cornwallis, Nov. 4, 1780, *Papers of Jefferson,* IV, p. 110.

30. Washington to Jefferson, Sept. 11, 1780, Jefferson to William Eaton, Sept. 7, 1780, Tench Tilghman to Jefferson, Sept. 21, 1780, Jefferson to Horatio Gates, Oct. 4, 1780, Jefferson to Edward Stevens, Nov. 10, 1780, *ibid.,* III, pp. 610–611, 639, 654, IV, pp. 10–11 and n., 111.

31. Jefferson to Washington, Oct. 22, 1780, Jefferson to Weedon, Oct. 22, 1780, Steps to Be Taken to Repel General Leslie's Army, Oct. 22, 1780, Jefferson to Robert Lawson, Oct. 23, 1780, Jefferson to Huntington, Oct. 25, 1780, Jefferson to Wood, Oct. 28, 1780, Jefferson to E. Stevens, Nov. 10, 1780, *ibid.*, pp. 59–60, 61, 61–63, 64, 67–68, 79, 111–112; Jones to Madison, Nov. 10, Dec. 8, 1780, *Papers of Madison*, II, pp. 169, 233.

32. Pendleton to Madison, Dec. 4, 1780, *Papers of Madison*, II, p. 222. See also Jones to Madison, Nov. 10, 1780, *ibid.*, p. 169.

33. Richard Elliott to Jefferson, Nov. 7, 1780, *Papers of Jefferson*, IV, pp. 97–98. See also Pendleton to Madison, Oct. 30, 1780, *Papers of Madison*, II, pp. 155–156; R. H. Lee to A. Lee, Oct. 29, 1780, R. H. Lee to Bland, Oct. 31, 1780, and R. H. Lee to S. Adams, Nov. 10, 1780, *Letters of R. H. Lee*, II, pp. 207, 209, 211.

34. Alexander J. Wall, "The Story of the Convention Army, 1777–1783," N.-Y. Hist. Soc., *Bulletin*, XI (1927), pp. 67–99. The name of the army comes from the fact that Gates, fearing British reinforcements were on the way, expedited negotiations by agreeing to "convention articles" of surrender rather than the usual "articles of capitulation."

35. Innes to [Wood], Mar. 11, 1780, Emmet Collection. See also *Journals of the Continental Congress*, XIII, p. 42; Phillips to Bland, Apr. 19, 1779, Washington to Wood, Dec. 4, 1779, *Bland Papers*, I, pp. 119–120, II, pp. 29–30; Honyman Diary, Feb. 3, 1779; and Jefferson to [John?] Harris, Mar. 19, 1780, *Papers of Jefferson*, III, pp. 318–319.

36. Phillips to Jefferson, June 18, Aug. 12, 25, 1779, Baron Riedesel to Jefferson, Dec. 4, 1779, *Papers of Jefferson*, III, pp. 3, 66, 74–75, 212–213.

37. Jefferson to Henry, Mar. 27, 1779, *ibid.*, II, p. 242. See also Jefferson to Riedesel, July 1779, *ibid.*, III, pp. 59–60; and R. Parker to R. H. Lee, Apr. 8, 1779, *SLM*, p. 328.

38. For the discussion in this and following paragraphs, see Emory G. Evans, "Trouble in the Back Country: Disaffection in Southwest Virginia During the American Revolution," in Ronald Hoffman, Thad W. Tate, and Peter J. Albert, eds., *An Uncivil War: The Southern Backcountry during the American Revolution* (Charlottesville, Va., 1985), pp. 179–212; Duane Meyer, *The Highland Scots of North Carolina, 1732–1776* (Chapel Hill, N. C., 1961), chap. 5; Mary B. Kegley and F. B. Kegley, *Early Adventurers on the Western Waters.* Vol. I: *The New River of Virginia in Pioneer Days, 1745–1800* (Orange, Va., 1980), chap. 11; Lewis Preston Summers, *History of Southwest Virginia, 1746–1870: Washington County, 1777–1870* (Richmond, Va., 1903), pp. 292–295, 301–304; and Ian Charles Cargill Graham, *Colonists from Scotland: Emigration to North America, 1707–1783* (Ithaca, N. Y., 1956), pp. 38–39.

39. Arthur Campbell to William Preston, July 3, 1780, "Preston Papers," *Branch Historical Papers*, No. 4 (1915), p. 317.

40. *Statutes,* X, pp. 268–270. See also Preston to Jefferson, Mar. 1780, Jefferson to Wood, June 9, 16, 1780, Wood to Jefferson, June 15, 1780, Jefferson to James Callaway, Aug. 1, 1780, Jefferson to Huntington, Sept. 14, 1780, and Jefferson to Va. Delegates in Congress, Oct. 27, 1780, *Papers of Jefferson,* III, pp. 340, 428–429, 453, 449–450, 519–520, 647–648, IV, pp. 76–77.

41. Preston to Jefferson, Aug. 8, 1780, *Papers of Jefferson,* III, p. 534. See also Jefferson to Huntington, Nov. 7, 1780, Gates to Jefferson, Nov. 1, 1780, Jefferson to Patrick Lockhart, Nov. 8, 1780, and John Smith to Zane, Nov. 16, 1780, *ibid.,* IV, pp. 99, 86–87, 103–104, 119–120.

42. Jefferson to Wood, Dec. 15, 1780, *ibid.,* pp. 210–211. See also Jefferson to Wood, Oct. 26, Nov. 3, 7, 1780, Jefferson to Huntington, Nov. 3, 1780, Jefferson to Washington, Nov. 26, 1780, Continental Board of War to Jefferson, Dec. 6, 1780, and Forsyth to the Agent Superintending the State Supplies, Dec. 6, 1780, *ibid.,* pp. 72–74, 95–96, 100–102, 92–93, 160–161, 181–182.

43. Jefferson to Wood, Oct. 28, Nov. 1, 1780, *ibid.,* pp. 79–80, 87–88; Clinton's Narrative, Cornwallis to Leslie, Nov. 12, 1780, Cornwallis to Clinton, Dec. 3, 1780, Willcox, ed., *American Rebellion,* pp. 230–231, 474, 476–479.

44. Jameson to Madison, Nov. 18, 1780, Jones to Madison, Nov. 24, 1780, *Papers of Madison,* II, pp. 186–187 and n. 10, 198–199; Jefferson to Gates, Nov. 19, 1780, Jefferson to Harrison, Nov. 24, 1780, Jefferson to Lawson, Nov. 24, 1780, Jefferson to E. Stevens, Nov. 26, 1780, *Papers of Jefferson,* IV, pp. 127, 150–151, 159.

45. Clinton to Cornwallis, Dec. 13, 1780, Willcox, ed., *American Rebellion,* p. 482. See also Alden, *American Revolution,* pp. 209–210.

46. J. Page to Bland, Jan. 21, 1781, Edmund Ruffin Collection, Alderman Lib. See also Honyman Diary, Jan. 29, 1781; Va. delegates to Jefferson, Jan. 23, 1781, and Madison to Pendleton, Jan. 23, 1781, *Papers of Madison,* II, pp. 295–296, 297.

47. Madison to Pendleton, Jan. 16, 1781, *Papers of Madison,* II, pp. 286–287; Jefferson to Harrison, Nov. 24, 1780, Washington to Jefferson, Dec. 9, 1780, Jan. 2, 1781, *Papers of Jefferson,* IV, pp. 150, 195, 299–300; Washington to Comte de Rochambeau, Dec. 23, 1780, Washington to Marquis de Lafayette, Dec. 26, 1780, Washington to Jefferson, Dec. 27, 1780, *Writings of Washington,* XXI, pp. 9, 19, 21; Freeman, *Washington,* V, p. 110 and n.

48. Jefferson to T. Nelson, Jan. 2, 1781, *Papers of Jefferson,* IV, p. 297. See also Jefferson to Steuben, Dec. 31, 1780, Jefferson to Harrison, Jan. 1, 1781, Jefferson to the County Lieutenants, Jan. 2, 1781, T. Nelson to Jefferson, Jan. 4, 1781, Jefferson to Jacob Wray, Jan. 15, 1781, Innes to Jefferson, Feb. 24, 1781, and William Tatham to William A. Burwell, Jan. 13, 1805, *ibid.,* pp. 254, 289, 294–296, 307, 377–378, 699, 273–274.

49. Clinton's Narrative, Willcox, ed., *American Rebellion,* pp. 235–237; Jefferson to Washington, Jan. 10, 1781, Jefferson to Greene, Jan. 16, 1781, Jefferson to the Va. Delegates in Congress, Jan. 18, 1781, *Papers of Jefferson,* IV, pp. 333–335, 379–380, 398–400.

50. Daniel Hylton's Deposition, Oct. 12, 1796, *Papers of Jefferson,* IV, p. 272; S. G. Tucker to Bland, Jan. 21, 1781, *Bland Papers,* II, pp. 54–56.

51. Jefferson's Diary of Arnold's invasion, Jan. 4, 5 [1781], *Papers of Jefferson,* IV, pp. 258–259. See also *ibid.,* pp. 256n–258n; and Malone, *Jefferson the Virginian,* pp. 337–340.

52. Jefferson to Weedon, Jan. 10, 1781, *Papers of Jefferson,* IV, pp. 335–336, quotation on p. 336. See also Jefferson to Washington, Jan. 10, 1781, *ibid.,* pp. 333–335; Honyman Diary, Jan. 29, 1781; Clinton's Narrative, Willcox, ed., *American Rebellion,* p. 237; and John Graves Simcoe, *Simcoe's Military Journal: A History of the Operations of a Partisan Corps, Called The Queen's Rangers, Commanded by Lieut. Col. J. G. Simcoe, During the War of the American Revolution* (New York, 1844), p. 161.

53. *Journal of the House of Delegates. March 1781 Session* (Virginia State Library, *Bulletin,* XVII [Richmond, Va., 1928]), p. 18; Jefferson to Weedon, Jan. 10, 1781, *Papers of Jefferson,* IV, pp. 335–336.

54. Jefferson to Weedon, Jan. 11, 1781, T. Nelson to Jefferson, Jan. 16, 1781, Jefferson to Va. Delegates in Congress, Jan. 18, 1781, Steuben to Jefferson, Jan. 21, 1781, *Papers of Jefferson,* IV, pp. 339, 382, 398–400, 422; Banister to Bland, Jan. 1781, *Bland Papers,* II, pp. 52–54.

55. Jefferson to Weedon, Jan. 10, 1781, Steuben to Jefferson, Jan. 12, 1781, *Papers of Jefferson,* IV, pp. 336, 345. See also Jefferson to Washington, Jan. 10, 1781, Jefferson to Va. Delegates in Congress, Jan. 18, 1781, and Steuben to Jefferson, Jan. 21, 1781, *ibid.,* pp. 335, 398–400, 422–423.

56. Madison to Pendleton, Jan. 23, 1781, *Papers of Madison,* II, p. 297. See also Madison to Pendleton, Jan. 16, 1781, *ibid.,* pp. 286–287; and *Papers of Jefferson,* IV, pp. 256–278.

57. Ward, *War of the Revolution,* ed. Alden, II, pp. 68–69; Alden, *South in the Revolution,* pp. 252–255.

58. Daniel Morgan to William Snickers, Jan. 26, 1781, Alden, *South in the Revolution,* p. 254. See also *Papers of Jefferson,* IV, p. 438n.

59. Jefferson to the County Lieutenants, Feb. 16, 1781, *Papers of Jefferson,* IV, p. 613. See also Jefferson to Gates, Feb. 17, 1781, *ibid.,* p. 637; and Ward, *War of the Revolution,* ed. Alden, I, chaps. 70–71.

60. Bland to Jefferson, Feb. 9, 1781, Jefferson to James Maxwell, Feb. 16, 1781, T. Nelson to Jefferson, Feb. 18, 19, 1781, *Papers of Jefferson,* IV, pp. 567–569, 631 and n., 650–651, 658–659.

Chapter 12. REFORM AND TAXES

1. "Virginia Commerce," p. 277; Johnson, "Government Regulation," p. 224; *Va. Gaz.* (Dixon and Hunter), June 1, 1775; J. Page to S. G. Tucker, Sept. 28, 1779, Tucker-Coleman Collection; Honyman Diary, June 28, Dec. 4, 1776, July 31, 1779; George Dabney to Charles Dabney, Apr. 18, 1779, Dabney Papers, University of North Carolina, Chapel Hill, N. C., microfilm, Foundation Lib.

2. *Va. Gaz.* (Dixon and Nicolson), July 14, 1779. See also Madison to Bradford, July 17, 1779, *Papers of Madison*, I, pp. 300–302.

3. *Va. Gaz.* (Dixon and Nicolson), July 24, 1779. See also *ibid.*, July 31, Aug. 7, 14, 1779.

4. Honyman Diary, July 31, 1779.

5. *Statutes*, X, p. 113; Abernethy, *Western Lands and the Revolution*, pp. 214–216; Jay to Jefferson, July 26, 1779, E. Randolph to Jefferson, Nov. 13, 1779, *Papers of Jefferson*, III, p. 57, 184–186; John Hatley Norton to Samuel & J. H. Delap, Dec. 9, 1778, prize case of the *Willis*, H.C.A. 32/491, bundle j.

6. R. Parker to R. H. Lee, Mar. 26, 1779, Revolutionary Lee Papers, Alderman Lib. See also R. Parker to R. H. Lee, Mar. 12, Apr. 8, 1779, *ibid.*

7. Pendleton to Woodford, Apr. 1, 1779, *Letters and Papers of Pendleton*, I, p. 278.

8. Washington to Mason, Mar. 27, 1779, *Papers of Mason*, II, p. 493 (punctuation supplied).

9. Mason to R. H. Lee, June 4, 19, 1779, *ibid.*, pp. 508, 524. See also *Statutes*, IX, p. 299, X, pp. 75, 164; and *Journal of the House of Delegates of . . . Virginia; Begun . . . the Fourth Day of October . . . 1779* (Richmond, Va., 1827), p. 27.

10. Meriwether Smith to Harrison, Dec. 12, 1779, Brock Collection, Box 2. See also *Statutes*, X, pp. 74–75, 113; Burnett, ed., *Letters of the Continental Congress*, IV, pp. lxiii–lxvi, V, lxiv; Cyrus Griffin to Burger Hall [Aug. 10, 1779], *ibid.*, IV, p. 360n; R. H. Lee to [Laurens], Aug. 7, 1779, and R. H. Lee to [Whipple], Aug. 8, 1779, *Letters of R. H. Lee*, II, pp. 103, 106.

11. Mason to Jefferson, Apr. 3, 1779, *Papers of Mason*, II, p. 495. See also Mason to Mercer, Feb. 6, 1778, *ibid.*, I, pp. 426–428; and *Papers of Jefferson*, II, p. 136n.

12. *Papers of Jefferson*, II, pp. 133–154; *Papers of Mason*, I, pp. 399–408, 408n–409n.

13. Mason to R. H. Lee, June 4, 19, 1779, *Papers of Mason*, II, pp. 507, 523. See also Land Warrant, July 10, 1779, *ibid.*, pp. 531–532.

14. Jefferson to Fleming, June 8, 1779, *Papers of Jefferson*, II, p. 288. See also *Journal of the House of Delegates, May 1779*, p. 61.

15. For the legislative history in this and following paragraphs, see Bill for Settling Titles to Unpatented Lands, *Papers of Jefferson*, II, pp. 155–167; *Statutes*, X, pp. 35–50, 237–238, 484–485; Mason to Mercer, Feb. 6, 1778, Mason to R. H. Lee, June 19, 1779, *Papers of Mason*, I, pp. 414–422, 426–427, II, pp. 522–524; Abernethy, *Western Lands and the Revolution*, pp. 224, 259, 305; Rowland, *Mason*, I, pp. 327–328; *Journal of the House of Delegates, May 1779*, pp. 38–40; and George Morgan to Va. Delegates in Congress, Nov. 16, 1780, *Papers of Madison*, II, pp. 176–178.

16. Pendleton to Woodford, July 26, 1779, *Letters and Papers of Pendleton*, I, p. 294. See also Abernethy, *Western Lands and the Revolution*, pp. 218–219; and *History of Virginia*, pp. 272–273.

17. Pendleton to Woodford, May 24, 31, 1779, *Letters and Papers of Pendleton*, I, pp. 286, 290. See also *Statutes*, X, p. 10.

18. *Statutes*, X, p. 19. See also *ibid.*, p. 12; Mason to R. H. Lee, June 4, 1779, *Papers of Mason*, II, p. 507; and *Papers of Jefferson*, II, pp. 186–188, 223n.

19. *Statutes*, X, pp. 79–81; Jefferson to Huntington, Dec. 30, 1779, *Papers of Jefferson*, III, p. 250.

20. *Papers of Jefferson*, I, pp. 353, 558–559; Stanley F. Chyet, "The Political Rights of the Jews in the United States, 1776–1840," *Critical Studies in American Jewish History: Selected Articles from American Jewish Archives*, II (Cincinnati, Ohio, 1971), pp. 27–88.

21. For the description in this and following paragraphs, see Bill No. 55, *Papers of Jefferson*, II, pp. 476–479; *Papers of Mason*, II, pp. 505–506; and *Statutes*, X, pp. 129–130.

22. Porterfield to Woodford, May 28, 1779, *Manuscripts*, p. 30.

23. *Statutes*, X, pp. 31, 42–43, 66–74; *Papers of Jefferson*, II, pp. 279–285. Evans, "Private Indebtedness," p. 354n, questions whether the amount received was so large.

24. Mason to R. H. Lee, June 4, 1779, *Papers of Mason*, II, p. 507.

25. Mason to R. H. Lee, June 19, 1779, *ibid.*, pp. 522–523.

26. Mason to R. H. Lee, June 4, 1779, *ibid.*, p. 507.

27. *Papers of Jefferson*, I, pp. 602–603. See also Jefferson to J. Page, Jan. 19, 23, Apr. 9, 1764, *ibid.*, pp. 13, 14, 17; *Va. Gaz.* (Dixon and Hunter), Nov. 15, 1776; R. H. Lee to [W. Lee], Jan. 25, 1778, *Letters of R. H. Lee*, I, p. 382; Custis to Washington, July 15, 1778, Butler Papers; and Honyman Diary, June 12, 1779.

28. *Papers of Jefferson*, I, pp. 598–599, II, pp. 271–272. See also Porterfield to Woodford, May 28, 1779, *Manuscripts*, p. 30; Honyman Diary, June 12, 1779; and *Journal of the House of Delegates, October 1779*, p. 35.

29. For the discussion in this and following paragraphs, see Robert Polk Thomson, "The Reform of the College of William and Mary, 1763–1780" (Amer. Phil. Soc., *Proceedings*, CXV, no. 1 [Philadelphia, 1971]), pp. 187–213; and Bill No. 80, *Papers of Jefferson*, II, pp. 535–543.

30. Jefferson to Samuel Stanhope Smith, Apr. 19, 1779, *Papers of Jefferson*, II, p. 253.

31. Pendleton to Woodford, June 21, 1779, *Letters and Papers of Pendleton*, I, p. 291. See also *Journals of the Council*, I, p. 296; and Bill No. 80, *Papers of Jefferson*, II, pp. 364–365.

32. *Papers of Jefferson*, II, p. 365. See also Board of War to Jefferson, Nov. 13, Dec. 1, 1779, Instructions to Inspector of Stores and Provisions, Jan. 25, 1780, *ibid.*, III, pp. 183, 209–210, 269–270; Elizabeth Commetti, "The Departments of the Quartermaster and Clothier-General, 1775–1780" (Ph.D. diss., University of Virginia, 1939), pp. 195, 220–221, 227; *Journal of the House of Delegates, May 1779*, p. 54; Board of War to Jefferson, Nov. 8, 1779, *Official Letters of Governors*, II, p. 58; and War Office Letter Book, Nov. 8, 11, 1779, Jan. 21, 1780.

33. War Office Letter Book, Nov. 11, 1779. See also Board of War to Jefferson, Nov. 13, 1779, Jan. 21, 1780, *Papers of Jefferson*, III, pp. 182–183, 265.

34. Board of War to T. Nelson, Dec. [1779], War Office Letter Book, p. 8. See also *ibid.*, Nov. 8, 1779.

35. *Journal of the House of Delegates, May 1779*, p. 53; *Journal of the House of Delegates, October 1779*, p. 17; Lawson to Speaker, Sept. 27, 1779, Griffin to Speaker, Dec. 14, 1779, Executive Communications, Box 3; *Statutes*, X, pp. 198–199; Jane Carson, *James Innes and his brothers of the F. H. C.* (Williamsburg, Va., 1965), pp. 107–108.

36. Innes to M. Page, Oct. 27, 1779, *Papers of Jefferson*, III, p. 122; Carson, *Innes*, pp. 110–112.

37. Henry to T. Smith, Mar. 15, 1779, War Office Letter Book, Nov. 1779–Mar. 1780 [2nd section], microfilm, reel 264, Va. State Lib.; T. Smith to Day, Feb. 26, 1779, Thomas Smith Letter Book; *Statutes*, X, pp. 15–16.

38. Board of Trade to Executive Council, Mar. 4, 1780, *Papers of Jefferson*, III, p. 309. See also Board of Trade to Jefferson, June 30, July 1, 1779, Jefferson to Board of Trade, July 1, Dec. 10, 1779, Jan. 26, 1780, *ibid.*, pp. 19, 23, 214, 270–271; and Mercer to Jefferson, Oct. 23, 1779, Executive Papers, Box 3.

39. Custis to Washington, Oct. 26, 1779, Rowland, *Mason,* I, pp. 337–338; *Papers of Mason,* II, pp. 607–613; *Statutes,* X, pp. 182–189.

40. *Statutes,* X, pp. 165–172, 189–191; *Papers of Mason,* II, pp. 598–606; *Papers of Jefferson,* III, p. 105n.

41. *Papers of Mason,* II, p. 549; George E. Lewis, *The Indiana Company, 1763– 1798: A Study in Eighteenth-Century Frontier Land Speculation and Business Venture* (Glendale, Calif., 1941), pp. 227–234.

42. Mercer to Jefferson, Jan. 8, 1780, *Papers of Jefferson,* III, p. 262. See also Bernard Gratz to M. Gratz, Oct. 28, 1779, Gratz Papers, Elting MSS, Hist. Soc. Pa.; and *Journal of the House of Delegates, October 1779,* pp. 27–29.

43. *Journal of the House of Delegates, May 1779,* p. 32; *Papers of Mason,* II, pp. 595–598.

44. Henry to de Gálvez, Jan. 14, 1779, Clinton Papers.

45. *Papers of Mason,* II, pp. 595–598, quotation on p. 596. See also Mason to R. H. Lee, Apr. 12, 1779, *ibid.,* pp. 497–500.

46. *Statutes,* X, pp. 203–207, quotation on p. 206. See also *ibid.,* pp. 140, 149–151, 157–158; Pendleton to Woodford, Nov. 1, 1779, *Letters and Papers of Pendleton,* I, p. 303; and *Papers of Mason,* II, pp. 541–542.

47. *Papers of Mason,* II, pp. 538–540; *History of Virginia,* p. 279; Cary to Jefferson, Dec. 18, 1779, *Papers of Jefferson,* III, pp. 230–231.

Chapter 13. "BARELY SUFFICIENT TO KEEP US JOGING ALONG"

1. Honyman Diary, Feb. 6, 1780. See also *ibid.,* Jan. 10, Feb. 29, Apr. 15, 1780; and James Madison's temperature record, Misc. MSS, Amer. Phil. Soc., microfilm, Foundation Lib.

2. *Journal of the House of Delegates, October 1779,* p. 102. See also Jefferson to Caswell, June 22, 30, 1780, Board of Trade to Jefferson, Dec. 18, 1779, Council Order respecting State Naval Vessels, Mar. 25, 1780, *Papers of Jefferson,* III, pp. 9, 20, 229, 331–332; *Statutes,* X, p. 217; Harold B. Gill, Jr., *The Apothecary in Colonial Virginia* (Williamsburg, Va., 1972), pp. 85–86; and Board of War to McClurg, Jan. 18, 1780, War Office Letter Book.

3. Cary to Jefferson, Dec. 18, 1779, Board of Trade to Jefferson, Feb. 18, 1780, Board of War to Jefferson, Apr. 5, 1780, Inventory of Supplies for the Virginia line, Apr. 7, 1780, Jefferson to Ambler, May 23, 1780, Council to Muter

[June 13–24, 1780], Appointment of James Maxwell as Commissioner of the Navy [before July 21, 1780], Jefferson to William Armistead, July 31, 1780, Muter to Jefferson, Mar. 6, 1781, *Papers of Jefferson*, III, pp. 230, 297–298, 344–345, 346–348, 387, 439, 498, 517, V, p. 80; *Journals of the Council*, II, pp. 278; Journal entries for May–June 1780, Virginia War Office Book, 1777–1780, pp. 42ff., microfilm, Clements Lib.

4. Jameson to Madison, May 21, 1780, *Papers of Madison*, II, p. 30. See also Benjamin Waller to Madison, Nov. 28, 1785, *ibid.*, VIII, pp. 426–428; Board of Trade to Jefferson, Mar. 25, 1780, Notice of Removal of Executive Office from Williamsburg to Richmond, Mar. 25, 1780, J. Page to Jefferson, Apr. 7, 1780, Jefferson to J. P. G. Muhlenberg, Apr. 12, 1780, Jefferson to Reed, Apr. 18, 1780, Thomas Blackburn to Jefferson, May 4, 1780, Jefferson to Wood, May 17, 1780, Muter to Jefferson, Dec. 1, 1780, *Papers of Jefferson*, III, pp. 332, 333–334 and n., 349, 351–352, 353–354, 369, 377, IV, p. 173; General Assembly resolution, May 24, 1780, *Calendar of Virginia State Papers*, I, p. 355; *Statutes*, X, p. 136; and *Journals of the Council*, II, p. 256.

5. Recollections dictated to Charles Campbell, *Jefferson Papers*, III, p. 334n. See also Jameson to Madison, May 21, 1780, *Papers of Madison*, II, p. 29.

6. Eliza Jacquelin Ambler to Mildred Smith [Dudley] [June 1780], Ambler Papers. See also *Statutes*, X, pp. 317–320; *Journal of the House of Delegates, October 1782*, pp. 33, 35, 41; Cary to Jefferson, Dec. 18, 1779, Thomas Turpin to Jefferson, Dec. 22, 1779, Jefferson to Huntington, June 9, 1780, Muter to James Kemp, Oct. 1, 1780, *Papers of Jefferson*, III, pp. 230–231, IV, pp. 224–225 and n., III, p. 427, IV, p. 3; and Jameson to Madison, Sept. 20, 1780, *Papers of Madison*, II, p. 94.

7. Ferguson, *Power of the Purse*, pp. 48–49; *Journals of the Continental Congress*, XVI, p. 197.

8. *Papers of Mason*, II, pp. 632, 633–637; *Statutes*, X, pp. 233–237.

9. Jefferson to Huntington, July 27, 1780, *Papers of Jefferson*, III, p. 511. See also Jefferson to Thomas Sim Lee, Jan. 30, 1780, Committee of Congress to Jefferson, June 2, 1780, and Jefferson to Mathews, Sept. 2, 1780, *ibid.*, pp. 279–280, 406–410, 584–585.

10. For the discussion of fiscal policy in this and following paragraphs, see Ferguson, *Power of the Purse*, pp. 51–69.

11. Jefferson to Madison, July 26, 1780, *Papers of Jefferson*, III, p. 507. See also Madison to Jefferson, May 6, 1780, *ibid.*, p. 370.

12. Griffin to Jefferson, June 9 [1780], *ibid.*, p. 424. See also *Journals of the Continental Congress*, XVI, p. 267. Maryland had fewer delegates present than its law required to cast a vote, and all of Georgia's congressmen were absent.

13. *History of Virginia*, pp. 277–278, quotation on p. 278. See also *Journal of the House of Delegates, May 1780*, p. 37; J. Jones to Washington, July 18, 1780, Ford, ed., *Letters of Jones*, p. 20; and Custis to Washington, July 26, 1780, Butler Papers.

14. *Journal of the House of Delegates, May 1780*, p. 59. See also *ibid.*, p. 39; Henry, II, p. 53; and *Statutes*, X, pp. 242, 254.

15. Jefferson to Madison, July 26, 1780, *Papers of Jefferson*, III, p. 506. See also Proclamation of the Act concerning Redemption of Continental Money, Aug. 28, 1780, *ibid.*, pp. 565–566; *Journal of the House of Delegates, May 1780*, pp. 36–37, 59; *Statutes*, X, pp. 241–254; and R. H. Lee to [S. Adams], Sept. 10, 1780, *Letters of R. H. Lee*, II, pp. 201–202.

16. R. H. Lee to Laurens, July 10, 1780, *Letters of R. H. Lee*, II, p. 188; *Journal of the House of Delegates, May 1780*, pp. 80–83; *Papers of Mason*, II, pp. 645–652; Jameson to Madison, Sept. 20, 1780, *Papers of Madison*, II, p. 94.

17. J. Jones to Madison, Nov. 18, 1780, *Papers of Madison*, II, p. 184. See also J. Jones to Madison, Nov. 5, 10, 1780, Madison to J. Jones, Nov. 21, 1780, Pendleton to Madison, Nov. 27, 1780, *ibid.*, pp. 161–162, 168, 190, 208–209; R. H. Lee to [S. Adams], Nov. 10, 1780, *Letters of R. H. Lee*, II, p. 212; Jefferson to E. Stevens, Nov. 26, 1780, *Papers of Jefferson*, IV, p. 159; *Statutes*, X, pp. 322–323, 347–350, 373–375; and Ferguson, *Power of the Purse*, p. 50.

18. *Papers of Mason*, II, pp. 627–629, quotation on p. 627. See also Jefferson to Harrison, June 8, 1780, Jefferson to Huntington, June 9, 30, July 27, 1780, *Papers of Jefferson*, III, pp. 423, 425–426, 471, 510; and Evans, *Nelson*, pp. 85–87.

19. Remarks on the Proposed Bill for regulating Elections of the Members of the General Assembly [ca. June 1, 1780], *Papers of Mason*, II, pp. 630, 631n.

20. Honyman Diary, Apr. 15, 1780; Custis to Washington, July 26, 1780, Butler Papers.

21. Bland, Sr., to Bland, Jr., Oct. 21, 1780, *Bland Papers*, II, p. 37. See also A. Drummond to J. Coles, Mar. 13 [1780], Carter-Smith Papers; and *Journal of the House of Delegates, May 1780*, pp. 76–77.

22. Jefferson to E. Stevens, Sept. 12, 1780, *Papers of Jefferson*, III, p. 640. See also Jefferson to Gates, Sept. 3, 1780, Advice of Council respecting Reinforcements of Militia, Sept. 4, 1780, Washington to Jefferson, Sept. 11, 1780, and Jefferson to North Carolina Board of War, Sept. 23, 1780, *ibid.*, pp. 588, 597–601, 638–640, 659.

23. Jefferson to Gates, Sept. 23, 1780, *ibid.*, p. 658. See also Gates to Jefferson, July 19, Oct. 6, 1780, Jefferson to Committee of Congress at Headquarters, July 22, 1780, Jefferson to Gates, Sept. 3, Oct. 15, 1780, and Jefferson to Va. Delegates in Congress, Oct. 27, 1780, *ibid.*, pp. 495–497, IV, pp. 16–17, III, pp. 500, 588, IV, pp. 40, 76–77.

24. E. Stevens to Jefferson, Nov. 10, 1780, *ibid.*, IV, p. 112.

25. E. Stevens to Jefferson, Nov. 18, 1780, Greene to Jefferson, Dec. 14, 1780, *ibid.*, pp. 126, 206. See also Jefferson to E. Stevens, Nov. 26, 1780, *ibid.*, p. 159.

26. J. Jones to Madison, Nov. 5, 1780, *Papers of Madison*, II, p. 161. See also J. Jones to Madison, Oct. 17, 1780, Pendleton to Madison, Oct. 17, 1780, *ibid.*, pp. 139, 141–142; and *Journal of the House of Delegates of . . . Virginia; Begun . . . the Sixteenth Day of October . . . 1780* (Richmond, Va., 1827), pp. 8, 66–67.

27. Mason to Jefferson, Oct. 6, 1780, *Papers of Jefferson*, IV, p. 19.

28. Jefferson to Harrison, Nov. 24, 1780, *ibid.*, p. 150. For this and the following paragraph, see also Greene to Jefferson, Nov. 20, 1780, *ibid.*, pp. 130–134; George Washington Greene, *The Life of Nathanael Greene, Major-General in the Army of the Revolution*, III (New York, 1871), pp. 54–63; Mason to Harrison, Oct. 13, 1780, *Papers of Mason*, II, p. 677; and *Statutes*, X, pp. 338–346, 376–377.

29. *Statutes*, X, pp. 326–337, quotation on p. 331. See also Mason to Jefferson, Oct. 18, 1780, Taylor to Jefferson, Dec. 5, 1780, *Papers of Jefferson*, IV, pp. 18–19, 180–181; and J. Jones to Madison, Nov. 10, 24, 1780, *Papers of Madison*, II, pp. 168, 198.

30. J. Jones to Madison, Nov. 18, 1780, *Papers of Madison*, II, p. 183 and n. 6.

31. Madison to J. Jones, Nov. 28, 1780, J. Jones to Madison, Dec. 8, Nov. 18, 1780, *ibid.*, pp. 209, 233, 183. See also J. Jones to Madison, Dec. 2, 1780, *ibid.*, pp. 218–219.

32. Jefferson to R. H. Lee, Sept. 13, 1780, *Papers of Jefferson*, III, p. 642. See also T. S. Lee to Jefferson, Aug. 28, 1780, Jefferson to Maxwell, Aug. 31, 1780, and Jefferson to T. S. Lee, Sept. 3, 1780, *ibid.*, pp. 565, 578–579, 590–591.

33. Jefferson to R. H. Lee, July 17, 1779, James Arbuckle to Jefferson, Dec. 22, 1780, *ibid.*, III, pp. 39–40, IV, pp. 221–222; *Statutes*, X, pp. 379–386.

34. J. Jones to Madison, Dec. 2, 1780, *Papers of Madison*, II, p. 219. See also J. Jones to Madison, Jan. 2, 1781, and Madison to Pendleton, Jan. 16, 1781, *ibid.*, pp. 269–270, 287.

35. Bland to Jefferson, Nov. 22, 1780, Madison to J. Jones, Nov. 25, 1780, Commission to John Laurens and Amendment to His Instructions, Dec. 23, 1780, *ibid.*, pp. 195–197, 202–206, 256–261.

36. J. Jones to Madison, Jan. 2, 1781, *ibid.*, p. 269.

37. Mason to J. Jones, July 27, 1780, *Papers of Mason*, II, pp. 661–662. See also J. Jones to Jefferson, June 30, 1780, John Walker to Jefferson, July 11, 1780, *Papers of Jefferson*, III, pp. 473, 484, 634n–636n; R. H. Lee to [Henry], Nov. 15,

Notes to Pages 256–259

1778, *Letters of R. H. Lee*, I, p. 452; Pendleton to Madison, Sept. 25, 1780, *Letters and Papers of Pendleton*, I, pp. 309–310; and Jensen, *Articles of Confederation*, pp. 225–238.

38. Mason to J. Jones, July 27, 1780, *Papers of Mason*, II, p. 656. See also Boyd Crumrine, *History of Washington County, Pennsylvania, with Biographical Sketches of Many of its Pioneers and Prominent Men* (Philadelphia, 1882), pp. 190–192; and *Statutes*, X, p. 533. A third representative on the negotiating team, Thomas Lewis, who was from the disputed area, did not attend.

39. *Journal of the House of Delegates, October 1779*, p. 106. See also Thomas Scott to Reed, Nov. 29, 1779, Huntington to Jefferson, Dec. 30, 1779, Jefferson to Huntington, Feb. 9, 1780, *Papers of Jefferson*, III, pp. 206–208, 248–249, 286–289; and Crumrine, *History of Washington County*, pp. 182–183 and map.

40. Mason to J. Jones, July 27, 1780, *Papers of Mason*, II, p. 655; Pennsylvania resolution, Crumrine, *History of Washington County*, p. 195. See also *ibid.*, p. 202.

41. Mason to Samuel Purviance, May 20, 1782, *Papers of Mason*, II, pp. 714–715. See also A Resolution to Suspend the Sale of Public Lands, July 4, 1780, Mason to J. Jones, July 27, 1780, *ibid.*, pp. 638–639, 655–663; and Bland to Jefferson, Nov. 22, 1780, *Papers of Jefferson*, IV, p. 137.

42. Committee Report, Sept. 6, 1780, *Papers of Jefferson*, III, pp. 633–634. See also *Papers of Madison*, II, pp. 72–77.

43. Madison to J. Jones, Oct. 17, Nov. 21, 1780, *Papers of Madison*, II, pp. 136, 191. See also Motion on Western Lands, Sept. 6, 1780, and Madison to J. Jones, Sept. 19, 1780, *ibid.*, pp. 77–78, 89–90.

44. Jones to Madison, Dec. 2, 1780, *ibid.*, pp. 220, 221; Jefferson to Washington, Sept. 26, 1780, Resolution, Jan. 2, 1781, *Papers of Jefferson*, III, pp. 665–666, IV, pp. 386–391.

45. Jefferson to the County Lieutenants, Jan. 19, 1781, Jefferson to the First Magistrate of Each County, Jan. 20, 1781, Greenbrier County Militia Officers to Jefferson, Jan. 29, 1781, Robert Ewing to Jefferson, Feb. 12, 1781, Steuben to Jefferson, Feb. 19, 1781, Littleberry Mosby to Jefferson, Feb. 24, 1781, Humphrey Brooke to Jefferson, Feb. 26, 1781, Weedon to Jefferson, Mar. 10, 1781, Beverley Winslow to Jefferson, Mar. 23, 1781, Jefferson to Muhlenberg, Apr. 3, 1781, Jefferson to Steuben, Apr. 3, 6, 1781, Jefferson to John Skinker and William Garrard, Apr. 14, 1781, *Papers of Jefferson*, IV, pp. 400–403, 414–415, 469, 587–588, 662, 700, V, pp. 10, 122–123, 224, 328–329, 332–333, 366, 451–452.

46. Innes to Jefferson, Feb. 21, 1781, *ibid.*, IV, p. 675; Pendleton to Madison, Apr. 23, 1781, *Letters and Papers of Pendleton*, I, p. 351. See also R. H. Lee to S. Adams, ca. Apr. 1781, *Letters of R. H. Lee*, II, p. 219; Charles Fleming to Jefferson, Jan. 17, 1781, T. Nelson to Jefferson, Jan. 22, 1781, Berkeley County Militia

Officers to Jefferson, Jan. 25, 1781, and William Clayton to Jefferson, Mar. 16, 1781, *Papers of Jefferson*, IV, pp. 385–386, 426–427, 451–452, V, pp. 154–155.

47. George Brooke to Jefferson, Jan. 25, 1781, *Papers of Jefferson*, IV, p. 443.

48. Proclamation Convening the General Assembly, Jan. 23, 1781, Jefferson's Circular Letter to Members of the Assembly, Jan. 23, 1781, *ibid.*, pp. 432, 433–434; *Journal of the House of Delegates, March 1781*, p. 6.

49. *Journal of the House of Delegates, March 1781*, p. 11.

50. William C. Rives, *History of the Life and Times of James Madison*, 2nd ed., I (Boston, 1866), pp. 278–279.

51. Walker to Jefferson, Mar. 8, 1781, William Davies to Jefferson, Mar. 18, 1781, *Papers of Jefferson*, V, pp. 101–102, 175–176; *Journal of the House of Delegates, March 1781*, pp. 31, 34–35, 44; *Statutes*, X, p. 396.

52. *Statutes*, X, pp. 391–392; Jefferson to Spotswood, Jan. 31, 1781, Steuben to Jefferson, Mar. 5, 1781, Jefferson to the Speaker of the House of Delegates, Mar. 1, 6, 1781, *Papers of Jefferson*, IV, p. 490, V, pp. 66–70, 34, 76–77 and n.; *Journal of the House of Delegates, March 1781*, pp. 12, 15–17, 41–42.

53. *Statutes*, X, p. 393.

54. *Ibid.*, pp. 393–395, quotation on p. 395. See also Mason to Jefferson, May 14, 1781, *Papers of Jefferson*, V, pp. 647–649; and *Journal of the House of Delegates, March 1781*, pp. 14–15, 19–23, 25, 30, 32, 34–35, 37, 38, 42, 48.

55. Greene to Jefferson, Apr. 28, 1781, Jefferson to Greene, Apr. 1, 1781, *Papers of Jefferson*, V, pp. 569, 314. See also Jefferson to R. H. Lee, Mar. 16, 1781, George Elliott to Jefferson, Mar. 22, 1781, and Jefferson to Greene, Mar. 24, Apr. 1, 1781, *ibid.*, pp. 161–162, 205–206, 229–231, 313–314.

56. *Journal of the House of Delegates, March 1781*, pp. 23–31, 38; *Statutes*, X, pp. 397–400.

57. Jefferson's Circular Letter to Members of the Assembly, Jan. 23, 1781, *Papers of Jefferson*, IV, p. 434.

58. *Journal of the House of Delegates, March 1781*, pp. 33–34.

59. *Ibid.*, pp. 30, 34–35, 39, 41; *Journal of the House of Delegates of . . . Virginia; Begun . . . the Seventh Day of May . . . 1781* (Richmond, Va., 1828), p. 18; Pendleton to Madison, Mar. 26, 1781, *Papers of Madison*, III, pp. 34–35 and n. 14.

60. Innes to Jefferson, Mar. 30, 1781, *Papers of Jefferson*, V, p. 293.

61. Phillips to Weedon, Apr. 6, 1781, *ibid.*, pp. 364–365. See also Jefferson

394 Notes to Pages 262–266

to Weedon, Apr. 4, 1781, Joseph Prentis to Jefferson, Apr. 8, 1781, Weedon to Phillips, Apr. 12, 1781, Steuben to Phillips, Apr. 30, 1781, *ibid.*, pp. 352, 383 and n., 457n–458n, 557n; Simcoe, *Journal*, p. 186; and *Journal of the House of Delegates, March 1781*, pp. 19, 24–25, 38–39, 44–45, 49.

62. *Journal of the House of Delegates, March 1781*, p. 15. See also *ibid.*, pp. 19, 26.

63. Jefferson to Timothy Pickering, Mar. 4, 1781, *Papers of Jefferson*, V, p. 59.

64. *Journal of the House of Delegates, March 1781*, pp. 22, 41. See also Muter to Jefferson, Mar. 2, 12, 1781, *Papers of Jefferson*, V, pp. 45–46, 133–134.

65. Davies to T. Nelson, July 14, Aug. 14, 1781, *Calendar of Virginia State Papers*, II, pp. 218, 329.

66. Davies to T. Nelson, July 17, 1781, *ibid.*, p. 224. See also *Journals of the Council*, II, p. 358.

67. Davies to T. Nelson, Aug. 14, 1781, *Calendar of Virginia State Papers*, II, p. 328. See also John Pierce to T. Nelson, Aug. 15, 1781, Edward Carrington to T. Nelson, Sept. 7, 1781, *ibid.*, pp. 332, 400–402; Lafayette to Davies, Aug. 25, 1781, *Lafayette in Virginia: Unpublished Letters from the Original Manuscripts in the Virginia State Library and the Library of Congress* (Historical Documents, Institut Français de Washington, Cahier II [Baltimore, Md., 1928]), p. 53; and *Journals of the Council*, II, p. 387.

Chapter 14. DEFEAT

1. Pendleton to Madison, Mar. 26, 1781, *Papers of Madison*, III, p. 34 and n. 12; *Journal of the House of Delegates, March 1781*, pp. 22–23; Ward, *War of the Revolution*, ed. Alden, II, p. 870; Washington to Jefferson, Feb. 21, 1781, Lafayette to Jefferson, Mar. 3, 16, 1781, Richard Claiborne to Jefferson, Mar. 14, 1781, Jefferson to R. H. Lee, Mar. 3, 1781, Jefferson to the Commander Officer of the French Squadron, Mar. 4, 1781, Jefferson to William Lewis, Mar. 4, 1781, *Papers of Jefferson*, IV, pp. 683–685, V, pp. 49–51, 159–160, 55–57, 142, 51–52, 55–56, 57.

2. Washington to Greene, Mar. 21, 1781, *Writings of Washington*, XXI, p. 346. See also Theodore Thayer, *Nathanael Greene: Strategist of the American Revolution* (New York, 1960), pp. 337–338; and Washington to Jefferson, Feb. 6, 1781, *Papers of Jefferson*, IV, pp. 543–544. See also *ibid.*, V, p. 24n.

3. Jefferson to Greene, Feb. 18, 1781, Greene to Jefferson, Feb. 28, 1781, *Papers of Jefferson*, IV, p. 647, V, pp. 22–23. See also Jefferson to Charles Magill, Feb. 18, 1781, *ibid.*, IV, pp. 649–650.

4. Greene to Jefferson, Mar. 31, 1781, Greene to Steuben, Apr. 6, 1781, *ibid.*, V, pp. 302, 276n–277n.

5. Steuben to Greene, Feb. 23, 1781, *ibid.*, IV, p. 696n. See also Greene to Steuben, Feb. 10, 1781, *ibid.*, pp. 576n–577n.

6. Maj. William North to Greene, Feb. 23, 1781, *ibid.*, p. 661n.

7. Walker to Jefferson, Mar. 9, 1781, *ibid.*, V, p. 108. See also Jefferson to Walker, Jan. 18 [1781], *ibid.*, IV, p. 400.

8. Simcoe, *Journal*, p. 160.

9. Steuben to Jefferson, Feb. 11, 1781, *Papers of Jefferson*, IV, p. 584. See also Jefferson to Harrison, Nov. 30, 1780, and Senf to Jefferson, Jan. 29, 1781, *ibid.*, pp. 168–169, 475–476.

10. Steuben to Washington, Feb. 15, 1781, John McAuley Palmer, *General Von Steuben* (New Haven, Conn., 1937), p. 253. See also Jefferson to Steuben, Feb. 12, 1781, *Papers of Jefferson*, IV, p. 593.

11. Jefferson to Steuben, Mar. 10, 1781, *Papers of Jefferson*, V, p. 120. See also Jefferson to Steuben, Feb. 12, 1781, Cary to Jefferson, Feb. 13, 1781, Jefferson to Turner Southall et al., Feb. 15, 1781, John Allen to Jefferson, Mar. 12, 1781, Jefferson to William Call, Apr. 12, 18, 1781, Senf to Steuben, Apr. 20, 1781, Jefferson to Steuben, Apr. 22, 1781, Steuben to Washington, Apr. 14, 1781, Greene to Washington, Mar. 18, 1781, and Greene to T. S. Lee, Apr. 7, 1781, *ibid.*, IV, pp. 592–594, 596–597, 621, V, pp. 126–127, 413, 487, 510–511, 536–537, 107n, 538n.

12. Davies to Steuben, Feb. 18, 1781, *ibid.*, IV, p. 661n. See also Jefferson to Steuben, Apr. 26, 1781, *ibid.*, V, p. 559.

13. Innes to Jefferson, Feb. 21, 1781, *ibid.*, IV, p. 676. For the description in this and following paragraphs, see Appendix I, "The Affair at Westover," *ibid.*, V, pp. 671–686.

14. Mary Willing Byrd to Steuben, Feb. 15, 1781, Innes to Steuben, Feb. 27, 1781, *ibid.*, pp. 688, 694–696. See also *ibid.*, p. 681n; Carson, *Innes*, p. 126; and *Journals of the Council*, II, p. 285.

15. M. W. Byrd to Jefferson, Feb. 23, 1781, *Papers of Jefferson*, V, p. 690. See also John Nicholas to Jefferson [ca. Feb. 20, 1781], *ibid.*, IV, p. 668.

16. Benedict Arnold to Muhlenberg, Mar. 14, 1781, *ibid.*, V, p. 699.

17. Jefferson to Lafayette, Mar. 8, 1781, Steuben to Jefferson, Mar. 9, 1781, *ibid.*, pp. 92, 106–108 and n.

18. *Ibid.*, p. 107. See also Jefferson to the Speaker of the House of Delegates, Mar. 1, 1781, Muhlenberg to Jefferson, Mar. 10, 1781, Walker to Jefferson, Mar. 17, 1781, Jefferson to Lafayette, Mar. 19, 1781, Lafayette to Jefferson, Mar. 20, 1781, and Jefferson to Huntington, Mar. 21, 1781, *ibid.*, pp. 33–37, 116–117, 173, 179–182, 188–189, 199.

19. Lafayette to Jefferson, Mar. 27, 1781, *ibid.*, p. 261. See also Greene to Jefferson, Mar. 16, 1781, Magill to Jefferson, Mar. 16, 1781, James Barron to Jefferson, Mar. 20, 1781, Jefferson to Huntington, Mar. 21, 1781, *ibid.*, pp. 156–157, 162–163, 187, 198–199; Adm. Arbuthnot to the Admiralty, Mar. 30, 1781, Adm. 1/146, fol. 625; Lafayette to Washington, Mar. 26, 1781, Louis Gottschalk, ed., *The Letters of Lafayette to Washington, 1777–1799* (New York, 1944), p. 167; Clinton's Narrative, Willcox, ed., *American Rebellion*, pp. 254–255; and Ward, *War of the American Revolution*, ed. Alden, II, pp. 870–871.

20. Arbuthnot to the Admiralty, Mar. 20, 1781, Adm. 1/486, fols. 575–581. See also Jefferson to Lafayette, Mar. 19, 1781, *Papers of Jefferson*, V, pp. 180–181.

21. Weedon to Steuben, Apr. 1, 1781, *Papers of Jefferson*, V, p. 276n. See also Steuben to Greene, Mar. 27, 30, 1781, R. H. Lee to Jefferson, Mar. 27, 1781, Weedon to Jefferson, Mar. 27, 1781, Council resolution, Mar. 29, 1781, and Weedon to Steuben, Apr. 3, 1781, *ibid.*, pp. 262–263 and n., 276n, 277n.

22. R. H. Lee to Jefferson, Apr. 9, 13, 1781, Mercer to Jefferson, Apr. 14, 1781, Jefferson to Steuben, Apr. 14, 1781, Weedon to Jefferson, Apr. 21, 1781, *ibid.*, pp. 394, 434–435, 446–448, 452–454, 529–530; Clinton to Gen. Phillips, Mar. 10, 1781, Willcox, ed., *American Rebellion*, pp. 495–496.

23. Washington to Lund Washington, Apr. 30, 1781, *Papers of Jefferson*, V, p. 530n. See also Henry Lee, Sr., to Jefferson, Apr. 9, 1781, and Edmund Read to Jefferson, Apr. 10, 1781, *ibid.*, pp. 393–394, 399.

24. Jefferson to the County Lieutenants, Apr. 12, 1781, *ibid.*, p. 415. See also Jefferson to Steuben, Apr. 3, 6, 26, 1781, and Steuben's Plan for Defensive Operations, Apr. 17, 1781, *ibid.*, pp. 332–333, 366–367, 560–561, 479–481.

25. Garrett Van Meter to Jefferson, Apr. 11, 1781, Jefferson to Van Meter, Apr. 27, 1781, *ibid.*, pp. 410, 566. See also Thomas Read to Jefferson, Apr. 4, 1781, Jefferson to H. Lee, Sr., Apr. 13, 1781, Jefferson to Samuel Cox, Apr. 14, 1781, George Skillern to Jefferson, Apr. 14, 1781, George Moffett to Jefferson, May 5, 1781, Samuel McDowell to Jefferson, May 9, 1781, Accomac County tax commissioners to Jefferson, May 15, 1781, and George Corbin to Jefferson, May 31, 1781, *ibid.*, pp. 344–345, 434, 444, 449–450, 603–605 and n., 621–622, 652–653, VI, pp. 44–47.

26. For the description in this and following paragraphs, see Thady Kelly to Innes, Apr. 18, 1781, Innes to Jefferson, Apr. 18, 20, 23, 1781, Jefferson to the County Lieutenants of Henrico and Certain Other Counties, Apr. 19, 1781, Jefferson to Henrico County lieutenant, Apr. 19, 1781, Jefferson to the Treasurer et al., Apr. 19, 1781, Jefferson to Huntington, Apr. 23, 1781, Jefferson to Weedon, Apr. 23, 1781, Steuben to Innes, Apr. 23, 1781, Jefferson to Steuben,

Apr. 24, 1781, Bolling Starke to Jefferson, Apr. 30, 1781, *ibid.*, V, pp. 485, 486n, 489, 506–507, 539–540, 496–497, 497, 502–503 and n., 538–539, 545–546, 543n–544n, 549–550, 579–580; Jameson to Madison, Apr. 28, 1781, *Papers of Madison*, III, pp. 90–91; and Simcoe, *Journal*, pp. 186–203.

27. Banister to Bland, May 16, 1781, *Bland Papers*, II, pp. 69–70. See also Ward, *War of the American Revolution*, ed. Alden, II, pp. 871–872; Honyman Diary, Apr. 30, 1781; and Jefferson to Washington, May 9, 1781, *Papers of Jefferson*, V, pp. 623–625.

28. Carrington to Davies, Apr. 16, 1781, Steuben to Washington, May 5, 1781, *Papers of Jefferson*, V, pp. 465n, 550n. See also Huntington to Jefferson, Apr. 9, 1781, Jefferson to Steuben, Apr. 14, 1781, and Davies to Jefferson, Apr. 16, 21, 1781, *ibid.*, pp. 392, 452–454 and n., 465, 515–516.

29. Banister to Bland, May 16, 1781, *Bland Papers*, II, pp. 69–70; Ward, *War of the American Revolution*, ed. Alden, II, pp. 471–472.

30. Journal of the Council, Apr. 25, 1781, *Papers of Jefferson*, V, p. 558n. See also Maxwell to Jefferson, Apr. 26, 1781, *ibid.*, pp. 557–558, quotation on p. 558.

31. Journal of the Council, Apr. 25, 1781, Maxwell to Jefferson, Apr. 26, 1781, *ibid.*, pp. 558n, 557–558; Simcoe, *Journal*, p. 201; Ward, *War of the American Revolution*, ed. Alden, II, pp. 871–872; Richard O'Brien to Andrew Monroe, Feb. 1822, Henry S. Randall, *The Life of Jefferson*, I (New York, 1858), pp. 324n–325n.

32. Lafayette to Washington, May 4, 1781, Gottschalk, ed., *Letters of Lafayette to Washington*, pp. 188–190, quotation on p. 189. See also Louis Gottschalk, *Lafayette and the Close of the American Revolution* (Chicago, 1942), pp. 210–224.

33. Honyman Diary, May 11, 1781. See also Pendleton to Madison, May 7, 1781, *Letters and Papers of Pendleton*, I, p. 354; and Simcoe, *Journal*, pp. 201–202.

34. For the description of British strategy in this and following paragraphs, see Ward, *War of the American Revolution*, ed. Alden, II, chaps. 73–74; Piers Mackesy, *The War for America, 1775–1783* (Cambridge, Mass., 1964), chaps. 22–23; Franklin Wickwire and Mary Wickwire, *Cornwallis: The American Adventure* (Boston, 1970), chap. 14; and William B. Willcox, "The British Road to Yorktown: A Study in Divided Command," *AHR*, LII (1946–1947), pp. 1–35.

35. Cornwallis to Germain, Apr. 23, 1781, Willcox, ed., *American Rebellion*, pp. 511–512.

36. Gottschalk, *Lafayette and the Close of the Revolution*, pp. 225–227; Lafayette to Washington, May 4, 1781, Gottschalk, ed., *Letters of Lafayette to Washington*, pp. 188–190; Banister to Bland, May 16, 1781, *Bland Papers*, II, pp. 69–70; Jefferson to Washington, May 9, 1781, David Ross to Jefferson, May 16, 1781, *Papers of Jefferson*, V, pp. 623–624, 660–661; Simcoe, *Journal*, p. 203.

37. Gottschalk, *Lafayette and the Close of the Revolution*, p. 231; Clinton to

[William Eden], May 11–June 10, 1781, Aukland MSS, King's College, Cambridge, reproduced in Benjamin F. Stevens, comp. and ed., *Facsimiles of Manuscripts in European Archives Relating to America, 1773–1783*, VII (London, 1891), p. 748; Lafayette to Washington, May 24, 1781, Gottschalk, ed., *Letters of Lafayette to Washington*, pp. 196–197; Lafayette to Jefferson, May 26, 1781, Jefferson to Washington, May 28, 1781, *Papers of Jefferson*, VI, pp. 18–19, 32–33.

38. Clinton to Phillips, Mar. 10, 1781, Willcox, ed., *American Rebellion*, p. 496. See also Lafayette to Jefferson, May 26, 1781, *Papers of Jefferson*, VI, pp. 18–19; and Wickwire and Wickwire, *Cornwallis*, p. 328.

39. Pendleton to Madison, May 28, 1781, *Papers of Madison*, III, p. 136. See also R. H. Lee to Va. delegates, June 12, 1781, *ibid.*, p. 158; and Gottschalk, *Lafayette and the Close of the Revolution*, pp. 226–237.

40. Gottschalk, *Lafayette and the Close of the Revolution*, pp. 238–243; Wickwire and Wickwire, *Cornwallis*, pp. 329–330; Henry P. Johnston, *The Yorktown Campaign and the Surrender of Cornwallis, 1781* (New York, 1881), p. 43; Simcoe, *Journal*, p. 211.

41. Davies to Steuben, May 12, 1781, *Papers of Jefferson*, VI, pp. 631–632. See also Jefferson to Steuben, Apr. 22, 1781, Robert Gemble to Steuben, May 2, 1781, and Steuben's Narrative of His Movements on Leaving Point of Fork, 1781, *ibid.*, V, pp. 536, 581n, VI, p. 633.

42. Jefferson to the Members of Assembly for Fluvanna and Certain Other Counties, May 1, 1781, Jefferson to certain county lieutenants, May 21, 1781, Jefferson to Ross, May 25, 1781, Samuel Patterson to Davies, May 27, 1781, Ross to Davies, May 27, 1781, Jefferson to Davies, May 31, 1781, Stephen Southall to Davies, May 31, 1781, *ibid*, V, pp. 585–586, 628n–629n, VI, pp. 3–4, 17–18, 22–23, 23n–24n, 48–49, 49n; *Journal of the House of Delegates, May 1781*, pp. 3–4.

43. Steuben to Lafayette, May 28, 1781, Palmer, *Steuben*, p. 274. See also *ibid.*, pp. 270–274, 281.

44. *Ibid.*, p. 269; Gottschalk, *Lafayette and the Close of the Revolution*, p. 240.

45. Lafayette to Washington, May 8, 1781, Gottschalk, ed., *Letters of Lafayette to Washington*, p. 191. See also Lafayette to Washington, May 25, July 18, 1781, *ibid.*, pp. 198, 204; Lafayette to Jefferson, May 26, 28, 31, 1781, *Papers of Jefferson*, VI, pp. 19, 26–27, 52; Pendleton to Madison, May 21, 1781, *Papers of Madison*, III, p. 128; and Gottschalk, *Lafayette and the Close of the Revolution*, pp. 240–241.

46. Jefferson to Washington, May 28, 1781, *Papers of Jefferson*, VI, pp. 32–33; *Journal of the House of Delegates, May 1781*, pp. 5–6.

47. Simcoe, *Journal*, p. 212. See also Wickwire and Wickwire, *Cornwallis*, pp. 330–334.

48. Steuben to Nash, June 5, 1781, *Papers of Jefferson*, VI, p. 627. See also Steuben's Narrative, *ibid.*, pp. 633–634; and Gottschalk, *Lafayette and the Close of the Revolution*, p. 252.

49. Simcoe, *Journal*, p. 223; *Journal of the House of Delegates, May 1781*, p. 29.

50. Steuben's Narrative, *Papers of Jefferson*, VI, p. 634. See also Palmer, *Steuben*, p. 279; and Wickwire and Wickwire, *Cornwallis*, pp. 332–333.

51. Steuben's Narrative, *Papers of Jefferson*, VI, p. 634; Lafayette to Washington, June 18, 1781, Gottschalk, ed., *Letters of Lafayette to Washington*, pp. 201–202.

52. Steuben's Narrative, *Papers of Jefferson*, VI, p. 635; Davies to Steuben, May 12, 1781, *ibid.*, p. 632.

53. Jefferson to Robert Andrews and the Rev. James Madison, June 3, 1781, Jefferson to Reed, June 3, 1781, Jefferson to the Surveyor of Monongalia County, June 1781, *ibid.*, pp. 72, 74, 76; Malone, *Jefferson the Virginian*, p. 355; *Journal of the House of Delegates, May 1781*, pp. 7, 10.

54. Harrison to J. Jones, June 8, 1781, Ford, ed., *Letters of Jones*, p. 82. See also Jefferson's Diary of Arnold's Invasion, and Jefferson to W. Fleming, June 9, 1781, *Papers of Jefferson*, IV, pp. 256–258, 261, 265, 267n, VI, p. 84.

55. Jefferson to W. Fleming, May 13, 1781, Jefferson to A. Lewis, May 13, 1781, *Papers of Jefferson*, V, p. 640; *Journals of the Council*, II, pp. 331, 341, 345–348, 353.

56. *Journal of the House of Delegates, May 1781*, pp. 10, 22, 30–31; W. Fleming to Harrison, June 7, 1781, *Letters of Governors*, III, p. 1; Harrison to [Steuben?], June 5, 1781, Myers Collection, N. Y. Pub. Lib., microfilm, Foundation Lib.

57. *Journal of the House of Delegates, May 1781*, p. 10; Harrison to J. Jones, June 8, 1781, Ford, ed., *Letters of Jones*, p. 83; J. Page to Harrison, Sept. 22, 1780, Jefferson, Diary of Arnold's Invasion, Gilmer to Jefferson, Apr. 13, 1781, *Papers of Jefferson*, III, pp. 655–666, IV, p. 261, V, pp. 430–431. See also *ibid.*, VI, pp. 78–79.

58. A. Stuart to Jefferson, Sept. 8, 1781, *Papers of Jefferson*, VI, p. 85n. See also Young to Davies, June 9, 1781, R. H. Lee to the Va. Delegates in Congress, June 12, 1781, *ibid.*, pp. 84–85, 85n–86n, 90–93; R. H. Lee to Washington, June 12, 1781, and R. H. Lee to [James Lovell], June 12, 1781, *Letters of R. H. Lee*, II, pp. 233–235, 235–238.

59. *Journal of the House of Delegates, May 1781*, p. 15. See also *ibid.*, pp. 29–30; Palmer, *Steuben*, p. 281; and Cary to Jefferson, June 19, 1781, *Papers of Jefferson*, VI, pp. 96–98.

60. *Statutes,* X, pp. 412–416, 437, quotations on p. 414; Evans, *Nelson,* p. 103.

61. *Statutes,* X, pp. 411–413, 416–421, 426–431, 433–434.

Chapter 15. VICTORY

1. Gottschalk, *Lafayette and the Close of the Revolution,* p. 244 and n.; Wickwire and Wickwire, *Cornwallis,* p. 334.

2. Lafayette to Washington, June 28, 1781, Gottschalk, ed., *Letters of Lafayette to Washington,* p. 203. See also Madison to Mazzei, July 7, 1781, *Papers of Madison,* III, p. 178; and Wickwire and Wickwire, *Cornwallis,* p. 335.

3. Clinton to [W. Eden], May 11–June 10, 1781, William B. Willcox, *Portrait of a General: Sir Henry Clinton in the War of Independence* (New York, 1964), p. 390.

4. Clinton to Cornwallis, May 29, 1781, Willcox, ed., *American Rebellion,* pp. 524–525.

5. For the description of British strategy in this and following paragraphs, see Ward, *War of the American Revolution,* ed. Alden, II, chaps. 73–74; Mackesy, *War for America,* chaps. 22–23; Wickwire and Wickwire, *Cornwallis,* chap. 14; and Willcox, "British Road to Yorktown," pp. 1–35.

6. For the description of events in this and following paragraphs, see Douglas Southall Freeman, *George Washington: A Biography.* Vol. V: *Victory with the Help of France* (New York, 1952), pp. 286–300; Gottschalk, *Lafayette and the Close of the Revolution,* pp. 251–268; Wickwire and Wickwire, *Cornwallis,* pp. 335–353; Willcox, *Portrait of a General: Clinton,* pp. 394–402; Palmer, *Steuben,* p. 282; and Simcoe, *Journal,* pp. 226–237.

7. Cornwallis to Clinton, June 11, 1781, Willcox, ed., *American Rebellion,* pp. 535–537, quotation on p. 536. Washington also expected the British to withdraw from Virginia to reinforce both New York and Charleston. Washington to Custis, July 26, 1781, *Writings of Washington,* XXII, p. 415. See also Wickwire and Wickwire, *Cornwallis,* pp. 338–340; and Willcox, *Portrait of a General: Clinton,* p. 404.

8. Willcox, *Portrait of a General: Clinton,* pp. 404–408; and Wickwire and Wickwire, *Cornwallis,* pp. 349–350, blame each other's principal character for misinterpreting the exchange of correspondence.

9. Cornwallis to Clinton, July 27, 1781, Willcox, ed., *American Rebellion,* pp. 552–553; Cornwallis to Clinton, Aug. 12, 1781, Charles Ross, ed., *Correspondence of Charles, First Marquis Cornwallis,* I (London, 1859), p. 112.

10. Lafayette to [T. Nelson?], July 1, 1781, *Lafayette in Virginia,* p. 18. See

also Gottschalk, *Lafayette and the Close of the Revolution*, pp. 273–275; Quarles, *Negro in the Revolution*, pp. 94–95; and Lafayette to Washington, July 20, 31, Aug. 25, 1781, Gottschalk, ed., *Letters of Lafayette to Washington*, pp. 205–210, 213–214, 223–224.

11. Lafayette to Washington, July 20, 30, 1781, Gottschalk, ed., *Letters of Lafayette to Washington*, pp. 205, 207, 211.

12. Lafayette to Washington, Aug. 6, 1781, *ibid.*, p. 215; Gottschalk, *Lafayette and the Close of the Revolution*, pp. 280–285.

13. Washington to Lafayette, July 13, 1781, *Writings of Washington*, XXII, p. 368.

14. Rochambeau to de Grasse, May 28, 1781, Henri Doniol, *Histoire de la Participation de la France à l'établissement des Etats-Unis d'Amérique: Correspondance diplomatique et documents*, V (Paris, 1892), p. 475. See also *Writings of Washington*, XXII, p. 202n; and Freeman, *Washington*, V: *Victory*, pp. 309–313.

15. Clinton to Cornwallis, Aug. 27, 1781, Willcox, ed., *American Rebellion*, p. 562. See also Clinton to Cornwallis, Aug. 2, 1781, Cornwallis to Clinton, Aug. 20, 1781, Benjamin F. Stevens, comp. and ed., *The Campaign in Virginia 1781: An Exact Reprint of Six Rare Pamphlets on the Clinton-Cornwallis Controversy . . .*, II (London, 1888), pp. 109–119, 130–136; and Willcox, *Portrait of a General: Clinton*, pp. 409–413.

16. For the description in this and following paragraphs, see Willcox, *Portrait of a General: Clinton*, pp. 414–424; Clinton to Cornwallis, Aug. 27, 1781, Clinton's narrative, Willcox, ed., *American Rebellion*, pp. 562, 330; and Gottschalk, *Lafayette and the Close of the Revolution*, pp. 296–298.

17. Davies to Steuben, July 12, 1781, Evans, *Nelson*, p. 106.

18. Lafayette to T. Nelson, Aug. 26, July 1, 1781, *Lafayette in Virginia*, pp. 54, 21. See also Lafayette to T. Nelson, July 27, 1781, Lafayette to Davies, Aug. 6, 1781, *ibid.*, pp. 33–34, 40; T. Nelson to Josiah Parker, July 26, 1781, *Calendar of Virginia State Papers*, II, p. 257; T. Nelson to the state auditors, and T. Nelson to the treasurer, July 30, 1781, *Official Letters of Governors*, III, pp. 15–16.

19. Lafayette to T. Nelson, Aug. 20, 25, 26, 1781, *Lafayette in Virginia*, pp. 52–54; *Journals of the Council*, II, pp. 377–379; Walker to Steuben, Apr. 17, May 31, 1781, *Papers of Jefferson*, VI, p. 44n; Jameson to T. Nelson, Aug. 28, 30, 31, 1781, T. Nelson to Barron, Aug. 31, 1781, T. Nelson to Maxwell, Aug. 31, 1781, T. Nelson to Harrison, Nov. 26, 1781, *Official Letters of Governors*, III, pp. 26–29, 100.

20. T. Nelson to Lafayette, Aug. 15, 1781, *Official Letters of Governors*, III, p. 24; Claiborne to T. Nelson, July 31, Aug. 23, 1781, *Calendar of Virginia State Papers*, II, pp. 275, 354. See also T. Nelson to Claiborne, July 25, 1781, Claiborne

to Davies, July 30, 1781, and Greene to Davies, Aug. 11, 31, 1781, *ibid.*, pp. 264, 271–272, 320–321, 372.

21. T. Nelson to Lafayette, Aug. 3, 1781, *Official Letters of Governors*, III, p. 20. See also Davies to T. Nelson, July 28, 1781, *Calendar of Virginia State Papers*, II, p. 263, *ibid.*, p. 287; and Evans, *Nelson*, p. 108.

22. Lafayette to Davies, Aug. 13, 1781, *Lafayette in Virginia*, p. 46. See also Lafayette to T. Nelson, Aug. 12, 1781, *ibid.*, p. 45; and Gottschalk, *Lafayette and the Close of the Revolution*, p. 285.

23. Lafayette to Washington, Aug. 11, 1781, Gottschalk, ed., *Letters of Lafayette to Washington*, p. 217; Washington to Lafayette, Aug. 27, 1781, *Writings of Washington*, XXIII, p. 52. See also Washington to Lafayette, Aug. 15, 1781, *ibid.*, XXII, pp. 501–502.

24. *Journals of the Council*, II, p. 381; Evans, *Nelson*, pp. 112–114; Proclamation, Sept. 5, 1781, T. Nelson to Ross, Sept. 12, 1781, T. Nelson to John Wells, Sept. 12, 1781, T. Nelson to Richard Morris, Sept. 26, 1781, Armistead to Davies, Sept. 25, 1781, Day to T. Nelson, Oct. 1, 1781, *Calendar of Virginia State Papers*, II, pp. 395–396, 416, 419, 488, 491, 517.

25. T. Nelson to Pierce, Sept. 19, 1781, *Calendar of Virginia State Papers*, II, pp. 467–468. See also Lewis Burwell to Davies, Sept. 11, 1781, and Pierce to Davies, Sept. 13, 1781, *ibid.*, pp. 414, 423.

26. Jameson to T. Nelson, Sept. 15, 1781, *ibid.*, p. 443. See also T. Nelson to Pierce, Sept. 19, 1781, Davies to T. Nelson, Sept. 23, 28, 1781, T. Nelson to Wells, Sept. 25, 1781, and T. Nelson to Jameson, Sept. 27, 1781, *ibid.*, pp. 467–468, 483, 490, 500, 503.

27. Evans, *Nelson*, pp. 114–117.

28. Jameson to T. Nelson, Sept. 19, 1781, Davies to Jefferson, Sept. 17, 1781, *Calendar of Virginia State Papers*, II, pp. 443, 449.

29. Jameson to T. Nelson, Sept. 17, 1781, T. Nelson to Jameson, Sept. 21, 1781, *ibid.*, pp. 448, 474–475. See also T. Nelson to Council, Sept. 5, 1781, Davies to T. Nelson, Sept. 15, 1781, *ibid.*, pp. 391, 442; and *Journals of the Council*, II, pp. 381ff.

30. *Journals of the Council*, II, pp. 397–398. See also *ibid.*, pp. 386–387; Jameson to T. Nelson, Aug. 15, 1781, *Calendar of Virginia State Papers*, II, p. 444; and Jameson to T. Nelson, Aug. 28, 1781, *Official Letters of Governors*, III, pp. 27, 93n.

31. T. Nelson to Maj. Hubbard, Sept. 20, 1781, Evans, *Nelson*, p. 115.

32. *Journals of the Council*, II, pp. 377, 378; T. Nelson to George Webb, Oct. 17, 1781, *Calendar of Virginia State Papers*, II, p. 552; a Petition and Remon-

strance from the Freeholders of Prince William County, Dec. 10, 1781, *Papers of Mason*, II, pp. 700–711.

33. S. G. Tucker to Mrs. Tucker, Sept. 15, 1781, Richard Butler Diary, Gottschalk, *Lafayette and the Close of the Revolution*, p. 305. See also Freeman, *Washington*, V: *Victory*, pp. 322–333.

34. Freeman, *Washington*, V: *Victory*, pp. 333–334; Gottschalk, *Lafayette and the Close of the Revolution*, pp. 307–315; Johnston, *Yorktown Campaign*, pp. 101–102.

35. For the discussion in this and following paragraphs, see Gottschalk, *Lafayette and the Close of the Revolution*, p. 300; Wickwire and Wickwire, *Cornwallis*, pp. 358–364; Willcox, *Portrait of a General: Clinton*, pp. 422–434; and Ward, *War of the Revolution*, ed. Alden, pp. 626–628.

36. Cornwallis to Clinton, Sept. 16–17, 1781, Willcox, ed., *American Rebellion*, p. 571. See also Wickwire and Wickwire, *Cornwallis*, p. 364; and Willcox, *Portrait of a General: Clinton*, pp. 428–429.

37. Minutes of council of war, Sept. 24, 26, 1781, Willcox, ed., *American Rebellion*, pp. 574, 576–577; Willcox, *Portrait of a General: Clinton*, p. 436n; Mackesy, *War for America*, pp. 425–427.

38. Freeman, *Washington*, V: *Victory*, pp. 345–350; Pendleton to Madison, Oct. 8, 1781, *Papers of Madison*, III, pp. 277–280.

39. Cornwallis to Clinton, Sept. 29, 1781, Willcox, ed., *American Rebellion*, p. 577. See also minutes of council of war, Sept. 24, 1781, and Cornwallis to Clinton, Oct. 20, 1781, *ibid.*, pp. 574, 583. For the description of the battle in this and following paragraphs, see Freeman, *Washington*, V: *Victory*, pp. 350–377; Wickwire and Wickwire, *Cornwallis*, pp. 369–388; and Simcoe, *Journal*, p. 252.

40. State of the army in Virginia, Oct. 18, 1781, Stevens, ed., *Clinton-Cornwallis Controversy*, II, p. 198.

41. Anonymous diary, Freeman, *Washington*, V: *Victory*, p. 367; Johann Conrad Doehla Journal, Wickwire and Wickwire, *Cornwallis*, pp. 377, 379.

42. Diary of Capt. John Davis, Evans, *Nelson*, p. 119.

43. Cornwallis to Clinton, Oct. 20, 1781, Willcox, ed., *American Rebellion*, p. 584.

44. Washington to Nathanael Greene, Oct. 16, 1781, *Writings of Washington*, XXIII, p. 231; Cornwallis to Clinton, Oct. 20, 1781, Willcox, ed., *American Rebellion*, p. 585.

45. Cornwallis to Clinton, Oct. 20, 1781, Willcox, ed., *American Rebellion*, pp. 585–586. See also Willcox, *Portrait of a General: Clinton*, p. 438.

46. For the discussion in this and the following paragraph, see Freeman, *Washington*, V: *Victory*, chap. 23.

Chapter 16. "THE MOST PAINFUL SUSPENSE WITH
REGARD TO EVENTS IN EUROPE"

1. Madison to E. Randolph, Sept. 10, 1782, *Papers of Madison*, V, p. 117. See also Samuel Flagg Bemis, *The Diplomacy of the American Revolution* (Bloomington, Ind., 1933), pp. 190–191; and Richard B. Morris, *The Peacemakers: The Great Powers and American Independence* (New York, 1965), pp. 251–257.

2. Freeman, *Washington*, V: *Victory*, pp. 398–401; Howard C. Rice, Jr., and Anne S. K. Brown, trans. and eds., *The American Campaigns of Rochambeau's Army, 1780, 1781, 1782, 1783*. Vol. I: *The Journals of Clermont-Crèvecoeur, Verger, and Berthier* (Princeton, N. J., 1972), p. 65n; Marquis de Chastellux, *Travels in North America in the Years 1780, 1781, and 1782*, trans. and ed. Howard C. Rice, Jr., II (Chapel Hill, N. C., 1963), pp. 374–375.

3. Article VIII, Freeman, *Washington*, V: *Victory*, p. 383n; Simcoe, *Journal*, p. 254. See also Freeman, *Washington*, V: *Victory*, pp. 384n, 513–515; and T. Nelson to [Va.] Delegates in Congress, Oct. 20, 1781, *Official Letters of Governors*, III, p. 88.

4. Harrison to John Smith, Jan. 10, 1782, *Official Letters of Governors*, III, p. 124. See also T. Nelson to Robert Lawson, Oct. 20, 1781, T. Nelson to Va. Delegates in Congress, Oct. 21, Dec. 15, 1781, Andrews to Weedon, Nov. 6, 1781, T. Nelson to Gloucester and Hanover county lieutenants, Dec. 11, 1781, Harrison to Morgan, Dec. 11, 1781, Davies to Harrison, Dec. 15, 1781, Harrison to Wood, Jan. 1, 1782, *ibid.*, pp. 88–89, 95, 108–109, 112, 118; Washington to president of Congress, Dec. 3, 29, 1781, Feb. 18, 1782, Washington to Abraham Skinner, Dec. 5, 1781, and Washington to George Clinton, May 5, 1782, *Writings of Washington*, XXIII, pp. 263n, 369, 372, 403–404, XXIV, pp. 4–6, 223.

5. Evelyn M. Acomb, trans. and ed., *The Revolutionary Journal of Baron Ludwig von Closen, 1780–1783* (Chapel Hill, N. C., 1958), p. 169. See also Rice and Brown, trans. and eds., *American Campaigns of Rochambeau's Army*, I, pp. 65–67, 157–158; Arnold Whitridge, *Rochambeau* (New York, 1965), pp. 235–238; Chastellux, *Travels*, ed. Rice, II, pp. 374–468; the Rev. J. Madison to Madison, June 15, 1782, *Papers of Madison*, IV, pp. 337–339; and Wythe to Jefferson, Dec. 31, 1781, *Papers of Jefferson*, VI, pp. 144–145.

6. Rutherfoord Goodwin, *A Brief & True Report Concerning Williamsburg in Virginia* (Williamsburg, Va., 1941), pp. 291, 298; Acomb, trans. and ed., *Journal of von Closen*, p. 208 and n.; Harrison to Washington, July 11, 1782, *Official Letters of Governors*, III, pp. 265–266; J. Jones to Madison, July 8, 1782, E. Randolph to Madison, July 18, 1782, the Rev. J. Madison to Madison, June 15, 1782, *Papers*

of Madison, IV, pp. 400 and n. 3, 424, 337–339; Rice and Brown, trans. and eds., *American Campaigns of Rochambeau's Army*, I, pp. 73, 84.

7. Rice and Brown, trans. and eds., *American Campaigns of Rochambeau's Army*, I, p. 64.

8. Harrison to Washington, July 11, 1782, Harrison to Rochambeau, June 26, 1782, *Official Letters of Governors*, III, pp. 266, 257–258.

9. *Journal of the House of Delegates of . . . Virginia; Begun . . . the First Day of October . . . 1781* (Richmond, Va., 1828), pp. 10, 14, 19, 51, 53, 59, 61, 71; Jacquelin Ambler to Madison, Dec. 22, 29, 1781, *Papers of Madison*, III, pp. 335–337, 341.

10. *Journal of the House of Delegates, October 1781*, pp. 3–6, 11, 22; *Evans, Nelson*, p. 121; Ambler to Young, Oct. 26, 1781, Ambler to Thomas Nicolson, Oct. 26, 1781, Webb to Jameson, Nov. 2, 1781, Webb to Claiborne, Nov. 9, 1781, Jameson to Harrison, Nov. 26, 1781, *Official Letters of Governors*, III, pp. 91–93, 95–96, 98–100.

11. Harrison to Greene, Jan. 21, 1782, Harrison to Davies, Apr. 24, 1782, Harrison to John Tyler, May 6, 1782, *Official Letters of Governors*, III, pp. 132, 197, 213.

12. Harrison to Arthur Campbell, Feb. 13, 1782, *ibid.*, p. 151. See also Harrison to Ross, Feb. 11, 1782, *ibid.*, pp. 149–150; *Statutes*, X, pp. 449–450, 458, 462–468; and *Journal of the House of Delegates, October 1781*, pp. 29, 37, 69.

13. *Virginia Gazette, or, the American Advertiser* (Richmond), Jan. 28, 1782. See also Selby, *Dunmore*, pp. 64–65; Harrison to Greene, Jan. 21, 1782, *Official Letters of Governors*, III, pp. 132–133; Jameson to Madison, Jan. 26, 1782, and Va. Delegates to Harrison, Feb. 15, 1782, *Papers of Madison*, IV, pp. 46, 65–67.

14. E. Randolph to Madison, Nov. 16, 1782, *Papers of Madison*, V, pp. 280–281. See also *Va. Gaz., or, American Advertiser*, Nov. 16, 1782.

15. Resolution of Thanks to Jefferson by the Virginia General Assembly, Dec. 12, 1781, *Papers of Jefferson*, VI, pp. 135–136. See also *Journal of the House of Delegates, October 1781*, pp. 17, 34, 37, 40, 48–52.

16. Jefferson to Monroe, May 20, 1782, *Papers of Jefferson*, VI, p. 185.

17. Pendleton to Madison, Dec. 3, 1781, *Letters and Papers of Pendleton*, II, p. 381.

18. [Dec. 10, 1781], *Papers of Mason*, II, pp. 700–711, quotations on pp. 704–705. See also *Journal of the House of Delegates, October 1781*, p. 34.

19. Pendleton to Madison, Dec. 3, 1781, *Letters and Papers of Pendleton*, II, p.

381; Prince William Co. Resolution [Dec. 10, 1781], *Papers of Mason*, II, pp. 706, 708.

20. T. Nelson to Tyler, Dec. 22, 1781, T. Nelson to the Senate, Jan. 12, 1782, Evans, *Nelson*, p. 122.

21. Pendleton to Madison, Dec. 31, 1781, *Letters and Papers of Pendleton*, II, p. 383. See also *Statutes*, X, pp. 478, 496; *Journal of the House of Delegates, October 1781*, pp. 53, 61–62, 67, 69; and Jameson to Harrison, Nov. 26, 1781, *Official Letters of Governors*, III, pp. 98–100.

22. Harrison to Greene, Jan. 21, 1782, Harrison to Tyler, Dec. 2, 1782, *Official Letters of Governors*, III, pp. 132, 391. See also Harrison to Robert Morris, Feb. 7, 1781, Harrison to Tyler, July 1, 1782, *ibid.*, pp. 144–145, 262; Morris to Harrison, Feb. 28, 1782, *Calendar of Virginia State Papers*, III, p. 79; Harrison to Va. Delegates, Feb. 9, 1782, Va. Delegates to Harrison, Feb. 25, 1781, and Jameson to Madison, Mar. 23, 1782, *Papers of Madison*, IV, pp. 58–62, 71, 117–119.

23. Harrison to Tyler, Dec. 20, 1782, *Official Letters of Governors*, III, pp. 409. See also Nov. 15, 1782, *ibid.*, p. 379; and *Journals of the Council*, III, pp. 130, 160–161, 189, 194.

24. Day to T. Smith, Aug. 17, 1778, Correspondence, T. Smith, Box 3.

25. Devereux Jarratt to John Coleman, Oct. 24, 1794, *The Life of the Reverend Devereux Jarratt* (Baltimore, Md., 1806), reprinted in Douglass Adair, ed., *WMQ*, 3rd Ser., IX (1952), p. 361.

26. *Statutes*, XII, pp. 339–340, 497; *Papers of Madison*, VIII, p. 446, n. 1.

27. J. Jones to Madison, June 14, 8, 1783, *Papers of Madison*, VII, pp. 144–145, 120. See also Main, *Political Parties*, p. 245.

28. *Papers of Mason*, II, p. 709. For the discussion in this and the next paragraph, see *Statutes*, X, pp. 455–457, 471–474, 501–517, XI, p. 75; and *Journal of the House of Delegates, October 1781*, pp. 31, 44, 61, 65.

29. J. Jones to Madison, May 25, 31, 1783, *Papers of Madison*, VII, pp. 75, 99. See also E. Randolph to Madison, May 5, 10, 21–24, 1781, J. Jones to Madison, May 21, 1782, *ibid.*, IV, pp. 208, 225, 265, 259–260; S. G. Tucker to Bland, May 2, 10, 1782, *Bland Papers*, II, pp. 79–82; S. G. Tucker to Bland, May 19, 1782, Emmet Collection; and *Statutes*, X, pp. 491–492, XI, pp. 66–71, 194.

30. J. Jones to Madison, June 8, 1783, *Papers of Madison*, VII, p. 120.

31. J. Jones to Madison, June 14, 1783, *ibid.*, p. 144. See also Instructions to Va. Delegates *in re* Settlement of Accounts, Dec. 28, 1782, *ibid.*, V, pp. 459–460; and Ferguson, *Power of the Purse*, p. 333.

32. Harrison to Robert Morris, Mar. 27, 1782, *Official Letters of Governors,* III, p. 184. See also Harrison to Robert Morris, Feb. 7, 1782, *ibid.,* pp. 144–145.

33. Committee report, Nov. 3, 1781, Madison to Jefferson, Nov. 18, 1781, *Papers of Madison,* III, pp. 304n, 307–308. See also Harrison to Tyler, May 6, 1782, *Official Letters of Governors,* III, p. 213.

34. Motion To Amend Arthur Lee's Motion on Western Lands of Apr. 18, 1781, A. Lee to S. Adams, Apr. 21, 1782, *Papers of Madison,* IV, pp. 158, n. 1, 202, n. 9. For the discussion in this and the next paragraph, see Madison to Pendleton, Apr. 23, 1781, E. Randolph to Madison, May 21–24, June 1, 1782, J. Jones to Madison, June 8, 1783, *ibid.,* pp. 178, 265, 305, VII, p. 119; Merrill Jensen, "The Creation of the National Domain, 1781–1784," *MVHR,* XXVI (1939–1940), pp. 323–342; and *Statutes,* XI, pp. 326–328.

35. *Journals of the Council,* III, pp. 228, 295, 316, 341, 345, 401, 421, 474; Harrison to William Moore, Mar. 22, 1781, Harrison to Speaker of House of Delegates, Nov. 25, 1782, *Official Letters of Governors,* III, pp. 176–177, 387.

36. Madison to E. Randolph, July 30, 1782, *Papers of Madison,* IV, p. 447.

37. E. Randolph to Madison, Dec. 13, 1782, Jan. 3, 1783, *ibid.,* V, p. 401, VI, p. 8. See also Madison to E. Randolph, Nov. 19, 1782, *ibid.,* V, p. 289; *Statutes,* X, pp. 409–410, 451, XI, p. 171; *Journal of the House of Delegates, October 1781,* pp. 49, 52, 54–55, 58; and Main, *Antifederalists,* p. 74.

38. E. Randolph to Madison, May 15, 24, June 28, 1783, J. Jones to Madison, May 31, June 14, 1783, Madison to Jefferson, Dec. 10, 1783, *Papers of Madison,* VII, pp. 46, n. 2, 73, 200, 99, 143, 401; Ferguson, *Power of the Purse,* p. 242; *Statutes,* XI, pp. 247–249, 350–352.

39. *Statutes,* IV, p. 132. See also Ballagh, *History of Slavery in Virginia,* pp. 119–120.

40. McColley, *Slavery and Jeffersonian Virginia,* pp. 141–162; *Statutes,* XI, pp. 39–40; David Brion Davis, *The Problem of Slavery in the Age of Revolution, 1770–1823* (Ithaca, N. Y., 1975), p. 197; Hilda Justice, comp., *Life and Ancestry of Warner Mifflin* (Philadelphia, 1905), p. 94; Samuel Shepherd, comp., *The Statutes At Large of Virginia, from October Session 1792, to December Session 1806, Inclusive,* III (Richmond, Va., 1835), p. 253; Fredrika Teute-Schmidt and Barbara Ripel Wilhelm, "Early Proslavery Petitions in Virginia," *WMQ,* 3rd Ser., XXX (1973), pp. 133–146; Jordan, *White Over Black,* pp. 347–349.

41. Morris, *The Peacemakers,* p. 412.

42. *Va. Gaz., or, American Advertiser,* Apr. 5, 1783. See also *ibid.,* Mar. 22, Apr. 26, 1783; and Peace proclamation, Apr. 21, 1783, *Official Letters of Governors,* III, p. 196.

43. Mason to A. Lee, Mar. 25, 1783, *Papers of Mason*, II, p. 766; Notes on debates, Mar. 12–15, 1783, Pendleton to Madison, Mar. 31, 1783, *Papers of Madison*, VI, pp. 328, 422; *Va. Gaz., or, American Advertiser*, Mar. 22, 1783; Clark to Harrison, Apr. 30, 1783, *Clark Papers, 1781–1784*, pp. 228–229.

44. Pendleton to Madison, Mar. 31, 1783, *Papers of Madison*, VI, p. 422; Mason to Henry, May 6, 1783, *Papers of Mason*, II, p. 771. See also Mason to William Cabell, May 6, 1783, Mason to Henry Tazewell, May 6, 1783, Mason to Arthur Campbell, May 7, 1783, *ibid.*, pp. 768–777; Evans, "Planter Indebtedness," pp. 511–533; Evans, "Private Indebtedness," pp. 349–374; and Notes on debates, Mar. 20, 1783, *Papers of Madison*, VI, p. 370.

45. Morris, *The Peacemakers*, p. 464.

46. Carleton to Washington, May 12, 1783, *State Papers and Public Documents of the United States*, 3rd ed., III (Boston, 1819), p. 190. See also *Statutes*, XI, p. 27; Harrison to Va. Delegates, Aug. 30, 1782, motion on slaves taken by the British, Sept. 10, 1782, Madison to E. Randolph, Apr. 15, 1783, and Va. Delegates to Harrison, Apr. 22, 1783, *Papers of Madison*, V, pp. 90, 111–112, VI, pp. 465, 478–479.

47. For the discussion in this paragraph, see Morris, *The Peacemakers*, pp. 411–437.

Bibliographical Essay

Research for this study was greatly eased by the extensive publication of materials in early American history in letterpress and microform editions over the past generation. Through the foresight of its director emeritus of research, Edward M. Riley, the Colonial Williamsburg Foundation sponsored either alone or in cooperation with others the filming of a number of these records and in addition amassed a complete collection of all that became available in whatever form. As the notes indicate, it is through this collection that most of the materials used for this study were viewed.

For the study of Revolutionary Virginia the most important printed source is Julian P. Boyd et al., eds., *The Papers of Thomas Jefferson*, vols. 1–6 (Princeton, N. J., 1950–1952). Whatever the criticism of the superabundant annotation in Boyd's work, the mine of local history in the early volumes of this series will forever be a godsend to scholars in the field. Because the Princeton edition is not yet complete, Paul Leicester Ford's older *The Works of Thomas Jefferson*, 12 vols. (New York, 1904–1905), is needed for pamphlet material, as is William Peden's edition of Jefferson's *Notes on the State of Virginia* (Chapel Hill, N. C., 1955). John C. Fitzpatrick's edition of *The Writings of George Washington from the Original Manuscript Sources, 1745–1799*, 39 vols. (Washington, D. C., 1931–

1944), of course, does not include letters to Washington, selections of which are printed in Stanislaus Murray Hamilton, ed., *Letters to Washington, and Accompanying Papers,* 5 vols. (Boston, 1898–1902) (through 1775), Louis Gottschalk, ed., *The Letters of Lafayette to Washington, 1777–1799* (New York, 1944), and C. W. Butterfield, ed., *Washington-Irvine Correspondence* (Madison, Wis., 1882), but which otherwise must be consulted in the George Washington Papers microfilm of the Library of Congress Presidential Papers series (Washington, D. C., 1964). The microfilm edition includes only Washington papers in the Library of Congress, less than two-thirds of those known to be extant. William T. Hutchinson and William M. E. Rachal, eds., *The Papers of James Madison,* vols. 1–7 (Chicago, 1962–1971), make a contribution similar to Boyd's for the years in which their subject was politically active, as does Robert A. Rutland, ed., *The Papers of George Mason, 1725–1792,* 3 vols. (Chapel Hill, N. C., 1970). No single edition exists of the papers of the all-important Lee brothers. James Curtis Ballagh, ed., *The Letters of Richard Henry Lee,* 2 vols. (New York, 1911–1914), has been supplanted by Paul Hoffman, ed., *Guide to the Microfilm Edition of the Lee Family Papers, 1742–1795* (Charlottesville, Va., 1966), which are materials at the University of Virginia. A complementary collection, the Lee Papers, 1769–1789, is at the American Philosophical Society, Philadelphia. Selections from the Virginia collection are also published in the *Southern Literary Messenger,* N.S., XXVII (1858). William Lee's papers are printed in Worthington Chauncey Ford, ed., *Letters of William Lee, 1766–1783,* 3 vols. (Brooklyn, N. Y., 1891). Lee family manuscripts, including William Lee Letter Books, 1769–1789, are at the Virginia Historical Society, Richmond, Va. A selection of Patrick Henry's few extant papers is woven into William Wirt Henry's worshipful but nonetheless useful biography of his grandfather, *Patrick Henry: Life, Correspondence and Speeches,* 3 vols. (New York, 1891). Edmund Pendleton's papers with virtually no annotation are in David John Mays, ed., *The Letters and Papers of Edmund Pendleton, 1734–1803,* 2 vols. (Charlottesville, Va., 1967). Other printed collections are Charles Campbell, ed., *The Bland Papers: Being a Selection from the Manuscripts of Colonel Theodorick Bland, Jr., of Prince George County, Virginia,* 2 vols. (Petersburg, Va., 1840–1843), R. A. Brock, ed., "Papers, Military and Political, 1775–1778, of George Gilmer, M.D., of 'Pen Park,' Albemarle County, Va." (Virginia Historical Society, *Collections,* N.S., VI [Richmond, Va., 1887]), pp. 69–140, Worthington C. Ford, ed., *Letters of Joseph Jones of Virginia, 1777–1787* (Washington, D. C., 1889), Frances Norton Mason, ed., *John Norton & Sons, Merchants of London and Virginia:*

Being the Papers from their Counting House for the Years 1750 to 1795 (Richmond, Va., 1937), "Preston Papers," *John P. Branch Historical Papers of Randolph-Macon College,* No. 4 (1915), pp. 288–346, and *Lafayette in Virginia: Unpublished Letters from the Original Manuscripts in the Virginia State Library and the Library of Congress* (Historical Documents, Institut Français de Washington, Cahier II [Baltimore, Md., 1928]). Some of William Woodford's letters are interspersed in the privately printed, but helpful, *The Life of Brigadier General William Woodford of the American Revolution,* 2 vols. (Richmond, Va., 1973) by Mrs. Catesby Willis Stewart, Colonel Robert Howe's are in "The Letters of Col. William Woodford, Col. Robert Howe and Gen. Charles Lee to Edmund Pendleton," *Richmond College Historical Papers,* I (1915), pp. 98–163, Charles Lee's are in *The Lee Papers* (New-York Historical Society, *Collections,* IV–VII [New York, 1872–1875]), and Silas Deane's are in the *Deane Papers, ibid.,* XIX–XXIII (New York, 1887–1891), and *The Deane Papers: Correspondence between Silas Deane, His Brothers, and their Business and Political Associates, 1771–1795* (Connecticut Historical Society, *Collections,* XXIII [Hartford, Conn., 1930]). Portions of the Leven Powell Letters at the Alderman Library, University of Virginia, Charlottesville, Va., have been published in Robert C. Powell, ed., *A Biographical Sketch of Col. Leven Powell, Including His Correspondence During the Revolutionary War* (Alexandria, Va., 1877). St. George Tucker's papers, which give many insights into the war at Williamsburg and Petersburg, are in the Earl Gregg Swem Library, College of William and Mary, Williamsburg, Va., and have been microfilmed. The influence of Philadelphia merchants in Virginia can be followed in E. James Ferguson et al., eds., *The Papers of Robert Morris, 1781–1784,* 6 vols. to date (Pittsburgh, Pa., 1973–), and Carter Braxton's connection with Morris in the Carter Braxton Business Papers, Historical Society of Pennsylvania, Philadelphia. Related Continental financial matters are superbly described in E. James Ferguson, *The Power of the Purse: A History of American Public Finance, 1776–1790* (Chapel Hill, N. C., 1961), and Clarence L. Ver Steeg, *Robert Morris, Revolutionary Financier, With an Analysis of His Earlier Career* (Philadelphia, 1954).

Similarly, almost all of the important official papers of the time are in print. The pre-Revolutionary legislative record is in John Pendleton Kennedy, ed., *Journals of the House of Burgesses of Virginia, 1770–1772* (Richmond, Va., 1905), Kennedy, ed., *Journals of the House of Burgesses of Virginia, 1773–1776, Including the Records of the Committee of Correspondence* (Richmond, Va., 1905), and H. R. McIlwaine, ed., *Legislative Journals of the Council of Colonial Virginia,* III (Richmond, Va., 1919). The original editions of the journals of the House of Delegates and the Senate may be found in Clifford K. Shipton, ed., *Early American Imprints, 1st Ser., 1639–1800*, microcards (Worcester, Mass.), and in William S. Jenkins, comp., *Records of the States of the United States of America*, microfilm (Washington, D. C., 1949). Peter Force, comp., *American Archives . . .* , 4th Ser., vols. I–VI, and 5th Ser., vols. I–III (Washington, D. C., 1837–1846, 1848–1853), which is a useful omnibus of contemporary material on the Revolution, excerpted from the journals of the Virginia conventions and the House of Delegates only the passages bearing directly on the rebellion. The delegates' journal for the special session of March 1781 is in the Virginia State Library, *Bulletin*, XVII (1928); the Senate's is not extant. The executive council's records are in H. R. McIlwaine and Wilmer L. Hall, eds., *Journals of the Council of the State of Virginia*, 3 vols. (Richmond, Va., 1931–1952). The gubernatorial papers of Henry, Jefferson, Nelson, and Harrison are in H. R. McIlwaine, ed., *Official Letters of the Governors of the State of Virginia*, 3 vols. (Richmond, Va., 1926–1929). Wm. P. Palmer et al., eds., *Calendar of Virginia State Papers and Other Manuscripts Preserved in the Capitol at Richmond*, 3 vols. (Richmond, Va., 1875–1883), contains a myriad of letters to and from executive departments, but the manuscript Executive Papers at the Virginia State Library should be consulted for materials not included in the calendar. The calendar is indexed in Earl G. Swem, comp., *Virginia Historical Index*, 2 vols. (Roanoke, Va., 1934–1936), which also is the avenue to the otherwise hopelessly jumbled contents of the first and second series of the *William and Mary Quarterly*, the *Virginia Magazine of History and Biography* (through volume XXXVIII), *Tyler's Quarterly Historical and Genealogical Magazine*, William Maxwell, ed., *Virginia Historical Register, and Literary Companion*, and the *Lower Norfolk County Virginia Antiquary*. Most of the material in these serials is genealogical, but they contain many nuggets such as "Correspondence of Col. William Aylett, Commissary General of Virginia," in *Tyler's Quarterly*, I (1920), pp. 87–110, 145–161, and "Letters of the Byrd Family," *VMHB*, XXXV, XXXIX (1927, 1931), passim. The *Index* also covers William Waller Hening, ed., *The Statutes at Large; Being a Collection of All the Laws of Virginia, from the First Session of the Legislature, in the Year 1619*, 13 vols. (New York, Philadelphia, and Richmond, Va., 1819–1823). The several *Virginia Gazettes* published during the Revolutionary years are indexed in Lester J. Cappon and Stella F. Duff, comps., *Virginia Gazette Index, 1736–1780*, 2 vols. (Williamsburg, Va., 1950). Publication of William J. Van Schreeven et al., comps., *Revolutionary Virginia: The Road to Independence*, 7 vols. (Charlottesville, Va., 1973–1983), makes a major contribution to the history of this period by pulling together not only the records of the Virginia conventions, but also of the county committees and the Committee of Safety. In volume IV, where I have had occasion to check closely, however, I have found transcription errors. The history of the most famous Virginia convention is in Hugh Blair Grigsby, *The Virginia Convention of 1776* (Richmond, Va., 1855). Continental records are in Worthington Chauncey Ford, ed., *Journals of the Continental Congress, 1774–1789, Edited from the Original Records in the Library of Congress*, 34 vols. (Washington, D. C., 1904–1937), and Papers of the Continental Congress, 1774–1789, microfilm, Library of Congress.

The war in the West is well documented in print in Reuben Gold Thwaites and Louise Phelps Kellogg, eds., *Documentary History of Dunmore's War, 1774* (Madison, Wis., 1905), Thwaites and Kellogg, eds., *The Revolution on the Upper Ohio, 1775–1777* (Madison, Wis., 1908), Thwaites and Kellogg, eds., *Frontier Defense on the Upper Ohio, 1777–1778* (Madison, Wis., 1912), James Alton James, ed., *George Rogers Clark Papers, 1771–1781* and *1781–1784* (Illinois State Historical Library, *Collections*, VIII, XIX [Springfield, Ill., 1912, 1926]), Milo M. Quaife, ed., *The Capture of Old Vincennes: The Original Narratives of George Rogers Clark and of his Opponent Gov. Henry Hamilton* (Indianapolis, Ind., 1927), "A Narrative of the Transactions, Imprisonment, and Sufferings of John Connolly, an American Loyalist and Lieut. Col. in His Majesty's Service," *Pennsylvania Magazine of History and Biography*, XII (1888), pp. 310–324, 407–420, XIII (1889), pp. 61–70, 153–167, 281–291, "The Haldimand Papers, 1762–1782," Michigan Pioneer and Historical Society, *Collections*, X (1888), pp. 210–672, John Heckewelder, *A Narrative of the Mission of the United Brethren among the Delaware and Mohegan Indians; from Its Commencement in the Year 1740 to the Close of the Year 1808* (Philadelphia, 1820), and William L. Saunders, ed., *The Colonial Records of North Carolina*, X (Raleigh, N. C., 1890).

Documentation at the Virginia State Library for the administrative history during the Revolution is voluminous, particularly the records of the Committee of Safety, the state agents, the board of trade, the public stores in Richmond, Fredericksburg, and Philadelphia, the state clothier, the board of war, the naval board, the public foundry, and the state ropewalk. Some of these records have been microfilmed. The vagaries of the supply system, both state and Continental, are analyzed in Robert Walter Coakley, "Virginia Commerce During the American Revolution" (Ph.D. diss., University of Virginia, 1949), Elizabeth Commetti, "The

Departments of the Quartermaster and Clothier-General, 1775–1780"
(Ph.D. diss., University of Virginia, 1939), Calvin B. Coulter, "The Virginia Merchant" (Ph.D. diss., Princeton University, 1944), and Victor
Leroy Johnson, *The Administration of the American Commissariat During the
Revolutionary War* (Philadelphia, 1941). The story of the Virginia navy is
in Robert Armistead Stewart, *The History of Virginia's Navy of the Revolution* (Richmond, Va., 1934), and Charles O. Paullin, *The Navy of the American Revolution* (Cleveland, Ohio, 1906). An overview of the executive's
struggle to fulfill its responsibilities despite its relative political weakness
is Emory G. Evans, "Executive Leadership in Virginia, 1776–1781:
Henry, Jefferson, and Nelson," in Ronald Hoffman and Peter J. Albert,
eds., *Sovereign States in an Age of Uncertainty* (Charlottesville, Va., 1981),
pp. 181–225.

For the British role, the most important resource is the Virginia Colonial Records Project sponsored by the Colonial Williamsburg Foundation, the Virginia State Library, and the University of Virginia, which
microfilmed virtually every record relating to early Virginia in the major
British depositories. Interlibrary loan requests for this material should
be addressed to the university. Because the film follows the cataloging
of the original depositories, users need first to consult Charles M. Andrews, *Guide to the Materials for American History, to 1783, in the Public
Records Office of Great Britain*, 2 vols. (Washington, D. C., 1912–1914),
Charles M. Andrews and Frances G. Davenport, *Guide to the Manuscript
Materials for the History of the United States to 1783, in the British Museum,
in Minor London Archives, and in the Libraries of Oxford and Cambridge*
(Washington, D. C., 1908), Bernard R. Crick and Miriam Alman, *A
Guide to Manuscripts Relating to America in Great Britain and Ireland* (Lon-
don, 1961), or some other such directory. The survey reports prepared
by the project staff for the guidance of the photographers provide an
excellent calendar of the material, also keyed to the original cataloging.
Most important for this study is the official correspondence of Governor
Dunmore and the secretary of state, Lord Dartmouth, C.O. 5/1333–
1334, 1336, 1349–1353, 1372–1375, Public Record Office. Microfilm of
Dunmore materials owned by the family is in the Swem Library, and
other correspondence is in the *Aspinwall Papers* (Massachusetts Historical
Society, *Collections*, 4th Ser., Pt. II, XL [Boston, 1871]). An exhaustive
account of Dunmore's governorships is Percy Burdelle Caley, "Dunmore: Colonial Governor of New York and Virginia, 1770–1782" (Ph.D.
diss., University of Pittsburgh, 1939). Military correspondence relating
to the early Virginia campaign is in Admiralty 1/485, 486, 487, P.R.O.

(found in the Virginia Colonial Records Project), A. S. Hamond Naval Papers, 1766–1825, microfilm, the originals of which are at the University of Virginia, and Clarence Edwin Carter, comp. and ed., *The Correspondence of General Thomas Gage . . . 1763–1775*, 2 vols. (New Haven, Conn., 1931). The 1779 campaign may be followed in the "Biographical Memoir of Sir George Collier, Knt., Vice-Admiral of the Blue," *The Naval Chronicle for 1814: Containing a General and Biographical History of the Royal Navy of the United Kingdom*, XXXII (1814), pp. 265–296, 353–400, and the 1781 campaign in John Graves Simcoe, *Simcoe's Military Journal: A History of the Operations of a Partisan Corps, Called The Queen's Rangers, Commanded by Lieut. Col. J. G. Simcoe, During the War of the American Revolution* (New York, 1844), and Charles Ross, ed., *Correspondence of Charles, First Marquis Cornwallis*, 3 vols. (London, 1859). The high command's correspondence during most of the war is in the Sir Henry Clinton Papers, 1776–1794, at the William L. Clements Library, University of Michigan, Ann Arbor, Mich., and the Carleton (or Dorchester) Papers in the P.R.O. The latter are calendared in Historical Manuscripts Commission, *Report on American Manuscripts in the Royal Institutions of Great Britain*, 4 vols. (London, 1904–1909). The Clinton-Cornwallis controversy may be followed in William B. Willcox, ed., *The American Rebellion: Sir Henry Clinton's Narrative of His Campaigns, 1775–1782, with an Appendix of Original Documents* (New Haven, Conn., 1954). Benjamin F. Stevens, comp. and ed., *The Campaign in Virginia 1781 . . .*, 2 vols. (London, 1888), and Stevens, comp. and ed., *Facsimiles of Manuscripts in European Archives Relating to America, 1773–1783*, 25 vols. (London, 1889–1898), contain additional material. The two most important British commanders may be interestingly compared in Franklin Wickwire and Mary Wickwire, *Cornwallis: The American Adventure* (Boston, 1970), and William B. Willcox, *Portrait of a General: Sir Henry Clinton in the War of Independence* (New York, 1964). The overall problems faced by the British are discussed in Piers Mackesy, *The War for America, 1775–1783* (Cambridge, Mass., 1964), and Eric Robson, *The American Revolution in its Political and Military Aspects, 1763–1783* (London, 1955). Detailed descriptions of battles are in Christopher Ward, *The War of the Revolution*, ed. John Richard Alden (New York, 1952), and John Richard Alden, *The South in the Revolution, 1763–1789* (Baton Rouge, La., 1957).

The correspondence of the French commanders is in Henri Doniol, *Histoire de la Participation de la France à l'établissement des Etats-Unis d'Amérique: Correspondance diplomatique et documents*, V (Paris, 1892). Accounts of Clermont-Crèvecoeur, Verger, and Berthier are in Howard C

Rice, Jr., and Anne S. K. Brown, trans. and eds., *The American Campaigns of Rochambeau's Army, 1780, 1781, 1782, 1783*, I (Princeton, N. J., 1972). Other useful personal accounts on the Patriot side are Jack P. Greene, ed., *The Diary of Colonel Landon Carter of Sabine Hall, 1752–1778*, 2 vols. (Charlottesville, Va., 1965), Edward Miles Riley, ed., *The Journal of John Harrower: An Indentured Servant in the Colony of Virginia, 1773–1776* (Williamsburg, Va., 1963), Howard R. Marraro, trans., *Memoirs of the Life and Peregrinations of the Florentine, Philip Mazzei, 1730–1816* (New York, 1942), Edmund Randolph, *History of Virginia*, ed. Arthur H. Shaffer (Charlottesville, Va., 1970), the Revolutionary portions of which reflect Randolph's first-hand experiences, and the manuscript diaries of Landon Carter's son Robert Wormeley Carter (originals at the Clements Library and the Swem Library), of William Cabell (original at the Virginia State Library), and of Robert Honyman, 1776–1782 (originals at the Library of Congress and Henry Huntington Library, San Marino, Calif.). The Huntington Library volume is published in Philip Padelford, ed., *Colonial Panorama, 1775: Dr. Robert Honyman's Journal for March and April* (Freeport, N. Y., 1971), and portions of the Library of Congress volume in Richard K. MacMaster, ed., "News of the Yorktown Campaign: The Journal of Dr. Robert Honyman, April 17–November 25, 1781," *VMHB*, LXXIX (1971), pp. 387–426.

A gossipy account of events from one loyalist point of view is the correspondence between James Parker of Norfolk and Charles Steuart, auditor for the American Board of Customs Commissioners. Parker's half of the correspondence is in the Charles Steuart Papers, National Library of Scotland, Edinburgh, and Steuart's, along with Parker's journal and loyalist claims, is in the Parker Family Papers, Liverpool Library, Liverpool, England. Microfilm copies are in the Foundation Library, CWF. Petitions of loyalists for compensation from the Loyalist Commission after the war are in Audit Office 12/54, 56, 97, 99, and Treasury 1/549, P.R.O., microfilm, Virginia Colonial Records Project. Loyalist activity is covered in Isaac Samuel Harrell, *Loyalism in Virginia: Chapters in the Economic History of the Revolution* (Philadelphia, 1926), Adele Hast, *Loyalism in Revolutionary Virginia: The Norfolk Area and the Eastern Shore* (Ann Arbor, Mich., 1982), George M. Curtis III, "The Goodrich Family and the Revolution in Virginia, 1774–1776," *VMHB*, LXXXIV (1976), pp. 49–74, and Emory G. Evans, "Trouble in the Back Country: Disaffection in Southwest Virginia During the American Revolution," in Ronald Hoffman, Thad W. Tate, and Peter J. Albert, eds., *An Uncivil War: The Southern Backcountry during the American Revolution* (Charlottesville, Va., 1985), pp. 179–212. For comparison with other colonies, see Robert McCluer Calhoon, *The Loyalists in Revolutionary America, 1760–1781* (New York, 1973), and for the activities of Dunmore, John Randolph, and others in Great Britain after their exile, Mary Beth Norton, *The British-Americans: The Loyalist Exiles in England, 1774–1789* (Boston, 1972).

Because of the numerous heroes, the secondary literature on Revolutionary Virginia is dominated by biography, culminating in the multivolume monuments by Dumas Malone, *Jefferson and His Time,* 6 vols. (Boston, 1948–1981), Douglas Southall Freeman, *George Washington: A Biography,* 7 vols. (New York, 1948–1957), and Irving Brant, *James Madison,* 6 vols. (Indianapolis, Ind., 1941–1961). Most important for this study are Malone's first volume, *Jefferson the Virginian* (1948), for discussion of the coming of the war and Jefferson's proposed reforms, Freeman's third and fifth volumes, *Planter and Patriot* (1951) and *Victory with the Help of France* (1952), and Brant's first, *James Madison, the Virginia Revolutionist* (1941), for Madison's role in the religious reforms and consistent support for Congress. David John Mays's *Edmund Pendleton, 1721–1803: A Biography,* 2 vols. (Cambridge, Mass., 1952) is the best account of the coming of the war in Williamsburg, the activities of the Committee of Safety, and the establishment of the new government. H. J. Eckenrode, *The Revolution in Virginia* (Boston, 1916), is especially good on the formation of the county committees. See also Emory G. Evans, *Thomas Nelson of Yorktown: Revolutionary Virginian* (Williamsburg, Va., 1975), Robert D. Meade, *Patrick Henry,* 2 vols. (Philadelphia, 1957–1969), Richard R. Beeman, *Patrick Henry: A Biography* (New York, 1974), John Richard Alden, *General Charles Lee: Traitor or Patriot?* (Baton Rouge, La., 1951), John McAuley Palmer, *General Von Steuben* (New Haven, Conn., 1937), Theodore Thayer, *Nathanael Greene: Strategist of the American Revolution* (New York, 1960), Don Higginbotham, *Daniel Morgan: Revolutionary Rifleman* (Chapel Hill, N. C., 1961), and Louis Gottschalk, *Lafayette and the Close of the American Revolution* (Chicago, 1942).

An antidote to the more worshipful approaches to Virginia history is the emphasis on the debt problem by some historians earlier in this century, particularly Harrell, *Loyalism in Virginia.* Serious objection has been raised to this view by Emory G. Evans, "Planter Indebtedness and the Coming of the Revolution in Virginia," *WMQ,* 3rd Ser., XIX (1962), pp. 511–533, Evans, "Private Indebtedness and the Revolution in Virginia, 1776 to 1796," *ibid.,* XXVIII (1971), pp. 349–374, and in studies of the overall debt problem by Aubrey C. Land, "Economic Behavior in a Planting Society: The Eighteenth-Century Chesapeake," *Journal of*

Southern History, XXXIII (1967), pp. 469–485, Jacob M. Price, "The Economic Growth of the Chesapeake and the European Market, 1697–1775," *Journal of Economic History,* XXIV (1964), pp. 496–511, Price, *France and the Chesapeake: A History of the French Tobacco Monopoly, 1674–1791, and of Its Relationship to the British and American Tobacco Trades* (Ann Arbor, Mich., 1973), and Price, *Capital and Credit in British Overseas Trade: The View from the Chesapeake, 1700–1776* (Cambridge, Mass., 1980). Joseph Albert Ernst, *Money and Politics in America, 1755–1775: A Study in the Currency Act of 1764 and the Political Economy of Revolution* (Chapel Hill, N. C., 1973), and Richard B. Sheridan, "The British Credit Crisis of 1772 and the American Colonies," *JEH,* XX (1960), emphasize the potential for economic conflict with the mother country adumbrated by the business cycles of the 1760s and early 1770s. The economic changes in the decades just prior to the Revolution that help explain the Virginians' initial expectations as to their future in the empire and their subsequent confidence in opting for independence may be seen in Paul G. E. Clemens, *The Atlantic Economy and Colonial Maryland's Eastern Shore: From Tobacco to Grain* (Ithaca, N. Y., 1980), David C. Klingaman, *Colonial Virginia's Coastwise and Grain Trade* (New York, 1975), Harold B. Gill, Jr., "Wheat Culture in Colonial Virginia," *Agricultural History,* LII (1978), pp. 380–393, Joseph A. Goldenberg, *Shipbuilding in Colonial America* (Charlottesville, Va., 1976), and Gaspar J. Saladino, "The Maryland and Virginia Wheat Trade from Its Beginnings to the American Revolution" (M.A. thesis, University of Wisconsin, 1960). The importance of the settlement of the Valley is seen in Freeman H. Hart, *The Valley of Virginia in the American Revolution, 1763–1789* (Chapel Hill, N. C., 1942), and Robert D. Mitchell, *Commercialism and Frontier: Perspectives on the Early Shenandoah Valley* (Charlottesville, Va., 1977).

The potential for conflict with the mother country and the promise that the West held for contemporaries is shown in Thomas Perkins Abernethy, *Western Lands and the American Revolution* (New York, 1937), Clarence Walworth Alvord, *The Mississippi Valley in British Politics,* 2 vols. (Cleveland, Ohio, 1917), Jack M. Sosin, *Whitehall and the Wilderness: The Middle West in British Colonial Policy, 1760–1775* (Lincoln, Nebr., 1961), Kenneth P. Bailey, *The Ohio Company of Virginia and the Westward Movement, 1748–1792* (Glendale, Calif., 1939), and William Stewart Lester, *The Transylvania Colony* (Spencer, Ind., 1935). John R. Alden, *John Stuart and the Southern Colonial Frontier* (Ann Arbor, Mich., 1944), describes British policy with the southern Indian tribes.

Recent studies, moreover, point out a number of problems that the

Tidewater planter elite was having in the generation before the Revolution maintaining control of a rapidly growing society: on the concern in Virginia with declining virtue, Gordon S. Wood, "Rhetoric and Reality in the American Revolution," *WMQ*, 3rd Ser., XXIII (1966), pp. 3–32; on the Robinson affair, Ernst, *Money and Politics*, chap. 6, and Jack P. Greene, "The Attempt to Separate the Offices of Speaker and Treasurer in Virginia, 1758–1766," *VMHB*, LXXI (1963), pp. 11–18; on the Chiswell affair, Carl Bridenbaugh, "Violence and Virtue in Virginia, 1766: or, The Importance of the Trivial," Mass. Hist. Soc., *Procs.*, LXXVI (1964), pp. 1–29; and on criticism of the county courts, A. G. Roeber, *Faithful Magistrates and Republican Lawyers: Creators of Virginia Legal Culture, 1680–1810* (Chapel Hill, N. C., 1981).

The trials of the religious establishment are recounted in Rhys Isaac, *The Transformation of Virginia, 1740–1790* (Chapel Hill, N. C., 1982), Wesley M. Gewehr, *The Great Awakening in Virginia, 1740–1790* (Durham, N. C., 1930), Thad W. Tate, "William Stith and the Virginia Tradition," in Lawrence H. Leder, ed., *The Colonial Legacy* (New York, 1973), III-IV, pp. 121–145, Carl Bridenbaugh, *Mitre and Sceptre: Transatlantic Faiths, Ideas, Personalities, and Politics, 1689–1775* (New York, 1962), H. J. Eckenrode, *Separation of Church and State in Virginia: A Study in the Development of the Revolution* (Richmond, Va., 1910), Robert B. Semple, *A History of the Rise and Progress of the Baptists in Virginia* (Richmond, Va., 1810, rev. ed. by G. W. Beale, 1894), and Thomas E. Buckley, *Church and State in Revolutionary Virginia, 1776–1787* (Charlottesville, Va., 1977).

The failure to resolve the greatest problem faced by that generation of Virginians is analyzed in James Curtis Ballagh, *A History of Slavery in Virginia* (Baltimore, Md., 1902), Robert McColley, *Slavery and Jeffersonian Virginia* (Urbana, Ill., 1964), and Winthrop D. Jordan, *White Over Black: American Attitudes toward the Negro, 1550–1812* (Chapel Hill, N. C., 1968), parts 3–5. See also Thad W. Tate, *The Negro in Eighteenth-Century Williamsburg* (Williamsburg, Va., 1965), and Benjamin Quarles, *The Negro in the American Revolution* (Chapel Hill, N. C., 1961).

The nature of the prewar political establishment is succinctly described by Charles S. Sydnor, *Gentlemen Freeholders: Political Practices in Washington's Virginia* (Chapel Hill, N. C., 1952), and Isaac, *Transformation of Virginia*, and massively documented by Jack P. Greene, *The Quest for Power: The Lower Houses of Assembly in the Southern Royal Colonies, 1689–1776* (Chapel Hill, N. C., 1963), Lucille Griffith, *The Virginia House of Burgesses, 1750–1774* (University, Ala., 1968), and Robert E. Brown and B. Katherine Brown, *Virginia 1705–1786: Democracy or Aristocracy?* (East

Lansing, Mich., 1964). But on Sydnor see Richard R. Beeman, "Social Change and Cultural Conflict in Virginia: Lunenburg County, 1746 to 1774," *WMQ*, 3rd Ser., XXXV (1978), pp. 455–476. The only persistent factionalism of the period is noted by Jackson T. Main, "Sections and Politics in Virginia, 1781–1787," *ibid.*, XII (1955), pp. 96–112, Main, *Political Parties before the Constitution* (Chapel Hill, N. C., 1973), and Marc Egnal,"The Origins of the Revolution in Virginia: A Reinterpretation," *WMQ*, 3rd Ser., XXXVII (1980), pp. 401–428. For a close social and economic analysis of Virginia after the war, consult Jackson Turner Main, *The Social Structure of Revolutionary America* (Princeton, N. J., 1965), and Main, "The Distribution of Property in Post-Revolutionary Virginia," *Mississippi Valley Historical Review*, XLI (1954–1955), pp. 241–258. See also Michael L. Nicholls, "Origins of the Virginia Southside, 1703–1753: A Social and Economic Study" (Ph.D. diss., College of William and Mary, 1972), and Richard R. Beeman, *The Evolution of the Southern Backcountry: A Case Study of Lunenburg County, Virginia, 1746–1832* (Philadelphia, 1984). See also Beeman, *The Old Dominion and the New Nation, 1788–1801* (Lexington, Ky., 1972), for politics after the war. Bernard Bailyn's *The Ideological Origins of the American Revolution* (Cambridge, Mass., 1967) details the assumptions that underlay the colonists' attitude toward the empire after the French and Indian War and with little break fed the nationalism born of independence. Caroline Robbins, *The Eighteenth-Century Commonwealthman: Studies in the Transmission, Development and Circumstance of English Liberal Thought from the Restoration of Charles II until the War with the Thirteen Colonies* (Cambridge, Mass., 1959), H. Trevor Colbourn, *The Lamp of Experience: Whig History and the Intellectual Origins of the American Revolution* (Chapel Hill, N. C., 1965), and J. G. A. Pocock, *The Machiavellian Moment: Florentine Political Thought and the Atlantic Republican Tradition* (Princeton, N. J., 1975), amplify this tradition. Gordon Wood analyzes constitution making during and after the war in *The Creation of the American Republic, 1776–1787* (Chapel Hill, N. C., 1969). Robert E. Shalhope, "Toward a Republican Synthesis: The Emergence of an Understanding of Republicanism in American Historiography," *WMQ*, 3rd Ser., XXIX (1972), pp. 49–80, summarizes the work of the school. For an important criticism, see Joyce Appleby, "The Social Origins of American Revolutionary Ideology," *Journal of American History*, LXIV (1978), pp. 935–958.

Index

Abatis, 308
Abingdon, Va., 219
Accokeek Mine, 169
Accomac (ship), 255
Accomack County, Va., 271
Act of Union (1707), 15, 27
Adams, John, 30, 39, 88, 94, 97, 98, 103, 116, 132, 322; on slavery, 108; on U. S. Constitution, 110–111; on Virginia constitution, 112–114
Adams, Samuel, 10, 30, 84, 94, 320
Adventure, The (ship), 175
Agnew, Rev. John, 93, 208
Agnew, Mrs. John, 208
Albany, N. Y., 228
Albemarle County, Va., 48, 145, 169, 234, 276, 315
Albemarle Sound, 149, 179
Albion (ship), 149
Aldermen, 161
Alexandria, Va., 10, 172, 175, 181, 220, 270
Allen's Creek, Va., 276, 289
Almon, John, 103
Ambler, Jacquelin, 48, 241, 246, 300
Amelia County, Va., 292
American Philosophical Society, 245
Amherst County, Va., 282
Ammunition, 19, 70, 186, 263, 269
Amsterdam, Netherlands, 173
André, Maj. John, 222
Andrews, Rev. Robert, 228, 238
Anglican church. *See* Church of England
Anglo-Saxons, 139–140, 237
Annapolis, Md., 92, 106, 265
Anticlericalism, 34–35

Antifederalism (in Va.), 319–321
Appalachian Mountains, 16, 120, 141, 184
Appomattox River, 165, 224, 272
Arbuthnot, Adm. Marriot, 204, 213, 269–270, 287, 291
Aristocracy, 114–116, 140–141, 160
Armistead, William, 177, 246, 263, 298
Arms, 45, 46, 48, 63, 64, 74–75, 167–169, 171, 175, 196, 205, 211, 213, 217, 218, 223, 224, 252, 269, 270, 273, 280, 284
Army, British, 50, 55, 59, 311, 314; at battle of Great Bridge, 69–75; Dunmore recruits for, 64–69, 93, 124–127; northern campaigns, 127, 128, 129, 133–135, 136–137; southern campaigns, 86, 88, 89–90, 93, 105–106, 126, 211–216; strategy, 133, 141, 201–202, 210, 216–217, 227, 274, 286–292; in Virginia, 204–210, 216–226, 265–285, 286–292; western campaign, 194–203; at Yorktown, 292–309. *See also* Regiments, British
Army, Continental, 49–50, 57, 127–129, 130, 131, 134–135, 137, 139, 176–177, 184, 217, 248, 260, 263, 266; with Lafayette, 276, 289–294, 297–298; in South Carolina, 211–215, 216; Virginians in, 131–132; at Yorktown, 300–309, 311–312
Army, Convention, 218–219, 220–221, 273, 276
Army, French: at Williamsburg, 312–313; at Yorktown, 300–309
Army, southern, 213–214, 225–226, 252–254

Arnold, Gen. Benedict, 226, 260, 262, 265–270, 303, 315; invades Virginia, 221–225, 259
Articles of Confederation, 53–54, 142, 154–155, 243–244, 320, 323
Artillery, 70, 72–73, 74, 82–83, 195, 273; British, 125, 272, 280, 302, 308; French, 305, 306–307; Virginia, 62, 90, 125, 132–133, 135, 211, 238, 240; at Yorktown, 303–309
Arundel, Dohicky, 125, 126
Arundel, H.M.S. (ship), 44, 55
Asbury, Francis, 322
Association: Continental, 10, 77; Virginia, 8, 10, 18, 77
Athens, Greece, 116
Auditors, 122, 141, 178, 224, 271–272. *See also* Board of Auditors
Augusta County, Va., 88, 169, 187, 271, 300
Austinville, Va., 167
Aylett, William: 94; as state agent, 171, 174–175; clashes with Braxton, 173–174, 175; commissary of purchases, 61; conflict of interest, 122, 123; criticized, 174–175; deputy commissary general for purchases, 177–178, 179–180, 181

Bachelor Mill Dam, Va., 70
Bacon, 178, 227
Bahamas, W. I., 85
Ball, John, 172
Ballendine, John, 168, 169
Baltimore, Md., 61, 92, 129, 170, 178, 252, 254, 300
Baltimore Iron Works, 169
Banister, John, 130, 150–151, 165, 190, 272–273, 275
Baptists, 135, 145; Regular, 33; Separate, 33–34
Barber of Seville, The, 151
Barbour, James, 177
Barley, 233
Barras, Jacques-Melchior Saint-Laurent, Comte de, 295, 301
Barron, Capt. James, 76, 92, 210–211, 240, 246, 254–255
Barron, Richard, 76
Battalions, 78, 208
Battersea (plantation), 272
Battut, Lt. John, 62, 73, 74, 82
Beall, Samuel, 173
Beaumarchais, Pierre Augustin Caron de, 151, 176, 180, 181

Bedford County, Va., 165, 169, 220
Beef, 62, 177, 178, 248, 253, 259, 261, 271, 298
Bellew, Capt. Henry, 74, 81, 82
Bellini, Charles, 238
Benezet, Anthony, 107
Bentley, Thomas, 191
Berkeley, Norborne, Baron de Botetourt, 8, 15
Berkeley County, Va., 4, 49, 169
Berkeley (plantation), 224
Bermuda, 69, 123, 166
Bermuda Hundred, Va., 274
Bird, Col. Henry, 199
Blacklist: rumors of, 3
Blacks, 38, 162, 208, 221, 292–293, 311, 313, 324; with Dunmore, 105, 126, 314; at Great Bridge, 70–74. *See also* Free blacks; Slaves
Blacksburg, Va., 219
Blackstone, Sir William, 159
Blackwater River, 149
Blaine, Ephraim, 181
Blair, George, 206
Blair, John, 49, 76
Bland, Richard, 38, 75, 90, 165; accused of loyalism, 50; declines election, 53; elected to Congress, 10; urges hanging Dunmore, 45
Bland, Theodorick, 165, 252, 255–256, 258, 273
Bland, Theodorick, Jr., 46, 129, 207, 218, 273
Bland, Theodorick the elder, 223
Blandford (plantation), 272
Blenheim (plantation), 218
Blockade: British, 58, 79, 136, 170, 175–176, 179, 180, 204; Dunmore proposes, 18, 21; by French, 226
Blockade runners, 170, 171–172, 179
Blonde, H.M.S. (ship), 216
Blue Licks, Ky., 202
Blue Ridge Mountains, 23, 33, 188
Board of Auditors (Va.), 241, 247
Board of Navy Commissioners (Va.), 121
Board of Trade (Va.), 239, 241, 245, 246
Board of War (Va.), 210, 239–242, 245, 246
Bondfield, John, 176
Bonetta, H.M.S. (ship), 311
Book of Common Prayer, 121
Boone, Daniel, 141, 202
Bordeaux, France, 173, 176, 180
Boston, Mass., 57, 106, 163, 218, 295; sends circular letter, 9; Tea Party, 8, 13

Botetourt, Lord. *See* Berkeley, Norborne,
  Baron de Botetourt
Botetourt County, Va., 139, 220, 271
Bottoms Bridge, Va., 275, 276, 289
Bounties, 131, 188; enlistment, 128, 132,
  135, 136, 137, 209, 214, 252, 254, 284–
  285; in the West, 153, 154, 190–191,
  194, 231, 244, 257, 321
Bowling Green, Va., 4
Bowman, Capt. Joseph, 191, 193
Boyd's Creek, Tenn., 200
Boykin, William, 81
Boykin affair, 81, 89
Bracken, John, 238
Brafferton, The, 237
Brandon (plantation), 275
Brandywine Creek, 134
Braxton, Carter, 110, 181; accepts Hen-
  ry's report, 53; animosity to R. H. Lee,
  39; clashes with Aylett, 173–174, 175;
  criticized, 228–229; disestablishment of
  Church of England, 145–147; and Fin-
  castle County bill, 143–144; goods con-
  fiscated, 178; mercantile contacts with
  other colonies, 32; Morris's partner,
  173–175; proposes assize courts, 156;
  opposes Henry, 5; opposes independ-
  ence, 91; opposes 40-to-1 plan, 249;
  pamphlet on constitution, 114–116;
  R. H. Lee and Henry attack, 139; on re-
  publican government, 140; runs for of-
  fice, 95; and Silas Deane, 151; on west-
  ern lands, 230, 232, 243
Braxton fleet, 181
Brent, George, 126
Brest, France, 288
Bretman, Thomas, 172
British Loyalist Commission, 59, 67
Brodhead, Col. Daniel, 201
Brooke, George, 259
Brown, John (of Norfolk), 69
Brown, John (of Williamsburg), 177, 263,
  272, 298, 320
Brunswick County, Va., 217
Brussels, Belgium, 315
Bruton Parish, 228
Bruton Parish Church, 97
Buckingham County, Va., 168
Bucktrout, Benjamin, 165
Buford, Col. Abraham, 213
Bullitt, Thomas, 190
Bunker Hill: battle of, 49, 73–74
Burgh, James, 119
Burgoyne, Gen. John, 133, 134–135, 188,
  308–309

Burke, Edmund, 13
Burke, Thomas, 159
Burwell, Lewis, 38, 49, 89
Burwell's Ferry, Va., 89
Burwell's Landing, Va., 2, 245, 271, 275,
  301
Butler, Col. Richard, 289–290
Byrd, Mary Willing, 268
Byrd, Thomas, 67
Byrd, William, III, 66, 268

Cabell, John, 79
Cabin Point, Va., 74, 224
Cahokia, Ill., 193, 199
Caldwell, Capt. William, 202
Call, Maj. Richard, 279–280
Callaway, James, 167
Callender, Capt. Eliezer, 170
Calvert, John, 83
Camden, S. C., 279; battle of, 215, 225–
  226, 252
Cameron, Alexander, 186–188, 199–200
Cameron, Allan, 57–58
Camm, John, 238
Campbell, Alexander, 77
Campbell, Archibald, 83
Campbell, Col. Arthur, 200, 202–203,
  219, 220, 314
Campbell, Col. William, 216, 219, 220
Canada, 7, 57, 89, 106, 133, 201, 303, 324
Cannon, 56, 62–63, 68–69, 70, 72, 73,
  74, 82, 90, 104, 106, 125, 171, 263, 267,
  280, 306–307, 308, 309
Cape Fear, N. C., 93, 270, 274
Cape Fear River Valley, 219
Cape Henry, Va., 171. *See also* Virginia
  Capes
Cap François, W. I., 172, 176
Capitol, 18, 48, 61, 95, 97, 99, 135, 207
Capitol Landing, Va., 167
Caribbean Sea, 170, 172, 294, 310, 311
Carleton, Sir Guy, 324
Carlisle Peace Commission, 136
Carnatic, India, 288
Caroline County, Va., 3, 50, 75, 90, 190,
  217, 244
Carrington, Edward, 272
Carrington, Paul, 75
Carter, Charles, of Corotoman, 95
Carter, Charles, of Ludlowe, 95
Carter, Charles, of Shirley, 119
Carter, Charles, of Stafford, 156, 165
Carter, Edward, 218
Carter, Landon, 38, 85, 140, 167
Carter, Robert, 43, 91, 119, 166, 169, 271

Carter, Robert Wormeley, 38, 42, 94, 95
Carter's Mountain, Va., 282
Cary, Archibald, 38, 66, 101–102, 165,
    167, 244, 281–282, 283–284; threatens
    Henry, 129
Cary, Richard, 148
Caswell, Gen. Richard, 215
Cattle, 24, 25, 165, 177, 178, 242, 274
Cavalry: British, 213, 215, 216–217, 225–
    226, 275, 279, 281–282, 291, 302, 306;
    Continental, 129, 207, 215, 216, 217,
    225–226, 289–290, 293; French, 306;
    Virginia, 91, 93, 128, 137, 207, 208,
    211, 213, 217, 218
Cedar Point, Md., 271
Charles I (of England), 316
Charles City County, Va., 95
Charleston, S. C., 124, 171, 186, 187, 216,
    221, 226, 227, 274, 279, 287, 290, 311,
    312, 314; Clinton besieges, 210, 211–
    214
Charlotte County, Va., 271
Charlotte County Courthouse, 281
Charlottesville, Va., 94, 211, 218, 236,
    239; government moves to, 276–277,
    282, 296
Charon, H.M.S. (ship), 222, 307
Chastellux, François-Jean de Beauvoir,
    Chevalier de, 300
Cheraw Hill, S. C., 225
Cheriton, Northampton County, Va., 171
Cherokee Indians, 158; attack along fron-
    tier, 187–188; Cameron incites, 199–
    200; Overhill, 186, 188
Cherrystone, Northampton County, Va.,
    171
Chesapeake Bay, 23, 76, 85, 86, 105, 126,
    133, 252, 265, 292, 293–296, 310, 311;
    British assault, 204–205, 206, 208, 210,
    216, 222–223, 226, 259, 269, 274, 275,
    293–296, 303; British blockade, 170,
    171, 175–176, 179, 180, 254–255;
    French in, 226, 287, 290, 293–296, 301
Chesapeake Bay islands, 106
Chesapeake region, 32, 287, 290
Chesterfield County, Va., 130, 167, 197,
    297, 314
Chesterfield County Courthouse, 252,
    272, 273, 275, 276
Chevallie, Pierre, 180
Chicago, Ill., 198
Chickahominy River, 275, 276, 289
Chickahominy River shipyard, 271
Chickamauga, Ga., 188

Chillicothe, Ohio, 199, 203
Chincoteague, Va., 171
Chiswell, Col. John, 36, 167
Chiswell Mines, 167, 219, 220
Choisy, Claude-Gabriel, Marquis de, 306,
    308
Chota, Tenn., 200; May 1776 conference,
    186–187
Chotank (plantation), 271
Chowan River, 179
Christian, Col. William, 187, 188, 202
Church of England, 33, 34, 35, 109–110;
    disestablishment of, 145–147; episco-
    pacy controversy, 35, 46. *See also* Protes-
    tant Episcopal Church
Cincinnati, Ohio, 192
Circuit courts. *See* Courts, assize
Citizenship: bill for, 233–234
City Point, Va., 272, 273
Claiborne, Maj. Richard, 297
Clark, George Rogers, 224, 257, 323; cap-
    tures Hamilton, 195–198; criticized,
    202–203; defends St. Louis, 198–199;
    Illinois campaign, 191–198; plans at-
    tack on Detroit, 189–191; represents
    Kentucky, 141, 142; retrenches in Ohio,
    200–201
Clarksville, Ky., 198
Clifford and Teysset, 173
Clinton, Sir Henry, 204, 207–208, 210,
    216, 222, 275, 294, 308; besieges
    Charleston, 211–214; dispute with
    Cornwallis, 286–292, 294–295, 302–
    303, 305; in Virginia, 86–88; replaces
    Howe, 136; southern expedition, 89–
    94, 105–106, 125, 126
Closen, Baron Ludwig von, 301, 312
Clothing, 158, 171, 223, 240, 252–253,
    254, 259, 261, 277
Cobham, Va., 69, 224, 291
Cocke, James, 247
Coke, Thomas, 322
Colle (plantation), 182, 218
College Landing, Va., 301
Collier, Sir George, 221, 227; invades Vir-
    ginia, 204–210
Collier-Mathew expedition, 204–208, 216
Collins, Lt. Henry, 1–2, 46
Colston, Raleigh, 172
Combined Fleet, 287
Commercial agent (Va.), 181–182, 239,
    241, 298, 299
Commissariat (Continental), 122–123,
    177–178, 263–264

Commissaries, 61, 175, 178, 180, 298–
    299; Continental, 122–123, 176, 177,
    179, 181, 263; Virginia, 217, 272, 299
Commissary general (Va.), 263, 298
Commissary of issues (Va.), 177
Commissary of military stores (Va.), 240
Commissary of prisoners (Va.), 240
Commissary of provisions (Va.), 61–62,
    263–264, 272
Commissary of purchases (Va.), 61, 177–
    178
Commissary of stores (Va.), 240, 246, 317
Commissioner of the navy (Va.), 239, 246,
    273, 317
Commissioner of trade (Va.), 246
Commissioner of war (Va.), 246, 263–264,
    267–268, 276, 284, 296, 297, 299, 317
Commissioners, 45, 79, 178, 184, 186,
    190, 314; peace, 87, 136
Commissioners of oyer and terminer
    (Va.), 148
Commissioners of public accounts (Va.),
    122
Commissioners of the navy (Va.), 121, 239
Commissioners of the poor (Va.), 146
Commissioners of the specific tax (Va.),
    233, 240
Commissions, Continental, 81, 88–89
Committee of Commerce (Continental),
    191
Committee of Safety (Va.), 69, 80, 87,
    122, 148, 170, 239; attacks Dunmore,
    63, 64; bypasses Henry, 63–64, 88–89;
    confronts Charles Lee, 90–94; contro-
    versy with Henry, 75–76, 81; estab-
    lished, 52–53; informed of burning of
    Norfolk, 82–84; and loyalists, 77; orga-
    nizes forces, 61–62; powers of, ex-
    panded, 78–79; and threat of black up-
    rising, 68
Committee of Secret Correspondence
    (Continental), 96
Committees of correspondence (Va.), 9–
    10
Common Sense, 84–85, 97, 113–114
Commonwealth (British), 116
Concord and Lexington, Mass.: battles of,
    4, 21, 235
Confederation, Continental, 107
Congress. *See* Continental Congress
Congress (ship), 175, 179
Connecticut, 138, 142, 181
Connolly, Dr. John, 92, 184; captures Fort
    Pitt, 17; schemes with Dunmore, 56–58

Constitution, U. S., 319
Continental Congress, 1, 88, 90, 124, 142,
    150–152, 155, 175, 181, 190, 208, 220–
    221, 226, 229, 240, 251, 255, 262, 310,
    312, 315, 318–319, 321, 323; accepts
    Virginia cession, 320–321; adopts Dec-
    laration of Independence, 98–99; ad-
    vises colonies to establish governments,
    98; appoints Washington, 49; burgesses
    call for, 8; Committee of Commerce,
    191; criticizes Virginia land office, 242–
    243; follows Virginia model, 10; 40-to-1
    plan, 248–251; orders Woodford south,
    211; proposes Provision Law, 247–248;
    rebuilds southern army, 214; receives
    western lands, 256–259; rejects Vir-
    ginia regiments, 78; reorganizes com-
    missariat, 177
Continental line, 217
Convention (Va.), Aug. 1774, 9, 10, 11,
    16, 17, 18, 19, 26
Convention (Va.), Mar. 1775, 1
Convention (Va.), July–Aug. 1775, 49–54,
    56, 57, 61, 62, 144, 184
Convention (Va.), Dec. 1775–Jan. 1776,
    66, 68, 69, 79, 80, 81, 83–84, 88, 92;
    recruits regiments, 77–78; supports
    Henry, 75–76, 88
Convention (Va.), May–June 1776, 91,
    93–99, 100–123, 138–139, 165, 172;
    adopts constitution, 110–121; adopts
    Declaration of Rights, 100–104, 106–
    110; authorizes iron foundry, 168–169;
    authorizes saltworks, 165–166; debates
    slavery, 107–108; elections for, 94–95;
    on ex post facto laws, 110; on freedom
    of religion, 108–110; on judiciary, 147–
    148; and western lands, 141, 142
Cooper River, 213
Cooper's plantation, Hampton, Va., 63
Corbin, Richard, 49, 139; acting gover-
    nor, 75; Henry seeks to capture, 4, 43;
    negotiates with Clinton, 87–88
Corbin, Richard, Jr., 46
Cork, Ireland, 75, 105, 182
Corn, 31, 199, 200, 215, 233, 248, 259,
    306
Cornstalk, Chief, 17, 186
Cornwallis, Charles, Earl, 86, 105, 200,
    219, 222, 225–226, 252, 270, 285, 313,
    314, 319, 321, 324; defeats Wayne at
    Green Spring, 290–291; dispute with
    Clinton, 286–292, 294–295, 302–303;
    leaves Virginia, 311; marches through

Virginia, 289–292; marches to Virginia, 274–279; raids Charlottesville, 279–282; southern campaign, 214–216; surrenders at Yorktown, 301–309
Council (colonial), 4, 9, 17, 43, 56, 66, 87, 114, 231, 321
Council (republican), 99, 121–122, 132, 141, 148, 177, 180, 187, 198, 224, 267, 270, 271, 282, 284, 312, 313, 316, 317; established, 117, 118, 119; establishes trade with Europe, 175–176; establishes West Indian trade, 170–172; and government reorganization, 239, 240, 241, 242, 246; prepares Virginia defense, 296–300; reacts to British invasions, 296, 297, 299, 300; seeks loans, 180–183; supports G. R. Clark, 190–191
"Country Shop," Warwick, Va., 167
County: commissioners, 76–77, 92, 122, 148; committees, 3, 4, 5, 10, 18–19, 38, 42, 45, 48, 50, 51, 52, 53, 76–77, 78–79, 148, 165; government, 148–149, 161–162; lieutenants, 296; sheriffs, 78–79, 120, 121, 148, 300
Courts, 34, 60, 76, 107, 117, 119–120, 132, 147, 156, 157, 159, 231, 234, 257, 284, 319, 323, 324; Admiralty, 69, 76, 119, 120, 148, 158, 247; appeals, 119–120, 122, 148, 157, 158; assize, 36, 156, 318; Chancery, 119, 148, 157, 158, 239; closed, 8, 9, 18; county (Va.), 9, 35–36, 76–77, 79, 117, 119, 148–149, 156–157, 180, 219, 255, 318, 322; General (colonial), 9, 36, 119–120, 148; General (republican), 156–157, 158, 242, 284; Jefferson influences, 119–120, 147–148, 156–157; military, 46, 81, 89, 127, 284; oyer and terminer, 284; Supreme (Va.), 114, 119
Cowpens, S. C.: battle of, 225–226, 263, 274, 279, 288
Cowper, Wells, 175
Crawford, William, 201
Crèvecoeur, J. Hector St. John, 108
Cromwell, Oliver, 116
Culpeper County, Va., 64, 73–74, 220
Cumberland County, Va., 48, 94, 143
Cumberland Gap, 141, 143, 188
Cumberland River, 141, 257
Cumberland shipyard, 245
Cunninghame, William, 27
Curaçao, W. I., 172
Curle, Col. William Roscoe Wilson, 262
Currency, 52, 152, 180, 248–249, 250, 259, 261, 284–285, 296, 318–319

Currency Act (British), 28
Custis, John Parke, 136, 252
Custis (ship), 175

Daingerfield, Col. William, 106
Dalton, John, 175
Dan River, 226, 274
Dark Ages, 139–140
Davies, Samuel, 33
Davies, Col. William, 263, 264, 267–268, 276, 277, 281, 296, 297, 317
Day, Benjamin, 241, 298, 317
Deane, Silas, 138, 173, 175, 180, 181, 205, 206, 228; affair, 151–152
Deane, Simeon, 181, 206
Debts, 163, 244, 323–324
Declaration of Independence, 96, 103
Declaration of Rights (Va.), 100–104, 106–110, 145, 147
Declaration of the Rights of Man and the Citizen, 103
DeCrome, M. Delaporte, 133
Deep Creek, 70
de Grasse, Admiral. See Grasse
Delap, S. and J., 173, 180
Delaware, 98, 103, 142, 249, 258
Delaware Bay, 46, 133, 181
Delaware line, 214
Delaware River, 256
Delight, H.M.S. (ship), 216
Denaturalization, 234
Denmark, 288
Depreciation, 249, 298, 318–319
Deputy commissary general for purchases (Continental), 122–123, 177–178, 263–264
Deputy quartermaster general (Continental), 297
d'Estaing, Admiral. See Estaing
Destouches, Charles-René-Dominique Sochet, Chevalier, 269–270
Detroit, Mich., 57, 141, 188, 191, 194, 198, 199, 200, 202, 323
Dewitt's Corner, S. C., 188
Dick, Charles, 167–168
Dickinson, John, 142
Dickson, Beverley, 42
Dictator, 116, 119, 315; proposals for appointment of, 129–130, 283–285
Digby, Adm. Robert, 288, 301, 302–303, 309
Digges, Dudley, 75, 122, 129, 282
Diligence (ship), 255
Dillard, Capt. Thomas, 191, 192
Dillwyn, George, 322

Dinwiddie County, Va., 33, 176
Disestablishment: of Church of England, 145–147
Dissenters, 33–34, 35, 108–110, 135, 138, 145–147, 162, 237
Dixon, John, 1, 49, 238
Dixon and Hunter, 99, 102
Dodge, John, 197, 200
Doncastle's Ordinary, Va., 4, 5
Donelson, John, 202–203
Draft, 132, 135–136, 209, 214
Dragging Canoe, Chief, 186, 188, 199–200
Dragoons, 129, 207, 279. *See also* Cavalry
Dumfries, Va., 10, 126, 177, 270
Dunkerque, France, 175
Dunmore, Earl of. *See* Murray, John, Earl of Dunmore
Dunmore, H.M.S. (ship), 56, 81, 125
Dunmore, Lady, 14, 18, 46, 47, 55
Dunmore County, Va., 10
Dunmore's *Virginia Gazette*, 58–59, 84
Dunmore's War, 17, 45, 79, 186
Dutch West Indies, 182

Eastern Shore, 23, 31, 50, 52, 77, 78, 90, 93, 170, 171, 179, 259; loyalists in, 59–60, 92, 106, 300
Eaton, William, 177, 217
Eaton's Station, Tenn., 187
Eclipse, solar, 192
Eden, Gov. Robert, 92–93, 94, 106, 126
Edenton, N. C., 174, 179
Edward III (of England), 149
Eilbeck (ship), 56
Elections, 38–39, 51, 53, 78, 94–95, 101–102, 111–112, 116, 117–118, 120, 122, 138, 228, 229, 251–252, 262
Elizabeth City County, Va., 228, 262
Elizabeth River, 62, 70, 72, 81, 83, 86, 104, 205, 226
Elk Hill, Va., 286
Ellegood, Lt. Col. Jacob, 69, 92
Ely's Ford, Va., 276
Emancipation proclamation, 66–67
Embargo, 50, 158, 178, 244
England, 139–140, 149
English Channel, 288
Engrossing, 244
Enlistments, 284–285
Entail, 140–141
Epaulement, 307, 308
Epidemics, 128, 253; smallpox, 59–60, 104, 105, 126, 131
Essex County, Va., 228

Estaing, Charles Henri Théodat, Comte d', 181, 218
Ethiopian Regiment, 67
Eveille (ship), 226
Everard, Thomas, 247
Executive, 118–119, 128; Nelson rejuvenates, 299; plural, 118–119
Ex post facto laws, 102
Express riders, 211, 222
Extradition, 234

Fairfax County, Va., 10, 18, 31, 95
Fairfax family, 24
Fairfax grant, 25
Falls of the Ohio, 192, 193, 199, 201
Falmouth (Portland), Me., 84
Falmouth, Va., 168
Fanny (ship), 182
Farmers General, 172
Fascines, 305
Fauquier, Gov. Francis, 8
Fauquier County, Va., 94, 191, 271
Ferguson, Maj. Patrick, 215–216
Feudalism, 139–140
Fincastle, Lord, 46, 143
Fincastle County, Va., 53, 68, 143–144, 187
Fincastle County bill, 143–144
Finnie, William, 3, 62, 211
Fish, 165
Fitzhugh, William, 156
Fleming, William, 139, 202, 229, 296; acting governor, 282, 283
Flora, William, 73
Florence, Italy, 182
Florida, 55, 56, 62
Flour, 62, 81, 171, 172, 173–174, 175, 181, 248, 273, 298
Fordyce, Capt. Charles, 73, 74
Forestalling, 244
Forsythe, Robert, 263
Fort Dunmore. *See* Fort Pitt
Fort Frederick, Md., 220–221
Fort Granby, S. C., 279
Fort Jefferson, Ky., 191, 198, 201
Fort Motte, S. C., 279
Fort Moultrie, S. C., 124
Fort Nelson, Ky., 201
Fort Nelson, Portsmouth, Va., 205
Fort Orange, St. Eustatius, W. I., 172
Fort Patrick Henry, Tenn., 188
Fort Pitt. Pa., 57, 201
Fort Sackville, Ind., 195
Fort Stanwix, N. Y.: treaty of, 231–232

Foundries, 167, 168, 169
Fowey, H.M.S. (ship), 4, 5, 43, 46, 48, 55,
    67, 106, 223
Foy, Capt. Edward, 43, 46–47
Fraise work, 308
France, 7, 11, 16, 39, 98, 103, 132–133,
    136, 138, 149, 166, 167, 169, 184, 206,
    210, 310; alliance with, 96, 136, 182,
    193, 228, 243, 288; extends aid, 151–
    152, 240, 252, 255; in Illinois, 189,
    192–200, 257; peace negotiations with,
    322–323, 324; trade with, 170, 172,
    173, 175–176, 180–182, 205, 298–299,
    316. See also Army, French; Cavalry,
    French; Navy, French
Francy, Lazare-Jean Théveneau de, 180
Franklin, Benjamin, 91, 98, 103, 107, 138,
    142, 182, 322; proposes confederation,
    53–54
Franklin County, Va., 167
Frederick County, Va., 4, 10, 25, 49, 169,
    191
Fredericksburg, Va., 25, 26, 50, 106, 159,
    167, 180, 211, 236, 275; arms manufac-
    tory at, 53, 167, 224, 270, 276; forms
    committee of correspondence, 10;
    troops at, 3, 4
Frederick Town, Md., 220–221, 311
Free blacks, 67, 132, 161, 321–322
Freedom of religion, 108–110, 120
French and Indian War, 7, 25, 28, 29, 30,
    32, 62, 66, 219, 231
French Broad River, 187, 200
French Corps, 133

Gabions, 305
Gage, Gen. Thomas, 4, 55, 57, 58
Galleys, 171, 245, 270, 314
Galloway, Joseph, 10
Gálvez, Gov. Bernardo de, 170, 189
Gambier, Adm. James, 204
Gambling, 34, 244
Gates, Gen. Horatio, 134, 214, 216, 220,
    225, 252, 266; defeated at Camden, 215
Gayton, Commodore George, 216
General Assembly, 87–88, 118, 122, 178,
    227, 251, 300–301, 312; abolishes slave
    trade, 158; adjourns to Charlottesville,
    276; adopts manumission, 321–322;
    agrees to import duty, 284; avoids
    draft, 132; considers land office bill,
    153–155, 229–232; criticizes peace
    treaty, 323; defends against Collier,
    208–209; defines treason, 149; demobi-
    lizes, 314; elects Harrison governor,

313–314; elects Jefferson governor,
    209; elects judges, 119–120; enacts citi-
    zenship bill, 233–234; enacts sequestra-
    tion bill, 234–235; forms committee of
    correspondence, 9–10; hears Indiana
    Company appeal, 232; impeaches Nel-
    son, 300, 315–316; and judiciary, 147–
    149, 156–157, 158; meets in Staunton,
    282–283; moves capital to Richmond,
    235–236; organizes Illinois County,
    193–194; punishes loyalists, 220; raises
    revenue, 152–156; recruiting, 254–255;
    recruits French, 132–133; recruits gar-
    rison regiments, 129; reduces govern-
    ment, 245–246; and revisal of Virginia
    law, 159–162; revises taxes, 232–233;
    sets Pennsylvania border, 256–257; spe-
    cial session of, 259–263; supports
    southern army, 213–214; tax reform,
    152–153; and western lands, 141–144,
    152–155, 158–159
General assessment for Christian reli-
    gions, 109–110, 146–147
Genoa, Italy, 182
Gentry, André, 300
George III (of England), 13, 87, 94, 120,
    310, 322; Americans denounce, 12;
    Henry compares to Caesar, 7; proclaims
    rebellion, 66
Georgia, 187, 188, 200, 215, 255, 274,
    314; recruits in Virginia, 131; resolu-
    tion for independence, 98, 99; western
    claims, 142
Germain, Lord George, 287
Germanna, Va., 167
German regiment (Va.), 77, 95, 124, 137
Germantown, Pa., 134
Germany, 182
Gibault, Fr. Joseph, 193
Gibraltar, 288, 310
Gibson, Col. George, 89, 134, 170, 189,
    191
Gibson, John, 57
Gibson's Lambs, 89
Gilmer, Dr. George, 48, 49, 166
Girty, Simon, 199, 201, 202
Glassford, John, 27
Glassford & Co., 31, 69
Glebes, 109, 145–147
Gloucester County, Va., 106, 128, 166,
    177, 241
Gloucester Point, Va., 290, 292, 305–306,
    308, 311, 312
Gnadenhütten, Ohio, 201
Gold Mine Creek, Va., 276

Goochland County, Va., 280
Goodrich, Bartlett, 69
Goodrich, Bridger, 69, 206, 208
Goodrich, John, 44–45, 69, 206
Goodrich, John, Jr., 69
Goodrich, William, 69
Goodrich family, 62, 69, 77, 93, 170, 182, 206, 216
Gosport, Va., 83, 205, 208
Government: balanced, 115; checks and balances, 119; contract theory of, 100–101, 108, 111; mixed, 114–115, 118; rotation in office, 102; separation of powers, 114, 119, 148, 161; unicameral, 113–114
Governor's Palace, 1, 4, 15, 18, 41, 43, 45, 61, 91, 99, 121, 128, 129, 246, 312; arms in seized, 46, 48
Gower, Granville Leveson-Gower, Earl, 15
Grain, 25, 31–32, 49, 50, 158, 169, 181, 210, 244, 248, 298, 299
Grand Union flag, 97
Grasse, François-Joseph-Paul, Comte de, 288–289, 299, 311; at Yorktown, 301–309; in Chesapeake, 293–296
Gratz, Michael, 180
Gratz family, 142, 177
Graves, Adm. Samuel, 4, 46, 55, 56
Graves, Adm. Thomas, 291, 294–295, 296, 302, 303, 309, 311
Great Awakening, 33–34
Great Bridge, Va., 64, 84, 92, 216, 269; battle of, 69–74, 80
Great Britain, 7, 12–14, 79, 87, 142, 149, 151, 155, 163, 165, 170, 172, 188, 204, 244, 287, 310, 321, 322–324; debts, 148, 155–156, 323–324; inaccurate reports from, 20; rumors of troop movements in, 3, 77; strategy, 96, 127, 136, 184, 186, 188–189, 198; suffrage, 12
Great Dismal Swamp, 205
Great Kanawha River, 17
Great Lakes, 23, 142, 184, 323
Great Wagon Road, 25
Green, Capt. Berryman, 297
Greenbriar Company, 231
Greene, Gen. Nathanael, 214, 253, 263, 272, 283, 293, 297, 311; commands southern army, 225, 261, 265, 266, 270, 274, 277, 280, 284, 290, 314
Green River, Ky., 137, 159
Greensburg, Pa., 202
Green Spring, Va.: battle of, 291
Gregory, Gen. Isaac, 269
Griffin, Cyrus, 249

Griffin, Samuel, 240
Gruel, James, et Cie., 175, 176
Grymes, Benjamin, Jr., 3
Grymes, John, 93
Grymes, John Randolph, 105
Grymes, Phillip, 299
Guilford Courthouse, N. C., 226; battle of, 274
Gulf of Mexico, 184
Gunboats, 201, 202
Gunpowder, 19, 44–45, 53, 62, 69, 70, 78, 122, 141, 165, 170–171, 176, 189, 195, 205, 223, 280; incident at Williamsburg, 1–5, 19, 41–42, 43, 53
Gwatkin, Rev. Thomas, 46, 238
Gwynn's Island, Va., 104–106, 124, 125, 126

Hagerstown, Md., 58
Halifax County Courthouse, 281
Hamilton, Alexander, 307, 308
Hamilton, Gov. Henry: attacks G. R. Clark, 194; G. R. Clark captures, 195–198; "Hair Buyer General," 188–189
Hamond, Capt. Andrew Snape, 85, 86, 104–106, 126
Hampden-Sydney Academy, 237
Hampshire County, Va., 271
Hampton, Va., 48, 58, 63, 76, 83, 170, 205, 207, 219, 262, 312; Leslie invades, 216, 221
Hampton River, 63
Hampton Roads, 56, 58, 76, 104, 295
Hancock, John, 99
Hand, Gen. Edward, 191–192
Hannastown, Pa., 202
Hanover County, Va., 18, 61, 75, 121, 133, 136, 166, 245, 313; committee, 4, 5; presbytery, 33, 237
Hanover County Courthouse, 276
Hanover Town, Va., 61
Hardy, Samuel, 296, 299
Hare, Lt. Charles, 268
Harris, Joseph, 58
Harrison, Benjamin, of Berkeley, 38, 48, 78, 95, 135, 149, 170, 190, 201, 224, 232, 256, 260, 262, 265, 281–282, 283, 313; animosity to R. H. Lee, 39, 150–152; complains of governor's powers, 316–317; criticizes G. R. Clark, 202–203; decides on independence, 91; dispute with Morris, 320; elected governor, 313–314; elected Speaker, 157; elected to Congress, 10; opposes assize courts, 156; opposes 40-to-1 plan, 249–

251; proclaims peace, 323; R. H. Lee
and Henry attack, 139
Harrison, Benjamin, Jr., 32, 46, 139
Harrison, Benjamin, of Brandon, 156
Harrison, Charles Henry, 156
Harrison, Richard, 170, 172
Harrodsburg, Ky., 141, 143, 189, 199
Harvie, John, 79, 234
Havana, Cuba, 198
Hawk, H.M.S. (ship), 63
Hawkins, John, 61–62, 177–178
Hay, 248
Hay, Maj. Jehu, 196, 197
Hayes, James, 322
Haywood, William, 176
Head of Elk, Md., 134, 265, 269, 300
Headrights, 153, 230–231
Helms, Capt. Leonard, 191, 193, 194
Hemp, 25, 233
Henderson, Richard, 141, 143, 144, 154,
  158–159, 243
Henley, Samuel, 46, 238
Henrico County, Va., 166
Henry, Patrick, 36, 38, 39, 44, 53, 111,
  124, 131, 133, 134, 149, 158, 180, 182,
  187, 188, 193, 198, 207, 208, 210, 229,
  241, 243, 261, 285, 300–301, 321, 323;
  alleges British corruption, 13; asks F. L.
  Lee to defend, 5; attacks Harrison and
  Braxton, 139; attempts to capture Richard Corbin, 4; Braxton proposes truce
  to, 5; called dictator, 127–130; calls for
  appointment of dictator, 283; calls for
  executive veto, 116; Committee of
  Safety bypasses, 63–64; controversy
  with Woodford, 75–76; criticizes hard
  money policy, 319; drafts remonstrance, 260; elected colonel, 50;
  elected governor, 119, 121; elected to
  Congress, 10; escorted to border, 5;
  founds navy, 76; gathers army, 61; imi-
  tates Davies, 33; marches to Williamsburg, 4; on Braxton's pamphlet, 114–
  115; on ex post facto laws, 109–110; on
  freedom of religion, 109–110; on independence, 95–97, 98; on *Thoughts on
  Government*, 113; opposes assize courts,
  156; opposes Congress, 320; opposes
  40-to-1 plan, 249; Parsons' Causes, 34;
  political alliances, 43; proposes emissary, 255; resigns, 88–89; resolves
  against Stamp Tax, 7; supports G. R.
  Clark, 190–191, 194
Henry County, Va., 220
Hessian fly, 181

Highland Scots, 74, 106, 219
Hillsborough, N. C., 214, 215, 274
Hite, Abraham, 177
Hite, Thomas, 177
Hival and Sons, 175
Hogpen (British fort), 70, 74
Holland, 116, 182, 288
Holston River, 187, 191
Holston River Valley, 219
Holt, James, 76
Holt, John Hunter, 58–59
Holt, William, 148
Honyman, Robert, 136, 176, 213, 214,
  228, 245, 251–252, 274
Hood, Adm. Samuel, 294–295, 296, 302,
  303
Hood's Landing, Va., 223, 224
Hood's Point, Va., 267, 272
Hooe's Ferry, Va., 245
Hopkins, Commodore Ezek, 85–86
Horse racing, 34, 244, 312
Horses, 25, 48, 62, 207, 213, 221, 261,
  263, 274, 276, 279, 284, 298, 313
Hospitals, 240, 246, 272, 312, 314
House of Burgesses: abolished, 95; adopts
  fast day resolution, 8; calls convention,
  9; calls for general congress, 8; extralegal session, 8; meets June 1775, 42;
  popularity, 40; resolves against Townshend Duties, 8; seeks Dunmore's return, 45; separates offices of Speaker
  and treasurer, 39
House of Delegates, 207, 265, 279, 315,
  320; Committee of the Whole, 190;
  Committee on Propositions and Grievances, 143, 144; Committee on Religion, 145–146; Committee on the State
  of the Country, 143, 145; compared to
  House of Burgesses, 300–301; considers land office bill, 230; constitution
  provides for, 116–118; impeaches Jefferson, 283; investigates Steuben's defeat, 284; politics in, 138–139, 150–
  152, 157–158; reconsiders moving capital, 262; retrenches in Ohio, 201; sets
  scale of depreciation, 318–319; supports G. R. Clark, 190–191; votes on
  impost, 321
Howe, Richard, Vicount, 87
Howe, Col. Robert, 74; at Norfolk, 80–85
Howe, Sir William, 86, 87, 106, 127, 129,
  135, 176, 178; Clinton replaces, 136–
  137; in Chesapeake Bay, 133–134
Hudson River Valley, 127, 133
Huger, Gen. Isaac, 225

Hughes, Joseph, 174–175
Hull, England, 166
Hunter, James, 168, 169; ironworks, 224, 270, 276
Husbandmen, 140
Hutchings, Joseph, 62, 64, 83
Hutchinson, Gov. Thomas, 20

Iberian Peninsula, 31
Illinois, 142, 189, 190, 192, 194, 200, 202
Illinois Company, 142, 243
Illinois County, 194
Illinois River, 199
Immigration, 234
Impost, 321
Impressment, 248, 255, 261, 265, 271, 284, 298, 300, 312, 316
Independence, 80–99, 149, 161, 163, 322–324
Independent companies: 1, 2, 3, 4, 18, 41–42, 131
India, 288, 310
Indiana, 142
Indiana Company, 142, 154, 189, 231–232, 242–243, 257
Indians, 58, 92, 141, 184. *See also* Cherokee Indians; Shawnee Indians
Indigo, 171
Inflation, 52, 150, 152, 179–180, 227, 229–235, 244, 247, 251–252, 298–299, 316
Inglis and Long, 172
Ingram, James, 69
Innes, Col. James, 41, 43, 49, 58, 240, 241, 246, 259, 268, 271, 272
Inoculation, 131; controversy over, 59–60
Inspector of stores and provisions (Va.), 246
Ireland, 79
Ironworks, 25, 167–169, 224, 270, 276
Irvine, Gen. William, 201
Isaac (slave), 247
Isle of Wight County, Va., 69, 166
Italy, 31
Ivy Creek, Va., 218

James City County, Va., 95, 228
James II (of England), 316
Jameson, David, 165, 214, 246, 247, 282, 296, 300, 316
James River, 2, 24, 63, 64, 88, 149, 165, 245, 268, 290, 292, 293, 301, 305; British invade via, 216–217, 221, 223, 224, 266, 271–272, 275, 280; fortified by Virginia, 216–217, 267

James River Valley, 31
Jamestown, Va., 26, 64, 117, 211, 290, 295, 301
Jamieson, Neil, 31, 69, 83, 93
Jarratt, Rev. Devereux, 33, 317
Jay, John, 256, 322, 324
Jefferson (ship), 254, 270, 273
Jefferson, Thomas, 21, 36, 94, 103, 107, 123, 132, 166, 168, 182, 187, 197–200, 227, 243, 244, 248, 250, 251, 300–301, 322; and slave trade, 158; calls special session, 259–263; criticizes Norfolk, 60–61; decides on independence, 91; defends against Arnold, 222–225; defends against Phillips, 270–274; drafts Declaration of Independence, 98; enters House of Delegates, 138–140; escapes Tarleton, 281–282; Fincastle County bill, 143–144; helps draft Virginia constitution, 110–121; impeachment, 283–284, 315; land office bill, 153–155; moves government to Richmond, 246–247; on capital crimes, 160; on Convention Army, 218–221; on debts, 30; on disestablishment of Church of England, 145–147; on general education, 160; on industry, 169–170; on southern campaign, 214–216; opposes North's resolution, 42; plans attack on Arnold, 265–270; prepares defense, 210–211; proposes capital move to Richmond, 235–236; proposes citizenship bill, 233–234; proposes confiscation of loyalist estates, 234–235; proposes judiciary, 147–148, 156–157; proposes land office bill, 229–232; proposes property tax revision, 232–233; proposes Sequestration Act, 155–156; reduces government, 245–246; reforms William and Mary, 236–239; reorganizes government, 239–242; repeal of primogeniture and entail, 140–141; resentment toward Henry, 283; revisal of the laws, 159–162; seeks supplies, 252–253; Statute for Religious Freedom, 146–147, 160; Steuben criticizes, 263; supports cession of western lands, 257–259; supports G. R. Clark, 190–191; tax reform, 152–153
Jenifer and Hooe, 172
Jenny (ship), 171
Jews, 162, 233–234
Johnson, Thomas, 142
Jonathan Smith (ship), 182
Jones, Emanuel, 238

Jones, Gabriel, 229
Jones, John Gabriel, 141, 142
Jones, Joseph, 75–76, 251, 253, 254, 255,
    258, 283, 319–320, 321
Jouett, Capt. John, Jr., 281
Judiciary, 119–120, 147–148
Justices of the peace, 117, 121–122, 148,
    161, 178, 316

Kalb, Johann, Baron de, 214, 215
Kaskaskia, Ill., 189, 191, 192, 193, 194,
    195, 198
Kemp's Landing, Va., 62, 68, 74, 84, 205;
    battle of, 64, 73; Leslie attacks, 216
Kentucky, 137, 141, 142, 143–144, 159,
    190, 191, 192, 199, 202, 203, 258
Kentucky County, 143–144, 194
Kentucky River, 199, 201
King, John, 175
King and Queen County, Va., 4
King's Ferry, N. Y., 204
King's Fisher, H.M.S. (ship), 56, 64, 81
King's Mountain, S. C.: battle of, 200,
    215–216, 220
King William County, Va., 61, 76, 94, 95
King William County Courthouse, 211

La Chavigny (ship), 175
Lafayette, James, 292–293
Lafayette, Marie-Joseph-Paul-Yves-Roch-
    Gilbert du Motier, Marquis de, 260,
    284, 286, 289; at Yorktown, 301–309;
    Cornwallis puzzles, 292–294; defends
    against Cornwallis, 275–281; defends
    Point of Fork, 276–277; follows Corn-
    wallis through Virginia, 289–292; orga-
    nizes Virginia defenses, 296–299; plans
    to attack Arnold, 265–270
La Fendant (ship), 210, 211
La Luzerne, Anne-César, Chevalier de, 210
La Mothe, Capt. William, 196, 202
Lancaster County, Va., 95, 271
Land: speculators, 120, 141–142, 230,
    258, 319; titles, 148–149
Land office bill, 153–155, 229–232
La Rochefoucauld, Louis-Alexandre, Duc
    de La Roche-Guyon et de, 103
Laurens, Henry, 30, 322
Lauzun, Armand-Louis de Gontaut, Duc
    de, 306
Lawson, Arthur, 64
Lawson, Col. Robert, 217, 240, 279, 281
Lawyers, 35, 36, 156–157
Lead, 45, 53, 68, 167, 169, 275
League of Armed Neutrality, 288

Lee, Arthur, 20, 262, 316, 320, 323; and
    Silas Deane, 151–152
Lee, Gen. Charles, 88, 113, 121, 122, 124,
    125, 127, 187; in Williamsburg, 89–94
Lee, Francis Lightfoot, 5, 38, 85, 91, 94–
    95, 150
Lee, Henry "Lighthorse Harry," 217, 280
Lee, Richard Henry, 21, 30, 38, 94, 97,
    110, 116, 118–119, 132–133, 135, 152,
    166, 180, 214, 229, 230, 235, 243, 256,
    270, 300–301, 314; animosity to Benja-
    min Harrison, 39, 150–152; animosity
    to Braxton, 39; attacks Harrison and
    Braxton, 139; calls for appointment of
    dictator, 283; decides on independence,
    91; elected Speaker, 260; elected to
    Congress, 10, 157–158; favors 40-to-1
    plan, 249–250; investigates Braxton
    and Morris, 173–174; on Braxton's
    pamphlet, 114–115; on unicameral as-
    sembly, 114; opposes Congress, 320;
    opposes impost, 321; proposes appoint-
    ment of junto, 315; publishes handbill
    on constitution, 112–113; publishes
    Thoughts on Government, 112–113; reso-
    lution for independence, 98; rumors of
    blacklist, 3; seeks to close courts, 9
Lee, Thomas Ludwell, 95, 97, 102, 106–
    107, 159
Lee, Gov. Thomas Sims, 221
Lee, William, 20, 21, 66, 151, 176, 182,
    315
Le Fier Roderique (ship), 180, 181, 210
Legge, William, Earl of Dartmouth, 1, 17,
    18, 19, 21, 74, 75
Leslie, Gen. Alexander, 216–217, 220,
    221, 222, 224, 252, 253, 275
Leslie, Capt. Samuel, 62, 63, 72–73, 74
Lewis, Gen. Andrew, 88, 97, 99, 106,
    127–128, 131, 187, 282, 299; attacks
    Gwynn's Island, 124–127; wins at Point
    Pleasant, 17
Lewis, Col. Charles, 187
Lewis, Fielding, 167–168, 170, 180
Lewis (ship), 255
Lexington, Ky., 202, 203
Lexington and Concord, Mass.: battles of,
    4, 21, 235
Liberty, 171, 254, 314
Liberty, H.M.S. (ship), 58
Licensing: of clergy, 33–34; of lawyers, 36
Licking River, 199, 202
Lincoln, Gen. Benjamin, 213, 226, 301,
    309
Linn, Benjamin, 189

Linn, William, 170, 189, 191
Liquor, 209, 210, 242, 248
Little Carpenter, Chief, 188
Liverpool, H.M.S. (ship), 74, 81
Livingston, Robert R., 98
Loan office (Va.), 155
Logan, Benjamin, 202
Logan (ship), 125
London, England, 84, 103, 173
Long Island, N. Y., 206
Long Island in Holston River, 187, 188
Loudoun County, Va., 136, 169, 271
Louisa County, Va., 280
Louis XV (of France), 11
Loyalists, 67, 68–69, 74, 86, 95, 105–106,
   112, 121–122, 148, 186–187, 201, 206,
   208, 215, 216, 221, 238, 284, 298–299,
   302–303, 314, 323; Charles Lee evacu-
   ates, 92–93; defeated at King's Moun-
   tain, 200; estates forfeited, 234–235; es-
   tates sequestered, 76–77, 155–156;
   General Assembly punishes, 220; in
   Norfolk, Portsmouth, and Eastern
   Shore, 59–61; in southwestern coun-
   ties, 59–61; in Virginia, 46–47; mer-
   chants depart, 149–150; Virginia lead-
   ers tolerant toward, 59; in western
   counties, 219–220
Loyal Land Company, 154, 231
Loyauté, Monsieur, 132–133
Lucille, 300
Lux & Bowly, 170
Lynch, Charles, 165, 167, 220
Lynching, 220
Lyne, Capt. George, 63, 241
Lyon, Rev. John, 300
Lyon (ship), 180, 181

McAlestor, Hector, 59, 69, 216
MacCartney, Capt. John, 55–56
McClurg, Dr. James, 139, 238, 246
McIntosh, Lachlan, 191
McKee, Alexander, 57, 201, 202
McKnight, Thomas, 69
McPherson, Maj. William, 289–290
Madeira Islands, 31
Madison, James, 120, 161, 214, 238–239,
   254–255, 256, 258, 300–301, 310–311,
   319, 321, 323; disestablishment of
   Church of England, 145–147; favors
   40-to-1 plan, 249; on freedom of reli-
   gion, 108–110; proposes assize courts,
   156–157
Madison, Rev. James, 133–134, 237, 245,
   256

Madrid, Spain, 256
Magazine, Williamsburg, Va., 42–43, 45,
   46, 62; Dunmore raids, 1–5, 7, 19, 21,
   41, 44, 53, 323
Magdalen, H.M.S. (ship), 1–2, 43, 46, 55
Magill, Maj. Charles, 266
Maisonville, François, 196
Malvern Hill, Va., 292
Manchester, Va., 223, 224, 273
Manufacturing, 25, 26–27, 31, 163, 166–
   170, 183
Manufacturing Society of Williamsburg,
   167
Manumission, 161, 321–322
Maria, H.M.S. (ship), 74–75
Marlboro Mine, 25, 169
Marriage of Figaro, The, 151
Marshall, Thomas, 133, 211
Martial law, 284
Martin, Gov. Josiah, 44, 75, 86
Martinique, W. I., 170, 172
Martin's Station, Ky., 199
Maryland, 57, 68, 91, 98, 134, 154–155,
   181, 209, 243, 254, 255, 256, 270, 301;
   border, 120; committee of safety, 92–
   94; declaration of rights, 103; ratifies
   Articles of Confederation, 320; refuses
   to advance boycott, 50; refuses to ratify
   Articles of Confederation, 142
Maryland line, 214
Mason, George, 21, 95, 150, 156–159,
   166, 181, 210–211, 213–214, 227, 229,
   251, 253, 300–301, 323; at third convention, 50–54; criticizes Nelson, 315–
   316; disestablishment of Church of England, 145–147; drafts constitution,
   110–121; drafts Declaration of Rights,
   100–104, 106–110; land office bill,
   153–155; on Committee of Safety, 53;
   partner of George Dalton, 175; proposes assize courts, 156; proposes cession of western claims, 256–259; proposes citizenship bill, 234; proposes
   confiscation of supplies, 178; proposes
   currency issue, 242; proposes land office bill, 229–232; proposes Provision
   Law, 247–248; proposes 40-to-1 plan,
   248–251; resolution for dictator, 129–
   130; supports G. R. Clark, 190–191;
   supports property tax revision, 232–
   233; supports sequestration bill, 234–
   235; supports Virginia land claims,
   242–243; tax reform, 152–153
Mason and Dixon Line, 256
Massachusetts, 84, 98, 103, 112, 131, 142

Massenbach (German officer), 91
Mathew, Maj. Gen. Edward, 204–208
Matoax (plantation), 223
Mattaponi Church, Va., 276
Matthews, Maj. Thomas, 205
Maxwell, James, 246, 273
Mazzei, Philip, 103, 182, 218, 238, 314
Meat, 81, 165, 244, 248, 299
Medical director general (Va.), 246
Mercer, George, 8
Mercer, Col. Hugh, 3, 50, 51, 89, 106, 126
Mercer, James, 42, 75, 168, 229
Mercer, Lt. Col. John, 306
Merchants, 189, 228–229, 244; British, 8,
    9, 26–32, 53, 77, 163; forced to depart,
    149–150; French, 172, 175–176, 180–
    181; in Norfolk, 50, 59–60, 69, 72;
    Scots, 27–30, 59–60; and Silas Deane
    affair, 151–152; in Virginia, 26–32,
    167, 172–183; in West Indies trade,
    171–172
Merckle, John, 173
Mercury, H.M.S. (ship), 46, 48, 55, 58, 86
Methodism, 33
Methodists, 322
Miami River, 202, 203
Michilimackinac (Mich.), 198
Middle Colonies, 31, 32, 35, 87, 94
Mifflin, Warner, 322
Militia, 68–74, 82, 95, 117, 121–122, 124,
    126, 128, 134, 135, 190, 200, 201, 207,
    209, 210–211, 213–214, 216–217, 222,
    224, 225–226, 244, 252–253, 259, 260,
    262, 268–274, 279, 284, 292, 296, 298,
    305–306, 311
Miller, Henry, 25
Miller, John, 169
Mills, 78, 83, 86, 105, 165, 275, 298
Mills Creek, Va., 63
Minden: battle of, 47
Mines, 28, 53, 68, 167, 169, 219, 220
Minorca, 288, 310
Minutemen, 52, 64, 73–74, 82, 128–129,
    135, 260
Mississippi Company, 154
Mississippi River, 7, 92, 120, 142, 170,
    189, 198, 255–256, 323
Mississippi River Valley, 186
Mitchell, Cary, 77
Mobile, Ala., 187
Molly (ship), 171
Monarchy, 116, 140, 161
Monongalia County, 143
Monroe, James, 46
Montagu, Capt. George, 5, 43, 46, 48, 55

Montagu, Capt. James, 56
Montesquieu, Charles-Louis de Secondat,
    Baron de la Brède et de, 11, 116
Montgomery, Capt. John, 193, 194, 199
Montgomery County, Va., 144, 219, 220
Monticello (plantation), 281, 282, 283
Moore, Augustine, 309
Moore, Bernard, 148
Moore, Samuel, 189
Moore's Creek, N. C.: battle of, 105
Moravians, 33
Morgan, Capt. Daniel, 49, 134, 225–226,
    263, 274, 292
Morgan, George, 189, 190, 192, 242
Morris, Richard, 178, 179, 254, 298, 299
Morris, Robert, 135, 139, 142, 170, 172–
    173, 176, 181, 191, 284; criticized, 227;
    dispute with Harrison, 320; proposes
    impost, 321; R. H. Lee investigates,
    173–174; and Silas Deane, 151–152
Morristown, N. J., 211, 295
Moseley, Edward Hack, Jr., 77
Moseley, Edward Hack, Sr., 77
Mount Vernon (plantation), 300
Muhlenberg, Gen. John Peter Gabriel,
    124, 217, 267, 271, 272
Murray, John, Earl of Dunmore, 55, 58,
    77, 82, 91, 108, 112, 119, 165–166, 167,
    184, 202, 206, 208, 243–244, 323;
    abandons Virginia, 124–127; appears
    scheming, 20–21; at Porto Bello, 48;
    believes opposition small, 21; character,
    15–16; confronts burgesses, 42–43; dis-
    misses assembly 1774, 8; Dunmore's
    War, 17, 45, 79, 186; early career, 14–
    15; emancipation proclamation, 66–67;
    Ethiopian Regiment, 67; fails to inform
    ministry, 18–19; flees Williamsburg,
    43–45; magazine incident, 1–5; occu-
    pies Norfolk, 68–69; on Gwynn's Is-
    land, 104–106; prorogues assembly, 9;
    quarrels with MacCartney, 55–56; raids
    Hampton Roads, 62–66; rendezvous
    with Clinton, 86–87; return rumored,
    128; returns to America, 314; schemes
    with Connolly, 56–58; summons as-
    sembly, 41; western claims, 15–17
Muter, George, 246, 263, 268, 269

Nansemond County, Va., 92
Nantes, France, 175–176, 228
Nash, Gov. Abner, 280
Navigation Acts, 324
Navy, British, 4–5, 19, 148, 213, 226, 268,
    269–270, 287–288; blockades, 170–

171, 175–176, 179, 180, 254; Dunmore flees to, 43–49; at Gwynn's Island, 104–106, 124–127; off Norfolk, 55–56, 58–60, 62–64, 68–75, 80–88; raids Virginia, 204–208, 216–225, 270–274, 275; threatens invasion, 133–134, 210–211; at Yorktown, 291–309, 311
Navy, Continental, 85–86
Navy, French, 210, 211, 226, 251, 265, 269, 270, 287–296, 301, 305–306, 311
Navy, Virginia, 76, 121, 171, 239, 245, 246, 254–255, 265, 271, 273
Neabsco Mine, 169
Neavill, John, 79
Nelson, Hugh, 207, 211
Nelson, Thomas, 56, 66, 87–88, 118–119, 121, 307
Nelson, Thomas, Jr., 97, 207, 210–211, 217, 222, 237, 240, 271, 291, 311, 319; appointed brigadier general, 133–135; appointed major general, 208; decides on independence, 91; elected governor, 283–284; favors Hugh Mercer, 50; General Assembly impeaches, 300, 315–316; opposes Jefferson for governor, 209; organizes Virginia defenses, 296–300; provides note to Henry, 5; resigns as governor, 313
Nelson, William, 240
Neville, Capt. John, 57
New Bern, N. C., 44, 207
Newcastle, Va., 293
New England, 90, 94, 127, 260
New Hampshire, 103
New Jersey, 69, 98, 111, 129, 133, 166, 177, 232, 260
New Kent County, Va., 5, 177
New Kent County Courthouse, 293
New London, Conn., 303
New Orleans, La., 7, 92, 170, 189, 191, 198, 243, 255
Newport, R. I., 57, 210, 226, 287, 291, 295
Newport News, Va., 216, 221, 262
New River Valley, 219
New Sides and New Lights, 33
Newton, Thomas, 83, 317
New York, 98, 105, 106, 129, 136, 204, 219, 287, 290, 291, 301, 303, 305, 314; western claims, 142, 256, 320
New York, N. Y., 59, 127, 163, 182, 210, 217, 228, 229, 269, 289, 291, 324
New York Gazette and Weekly Mercury, 103
Nicholas, George, 3, 46, 48, 63, 283, 315
Nicholas, Robert Carter, 1, 36, 38, 66, 69,

90, 97, 140; considers North's resolution, 42; counsels patience, 44; disestablishment of Church of England, 145–147; establishes manufacturing society, 167; hostility to Randolphs, 39, 47; investigates Dunmore's flight, 45; on slavery, 107–108; opposes assize courts, 156; opposes independence, 94–95; orders arms, 44–45; rejects Henry's aid, 5; wants to censure Henry, 5; West Augusta bill, 143
Nicholson (ship), 171
Nitrates, 165
Nolichucky River, 188
Nomini Hall (plantation), 166
Norfolk, Va., 31, 57, 69–70, 72–74, 77, 79, 80, 92, 93, 104, 112, 126, 172, 204, 246; burning of, 81–84; Dunmore occupies, 68–74; forms committee of correspondence, 10; loyalists in, 59–61; merchants aid Dunmore, 50; not rebuilt, 205–206; prewar politics, 59; representation, 117; reputation injured, 59, 60–61; Scots in, 27
Norfolk County, Va., 10, 70, 95
Norfolk *Virginia Gazette*, 58–59
Norman Conquest, 140
North, Frederick, Lord, 15, 41, 44
North America, 310
Northampton County, Va., 68, 165, 171, 271
North Anna River, 276
North Carolina, 33, 69, 86, 90, 105, 124, 171, 176, 177, 179, 191, 205–206, 207, 209, 213, 215, 219, 221, 245, 252, 255, 270, 280, 284, 287, 298; border, 120; declaration of rights, 103; resolution for independence, 98; troops at Great Bridge, 70–74; troops from, 269; western claims, 142
Northern Neck, 23, 24, 25, 39, 134
North Sea, 287
Northumberland County, Va., 166, 271
Northwest Territory, 321
Norton, John Hatley, 173, 178, 229
Norton and Beall, 175, 176
Notes on Virginia, 85

Oats, 233
Ocracoke Inlet, 171
Ocracoke Sound, 245
Offley Hoo (plantation), 313
O'Hara, Brig. Charles, 309
Ohio Company, 153, 154, 157, 231–232
Ohio Country, 57, 184

Ohio County, 143
Ohio River, 142, 170, 186, 189, 192, 198, 199, 200, 202, 243, 244, 256, 321
Ohio Valley, 141
Old, John, 169
Old Albemarle County Courthouse, Va., 277, 286
Old Point Comfort, Va., 291, 292
Oligarchy, 116
Orangeburg, S. C., 279
Orange County, Va., 109
Ordinaries, 242
Ordnance, 167–169
Orphans, 255
Osborne's, Va., 273, 275
Otter, H.M.S. (ship), 44, 55, 58, 63, 81, 125, 126, 206
Oucanastota, Chief, 188
Our Lady of Mt. Carmel and St. Anthony (ship), 228
Oxford Mine, 169

Pacolet River, 225
Pagan Creek, Va., 217
Page, John, 61, 90, 94, 123, 128, 133, 165, 170–171, 180, 187, 235, 237, 241, 246, 314, 317; as lieutenant governor, 121–122; elected to Council, 119; opposes Jefferson for governor, 209
Page, Mann, 134
Page, Mann, Jr., 3, 150–151
Paine, Thomas, 84–85, 97, 113, 114, 115
Palace. *See* Governor's Palace
Pamunkey River, 61, 272, 293
Paris, France, 228
Paris, Treaty of: 1763, 7, 120; 1783, 159, 322–324
Parker, James, 18, 59–60, 69, 83, 88, 125, 206, 216
Parker, Sir Peter, 104
Parker, Richard, 229
Parker, Maj. Thomas, 104
Parliament, 165, 322; alleged corruption, 11–13; asserts right to tax colonies, 7–8, 14; limits colonial currency, 28; supremacy, 111; united on colonial policy, 13
Parole, 262
Parrish, John, 322
Parsons' Causes, 34
Pasteur, Capt. John, 170, 171
Patriot (ship), 254
Paymasters general (Va.), 314
Peace commission (British), 87, 90, 136
Peace negotiations, 322–324

Pendleton, Edmund, 5, 36, 38, 39, 42, 111, 118–119, 135, 152, 165, 190, 217, 229, 232, 235, 239, 244, 251, 259, 300–301, 315–316, 323; bypasses Henry, 63–64, 88–89; chairs Caroline County committee, 3; chairs Committee of Safety, 61, 75; Charles Lee criticizes, 90; citizenship bill, 232–233; contributes to Declaration of Rights, 108–110; debates Jefferson, 139–140; elected to Congress, 10; opposes closing courts, 9; president of Convention, 95; proposes judiciary, 156–157; resolution for independence, 96–97; retires as Speaker, 150–151; revisal of the laws, 158–159; soothes dissension, 5–6
Penet, D'Acosta Frères et Cie., 176, 182
Penet, Pierre, 175, 176, 182
Penet, Windel et Cie., 169
Pennsylvania, 91, 98, 120, 186, 209; adopts unicameral assembly, 114; border, 143, 256; conflict with Virginia, 57; declaration of rights, 103; landless state, 142
Pennsylvania Evening Post, 97
Pennsylvania line, 276, 279, 286, 289, 290–291, 292, 293, 297–298
Pensacola, Fla., 187
Peoria, Ill., 199
Perseus, H.M.S. (ship), 181
Petersburg, Va., 175, 178, 179, 211, 213, 216, 241, 267, 275, 298; Arnold threatens, 223–224; Phillips raids, 272–273
Peyster, Maj. Arent Schuyler de, 198, 202
Peyton, John, 240
Philadelphia, Pa., 1, 59, 61, 84, 97, 127, 129, 133, 135, 136, 139, 141, 163, 167, 174, 180, 210, 211, 224, 228, 243, 245, 249, 283, 284, 285, 291, 303
Phillips, Josiah, 206
Phillips, Gen. William, 218, 262, 291; arrives in Chesapeake, 269–270; burns Cedar Point, Md., 270–271; raids along James River, 271–275
Phripp, Matthew, 59, 77, 175
Piankatank River, 104
Piedmont, 23, 24–25, 26, 27, 29, 31, 33, 39, 61–62
Pigeon Quarter, Yorktown, Va., 305
Pierce, John, 177, 263–264, 298
Pinkney, John, 43, 58, 85
Piqua, Ohio, 199
Pittsburgh, Pa., 17, 120, 188, 190, 193, 201, 202, 256; conferences with Indians, 56, 184, 186

Pittsylvania County, Va., 143, 220
Pleasant, Robert, 173
Pliarne, Emanuel de, 175
Pocahontas Bridge, Va., 272
Point of Fork, Va., 272, 275, 284, 286;
   British raid, 276–281
Point Pleasant, Va., 57; battle of, 17
Pollock, Oliver, 170, 198
Pork, 62, 177, 178, 248, 254
Porterfield, Col. Charles, 211, 213, 215
Portland, Me., 84
Porto Bello (plantation), 48
Portsmouth, Va., 55, 68–74, 77, 83, 86,
   93, 104, 128, 176, 205, 207, 210–211,
   217, 221, 223, 224, 226, 265, 267, 268,
   271, 275, 290, 291–293, 296, 312;
   forms committee of correspondence,
   10; loyalists in, 59–61
Potomac River, 57, 120, 126, 168, 175,
   245
Powhatan County, Va., 24
Preemption rights, 230
Prentis, Robert, 49
Presbyterianism, 33
Presbyterians, 33, 110
Preston, Col. William, 219, 220
Price, Rev. Thomas, 97
Prices, 28–30, 34, 68, 123, 132, 135–136,
   153, 154, 166, 171, 173–174, 177, 178,
   179, 180–181, 209, 228, 231, 234, 242,
   248, 249, 261; regulation of, 227
Primogeniture, 141, 160
Prince Edward County, Va., 237, 300
Prince Edward County Courthouse, 281
Princess Anne County, Va., 64, 70, 92, 95
Princeton College, 109
Prince William County, Va., 18, 31, 132,
   169, 240, 315
Prisoners of war, 73–74, 81–82, 196–199,
   206, 211, 218–219, 220–221, 262, 311–
   312
Privateers, 206, 208, 254, 310, 314
Privy Council (British), 157
Privy Council (Va.) *See* Council (republi-
   can)
Proclamation of 1763 (British), 16, 142,
   186
Prohibitory Act (British), 87
Protestant Episcopal Church, 237
Provision Law, 247–248, 253–254, 260,
   261, 263–264
Public Store, 61, 136, 167, 171, 174, 177,
   207, 209, 240, 247, 263, 298
"Public Taylors Shop," 167
Public virtue, 115, 123

Purdie, Alexander, 42, 44, 49, 85, 99,
   102, 165, 178
Purifying declaration, 320
Purveyors of the state hospitals (Va.), 240

Quakers, 33, 107, 322
Quartermaster (Continental), 272
Quartermaster general (Continental),
   177, 240, 247, 297
Queen's Creek, Williamsburg, Va., 167
Queen's Own Loyal Regiment, 67, 69,
   106, 126
Queen's Rangers, 279, 311

Rainbow, H.M.S. (ship), 204, 205, 208
Raisonable, H.M.S. (ship), 204–205
Raleigh Tavern, 8, 9, 42, 88
Ralls, Capt. George, 171–172
Ramsey's Mill, N. C., 274
Ramsour's Mill, N. C., 274
Randolph, Edmund, 47, 109, 111, 155,
   228–229, 237, 243, 244, 249, 320; ap-
   pointed to admiralty court, 76; history
   of Virginia, 95, 116–117
Randolph, John, 39, 44, 47
Randolph, Peyton, 1, 2, 36, 38, 48, 53,
   300–301; elected to Congress, 10; hos-
   tility to Nicholas, 39; opposes North's
   resolution, 42; president of Congress,
   10; quiets public outrage, 3; resigns as
   president of Congress, 41–42
Randolph, Susan, 47
Rapidan River, 276, 286
Rawdon, Francis Rawdon-Hastings, Lord,
   274, 279
Receiver general, 4, 5, 43, 46, 49, 87, 139
Reciprocity, 234
Recruiting, 130–132, 135, 254–255, 260
Redoubts No. Nine and Ten, Yorktown,
   Va., 307, 308
Regiments, British: Ethiopian, 67; 14th,
   55, 62, 64, 69, 72, 73, 126; Queen's
   Own Loyal, 67, 69, 106, 126; Queen's
   Rangers, 279, 311; Royal Highlanders,
   205; 71st Highlanders, 279–280
Regiments, Virginia: half-pay for officers,
   209, 314; reduced, 137, 314; 1st, 50,
   63–64, 75–76, 78, 81, 88–89, 127, 128,
   134, 187; 2nd, 51, 62, 63, 64, 66, 78,
   80, 127, 128, 131, 136, 138; 3rd, 51, 89,
   128; 4th, 171; 5th, 171; 6th, 171; 7th,
   128; 8th, 77, 95, 124, 137; 9th, 134,
   171. *See also* Militia; Minutemen; State
   artillery regiment; State garrison regiment

Religious freedom, 108–110, 120, 161–
    162; Jefferson's statute for, 146–147
Remembrancer, The, 103
Republicanism, 85, 100–101, 112, 115,
    116, 140, 160, 161
Requisitions, 247, 251
Reveley, John, 168, 169
Revenge (ship), 171
Revolution, American, 12, 16, 21, 24, 25,
    29, 30, 33, 36, 40, 47, 60, 69, 103, 123,
    161, 167, 203, 237, 285, 323; compared
    to Chinese, French, and Russian revolu-
    tions, 116; effects of, in Virginia, 317–
    322; radicalism of, 115–116; religious
    freedom debated, 108–110; slavery de-
    bated, 106–108
Revolution, French, 103, 116
Revolution, Glorious, 11, 13–14, 15, 33,
    149
Rhode Island, 98, 165, 166, 169, 301, 321
Richardson, Archibald, 179
Richmond, Va., 75, 167, 201, 216, 219,
    227, 253, 262, 266, 275, 276, 282, 289,
    292, 293–294, 296, 298, 313, 314, 320,
    322; Arnold attacks, 223–224; capital
    moved to, 235–236, 246
Richmond County, Va., 94
Rickman, William, 139
Riedesel, Friedrich Adolph von, Baron of
    Eisenbach, 218–219
Rittenhouse, David, 256
Rivanna River, 272, 280
Rivington, James, 229
Roanoke River, 216
Robertson, Charles, 77
Robertson, Gen. James, 303
Robinson, John, 38; scandal, 28–29, 36,
    39, 152
Robinson, William, 62
Robin's Point, Gloucester, Va., 166
Rochambeau, Jean-Baptiste-Donatien de
    Vimeur, Comte de, 226, 289, 291, 294–
    295; at Williamsburg, 300–301, 312–
    313; at Yorktown, 301–309
Rocheblave, Mme. de, 192
Rocheblave, Phillippe de Rastel, Chevalier
    de, 189, 192, 193, 202
Rockbridge County, Va., 271
Rockfish Gap, 25
Rodney, Sir George, 291, 294
Roebuck, H.M.S. (ship), 85, 87, 104, 126
Rogers, Col. David, 191
Roman Catholics, 162
Roman republic, 91, 100, 116, 130
Romulus, H.M.S. (ship), 216

Ropewalk, 167, 314
Rose, Duncan, 179, 241
Ross, Alexander, 92
Ross, David, 169, 246, 275, 277, 298
Ross, John, 228
Roultrac (ship), 176
Royal Gazette (New York), 229
Royal Highlanders, 205
Rubsamen, Jacob, 165, 167
Rudelle's Station, Ky., 199
Rum, 135, 227, 248, 280
Russell, Col. William, 187
Russia, 288
Rye, 233

St. Augustine, Fla., 55, 126, 186, 187
St. Clair, Arthur, 184, 186
St. Eustatius, W. I., 170, 171, 172
St. George's Island, Md., 126
St. Louis, Mo., 194, 198, 199
Saint Simon, Adm. *See* Saint-Simon-
    Montbléru
Saint-Simon-Montbléru, Claude-Anne de
    Rouvroy, Marquis de, 295, 301, 306–
    308
Salt, 82, 170, 174, 206, 244, 248, 253;
    price of, 178, 227; shortage of, 123,
    165–166
Saltpeter, 53, 78, 165, 280
Saltworks, 165, 166, 169
Sandwich, John Montagu, Earl of, 288
Sandy Hook, N. Y., 222
Sandy Point, Va., 64, 268
Santo Domingo, W. I., 172
Saratoga, N. Y.: battle of, 134, 157, 210,
    214, 218, 227
Savannah, Ga., 186
Scandinavia, 217
Schaw, John, 59
Scots, 15, 53, 59–60, 61, 106; merchants
    forced to depart, 149–150; in tobacco
    trade, 27–30. *See also* Highland Scots
Scott, Col. Charles, 48, 70, 72, 207, 211,
    213
Seaford, H.M.S. (ship), 171
Sectaries, German, 33
Senate (Va.), 129, 244, 249, 283, 315; es-
    tablished, 117–118; Fincastle County
    bill, 144; resists House of Delegates,
    261
Senf, John Christian, 217, 267
Sequestration Act, 155–156
Sequestration bill, 234–235
Seven Years' War, 219. *See also* French and
    Indian War

Sevier, John, 141, 200, 203, 215–216
Shawnee Indians, 17, 52, 199, 231
Shedden, Robert, 93
Shelby, Isaac, 215–216
Shenandoah River, 25
Shenandoah Valley, 23, 24, 25, 31, 33
Sheriffs, 78–79, 120, 121, 148, 300
Sherman, Roger, 98
Shipyard, 245, 271
Shirtmen, 42, 59, 61, 74, 80, 81, 83, 125
Shockoe Hill, Richmond, Va., 247
Shoemakers, 167
Simcoe, Lt. Col. John Graves, 271–272, 285, 286, 311; at Gloucester Point, 305–306; driven back at Spencer's Ordinary, 289–290; raids Point of Fork, 276–281
Slaughter, Col. George, 199
Slavery, 99, 322; abolition of debated, 106–108, 254; Jefferson on, 160–161
Slaves, 20, 24, 25, 34, 56, 58, 63, 64, 72, 141, 153, 167, 180, 235, 267, 284, 302, 313, 321; Dunmore emancipates, 66–67; Dunmore threatens to incite, 2–3, 4, 58; freed by British, 224, 268, 271, 274, 275, 324; manumission of, 161, 321–322; taxed, 152, 232–233, 242, 252; uprising rumored, 2, 67–68
Slave trade, 99, 120, 158, 160
Smallpox, 59–60, 104, 105, 126, 131
Smallwood, Gen. William, 224
Smith, Meriwether, 96, 97, 156, 228, 229, 243
Smith, Samuel Stanhope, 237–238
Smith, Thomas, 177, 179, 180, 182, 207, 241
Smith, Maj. William, 191
Smithfield, Va., 176, 207, 217, 224
Smollett, Tobias, 47
Smyth, J. F. D., 57, 58
Solebay, H.M.S. (ship), 208
South: opposes 40-to-1 plan, 249
South Africa, 288
South Anna River, 276, 286
South Carolina, 69, 90, 99, 104, 188, 200, 211, 215, 222, 225, 255, 274, 277, 315; ratification of state constitution, 111; recruits in Virginia, 131; resolution for independence, 98; western claims, 142
South Carolina line, 217
South Quay, Va., 149, 176, 179
Southside, 23, 25–26, 33, 39, 63, 77
Sovereignty, 111
Spain, 180, 182, 255, 310; declares war on Britain, 288
Speculators. *See* land speculators

Speirs, Alexander, 27
Spencer's Ordinary, 289
Spies, 104, 292–293
Spotsylvania County, Va., 18
Spotswood, Gen. Alexander, 261
Spotswood, Gov. Alexander, 167
Sprowle, Andrew, 56, 69, 83, 93
Squatters, 144
Squire, Capt. Matthew, 56, 58, 63, 81
Stadler, John, 91
Stafford County, Va., 10, 95, 169
Stamp Act, 7–8, 9, 13, 29
Stamp Act Congress, 8
Starke, Bolling, 176, 179, 271–272
State agent (Va.), 177, 181–182, 241, 314, 316, 317
State Artillery Regiment (Va.), 132–133, 210–211, 238, 314
State Garrison Regiment (Va.), 129, 136, 210–211, 215, 246, 314
Staten Island, N. Y., 127
Statute for Religious Freedom, 146–147, 160
Statute Staple (British), 149
Staunton, Va., 25, 236, 282–283
Stephen, Gen. Adam, 128, 187
Stephenson, Capt. Hugh, 49
Steuben, Friedrich Wilhelm Augustus, Baron von, 262, 263, 286, 289; alienates officers, 267–268; defends against Phillips, 270–274; defends Point of Fork, 276–281; legislature investigates defeat, 284; plans attack on Arnold, 266–270
Stevens, Gen. Edward, 72, 73, 215, 253
Stuart, Henry, 186, 188
Stuart, John, 58, 186
Stuart kings (British), 11
Sub-clothier (Va.), 240, 247
Subversion, 149
"Suffering traders," 231–232
Suffolk, Va., 70, 74, 84, 91, 175, 176, 179, 221
Suffolk County Resolves (Mass.), 10–11
Suffrage, 36, 38, 102, 116–117, 118
Sugar, 31, 227
Sulfur, 53, 78, 165, 280
Superintendent of finance (Continental), 320
Superintendent of Indian affairs for southern department (British), 58, 186
Surinam, W. I., 172
Surry County, Va., 291
Sweden, 182, 288
Swift, H.M.S. (ship), 268

Swift Run Gap, 25
Switzerland, 182
Sycamore Shoals, N. C., 187, 216

Tailors, 61, 167
Tait, James, 165
Tangier Island, Va., 254
Tanyard, 167, 314
Tarleton, Lt. Col. Banastre, 215, 275, 286, 292; defeated at Cowpens, 225–226; raids Charlottesville, 281–282, 285; at Waxhaws, 213; at Yorktown, 302–303, 306
Tarpley, Thompson & Company, 172
Taxes, 28, 52, 144, 209, 214, 247, 248–250, 319, 320, 321; on church property, 109, 145–147; by Parliament, 7–10, 14, 41, 44, 60; on personal property, 152–153, 232–233; poll, 136, 152, 242, 252; specific, 233, 240, 242, 249, 250, 253
Tayloe, John, 85, 119, 169
Taylor, John, of Caroline, 260
Taylor's Ferry, Va., 216
Tempest (ship), 270, 273
Tennessee, 141, 186, 203
Tennessee River, 187, 192, 199
Textiles, 166–167
Thetis (ship), 255, 271
Thistle Distillery, 83
Thoughts on Government, 113
Tidewater, 23, 24, 25, 26, 27, 38, 39, 58, 69, 77, 90, 94, 125, 128, 145, 157, 169, 298
Tilly, Capt. Arnaud de Gardeur de, 226, 265
Tithables, 152
Tobacco, 34, 50, 84, 150, 163, 205, 206, 208, 214, 223, 224, 233, 241, 242, 244, 248, 270–271, 273; inspection, 79, 158; prices, 181, 227; trade, 11, 26–31, 52, 172–173, 175, 176, 179–181, 183
Todd, Col. John, 194, 198
Toleration Act (British), 33
Tonyn, Gov. Patrick, 55
Townshend Duties, 8, 13, 29
Transylvania, 141
Transylvania Company, 143, 154, 158–159, 232
Travis, Lt. Edward, 73
Treason, 149
Treasury (Va.), 122, 296
Treaty of Paris. *See* Paris, Treaty of
Tredell's Landing, Va., 301, 305

Trent, William, 232, 242–243
Tryon, Gov. William, 86
Tucker, Robert, 83
Tucker, St. George, 103–104, 107, 108, 123, 171, 174, 223, 299, 300
Tucker, Thomas Ludwell, 174
Tucker's Point, Va., 86, 104, 105, 126
Tucker's windmill, 83, 86
Turberville, Maj. George, 268
Tuscany, Italy, 182
Tyler, John, 260
Tyree's plantation, Va., 290

United States of America, 235, 243, 322–324
United States Post Office, 247

Valley Forge, Pa., 135, 175, 176
Van Bibber, Abraham, 170, 171–172
Vandalia, 142
Vandalia Company, 154, 257
Van Horne, Hannah, 47
Vaudreuil, Louis-Philippe de Rigaud, Marquis de, 211
Venice, Italy, 116
Vermont, 103, 114
Vigo, Francis, 194
Ville de Paris (ship), 301
Vincennes, Ind., 192, 193, 194, 195, 197, 198, 201
Vioménil, Antoine-Charles de Houx, Baron de, 301, 307
Virginia, 181, 205–206, 209; Antifederalism in, 319–321; boycotts British goods, 8; business cycles, 29–30; cargo trade, 21–31; cavalry, 91, 93, 128, 137, 207, 208, 211, 213, 217, 218; cession of western claims, 256–259; charter (1690), 120; cities, 26; conflict of interest, 122–123, 172; conflict with Pennsylvania, 57; constitution, 110–121, 194, 232; counties elect convention delegates, 9; courts close, 8–9; criticism of courts, 35–38; debts, 21–31; debt to Continent, 320; Declaration of Rights, 100–104, 106–110, 194; diversification, 31; elections, 38; geography, 23–24; government, 36–40; grain trade, 30–31; Lafayette plans to attack Arnold, 265–270; land claims, 142; land office, 257; Leslie invades, 216–221; loyalists in, 46–47, 59–61; paper currency, 28; politics, 138–139, 317–318; population, 24; religious unrest, 32–34; resolution

for independence, 97; social structure, 24–26; suffrage, 38; supply system disintegrates, 263–264; tobacco production, 26–27; war debt, 153
Virginia, University of, 239
Virginia Capes, 23, 47–48, 74, 88, 104, 105, 126, 133, 176, 181, 204, 269, 270, 311; battle of, 295–296, 302, 303. *See also* Cape Henry, Va.
Virginia Gazette, 18–19, 21, 65, 66, 81, 85, 91, 102, 103, 127, 149, 165, 177; Dunmore seizes, 58–59; prints Declaration of Independence, 99; quoted, 42, 58, 67, 88, 97, 114, 135, 188, 228. *See also* Dunmore's *Virginia Gazette*; Norfolk *Virginia Gazette*
Virginia Gazette, or, the American Advertiser, 322
Volunteer companies. *See* Independent companies

Wabash Company, 142, 243
Wabash River, 195
Wadsworth, Jeremiah, 181
Wagons, 62, 70, 74, 93, 211, 213–214, 221, 245, 253, 259, 261, 271, 275, 284
Walker, John, 258, 266–267, 284, 296
Walker, Thomas, 184, 232
Waller, Benjamin, 49, 247
Waller's Grove, Williamsburg, Va., 48, 61, 97
Warren, James, 84, 113
Warwick, Va., 167, 245
Warwick County, Va., 228
Washington, George, 38, 47, 48, 57, 77, 84–85, 88, 97, 111, 119, 124, 127, 129, 136, 152, 170, 176, 185, 204, 211, 216–217, 222, 226, 229, 232, 252, 255, 260, 265–266, 267, 271, 272, 279, 283, 286, 289, 291; arrives in Williamsburg, 300–301; at Alexandria, 3; at Brandywine Creek and Germantown, 134; criticizes Henry, 50; elected to Congress, 10; leaves Virginia, 311; plans Yorktown campaign, 293–298; uniform, 18; wins battle of Yorktown, 301–309
Washington, John Augustine, 112, 157
Washington, Lund, 271
Washington County, Va., 143, 200, 219, 220, 314
Washington Iron Works, 167
Watauga Fort, N. C., 187
Watauga settlements, 186–187, 191
Waxhaws, S. C.: battle of, 213
Wayles, John, 30

Wayne, Gen. Anthony, 276, 279, 286, 289; Cornwallis defeats at Green Spring, 290–291; quarrels with Nelson, 297
Weapons, 46, 48, 127, 207, 218, 252, 275
Weather, 245
Webb, George, 282
Webb, Thomas, 172
Weedon, Gen. George, 128, 217, 270, 276; at Gloucester Point, 305, 306
Wesleyans, 33
West Augusta: County bill, 143–144; District of, 117, 143
Western lands, 102, 120, 137, 141–144, 242–243, 320; Mason proposes sale, 153–155; Virginia cedes to Congress, 258–259
West Florida, 314
Westham, Va., 168
Westham foundry, 168–169, 223, 224
West Indies, 55, 67, 68, 79, 133, 136, 165, 288, 295, 303, 310; Dutch, 182; French, 28; Spanish, 28; trade with, 170, 171–172, 174, 175
Westmoreland County, Va., 136
Westover (plantation), 223–224, 272, 275; "black affair" of, 268
West Point, N. Y., 204, 221
West Point, Va., 312
West Virginia, 142, 231
Wethersfield, Conn., 289
Wharton, Samuel, 142
Wharton, Thomas, 142
Wheat, 25, 31, 32, 233
Wheeling, Va., 170, 202
Wheeling River, 57
Whiting, Thomas, 241
Wicomico, Va., 208
William, H.M.S. (ship), 81
William (ship), 56
William and Mary, College of, 47, 61, 75, 103, 127, 154, 245, 312; board of visitors, 236, 237, 238; charter, 238; Jefferson reforms, 236–239; representation, 117; student company, 133–134, 207
Williamsburg, Va., 17, 18, 24, 26, 58, 59, 61, 62, 63, 64, 66, 68, 70, 74, 80, 83, 88, 124, 127, 129, 133, 141, 144, 173, 177, 178, 207, 210–211, 224, 240, 246, 271, 275, 289–290, 300–302, 312; capital moved to Richmond, 246; forms committee of correspondence, 10; gunpowder incident at, 1–5, 19, 41–42, 43, 53; hustings court, 36, 49; independence celebrated at, 99; Indian delegation visits, 188; Leslie threatens, 216; Manufac-

turing Society, 167; Public Taylors
Shop, 167; regulates prices, 227; representation, 117; troops unruly at, 45–49,
112; victory at Saratoga celebrated,
134–135
Williamson, Col. David, 201
Willing, Capt. James, 191
Willing, Thomas, 191
Willing and Morris, 32, 172–173
Willis, Lewis, 3
Willis (ship), 228
Willoughby, John, 77
Willoughby's Point, Va., 204
Wilmington, N. C., 219, 274, 288
Wilson, James, 104
Winchester, Va., 25, 56, 207, 311
Winemaking, 238
Wood, Capt. James, 56, 137, 158, 184,
218, 220–221
Woodford, Col. William, 63–64, 67, 77,
79–85, 91, 93, 112, 232; at Great
Bridge, 69–74; captured at Charleston,
211–214; controversy with Henry, 75–
76; elected colonel, 51; favors Hugh
Mercer, 50; occupies Norfolk, 74; resigns, 127–128

Woolman, John, 107
Wormeley, Ralph, Jr., 93
Wormeley Creek, 303, 305
Wormeley family, 299
Wray, Jacob, 222
Wythe, George, 38, 39, 107, 120, 138,
172, 238; decides on independence, 91;
elected Speaker, 150; revisal of the
laws, 159; supports G. R. Clark, 190–
191
Wythe County, Va., 167

Yadkin River Valley, 219
Yates and Payne, 180
Yohogania County, Va., 143
York, Pa., 134
York County, Va., 4–5, 36, 122, 166, 228
York River, 211, 245, 293, 302
Yorktown, Va., 42, 43, 45, 48, 50, 128,
165, 173, 180, 207, 211, 229, 241, 245,
265, 271, 289, 290, 293, 294, 312; battle
of, 301–309, 310, 314, 318
Yorktown Creek, 305

Zane, Isaac, 169